LET'S GO

■ PAGES PACKED WITH ESSENTIAL INFORMATION

"Value-packed, unbeatable, accurate, and comprehensive."

—*The Los Angeles Times*

"The guides are aimed not only at young budget travelers but at the independent traveler; a sort of streetwise cookbook for traveling alone."

—*The New York Times*

"Unbeatable; good sight-seeing advice; up-to-date info on restaurants, hotels, and inns; a commitment to money-saving travel; and a wry style that brightens nearly every page."

—*The Washington Post*

■ THE BEST TRAVEL BARGAINS IN YOUR BUDGET

"All the dirt, dirt cheap."

—*People*

"Let's Go follows the creed that you don't have to toss your life's savings to the wind to travel—unless you want to."

—*The Salt Lake Tribune*

■ REAL ADVICE FOR REAL EXPERIENCES

"The writers seem to have experienced every rooster-packed bus and lunar-surfaced mattress about which they write."

—*The New York Times*

"[Let's Go's] devoted updaters really walk the walk (and thumb the ride, and trek the trail). Learn how to fish, haggle, find work—anywhere."

—*Food & Wine*

"A world-wise traveling companion—always ready with friendly advice and helpful hints, all sprinkled with a bit of wit."

—*The Philadelphia Inquirer*

■ A GUIDE WITH A SPIRIT AND A SOCIAL CONSCIENCE

"Lighthearted and sophisticated, informative and fun to read. [Let's Go] helps the novice traveler navigate like a knowledgeable old hand."

—*Atlanta Journal-Constitution*

"The serious mission at the book's core reveals itself in exhortations to respect the culture and the environment—and, if possible, to visit as a volunteer, a student, or a teacher rather than a tourist."

—*San Francisco Chronicle*

LET'S GO PUBLICATIONS

TRAVEL GUIDES

Australia 8th edition
Austria & Switzerland 12th edition
Brazil 1st edition
Britain 2006
California 10th edition
Central America 9th edition
Chile 2nd edition
China 5th edition
Costa Rica 2nd edition
Eastern Europe 12th edition
Ecuador 1st edition
Egypt 2nd edition
Europe 2006
France 2006
Germany 12th edition
Greece 8th edition
Hawaii 3rd edition
India & Nepal 8th edition
Ireland 12th edition
Israel 4th edition
Italy 2006
Japan 1st edition
Mexico 21st edition
Middle East 4th edition
New Zealand 7th edition
Peru 1st edition
Puerto Rico 2nd edition
South Africa 5th edition
Southeast Asia 9th edition
Spain & Portugal 2006
Thailand 2nd edition
Turkey 5th edition
USA 23rd edition
Vietnam 1st edition
Western Europe 2006

ROADTRIP GUIDE

Roadtripping USA

ADVENTURE GUIDES

Alaska 1st edition
Pacific Northwest 1st edition
Southwest USA 3rd edition

CITY GUIDES

Amsterdam 4th edition
Barcelona 3rd edition
Boston 4th edition
London 15th edition
New York City 15th edition
Paris 13th edition
Rome 12th edition
San Francisco 4th edition
Washington, D.C. 13th edition

POCKET CITY GUIDES

Amsterdam
Berlin
Boston
Chicago
London
New York City
Paris
San Francisco
Venice
Washington, D.C.

LET'S GO PUERTO RICO

JULIANA TOLLES EDITOR

RESEARCHER-WRITERS
LUCAS LAURSEN
LAUREN TRUESDELL

JESSICA HUANG MAP EDITOR
ASHLEY E. ISAACSON MANAGING EDITOR

ST. MARTIN'S PRESS ✖ NEW YORK

Maps by David Lindroth copyright © 2006 by St. Martin's Press.

Distributed outside the USA and Canada by Macmillan.

ISBN: 0-312-34884-3
EAN: 978-0-312-34884-7
Second edition
10 9 8 7 6 5 4 3 2 1

Let's Go: Puerto Rico is written by Let's Go Publications, 67 Mount Auburn St., Cambridge, MA 02138, USA.

CONTENTS

HOW TO USE THIS BOOK

COVERAGE LAYOUT. *Let's Go: Puerto Rico* launches out of **San Juan.** From this bustling capital city venture to the **Northeast** for trips to the rainforest and beautiful beaches. Head all the way to the east coast for the city of Fajardo and transportation to the idyllic Caribbean islands of **Vieques** and **Culebra.** Back on the mainland, the journey continues through the sleepy coastal towns of the undiscovered **Southeast,** ending in Puerto Rico's southern jewel, Ponce. Next, trek west through the cactus forests and salt flats of the **Southwest** for relaxed ocean fun, with a brief foray to the isolated reserve of Isla Mona. Then, head north into the rugged karst landscape of the **Northwest** for world-class surfing. Lastly, travel through the seldom-visited, mountainous center of the island on the winding series of roads called the **Ruta Panorámica.**

TRANSPORTATION INFO. For making connections between destinations, information is generally listed under both the arrival and departure cities. Parentheticals usually provide the trip duration followed by the frequency, then the price. Travelers to Puerto Rico must choose between driving and going by *carros públicos* (public cars). For more information on this and of general travel concerns, consult **Essentials** (p. 8).

COVERING THE BASICS. The first chapter, **Discover Puerto Rico** (p. 1), contains highlights of the island, complete with **Suggested Itineraries.** The **Essentials** (p. 8) section contains practical information on planning a budget, making reservations, and other useful tips for traveling in Puerto Rico. Take some time to peruse the **Life and Times** section, which briefly sums up the history, culture, and customs of Puerto Rico. The **Appendix** (p. 309) has climate information, as well as a Spanish pronunciation guide and glossary. For study abroad and volunteer opportunities in Puerto Rico, **Beyond Tourism** (p. 84) is all you need.

PRICE DIVERSITY. Our researchers list establishments in order of value from best to worst, with absolute favorites denoted by the *Let's Go* thumbs-up (🖐). Since the cheapest price does not always mean the best value, we have incorporated a system of price ranges for food and accommodations; see p. viii.

SCHOLARLY ARTICLES. Four contributors with unique local insight wrote articles for *Let's Go: Puerto Rico.* **María Pilar Barreto** discusses her experience volunteering in a San Juan public library (p. 89). Education policy specialist **Adrián Cerezo** explains Puerto Rico's unusual public transportation system (p. 75). Harvard PhD **Camille Lizarribar** explores Puerto Rico's traditional Roman Catholic icons, *santos y palos* (p. 78). Harvard PhD candidate **Iliana Pagán Teitelbaum** discusses Puerto Rico's complicated political relationship with the US (p. 71).

PHONE CODES AND TELEPHONE NUMBERS. The area code for all of Puerto Rico is ☎787. Phone numbers in text are preceded by the ☎ icon.

A NOTE TO OUR READERS. The information for this book was gathered by *Let's Go* researchers from May through August of 2005. Each listing is based on one researcher's opinion, formed during his or her visit at a particular time. Those traveling at other times may have different experiences since prices, dates, hours, and conditions are always subject to change. You are urged to check the facts presented in this book beforehand to avoid inconvenience and surprises.

Puerto Rico Chapter Divisions

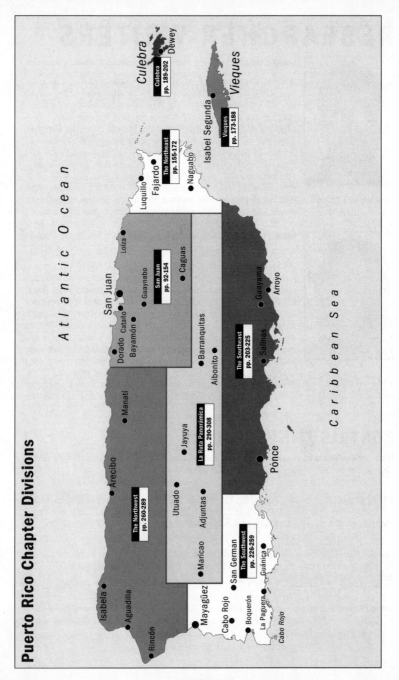

Atlantic Ocean

Caribbean Sea

Culebra
Dewey

Culebra
pp. 189-202

Vieques

Isabel Segunda

Vieques
pp. 173-188

Luquillo
Fajardo
Naguabo

The Northeast
pp. 155-172

Loiza

San Juan

Guaynabo

San Juan
pp. 92-154

Caguas

Catano
Dorado

Bayamón

Guayama
Arroyo

Manati

Barranquitas

Salinas

The Southeast
pp. 203-225

Aibonito

Jayuya

La Ruta Panorámica
pp. 290-308

Arecibo

Ponce

Utuado

The Northwest
pp. 260-289

Adjuntas

Maricao

San German

The Southwest
pp. 226-259

Guánica

Isabela

Aguadilla

Mayagüez

Rincón

Cabo Rojo

Boquerón

La Paguera

Cabo Rojo

VII

RESEARCHER-WRITERS

Lucas Laursen *Northwest, Southwest, Ruta Panorámica*

A veteran researcher of *Let's Go Southwest USA Adventure Guide: 2004*, Lucas brought his outdoors expertise to the wild side of Puerto Rico. When he wasn't politely declining declarations of love from locals, this adventurous astrophysics major was surfing with beach bums in Rincón, chatting with *mundillo* artisans, or going door-to-door in search of the island's inside stories. Lucas also discovered Puerto Rico's cheap eats, living on tuna fish, fresh mangos, and *panadería* treats. Neither computer failures, nor car breakdowns, nor vicious stray dogs could faze this intrepid California native, who maintained his tenacious attention to detail and passion for polished prose throughout his trip.

Lauren Truesdell *Culebra, Northeast, San Juan, Southeast, Vieques*

A former associate editor of *Let's Go Eastern Europe: 2004* and managing editor for the *Let's Go 2005* series, Lauren headed out on the road to rate beaches on Vieques and *mojitos* in San Juan. Summitting El Yunque mountain, braving the madness of Expreso de Diego, and covering her first cockfight were all in a day's work for this down-to-earth researcher. Although her ability to squash mosquitoes in mid-air and merge across six lanes of rush hour traffic are impressive, this New Yorker is truly remarkable for her wry, witty prose and unbeatable good humor. Whether she was sampling traditional Puerto Rican *postres* or grinning like a little kid in the copilot's seat on a flight from Vieques, Lauren searched out unique experiences to share with our readers.

CONTRIBUTING WRITERS

María Pilar Barreto is a candidate for an A.B. in Latin American Studies at Harvard University and is a native of Guaynabo, Puerto Rico.

Adrián Cerezo directs the Community-Based Education Center at Sacred Heart University in San Juan. He has a BA in clinical psychology from Sacred Heart and received a Distinguished Alumni Award in 1998 for his contributions to the field of education.

Camille Lizarribar has a PhD in Comparative Literature from Harvard University and a JD from Harvard Law. She most recently worked as a clerk for a Judge at the Federal district court in San Juan.

Iliana Pagán Teitelbaum received her BA in Latin American Studies from the University of Puerto Rico. She expects to receive a PhD in Romance Languages and Literatures from Harvard University.

ACKNOWLEDGMENTS

TEAM PR THANKS: Lucas and Lauren for their dedication, mad driving skills, and funny stories; these amazing ▩RWs handled every obstacle with grace and poise. Ashley for her enduring patience and tireless editing. Jess for making great maps with a smile. Prod, especially Alex, for showing us love when Frame did not. The ME team for wisdom, moral support, and screaming contests. Adrienne for answering our thousands of questions.

JULIANA THANKS: Ashley for her unwavering confidence in me. Lucas and Lauren for being simply the best. Jess for taking all my crazy map requests in stride. My fellow Let's Goers for making late nights a blast with salsa, snacks, and Latin lovin'; this wouldn't have been half as much fun without you. Fourth floor Wolbach for the swinging parties, deadline commiseration, and tasty baked goods; I have such fond memories. Alex, Debra, and Victor for their encouragement. Yannis for opening my eyes to new perspectives and sharing your enthusiasm for life; your love, kindness, and humor make everything, even a bad day, more enjoyable. Mom, Dad, and Lydia for their constant love and support in everything that I do.

JESS THANKS: Juliana and Ashley, the ever-patient, all-star editing team. Lucas and Lauren for doing their best to humor my requests and heroically attempting to label nameless streets. Katherine, Kelly, and David for feeding me yogurt and muffins and keeping me sane during the late nights. Mom, Dad, and the sibs for their steadfast support.

ASHLEY THANKS: The heart and soul of the book, ▩Juliana ("Seertu"), for self-sufficient intelligence and dedication. ▩LT and ▩Lucas, the least-stressful RWs ever. Jess and all MEs.

Editor
Juliana Tolles
Managing Editor
Ashley Eva Isaacson
Map Editor
Jessica Huang
Typesetter
Ansel S. Witthaus

LET'S GO

Publishing Director
Seth Robinson
Editor-in-Chief
Stuart J. Robinson
Production Manager
Alexandra Hoffer
Cartography Manager
Katherine J. Thompson
Editorial Managers
Rachel M. Burke, Ashley Eva Isaacson, Laura E. Martin
Financial Manager
Adrienne Taylor Gerken
Publicity Manager
Alexandra C. Stanek
Personnel Manager
Ella M. Steim
Production Associate
Ansel S. Witthaus
IT Director
Jeffrey Hoffman Yip
Director of E-Commerce
Michael Reckhow
Office Coordinator
Matthew Gibson

Director of Advertising Sales
Jillian N. London
Senior Advertising Associates
Jessica C.L. Chiu, Katya M. Golovchenko, Mohammed J. Herzallah
Advertising Graphic Designer
Emily E. Maston

President
Caleb J. Merkl
General Manager
Robert B. Rombauer
Assistant General Manager
Anne E. Chisholm

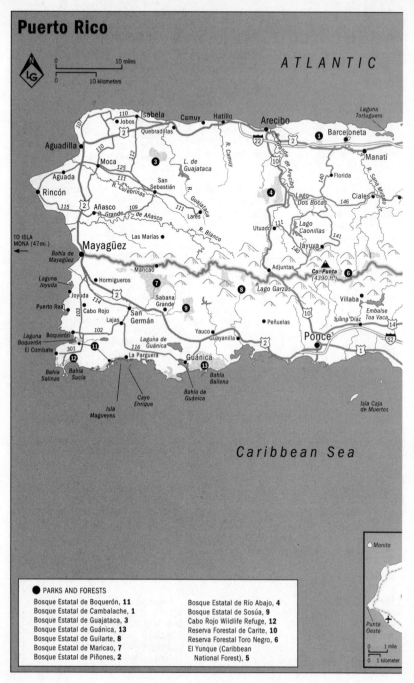

Puerto Rico

ATLANTIC

Caribbean Sea

PARKS AND FORESTS

Bosque Estatal de Boquerón, 11
Bosque Estatal de Cambalache, 1
Bosque Estatal de Guajataca, 3
Bosque Estatal de Guánica, 13
Bosque Estatal de Guilarte, 8
Bosque Estatal de Maricao, 7
Bosque Estatal de Piñones, 2

Bosque Estatal de Río Abajo, 4
Bosque Estatal de Sosúa, 9
Cabo Rojo Wildlife Refuge, 12
Reserva Forestal de Carite, 10
Reserva Forestal Toro Negro, 6
El Yunque (Caribbean
    National Forest), 5

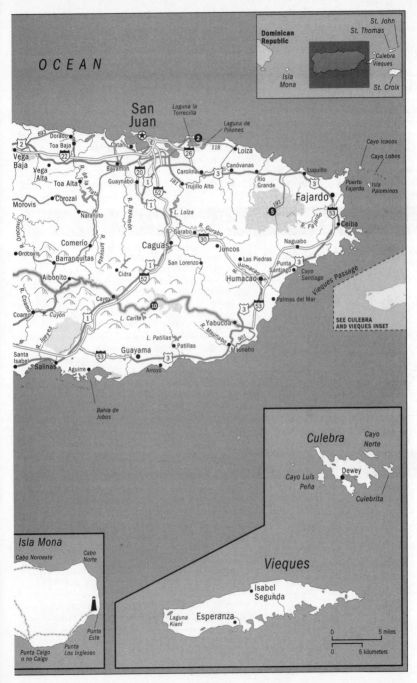

1 2 3 4 5

PRICE RANGES>>PUERTO RICO

Our researchers list establishments in order of value from best to worst; our favorites are denoted by the Let's Go thumbs-up (◼). Since the best value is not always the cheapest price, we have incorporated a system of price ranges for quick reference. Our price ranges are based on a rough expectation of what you will spend. For **accommodations,** we base our price range off the cheapest price for which a single traveler can stay for one night. For **restaurants** and other dining establishments, we estimate the average price of a full entree without beverages or appetizers. The table below tells you what you will *typically* find in Puerto Rico at the corresponding price range.

ACCOMMODATIONS	RANGE	WHAT YOU'RE *LIKELY* TO FIND
❶	under $40	Primarily campgrounds or large fields in which you can pitch a tent. As low as $10. Toilets, water, and often showers. Some have security guards.
❷	$40-60	Inexpensive guesthouses. These vary from unadorned spare bedrooms to suprisingly well-equipped, comfortable accommodations. Some cheaper hotels with smaller rooms. Also, rustic cabins and villas for larger groups.
❸	$61-89	Small, independent hotels. Rooms should be clean and have a private bath; some may have a kitchenette.
❹	$90-130	Nicer guesthouses, small hotels and and most *paradores*. You should expect attentive staff, daily maid service, A/C, TV and sometimes a pool.
❺	over $130	Large chain hotels, resorts, and realtor-owned vacation rentals. Expect the best, because you're paying for it.
FOOD	RANGE	WHAT YOU'RE *LIKELY* TO FIND
❶	under $6	*Panaderías* and *cafeterías* serving sandwiches and typical Puerto Rican food. Usually only open for lunch. No tips.
❷	$6-10	Inexpensive sit-down restaurants with waitstaff and relatively expensive *cafeterías* serving dinner.
❸	$11-15	The vast majority of tourist-oriented restaurants fall into this category. Almost all have a waitstaff, a sit-down dining area, and a full menu with appetizers and desserts.
❹	$16-20	A somewhat fancy eatery, including most seafood restaurants. All of the amenities from above, but slightly classier.
❺	over $20	The best restaurants in Puerto Rico. Expect either a very hip atmosphere or some of the best food on the island. Make a reservation; dress nicely.

DISCOVER
PUERTO RICO

From the rumble of *reggaetón* to the beat of *bomba*, life on Puerto Rico pulsates to a constant cacophony of sound and movement. Hordes of cars weave across the island, commerce bustles at the pace of a developed metropolis, and a dazzling array of local festivals offers endless excuses to party. Puerto Rico is remarkable for the sheer amount of stuff that it has managed to squeeze onto a plot of land the size of Connecticut. In addition to four million people, this little island is home to some of the world's most beautiful beaches, the only rainforest in the US, acres of coral reef, the world's third-largest underground cave system, nine protected nature reserves, the world's largest radio telescope, and species of wildlife found nowhere else on the planet.

It's no wonder that the affection Puerto Ricans feel for their enchanted isle is displayed proudly in many Puerto Rican flags and "Borinquén Querida" bumper stickers. Puerto Ricans stand at the intersection of the cultural and economic worlds of the United States and Latin America—the language is Spanish, the culture is Latin, but Americanization and commercial development have penetrated most of the cities. Instead of choosing between these two worlds, Puerto Ricans have unified their diverse heritage—Taíno, African, and Spanish—to create a vibrant culture that is uniquely Puerto Rican, or more accurately, Boricua. The island's original Taíno name still serves as a password for the lively spirit that is Puerto Rico.

FACTS AND FIGURES

OFFICIAL NAME: Estado Libre Asociado de Puerto Rico (Free Associated State of Puerto Rico).	**PERCENTAGE OF US RUM PRODUCED IN PUERTO RICO:** 70.
CAPITAL: San Juan.	**POPULATION OF PUERTO RICANS IN THE US:** 3.9 million.
POPULATION DENSITY: 1137 people per sq. mi.	**NUMBER OF CITIES THAT CLAIM COLUMBUS LANDED THERE:** 5 (Combate, Guayanilla, Mayagüez, Boquerón, Añasco).
PER CAPITA GDP: $17,700.	

WHEN TO GO

Travelers to Puerto Rico usually find themselves faced with a choice between perfect weather and steep discounts. No matter when you travel it will be low season on one part of the island. Most travelers escape to Puerto Rico between December and April when the weather up north is miserable and the island's climate is at its prime. As a result, hotels in San Juan, Culebra, and Vieques raise their rates during this season. If you want to travel during this time, the best solution is to go to the parts of the island that are rarely visited by foreigners, such as the southern and western coasts or the central mountains. The high season on these parts of the island is from May to November. Puerto Ricans travel during school vacations—primarily Christmas (late Dec.), *Semana Santa* (the week before Easter), and summer (June-Aug.)—filling up accommodations and beaches nearly everywhere outside of San Juan. It may be best not to make travel plans these times, but if you do, make reservations in advance. Also, during the summer Puerto Rico is at its hottest and most humid. **Hurricane season** officially lasts from June to November, but most storms are in August and September. Traveling during this time is risky; a hurricane will almost certainly ruin any vacation, but if there is no hurricane (most of the time) travelers will enjoy empty beaches and steep hotel discounts. **Surf season** in Puerto Rico runs from November to mid-April.

WHAT TO DO

Puerto Rico easily has enough cultural and natural attractions to keep anyone busy for weeks. Whether you're looking for a taste of Latin culture and Caribbean history, an outdoor adventure, or just a relaxing vacation on the beach, Puerto Rico will not disappoint.

IN THE SEA

Puerto Rico is a great place to swim with sharks, turtles, manatees, barracudas, dolphins, whales, lobsters, and hundreds of brightly colored fish. Everyone agrees that Puerto Rico's best diving is at **Isla Mona** (p. 248), which boasts hundreds of dive sites and visibility up to 180 ft. However, the 4hr. journey takes a lot of planning, and even more moolah. For a similar, but more accessible experience, try Rincón, where boats leave almost daily for **Isla Desecheo** (p. 288), an offshore island surrounded by thriving reefs. A completely different dive experience awaits off the southwestern coast of Puerto Rico. Six miles offshore a dramatic sea wall starts at 60 ft. then seems to disappear completely as a sheer cliff descends to over 150 ft. The best place to access The Wall is the spirited *pueblo* of **La Parguera** (p. 232). Finally, one of Puerto Rico's most unique dive spots is just off the coast of **Aguadilla** (p. 272), where hundreds of old tires have been transformed into an artificial reef. Visitors who want a slightly cheaper glimpse of the island's underwater world are in luck—some of the best snorkeling opportunities can be found off the coasts of **Vieques** (p. 173), **La Parguera** (p. 232), and **Isla Caja de Muertos** (p. 215). Culebra (p. 189), Isabela (p. 272), Isla Mona (p. 248), Rincón (p. 280), and San Juan (p. 92) also offer snorkeling spots of varying quality.

ON THE SAND

If it's beaches you're after, you've come to the right place. From Culebra to San Juan to Isla Mona, Puerto Rico has some of the most gorgeous beaches in the world. And the winner is...**Playa Flamenco** (p. 197), Culebra's public beach. With an enormous crescent of white sand, aquamarine water, and medium-sized waves, Flamenco is the stuff of Caribbean dreams. Culebra's other beaches are equally stunning, if not more so, but a bit more difficult to reach. The many beaches of **Vieques** (p. 173) come in a close second. Back on the mainland, the prized patches of sand can be found in southwest Puerto Rico. **Balneario Boquerón** (p. 244), **La Playuela** (p. 243), and **El Combate** (p. 242) could all tempt you to extend your vacation. Luquillo's **Balneario Monserrate** (p. 163) receives a lot of public acclaim, much of it deserved, but it must share the spotlight with fellow north coast all-star beaches **Balneario Seven Seas** (p. 168), **Balneario Cerro Gordo** (p. 146), and **Balneario Puerto Nuevo** (p. 266). In terms of aesthetics alone, the dramatic coastline of northwest Puerto Rico is incomparable, although the rough waves in the area make it difficult to swim. Almost any northern coastline drive will reveal spectacular beaches, but easily accessible areas include **Playa Jobos** (p. 276), in Isabela; **Bosque Estatal de Piñones** (p. 147), near San Juan; and **Las Ruínas** (p. 277), near Aguadilla. And, of course, if you're looking for one of the best metropolitan beaches in the world, the coastline around **San Juan** (p. 92) cannot be beat.

IN DA CLUB

This island knows how to party—on Friday and Saturday nights San Juan's nightlife competes with the best in the world. Traffic slows to a crawl as thousands of hip, young *sanjuaneros* prowl the streets for the biggest and best party. **Old San Juan** (p. 140), and Calle San Sebastián in particular, is without a doubt the hippest scene on the island. If it's big clubs that you're after, **Santurce** (p. 141) and **Isla Verde** (p. 141) offer anything and everything: salsa, reggae, pop, gay, straight, ritzy, and low-key. But San Juan is not the be-all and end-all of Puerto Rico's nightlife. **Ponce** (p. 203) has a lively bar scene and one of the best gay clubs on the island. During the surf season, **Rincón** (p. 280) and **Playa Jobos** (p. 278) host a good party any night of the week. University students liven things up in **Mayagüez** (p. 254), and head out to the coastal towns of **La Parguera** (p. 232) and **Boquerón** (p. 244) on weekend nights. Only in Vieques, Culebra, and La Ruta Panorámica will you have trouble finding hopping nightlife.

BACK THROUGH TIME

Puerto Rico's colorful history as the home of the Taíno people, an early Spanish colony, and a melting pot of cultures and traditions has left a legacy of great historical sights. If you can tear yourself away from the beach, take the opportunity to wander down to the dungeon of the 16th-century Spanish fort **Castillo San Cristóbal** (p. 121) in Old San Juan. In the same part of town, **Museo de Las Americas** (p. 130) and **Museo de la Raíz Africana** (p. 130) offer visitors a peek at the Spanish and African heritage that have shaped Puerto Rican art, crafts, music, and religion today. In more recent history, the **Museo Felisa Rincón de Gautier** tells the story of how a high-school dropout became the first female mayor in the western hemisphere and changed the face of the island's capital. Outside of San Juan, the first stop for history buffs is the city of **Ponce** (p. 203), which is home to a variety of museums, including the **Museo de la Música Puertorriqueña,** which takes visitors through the history of Puerto Rico's musical beats. Last, but not least, is the remarkable collection of religious paintings and *santos* in the centuries-old **Porta Coeli Chapel and Museum of Religious Art** (p. 241) in San Germán.

IN THE WILD

Find San Juan a bit tame? Is Vieques too "laid-back" for your vacation? Never fear; Puerto Rico has some first-rate adventures that offer an all-natural adrenaline rush. Start your engines and head to Arecibo's **Camuy Caves** (p. 269), the world's third-largest underground cave system. Several tour operators lead expeditions that kick the action up a notch with spelunking, rapelling, rafting, and hiking. For an entirely different wild side of Puerto Rico, arrange a trip out to the deserted island of **Isla Mona** (p. 248), where enormous iguanas and hordes of hermit crabs greet visitors. Puerto Rico's rugged **Ruta Panorámica** (p. 290) is the gateway to many of the island's isolated nature reserves, where you can have the call of the *coquí* and the mountain views all to yourself. The rough road may require some crafty driving skills, but the panoramic views, ample hiking, and numerous lakes make the trip worthwhile. For a shorter stint in Puerto Rico's wilds, try the beautiful **El Yunque** forest (p. 155), where you can summit a mountain in an afternoon.

■ LET'S GO PICKS

BEST PLACE TO SALSA THE NIGHT AWAY: San Juan's many glitzy clubs, especially **Club Habana** (p. 141) and **Rumba** (p. 140).

BEST PLACE TO BE AWE-INSPIRED BY NATURE: The peak of **El Yunque Mountain** (p. 160), where on a clear day the views extend to the Caribbean Ocean; **Isla Mona** (p. 248) where animals still rule the roost; and **Cabo Rojo Lighthouse** (p. 243), where earth meets land in the most dramatic way possible.

BEST WAY TO GLOW IN THE DARK: Swimming in the bioluminescent bays of **Vieques** (p. 187), **Fajardo** (p. 170), and **La Parguera** (p. 235)

BEST PLACE TO HANG TEN: The popular surf breaks off the coast of **Jobos** (p. 276) and **Rincón** (p. 286).

BEST PLACE TO PLAY BALL WITH THE TAÍNOS: Utuado's **Parque Indígena Caguana** (p. 304) has a host of *batey* fields. Ponce's **Parque Indígena Tibes** (p. 217) has even more, but they actually predate the Taínos. Jayuya's **Museo El Cemí** (p. 303) comes in a distant third.

BEST SUNSETS: The lighthouse at **Rincón** (p. 285), the coastline of **Boquerón** (p. 244), or, if you're in the mood for adventure, Playa Sardinera on **Isla Mona** (p. 248).

BEST PLACE TO LOSE TEN BUCKS AND GAIN LOCAL CREDIBILITY: Betting on a cockfight with the *sanjuaneros* at Isla Verde's **Club Gallístico** (p. 137).

BEST PLACE TO GET SLOSHED: San Juan's **Festival de la Calle San Sebastián** (p. 138), where the drinking never seems to stop.

BEST PLACE TO SEE MACHO PUERTO RICAN MEN WEAR DRESSES: Ponce's **Carnaval** (p. 209), where machismo takes a backseat to tradition.

BEST LOCAL FLAVOR: The fresh fruit and even fresher *batidas* in Isla Verde's **Plaza del Mercado** (p. 125).

BEST PLACE TO HAVE A CAR ACCIDENT: Highway 3, the highly congested road that connects San Juan to Fajardo. Or perhaps Hwy. 2 or maybe Hwy. 5...or just about anywhere.

SUGGESTED ITINERARIES

BEST OF PUERTO RICO (5 WEEKS)

DISCOVER

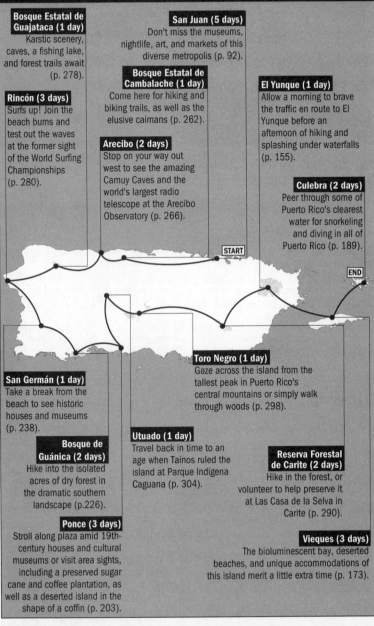

Bosque Estatal de Guajataca (1 day)
Karstic scenery, caves, a fishing lake, and forest trails await (p. 278).

San Juan (5 days)
Don't miss the museums, nightlife, art, and markets of this diverse metropolis (p. 92).

Rincón (3 days)
Surfs up! Join the beach bums and test out the waves at the former sight of the World Surfing Championships (p. 280).

Bosque Estatal de Cambalache (1 day)
Come here for hiking and biking trails, as well as the elusive caimans (p. 262).

El Yunque (1 day)
Allow a morning to brave the traffic en route to El Yunque before an afternoon of hiking and splashing under waterfalls (p. 155).

Arecibo (2 days)
Stop on your way out west to see the amazing Camuy Caves and the world's largest radio telescope at the Arecibo Observatory (p. 266).

Culebra (2 days)
Peer through some of Puerto Rico's clearest water for snorkeling and diving in all of Puerto Rico (p. 189).

START

END

San Germán (1 day)
Take a break from the beach to see historic houses and museums (p. 238).

Toro Negro (1 day)
Gaze across the island from the tallest peak in Puerto Rico's central mountains or simply walk through woods (p. 298).

Bosque de Guánica (2 days)
Hike into the isolated acres of dry forest in the dramatic southern landscape (p.226).

Utuado (1 day)
Travel back in time to an age when Taínos ruled the island at Parque Indígena Caguana (p. 304).

Reserva Forestal de Carite (2 days)
Hike in the forest, or volunteer to help preserve it at Las Casa de la Selva in Carite (p. 290).

Ponce (3 days)
Stroll along plaza amid 19th-century houses and cultural museums or visit area sights, including a preserved sugar cane and coffee plantation, as well as a deserted island in the shape of a coffin (p. 203).

Vieques (3 days)
The bioluminescent bay, deserted beaches, and unique accommodations of this island merit a little extra time (p. 173).

DISCOVER

WHIRLWIND TOUR (1 WEEK)

Arecibo (1 day)
Rent a car and head out to the Camuy Caves; the adventurous can book a tour for tubing or rapelling. Don't miss the famous Arecibo Observatory (p. 266).

Old San Juan (2 days)
Explore the colonial forts, many museums, upscale restaurants, and hopping nightlife in Puerto Rico's capital city (p. 92).

Culebra (2 days)
Allow a few hours for the ferry and get ready to enjoy superb beaches, snorkeling, and swimming on this laid-back island, which boasts only six stop signs (p. 189).

START

END

El Yunque (½ day)
Head east for an afternoon of hiking in a tropical rainforest (p. 155).

Utuado (½ day)
Start the day early at Utuado's Parque Indígena Caguana to see the drawings that the island's early residents left behind (p. 304).

Luquillo (½ day)
Enjoy eats from the food stands on the beautiful public beach of Luquillo (p. 161).

Fajardo (½ day)
Catch a nighttime tour of a bioluminescent bay in Fajardo (p. 164).

THE GREAT OUTDOORS (2 WEEKS)

Bosque Estatal de Guajataca (1 day)
Explore the caves and well-maintained trails of the forest or try your hand at fishing in the lake (p. 278).

Bosque Estatal de Cambalache (1 day)
Enjoy the hiking and mountain biking trails. If you're lucky, you may catch a glimpse of the caimans (p. 262).

El Yunque (2 days)
Warm up your walking legs in the tropical rainforest by hiking to the top of El Yunque mountain, camping with the *coquís*, or trying the National Recreation Trail (p. 155).

END

START

Isla Mona (3 days)
This deserted island reserve, with its giant iguanas and tiny hermit crabs, is the highlight of the tour. (p. 248).

Toro Negro (2 days)
Check out the trails and look down from the highest point in Puerto Rico (p. 298).

Bosque Estatal de Carite (2 days)
Save Puerto Rico's forest with the volunteers at Las Casas de la Selva in Carite (p. 290).

Bosque de Guánica (2 days)
Wander in the cactus forests of the south or stick to the shore for beaches and diving (p. 226).

Cañón San Cristóbal (1 day)
Descend into this dramatic canyon with a guide (p. 298).

PUBLIC TRANSPORTATION (2 WEEKS)

San Juan (5 days)
Begin here, in Puerto Rico's most public-transportation-friendly city. See below for details.

Culebra (4 days)
Hop on an early-morning ferry to enjoy Puerto Rico's best beach: Playa Flamenco. If you stay in Dewey, you won't have to worry about transportation. Make sure to allow a day for transportation back to San Juan (p. 189).

START

END

Fajardo (1 day)
Transportation by *público* from Ponce to San Juan, and then from San Juan to Fajardo, will probably take most of day, but save the evening for a tour through the eerie glow of Fajardo's bioluminescent bay (p. 164).

Isla Caja de Muertos (1 day)
Book a tour out to Puerto Rico's own Coffin Island, where the pirate Cofresí is rumored to have buried his gold dubloons (p. 215).

Ponce (3 days)
Allow a morning for transportation via *público* to this southern star, home to historic houses, cultural museums, and a lively oceanside boardwalk (p. 203).

San Juan

Old San Juan (2 days)
Walkable Old San Juan has a wide variety of museums and historical sights, with restaurants conveniently placed for hungry sightseers (p. 96).

Isla Verde (1 day)
Catch rays at the beaches of Isla Verde. Ocean Park and Condado also offer accessible alternatives (p. 133).

Cataño (½ day)
Catch the ferry over to the Bacardi Rum factory for a tour and free samples (p. 145).

Bosque Estatal de Piñones (1 day)
Take the B40 bus or hire a *público* to Piñones, where you can rent a bike to traverse the forest. Check out the budget-friendly food stands and lonely beaches before heading home (p. 150).

Río Piedras (½ day)
Hit Plaza del Mercado and Paseo de Diego for some unbeatable bargains on fresh food and outlet clothing (p. 97).

ESSENTIALS

PLANNING YOUR TRIP

> ### ENTRANCE REQUIREMENTS
> **Passport** (p. 9). Required for citizens of every country except the US (US citizens should bring government-issued identification to prove citizenship).
> **Visa** (p. 11). Required for citizens of every country except those from the US, Canada, Bermuda, or one of the 27 countries participating in the US Visa Waiver Program.
> **Work Permit** (p. 10). Required for all foreigners planning to work in Puerto Rico.

EMBASSIES AND CONSULATES

US CONSULAR SERVICES ABROAD

For immigration purposes, Puerto Rico is treated as part of the US. Contact the nearest US embassy or consulate for information regarding visas to Puerto Rico. The **US State Department** provides contact info for **US embassies and consulates abroad** at http://usembassy.state.gov.

Australia: Moonah Pl., Yarralumla (Canberra), ACT 2600 (☎02 6214 5600; fax 6214 5970; http://canberra.usembassy.gov). **Consulates:** 553 St. Kilda Rd., Melbourne, VIC 3004 (☎03 9526 5900; fax 9510 4646; http://melbourne.usconsulate.gov); 16 St. George's Terr., 13th fl., Perth, WA 6000 (☎08 9202 1224; fax 9231 9444; http://perth.usconsulate.gov); MLC Centre, 19-29 Martin Pl., 59th fl., Sydney, NSW 2000 (☎02 9373 9200; fax 9373 9184; http://sydney.usconsulate.gov).

Canada: 490 Promenade Sussex Dr., Ottawa, ON K1N 1G8 (☎613-238-5335; fax 688-3091; http://canada.usembassy.gov). **Consulates:** 615 Macleod Trail SE, Calgary, AB T2G 4T8 (☎403-266-8962; fax 264-6630); Purdy's Wharf Tower II, ste. 904, 1969 Upper Water St., Halifax, NS B3J 3R7 (☎902-429-2480; fax 423-6861); 1155 Alexandre St., Montreal, QC H3B 3Z1, Mailing Address: P.O. Box 65, Station Desjardins, Montréal, QC H5B 1G1 (☎514-398-9695; fax 398-0973); 2 Place Terrasse Dufferin, Québec City, QC G1R 4T9, Mailing Address: B.P. 939, Québec City, QC G1R 4T9 (☎418-692-2095; fax 692-4640); 360 University Ave., Toronto, ON M5G 1S4 (☎416-595-1700; fax 595-0051; http://www.usconsulatetoronto.ca); 1095 W. Pender St., Vancouver, BC V6E 2M6 (☎604-685-4311; fax 685-5285; http://vancouver.usconsulate.gov); 201 Portage Ave., ste. 860, Winnipeg, MB R3B 3K6 (☎204-940-1800; fax 940-1809; http://winnipeg.usconsulate.gov).

Ireland: 42 Elgin Rd., Ballsbridge, Dublin 4 (☎1 668 8777; fax 668 9946; http://dublin.usembassy.gov).

New Zealand: 29 Fitzherbert Terr., Thorndon, Wellington. Mailing Address: P.O. Box 1190, Wellington (☎4 462 6000; fax 499 0490; http://wellington.usembassy.gov). **Consulates:** Citibank Building, 3rd fl., 23 Customs St., Auckland, Mailing Address: Private Bag 92022, Auckland (☎9 303 2724 ext. 225, 226, 250; fax 366 0870).

UK: 24 Grosvenor Sq., London W1A 1AE (☎020 7499 9000; fax 491 2485; http://london.usembassy.gov). **Consulates:** Danesfort House, 223 Stranmills Rd., Belfast, N. Ireland BT9 5GR (☎028 9038 6100; fax 9068 1301); 3 Regent Terr., Edinburgh, Scotland EH7 5BW (☎0131 556 8315; fax 557 6023).

CONSULAR SERVICES IN PUERTO RICO

Only the UK and Canada have consulates in Puerto Rico. Other countries have embassies in Washington, D.C., which serve travelers in Puerto Rico.

Australia: 601 Massachusetts Ave., Washington, D.C. 20036 USA (☎202-797-3000; fax 797-3168; www.austemb.org).

Canada: 501 Pennsylvania Ave. NW, Washington, D.C. 20001 USA (☎202-682-1740; fax 682-7701; www.canadianembassy.org). **Consulates:** Av. Ponce de León 273, Oficina 1350, San Juan, 00917 PR (☎250-0367).

Ireland: 2234 Massachusetts Ave. NW, Washington, D.C. 20008 USA (☎202-462-3939; fax 232-5993; www.irelandemb.org).

New Zealand: 37 Observatory Circle NW, Washington, D.C. 20008 USA (☎202-328-4800; fax 667-5227; www.nzemb.org).

UK: 3100 Massachusetts Ave., Washington, D.C., 20008 USA (☎202-588-7800 or 202-588-6500; fax 588-7850; www.britainusa.com/consular/embassy). **Consulates:** Av. Chardón 350, San Juan, 00918 PR (☎758-9828); 3100 Massachusetts Ave., 20008 USA.

TOURIST OFFICES

The **Puerto Rican Tourism Company** (**PRTC;** ☎800-866-7872; www.gotopuertorico.com), the island's official tourist center, has offices in Aguadilla (p. 272), Boquerón (p. 244), Ponce (p. 203), and San Juan (p. 92). In addition, there are regional offices in countries around the world. Any office will send you a complimentary issue of *¡Qué Pasa!* magazine (p. 101). Most municipal Alcaldías (Mayor's Offices), located on or near the plazas of municipal centers, can provide packets of historical information about the municipality.

Canada: 41-43 Colbourne St., ste. 301, Toronto, ON M5E 1E3 (☎416-368-2680, in Canada 800-667-0394).

UK: 67a High St., Walton-on-Thames, Surrey, KT 12 1DJ (☎01932 253 302).

US: 3575 W. Cahuenga Blvd., ste. 405, Los Angeles, CA 90068 (☎322-874-5991; 800-874-1230); 901 Ponce de León Blvd., Ste. 101, Coral Gables, FL 33134 (☎305-445-9112 or 800-815-7391); 666 Fifth Ave., New York, NY 10103 (☎212-586-6262 or 800-223-6530).

DOCUMENTS AND FORMALITIES

PASSPORTS

REQUIREMENTS
Citizens of all countries except the US need valid passports to enter Puerto Rico and to re-enter their home countries. Puerto Rico does not allow entrance if the holder's passport expires in under six months; returning home with an expired passport is illegal and may result in a fine. US citizens need to carry valid government ID, such as a driver's license, to prove their citizenship.

NEW PASSPORTS
Citizens of Australia, Canada, Ireland, New Zealand, the UK, and the US can apply for a passport at any passport office or at selected post offices and courts of law. Citizens of these countries may also download passport applications from the official website of their country's government or passport office. Any new passport or renewal applications must be filed well in advance of the depar-

ture date, though most passport offices offer rush services for a very steep fee. Note, however, that "rushed" passports still take up to two weeks to arrive.

PASSPORT MAINTENANCE

Photocopy the page of your passport with your photo, as well as your visas, traveler's check serial numbers, and any other important documents. Carry one set of copies in a safe place, apart from the originals, and leave another set at home. Consulates also recommend that you carry an expired passport or an official copy of your birth certificate in a part of your baggage separate from other documents.

If you lose your passport, immediately notify the local police and the nearest embassy or consulate of your home government. To expedite its replacement, you must show ID and proof of citizenship; it also helps to know all information previously recorded in the passport. In some cases, a replacement may take weeks to process, and it may be valid only for a limited time. Any visas stamped in your old passport will be irretrievably lost. You must apply for a replacement visa from the US consulate abroad that issued the original.

VISAS AND WORK PERMITS

VISAS

US Citizens do not need a passport or visa to enter Puerto Rico, just proof of citizenship. As of August 2005, citizens of Canada, Bermuda, and countries participating in the US Visa Waiver Program (www.travel.state.gov for a list of these countries) can enter the Puerto Rico without a visa, provided they present a valid passport, are traveling only for business or pleasure, and are staying for less than 90 days. In addition, travelers under the Visa Waiver Program must provide proof of intent to leave (such as a return plane ticket) and complete an I-94 form (provided to travelers at their port of entry). If you lose your I-94 form, you must replace it through **US Citizenship and Immigration Services** (**USCIS**; ☎800-375-5283; http://uscis.gov). Travelers not from the US, Canada, Bermuda, or Visa Waiver Program countries must obtain a visa before traveling to Puerto Rico.

With the exception of US citizens, all travelers planning to spend longer than 90 days (180 days for Canadians) in Puerto Rico must receive a visa from a US embassy or consulate in their home country before traveling to the island (to locate a US embassy or consulate, visit http://usembassy.state.gov). Visas cost around $100 and usually allow business or pleasure travelers to spend from six months to a year in Puerto Rico. Visa extensions can sometimes be obtained by filing an I-539 form with the USCIS. Call the forms request line at ☎800-870-3676 for more details.

Double-check entrance requirements at the nearest embassy or consulate of the United States (listed under **US Consular Services Abroad,** <u>p. 8</u>) or at www.travel.state.gov for up-to-date info before departure.

WORK PERMITS

Admission as a visitor does not include the right to work, which is authorized only by a work permit. US citizens can work in Puerto Rico without any type of work permit or visa. If you are not a US Citizen, you need a work permit or "green card" to work in Puerto Rico. Normally you must have a job offer before you can obtain the permit. First, your potential employer in Puerto Rico must file an I-129 Petition for Non-immigrant Worker with the USCIS and receive a notice of approval. In order to obtain approval, your employer will usually have to demonstrate that you have skills that locals lack. Next, you must apply for a temporary worker visa by filing a DS-156 and submitting the approval form received by your employer to the US embassy or consulate in your home country. You must also provide a passport, photograph, and I-797 form. Temporary work visas cost around $100. Visit http://travel.state.gov/visa/temp/types/types_1271.html for more details. Obtaining a work visa may seem complex, but it's critical that you go through the proper channels—the alternative is potential deportation. Travelers who wish to work on a cruise ship must obtain a US C1-D visa from the nearest US consulate.

IDENTIFICATION

When you travel, always carry at least two forms of identification on your person, including a photo ID; a passport and a driver's license or birth certificate is usually an adequate combination. Never carry all of your IDs together; split them up in case of theft or loss, and keep photocopies of all of them in your luggage and at home.

STUDENT, TEACHER, AND YOUTH IDENTIFICATION

Puerto Rican businesses rarely offer student discounts, but the following cards may be useful for the emergency helpline and insurance benefits that they provide.

The **International Student Identity Card (ISIC),** the most widely accepted form of student ID, provides access to a 24hr. emergency helpline and insurance benefits for US cardholders (see **Insurance,** p. 20). Applicants must be full-time secondary or post-secondary school students at least 12 years of age. Because of the proliferation of fake ISICs, some services (particularly airlines) require additional proof of student identity. The **International Teacher Identity Card (ITIC)** offers teachers the same insurance coverage as the ISIC. For travelers who are under 26 years old but are not students, the **International Youth Travel Card (IYTC)** also offers many of the same benefits as the ISIC.

Each of these identity cards costs $22 or equivalent. ISICs and ITICs are valid until the new year unless purchased between September and December, in which case they are valid until the beginning of the following new year. Thus, a card purchased in March 2006 will be valid until December 31, 2006, while a card purchased in November 2006 will be valid until December 31, 2007. IYTCs are valid for one year from the date of issue. To learn more about ISICs, ITICs, and IYTCs, visit www.myisic.com. Many student travel agencies issue the cards; for a list of issuing agencies or more information, see the **International Student Travel Confederation (ISTC)** website (www.istc.org).

The **International Student Exchange Card (ISE Card)** is a similar identification card available to students, faculty, and youths ages 12 to 26. The card provides discounts, medical benefits, access to a 24hr. emergency helpline, and the ability to purchase student airfares. An ISE Card costs $25; call ☎800-255-8000 for more info, or visit www.isecard.com.

CUSTOMS

Upon entering Puerto Rico you must declare certain items from abroad and pay a duty on those articles if their value exceeds $10,000. Upon returning home, you must declare all articles acquired abroad and pay a duty on the value of articles in excess of your home country's allowance. In order to expedite your return, make a list of any valuables brought from home and register them with customs before traveling abroad, and be sure to keep receipts for all goods acquired abroad. If you are flying back through the US, your baggage will be inspected by the US Department of Agriculture. You are allowed to take avocado, papaya, coconut, and plantain through the US, but not mango, soursop, passion fruit, or a potted plant.

MONEY

CURRENCY AND EXCHANGE

The currency chart below is based on August 2005 exchange rates between local currency and Australian dollars (AUS$), Canadian dollars (CDN$), European Union euros (EUR€), New Zealand dollars (NZ$), and British pounds (UK£). Check the currency converter on websites like www.xe.com or www.bloomberg.com, or a large newspaper for the latest exchange rates.

CURRENCY		
AUS$1 = US$0.79	US$1 = AUS$1.28
CDN$1 = US$0.81	US$1 = CDN$1.23
EUR€1 = US$1.21	US$1 = EUR€0.83
NZ$1 = US$0.72	US$1 = NZ$1.39
UK£1 = US$1.82	US$1 = UK£0.55

As a general rule, it's cheaper to convert money in Puerto Rico than at home. While currency exchange will probably be available in your arrival airport, it's wise to bring enough foreign currency to last for the first 24 to 72 hours of your trip.

When changing money abroad, try to go only to banks that have at most a 5% margin between their buy and sell prices. In Puerto Rico, the ubiquitous **Banco Popular** usually offers competitive rates. Since you lose money with every transaction, **convert large sums**, but **no more than you'll need.** However, there is little need to convert foreign currency in Puerto Rico as traveler's checks and credit cards are widely accepted and ATMs are everywhere.

If you use traveler's checks or bills, carry some in small denominations (about $50) for times when you are forced to exchange money at disadvantageous rates, but bring a range of denominations since charges may be levied per check cashed. Store your money in a variety of forms; ideally, at any given time you will be carrying some cash, some traveler's checks, and an ATM and/or credit card.

TRAVELER'S CHECKS

Traveler's checks are one of the safest and least troublesome means of carrying funds. American Express and Visa are the most-recognized brands. Many banks and agencies sell them for a small commission. Check issuers provide refunds if the checks are lost or stolen, and many provide additional services, such as toll-free refund hotlines abroad, emergency message services, and assistance with lost and stolen credit cards or passports. Traveler's checks are readily accepted in most tourist areas of Puerto Rico, such as San Juan and other big cities. They are less useful in the rural areas and usually not accepted at small establishments. Ask about toll-free refund hotlines and the location of refund centers when purchasing checks, and always carry emergency cash.

American Express: Checks available with commission at select banks, at all AmEx offices, and online (www.americanexpress.com; US residents only). American Express cardholders can also purchase checks by phone (☎800-721-9768). Checks available in Australian, British, Canadian, European, Japanese, and US currencies, among others. American Express also offers the Travelers Cheque Card, a prepaid reloadable card. Cheques for Two can be signed by either of two people traveling together. For purchase locations or more information, contact AmEx's service centers: in Australia ☎800 688 022, in New Zealand 423 74 409, in the UK 0800 587 6023, in the US and Canada 800-221-7282; elsewhere, call the US collect at 1-801-964-6665.

Travelex: Thomas Cook MasterCard and Interpayment Visa traveler's checks available. For information about Thomas Cook MasterCard in Canada and the US call ☎800-223-

7373, in the UK 0800 622 101; elsewhere call the UK collect at +44 1733 318 950. For information about Interpayment Visa in the US and Canada call ☎800-732-1322, in the UK 0800 515 884; elsewhere call the UK collect at +44 1733 318 949. For more information, visit www.travelex.com.

Visa: Checks available (generally with commission) at banks worldwide. For the location of the nearest office, call the Visa Travelers Cheque Global Refund and Assistance Center: in the UK ☎0800 515 884, in the US 800-227-6811, elsewhere, call the UK collect at +44 2079 378 091. Checks available in British, Canadian, European, Japanese, and US currencies, among others. Visa also offers TravelMoney, a prepaid debit card that can be reloaded online or by phone. For more information on Visa travel services, see http://usa.visa.com/personal/using_visa/travel_with_visa.html.

CREDIT, DEBIT, AND ATM CARDS

Credit cards are widely accepted throughout Puerto Rico, although small establishments only accept cash. Major credit cards—**MasterCard** (including European counterparts **Euro Card** and **Access**) and **Visa** (including European counterpart **Carte Bleue**)—are the most prevalent and can be used to extract cash advances in dollars from associated banks and teller machines. **American Express** is slightly less prevalent and **Discover** and **Diner's Club** are much less common.

Where they are accepted, credit cards often offer superior exchange rates—up to 5% better than the retail rate used by banks and other currency exchange establishments. Credit cards may also offer services such as insurance or emergency help, and are sometimes required to reserve hotel rooms or rental cars.

The use of **ATM cards** is widespread in Puerto Rico. Depending on the system that your home bank uses, you can most likely access your personal bank account from abroad. ATMs get the same wholesale exchange rate as credit cards, but there is often a limit on the amount you can withdraw per day (usually around $500). There is typically also a surcharge of $1-5 per withdrawal.

Debit cards are as convenient as credit cards but have a more immediate impact on your funds. A debit card can be used wherever its associated credit card company (usually MasterCard or Visa) is accepted, yet the money is withdrawn directly from the holder's checking account. Debit cards often also function as ATM cards and can be used to withdraw cash from associated banks and ATMs throughout Puerto Rico. Ask your local bank about obtaining one.

The two major international money networks are **MasterCard/Maestro/Cirrus** (for ATM locations ☎800-424-7787 or www.mastercard.com) and **Visa/PLUS** (for ATM locations ☎800-843-7587 or www.visa.com). Most ATMs charge a transaction fee ($1-5) that is paid to the bank that owns the ATM.

GETTING MONEY FROM HOME

If you run out of money while traveling, the easiest and cheapest solution is to have someone back home make a deposit to your bank account. Failing that, consider one of the following options.

WIRING MONEY

It is possible to arrange a **bank money transfer,** which means asking a bank back home to wire money to a bank in Puerto Rico. This is the cheapest way to transfer cash, but it's also the slowest, usually taking several days or more. Note that some banks may only release your funds in local currency, potentially sticking you with a poor exchange rate; inquire about this in advance. Money transfer services like **Western Union** are faster and more convenient than bank transfers—but also much pricier. Western Union can be found in almost every **Pueblo** supermarket in Puerto Rico. To find locations worldwide, visit www.westernunion.com, or call in Puerto Rico ☎800-325-4045, in Australia 800 173 833, in Canada and the US 800-325-6000,

TOP TEN LIST

TOP 10 WAYS TO SAVE IN PUERTO RICO

Puerto Rico is one of the cheapest Caribbean vacation destinations. Here are some ways to sweeten the deal.

1. Buy food at grocery stores and open-air markets instead of eating at a restaurant. Many guesthouses and *paradores* have kitchenettes for cooking.

2. Camp. You can't beat $10-per-night accommodations in the heart of the Puerto Rican forest.

3. Be on the lookout for days when you can get into sights and museums free. In San Juan, this is pretty much every day.

4. Drink tap water. It's safe and the savings add up fast.

6. Take *públicos* or walk as much as possible. It may take some extra time, but the savings will let you extend your vacation.

7. Choose accommodations in less-touristed urban centers. Use them as a base to explore the surrounding area. Examples include Hatillo in the west and Fajardo in the east, just a short drive from popular attractions.

8. Find free Internet access in libraries and universities. Another option is to stay at hotels where free wireless is included.

9. Bring your own snorkel and dive equipment. It may take up precious space in your luggage, but rental prices are steep.

10. Build outdoors experiences into your itinerary. Entrance to most Puerto Rican reserves and public beaches is free.

in the UK 0800 833 833. To wire money using a credit card (Discover, MasterCard, Visa), call in Canada, the US and Puerto Rico ☎ 800-225-5227, in the UK 0800 833 833. Money transfer services are also available to **American Express** cardholders and at selected **Thomas Cook** offices.

COSTS

The cost of your trip will vary considerably, depending on where you go, how you travel, and where you stay. The most significant expenses will probably be your round-trip **airfare** to Puerto Rico (see **Getting to Puerto Rico: By Plane,** p. 24) **accommodations,** and **car rental.** Before you go, spend some time calculating a reasonable daily **budget.**

STAYING ON A BUDGET

Your budget in Puerto Rico will vary depending on whether you stay in a large city, like San Juan, or in rural areas where it is possible to camp. To give you a general idea, a bare-bones day in San Juan (sleeping in cheaper guesthouses, buying food at supermarkets) would cost around $55-65; a slightly more comfortable day (sleeping in guesthouses and the occasional budget hotel, eating one meal per day at a restaurant, going out at night) would cost $90-100; and for a luxurious day, the sky's the limit.

In rural areas, a bare-bones day (camping and buying food at supermarkets) would cost about $25-35; a more comfortable day (staying at guesthouses or vacation centers, eating one meal per day at a restaurant, and catching some nightlife) would cost $100-110; and for a luxurious day, you can spend just as much as you would in any major city. Don't forget to factor emergency reserve funds (at least $200) into your budget.

TIPS FOR SAVING MONEY

Some simpler ways include splitting accommodation and food costs with trustworthy fellow travelers, and buying food in supermarkets rather than eating out, and doing your laundry in the sink (unless you're explicitly prohibited from doing so). Choosing *paradores* that include meals, laundry, and Internet can be a good way to save. Museums often have certain days once a month or once a week when admission is free; plan accordingly. San Juan also has frequent **festivals** with free live music and entertainment.

Wise travelers **pay close attention to high season.** The high season in San Juan and the eastern islands is from November to May. Hotels in these areas typically raise their rates during this time. West coast hotels, on the other hand, charge more from June to October, the high season on that part of the island. The weather is pleasant year-round throughout

Puerto Rico, though, so choose your destination accordingly. Travelers willing to brave the risk of hurricane season will find that everything gets cheaper in September and October. Of course **camping** is by far the most budget-friendly option; Culebra and Vieques have exceptionally nice campgrounds.

For getting around quickly, bikes are the most economical option, but bike rental is often hard to find in Puerto Rico. Don't forget about walking; you can learn a lot about a city by seeing it on foot, and Old San Juan is very walkable. Budget travelers with flexible schedules and travel plans may consider traveling by **públicos**—informal public vans that carry passengers between town centers for about $1-5—instead of renting a car. *Público* drivers wait for passengers in public squares starting around 6am, but don't leave until their vans are full, making departure times somewhat irregular. Visitors who plan to travel by *público* should note that these vans do not normally take passengers outside of town centers to sights, beaches, or nature reserves.

With each bottle of water priced around $1, staying hydrated can add up quickly. Cut costs by filling **water bottles** in hotel sinks or potable water cisterns and requesting **agua de pluma** (tap water) in restaurants. Drinking at bars and clubs can also become expensive. It's cheaper to buy alcohol at a supermarket and make your own *cuba libres* before going out. That said, don't go overboard. You shouldn't pinch pennies at the expense of your health or a great travel experience.

TIPPING AND BARGAINING

In Puerto Rico, it is customary to tip waitstaff and cab drivers 15-20% (at your discretion). Tips are usually not included in restaurant bills. It is unnecessary to tip at most *cafeterías, panaderías,* and other small eateries where you pick up food at the counter. Porters expect at least $1 per bag. Though not obligatory, it is also nice to give *público* drivers a small tip; about 10% should suffice. **Bargaining** is generally frowned upon and fruitless in Puerto Rico, but it does not hurt to ask hotel or guest house owners if they can offer a discount—many will lower rates if they are not full, especially if you are staying that night.

TAXES

Get ready to shop; Puerto Rico has **no sales tax, restaurant tax,** or **Value-Added Tax.** There is a 9% **accommodations tax,** but unofficial guesthouses frequently do not charge a tax. *Let's Go* indicates if tax is included in most accommodations listings.

PACKING

Pack lightly: Lay out only what you absolutely need, then take half the clothes and twice the money. The Travelite FAQ (www.travelite.org) is a good resource for tips on traveling light. The online **Universal Packing List** (http://upl.codeq.info) will generate a customized list of suggested items based on your trip length, the expected climate, your planned activities, and other factors. If you plan to do a lot of hiking, also consult **The Great Outdoors,** p. 43. Some frequent travelers keep a bag packed with all the essentials: passport, money belt, hat, socks, etc. Then, when they decide to leave, they know they haven't forgotten anything.

   Luggage: If you plan to cover most of your itinerary on foot, a sturdy **frame backpack** is unbeatable. (For the basics on buying a pack, see p. 45.) Toting a **suitcase** or **trunk** is fine if you plan to live in one or two cities and explore from there, but not a great idea if you plan to move around frequently. In addition to your main piece of luggage, a **daypack** (a small backpack or courier bag) is useful.

   Clothing: No matter when you're traveling, it's a good idea to bring a rain jacket (Gore-Tex® is both waterproof and breathable), sturdy shoes or hiking boots, and thick socks.

Flip-flops or waterproof sandals are must-haves for grubby guesthouse showers, and extra socks are always a good idea. If you plan to visit religious or cultural sites, remember that you will need modest and respectful dress. In Puerto Rico's mild climate, jeans paired with a tank top (women) or light button-down shirt (men) are everyday dress. No matter how steamy the weather gets, Puerto Rican locals will not wear shorts—wearing them will mark you as a tourist. A long-sleeved t-shirt or a light jacket may come in handy for cooler nights in the mountains, though during the summer it's almost never needed. Puerto Ricans dress up to go out—women wear tight pants (usually jeans) with shirts that redefine scandalous and men wear slacks and button-down shirts. You may want to bring a nicer outfit for going out, along with a nice pair of shoes.

Sleepsack: Some *centros vacacionales* require that you provide your own linen. Save cash by making your own sleepsack: fold a full-size sheet in half the long way, then sew it closed along the long side and one of the short sides.

Toiletries: Condoms, deodorant, razors, tampons, and toothbrushes are often available, but it may be difficult to find your preferred brand; bring extras. Contact lenses are likely to be expensive and difficult to find, so bring enough extra pairs and solution for your entire trip. Also bring your glasses and a copy of your prescription in case you need emergency replacements.

Converters and Adapters: In Puerto Rico, as in the rest of the US, electricity is 110 volts AC. 220/240V electrical appliances will likely self-destruct when plugged into 110V current. Visit a hardware store for an **adapter** (which changes the shape of the plug) and a **converter** (which changes the voltage; $20). Don't make the mistake of using only an adapter, unless appliance instructions explicitly state otherwise.

First-Aid Kit: For a basic first-aid kit, pack bandages, a pain reliever, antibiotic cream, a thermometer, a multifunction pocketknife (make sure to put this in your checked luggage), tweezers, moleskin, decongestant, motion-sickness remedy, diarrhea or upset-stomach medication (Pepto Bismol® or Imodium®), an antihistamine, sunscreen, insect repellent, and burn ointment.

Film: Film and developing in Puerto Rico are slightly more expensive than elsewhere (about $5 to purchase a roll of 24 color exposures), so consider bringing along enough film for your entire trip and developing it at home. Less serious photographers may want to bring a disposable camera or two. Despite disclaimers, airport security X-rays can fog film, so buy a lead-lined pouch at a camera store or ask security to hand-inspect it. Always pack film in your carry-on luggage, since higher-intensity X-rays are used on checked luggage. If you don't want to bother with film, consider using a digital camera. Although it requires a steep initial investment, a digital camera means you never have to buy film again. Just be sure to bring along a large enough memory card and extra (or rechargeable) batteries. For more info on digital cameras, visit www.shortcourses.com/choosing/contents.htm.

Other Useful Items: For safety purposes, you should bring a **money belt** and a small **padlock.** Basic **outdoors equipment** (plastic water bottle, compass, waterproof matches, pocketknife, sunglasses, sunscreen, hat) may also prove useful. **Quick repairs** of torn garments can be done on the road with a needle and thread; also consider bringing electrical tape for patching tears. If you want to do laundry by hand, bring detergent, a small rubber ball to stop up the sink, and string for a makeshift clothes line. Other things you're liable to forget include: an umbrella, sealable **plastic bags** (for damp clothes, soap, food, shampoo, and other spillables), an **alarm clock,** safety pins, rubber bands, a flashlight, earplugs, garbage bags, and a small calculator. A **cell phone** can be a lifesaver (literally) on the road; see p. 37 for information on acquiring one that will work in Puerto Rico.

Important Documents: Don't forget your passport, traveler's checks, ATM and/or credit cards, adequate ID, and photocopies of all of the aforementioned in case these documents are lost or stolen. Also check that you have any of the following that might apply to you: a driver's license (p. 11); travel insurance forms (p. 16); ISIC (p. 5).

SAFETY AND HEALTH

GENERAL ADVICE

In any type of crisis situation, the most important thing to do is **stay calm.** Your country's embassy abroad (p. 9) is usually your best resource when things go wrong; registering with that embassy upon arrival in the country is often a good idea. The government offices listed in the **Travel Advisories** box (p. 18) can provide information on the services they offer their citizens in case of emergencies abroad. For information on transportation and driving safety, see **Getting Around,** p. 28.

LOCAL LAWS AND POLICE

In an emergency, the Puerto Rican police are good resource for help. To reach them or other emergency personnel anywhere in Puerto Rico, dial ☎**911.** In a few remote areas 911 may not work. If it does not, the Puerto Rico police department phone number is listed in every practical information section of this guide; it is generally the regional prefix plus 2020.

IN CASE OF EMERGENCY, DIAL ☎911.

DRUGS AND ALCOHOL

The legal drinking age in Puerto Rico is 18, although many establishments do not ask for identification. *Let's Go* does not recommend underage drinking. It is illegal to drive with a blood alcohol level over 0.8%. Some cities have specific rules about drinking in public. It is illegal to drink in the streets of Old San Juan and some other Puerto Rican cities. It is also illegal to drink out of a bottle on the street in many cities. Narcotics such as marijuana, heroin, and cocaine are highly illegal in Puerto Rico, and this prohibition is strictly enforced. If you carry prescription drugs while traveling, keep a copy of the prescription with you.

SPECIFIC CONCERNS

HURRICANES

Hurricane season in Puerto Rico officially runs from June 1 to November 30, but poses the most significant threat from August to October. On average, a hurricane brushes by San Juan every 3.85 years. Travelers should be aware that hurricanes sometimes cause serious flooding and take lives. In the event of a hurricane, travelers should stay tuned to radio and TV stations for warnings from the US National Weather Service (NWS). If instructed to remain where they are, travelers should wait out the storm indoors and away from windows. Travelers may be advised to stock up on cash, water, and canned food before a hurricane arrives. For more advice, visit http://www.nws.noaa.gov.

TERRORISM

In light of the September 11, 2001 terrorist attacks in the eastern US, the US government frequently puts the nation, and its territories, on an elevated terrorism alert. Puerto Rico has not had any attacks—or threats of attacks—but like the rest of the US the island has taken precautions. Monitor developments in the news and stay on top of any local, state, or federal terrorist warnings. The box on **travel advisories** lists offices to contact and webpages to visit to get the most updated list of your home country's government's advisories about travel.

 TRAVEL ADVISORIES. The following government offices provide travel information and advisories by telephone, by fax, or via the web:

Australian Department of Foreign Affairs and Trade: ☎ 1300 555 135; www.dfat.gov.au.

Canadian Department of Foreign Affairs and International Trade (DFAIT): Call ☎ 800-267-8376; www.dfait-maeci.gc.ca. Call for their free booklet, *Bon Voyage...But.*

New Zealand Ministry of Foreign Affairs: ☎ 044 398 000; www.mft.govt.nz/travel/index.html.

United Kingdom Foreign and Commonwealth Office: ☎ 020 7008 1500; www.fco.gov.uk.

PERSONAL SAFETY

EXPLORING AND TRAVELING

To avoid unwanted attention, try to blend in as much as possible. Respecting local customs (in some cases, dressing more conservatively than you would at home) may placate would-be hecklers. Familiarize yourself with your surroundings before setting out, and carry yourself with confidence. Check maps in shops and restaurants rather than on the street. If you are traveling alone, be sure someone at home knows your itinerary, and never admit that you're by yourself. When walking at night, stick to busy, well-lit streets and avoid dark alleyways. Some travelers find it helpful to look for children playing, women walking in the open, and other signs of an active community to in order gauge the safety of an area. If you ever feel uncomfortable, leave the area as quickly and directly as you can.

San Juan has its share of crime, but it's no less safe than other large metropolitan areas such as London or New York. Most incidents are limited to specific areas; travelers often feel most comfortable in Old San Juan, Condado, Ocean Park, and Isla Verde. It is best not to be out alone, especially at night, in the neighborhoods of Santurce, Hato Rey, and Río Piedras. Travelers should also take caution in the metropolitan areas of Ponce, Mayagüez, Arecibo, Fajardo, and Aguadilla. Unlike other major tourist destinations, Puerto Rico does not have a history of crime specifically targeting foreigners; the biggest problem is being in the wrong place at the wrong time.

There is no sure way to avoid all the threatening situations you may encounter while traveling, but a good **self-defense course** will give you concrete ways to react to unwanted advances. **Impact, Prepare, Model Mugging** can refer you to local self-defense courses in the US. Visit www.modelmugging.org for a list of nearby chapters. Workshops (2-4hr.) start at $50; full courses (20hr.) run US $350-500.

If you are using a **car,** learn local driving signals and wear a seatbelt. Children under 40 lbs. should ride only in specially-designed carseats, available for a small fee from most car rental agencies. Study route maps before you hit the road, and if you plan on spending a lot of time driving, consider bringing spare parts. If your car breaks down, wait for the police to assist you. For long drives in desolate areas, invest in a cellular phone and a roadside assistance program (p. 32). Park your vehicle in a garage or well-traveled area, and use a steering wheel locking device in larger cities. **Sleeping in your car** is one of the most dangerous (and often illegal) ways to get your rest. For info on the perils of **hitchhiking,** see p. 35.

POSSESSIONS AND VALUABLES

Never leave your belongings unattended; crime occurs in even the most demure-looking guesthouse or hotel. Always lock your hotel room. Carry your backpack in front of you where you can see it.

There are a few steps you can take to minimize the financial risk associated with traveling. First, **bring as little with you as possible.** Second, buy a few combination **padlocks** to secure your belongings either in your pack or in a hotel. Third, **carry as little cash as possible.** Keep your traveler's checks and ATM/credit cards in a **money belt**—not a "fanny pack"—along with your passport and ID cards. Fourth, **keep a small cash reserve separate from your primary stash.** This should be about $50 (US$ are best) sewn into or stored in the depths of your pack, along with your traveler's check numbers and important photocopies.

In large cities **con artists** often work in groups and may involve children. Beware of certain classics: sob stories that require money, rolls of bills "found" on the street, mustard spilled (or saliva spit) onto your shoulder to distract you while they snatch your bag. **Never let your passport and your bags out of your sight.** Beware of **pickpockets** in city crowds, especially on public transportation. Also, be alert in public telephone booths: If you must say your calling card number, do so very quietly; if you punch it in, make sure no one can look over your shoulder.

Unfortunately, petty thieves in Puerto Rico have learned that travelers like to swim in the ocean and leave all of their valuables on the beach. Do not take anything valuable to the beach. This includes wallets, cell phones, cash, and jewelry. If you are traveling with a group, have one person stay on the beach and watch your stuff while the others swim. If you are traveling alone, the best thing to do is to put your hotel/car key in a waterproof bag, keep it with you when you enter the water, and leave absolutely nothing valuable on the beach. Another option is to ask a nearby beachgoer to watch your stuff while you swim, but this requires a bit of trust and a lot of luck. Less-frequented beaches have become targets for carjackings, especially along the north coast. When parking at the beach, do not leave anything in sight in your car or store valuables in your trunk.

If you will be traveling with electronic devices, such as a laptop computer or a PDA, check whether your homeowner's insurance covers loss, theft, or damage when you travel. If not, you might consider purchasing a low-cost separate insurance policy. **Safeware** (☎ 800-800-1492; www.safeware.com) specializes in covering computers and charges $90 for 90-day international travel coverage up to $4000.

PRE-DEPARTURE HEALTH

In your **passport,** write the names of any people you wish to be contacted in case of a medical emergency, and list any allergies or medical conditions. Matching a prescription to a foreign equivalent is not always easy or safe, so if you take prescription drugs, consider carrying up-to-date, legible prescriptions or a statement from your doctor stating the medication's trade name, manufacturer, chemical name, and dosage. While traveling, be sure to keep all medication with you in your carry-on luggage. For tips on packing a **first-aid kit** and other health essentials, see p. 15.

IMMUNIZATIONS AND PRECAUTIONS

There are no required inoculations for entry into Puerto Rico, but travelers over two years old should make sure that the following vaccines are up to date: MMR (for measles, mumps, and rubella); DTaP or Td (for diphtheria, tetanus, and pertussis); IPV (for polio); Hib (for *haemophilus* influenza B); and HepB (for Hepatitis B). Visitors from certain African nations require an International Vaccination Certificate for Yellow Fever. For recommendations on immunizations and prophylaxis, consult the CDC (see below) in the US or the equivalent in your home country, and check with a doctor for guidance.

INSURANCE

Travel insurance covers four basic areas: medical/health problems, property loss, trip cancellation/interruption, and emergency evacuation. Though regular insurance policies may well extend to travel-related accidents, you might consider purchasing separate travel insurance if the cost of potential trip cancellation, interruption, or emergency medical evacuation is greater than you can absorb. Prices for travel insurance purchased separately generally run about $50 per week for full coverage, while trip cancellation/interruption may be purchased separately at a rate of $3-5 per day depending on length of stay.

Medical insurance (especially university policies) often covers costs incurred abroad; check with your provider. **Canadian** provincial health insurance plans increasingly do not cover foreign travel; check with the provincial Ministry of Health or Health Plan Headquarters for details. **Homeowners' insurance** (or your family's coverage) often covers theft during travel and loss of travel documents (passport, plane ticket, railpass, etc.) up to $500.

ISIC and **ITIC** (p. 11) provide basic insurance to US cardholders, including $100 per day of in-hospital sickness for up to 100 days and $10,000 of accident-related medical reimbursement (see www.isicus.com for details). Cardholders have access to a toll-free 24hr. helpline for medical, legal, and financial emergencies overseas. **American Express** (☎800-338-1670) grants most cardholders automatic collision and theft car rental insurance on rentals made with the card.

USEFUL ORGANIZATIONS AND PUBLICATIONS

The US **Centers for Disease Control and Prevention** (**CDC;** ☎877-FYI-TRIP/877-394-8747; www.cdc.gov/travel) maintains an international travelers' hotline and an informative website. The CDC's comprehensive booklet *Health Information for International Travel* (The Yellow Book), a biannual rundown of disease, immunization, and general health advice, is free online or $29-40 via the Public Health Foundation (☎877-252-1200). Consult the appropriate government agency of your home country for consular information sheets on health, entry requirements, and other issues for various countries (see the listings in the box on **Travel Advisories,** p. 18). For quick information on health and other travel warnings, call the **Overseas Citizens Services** (M-F 8am-8pm ☎888-407-4747, outside the US 202-501-4444), or contact a passport agency, embassy, or consulate abroad. For information on medical evacuation services and travel insurance firms, see the US government's website at http://travel.state.gov/travel/abroad_health.html or the **British Foreign and Commonwealth Office** (www.fco.gov.uk). For general health info, contact the **American Red Cross** (☎800-564-1234; www.redcross.org).

STAYING HEALTHY

Common sense is the simplest prescription for good health while you travel. Drink lots of fluids to prevent dehydration and constipation, and wear sturdy, broken-in shoes and clean socks. You may want to bring a compact **first aid kit** (p. 16) and allergy sufferers should obtain a full supply of any necessary medication before the trip. Always carry medications in carry-on luggage.

ONCE IN PUERTO RICO

ENVIRONMENTAL HAZARDS

To avoid **heat exhaustion and dehydration,** take extra precautions when hiking in Puerto Rico's central mountains and visiting the island's many beaches. Heat exhaustion leads to nausea, excessive thirst, headaches, and dizziness. Avoid it by drinking plenty of fluids, eating salty foods (e.g., crackers), abstaining from dehydrating beverages (e.g., alcohol and caffeinated beverages), and always wearing sunscreen. Continuous heat stress can eventually lead to heatstroke, characterized by a rising temperature, severe headache, delirium, and cessation of sweating. Victims should be cooled off with wet towels and taken to a doctor. Visitors should be especially careful to avoid **sunburn,** a common problem for travelers in Puerto Rico. Always wear sunscreen (SPF 30 is good) when spending excessive amounts of time outdoors. If you get sunburned, drink more fluids than usual and apply an aloe-based lotion. Severe sunburns can lead to sun poisoning, a condition that affects the entire body, causing fever, chills, nausea, and vomiting. Sun poisoning should always be treated by a doctor.

INSECT-BORNE DISEASES

Many diseases are transmitted by insects—mainly mosquitoes, fleas, ticks, and lice. Be aware of insects in wet or forested areas, especially while hiking and camping; wear long pants and long sleeves, tuck your pants into your socks, and use a mosquito net. Use insect repellents such as DEET and soak or spray your gear with permethrin (licensed in the US only for use on clothing). **Mosquitoes**—responsible for diseases including **dengue fever**—can be particularly dangerous in wet, swampy, or wooded areas, which can be found in rural areas of Puerto Rico. Dengue fever is transmitted by *Aedes* mosquitoes, which bite during the day rather than at night. The incubation period is 3-14 days, usually 4-7 days. Early symptoms include a high fever, severe headaches, swollen lymph nodes, and muscle aches. Many patients also suffer from nausea, vomiting, and a pink rash. If you experience these symptoms, see a doctor immediately, drink plenty of liquids, and take fever-reducing medication such as acetaminophen (Tylenol). *Never take aspirin to treat dengue fever.* There is no vaccine available for dengue fever. **Ticks**—which can carry Lyme and other diseases—can be particularly bad in rural and forested regions, such as the central mountains and national forests of Puerto Rico.

FOOD- AND WATER-BORNE DISEASES

Prevention is the best cure: be sure that your food is properly cooked and the water you drink is clean. Watch out for food from markets or street vendors that may have been cooked in unhygienic conditions. Other culprits are raw shellfish, unpasteurized milk, and sauces containing raw eggs. Always wash your hands before eating or bring a quick-drying, purifying liquid hand cleaner.

> **Traveler's diarrhea:** Results from drinking fecally-contaminated water or eating uncooked and contaminated foods. Symptoms include nausea, bloating, and urgency. Try quick-energy, non-sugary foods with protein and carbohydrates to keep your strength up. Over-the-counter anti-diarrheals (e.g., Imodium) may counteract the problems. The most dangerous side effect is dehydration; drink 8 oz. of water with ½ tsp. of sugar or honey and a pinch of salt, try uncaffeinated soft drinks, or eat salted crackers. If you

develop a fever or your symptoms don't go away after 4-5 days, consult a doctor. Consult a doctor immediately for treatment of diarrhea in children.

Dysentery: Results from a serious intestinal infection caused by certain bacteria in contaminated food or water. The most common type is bacillary dysentery. Symptoms include bloody diarrhea (sometimes mixed with mucus), fever, and abdominal pain and tenderness. Bacillary dysentery generally only lasts a week, but it is highly contagious. Amoebic dysentery, which develops more slowly, is a more serious disease and may cause long-term damage if left untreated. A stool test can determine which kind you have; seek medical help immediately. Dysentery can be treated with the drugs norfloxacin or ciprofloxacin (commonly known as Cipro). If you are traveling in high-risk (especially rural) regions, consider obtaining a prescription before you leave home. Dehydration can be a problem; be sure to drink plenty of water or eat salted crackers.

Cholera: An intestinal disease caused by a bacteria in contaminated food. Symptoms include severe diarrhea, dehydration, vomiting, and muscle cramps. See a doctor immediately; if left untreated, it may be deadly within hours. Antibiotics are available, but the most important treatment is rehydration. No vaccine is available in the US.

Hepatitis A: A viral infection of the liver acquired primarily through contaminated water, including through shellfish from contaminated water. Symptoms include fatigue, fever, loss of appetite, nausea, dark urine, jaundice, vomiting, aches and pains, and light stools. The risk is highest in rural areas and the countryside, but it is also present in urban areas. Ask your doctor about the Hepatitis A vaccine (Havrix or Vaqta) or an injection of immune globulin (IG; formerly called gamma globulin).

Giardiasis: Transmitted through parasites (microbes, tapeworms, etc. in contaminated water and food) and acquired by drinking untreated water from streams or lakes. Symptoms include diarrhea, abdominal cramps, bloating, fatigue, weight loss, and nausea. If untreated it can lead to severe dehydration. Giardiasis occurs worldwide.

Schistosomiasis: Also known as bilharzia; a parasitic disease caused when the larvae of flatworm penetrate unbroken skin. Symptoms include an itchy localized rash, followed in 4-6 weeks by fever, fatigue, painful urination, diarrhea, loss of appetite, and night sweats. To avoid it, try not to swim in fresh water; if exposed to untreated water, rub the area vigorously with a towel and apply rubbing alcohol.

OTHER INFECTIOUS DISEASES

Rabies: Transmitted through the saliva of infected animals; fatal if untreated. By the time symptoms (thirst and muscle spasms) appear, the disease is in its terminal stage. If you are bitten, wash the wound thoroughly, seek immediate medical care, and try to have the animal located. A rabies vaccine, which consists of 3 shots given over a 21-day period, is available and recommended for developing world travel, but is only semi-effective. Rabies is found all over the world, and in Puerto Rico is often transmitted through stray dogs and mongeese.

Hepatitis B: A viral infection of the liver transmitted via blood or other bodily fluids. Symptoms, which may not surface until years after infection, include jaundice, loss of appetite, fever, and joint pain. It is transmitted through activities like unprotected sex, injections of illegal drugs, and unprotected health work. A 3-shot vaccination sequence is recommended for health-care workers, sexually-active travelers, and anyone planning to seek medical treatment abroad; it must begin 6 months before traveling.

AIDS and HIV: For detailed information on Acquired Immune Deficiency Syndrome (AIDS) in Puerto Rico, call the US Centers for Disease Control's 24hr. hotline at ☎800-342-2437, or contact the Joint United Nations Programme on HIV/AIDS (UNAIDS), 20 Ave. Appia, CH-1211 Geneva 27, Switzerland (☎+41 22 791 3666; fax 22 791 4187).

Sexually transmitted diseases (STDs): Gonorrhea, chlamydia, genital warts, syphilis, herpes, and other STDs are easier to catch than HIV and can be just as deadly. **Hepatitis B** and **C** can also be transmitted sexually. Though condoms may protect you from some STDs, oral or even tactile contact can lead to transmission. If you think you may have contracted an STD, see a doctor immediately.

OTHER HEALTH CONCERNS

MEDICAL CARE ON THE ROAD

Puerto Rico has one of the best medical systems in the Caribbean. Every municipal center has some kind of health clinic or hospital, and all large cities have major hospitals with 24hr. emergency rooms. Travelers who have a minor medical problem in Puerto Rico can visit any hospital **clinic** and wait to see a doctor. Most hospitals have English-speaking doctors; smaller hospitals that do not should be able to find a translator. In an emergency, dial ☎ **911** from any phone and an operator will send out paramedics, a fire brigade, or the police as needed. Alternatively, go directly to the nearest emergency room for immediate service. Puerto Rican hospitals take many American medical insurance plans, but other travelers will have to pay for medical service. Almost all cities and towns have standard pharmacies. Culebra has much more limited medical services and in a real emergency you will have to be evacuated to Fajardo. Isla Mona has no medical services and is very remote.

If you are concerned about obtaining medical assistance while traveling, you may wish to employ special support services. The *MedPass* from **GlobalCare, Inc.,** 6875 Shiloh Rd. E., Alpharetta, GA 30005, USA (☎ 800-860-1111; fax 678-341-1800; www.globalcare.net), provides 24hr. international medical assistance, support, and medical evacuation resources. The **International Association for Medical Assistance to Travelers** (**IAMAT;** US ☎ 716-754-4883, Canada 519-836-0102; www.iamat.org) has free membership, lists English-speaking doctors worldwide, and offers detailed info on immunization requirements and sanitation. If your regular **insurance** policy does not cover travel abroad, you may wish to purchase additional coverage (see **Insurance,** p. 20).

Those with medical conditions (such as diabetes, allergies to antibiotics, epilepsy, or heart conditions) may want to obtain a **MedicAlert** membership (first year $35, annually thereafter $20), which includes a stainless steel ID tag, among other benefits, like a 24hr. collect-call number. Contact the MedicAlert Foundation, 2323 Colorado Ave., Turlock, CA 95382, USA (☎ 888-633-4298, outside US ☎ 209-668-3333; www.medicalert.org).

DRUG NAME IN ENGLISH	SPANISH TRANSLATION
acetaminophen	acetaminofén
antihistamine	antihistimíno
aspirin	aspirina
antibiotic ointment	crema antibiotica
ibuprofen	ibuprofén
penicillin	penicilina

WOMEN'S HEALTH

Women traveling in unsanitary conditions are vulnerable to **urinary tract (including bladder and kidney) infections.** Over-the-counter medicines can sometimes alleviate symptoms, but if they persist, see a doctor. **Vaginal yeast infections** may flare up in hot and humid climates. Wearing loosely fitting trousers or a skirt and cotton underwear will help, as will remedies like Monostat or Gynelotrimin. Bring supplies from home if you are prone to infection, as they may be difficult to find on the road. **Tampons, pads,** and reliable **contraceptive devices** are widely available in Puerto Rico, though your favorite brand may not be stocked—bring extras of anything you can't live without. **Abortion** is legal in Puerto Rico. Planned Parenthood's affiliate in Puerto Rico is PRO-FAMILIA, Urbanización El Vedado, Calle Padre Las Casas 117, Hato Rey, San Juan, PR 00919 (☎ 787-765-7373 or 787-767-6960).

GETTING TO PUERTO RICO

BY PLANE

When it comes to airfare, a little effort can save you a bundle. If your plans are flexible enough to deal with the restrictions, courier fares are the cheapest. Tickets bought from consolidators and standby seating are also good deals, but last-minute specials, airfare wars, and charter flights often beat these fares. The key is to hunt around, to be flexible, and to ask persistently about discounts. Students, seniors, and those under 26 should never pay full price for a ticket.

AIRFARES

Puerto Rico is the airline hub of the Caribbean and flights are relatively inexpensive year-round, especially from the US East Coast. Only San Juan's Luis Muñoz Marín International Airport has flights to destinations outside of the US. Most travelers will end up connecting somewhere on the US East Coast, though **Iberia** also offers direct flights to Madrid.

Airfares to Puerto Rico peak between December and April; holidays are also expensive. The cheapest times to travel are September and October, during the height of hurricane season. Midweek (M-Th morning) round-trip flights run $40-50 cheaper than weekend flights, but they are generally more crowded and less likely to permit frequent-flier upgrades. Not fixing a return date ("open return") or arriving in and departing from different cities ("open-jaw") can be pricier than round-trip flights. Patching one-way flights together is the most expensive way to travel.

If Puerto Rico is only one stop on a more extensive globe-hop, consider a round-the-world (RTW) ticket. Tickets usually include at least five stops and are valid for about a year; prices range $1200-5000. Try **Northwest Airlines/KLM** (☎ 800-225-2525; www.nwa.com) or **Star Alliance,** a consortium of 16 airlines including United Airlines (www.staralliance.com).

Fares for roundtrip flights to San Juan from the US or Canadian east coast cost $250-600 in the high season (Nov.-May) and $250-500 in the low season (June-Oct.); from the US or Canadian west coast $700-900/600-800; from the UK, UK550-650₤/UK500-550₤; from Australia AUS$3000-3400/AUS$2300-2600; from New Zealand NZ$2800-3300/NZ$2600-2800.

BUDGET AND STUDENT TRAVEL AGENCIES

While agents specializing in flights to Puerto Rico can make your life easy and help you save, they may not find you the lowest possible fare—they get paid on commission. Travelers holding **ISICs** and **IYTCs** (p. 11) qualify for discounts from student travel agencies. Most flights from budget agencies are on major airlines, but in peak season some may sell seats on less reliable chartered aircraft.

CTS Travel, 30 Rathbone Pl., London W1T 1GQ, UK (☎020 7290 0630). A British student travel agency with offices in 39 countries including the US, Empire State Building, 350 Fifth Ave., Ste. 7813, New York, NY, USA 10118 (☎877-287-6665).

STA Travel, 5900 Wilshire Blvd., Ste. 900, Los Angeles, CA 90036, USA (24hr. reservations and info ☎800-781-4040; www.sta-travel.com). A student and youth travel organization with over 150 offices worldwide (check their website for a listing of all their offices), including US offices in Boston, Chicago, Los Angeles, New York, Seattle, San Francisco, and Washington, D.C. Ticket booking, travel insurance, railpasses, and more. Walk-in offices are located throughout Australia (☎03 9349 4344), New Zealand (☎09 309 9723), and the UK (☎08701 600 599).

Travel CUTS (Canadian Universities Travel Services Limited), 187 College St., Toronto, ON M5T 1P7, Canada (☎800-592-2887; www.travelcuts.com). Offices across Canada and the US including Los Angeles, New York, Seattle, and San Francisco.

USIT, 19-21 Aston Quay, Dublin 2, Ireland (☎01 602 1904; www.usit.ie). Ireland's leading student/budget travel agency has 20 offices throughout Northern Ireland and the Republic of Ireland. Offers programs to work, study, and volunteer worldwide.

✈ **FLIGHT PLANNING ON THE INTERNET.** The Internet may be the budget traveler's dream when it comes to finding and booking bargain fares, but the array of options can be overwhelming. Many airline sites offer special last-minute deals on the Web. The are no good websites with a consolidated list of airlines that fly to Puerto Rico, but check out the following websites. **STA** (www.sta-travel.com) and **StudentUniverse** (www.studentuniverse.com) provide quotes on student tickets, while **Orbitz** (www.orbitz.com), **Expedia** (www.expedia.com), and **Travelocity** (www.travelocity.com) offer full travel services. **Priceline** (www.priceline.com) lets you specify a price, and obligates you to buy any ticket that meets or beats it; **Hotwire** (www.hotwire.com) offers bargain fares, but won't reveal the airline or flight times until you buy. Other sites that compile deals include www.bestfares.com, www.flights.com, www.lowestfare.com, www.onetravel.com, and www.travelzoo.com. Increasingly, there are online tools available to help sift through multiple offers; **SideStep** (www.sidestep.com; download required) and **Booking Buddy** (www.bookingbuddy.com) let you enter your trip information once and search multiple sites. An indispensable resource on the Internet is the **Air Traveler's Handbook** (www.faqs.org/faqs/travel/air/handbook), a comprehensive listing of links to everything you need to know before you board a plane.

COMMERCIAL AIRLINES

The commercial airlines' lowest regular offer is the **APEX** (Advance Purchase Excursion) fare, which provides confirmed reservations and allows "open-jaw" tickets. Generally, reservations must be made seven to 21 days ahead of departure, with a seven- to 14-day minimum-stay and up to 90-day maximum-stay restrictions. These fares carry hefty cancellation and change penalties (fees rise in summer). Book peak-season APEX fares early. Use **Expedia** (www.expedia.com) or **Travelocity** (www.travelocity.com) to get an idea of the lowest published fares, then use the resources outlined here to try and beat those fares. Low-season fares should be appreciably cheaper than the **high season** (Nov.-May) ones listed here.

Basic round-trip fares from the US to Puerto Rico range from roughly $250-800: to San Juan, $250-600; to Mayagüez, $600-1200; to Aguadilla $200-600; to Ponce, $600-800. From the UK and Ireland, fares range from roughly UK£500-650. From Australia and New Zealand, they are roughly AUS$2300-3400; from New Zealand NZ$2600-3300.

Note that flights to cities other than San Juan occur on an intermittent schedule. Standard commercial carriers like American and United will probably offer the most convenient flights, but they may not be the cheapest, unless you manage to grab a special promotion or airfare war ticket. You will probably find flying "discount" airlines like Jet Blue Airlines, Song Airlines, or Spirit Airlines, a better deal, if any of their limited departure points is convenient for you.

Air Flamenco (☎724-6464) flies from Isla Grande Airport on demand only to Culebra and sporadically to Fajardo and Vieques.

Air St. Thomas (☎800-522-3084) flies to St. Barths, St. Thomas, and Virgin Gorda.

Air Sunshine (from Puerto Rico ☎888-879-8900, from North America ☎800-327-8900; www.airsunshine.com) flies to St. Croix, St. Thomas, Tortola, and Vieques.

American Airlines (☎800-433-7300; www.aa.com), is the largest airline flying out of San Juan. Flights go throughout North America. Also to Scotland, England, and New Zealand and Australia. In the Caribbean to Mayagüez, Santo Domingo, Tortola, St. Thomas, St. Maarten, St. Lucia, St. Kitts, and St. Croix.

ATA (☎800-225-2995; www.ata.com) has direct flights to Chicago and Orlando, with North American connections.

Cape Air (☎800-352-0714; www.flycapeair.com) flies to Mayagüez, Ponce, St. Croix, St. Thomas, Tortola, Vieques.

Continental Airlines (☎800-523-3273; www.continental.com) has direct flights to Houston and Newark, where North American, UK, and Ireland connections can be made.

Copa (☎800-359-2672; www.copaair.com) flies to a variety of destinations in Central and South America.

Delta Airlines (☎800-221-1212; www.delta.com) flies direct to Atlanta, New York, and Orlando, where connections to North America and New Zealand can be made. Connections to Europe are offered on a seasonal basis.

Iberia (☎800-772-4642; www.iberia.com) has direct flights to Madrid with connections to cities throughout Europe.

Jet Blue Airlines (☎800-538-2583; www.jetblue.com). This budget airline offers great deals to major cities across the US.

Liat Airline (from the Caribbean ☎888-844-5428, from outside the Caribbean 868-624-4727; www.liatairline.com). Service to various Caribbean isles.

M&N Airlines (☎722-5980) flies from Isla Grande Airport to Vieques.

Northwest Airlines (☎800-225-2525; www.nwa.com) flies to direct to Newark, with North American and British connections.

Song Airlines (☎800-359-7664; www.flysong.com) is Delta's budget spin-off. From San Juan flights go to Boston, JFK in New York, and Orlando, with US connections.

Spirit Airlines (☎800-772-7117; www.spiritair.com). This budget airline flies directly to Fort Lauderdale and Orlando, with US connections.

Sun Country Airlines (☎ 800-359-6786; www.suncountry.com) flies directly to Minneapolis/St. Paul, with other US connections.

United Airlines (☎ 800-864-8331; www.ual.com) flies direct to Chicago and Philadelphia, with connections to the US, Australia, Europe, and New Zealand.

US Airways (☎ 800-428-4322; www.usair.com) flies to Newark, New York and Philadelphia with connections to the US, Australia, Europe, and New Zealand.

Vieques Air Link (☎ 888-901-9247 or 741-8331) flies to Vieques from San Juan.

STANDBY FLIGHTS

Traveling standby requires considerable flexibility in arrival and departure dates and cities. Companies dealing in standby flights sell vouchers rather than tickets, along with the promise to get you to your destination (or near your destination) within a certain window of time (typically 1-5 days). You call in before your specific window of time to hear your flight options and the probability that you will be able to board each flight. You can then decide which flights you want to try to make, show up at the appropriate airport at the appropriate time, present your voucher, and board if space is available. Vouchers can usually be bought for both one-way and round-trip travel. You may receive a monetary refund only if every available flight within your date range is full; if you opt not to take an available (but perhaps less convenient) flight, you can only get credit toward future travel. Carefully read agreements with any company offering standby flights as tricky fine print can leave you in the lurch. It is difficult to receive refunds, and clients' vouchers will not be honored when an airline fails to receive payment in time.

TICKET CONSOLIDATORS

Ticket consolidators, or **"bucket shops,"** buy unsold tickets in bulk from commercial airlines and sell them at discounted rates. The best place to look is in the Sunday travel section of any major newspaper (such as *The New York Times*), where many bucket shops place tiny ads. Call quickly, as availability is typically extremely limited. Not all bucket shops are reliable, so insist on a receipt that gives full details of restrictions, refunds, and tickets, and pay by credit card (in spite of the 2-5% fee) so you can stop payment if you never receive your tickets. Other consolidators worth trying are **Rebel** (☎ 800-732-3588; www.rebeltours.com) and **CheapTickets** (www.cheaptickets.com). More consolidators on the web include **Flights.com** (www.flights.com) and **TravelHUB** (www.travelhub.com). Keep in mind that these are just suggestions to get you started in your research; *Let's Go* does not endorse any of these agencies. As always, research companies before you hand over your credit card number. For more info, see www.travel-library.com/air-travel/consolidators.html. To check on a company's service record in the US, contact the Better Business Bureau (☎ 703-276-0100; www.bbb.org).

CHARTER FLIGHTS

Charters are flights a tour operator contracts with an airline to fly extra loads of passengers during peak season. Charter flights fly less frequently than major airlines, make refunds particularly difficult, and are almost always fully booked. Schedules and itineraries may also change or be canceled at the last moment (as late as 48hr. before the trip, and without a full refund), and check-in, boarding, and baggage claim are often much slower. However, these flights can also be cheaper. Discount clubs and fare brokers offer members savings on last-minute charter and tour deals. Study contracts closely; you don't want to end up with an unwanted overnight layover.

BY BOAT

FERRIES

Unfortunately no public boats make the trip between Puerto Rico and the Virgin Islands. However, there is a private ferry between Mayagüez, Puerto Rico and **Santo Domingo, Dominican Republic.** For more information see **Mayagüez**, p. 254.

CRUISE SHIPS

Every year hundreds of cruise ships drop off travelers in San Juan bay to spend the day wandering the streets of Old San Juan. Cruises generally depart from a major port (New York, Miami, Fort Lauderdale) and spend four to seven days traveling throughout the Caribbean. Some cruise ships depart from European ports to head to the Caribbean, but these are much more expensive. Nights, and some days, are spent onboard the ship, while most days are spent at various destination islands.

Despite popular conception, vacationing by cruise ship is no longer reserved for the rich and famous. During hurricane season (June-Oct.), a seven-night cruise can be as cheap as $200 per person. Though there are fewer ships to choose from, they are also much less expensive. Also, there is always the possibility that a hurricane will delay or ruin your cruise. All of the major online travel agents (www.expedia.com, www.orbitz.com, www.travelocity.com) offer highly discounted cruise prices (4-night cruises $200-800, 7-night cruises $300-1000). The individual cruise ship sites list regular fares with the occasional super special thrown in. Typically a cruise price includes accommodations, onboard meals and entertainment, and port taxes. However, travelers have to pay for their own transportation to the port of departure, meals and entertainment in the port city, casinos, gratuities, and alcoholic beverages. Price also varies with the type of accommodation: a suite or a cabin with a window is much more expensive than an interior cabin.

Carnival (www.carnival.com) and **Royal Caribbean** (www.rccl.com) use San Juan as a home port year-round. **Princess** (www.princess.com) uses San Juan as a home port only during the high season. The other major cruise lines that stop in San Juan include: **Celebrity** (www.celebrity.com), **Costa Cruise** (www.costacruise.com), **Cunard** (www.cunard.com), **Holland America** (www.hollandamerica.com), **Norwegian Cruise Line** (www.ncl.com), **P&O Cruises** (www.pocruises.com), **Radisson Seven Seas Cruises** (www.rssc.com), **Seabourn** (www.seabourn.com), **Silversea** (www.silversea.com), and **Windstar Cruises** (www.windstarcruises.com). The following websites also sell discounted cruises: www.bestpricecruises.com, www.1-800-cruises.com, www.cruisehotfares.com, www.beatanycruiseprice.com, www.caribbean-online.com, and www.acruise2go.com.

GETTING AROUND PUERTO RICO

BY PLANE

Most of Puerto Rico's internal flights connect San Juan, Fajardo, Culebra, and Vieques. All of the airlines flying to the Spanish Virgin Islands use tiny planes and

✈ **ONE-WAY TICKET TO PARADISE.** There are several options for getting to the offshore islands of Vieques and Culebra. The fastest route is to fly directly from San Juan's Luis Muñoz Marín International Airport, but this is also the most expensive ($75 one-way). Slightly cheaper is to fly from Isla Grande airport, just outside Puerta de Tierra ($45 one-way). Larger groups may find it convenient to take a taxi from San Juan to Fajardo ($65 for four people), then either fly to an island ($35-40) or take the ferry ($2-2.25). By far the most economical option is to take a *público* from Río Piedras to Fajardo ($3.50), then hop on the ferry. Allow at least 4hr. for the ride from Río Piedras to Fajardo. Ask the driver to take you all the way to the *la lancha* (the dock).

charge comparable rates. Note that flying into San Juan's international airport is significantly more expensive than flying into San Juan Isla Grande Airport. For information about flights see **San Juan** (p. 93), **Fajardo** (p. 164), **Culebra** (p. 189), **Vieques** (p. 173), **Mayagüez** (p. 254), or **Ponce** (p. 203). Unless you're in a big hurry, it's much more economical to rent a car or take a *público* than it is to fly.

BY PÚBLICO

There is no island-wide bus or train service. Instead, Puerto Ricans travel on *carros públicos* (also called *guaguas públicas*), private vehicles that transport groups of people between city centers. It is possible, albeit difficult, to travel to many cities using *públicos* alone, as long as you get used to the system. Be prepared to spend several hours each day waiting for a bus to your destination city and do not plan on visiting sights or parks outside of city centers.

On the plus side, *públicos* are cheap; the longest ride shouldn't cost more than $10. On the negative side, they are extremely slow, they have no schedule, and vehicles have absolutely no quality standards. Generally *públicos* wait either by a town's central plaza or in a *público* terminal starting early in the morning, then leave when they are full. This means that travelers have to wake up at the crack of dawn, then sit in a stuffy van waiting for enough people to show up so they get to leave. Drivers usually leave for the day when passengers stop showing up, but this time varies, so if you come after 10am all the vehicles may be gone. The system is time-consuming and frustrating but relatively comprehensive. *Públicos* leave from almost every municipal center and travel to adjacent municipalities and smaller *barrios* within the municipality. The destination of the vehicle is usually written on the front of the windshield. For a higher price, most *público* drivers will act as taxi drivers and take you wherever you want to go, but beware that if a *público* drops you off at the beach, you may end up stranded. It is also possible to flag down a *público* mid-route, especially along Hwy. 3 (*públicos* traveling between San Juan and Fajardo) and Hwy. 2 (*públicos* traveling between San Juan and Arecibo). The best strategy is to wait at one of the big cement benches on the side of the road. It is polite to tip a *público* driver at least 10% per person and more if you have bags.

Let's Go lists *público* routes in the transportation section of each town, but information changes frequently so it's a good idea to stop by the *público* station the night before you leave to get an update. The transport times listed in *Let's Go* are estimates provided by *público* drivers and they are almost always overly optimistic. Theoretically it takes 1hr. to get from San Juan to Fajardo, but on a *público* it can take up to 4hr. when you include traffic and frequent stops to pick up additional passengers. Do not take a *público* when you are in a hurry.

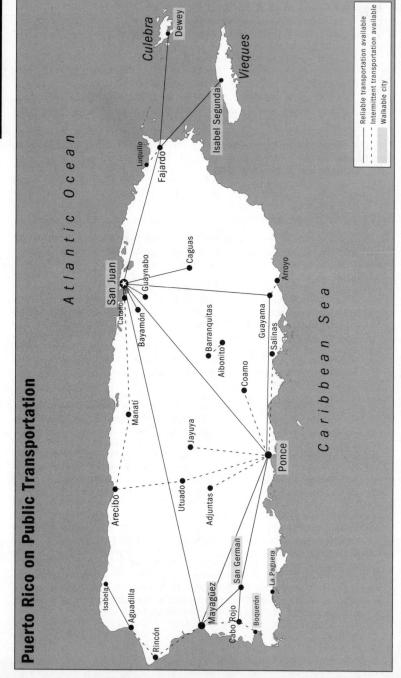

Puerto Rico on Public Transportation

Reliable transportation available
Intermittent transportation available
Walkable city

Atlantic Ocean

Caribbean Sea

Culebra
Dewey
Vieques
Isabel Segunda
Luquillo
Fajardo
San Juan
Caguas
Guaynabo
Arroyo
Cataño
Bayamón
Barranquitas
Guayama
Aibonito
Salinas
Coamo
Manatí
Jayuya
Ponce
Arecibo
Utuado
Adjuntas
Isabela
Aguadilla
Rincón
Mayagüez
San Germán
Cabo Rojo
Boquerón
La Paguera

BY CAR

Driving is the favorite transportation method for most locals and visitors in Puerto Rico. Roads are usually paved, but poorly maintained. Watch out for narrow and washed-out roads in the central mountains and reckless drivers just about everywhere. Read **On The Road,** p. 33.

DRIVING DISTANCES (IN MILES)

	Aguadilla	Albonito	Arecibo	Cabo Rojo	Fajardo	Luquillo	Mayagüez	Ponce	San Germán	San Juan
Aguadilla		95	33	26	112	108	17	63	31	81
Albonito	95		61	72	59	62	78	32	66	42
Arecibo	33	61		58	79	73	49	52	62	48
Cabo Rojo	26	72	58		131	131	9	41	7	111
Fajardo	112	59	79	131		7	129	89	125	34
Luquillo	108	62	73	131	7		124	90	124	28
Mayagüez	17	78	49	9	129	124		46	14	98
Ponce	63	32	52	41	89	90	46		34	70
San Germán	31	66	62	7	125	124	14	34		104
San Juan	81	42	48	111	34	28	31	98	70	

RENTING

Though car rental can be expensive, driving is the most efficient way to get around in Puerto Rico. A car is a must for travelers who want to visit beaches outside the city center, hike national parks, or move about in a timely manner. Unfortunately it is impossible to rent a car in Puerto Rico if you are under 21 and pricey to do so at any age. Most travelers will rent a car in San Juan, then use it to get around the island, though there are car rental agencies in every major city. If you will spend most of your time in San Juan or other cities, a compact car works best to navigate the narrow, congested streets. If you plan to drive the Ruta Panorámica, a car with four-wheel drive may be the optimal choice for navigating the sharp turns and steep hills, though it's possible to get almost everywhere without four-wheel drive.

You can generally make reservations before you leave by calling major international offices in your home country. However, occasionally the price and availability information they give doesn't jive with what the local offices in your country will tell you. Try checking with both numbers to make sure you get the best price and accurate information. Local desk numbers are included in town listings; for home-country numbers, call your toll-free directory.

To rent a car from in Puerto Rico, you need to be at least 21 years old. Some agencies require renters to be 25, and most charge those aged 21-24 an additional insurance fee (around $5-10 per day). Policies and prices vary from agency to agency. Small local operations occasionally rent to people under 21, but be sure to ask about the insurance coverage and deductible, and always check the fine print.

INTERNATIONAL AGENCIES

All of the following rental agencies have offices at the Luis Muñoz Marín Airport.

Alamo: ☎800-462-5266, Puerto Rico 787-791-1805; www.alamo.com

Avis: ☎800-331-1212, Puerto Rico 787-791-2500; www.avis.com.

Budget: ☎800-527-0700, Puerto Rico 787-791-3685; www.budget.com.

Dollar: ☎800-800-4000, Puerto Rico 787-791-5500; www.dollar.com.

Hertz: ☎800-654-3131, Puerto Rico 787-791-0840; www.hertz.com.

National: ☎800-227-7368, Puerto Rico 787-791-1805; www.nationalcar.com.

Payless Car Rental: ☎800-729-5377, Puerto Rico 787-625-8880; www.paylesscar-rental.com.

Thrifty: ☎800-847-4398, Puerto Rico 787-253-2525; www.thrifty.com.

PUERTO RICAN AGENCIES

AAA Car Rental: ☎787-726-7350 or 787-726-7355; www.aaacarrentalpr.com.

Charlie Car Rental: ☎800-289-1227, Puerto Rico 800-289-1227; www.char-liecars.com.

L&M Car Rental: ☎800-666-0807, Puerto Rico 787-791-1160; www.lmcarrental.com.

COSTS AND INSURANCE

Rental car prices start at around $40 a day from national companies, $30 from local agencies. Expect to pay more for larger cars and for four-wheel drive. Cars with **automatic transmission** can cost up to $10 a day more than cars with manual transmission (stick shift), and in some places, automatic transmission is hard to find in the first place. It is often difficult to find an automatic four-wheel drive.

Many rental packages offer unlimited miles, while others offer a limited number of miles per day with a surcharge per mile after that. Return the car with a full tank of gasoline (petrol) to avoid high fuel charges at the end. Be sure to ask whether the price includes **insurance** against theft and collision, tax, and special airport fees. Remember that if you are driving a conventional vehicle on an **unpaved road** in a rental car, you are almost never covered by insurance; ask about this before leaving the rental agency. Be aware that cars rented on an **American Express** or **Visa/MasterCard Gold or Platinum** credit card in Puerto Rico might *not* carry the automatic insurance that they would in some other countries; check with your credit card company. Insurance plans from rental companies almost always come with a **deductible** of around $500 for conventional vehicles; excess ranges up to around $800 for younger drivers and for four-wheel drive. This means that the insurance bought from the rental company only applies to damages over the excess; damages up to that amount must be covered by your existing insurance plan. Some rental companies in Puerto Rico require you to buy a **Collision Damage Waiver (CDW),** which will waive the excess in the case of a collision. **Loss Damage Waivers (LDWs)** do the same in the case of theft and vandalism.

National chains often allow one-way rentals (picking up in one city and dropping off in another). There is usually a minimum hire period and sometimes an extra drop-off charge of several hundred dollars

DRIVING PERMITS AND CAR INSURANCE

INTERNATIONAL DRIVING PERMIT (IDP)

If you plan to drive a car while in Puerto Rico, you must 18. Puerto Rico accepts unexpired International Driving Permits or driver's licenses from any country that imposes requirements similar to Puerto Rico (including the US, Canada, and many

European countries) for up to 120 days. Visitors staying longer than 120 days must apply for a Puerto Rican license.

Your International Driver's Permit, valid for one year, must be issued in your own country before you depart. An application for an IDP usually requires one or two photos, a current local license, an additional form of identification, and a fee. It may be a good idea to get an IDP, in case you're in a situation (e.g., an accident or stranded in a small town) where the police do not know English; information on the IDP is printed in 11 languages, including Spanish. To apply, contact your home country's automobile association. Be careful when purchasing an IDP online or anywhere other than your home automobile association. Many vendors sell permits of questionable legitimacy for higher prices.

CAR INSURANCE
Most credit cards cover standard insurance. If you rent, lease, or borrow a car, you will need a **Green Card,** or **International Insurance Certificate,** to certify that you have liability insurance and that it applies abroad. Green cards can be obtained at car rental agencies, car dealers (for those leasing cars), some travel agents, and some border crossings. Rental agencies may require you to purchase theft insurance in countries that they consider to have a high risk of auto theft.

ON THE ROAD
Puerto Rican drivers can be classified somewhere between confident and reckless. Traffic is heavy; many people disregard speed limits, neglect to signal turns, and cut off other cars. Markers such as stop signs are treated more like suggestions than laws. Aggressive urban drivers will feel right at home.

 NO HABLO SPANISH. It seems that everyone in Puerto Rico speaks English—until you hit the road. All Puerto Rican road signs are in Spanish and if you get pulled over, the cop probably won't speak English either. Not that this prevents English-speakers from driving. Most of the road signs have the same design that you'll find in the US or Europe and an 8-sided red sign isn't hard to decipher in any language. However, it's a good idea to brush up on your Spanish vocabulary before you get on the road. See the **Glossary,** p. 310.

Puerto Rico's road system is very similar to that of the US. In this book "Rte." (as in "Rte. 1") refers to small, one-lane roads, and "Hwy." (as in "Hwy. 7") to highways and expressways; Puerto Ricans call almost all roads *carreteras*. Roads are fairly easy to navigate, though signage varies. In San Juan remember that all signs pointing to "San Juan" eventually lead to Old San Juan. Puerto Rico has several good road maps, available for sale at most gas stations and drug stores. Hwy. 22, Hwy. 30, Hwy. 52, and Hwy. 53 are the island's only **toll roads.** These freeways have intermittent toll booths charging $0.30-1. Use the lane with the green "C" if you have correct change and the lane with the red "A" if you do not.

One confusing aspect of Puerto Rico's road system is the use of the **metric system** and the **imperial system.** Gas is measured in liters and the distance markers on the side of the road measure kilometers traveled. However, the speed limit is posted in miles per hour. Gasoline (petrol) prices vary, but average about $0.50 per liter in cities and from $0.55 per liter in outlying areas.

Carjackings are common in Puerto Rico, especially in big cities. If you are in a big city hotel without a parking lot, it's a good idea to put your car in a garage. Ask the hotel receptionist for regional advice. Never leave anything visible in your car; people have been known to **break in** for something as small as a couple of tapes. Carjackings frequently occur at **beaches,** especially deserted beaches. When driv-

> ⚠ **DRIVING PRECAUTIONS.** When traveling in the summer or in the desert, bring substantial amounts of **water** (a suggested 5 liters of water per person per day) for drinking and for the radiator. For long drives to unpopulated areas, register with police before beginning the trek, and again upon arrival at the destination. Check with the local automobile club for details. When traveling for long distances, make sure tires are in good repair and have enough air, and get good maps. A **compass** and a **car manual** can also be very useful. You should always carry a **spare tire** and **jack, jumper cables, extra oil, flares,** and a **flashlight.** If you don't know how to **change a tire,** learn before heading out, especially if you are planning on traveling in deserted areas. Blowouts on dirt roads are exceedingly common. If you do have a breakdown, **stay in your car;** if you wander off, it is less likely that trackers will find you.

ing, keep doors locked. To help drivers avoid nighttime carjackings, Puerto Rico has passed a law that cars are not required to stop at red lights between midnight and 6am. While driving, be sure to buckle up—seat belts are **required by law** in Puerto Rico. The **speed limit** varies from region to region. Most of the highways have a limit of 65 mph, while residential areas can post limits as low as 20 mph.

DANGERS

Central mountain roads tend to be narrow with sharp curves, poor visibility, sharp curves, and frequent one-lane washouts. Throughout the island most roads are paved, but most are poorly maintained and have accumulated their share of potholes. Never drive in the mountains at night or during a rainstorm. Probably the greatest danger is not the roads themselves, but rather the local drivers, who often use the whole road in narrow spots and drive at high speeds around sharp turns. Drivers are also reckless on the roads around large cities such as San Juan, where signaling turns is uncommon practice and speed limits are frequently exceeded.

CAR ASSISTANCE

Most automobile clubs offer free towing, emergency roadside assistance, and travel-related discounts in exchange for a modest membership fee. US or Canadian residents traveling to Puerto Rico should consider contacting the **American Automobile Association (AAA;** ☎800-564-6222; www.aaa.com), which offers service in Puerto Rico; call ☎787-620-7805 for roadside assistance. Membership costs vary depending on which branch you join ($50-60 for the first year; less for renewals and additional family members).

BY TAXI

All major Puerto Rican cities have taxi services, which are listed in the **Practical Information** sections. Puerto Rican taxi drivers usually give passengers a fair deal, but they rarely use a meter. Agree on a price before you get in the cab just to be certain. San Juan taxis use regulated fares; see p. 99 for more information.

BY BICYCLE

Many travelers harbor romantic visions of biking around a Caribbean island, but that is really much more feasible on less-developed islands. Heavy traffic and a huge mountain range running through the center of Puerto Rico make it difficult to ride anywhere. Furthermore, the only bike rental stores are in San Juan and on Vieques and Culebra. For serious bikers, the best place to ride is on the southern half of the island where there are flat roads with less traffic. Many travelers try to get around Culebra and Vieques on bikes, but both islands have mountains (or at least large hills) in the middle. In Puerto Rico, it is advisable to use bikes as a form of recreation rather than a mode of transportation.

BY THUMB

> **!** Let's Go never recommends hitchhiking as a safe means of transportation, and none of the information presented here is intended to do so.

Let's Go strongly urges you to consider the risks before you choose to hitchhike. Hitching means entrusting your life to a stranger and risking assault, sexual harassment, theft, and unsafe driving. For women traveling alone (or even in pairs), hitching is just too dangerous. A man and a woman are a less dangerous combination; two men will have a harder time getting a lift, while three men will go nowhere. Hitchhiking in Puerto Rico is dangerous and seldom done.

KEEPING IN TOUCH

BY EMAIL AND INTERNET

Internet access is widespread in Puerto Rico. Cybercafes have even sprung up in the small towns of Puerto Rico's central mountains. Logging on will usually cost about $1 per 10min. Though in some places it's possible to forge a remote link with your home server, in most cases this is a much slower (and thus more expensive) option than taking advantage of free **web-based email accounts** (e.g., www.hotmail.com and www.yahoo.com). **Internet cafes** and the occasional free Internet terminal at a public library or university are listed in the **Practical Information** sections of major cities. For lists of additional cybercafes in Puerto Rico, check out www.netcafeguide.com.

Increasingly, travelers find that taking their **laptop computers** on the road with them can be a convenient option for staying connected. Laptop users can call an Internet service provider via a modem using long-distance phone cards specifically intended for such calls. They may also find Internet cafes that allow them to connect their laptops to the Internet. And most excitingly, travelers with wireless-enabled computers may be able to take advantage of an increasing number of Internet "hot spots," where they can get online for free or for a small fee. Newer computers can detect these hot spots automatically; otherwise, websites like www.jiwire.com and www.wi-fihotspotlist.com can help you find them. For information on insuring your laptop while traveling, see p. 19. Travelers should be aware the extreme heat and humidity in Puerto Rico can damage laptops.

BY TELEPHONE

CALLING HOME FROM PUERTO RICO

You can usually make **direct international calls** from pay phones, but if you aren't using a phone card, you may need to drop your coins as quickly as your words. **Prepaid phone cards** are a common and relatively inexpensive means of calling abroad. Each one comes with a Personal Identification Number (PIN) and a toll-free access number. You call the access number and then follow the directions. To purchase prepaid phone cards, check online for the best rates; www.callingcards.com is a good place to start. Online providers generally send your access number and PIN via email, with no actual "card" involved. You can also call home with prepaid phone cards purchased in Puerto Rico (see **Calling Within Puerto Rico,** below).

PLACING INTERNATIONAL CALLS. To call Puerto Rico from home or to call home from Puerto Rico, dial:

1. The **international dialing prefix.** To call from **Australia,** dial 0011; **Canada** or the **US,** 011; **Ireland, New Zealand,** or the **UK,** 00; **Puerto Rico,** 011.
2. The **country code** of the country you want to call. To call **Australia,** dial 61; **Canada** or the **US,** 1; **Ireland,** 353; **New Zealand,** 64; the **UK,** 44; **Puerto Rico,** 1.
3. The **city/area code.** The area code for the entirety of **Puerto Rico** is ☎ 787.
4. The **local number.**

Another option is to purchase a **calling card,** linked to a major national telecommunications service in your home country. Calls are billed collect or to your account. To obtain a calling card, contact the appropriate company listed below. Where available, there are often advantages to purchasing calling cards online, including better rates and immediate access to your account. To call home with a calling card, contact the operator for your service provider in Puerto Rico by dialing the appropriate toll-free access number (listed below in the third column).

COMPANY	TO OBTAIN A CARD:	TO CALL ABROAD:
AT&T (US)	800-364-9292 or www.att.com	800-225-5288
Canada Direct	800-561-8868 or www.infocanadadirect.com	800-496-7123
MCI (US)	800-777-5000 or consumer.mci.com	800-888-8000
Telecom New Zealand Direct	www.telecom.co.nz	ATT 800-248-0064; MCI 800-666-5494; Sprint 800-659-0064
Telstra Australia	13 22 00 or www.telstra.com	MCI 888-343-5067; Sprint 888-311-9050

Placing a **collect call** through an international operator can be quite expensive, but may be necessary in case of an emergency. You can frequently call collect without even possessing a company's calling card just by calling its access number and following the instructions.

CALLING WITHIN PUERTO RICO

There are several different phone areas on the island, meaning that calling from the east coast to the west coast (or from San Juan to either coast) is long-distance. The simplest way to call within the country is to use a coin-operated phone. Puerto Rican pay phones cost $0.25-0.50 for local calls, and start at $1 for long-distance calls. **Prepaid phone cards**—available at newspaper kiosks, convenience stores, and drugstores—which carry a certain amount of phone time depending on the card's denomination, usually save time and money in the long run. The computerized phone will tell you how much time, in units, you have left on your card. Another kind of prepaid telephone card comes with a PIN and a toll-free access number. Instead of inserting the card into the phone, you call the access number and follow the directions on the card. These cards can be used to make international as well as domestic calls. Phone rates typically tend to be highest in the morning, lower in the evening, and lowest on Sunday and late at night.

 AREA CODE. You must use the area code (☎787) before dialing any number in Puerto Rico, local or long-distance. For directory assistance call ☎511.

CELLULAR PHONES

Although cell phones have spotty service in Puerto Rico's central mountains, they have fairly consistent reception in coastal regions and can be a useful emergency communication tool for drivers. However, cell phones are not as cost-effective as phone cards. They probably don't make sense for visitors who will not be making frequent calls or using a cell phone as a safety precaution when traveling by car. Travelers who own cell phones with coverage in the US will likely also have Puerto Rico included in their calling plan; check with your carrier before traveling.

The international standard for cell phones is **Global System for Mobile Communication (GSM).** To make and receive overseas calls from Puerto Rico (except those to the United States and Canada) you will need a **GSM-compatible phone** and a **SIM (Subscriber Identity Module) card,** a country-specific, thumbnail-sized chip that gives you a local phone number and plugs you into the local network. However, most **phones available for sale in Puerto Rico are not GSM-compatible** so if you are planning to make calls to places other than the US or Canada, you must make certain you are purchasing a GSM-compatible phone. It may be easiest to purchase one before you leave your home country. Many SIM cards are **prepaid,** meaning that they come with calling time included and you don't need to sign up for a monthly service plan. Incoming calls are frequently free. When you use up the prepaid time, you can buy additional cards or vouchers (usually available at convenience stores) to get more. For more information on GSM phones, check out www.telestial.com, www.orange.co.uk, www.roadpost.com, or www.planetomni.com. Companies like **Cellular Abroad** (www.cellularabroad.com) rent cell phones that work in a variety of destinations around the world, providing a simpler option than picking up a phone in-country.

TIP **GSM PHONES.** Having a GSM phone doesn't mean you're necessarily good to go when you travel abroad. The majority of GSM phones sold in the United States operate on a different **frequency** (1900) than international phones (900/1800) and will not work abroad. Tri-band phones work on all three frequencies (900/1800/1900) and will operate through most of the world. Some GSM phones are **SIM-locked** and will only accept SIM cards from a single carrier. You'll need a **SIM-unlocked** phone to use a SIM card from a local carrier.

TIME DIFFERENCES

Puerto Rico is 4hr. behind Greenwich Mean Time (GMT), and does not observe Daylight Savings Time.

The following table applies from late October to early April.

4AM	5AM	6AM	7AM	8AM	NOON	10PM
Vancouver Seattle San Francisco Los Angeles	Denver	Chicago	New York Toronto	**SAN JUAN** New Brunswick	London	Sydney Canberra Melbourne

This table is applicable from early April to late October.

4 AM	5 AM	6 AM	7 AM	8 AM	NOON	9 PM
Vancouver Seattle San Francisco Los Angeles	Denver	Chicago	**SAN JUAN** New York Toronto	New Brunswick	London	Sydney Canberra Melbourne

BY MAIL

Sending a postcard within Puerto Rico costs $0.23, while sending letters (up to 1 oz) domestically costs $0.37 and requires about 6 days.

SENDING MAIL HOME FROM PUERTO RICO

Airmail is the best way to send mail home from Puerto Rico. **Aerogrammes,** printed sheets that fold into envelopes and travel via airmail, are available at post offices. Write "airmail," "par avion," or "por avión" on the front. Most post offices will charge exorbitant fees or simply refuse to send aerogrammes with enclosures. **Surface mail** is by far the cheapest and slowest way to send mail. It takes one to two months to cross the Atlantic and one to three to cross the Pacific—good for heavy items you won't need for a while, such as souvenirs or other articles you've acquired along the way that are weighing down your pack. These are standard rates for mail from Puerto Rico to:

Australia: Allow 8 days for regular airmail home. Postcards/aerogrammes $0.70. Letters up to 1 oz. $0.80; packages up to 1 lb. $14.70, up to 4 lb. $26.75.

Canada: Allow 6 days for regular airmail home. Postcards/aerogrammes $0.50. Letters up to 1 oz. $0.60; packages up to 1 lb. $13.25, up to 4 lb. $15.50.

Ireland: Allow 10 days for regular airmail home. Postcards/aerogrammes $0.70. Letters up to 1 oz. $0.80; packages up to 1 lb. $14.00, up to 4 lb. $20.25.

New Zealand: Allow 7 days for regular airmail home. Postcards/aerogrammes $0.70. Letters up to 1 oz. $0.80; packages up to 1 lb. $12.50, up to 4 lb. $24.25.

UK: Allow 5 days for regular airmail home. Postcards/aerogrammes $0.70. Letters up to 1 oz. $0.80; packages up to 1 lb. $16.00, up to 4 lb. $28.00.

US: Allow 5 days for regular airmail. Postcards/aerogrammes $0.23. Letters up to 1 oz. $0.37; packages up to 1 lb. $3.75, up to 4 lb. $7.20.

SENDING MAIL TO PUERTO RICO

To ensure timely delivery, mark envelopes "airmail," "par avion," or "por avión." In addition to the standard postage system whose rates are listed below, **Federal Express** (www.fedex.com; Australia ☎ 13 26 10, Canada and the US 800-463-3339, Ireland 1800 535 800, New Zealand 0800 733 339, the UK 0800 123 800) handles express mail services from most countries to Puerto Rico. Mail is more reliable in large metropolitan areas; allow extra time for mail to reach rural areas.

There are several ways to arrange pick-up of letters sent to you while you are abroad. Mail can be sent via **General Delivery** or **Lista de Correos** in almost any city or town in Puerto Rico with a post office, and it is somewhat reliable (your best bet is to send packages as "certified mail"). Address General Delivery letters like so:

Ricky MARTIN
General Delivery
City, PR POSTAL CODE

The mail will go to a special desk in the central post office, unless you specify a post office by street address or postal code. It's best to use the largest post office, since mail may be sent there regardless. It is usually safer and quicker, though more expensive, to send mail express or registered. Bring your passport (or other photo ID) for pick up. If the clerks insist that there is nothing for you, have them check under your first name as well. *Let's Go* lists post offices in the **Practical Information** section for each city and most towns.

American Express's travel offices throughout the world offer a free **Client Letter Service** (mail held up to 30 days and forwarded upon request) for cardholders who contact them in advance. Some offices provide these services to non-cardholders (especially AmEx Travelers Cheque holders), but call ahead to make sure. *Let's Go* lists AmEx locations for most large cities in **Practical Information** sections; for a complete list, call ☎ 800-528-4800 or visit www.americanexpress.com/travel.

ACCOMMODATIONS

With the exception of a couple of dorm-style rooms in Rincón, there are no youth hostels in Puerto Rico. Most travelers will end up staying in a combination of hotels, guesthouses, and *paradores*. Groups of visitors staying in one place for a week or more can save money by contacting a realtor for vacation homes.

GUESTHOUSES

Guesthouses are usually the most affordable type of accommodation in Puerto Rico, with a single room costing about $50-100, depending on the region. Generally owned by a private individual (as opposed to a company or chain), guesthouses range from ramshackle rooms rented out on the second floor of a residence to charming hotel-style accommodations complete with a reception area and complimentary breakfast. Most accommodations of this type do not have 24hr. reception, so it is best to have a reservation if you plan to arrive late. Guesthouse rooms almost always have private bathrooms with hot water, but the furniture may be old or mismatched and the room itself may be aging. Guesthouse rooms rarely have daily maid service; instead, rooms are cleaned after a guest leaves. The most important quality in a guesthouse is safety; even though locks are standard, you will still be trusting your life, and all your possessions, to the owner. Rooms are typically priced by the number of beds instead of the number of occupants, so a single person will pay the same as two people staying in one double bed and two people staying in separate beds will have to pay the price of a quad. Few guesthouses accept credit cards. Guesthouses are not always endorsed by the government, and thus they do not always charge the 9% accommodations tax.

PARADORES

Not found in major cities, *paradores* (roughly translated "country inns") are small, independent hotels that are endorsed by the Puerto Rican Tourism Company (PRTC). A single room usually runs about $50-75 and the PRTC dictates that rates cannot change by season, making west coast *paradores* an excellent bargain during summer months (the high season on that part of the island). *Paradores* usually have 24hr. reception, daily maid service, an English-speaking staff, a restaurant, corporate discounts, and sometimes offer tours. Most also have a pool. Located primarily in the central mountains and on the west coast, *paradores* are very popular vacation destinations for Puerto Ricans. The Puerto Rican Tourism

Company web site (www.gotopuertorico.com) and *¡Qué Pasa!* magazine both have a complete list of *paradores*.

ACCOMMODATIONS FOR GROUPS

VACATION RENTALS

Travelers staying for at least three days should consider consulting a realtor for information about vacation rentals. Most vacation rentals are either winter homes that the owners rent out during the rest of the year or permanent vacation homes that realtors rent out on a rotating basis. These units range from timeshare condos in San Juan to luxurious houses on Culebra and Vieques. Most vacation rentals are quite classy and come with bedding, linens, and a fully equipped kitchen. Some also have air conditioning, pools, cable TV, and even jacuzzis. Always make sure you know exactly what amenities are included before reserving a vacation home, as units vary greatly and it is usually impossible to see a unit before reserving. Prices range between $100-$500 per day for anywhere from 2-6 beds. Vacation rentals rarely have daily maid service, but usually offer unparalleled privacy and a remarkably good deal for larger groups. *Let's Go* includes realtor information in San Juan, Luquillo, Vieques, Culebra, and Rincón. Many properties are also listed on the web. Search for "Puerto Rico vacation rentals" or try the following web sites: www.vacationhomes.com, www.prwest.com, www.surf-sun.com, www.10kvacationrentals.com, and www.a1vacationrentals.com.

CABINS AND VACATION CENTERS

When Puerto Ricans travel, they frequently take the whole extended family. Several no-frills accommodations cater directly to these large groups. The Puerto Rican **Compañía de Parques Nacionales (CPN)** sponsors **centros vacacionales** (vacation centers) at beaches in Arroyo (p. 222), Boquerón (p. 244), Añasco, and Humacao, and in the forest near Maricao (p. 307). These vacation centers usually have two types of cabins. **Cabañas** are basic concrete structures with two bedrooms, bunk beds, a tiny kitchen area, no air conditioning, and no hot water. **Villas** have a similar structure, but are slightly more expensive and come with air conditioning and hot water. Almost all vacation center structures accommodate six people in a very small space. In addition to rooms, most complexes also contain a pool, basketball courts, and a large beach. These are a great bargain for groups of travelers who plan to spend most of their time outside and don't mind cramped, cement rooms. All villas and cabins come with a full kitchen, but they do not include sheets, towels, or kitchen supplies. In 2005 the National Parks Company charged $65 per night for *cabañas* or $110 for *villas* plus 9% tax, with occasional promotional discounts. During low season on the west coast (Nov.-May) it is usually possible to show up and get a room, but during major holidays (*Semana Santa*, Christmas) and summer (May-Aug.) you must reserve well in advance either at the specific vacation center or at the San Juan office of the CPN, Apartado 9022089, San Juan, PR 00902-2089 (☎787-622-5200; fax 982-2107; www.parquesnacionalespr.com). Several private individuals have opened *cabañas* with a similar design; again, travelers must bring their own towels, linens, and kitchen equipment.

OTHER TYPES OF ACCOMMODATIONS

HOTELS

When Puerto Ricans refer to hotels, they typically mean the large American chains. These hotels are not listed in *Let's Go*, but if you feel like breaking the bank, most major chains have web sites with full information. **Hotel singles** in Puerto Rico cost about $200 per night, doubles $300. However, many offer discounts for military personnel, businesses, AAA members, frequent fliers, and a variety of other groups. Check the websites for more details.

There are also a few **small hotels** in most urban areas (and quite a few in San Juan) that charge much more reasonable rates (singles $65-140 per night). These hotels usually have the regular amenities—bathrooms, daily maid service, 24hr. reception, sometimes continental breakfast—but few of the perks, like casinos and pools. These small hotels can fill up fast, so it is best to reserve in advance, especially during high season. Hotel employees almost always speak some English.

UNIVERSITY DORMS

Many **colleges** and **universities** open their residence halls to travelers when school is not in session; some do so even during term-time. Getting a room may take a couple of phone calls and require advanced planning, but rates tend to be low and many offer free local calls and Internet access. For more information contact the University of Puerto Rico (In San Juan ☎787-764-0000, www.uprrp.edu; Aguadilla ☎787-890-2681, www.uprm.edu; Bayamón ☎787-786-2885; Cayey ☎787-738-2161; Mayagüez ☎787-832-4040, www.uprm.edu; Ponce ☎787-844-8181; Utuado ☎787-894-2828, http://upr-utuado.upr.clu.edu), which has campuses in most major Puerto Rican cities.

HOME EXCHANGES AND HOSPITALITY CLUBS

Home exchange offers the traveler various types of homes (houses, apartments, condominiums, villas, even castles in some cases), plus the opportunity to live like a native and to cut down on accommodation fees. For more information, contact HomeExchange.Com, P.O. Box 787, Hermosa Beach, CA 90254, USA (☎800-877-8723; fax 310-798-3865; www.homeexchange.com).

Hospitality clubs link their members with individuals or families abroad who are willing to host travelers for free or for a small fee to promote cultural exchange and general good karma. In exchange, members usually must be willing to host travelers in their own homes; a small membership fee may also be required. **Global-Freeloaders.com** (www.globalfreeloaders.com) and **The Hospitality Club** (www.hospitalityclub.org) are good places to start. **Servas** (www.servas.org) is an established, more formal, peace-based organization, and requires a fee and an interview to join. An Internet search will find many similar organizations, some of which cater to special interests (e.g., women, GLBT travelers, or members of certain professions). As always, use common sense when planning to stay with or host someone you do not know.

LONG-TERM ACCOMMODATIONS

Travelers planning to stay in Puerto Rico for extended periods of time may find it most cost-effective to rent an apartment. A basic one-bedroom (or studio) apartment in San Juan will range $700-1000 per month. Besides the rent itself, prospective tenants usually are also required to front a security deposit (frequently one month's rent) and the last month's rent.

There are no special requirements for foreigners renting an apartment in Puerto Rico. Because the island is a major tourist destination, almost every rental group is used to dealing with foreign renters. However, the sublet and rental markets are geared toward tourists looking for a vacation rental by the sea; it takes a little extra work to find cheaper, hole-in-the wall accommodations.

You can start you apartment search at http://puertorico.craigslist.org, www.yellowpages-caribbean.com/Countries/Puerto_Rico or in the classifieds of Puerto Rican newspapers, such as the *Puerto Rico Herald*. Many vacation rental and real estate agencies (listed at the beginning of each major city) rent out vacation properties by the month ($1500-2000 for one bedroom) during the low season.

CAMPING

Camping in Puerto Rico can be a rewarding way to slash travel costs. Camping areas are generally in beautiful locations, either steps from the beach or deep in a tropical forest, and offer the same views as 5-star hotels. Puerto Rico's temperate climate makes camping feasible year-round. During the winter months (Nov.-May) very few Puerto Ricans go on vacation and most of the campgrounds are completely empty. The exceptions are major holidays, such as Christmas and *Semana Santa*. During summer months Puerto Ricans flock to campgrounds around the island and it is advisable to make reservations in advance.

Women and solo travelers may feel less comfortable camping and should consider picking campgrounds with guards or other security measures. Camping with trusted fellow travelers is ideal. All campers should be sure to park their cars in a visible place, lock up valuables, and carry cash reserves in several places.

There are two principal organizations that maintain camping areas in Puerto Rico. The **Departamento de Recursos Naturales y Ambientales** operates campgrounds at reserves primarily in the Cordillera Central, while the **Compañía de Parques Nacionales** allows camping at several of the public beaches *(balnearios)* throughout the island (see below). It is possible to camp in El Yunque, but you must first obtain a permit from park rangers. Puerto Rico has very few private campgrounds and those that do exist tend to be more expensive and have fewer amenities than public camping areas. There are no camping areas in the San Juan area, though some people have been known to camp illegally in the Piñones area. For more information on outdoor activities in Puerto Rico, see **The Great Outdoors**, p. 43.

DEPARTAMENTO DE RECURSOS NATURALES Y AMBIENTALES (DRNA). Puerto Rico's DRNA operates camping areas in **Cambalache, Carite, Guajataca, Guilarte, Isla Mona, Lago Luchetti, Río Abajo, Sosúa,** and **Toro Negro.** Good news first: most DRNA campgrounds are relatively safe, well-located, and well-equipped with a gate, rustic showers, flush toilets (bring your own toilet paper), running water, covered picnic tables, outdoor grills, and trash cans. The bad news is that the camping process is enormously bureaucratic. Campers must first **get a permit** and **make a reservation** with a regional DRNA office (see list below). To get a permit, you must pay $4 per person and provide the exact dates you want to camp. DRNA officials ask that campers reserve at least two weeks in advance, but they sometimes make exceptions during low season. After obtaining a permit, campers need to check into the reserve's office during opening hours (usually M-F 7am-3:30pm) to get a key; campgrounds do not have attendants and campers use their own key for the front gate and the bathrooms. A car is required to access most DRNA camping areas. Finally, few DRNA officers speak English. If you can handle this governmental runaround, most campgrounds are gorgeous and peaceful, especially in the slow winter months. The main DRNA office is located in **San Juan** (☎787-724-8774; www.gobierno.pr/drna) next to the Club Náutico on Puerta de Tierra (p. 135). Regional offices are in: **Aguadilla** (p. 272), **Arecibo** (p. 266), **Mayagüez** (p. 254), and **Ponce** (p. 203). For complete information (in Spanish), check the DRNA web site at www.gobierno.pr/drna.

COMPAÑÍA DE PARQUES NACIONALES (CPN). The National Parks Company's oceanfront campgrounds afford travelers the opportunity to enjoy a million-dollar view for a few bucks. The CPN allows camping at seven public beaches around Puerto Rico, including **Cerro Gordo** (near Dorado), **La Monserrate** (in Luquillo), **Seven Seas** (in Fajardo), **Punta Guilarte** (near Arroyo), **Tres Hermanos** (near Añasco),

Cavernas de Camuy (Camuy), and incredible beach campgrounds on **Vieques**. These campgrounds almost always consist of big grassy fields that transform into a sea of tents during big holidays. Camping areas usually have some type of picnic tables, outdoor showers, and flush toilets, though some bathrooms are not cleaned regularly. Only some CPN camping areas have 24hr. surveillance and unfortunately some of the others (Cerro Gordo and La Monserrate) have reputations for being less than safe. **Never camp alone at a camping area without a guard.** The CPN charges campers $10 per tent for up to six people, except at Playa Flamenco in Culebra, which recently increased prices to $20 per tent. Fortunately, the CPN is much less bureaucratic than the DRNA and travelers can usually arrive any time and camp without a reservation. For more information contact the CPN main office in San Juan, Apartado 9022089, San Juan, PR 00902-2089 (☎787-622-5200; fax 982-2107). Spanish speakers can find additional information on the CPN web site at www.parquesnacionalespr.com.

THE GREAT OUTDOORS

The **Great Outdoor Recreation Pages** (www.gorp.com) provides excellent general information for travelers planning on camping or spending time in the outdoors.

> **LEAVE NO TRACE.** *Let's Go* encourages travelers to embrace the "Leave No Trace" ethic, minimizing their impact on natural environments and protecting them for future generations. Trekkers and wilderness enthusiasts should set up camp on durable surfaces, use cookstoves instead of campfires, bury human waste away from water supplies, bag trash and carry it out with them, and respect wildlife and natural objects. For more detailed information, contact the **Leave No Trace Center for Outdoor Ethics,** P.O. Box 997, Boulder, CO 80306 (☎800-332-4100 or 303-442-8222; www.lnt.org).

USEFUL RESOURCES

A variety of publishing companies offer hiking guidebooks to meet the educational needs of novice or expert. For information about camping, hiking, or biking, write or call the publishers listed below to receive a free catalog.

National Geographic Society, P.O. Box 6916, Hanover, PA, 17331, USA (US or Canada ☎800-437-5521, elsewhere 717-633-3319; www.nationalgeographic.com). Carries a selection of books and maps on the Caribbean, Puerto Rico included.

Sierra Club Books, 85 Second St., 2nd fl., San Francisco, CA 94105, USA (☎415-977-5500; www.sierraclub.org). Publishes general resource books on hiking and camping; all titles run $14-20.

The Mountaineers Books, 1001 SW Klickitat Way, ste. 201, Seattle, WA 98134, USA (☎206-223-6303; www.mountaineersbooks.org). Over 600 titles on hiking, biking, mountaineering, natural history, and conservation.

Wilderness Press, 1200 5th St., Berkeley, CA 94710, USA (☎800-443-7227 or 510-558-1666; www.wildernesspress.com). Carries over 100 hiking guides and maps, including guides to surfing hot spots.

NATIONAL PARKS

Puerto Rico has a system of *Bosques Estatales* (State Forests) and **El Yunque** is part of the US National Park system. The entire island of Isla Mona is a nature preserve and research center. These parks and reserves preserve Puerto Rico's amazing tropical rainforests and unique wildlife. Unfortunately, the Puerto Rican government does not have the financial resources maintain extensive trail networks for tourists. Visitors to parks—with the exception of El Yunque, which has several well-groomed trails—must choose between sticking to a few short, paved routes or hiring a guide to take them deeper into the forest. The good news is that visitors to Puerto Rican reserves face few environmental hazards—the biggest risk for hikers is getting lost.

There are no entrance for fees national parks, although tours and camping require small fees. The **DRNA** (p. 42) is in charge of administrating state parks and some campgrounds. The **US Fish & Wildlife Service** (www.fws.gov/southeast) is in charge of national parks.

WILDERNESS SAFETY

Staying **warm, dry,** and **well-hydrated** is key to a happy and safe wilderness experience. For any hike, prepare yourself for an emergency by packing a first-aid kit, a reflector, a whistle, high-energy food, extra water, raingear, a hat, mittens, and extra socks. Cotton is a bad choice for clothing as it dries painfully slowly.

Check **weather forecasts** often and pay attention to the skies when hiking, as weather patterns can change suddenly. Always let someone—a friend, your guesthouse owner, a park ranger, or a local hiking organization—know when and where you are going. Know your physical limits and do not attempt a hike beyond your ability. See **Safety and Health,** p. 17, for information on outdoor medical concerns.

WILDLIFE

LAND ANIMALS. Puerto Rico is lucky to have very few dangerous animals. There are no poisonous snakes and the most threatening land animal is the **rabid mongoose.** This species was originally imported to control the rat population and now runs wild, especially in El Yunque. If you see a small, furry, weasel-like animal, chances are it's a mongoose. Simply walk away as quickly as possible. **Mosquitoes** and other flying nuisances are especially bothersome in rural areas of Puerto Rico and may carry tropical diseases. Insects reach peak annoyance levels between May and November and travelers will probably want to bring bug repellent containing **DEET.**

CREATURES OF THE SEA. Jellyfish and sea lice patrol the seas around Puerto Rico, but few have fatal stings. To protect yourself from jellyfish stings, wear protective clothing (a wet suit or lycra) when spending extensive amounts of time in the water. The Portuguese Man-of-War has been known to inhabit Caribbean waters. Purplish-blue in color with tentacles up to 30 ft. long, the Portuguese Man-of-War also has a painful and potentially dangerous sting, which can cause anaphylactic shock, interference with heart and lung function, and even death. If you are stung by a Portuguese Man-of-War, rinse the sting with salt or fresh water and apply a cold compress to the affected area. If pain persists or if breathing difficulty develops, consult a medical professional. Shark attacks in Puerto Rico are extremely rare—Puerto Rico has had eight unprovoked shark attacks since 1749, and only two were fatal. Still, sharks—especially small nurse sharks—do patrol the Caribbean. Surfers and spearfishers are at greatest risk, and swimmers are advised to stay out of the water at dawn and dusk when sharks move toward shore to feed. Experts also advise against wearing high-contrast clothing or shiny jewelry and to avoid excessive splashing, all of which can attract sharks.

CAMPING AND HIKING EQUIPMENT

WHAT TO BUY

Good camping equipment is both sturdy and light. North American suppliers tend to offer the most competitive prices.

Sleeping Bags: Most sleeping bags are rated by season; "summer" means 30-40°F (around 0°C) at night; "four-season" or "winter" often means below 0°F (-17°C). Bags are made of **down** (warm and light, but expensive, and miserable when wet) or of **synthetic** material (heavy, durable, and warm when wet). Prices range $50-250 for a summer synthetic to $200-300 for a good down winter bag. **Sleeping bag pads** include foam pads ($10-30), air mattresses ($15-50), and self-inflating mats ($30-120). Bring a **stuff sack** to store your bag and keep it dry.

Tents: The best tents are free-standing (with their own frames and suspension systems), set up quickly, and only require staking in high winds. Low-profile dome tents are the best all-around. 2-person tents start at $100, 4-person at $160. Make sure your tent has a rain fly and seal its seams with waterproofer. Other useful accessories include a **battery-operated lantern,** a plastic **groundcloth,** and a nylon **tarp.**

Backpacks: Internal-frame packs mold well to your back, keep a lower center of gravity, and flex adequately to allow you to hike difficult trails, while **external-frame** packs are more comfortable for long hikes over even terrain, as they carry weight higher and distribute it more evenly. Make sure your pack has a strong, padded hip-belt to transfer weight to your legs. There are models designed specifically for women. Any serious backpacking requires a pack of at least 4000 in^3 (16,000cc), plus 500 in^3 for sleeping bags in internal-frame packs. Sturdy backpacks cost anywhere from $125 to 420—your pack is an area where it doesn't pay to economize. On your hunt for the perfect pack, fill up prospective models with something heavy, strap it on correctly, and walk around the store to get a sense of how the model distributes weight. Either buy a **rain cover** ($10-20) or store all of your belongings in plastic bags inside your pack.

Boots: Be sure to wear hiking boots with good **ankle support.** They should fit snugly and comfortably over 1-2 pairs of **wool socks** and a pair of thin **liner socks.** Break in boots over several weeks before you go to spare yourself blisters.

Other Necessities: Synthetic layers, like those made of polypropylene or polyester, and a pile jacket will keep you warm even when wet. A **space blanket** ($5-15) will help you to retain body heat and doubles as a groundcloth. Plastic **water bottles** are vital; look for shatter- and leak-resistant models. Carry **water-purification tablets** for when you can't boil water. Although most campgrounds provide campfire sites, you may want to bring a small **metal grate** or **grill.** For those places that forbid fires or the gathering of firewood, you'll need a **camp stove** (the classic Coleman starts at $50) and a propane-filled **fuel bottle** to operate it. Also bring a **first-aid kit, pocketknife, insect repellent,** and **waterproof matches** or a **lighter.**

WHERE TO BUY IT

The online/mail-order companies listed below offer lower prices than many retail stores. A visit to a local camping or outdoors store will give you a good sense of the look and weight of certain items before you buy.

Campmor, 28 Parkway, P.O. Box 700, Upper Saddle River, NJ 07458, USA (☎800-525-4784; www.campmor.com).

Cotswold Outdoor, Unit 11 Kemble Business Park, Crudwell, Malmesbury Wiltshire, SN16 9SH, UK (☎08704 427 755; www.cotswoldoutdoor.com).

ESSENTIALS

Discount Camping, 880 Main North Rd., Pooraka, South Australia 5095, Australia (☎08 8262 3399; fax 8260 6240; www.discountcamping.com.au).

Eastern Mountain Sports (EMS), 1 Vose Farm Rd., Peterborough, NH 03458, USA (☎888-463-6367; www.ems.com).

Gear-Zone, 8 Burnet Rd., Sweetbriar Rd. Industrial Estate, Norwich, NR3 2BS, UK (☎1603 410 108; fax 1603 413 537; www.gear-zone.co.uk).

L.L. Bean, Freeport, ME 04033, USA (US and Canada ☎800-441-5713; UK 0800 891 297; www.llbean.com).

Mountain Designs, 443a Nudgee Rd., Hendra, Queensland 4011, Australia (☎07 3856 2344; www.mountaindesigns.com).

Oceanic Worldwide, 2002 Davis St., San Leandro, CA 94577, USA (☎510-562-0500, fax 569-5404; www.oceanicworldwide.com).

Recreational Equipment, Inc. (REI), Sumner, WA 98352, USA (US and Canada ☎800-426-4840; elsewhere 253-891-2500; www.rei.com).

ORGANIZED ADVENTURE TRIPS

Organized adventure tours offer another way of exploring the wild. Activities include hiking, biking, skiing, canoeing, kayaking, rafting, climbing, photo safaris, and archaeological digs. Tourism bureaus often can suggest parks, trails, and outfitters. Organizations that specialize in camping and outdoor equipment like REI and EMS (see above) also are good source for info. One of the greatest adventures in Puerto Rico is exploring the limestone caves along the northern coast, either by foot, in a kayak, or by rapelling. See **Parque de las Cavernas del Río Camuy,** p. 269, for more information. Tours endorsed by the **Puerto Rico Tourism Company** (www.gotopuerto.com) are listed on its website. *Let's Go* also lists local tours in the **Practical Information** section in each town.

ENVIRONMENTALLY RESPONSIBLE TOURISM. The idea behind responsible tourism is to leave no trace of human presence behind. A campstove is a safer (and more efficient) way to cook than using vegetation. If you must make a fire, keep it small and use dead branches or brush rather than cutting vegetation. Make sure your campsite is at least 150 ft. from water supplies or bodies of water. If there is no toilet, bury human waste (but not paper) at least 4 in. deep and above the high-water line, and 150 ft. or more from any water supplies. Always pack your trash in a plastic bag and carry it to the next trash receptacle. For more information, contact one of the organizations below:

Earthwatch, 3 Clock Tower Pl. #100, Box 75, Maynard, MA 01754, USA (☎800-776-0188 or 978-461-0081; www.earthwatch.org).

International Ecotourism Society, 28 Pine St., Burlington, VT 05402, USA (☎802-651-9818; www.ecotourism.org).

National Audubon Society, Nature Odysseys, 700 Broadway, New York, NY 10003, USA (☎212-979-3000; www.audubon.org).

Tourism Concern, Stapleton House, 277-281 Holloway Rd., London N7 8HN, UK (☎020 7753 3330; www.tourismconcern.org.uk).

United Nations Environment Program (UNEP; ☎+33 1 44 37 14 41; www.uneptie.org/pc/tourism).

ACAMPA (☎787-706-0695; acampapr.com). Camping, hiking, backpacking, caving, rapelling, and customized nature tours around the island. Also offers 1-4 expeditions to Isla Mona. Day tours $75. 4-day expeditions $497.

Adventuras Tierra Adentro, (☎787-766-0470; www.aventuraspr.com). Daytrips canyoning in El Yunque and caving in Río Camuy caves. $150 per person, group rates available.

AdvenTours (☎787-889-0251 or 831-6447; www.adventours.tk). Offers a variety of tours leaving from San Juan, Mayagüez, and Luquillo and traveling throughout the island. Activities include city tours, hiking, kayaking, biking, bird-watching, and backpacking. Also offers specialty tours to coffee plantations, ecotours, and Hatha Yoga. Guides available in English, French, German, and sign language. Anywhere from $200-1000 depending on the number of days.

Expediciones Palenque (☎787-823-4354; www.expedicionespalenque.com). Has 1-day trips to Ciales, Arecibo, Utuado, Adjuntas, Jayuya, and Camuy ($75-85), as well as 3- to 5-day backpacking and rock-climbing trips ($150-300).

Las Tortugas Adventures (☎787-725-5169; www.kayak-pr.com). Based in San Juan. One of the island's most comprehensive kayak tour operators. Offers daytrips to Cayo Santiago, Río Espíritu Santo, Laguna de Piñones, Lago Matrullas, Fajardo's bioluminescent bay, and Isla Cardona. Trips cost around $40-70. Also has multi-day and snorkeling packages. Transport from San Juan available at additional cost.

Caradonna Dive Adventures (☎407-774-9000 or 800-330-3322; www.caradonna.com). Offers 7-night scuba dive packages at several resorts around the island. $740-1200. Some prices include airfare from Miami.

SPECIFIC CONCERNS

SUSTAINABLE TRAVEL

As the number of travelers on the road continues to rise, the detrimental effect they can have on natural environments becomes an increasing concern. With this in mind, *Let's Go* promotes the philosophy of **sustainable travel.** Through sensitivity to issues of ecology and sustainability, today's travelers can be a powerful force in preserving and restoring the places they visit.

Ecotourism, a rising trend in sustainable travel, focuses on the conservation of natural habitats and using them to build up the economy without exploitation or overdevelopment. Travelers can make a difference by doing advance research and by supporting organizations and establishments that pay attention to their impact on their natural surroundings and strive to be environmentally friendly.

The best way to become involved in preserving Puerto Rico's unique species of flora and fauna is to volunteer with one of the organizations listed in the **Beyond Tourism** chapter (p. 84). In general, travelers should avoid driving off-road and use public transportation or travel on foot whenever possible. Also, avoid visiting Culebra's beaches at night during turtle breeding season.

Although many companies and nonprofits in Puerto Rico claim that their activities are "ecotourism," Puerto Rico has yet to decide on a formal definition for the word. According to the Puerto Rico Tourism Company's ecotourism manager, only **Casa Pueblo** (p. 86) and the **Cabo Rojo Committee for Health & the Environment** qualify by international standards. Check out the organizations below general information on ecotourism in Puerto Rico.

Caribbean Alliance for Sustainable Tourism, 1000 Ponce de León 5th fl., San Juan, PR 00907 (☎787-725-9139). Nonprofit working with hotel and tourism sectors to reduce waste and improve land-use. Lists establishments certified as "green globe."

Caribbean Conservation Corporation, 4424 NW 13th St, ste. A-1, Gainesville, FL, USA 32609 (☎800-678-7853 or 352-373-6441; http://cccturtle.org). Mainly concerned with preserving sea turtle species in the Caribbean.

Fideicomiso de Conservación (Conservation Trust), Casa Ramón Power y Giralt, 155 C. Tetuán, San Juan Antiguo, PR 00901 (☎787-722-5834; www.fideicomiso.org). A Puerto Rican private nonprofit dedicated to preserving natural land areas.

RESPONSIBLE TRAVEL

The impact of tourist dollars on the destinations you visit should not be underestimated. The choices you make during your trip can have potent effects on local communities—for better or for worse. Travelers who care about the destinations and environments they explore should become aware of the social and cultural implications of the choices they make when they travel. Simple decisions such as buying local products instead of globally available products, paying a fair price for products or services, and attempting to say a few words in Spanish can have a strong, positive effect on the community.

Community-based tourism aims to channel tourist dollars into the local economy by emphasizing tours and cultural programs that are run by members of the host community and that often benefit disadvantaged groups. This type of tourism also benefits the tourists themselves, as these tours often take them beyond the traditional tours of the region. The coastal regions of Puerto Rico and the eastern islands are heavily dependent upon tourism, particularly tours of natural areas. In general, travelers should look for tours offered by local guides, such as Tanamá Expeditions (p. 305) or Las Casas de la Selva (p. 292), rather than those run out of large hotels and resorts. An excellent resource for general information on community-based travel is *The Good Alternative Travel Guide* (UK£10), a project of **Tourism Concern** (☎+44 020 7133 3330; www.tourismconcern.org.uk).

TRAVELING ALONE

There are many benefits to traveling alone, including greater interaction with locals. On the other hand, any solo traveler is a more vulnerable target of harassment and street theft. As a lone traveler, try not to stand out. Look confident, and be especially careful in deserted or very crowded areas. Stay away from areas that are not well-lit. If questioned, never admit that you are traveling alone. Maintain regular contact with someone at home who knows your itinerary, and always research your destination before traveling. For more tips, pick up *Traveling Solo* by Eleanor Berman (Globe Pequot Press, $18), visit www.travelaloneandloveit.com, or subscribe to **Connecting: Solo Travel Network,** 689 Park Rd., Unit 6, Gibsons, BC V0N 1V7, Canada (☎800-557-1757; www.cstn.org; membership $30-55).

WOMEN TRAVELERS

Women exploring on their own inevitably face some additional safety concerns, but it's easy to be adventurous without taking undue risks. If you are concerned, consider staying in guesthouses which offer single rooms that lock from the inside or in religious organizations with rooms for women only. Stick to centrally located accommodations and avoid solitary late-night treks or subway rides.

Always carry extra money for a phone call, bus, or taxi. **Hitchhiking** is never safe for lone women, or even for two women traveling together. Look as if you know where you're going and approach older women or couples for directions if you're lost or uncomfortable.

Generally, the less you look like a tourist, the better off you'll be. Dress conservatively, especially in rural areas. Wearing a conspicuous **wedding band** sometimes helps to prevent unwanted overtures.

Your best answer to verbal harassment and kissing noises—both common in Puerto Rico—is no answer at all; feigning deafness, sitting motionless, and staring straight ahead at nothing in particular will do a world of good that reactions usually don't achieve. The extremely persistent can sometimes be dissuaded by a firm, loud, and very public "¡Déjeme en paz!" (Leave me alone!). Don't hesitate to seek out a police officer or a passerby if you are being harassed. Memorize the emergency numbers in places you visit, and consider carrying a whistle on your keychain. A self-defense course will both prepare you for a potential attack and raise your level of awareness of your surroundings (see **Personal Safety**, p. 18). Be sure you are aware of the health concerns that women face when traveling (p. 23).

GLBT TRAVELERS

Puerto Rico is one of the Caribbean's premier GLBT destinations. The Condado area of San Juan is known for its active gay scene and has accommodations, restaurants, and nightlife venues geared specifically toward gay travelers. GLBT travelers should have no problems traveling throughout the island, though urban areas are more accustomed to alternative sexuality than rural areas. For the latest info on Puerto Rico's gay scene do not miss **Puerto Rico Breeze** (www.puertoricobreeze.com), a Spanish/English newsletter that includes articles, advertisements, and a calendar of events related to the island's gay scene (available online and at most gay-friendly establishment in San Juan). Listed below are contact organizations, mail-order bookstores, and publishers that offer materials addressing some specific concerns. **Out and About** (www.planetout.com) offers a bi-weekly newsletter and a comprehensive web site addressing gay travel concerns. The online newspaper **365gay.com** also has a travel section (www.365gay.com/travel/travelchannel.htm).

Gay's the Word, 66 Marchmont St., London WC1N 1AB, UK (☎+44 020 7278 7654; www.gaystheword.co.uk). The largest gay and lesbian bookshop in the UK, with both fiction and non-fiction titles. Mail-order service available.

Giovanni's Room, 1145 Pine St., Philadelphia, PA 19107, USA (☎215-923-2960; www.queerbooks.com). An international lesbian/feminist and gay bookstore with mail-order service (carries many of the publications listed below).

International Lesbian and Gay Association (ILGA; ☎+32 2 502 2471; www.ilga.org). Provides political information, such as homosexuality laws of individual countries.

FURTHER READING: GLBT.

Spartacus 2004-2005: International Gay Guide. Bruno Gmunder Verlag ($33).

Damron Men's Travel Guide, Damron Accommodations Guide, Damron City Guide, and *Damron Women's Traveller.* Damron Travel Guides ($18-24). For info, call ☎800-462-6654 or visit www.damron.com.

Ferrari Guides' Gay Travel A to Z, Ferrari Guides' Men's Travel in Your Pocket, Ferrari Guides' Women's Travel in Your Pocket, and *Ferrari Guides' Inn Places.* Ferrari Publications ($16-20).

The Gay Vacation Guide: The Best Trips and How to Plan Them, Mark Chesnut. Kensington Books ($15).

Gayellow Pages USA/Canada, Frances Green. Gayellow Pages ($16). They also publish smaller regional editions. Visit Gayellow pages online at www.gayellow-pages.com.

GLBT CRUISES

Several cruise companies cater exclusively to gay and lesbian travelers; other companies book groups of gays and lesbians to cruise around on borrowed boats. Both allow groups of gay and lesbian travelers to experience the Caribbean in a comfortable environment. **RSVP Vacations** (☎800-328-7787; www.rsvp.net) and **Pied Piper Travel** (☎800-874-7312; www.piedpipertravel.com) offer cruises for both men and women; **Olivia Cruises and Resorts** (☎800-631-6277; www.olivia.com) offers cruises exclusively for women. GLBT cruises leave less frequently than others, so it's best to plan early.

TRAVELERS WITH DISABILITIES

Puerto Rico is just as accessible to travelers with disabilities as the rest of the US. In big cities, most hotels and restaurants are wheelchair-accessible, though this may not be the case in smaller towns or rural areas. All hotels endorsed by the Puerto Rican Tourism Company (listed in *¡Qué Pasa!*) are required to have at least one wheelchair-accessible room. However, these hotels tend to be more expensive than guesthouses. Also, handicapped visitors will likely have to rent a car, as the *público* system does not accommodate such passengers, making travel around Puerto Rico more expensive.

Those with disabilities should inform airlines and hotels when making reservations; some time may be needed to prepare special accommodations. Major airlines will accommodate disabled passengers if notified at least 72hr. in advance. Call ahead to restaurants, museums, and other facilities to find out if they are handicapped-accessible. **Guide dog owners** should inquire as to the quarantine policies of Puerto Rico. Playa Monserrate, Luquillo's public *balneario*, has Puerto Rico's only **handicapped-accessible beach** (p. 163). Bosque Estatal de Cambalache, between Manatí and Arecibo, has a **wheelchair-accessible trail** (p. 262). **Wheelchair Getaways** of San Juan offers car rental for wheelchair-bound customers (☎800-868-8028, Puerto Rico 787-883-0131). For information on transportation availability in individual cities, contact the Puerto Rican chapter of the Easter Seals Society (☎787-767-6710 or 800-221-6827; www.pr.easter-seals.org).

If you are planning to go to El Yunque, the only park on the island run by the National Park Service, obtain a free **Golden Access Passport,** which is available at all park entrances and from federal offices whose functions relate to land, forests, or wildlife. The Passport entitles disabled travelers and their families to free park admission and provides a lifetime 50% discount on all campsite and parking fees.

USEFUL ORGANIZATIONS

Accessible Journeys, 35 W. Sellers Ave., Ridley Park, PA 19078, USA (☎800-846-4537; www.disabilitytravel.com). Designs tours for wheelchair users and slow walkers. The site has tips and forums for all travelers.

Flying Wheels, 143 W. Bridge St., P.O. Box 382, Owatonna, MN 55060, USA (☎507-451-5005; www.flyingwheelstravel.com). Specializes in escorted trips to Europe and the Middle East for people with physical disabilities; plans custom trips worldwide.

Mobility International USA (MIUSA), P.O. Box 10767, Eugene, OR 97440, USA (☎541-343-1284; www.miusa.org). Provides a variety of books and other publications containing information for travelers with disabilities.

Society for Accessible Travel and Hospitality (SATH), 347 Fifth Ave., Ste. 610, New York, NY 10016, USA (☎212-447-7284; www.sath.org). An advocacy group that publishes free online travel information and magazine *OPEN WORLD* (annual subscription $13, free for members). Annual membership $45, students and seniors $30.

MINORITY TRAVELERS

Because the vast majority of Puerto Ricans have darker skin and are of mixed Taíno, African, and European ancestry, there is relatively little discrimination on the island. Minority travelers will most likely not experience hostility or outright discrimination, but some minor harassment is not unheard of. Most likely, minority travelers will experience more curiosity than aggressiveness.

DIETARY CONCERNS

Vegetarians will not find it easy to survive on Puerto Rican food. Traditional island food centers around meat, beans cooked with lard, and sandwiches filled with chicken, beef, or pork. In San Juan the tourist-oriented restaurants will usually have at least one vegetarian option; unfortunately, there's not much variety and these restaurants tend to be more expensive. Outside of San Juan, some options include *mofongo* without meat inside, pizza *empanadillas*, and cheese sandwiches. Most major cities have at least one vegetarian *cafetería*, but these are typically only open for lunch. Vegetarians who eat fish are in luck—a variety of seafood options are available in many restaurants.

The travel section of the The Vegetarian Resource Group's website, at www.vrg.org/travel, has a comprehensive list of organizations and websites that are geared toward helping vegetarians and vegans traveling abroad. For more information, visit your local bookstore or health food store, and consult *The Vegetarian Traveler: Where to Stay if You're Vegetarian, Vegan, or Environmentally Sensitive*, by Jed and Susan Civic (Larson Publications; $16). Vegetarians will also find numerous resources on the web; try www.vegdining.com and www.happycow.net for starters. Memorizing the phrases "sin carne" (without meat) and "soy vegetariano(a)" (I am a vegetarian) or "No como carne" (I do not eat meat) may also be helpful.

Travelers who keep **kosher** should contact synagogues in larger cities for information on kosher restaurants. Your own synagogue or college Hillel should have access to lists of Jewish institutions across the nation. If you are strict in your observance, you may have to prepare your own food on the road. A good resource is the *Jewish Travel Guide*, edited by Michael Zaidner (Vallentine Mitchell; $18). A listing of halal restaurants can be found at www.zabihah.com.

OTHER RESOURCES

Let's Go tries to cover all aspects of budget travel, but we can't put *everything* in our guides. Listed below are books and websites that can serve as jumping-off points for your own research.

USEFUL PUBLICATIONS

The following publications are available in Puerto Rico.

- 🕮 **¡Qué Pasa!** (☎800-246-8677; www.gotopuertorico.com). The official publication of the Puerto Rican Tourism Company (PRTC) includes accommodations, restaurants, nightlife options, feature articles, and maps. Call to have a copy mailed home or pick up a copy at any tourist office or hotel. Free. The PRTC also publishes **Go To Puerto Rico**, another magazine describing hotels and restaurants throughout the island. Free.

- **The San Juan Star** It may not be the best newspaper in Puerto Rico, but The San Juan Star is the only island paper to come out with a daily English edition. Also has a Spanish language version. $0.45.

- **Places to Go** (www.coral-publications.com). Puerto Ricans' favorite travel guide is a color brochure listing hotels and restaurants in every city on the island. Available in English and Spanish at most tourist businesses and offices on the island. Also publishes the less-popular *Bienvenidos* magazine. Free.

El Boricua (www.elboricua.com). A monthly bilingual publication on Puerto Rican cultural and current events. Publishes the work of Puerto Rican poets.

Puerto Rican Telephone Tourist Quick Guide (www.superpagespr.com). It's hard to find, but this is one of Puerto Rico's most helpful publications. Includes tourism-related articles and an abbreviated version of the Yellow Pages designed for tourists. Free.

WORLD WIDE WEB

Almost every aspect of budget travel is accessible via the web. In 10min. at the keyboard, you can make a car rental reservation, get advice on travel hot spots from other travelers, or find out how long it takes to drive from San Juan to Ponce.

Listed here are some regional and travel-related sites to start off your surfing; other relevant websites are listed throughout the book. Because website turnover is high, use search engines (such as www.google.com) to strike out on your own.

WWW.LETSGO.COM *Let's Go's* website features a wealth of information and valuable advice at your fingertips. It offers excerpts from all our guides as well as monthly features on new hot spots in the most popular destinations. In addition to our online bookstore, we have great deals on everything from airfares to cell phones. Our resources section is full of information you'll need before you hit the road, and our forums are buzzing with advice from other travelers. Check back often to see constant updates, exciting new tips, and prize giveaways. See you soon!

THE ART OF TRAVEL

BootsnAll.com: www.bootsnall.com. Numerous resources for independent travelers, from planning your trip to reporting on it when you get back.

How to See the World: www.artoftravel.com. A compendium of great travel tips, from cheap flights to self defense to interacting with local culture.

Travel Intelligence: www.travelintelligence.net. A large collection of travel writing by distinguished travel writers.

Travel Library: www.travel-library.com. A fantastic set of links for general information and personal travelogues.

World Hum: www.worldhum.com. An independently produced collection of "travel dispatches from a shrinking planet."

INFORMATION ON PUERTO RICO

Atevo Travel: www.atevo.com/guides/destinations. Detailed introductions, travel tips, and suggested itineraries.

Caribbean National Forest: www.southernregion.fs.fed.us/caribbean/index.htm. The official web site of El Yunque, with flora and fauna descriptions, forest facts, and recreation information.

CIA World Factbook: www.odci.gov/cia/publications/factbook/index.html. Tons of vital statistics on Puerto Rico's geography, government, economy, and people.

Escape to Puerto Rico: http://escape.topuertorico.com. A variety of island-specific info, including a current event discussion forum, Puerto Rico e-cards, a search engine for island restaurants, and a history quiz.

Geographia: www.geographia.com. Highlights, culture, and people of Puerto Rico.

Music of Puerto Rico: www.musicofpuertorico.com. The ultimate site for anything you ever wanted to know about Puerto Rican music, including sound clips of popular songs in every genre.

PlanetRider: www.planetrider.com. A subjective list of links to the "best" websites covering the culture and tourist attractions of Puerto Rico.

Puerto Rico Herald: www.puertorico-herald.org. The island's only online English-language newspaper. A great source for current events.

Puerto Rico Magazine: www.prmag.com. Puerto Rico's first online travel magazine. Includes photos, maps, travel tips, island info, travel stores, and an online chat room.

Puerto Rican Tourism Company: www.gotopuertorico.com. The island's official tourism website includes information on the Puerto Rico's history, culture, entrance requirements, and current happenings. Contains top 10 destination lists and lists of various hotels and restaurants.

Super Pages: www.superpagespr.com. Puerto Rico's Yellow Pages search engine.

US State Department: www.state.gov. Information about the current governmental initiatives in the US (of which Puerto Rico is a commonwealth) as well as passports, visas, and other entrance requirements.

World Travel Guide: www.travel-guides.com. Helpful practical info.

LIFE AND TIMES

Puerto Rico is a brilliant mosaic of the cultures that have influenced the island's traditions over nearly two millennia of history. The Amerindian **Taíno** civilization gave the island the name of **Borikén,** which is related to the modern-day *Borinquén*, an affectionate name for Puerto Rico. West Africans, who came to Puerto Rico both as slaves and free persons, introduced the beat of **bomba y plena** and the religious tradition of **santería.** By far the most influential group to inhabit Puerto Rico was the Spanish colonists, who left the island with the legacy of the **Spanish** language, **Roman Catholicism,** the music of **danza** and **décima,** and traditional Spanish foods, such as **flan** and **bistec empanado.** The perceived importance of Puerto Rico's hispanic heritage is one of the reasons Puerto Ricans have consistently voted against becoming a US state. Despite their diverse heritage Puerto Ricans are clearly united by their of love *Borinquén Querida* (beloved Puerto Rico) and are happy to introduce visitors the wonders of their island home.

LAND

The island of Puerto Rico lies where the Caribbean Sea meets the Atlantic Ocean, 123 mi. southeast of Florida, between the **Greater Antilles** to the east and the smaller islands of the **Lesser Antilles** to the west. Besides the main island, three smaller islands are also included in Puerto Rico's land area—Isla Mona to the west and Vieques and Culebra to the east. While the main island only measures 100 mi. east to west and 35 mi. north to south, it has a whopping 700 mi. of coastline (when all of the contours are accounted for)—good news for visitors seeking sand and surf.

Three primary geographic regions cover Puerto Rico—the mountainous interior, the coastal plains, and the northern plateau (karst country). The **mountainous interior,** dominated by the **Cordillera Central,** occupies 75% of the island's land area and includes Puerto Rico's highest peak, **Cerro de Punta** (1388m). It is surrounded by **coastal plains**—the most fertile land on the island. Most crops were grown in this area; however, only 5% of the island is farmable and today less than 1% of the island's GDP comes from agriculture. Northern Puerto Rico is studded with rugged **karst country,** where water has dissolved limestone to form a series of narrow canyons and deep **caves** (p. 260). In this environment, the underground Río Camuy has created the third-largest system of subterranean caves in the world (p. 269). **Isla Mona,** 50 mi. west of Puerto Rico, has an entirely different composition (p. 248).

Puerto Rico contains over 1000 **streams** and 45 **rivers,** but they are all relatively small and unnavigable. No significant natural lakes exist on the island, but several rivers have been dammed to create artificial reservoirs. As a result of its strategic position at the mouth of the Caribbean, Puerto Rico (literally "rich port") has several shipping **ports;** Ponce and Mayagüez are among the largest.

CLIMATE

It's not hard to guess why many North Americans spend the winter here. The mild, **tropical climate** is pretty much perfect year-round. The locals start grumbling when the temperature falls below 70°F. Even winter cold fronts, called **nortes,** only drop the mercury to about 60°F. The temperature does vary slightly around the island; temperatures in the mountains usually hover about 5-9°F lower than those on the coast (see **Climate Chart,** p. 309). Northeastern trade winds drop all of the rain on the northern side of the island before clouds hit the mountains, leaving the south relatively arid and dry. Officially the **dry season** runs from December to March.

The much more important season to keep in mind is **hurricane season,** which officially runs from June 1 to November 30, but only poses a significant threat from August to October. Hurricanes have plagued Puerto Rico throughout its history, destroying crops and taking lives. On average, a hurricane brushes by San Juan every 3.85 years. Hurricane George, the worst storm in recent history, hit the island on September 21, 1998, causing almost $2 billion in damage.

FLORA AND FAUNA

PLANTS

PLANT HABITATS. Due to industrialization, the vast majority of primary forest on Puerto Rico has been destroyed; however, much of it has been recultivated and **national reserves** now protect 90,000 acres of land. **El Yunque** (p. 155) contains 75% of the island's scant virgin forest, including orchids, giant ferns, bamboo, and 240 species of trees. The reserve has both high altitude dwarf cloud forest and slightly lower altitude **rainforest,** consisting of sierra palms and epiphytes, plants that use other plants to climb high into the canopy. **Subtropical wet forests** abound at even lower elevations and, strangely, on mountains above 3000 feet. This vegetation, including open-crowned and canopy trees, can be found at Reserva Forestal Toro Negro (p. 298) and Bosque Estatal de Guilarte (p. 307). At an even lower elevation, **subtropical moist forest**—most adapted to flooding caused by hurricanes—is the most common type of vegetation on the island; it can be found in Bosque Estatal de Guajataca (p. 278). Southwest Puerto Rico is covered by an entirely different dry forest, defined by low rainfall and arid vegetation, including both bunch grass and many varieties of cacti. Although it's not indigenous, the brightly colored **flamboyán tree** is one of the most famous plants on the island. The flowering tree blooms from June to August at elevations below 2000 ft., especially along the Ruta Panorámica (p. 290). Several types of **mangroves** grow on the calm waters around the southwest coast, the east coast, and Vieques. Mangroves develop extensive root systems that attract corals, sponges, oysters, and many fish.

ENDANGERED PLANTS. Puerto Rico is home to over 40 species of endangered trees, ferns, cacti, and orchids. However, it is often difficult to identify endangered species, which are only distinguished from their relatives by subtle physical variations. One of the easiest endangered plants of identify is the **Higo Chumbo** cactus. Now found only on the islands of Mona, Monito, and Desecheo, it is a narrow, night-blooming cactus that produces green, cone-shaped flowers.

ANIMALS

COMMON ANIMALS. Don't come looking for lions, tigers, and bears—because of the way the way Puerto Rico was formed, most animals reached the island by swimming, flying, or floating. The most famous animal in Puerto Rico is the **coquí,** a one-inch-long tree frog famous for its loud, distinct "ko-kee" call. Of the 16 species of *coquí*, 13 are endemic to Puerto Rico. The *coquí* is quite a tease—the first sound of the famous *coquí* call serves as a warning for other frogs to go away, but the second sound, the "kee" of male frogs, serves as an invitation for females to come reproduce. Puerto Ricans love their little mascot, and the *coquí*'s image appears on merchandise throughout the island. The frogs themselves reside in any forest area. Beyond that, Puerto Rico is home to hundreds of bird species and a variety of reptiles native to the island's various habitats.

Many of Puerto Rico's unique animals do not make their home on the island itself. The seas around Puerto Rico are teeming with manta rays, octopus, barracudas, bananafish, and nurse sharks, among others. The **coral reefs** that surround the island make for lively underwater communities of fish, crustaceans, and echinoderms—perfect for travelers interested in snorkeling and diving. In Vieques, Fajardo, and La Parguera, mangroves support populations of tiny, luminescent creatures called **dinoflagellates;** when the water is disturbed by a boat or swimmer these critters make the seawater around them glow (see **Feet on Fire,** p. 187). Farther offshore, **Humpback whales** are often sighted en route to their breeding grounds in the Virgin islands between December and May (p. 288).

Puerto Rico's most incredible wildlife is found on small **Isla Mona,** 50 mi. west of the mainland. This uninhabited island is home to an astounding 700 species of animals, including the 4 ft. **Mona Iguana** and **Isla Mona Boa,** neither of which is found anywhere else in the world. The island has been referred to as the Galapagos of the Caribbean (p. 248).

ENDANGERED ANIMALS. One bird of note, the **Puerto Rican parrot,** is among the 10 most endangered species in the world—the population once dropped as low as 14 parrots. Scientists have been working for 34 years to save the species, which initially declined due to deforestation and intense (human) population growth. Initial results have been moderately successful and by 2005 approximately 40 had been released into the wild from captivity breeding programs. The Puerto Rican parrot—identifiable by its bright green body, red forehead, wide white eye-rings, and its noisy squawks and squeals—can be found in El Yunque. In the island of Culebra, endangered **leatherback** and **hawksbill sea turtles** come ashore to lay their eggs. Leatherbacks are the largest variety of sea turtles, reaching up to six feet long and weighing close to a ton. Hawksbills are slightly smaller, weighing in at about 300 pounds, and can be identified by their beak-like mouths and colorful, patterned shells. Visitors should never disturb turtle nests and should not visit the beaches at night.

DANGEROUS ANIMALS. Travelers are advised to be wary of **mongeese**—small, furry mammals that look like weasels—as they have been known to carry **rabies.** **Tarantulas, scorpions,** and **centipedes** found in the forest may sting, but are only harmful to travelers with allergies to these creatures. None of Puerto Rico's snakes are poisonous.

HISTORY

BEFORE THE SPANISH (PRE-1493)

The first inhabitants of the area now known as Puerto Rico, the Arcaicos, likely came to the island from North America and settled around Loíza. They were soon followed by the Igneris people, who came up from Venezuela around AD 300 and inhabited the coastal areas. However, the Ostinoids replaced both of these tribes and, by AD 1000, the Ostinoids had evolved into the **Taíno** civilization, the most influential group in the island's ancient history. Known for making grinding tools and jewelry, this peaceful people lived in communities of 300-600 inhabitants, governed by one *cacique* (chief). After nearly 500 years alone on the island, the Taínos were invaded by the **Caribs** of South America. These attacks sent many Taínos scrambling to

AD 600
The Taínos, the first permanent inhabitants of Puerto Rico, refer to their island home as "Borikén," which means "land of the lords."

the central mountains in retreat, but this incident was to be merely a precursor to a more lasting invasion.

SPANISH EMPIRE IN THE NEW WORLD (1493-1835)

CARIBBEAN TREASURE: A RICH PORT. Puerto Rico changed forever on November 19, 1493 when explorer **Christopher Columbus,** representing the Spanish government, landed on the island. After dubbing the island "San Juan Bautista," Columbus moved on to find greater treasures on other islands. One man on this initial voyage, **Juan Ponce de León,** didn't dismiss the island so quickly—he returned in July 1508 to settle down. The Taínos, possibly looking for allies against the Caribs, or possibly living up to their peaceful reputation, were hospitable to Ponce de León and allowed him to explore the northern coast in search of gold. On August 12, 1508 the Spaniard established the first European settlement on the island, Caparra.

This peaceful arrangement did not last. Under the auspices of the *Repartimiento de Indos* (Distribution of Indians) ordinance, Ponce de León instituted a system to control the native population by selecting an *hidalgo* (aristocrat) to control each village, encouraging intermarriage between Europeans and Taínos, and converting the local population to **Spanish Catholicism.** This plan was intended to civilize the Taínos and prepare them to be slaves for the Spaniards. Not surprisingly, the 30,000 Taínos did not like the arrangement, which worsened when they began dying from **smallpox, whooping cough,** and other European diseases. In 1511 the Taínos joined with the Caribs to rebel against the Spaniards, but they could not hold out against the European pistols, and by 1550 the few Native Americans who remained retreated to the central mountains.

MORE TROUBLE IN PARADISE. Meanwhile, the Spaniards confronted difficulties of life on an undeveloped Caribbean island. The island was plagued by persistent disease, unreliable crops, and hurricanes. The Spanish also soon discovered that a settlement on a flat, swampy terrain was susceptible to both malaria-carrying mosquitoes and attacks. Thus, they moved the capital to an island in front of a large, protected bay—this became known as San Juan. (In an unexplained mix-up, the capital city took the island's name and the island became "Puerto Rico"). When the Spaniards realized that other European powers might attack the island in an attempt to disrupt Spanish trade, they constructed several forts, including La Fortaleza (p. 122), El Morro (p. 119), and San Cristóbal (p. 121). This foresight prepared the island to withstand attacks from French, English, and Dutch forces. Most of the attackers didn't get beyond the forts of San Juan; those with the ingenuity to attack other spots on the island were quickly conquered by tropical diseases. At this time also the Spanish began importing

1300s
The violent Caribs land on Puerto Rico, threatening the Taínos' domination.

1492
Christopher Columbus first sails the ocean blue.

1493
After a successful first try, Columbus takes another crack at it—this time prepared for colonization with 17 ships and 1500 men.

1510
Taíno chief Urayoán commands his warriors to drown Spaniard Diego Salcedo to determine if the Taínos' Spanish conquerors are immortal. They are not.

1518
Portuguese and Dutch ships bring the slave trade to Puerto Rico.

1522
Iglesia San José is founded—now the oldest church still in use in the US.

LIFE AND TIMES

West African slaves to replace the labor of the rapidly dwindling native population.

THE EMERGENCE OF A PEOPLE. Bound by the rules of a mercantile economy, Puerto Rican islanders were commanded to trade only with the Spanish—they would send raw materials to Spain and receive finished goods in return. Because the Spanish placed heavy taxes on Puerto Rican goods, the Spanish profited while the islanders lived in poverty. To remedy the situation, inhabitants outside of San Juan, hidden from the watchful eye of the Spanish, began clandestine trade with other nations. When Spanish royalty got wind of this illegal trade in the 1760s, it sent Spaniard **Alejandro O'Reilly** to put an end to it. Upon arrival, O'Reilly found a population of 50,000 people with no government infrastructure. He responded by lowering taxes, building roads and schools, and developing the sugar cane industry. The changes were a success—within 50 years the population tripled and a Puerto Rican identity began to develop.

A REVOLUTIONARY WORLD. In the late 18th century, the eruption of revolutions around Latin America began to affect Puerto Rico. A 1791 slave rebellion on the neighboring island of Hispaniola caused foreign nations to turn to Puerto Rico for sugar and rum imports; this marked the beginning of the island's close relationship with the US. By 1830 the population had soared to 330,000, and Puerto Rico and Cuba were the only two remaining Spanish colonies. The Spanish monarchy's fear of losing the islands prompted a series of reforms. In 1809 Puerto Rico was officially allowed to send a non-voting representative to the Spanish *Cortes* (Spanish Parliament), and the mercantilist trade system slowly came to an end as Spain cut tariffs and opened ports to foreign trade. Many white Spaniards migrated to the island and developed an agricultural industry, with large haciendas producing the cash crops of **sugar cane, coffee,** and **tobacco.**

FROM COLONY TO PROVINCE TO NATION TO COLONY (1835-1898)

REVOLUTIONARY PUERTO RICO. In spite of these preventative measures, a minor revolution erupted in 1835 and three years later native islander Buenaventura Quiñones was exiled for planning a second revolution. A revolution initiated in the town of Lares in September 1868 declared the island republic and elected a president, but failed to gain popular support, and faded after a month and a half. Perhaps the most lasting contribution of the movement was the rallying cry "Viva Puerto Rico Libre!" which became the known as the **Grita de Lares** (Cry of Lares). These revolutions failed, but changes came about nonetheless. In late September 1868 the Spanish military overthrew the monarchy and a civil war broke out in Cuba. As a consequence of the turmoil, Madrid felt the call to improve its relationship with Puerto Rico. Over the next 20

LIFE AND TIMES

1533
The Spaniards begin constructing La Fortaleza to protect the island from English, Dutch, and French invaders—but construct it too far inland.

1539
The Spaniards realize their mistake and begin constructing El Morro.

1600-1785
Twelve hurricanes strike the island.

1791
A slave rebellion on Hispaniola.

1809
Puerto Rico finally gets a representative in the Spanish *Cortes* (parliament).

1835
For the first time Puerto Ricans lead a minor revolution against Spanish rule.

1873
Slavery is abolished in Puerto Rico.

years Puerto Ricans were granted the rights to participate in the Spanish parliament, to form municipal councils, and to develop political parties. Moreover, the island finally achieved the status of a "province."

A TEMPORARY VICTORY. In 1881 the election of the liberal **Práxedes Mateo Sagasta** as Prime Minister marked a new era in the Spanish government. Taking advantage of this opportunity, Puerto Rican **Luis Muñoz Rivera,** leader of the Autonomist Party, went to Madrid to politely ask for Puerto Rico's independence. In 1897 Mateo Sagasta granted Puerto Rico political and administrative autonomy, but retained a military presence on the island. For the next year, Puerto Rico enjoyed its brief stint as a relatively independent state.

ENTER THE US. Meanwhile, Spain was battling rebel forces in Cuba and their supporters in Puerto Rico. Independence fighters looked to the increasingly powerful US for assistance and began corresponding with US President **William McKinley.** On February 15, 1898, the **US battleship Maine** mysteriously exploded in Havana's harbor. American journalists blamed the Spanish (although the accident remained a mystery) and public opinion persuaded President William McKinley to press for war. McKinley requested that Spain withdraw immediately from the island and on April 20, 1898 the US congress authorized the use of force in the Caribbean.

US troops attacked San Juan on May 12, 1898 with limited success, but within three months the Spanish forces surrendered in Cuba and the war was essentially over. When US troops landed at Guánica on July 25, the Spaniards barely put up a fight. Consequently, on December 10, 1898 Spain signed the **Treaty of Paris,** which granted Cuba independence and ceded Puerto Rico and Guam to the US. Puerto Rico was subject to outside government once again.

SUGARVILLE, USA (1898-1942)

A ROCKY START. The first two years of American control were a difficult time for the Puerto Ricans. The inhabitants of the island who had hoped for greater liberty under US control were disappointed when the US government placed the Puerto Rico under **military rule** and limited free speech in the press. Additional problems ensued when the Americans separated the **Catholic Church** from the state, necessitating a complete restructuring of the religiously-based educational system. On the economic front, American corporations bought out local businessmen to take the reins of the sugar and tobacco industries. However, a hurricane devastated crucial coffee crops in 1899. Americans did provide food for the hungry, import new vaccines, and build a network of roads on the island, but the first two years of US rule constituted a rough patch in the history of the island.

THE BOOM... This tenuous situation could not last, and in 1900 the US passed the **Foraker Act,** which formally established a gov-

1897
Luis Muñoz Rivera requests Puerto Rico's independence—and his wish is granted. Who knew all he had do was ask nicely?

March 1898
Puerto Rican members of the Cuban revolutionary movement correspond with President McKinley in hopes of being included in US plans to attack Spanish colonies.

April 1898
US Congress authorizes the use of force in the Caribbean.

December 1898
The US wins the Spanish-American war and takes control of Puerto Rico.

1900
The US government appoints Puerto Rico's first governor.

1903
The Universidad de Puerto Rico is founded.

1917-1919
20,000 Puerto Ricans fight under the US flag in WWI.

ernor for the island, appointed by the US president, who would control a house of delegates (with elected representatives) and an upper legislature (with appointed officials). Residents of Puerto Rico would be taxed according to US laws, but they would not be considered American citizens. The 1917 **Jones Act** expanded the legislature to two houses of elected representatives and gave Puerto Ricans American citizenship, just before they would be eligible for the WWI draft.

At this time, the island experienced an economic boom. As a result of the fact that Puerto Rican industry was not taxed or charged duties for trading with the US, American investment increased. The Puerto Rican sugar industry grew and by 1920, 75% of islanders depended on sugar for income. Wages rose, disease decreased, education expanded, the government spent $50 billion on developing roads, and suddenly the population was increasing rapidly.

...AND THE BUST. Everything came crashing to an end in the 1930s. Devastating hurricanes in 1928 and 1932 ruined the agricultural income; then, the Great Depression came rolling onto the island. As unemployment rose to 65%, many Puerto Ricans attempted to solve their problems by migrating to the US. Others became increasingly dissatisfied with US control and joined the independence movement. The **Puerto Rican Nationalist Party (Partido Nacionalista Puertorriqueño; PNP),** headed by **Pedro Albizu Campos,** led protests for Puerto Rican independence. In 1936 the party was set back when four members were killed and others were jailed for murdering a chief of police, but the demonstrations continued. A year later, at the **Masacre de Ponce,** 19 people were killed at a PNP protest.

A more peaceful solution to the island's problems emerged in 1938 when **Luis Muñoz Marín** (grandson of revolutionary Luis Muñoz Riviera; see p. 59), founded the **Popular Democratic Party (Partido Popular Democrático; PPD).** Marín was less concerned with the status of the island as a colony than he was about improving the quality of life for Puerto Ricans. This plan was well received; in 1940 the PPD won control of the legislature and Muñoz Marín became president of the senate. With this position he attempted to end the sugar monopolies and diversify the economy. Though Muñoz Marín took the first steps toward reviving the economy, it would take a powerful outsider to finish the job.

OPERATION SAVE PUERTO RICO (1942-1999)

LET THE GOOD TIMES ROLL. In the early 1940s a few changes permanently transformed Puerto Rico, "the poorhouse of the Caribbean," into a developed country. The first was that **Americans began to drink rum** when WWII cut off their whiskey supply. Suddenly rum became a major Puerto Rican export. The second, much more significant change, came when American President **Franklin Delano Roosevelt** devised a

---

LIFE AND TIMES

1929
The Great Depression sends Puerto Rico's economy into a tailspin.

1934
The US passes a law stating that Puerto Rican sugar production must be cut in half.

1938
Luis Muñoz Marín founds the Popular Democratic Party, which later favors commonwealth status.

1939
The US Navy purchases 27,000 acres on Vieques Island.

1940s
President Franklin Delano Roosevelt encourages economic development on Puerto Rico with Operation Bootstrap.

1948
Puerto Rico participates in its first Olympic games with its own team but with the US flag as its banner. The resulting controversy spurs the commonwealth to choose a Puerto Rican flag.

plan to shift the island's economy away from agriculture toward the more lucrative manufacturing and tourism industries. This was **Operation Bootstrap,** the most successful economic revival campaign in the island's history. The American government encouraged US manufacturers to move to Puerto Rico, where revenue was partially free from US income tax and cheap labor was available. By 1964 over 2000 American companies had relocated to Puerto Rico. Net income per capita soared from $121 in 1940 to $1900 in the early 1970s. **Tourism** boomed and Puerto Rico entered the fast lane.

OFFICIAL STATUS AT LAST. Political improvements soon followed. In 1948 the US offered the island a constitutional government that Puerto Ricans approved in a 1951 vote, and in 1952 Puerto Rico became an official **commonwealth of the US.** As a commonwealth, Puerto Rico was similar to a US state, but residents could not vote in presidential elections, were not represented in Congress, and did not pay income taxes. Many Puerto Ricans, especially *independentistas* (supporters of independence), protested the island's new status. These opponents attempted to assassinate both Muñoz Marín and US President **Harry Truman** by opening fire on the governor's mansion on the day the bill was signed, **July 25, 1952.** Two years later, they started shooting in the US House of Representatives, reviving the old Cry of Lares as they shouted "Viva Puerto Rico Libre!" The attack wounded five American legislators.

The violence subsided, but the issue continued to loom large in Puerto Rican politics as two parties competed for power. The **New Progressive Party (Partido Nuevo Progresista; PNP),** founded in 1968, advocated for statehood; the PPD supported the commonwealth; and a small but vocal minority continued to argue for independence. Responding to this controversy, in 1962 Muñoz Marín and US President John F. Kennedy created a **"three-point program"** that would first study the benefits of the options, then allow Puerto Ricans to vote on the issue. In July 1967, with voter turnout lowered to 65.8% by *independentista* boycotts, 60.5% of Puerto Ricans voted to maintain commonwealth status, 38.9% cast their ballots for statehood, and 6% voted for independence.

During this time, Operation Bootstrap continued to support Puerto Rico's economy, generating improvements in education, literacy, life expectancy, and wages. Combined with a growing tourism industry of 100,000 visitors per year, this made the 1960s in Puerto Rico a time of plenty.

THE SHIFTY SEVENTIES. Puerto Rico's economic health declined throughout the 1970s as the US recession increased the cost of imported fuels and consumer goods. Unemployment on the island rose to an astounding 25% in 1975.

THE WATERGATE OF PUERTO RICO. Controversy wracked the island in 1978 when two alleged terrorists, both under 25 years old, were shot and killed by policemen on the mountaintop of **Cerro Maravilla** (p. 301) as they were attempting to blow

1952
Puerto Rico officially becomes a commonwealth of the US.

1954
In the name of independence several Puerto Ricans open fire in the US House of Representatives.

1967
For the first time Puerto Ricans are allowed to vote on their status—and the majority chooses a commonwealth.

1971
The US Army takes over the much of the island of Culebra for training and testing purposes.

1978
The police shoot and kill two young men accused of blowing up a TV tower in support of independence.

1986
US President Ronald Reagan decides it's a good idea to train soldiers in El Yunque.

September 1998
Hurricane George devastates Puerto Rico, causing $2 billion in damage.

1999
A stray naval bomb on Vieques accidentally kills civilian guard David Sanes.

November 2004
Sila Calderón elected the first female governor of Puerto Rico.

up a television tower as a sign of support for independence. In his 1980 reelection campaign, governor Carlos Romero Barceló called the policemen who were involved heroes and used the incident to further his political agenda, but an investigation later uncovered that the boys had surrendered and were kneeling when the police shot them. Ten members of the Puerto Rican police were convicted and many regard the event as a triumph of the Puerto Rican legal system.

ENVIRONMENTAL AND MILITARY CONCERNS. Environmental issues became prominent due to continued population growth and industrial pollution. New organizations developed around these issues, such as the **Conservation Trust of Puerto Rico,** a nonprofit created to protect the island's natural resources.

The foremost issue of the 1980s became the US military presence on the island. Puerto Rico's strategic position at the edge of the Greater Antilles and its proximity to Cuba made it an ideal position for the American military. The two most prominent bases were the **Roosevelt Roads Naval Station,** located on the eastern coast, and the enormous naval base that occupied two-thirds of **Vieques.** Puerto Ricans protested the bases from the start, and alarm grew throughout the 1980s when nuclear weapons were placed on the island.

MORE VICTORIES FOR THE COMMONWEALTH. In March 1998 the US House of Representatives narrowly passed a bill finally allowing Puerto Rico to have a federally authorized binding referendum on statehood status—if the advocates of statehood won, then Puerto Rico would be admitted into the Union. However, on December 13, 1998, when the vote was held, almost 80% of the population turned up to vote and 51% chose to retain commonwealth status.

PUERTO RICO TODAY

In 2000, Puerto Ricans elected the island's first female governor, **Sila Calderón,** who focused her campaign on the US military presence in Puerto Rico and especially on the island of Vieques. In April 1999 a bombing accident on the island accidentally killed a Puerto Rican security guard, prompting extensive protests. Finally, in June 2001 US President **George W. Bush** announced that the Navy would leave **Vieques** by May 2003. The Navy kept its end of the bargain, but chose in 2004 to also close the **Roosevelt Roads Navy Base,** dealing a tough blow to the island's economy with the loss of 6000 jobs. The unexploded bombs and other environmental hazards left on Vieques prompted Calderón to call for the former bombing range to be placed on the US **Environmental Protection Agency (EPA)** Superfund National Priorities list of most hazardous waste sites. In 2005, the EPA took this step and a cleanup of the former Navy sites is in the works.

In the 2004 elections former Puerto Rican Representative to the US House of Representatives **Aníbal Acevedo Vilá** (PPD) defeated former Governor Pedro Rosselló (PNP) to assume the Governor's seat. The excruciatingly narrow margin of victory, 0.2 percent of the vote, produced a politically contentious recount. In the same election, the PNP party was given a majority in the Puerto Rican legislature, splitting control of the government. Acevedo has also pledged in to push for another vote on Puerto Rico's status with respect the

US. The revival of this question, combined with an **unemployment rate** still hovering around 11%, shows that Puerto Rico has many domestic issues to confront as it looks toward the future.

GOVERNMENT

On July 25, 1952 Puerto Rico officially became a commonwealth of the United States. Ever since that day people have been asking, "What does that mean?" In many ways Puerto Rico resembles a state—the national American government handles foreign relations, defense, the postal service, and customs; Puerto Ricans are US citizens who are eligible for the draft; and the commonwealth is led by a **governor** who is popularly elected to a four-year term. Like the US, the Puerto Rican government is divided into **executive, legislative,** and **judicial branches,** with the governor choosing a cabinet and the judicial branch consisting of a supreme court and superior courts. However, some crucial differences fuel the intense debate over potential statehood status. Although Puerto Rico sends a representative to the **US House of Representatives** (until 2008 the seat will be held by **Luis G. Fortuño** of the PNP), this representative cannot vote. While Puerto Ricans are citizens, they cannot vote in the US presidential elections and they don't have to pay federal taxes.

Additional aspects of Puerto Rico's government differ from a US state more in details and name than in functionality. The legislative branch of the government consists of two houses elected to four-year terms on the same cycle as the governor. In an interesting quirk, at least one-third of the legislators must be from the minority party and if that does not happen, the houses are enlarged to make space for more representatives. Until November 2008, **the PNP will control both houses of the legislature.** On a more local level, the island is divided into 78 municipalities, each with a mayor and an assembly.

> **THE POLITICAL PARTIES OF PUERTO RICO.** When conversing with locals, knowledge of the Puerto Rican political parties will quickly prove that you're the most educated tourist around. And it ain't that hard:
> **New Progressive Party** (*Partido Nuevo Progresista*; PNP). Endorses statehood.
> **Popular Democratic Party** (*Partido Popular Democrático*; PPD). Supports commonwealth status.
> **Puerto Rican Independence Party** (*Partido Independentisto Puertorriqueño*; PIP). Endorses independence.

ECONOMY

Puerto Rico is the economic success story of Latin America, thanks to **Operation Bootstrap.** Within 60 years, Puerto Rico transformed from one of the poorest islands in the Caribbean, with a single-crop agricultural economy, to one of the most prosperous, with a diversified industrial economy. The US is by far the island's largest trading partner and major exports include apparel, electronics, rum, and pharmaceuticals—Puerto Rico produces 50% of US pharmaceuticals. Today, the $69 billion **GDP** breaks down as 54% services, 45% industry, and 1% agriculture. Increasing **tourism** has also played an important role in Puerto Rico's economic success.

But life on the island isn't all peachy. With a **per capita GDP** of **$17,700,** Puerto Rico remains much poorer than even the poorest US state. Unemployment hovered around 11% in 2005, over twice as high as the mainland. So while

Puerto Ricans certainly have nothing to complain about in comparison to some countries in Latin America, it's not easy being the underdeveloped cousin of the US.

PEOPLE

DEMOGRAPHICS

Like most Latin Americans, Puerto Ricans are an ethnic mix of their Spanish, African, and Native American ancestors. Today, 80.5% of islanders identify themselves as white (of primarily Spanish origin), 8% as black, 0.4% as Indian, and the remaining 10.4% as mixed or other. However, almost everyone on the island has a dark complexion and darker hair, regardless of their self-classification. The African heritage is most prominent on the coast, especially the town of Loíza, and people of Amerindian ancestry remain predominantly in the central mountains. As Puerto Rico was too poor a country throughout much of its history to afford many African slaves, Puerto Rico's strong African cultural heritage stems more from free blacks than slaves. Racial discrimination is rare in Puerto Rico.

Puerto Rico's population is most notable for its sheer size—the island is one of the most densely populated regions in the world. This population trend began in the early 19th century, when many Latin Americans immigrated to Puerto Rico in order to escape revolutions in their own countries. A high birth rate continued to push population numbers up until the mid-20th century. After the beginning of Operation Bootstrap the birth rate began to decline, but the death rate also declined and life expectancy rose accordingly—keeping population numbers steady. Furthermore, as Puerto Rico became relatively prosperous, residents of neighboring islands Cuba and Hispaniola began immigrating in floods. The resulting population of around 4 million (as of the July 2004 census) on an island only three times as large as Rhode Island produces a staggering population density of 1127 persons per square mile, higher than any of the 50 US states. Luckily, the annual growth rate has finally fallen to 0.47% and the population seems to be leveling out.

Operation Bootstrap encouraged Puerto Ricans to move to the cities, and today 71% of the population lives in urban areas, with almost one third of the total population in the greater San Juan area. In addition to the island population, currently almost three million Puerto Ricans live in the US, at least one third of them in New York City (the so-called "Nuyoricans").

LANGUAGE

Spanish and English are both official languages of Puerto Rico, but the vast majority of islanders prefer to speak Spanish. In San Juan almost everyone speaks English, but it is polite for visitors who speak some Spanish to initiate conversations in that language; many Puerto Ricans will answer in English. English continues to be much less common in rural areas of the island, but almost everyone in the tourist industry speaks English—non-Spanish speakers will probably not have problems getting around.

The issue of language plays an important role in Puerto Rico's relationship with the US, as many Puerto Ricans oppose statehood because they do not want to sacrifice their Hispanic culture. In 1991, when statehood once again dominated the headlines, the Puerto Rican government officially abolished English as an official language in an attempt to prevent US cultural domination. The legislature revoked this policy two years later, but only after making a strong statement that Spanish is in Puerto Rico to stay.

RELIGION

Eighty-five percent of Puerto Ricans remain true to their Spanish roots and identify themselves as Roman Catholic, although most major religions are represented on the island. As a commonwealth of the United States, Puerto Rico maintains a strict separation of church and state. **Santería,** a blend of Catholicism and the religion of the Yoruba people who were brought to the Caribbean as slaves from Nigeria, continues to be important to the island's African community. *Santería* first emerged in the slavery era when Africans continued practicing their own religions but substituted the names of Catholic saints to appease their masters. Practitioners of *santería* generally worship a hierarchy of saints and believe that it is possible to foretell the future.

CULTURE

FOOD

The wealth and diversity of restaurants in Puerto Rico, and especially San Juan, make it easy to visit the island without ever sampling regional cuisine. Don't make that mistake. Though similar to many other Latin American cuisines, Puerto Rican food (**comida criolla** or **cocina criolla**) offers a unique blend of spices and tastes.

MAIN DISHES. The Puerto Rican day starts with **desayuno** (breakfast), a casual meal enjoyed before work frequently in a **cafetería.** For many locals, breakfast consists of a cup of hot coffee with milk and toast. Most restaurants also serve a larger American breakfast, including fried eggs, scrambled eggs with ham, bacon, oatmeal, pancakes, and, from Spain, *tortillas españolas* (Spanish omelets; a mix of eggs, potatoes, and onions). Unlike Americans, Puerto Ricans also enjoy a good sandwich for breakfast.

Sandwiches make a reappearance for **almuerzo** (lunch) and this is one of the cheapest ways to fill up. Puerto Rican sandwiches are typically served on *pan de agua*, a fresh, tasty local version of French bread, and made with some kind of meat, cheese, lettuce, tomato, and mayonnaise or butter, then grilled in a press and served hot. Local favorites are the *cubano* and the *media noche*, two sandwiches

ON THE MENU

FRUITS OF PARADISE

Puerto Rico is full of *batida* (smoothie) and *piragua* (shaved ice) stands that offer fruity refreshment to thirsty travelers. However, several popular Puerto Rican fruits may be unfamiliar to visitors from outside the Caribbean:

Acerola: Known to some in English as the West Indian cherry or haw fruit, the *acerola* is a soft, bright red, cherry-like fruit that tastes like a cross between an apple and a cherry. It is one of the more common and cheaper fruit juices on the island.

Parcha: The *parcha*, or passion fruit, has a tart taste, which mixes well with the sweeter elements of *batidas*. The fruit has a hard purple or yellow rind, with many black seeds inside.

Guanábana: In English, soursop. The Puerto Rican variety is the largest type. The fruit has a white, pulpy interior; the shape of a pear; and the skin of a lime. It can be identified by its acidic, fruity flavor with hints of nuts.

Guayaba: Guava, round with yellow skin and pink flesh, offers a sweet and slightly acidic kick when its juice is added to drinks. The many hard seeds make it difficult to eat the fruit itself.

Plátanos: Plantains look like large, rough bananas, but the similarities end there. Raw, green plantains, known as *verdes*, have a slightly bitter, crunchy taste. Deep-fried and mashed plantains, which can appear as *amarillos* (sweet variety) or *tostones* (dry variety) taste like a hearty bread.

made with roasted pork, *pepinillas*, ham, and swiss cheese. The local fast-food chain **El Mesón Sandwiches,** based in Aguadilla, makes terrific sandwiches and has a couple of vegetarian options.

Most Puerto Ricans head to a *cafetería* or an American fast-food restaurant for a quick lunch on the go. A **traditional lunch** includes a heaping pile of rice, either plain or served with pigeon peas, chick peas, or red beans. Next step is the meat; some common options include: *biftec encebollado* (strips of beef with onions), fried pork chops, fried chicken, chicken breast, breaded Spanish steak, and fried seafood. Finally, add either *tostones* (dry, fried plantains; good with salt) or *amarillos* (fried sweet plantains) and a small salad to complete the meal.

Cena (dinner) tends to be a more formal affair eaten at home with the family, and smaller towns may not have any restaurants open late at night except fast food. You can't leave Puerto Rico without trying the famous *mofongo*, mashed plantain served with meat or fish inside. This traditional dish has been referred to as "the poor man's food" (despite the fact that it can be quite pricey) and one serving will leave you stuffed for days. **Soups** are another popular option—many are hearty enough to serve as a meal in themselves. *Asopao* is a thick stew served with either fish or chicken and occasionally pigeon peas. *Soncocho* is a salty, thinner fish soup. Travelers with adventurous palates may want to try less traditional options such as *sopón de garbanzos con patas de cerdo* (chickpea soup with pig feet).

Puerto Ricans love their **seafood,** though it's surprisingly expensive given that the island is surrounded by water. The unofficial national fish is red snapper, served in most nice restaurants as a whole fish, head and all. On the coast you will find an abundance of seafood restaurants serving up shrimp, conch, octopus, trunk fish, crab, and of course, lobster.

A few popular **spices** dominate Puerto Rican cuisine. The basic flavoring of most stews and soups is *sofrito*, olive oil seasoned with sweet chili peppers, onions, bell peppers, tomatoes, cilantro, oregano, and garlic. Meat dishes are typically marinated with the more simplified *adobo*, a mixture of vinegar, oil, black pepper, oregano, salt, and garlic. Many cooks also add a bit of *achiote*, a cooking oil made out of annatto seeds, to give the food a slight orange tint.

Vegetarians, especially those who do not eat fish, will have a hard time sampling local cuisine. Most beans are cooked with pork, many dishes are fried in lard, and almost everything comes with meat inside. There are **vegetarian cafeterías** in most big cities, but these typically only stay open for lunch. Puerto Rican restaurants can usually conjure up some type of vegetarian option, but be prepared for lots of plain *mofongo* and frozen vegetable medley.

SNACKS. Puerto Rico is not the place to travel if you want to lose weight as it's hard to resist the delectable **fried snacks.** Roadside stands, food kiosks, and some restaurants sell *empanadillas*, fritters filled with meat, seafood, or cheese. For even more calories, try an *alcapuria*, fried plantains stuffed with beef or pork, or a *pinono*, a fried plantain wrapped around ground beef. To round out the fried family, *sorullitos de maíz* are tasty fried sticks of ground corn. Puerto Ricans go crazy for *pinchos*, hunks of meat barbecued on a stick like a kebab.

A couple of popular **frozen snacks** provide a great way to cool off during the day. Street vendors, mostly in big cities, sell *piraguas*, shaved ice with flavored syrup on top. Private individuals put up signs advertising the sale of *limbers*, frozen fruit juice. Puerto Ricans also enjoy their **pastries,** and at any *repostería* you'll find *quesitos* (long pastries filled with white cheese) and *pan mallorca* (sweet bread).

DESSERTS. The combination of Puerto Rico's Latin heritage and its plethora of fresh fruits make for some delicious post-meal treats. The most common dessert is the popular *flan* (egg custard) served plain or with coconut or vanilla flavoring.

Another dessert common throughout Latin America is *tres leches*, a sweet cake covered with condensed milk sauce. The **fruit** in Puerto Rico is so tasty that it is often served for dessert; look for *guayaba con queso* (guava with cheese). Puerto Ricans also serve a variety of fruit-flavored *helado*, a smooth **ice cream** that resembles Italian *gelato*.

EATERIES. The cheapest place to dine is at one of the many **panaderías y reposterías** (bakery and pastry shops) found throughout the island. The local eateries generally have long hours (typically open daily 7am-9pm), but rarely have English menus, and many are so small that they don't have tables. Another cheap option is the ubiquitous *cafetería*, found even in Old San Juan. At some *cafeterías*—those open for lunch only—you order from the glass counter filled with steaming hot entrees. Those open for dinner and breakfast as well often are informal sit-down restaurant with $5-6 lunch specials. Formal, sit-down restaurants are the most expensive option; even outside of San Juan it's hard to find an entree for less than $12. The Puerto Rican Tourism Company has recognized many of the best **comida criolla** restaurants around the island and **mesones gastronómicos.** These fancy eateries are a great place to splurge on a quality Puerto Rican meal; check *¡Qué Pasa!* (p. 101) for a complete list.

RUM

AND (SOMETIMES) OTHER BEVERAGES. Rum is more than a drink in Puerto Rico, it's part of being Puerto Rican. In the early 20th century Puerto Rico's thriving sugar industry produced truckloads of rum, and though the sugar industry has declined, the rum industry continues to thrive with sugar cane from the Dominican Republic. The three primary brands produced in Puerto Rico are **Bacardi, Don Q,** and **Palo Viejo.** Bacardi has been based in Puerto Rico since the 1961 Cuban Revolution and continues to be the world's best-selling rum. However, Puerto Ricans prefer Don Q, which is still produced near **Ponce** at the Serallés Distillery. Rum connoisseurs declare that Palo Viejo is the best Puerto Rican rum, but it is not as widespread. The perennial bar favorite is the **Cuba libre,** commonly known as a rum and coke. And, of course, Puerto Rico is the birthplace of the **piña colada,** a blended mix of rum, pineapple juice, and coconut juice. During the Christmas season locals make **coquitos,** a mix of eggnog and rum named after the island's favorite frog. Over the last few years, new **alcohol taxes** have considerably raised the price of drinking, but that doesn't seem to stop anyone.

ON THE MENU

YO HO HO AND A BOTTLE OF RUM

Rum is the drink of choice in Puerto Rico. The following curious concoctions may tempt you to try a little of the local spirit:

Piña Colada. Supposedly invented on the island, it requires 1½ oz. white rum, 1 oz. coconut cream, 2 oz. pineapple juice, and ice. Blend well, then throw on a pineapple or a cherry for garnish.

Coquito. Named after the island's tiny frogs, Puerto Rico's Christmas concoction makes an excellent drink year-round. For a full batch, mix 28 oz. coconut milk, 14 oz. condensed milk, 2 egg yolks, 2 cups of Bacardi rum and blend well.

Puerto Rican Sunrise. This Puerto Rican version of the popular tequila sunrise is refreshingly easy to make. Mix equal parts of white rum with orange juice, and grenadine, then stir. For a tropical twist, replace the orange juice with passion fruit juice.

Fuzzy Pirate. Though it's not quite as well known as other beverages, the Fuzzy Pirate is a light and fruity treat. Just take 1 oz. of peach schnapps, 5 oz. cranberry juice, 1 oz. of spiced rum, and add a dash of orange curacao. Serve over ice.

Cuba Libre. The name may be Cuban, but this common drink is popular on the island of enchantment. Plus, it's one of the easiest mixed drinks to make—just mix rum and coke, and add a lime. The quantities are up to your discretion.

But you can't survive on rum alone; sometimes Puerto Ricans drink **beer** as well. The locally produced **Medalla,** a light beer, is the cheapest and most authentic option. When it's too early for alcohol, many Puerto Ricans enjoy their **café con leche,** coffee served with a lot of milk and sugar. Although coffee production has decreased significantly over the last 50 years, the towns of **Yauco** and **Maricao** are still known for their fine brews. Another popular beverage is **mavi,** a fermented drink made from the bark of a mavi tree and often served out of a large barrel.

CUSTOMS AND ETIQUETTE

Though many Puerto Ricans have spent time in the US, most retain a more Latin American sense of customs and etiquette. Puerto Ricans are generally very polite and friendly to travelers who treat them with similar respect. Most go out of their way to welcome foreigners.

GREETINGS. The common greetings in Puerto Rico are *buenos días* (good morning; used anytime before lunch), *buenas tardes* (good afternoon; before dinner), and *buenas noches* (good night; after dinner). It is polite to begin every conversation, in a personal or professional setting, with these phrases. Female friends often greet each other with a peck on the cheek or a quick hug. Sometimes men shake hands with women in a business situation, but the standard greeting between a man and a woman is a quick kiss on the cheek.

MEALTIME. Unless otherwise stated, Puerto Rican restaurants expect customers to come in and seat themselves. However, American chains in Puerto Rico (Chili's, Pizzeria Uno's, Denny's) generally ask that customers wait to be seated. Most waiters say **buen provecho** (enjoy your meal) when they deliver food. It is polite to say *buen provecho* to anyone already eating when you enter a restaurant that is not too crowded, especially smaller Puerto Rican establishments. Waitstaff expect a 15% tip for sit-down service (20% for good service in a city), but it is unnecessary to tip at most *panaderías*. Customers sitting down and eating at any restaurant (even a *panadería*) should pay after they eat, unless a sign says otherwise.

TIMING. Puerto Ricans, especially those outside of San Juan and in every form of bureaucracy, have a much more laid back sense of time than most Europeans and North Americans. Things get done when they get done. Restaurants, bars, and clubs in Puerto Rico **do not maintain strict closing hours.** Most will stay open as long as people are still around, even if this means staying open until 8am the next morning. On the flip side, if an establishment is empty, it will likely close early. Smaller establishments, even museums and stores, frequently change opening hours and will close if someone who's supposed to work happens to be sick or unavailable.

CHURCHES. It is respectful to wear **pants or a skirt** and cover you shoulders when visiting Catholic churches in Puerto Rico. Church workers and worshippers also appreciate quiet voices.

THE ARTS

For a small island, Puerto Rico lays claim to a remarkably impressive tradition of art and culture. The **Instituto de Cultura Puertorriqueña** (www.icp.gobierno.pr), founded in 1955, has worked over the last 50 years to preserve Puerto Rico's cultural heritage for the public. This organization runs many of the island's museums. Check their online calendar for a list of upcoming events.

VISUAL ART

HISTORY. San Juan's new **Museo de Arte** (p. 132) is the island's manifestation of a rich tradition of visual art. Most Puerto Rican artists have been strongly influenced by the island and their works tend to focus on the nature, history, and culture of Puerto Rico. The first prominent Puerto Rican artist, **José Campeche,** was born in 1751 in San Juan as the son of a freed slave. Despite the fact that he never left Puerto Rico to be trained in the European schools, Campeche became an internationally renowned artist. Some of his most important works include: *San Francisco, San Juan Bautista,* and *La Sacra Familia.* The next prominent Puerto Rican artist, **Francisco Oller,** studied in Paris and was deeply influenced by the 19th-century Impressionist movement, particularly the work of Paul Cézanne. Upon returning to Puerto Rico in 1853, Oller used these European styles to portray nationalist scenes of Puerto Rican lands and people. In addition to depicting Puerto Rico's flora and fauna, Oller also painted works of social commentary about life on the island, including *El velorio* (The Wake; 1893), a representation of a child's wake. Oller's hometown, Bayamón, maintains a museum devoted to the great painter (p. 150), and many of his works can be found in San Juan's Museo de Arte.

As Puerto Rico's economy began to flourish in the 1940s, so did its art scene. Around this time the government began subsidizing **poster art,** graphic arts that dealt with social and political themes on the island, and that later was used to produce announcements for cultural events and festivals. Prominent poster artist and painter **Lorenzo Homar** worked with fellow artists to found the **Centro de Arte Puertorriqueño** (Center for Puerto Rican Art), designed the symbol for the Institute of Puerto Rican Culture, and established and ran a graphic arts workshop at the Institute. Pennsylvania native **Jack Delano** was captivated by the spirit and poverty of the island when he visited Puerto Rico in 1941. Since then Delano has published several books of island photography.

TODAY. Though he was born in Brooklyn, **Rafael Tufiño Figueroa** moved to La Perla at an early age and is considered to be one of the island's most important contemporary artists. Tufiño used his background as inspiration to paint scenes of poverty in Puerto Rico. In one of his most famous works, *La perla* (1951), Tufiño uses strong colors and lines to depict life in San Juan's most infamous slum. *Luquillense* artist **Tomás Batista** is one of the first Puerto Ricans to become famous for sculpture, primarily woodwork. Trained in New York and Spain, Batista has spent much of his artistic time creating busts of notable Puerto Ricans that he had admired during his childhood, such as Eugenio de Hostos and Ramón Emeterio Betances. Batista has also created many of the statues adorning plazas in cities around the island, including Río Piedras, Ponce, and Luquillo.

ARTS AND CRAFTS

The sheer number of artisans at any island festival demonstrates that *artesanía* is alive and well in Puerto Rico. One common form of folk art is the **santo,** a small religious figure carved out of wood by a *santero.* The tradition of making *santos* began in the 16th century, when Catholic Spanish colonizers placed saints on their mantels to protect their homes from harm (see **Santos de Palos,** p. 78). *Santos* vary greatly: larger ones are placed in churches while smaller ones remain in the home; in terms of quality, a high-quality *santo* is more complex, yet still carved out of one piece of wood. *Santos* can be found at many tourist shops in Old San Juan in addition to almost any crafts fair.

Another popular Puerto Rican craft is the **vejigante mask,** a colorful mask with horns worn during *carnaval* celebrations. Some historians believe that *vejigante* mask-making originated in Spain, where the *vejigante* represents the Moors who fought with St. James. Others believe that it came from Africa with the slaves. Regardless, the art form now integrates both African and Spanish influences in a uniquely Puerto Rican tradition. There are two types of *vejigante* masks, each associated with a regional **carnaval** celebration. In **Ponce,** the masks are made out of **papier-maché** and contain larger horns painted with bright colors, frequently red and black (the colors of Ponce) or yellow and red (the colors of the Spanish flag). In the small northern town of **Loíza** the masks are made out of **coconut shells** and have smaller horns, teeth made out of bamboo, and exaggerated features to frighten spirits. Both types of masks are worn with a large coverall outfit with wide sleeves designed to look like wings. Several stores in Old San Juan and Ponce sell authentic *vejigante* masks, which start at around $25, but be prepared to shell out more for masks that are larger, have more horns, or are made by famous artists.

Finally, Puerto Ricans also excel in the art of **mundillo,** which is an elaborate kind of lace originally from Spain. Typically women will spend hours, or even days, crocheting the intricate lace, which is then used to make baby clothes, doilies, hats, or other items. This tradition is found primarily in the northwestern town of **Moca** (p. 279), where visitors can find *mundillo* makers at work in their homes. You can also stop by the **Museo de Arte** in **San Juan** (p. 132) to see the world's largest piece of *mundillo.*

LITERATURE

Puerto Rico's literary tradition originated in the mid-19th century, when people began writing about social and political themes distinct to the island. The first noted Puerto Rican author, **Manuel Alonso Pacheco,** is best remembered for his work *El Jíbaro* (1849). This half-prose, half-poetry work discussed the life of rural peasants. **Alejandro Tapía y Rivera,** contemporary to Pacheco and namesake of Old San Juan's theater, was known primarily as a playwright but also composed the allegorical poem *The Satanic: Grandiose Epic Dedicated to the Prince of Darkness.* However, the most internationally well-known author during this area was philosopher, teacher, and political activist **Eugenio María de Hostos,** who composed everything from social essays to children's stories. He spent his life traveling throughout Latin America working for reform and the independence of Puerto Rico and Cuba. During this time he wrote his famous book *La reseña historia de Puerto Rico* (The Recent History of Puerto Rico; 1873).

Puerto Rican literature shifted focus after the American occupation of the island. During the first few decades of the 20th century the so-called **Generation of '98** began writing about the juxtaposition of American influence and traditional Latin American life. Most of these writers, including **Cayetano Coll y Toste,** **José de Diego,** and **Luis Muñoz Rivera,** were better-known for their political work, but a few became renowned for their literary talents as well. In 1898 **Manuel Zeno-Gandia** penned **Puerto Rico's first novel,** *La charca* (The Pond), a story about the difficulty of life in the countryside.

The literary scene shifted after the Depression with the **Generation of the 30s.** The movement was ushered in by academic **Antonio S. Pedreira,** whose book *Insularism* (1979) looked at Puerto Rican values and culture under the influence of the US. Novelist **Enrique Laguerre** wrote about similar themes, focusing on the decline of Puerto Rico's agriculture. Around this time **Julia de Burgos** emerged as Puerto Rico's most famous female poet. After personally distributing her first works around the island and then moving to the US, de Burgos

COMMONWEALTH OR COLONY?

Puerto Rico's Convoluted Relationship with the US

Tourists are often surprised to hear Spanish spoken on the streets of Puerto Rico. Puerto Ricans, patriotically known as Boricuas (for the indigenous name of the island, Borikén) are US citizens, but many identify themselves as part of a Latin American nation that is divided between support of the status quo, statehood, and independence. The political status issue brings Puerto Ricans to an intense debate—elections regularly draw 80% voter participation.

In its 1952 constitution Puerto Rico was labeled a Commonwealth or, as it is called in Spanish, *Estado Libre Asociado* (ELA; Free Associated State). To many, the ELA is a misnomer since Puerto Rico—an unincorporated territory of the US since 1898 and one of the longest standing colonies on earth, according to the United Nations—is neither free nor a state, and it lacks the power of a true "associate." Puerto Rico's economic dependency on the US interferes with the resolution of the ever-present political status problem. Democratic efforts such as referenda have been ineffective in clarifying the island's status. For example, fearing a vote for complete independence, President Wilson canceled the 1916 referendum on the imposition of US citizenship and military draft; in the 1993 political status referendum, options were ill-defined, so the majority of Puerto Ricans voted "None of the above."

Views on the political status of the nation depend on the degree of knowledge of Puerto Rican history and economics. Both the right-wing statehooders (who want Puerto Rico to become the 51st US state) and the left-wing *independentistas* (who favor Puerto Rico becoming an independent country) denounce the exploitation brought on by the colonial status of the island. Statehooders and the center-right status quo supporters differ only in the degree of political autonomy to be surrendered in exchange for US economic benefits. In their campaigns, all three groups emphasize the preservation of Puerto Rican nationality and culture, including the Spanish language, the Puerto Rican flag, and Puerto Rican representation in the Olympics and the Miss Universe pageant.

After four centuries under Spanish rule and one century under US domination, Puerto Ricans (on the island or in the US) are proud of their resistance and of their flexibility as a people. The Puerto Rican celebration of American Independence Day on July 4th can seem particularly confusing to outsiders. Some Puerto Ricans cheer the US liberation from British colonial domination, while others demand the same freedom for Puerto Rico. Because a colonial government controls education, many aspects of Puerto Rican history are not taught in school. That is one reason why the independence movement, a majority from the 1920s to the 1950s, has diminished to a small minority of the population. Still alive despite decades of criminalization, persecution, and infiltration by the FBI, the independence option is considered viable by less than 10% of the population, with only 5% voting for the Independence Party in what most *independentistas* consider to be fake colonial elections.

The environmental and economic effects of the US colonial regime have been devastating. As multinational corporations profit $26 billion annually from the island, 60% of Puerto Ricans live in poverty and the per capita income is a third of the US average, or half that of the poorest state in the US. Many US industries have polluted land and water with impunity. The railroad that circumnavigated the island shut down in 1957, making Puerto Ricans dependent on cars. Fertile agricultural lands have been paved over in order to build giant car lots, shopping malls, and housing developments. Puerto Rico has been forced to rely on imports, and town centers are dying out as local merchants fail to compete with Wal-Mart.

With no vote in the US congress or the UN, Puerto Rico has been repeatedly utilized as an "Experimental Island." In 1930s experiments for the Rockefeller Institute, American Dr. Cornelius P. Rhoads was accused of injecting cancerous cells into unknowing Puerto Ricans, killing eight people. In places like Vieques and El Yunque Rainforest, the US military has experimented with live artillery, napalm, and depleted uranium.

After decades of being not-quite-equal "associates" with the US, Puerto Ricans remain divided to this day as to what the best political alternative should be. The historical tension of a US-Puerto Rico relationship that seems unjust to some, but convenient or indispensable to others, has become part of daily life for Puerto Ricans.

Iliana Pagán Teitelbaum received her BA in Latin American Studies from the University of Puerto Rico. She is currently finishing her dissertation and expects to receive a PhD in Romance Languages and Literatures from Harvard University.

attained international acclaim for her English-language poem *Farewell from Welfare Island* (1953).

In the mid-20th century Puerto Rican literature focused its critical lens on the lives of Puerto Ricans in New York. Foremost among this trend was Nuyorican **Pedro Juan Soto** who authored *Spiks* (1956) and *Usmail* (1958). In the latter half of the 20th century a number of Puerto Rican playwrights have started turning the themes of identity into dramatic works. **René Marques** gained notice for his play *La Carreta* (The Oxcart; 1970), which depicts a poor mountain family in Puerto Rico and their immigration to New York. Puerto Rico's most recent player in the international literary scene is **Esmeralda Santiago**, a Nuyorican who narrates her Puerto Rican childhood in *When I Was Puerto Rican* (1993).

MUSIC

From the gentle rhythm of salsa to the pounding thuds of reggaeton, this tiny island plays a disproportionately large role in the international music scene.

SALSA

The history of salsa is an unwilling love story between Cuban beats, Puerto Rican rhythms, and New York streets. Both Cubans and Puerto Ricans would like to claim to be the sole inventors of this contagious music, but most can agree that this popular genre of music originated among Caribbean immigrant populations in New York in the 1950s and only became identified by the term *salsa* in the 1970s. Over the last 50 years, salsa has evolved to become the most popular form of music in Puerto Rico.

WHAT STARTS AS MAMBO... Throughout the 1920s Puerto Ricans and Cubans immigrated en masse to New York, and they brought their music with them. In the 1940s Latin music became increasingly popular and mambo developed as a combination of Cuban, Dominican, and Puerto Rican rhythms with a bit of American jazz and big band music thrown in. The undisputed king of this era was Puerto Rican Tito Puente, who founded an orchestra in New York. Other popular Puerto Rican artists of the 1940s included Tito Rodríguez, Charlie Palmieri, and Rafael Muñoz.

...SOON BECOMES SALSA. By the 1960s New York was in love with the Latin/Caribbean-influenced music. Big bands used congas, *timbales*, bass, *güiro* (an open-ended wooden box with a wooden striker), bells, bongos, maracas, drums, a horn section, and several singers to create a new, rhythmic sound. As the music became increasingly popular, the word "salsa" made its appearance. In 1962 Joe Cuba released a song claiming that you need "salsa" to dance; this is the first recognized mention of the word *salsa* (sauce)—in relation to music. After Carlos Santana released the disc *Oye Como Va* in 1969, Latin music swept across the country and there was no turning back. In 1976 Billboard published a 24-page article on the salsa explosion, solidifying salsa's position as a recognized musical genre.

It's had its ups and downs in the US, but salsa has been a driving force in Puerto Rico's music scene. In 1962 **El Gran Combo** brought New York sounds of salsa to Puerto Rico and continued producing hits for the next 30 years. **Gilberto Santa Rosa** has been another consistently popular Puerto Rican salsa star. Despite the fact that the younger generation is turning to the more contemporary music, such as rap and *reggaetón*, salsa continues to dominate Puerto Rican music. Current popular Puerto Rican salsa artists include **Ismael Miranda, Tito Nieves,** and **Cheo Feliciano.**

CLASSICAL

DANZA. For centuries, Puerto Rican musicians had been influenced by Spanish classical music traditions and in the mid-19th century they began incorporating Caribbean rhythms to create *danzas*, a uniquely Puerto Rican style of minuet or waltz with an Afro-Caribbean slant. *Danza* spread to urban areas throughout the late 19th century, becoming Puerto Rico's most popular form of music and one of the first genres of island music to be recognized internationally. Many *danzas* continue to be popular today, including the island's national anthem **La Borinqueña.**

THE 20TH CENTURY. Puerto Rico's music scene changed forever when Spaniard **Pablo Casals** immigrated to Puerto Rico, his mother's homeland, in 1956. The talented cellist, composer, and conductor founded the renowned **Casals Classical Music Festival** (p. 138) in 1957, then served as the first conductor of the **Puerto Rican Symphony Orchestra.** The Symphony Orchestra continues to perform 48 weeks per year, primarily in San Juan's Luis Ferré Centro de Bellas Artes (p. 137). In 1959 Casals recruited a prestigious faculty to teach at Puerto Rico's first music conservatory, which continues to produce talented musicians today. Other notable contemporary Puerto Rican composers include **Roberto Sierra, Ernesto Cordero,** and **Luis Manuel Álvarez.**

LIFE AND TIMES

FOLK

Salsa may be better-known internationally, but the real heart of Puerto Rico's music scene lies in its folk legacy. First popularized in the countryside, the island's folk music borrows from **Spanish and Moorish traditions.** It centers on the **décima,** a 10-line rhyming verse with six to eight syllables per line. These stanzas can be either traditional songs or improvised, but both usually tell some kind of story about love, tragedy, or life lessons. The most common type of décima is the **seis,** a simple melody performed with one or two singers, a row of male dancers facing a row of female dancers, and a band consisting of a *cuatro* (a Puerto Rican guitar), a *güiro*, a *tiple* (another type of Puerto Rican guitar), and sometimes bongo drums, maracas, claves, and a bass.

BOMBA Y PLENA

Puerto Rico has two traditional forms of music that originate directly from the island's African population. **La Bomba** came from Africa in the late 17th century and became especially popular in the small, primarily Afro-Caribbean town of Loíza. In this complex song and dance, a group of people create a circle around three different drums. Everyone takes turns drumming and dancing in the center; a **caller** or main singer is echoed by the larger chorus, as dancers take turns moving to the rhythm of the drums. In some regional variations only women sing or only men sing, but the basic idea remains the same. The best place to experience *bomba* music is at Loíza's carnival in late July (p. 148). **La Plena** originated in the southern sugar cane zones around Ponce in the early 20th century and served as a form of protest for peasants of all races. Referred to as a **periódico cantado** (a sung newspaper) the *plena* usually discusses, and sometimes satirizes, current events. In a *plena* one primary caller sings and then a chorus responds, but unlike the *bomba*, the *plena* does not require dancing. The most important instrument for singing a *plena* is the *pandero*, a handheld drum that looks like a tambourine without the bells; other common instruments include *cuatros*, *güiros*, guitars, accordions, cowbells, and maracas. In the 21st century, the *plena* has emerged as a popular expression of Puerto Rican culture.

POP

When the **Latin Invasion** hit the United States in the late 1990s, most of the invaders came from Puerto Rico. Long popular throughout Latin America, Puerto Rican **Ricky Martin** hit the English-language market with his hit single *Livin' La Vida Loca*. When Martin shook his bonbon at the 1999 Grammys, the world became transfixed, even though Martin had been performing since 1984 as a member of the boy band **Menudo,** Puerto Rico's version of the Backstreet Boys.   Celebrity couple **Marc Anthony** and **Jennifer Lopez** (a.k.a. **J. Lo**) are also of Puerto Rican descent and started their careers singing in Spanish. The local band **Algarete** has won many Puerto Rican hearts, although the four Boricuas have not yet made it in the international music scene.

FILM

The first Puerto Rican movie appeared 1912 when **Rafael Colorado D'Assoy** produced *Un drama de Puerto Rico*. However, not much came of the island's film industry until the 1950s when *Maruja* was the first film to be distributed in the US. Other important films of the era included *Una voz en la montaña* (1952), directed by Amilcar Tirado, and *Modesta* (1956), which won first prize at the Venice Film Festival. Unfortunately the industry slowly died in the 60s and 70s as Puerto Rican filmmakers instead turned to joint productions in other countries.

Puerto Rico's film industry took a 180 in 1980 when **Jacobo Morales** wrote, directed, and starred in *Dios los cría* (God Created Them). The movie, which related five stories questioning contemporary Puerto Rican society, was well received by critics and fans alike. Morales's second major film, *Lo Que Le Pasó A Santiago* (What Happened to Santiago) did even better, winning the **1989 Academy Award** for best foreign film. Morales is still considered to be Puerto Rico's greatest film director.

In the mid-1980s, director **Marcos Zurinaga's** first major movie, *La gran fiesta* (The Great Party; 1986), recounted the last days of San Juan's Casino, a great meeting spot of the rich and famous. Zurinaga directed two more major films, *Tango Bar* (1988) and *The Disappearance of García Lorca* (1997), a mysterious look into the final days of Spanish poet Federico García Lorca. Puerto Rico's most financially successful film of all time was **Luis Molina's** 1993 comedy *La guagua aérea* (The Aerial Bus), which uses the pretext of a crowded flight to New York in the 1960s to explore the multitude of reasons that Puerto Ricans immigrate. Quite a few Puerto Ricans have made their names in the American entertainment industry, including Nuyoricans **Jimmy Smits, Rita Moreno, Jennifer Lopez, Michael DeLorenzo,** and **Benicio del Toro.**

Ironically, the most famous **Hollywood movie** related to Puerto Rico had nothing to do with the island itself. The 1961 film *West Side Story* took William Shakespeare's classic *Romeo and Juliet* and remade it in 1960s New York City, with a gang of second-generation white Americans, "the Jets," as the Montagues and a gang of Puerto Ricans, "the Sharks," as the Capulets. While the movie did bring international attention to the growing **Puerto Rican diaspora** in New York City, many Puerto Rican immigrants disliked the film. They complained that the movie confused Mexican and Puerto Rican culture; that it only portrayed poor Puerto Ricans and characterized them as lawless and prone to criminal activity; and that an American actress of European descent was cast as the Puerto Rican love interest (María), while the rougher Puerto Rican female character was portrayed by Puerto Rican native **Rita Moreno.** Despite the criticism, the film was an overwhelming success, winning **10 Academy Awards.** The classic film continues to be one of the most widely viewed representations of Nuyoricans in American culture.

An Alternative Way to Explore Puerto Rico's Museum Culture

Signs of Puerto Rico's singular relationship with the United States are carved everywhere in the island. Carved in cement, literally. As in the continental US, cities have given way to suburbs and people have become dependant on cars to move from home to work, to school, and to shop. Today a great proportion of the island's land area is carved by streets and highways. At last count there where 2.2 million cars in Puerto Rico (about six for every ten residents)—three times the proportion of the US and many more times that of the European Community.

Sprawl and lack of urban planning have made it almost impossible to design a public transportation system that competes with the car. But in a country where the average per capita income is about $12,500, not everybody can afford a car. That is why many low-income families, students, recent immigrants, and elderly persons keep alive a network of *pisa y corre* (roughly translated to "stop and go") public vans, also know as *carros públicos* (public cars) to move from town to town every day. For $3-20 a traveler can tour all the towns of Puerto Rico and get a closer look at Puerto Rican culture along the way.

One great advantage of *pisa y corre* transportation is that the vans usually travel directly between town plazas. Because most of the museums, cultural centers, traditional stores, and market places are centered around theses plazas, you will get right to the action. If you ask, people will tell you how to walk from the van stop to any cultural spot or hotel in the area. If you are planning to go to a place between towns, talk to the van drivers and make sure the *pisa y corre* does drive past the area. To request a van stop tell the driver *"me deja"* (leave me here) and you will be dropped off.

Pisa y corre vans are not intended for tourism, and because the presence of a foreigner provides diversion from the drag of the daily commute, fellow riders and the driver will usually share information about the cultural highlights of a town, lessons and opinions about any sub-

ject imaginable, and a collection of life histories to fill many volumes. In other words, this is not the way to travel incognito. No matter how you look, people in small towns will know that you are new there, and at least somebody will want to know what you are doing. So, in a sense, *pisa y corre* transportation is a cultural activity.

The following is a possible museum trip using the *pisa y corre:*

On any given day (except Sunday) you can spend a morning in Río Piedras exploring the centennial campus of the University of Puerto Rico, with its small but beautiful museum. Then walk to the plaza and take the *pisa y corre* to Caguas. The van will take Rte. 1, the historic first road to cross Puerto Rico from north to south.

When you arrive in Caguas (p. 149) you will be able to visit museums about *trovadores*, tobacco, and others on subjects related to the history and people of the town. From there take the bus to Cayey.

In Cayey ask around for directions to the college campus and visit their museum, which houses an impressive collection of modern print art. The main gallery is dedicated to the painter Ramón Frade and his masterful representations of everyday people and landscapes in early 20th century Puerto Rico. Next take the van to Guayama.

Right in Guayama you will find the Casa Cautiño Museum, a property co-managed by the Puerto Rican Institute of Culture and the Municipality of Guayama. It is an amazing example late 19th-century architecture that houses a collection of furniture and decorative arts of the same period. From there, on to Ponce...

Ponce is a good place to finally relax and spend the night. There are superb hotels close to the plaza where you can plan your visits to the city's many museums and cultural attractions.

Those who travel by *pisa y corre* soon discover that asking people is the best way to get around and, if you are lucky, to find some unexpectedly beautiful places and experiences.

Adrián Cerezo *is an education policy and non-formal education specialist currently directing the Community Based Education Center at Sacred Heart University in San Juan. He has a BA in clinical psychology from Sacred Heart University. In 1998 Cerezo received a Distinguished Alumni Award for his contributions to education.*

SPORTS AND RECREATION

DRY LAND SPORTS

BASEBALL. Forget soccer: Puerto Ricans shed their Latin American ties and choose baseball as the island's most popular sport. Every year from November to January six regional teams (Santurce, Bayamón, Carolina, Caguas, Mayagüez, and Ponce) play five to six games per week in competition for the series title. In February, the winning team participates in the **Caribbean Series**, playing against the Dominican Republic, Venezuela, and Mexico. Most of the top Puerto Rican baseball players eventually head to the US to play in the major leagues. The result: this little island has had an enormous impact on American baseball. Ever heard of **Roberto Alomar, Bernie Williams, Juan Gonzalez, Carlos Delgado,** or **Iván Rodríguez?** All are Puerto Rican, along with over 200 other players in Major League Baseball history. The trend has become so strong that in the 1997 All-Star Game a Puerto Rican either scored or batted in every single run.

Puerto Rico's most famous baseball player of all time, **Roberto Clemente,** also had a long and illustrious career in the Major Leagues. During his 18 years with the Pittsburgh Pirates, Clemente led the team to two World Series and was the National League MVP in 1966, the World Series MVP in 1971, and the National League Batting Champion four times. Although Clemente was killed over 30 years ago taking medical and food supplies to earthquake-stricken Nicaragua, and Puerto Ricans still hold him high esteem.

COCKFIGHTING. Though it's illegal in most of the US, cockfighting continues to be a popular tradition in Puerto Rico. Almost every city on the island has a cockfight arena, and fights are typically held every weekend, with as many as 40-50 games per day. Hordes of locals, primarily men, gather to watch, and bet on, the fight between two spur-wearing roosters. Though the tradition is primarily rural and private, San Juan does have one cockfight arena open to the public (see **Club Gallístico,** p. 137).

BOXING. Puerto Rico has produced some of the world's best professional boxers. In the 1930s **Sixto Escobar** became the first Puerto Rican world boxing champion. Most recently **Felix "Tito" Trinidad** ruled the ring as the champion of welterweight and middleweight boxing after he beat superstar Oscar de la Hoya in 1999. With an impressive 41-1 record Trinidad retired in January 2003 to pursue other activities, despite de la Hoya's request for a rematch. In 2000 **John "The Quietman" Ruíz,** raised in Massachusetts and Puerto Rico by Puerto Rican parents, became the first Latino heavyweight champion. Over the past 70 years Puerto Ricans have won six **Olympic medals** in boxing.

BASKETBALL. Puerto Rico also has an active basketball league, with 16 amateur and six professional teams. Internationally, the island has not fared so well since their gold medal at the 1991 PanAm games. However, several Boricuas have played for the NBA, including **Ramon Ramos, José Ortíz, Butch Lee, Carlos Arroyo,** and **Daniel Santiago.**

GOLF. Golf is the chosen sport of many tourists, and manicured green courses are spread across the island—most often with luxury resort complexes in tow. Both the ladies and senior PGA tours end at one of Puerto Rico's magnificent golf courses. However, tourists don't have all the fun; 90% of the active members of the **Puerto Rico Golf Association** are Puerto Rican. Puerto Rican golfers have also made their name internationally: the PGA Hall of Fame inducted Boricua **Juan "Chi Chi" Rodríguez** in 1992 after a long career. **Kitty Michaels** is a well-known female golfer.

WATER SPORTS

With over 700 mi. of coastline and year-round water temperatures of 74-80°F, Puerto Rico is a paradise for water sports lovers. From scuba diving to deep-sea fishing to surfing, Puerto Rico offers it all, with world-class conditions. Even beginners can dabble the many activities listed below.

> **SEA WARNINGS** Puerto Rico has its share of **fearsome sea creatures.** The ones you are most likely to run across are **jelly fish, sea urchins,** and **sea lice** (tiny jellyfish). While encounters with them may be painful, most of these animals will do little permanent harm. When spending extensive amounts of time in the water (diving, surfing, windsurfing) it's best to wear a lycra or wet suit. There are **sharks** around Puerto Rico, but attacks are extremely rare. If you don't bother them, they most likely won't bother you. For more information, see **Environmental Hazards,** p. 21.

SCUBA DIVING AND SNORKELING

Many people visit Puerto Rico exclusively for its superb diving and snorkeling. Numerous reefs surround the island, providing an arena to swim with hundreds of fish species. **Snorkeling** is relatively inexpensive and easy to learn. Snorkelers wear fins, a mask, and a snorkel (a short tube extending from the mouth out of the water). They swim on top of the water observing the marine life below. More advanced snorkelers can hold their breath while diving underwater (skin diving). Puerto Rico's best snorkeling is on Culebra, closely followed by Vieques and the islands off Fajardo, but there are many snorkeling spots around the island.

Scuba diving involves swimming underwater for longer periods of time with a tank of oxygen (a Self-Contained Underwater Breathing Apparatus; **SCUBA**) attached to your back, producing the incredible sensation of breathing underwater and swimming with the fish. Today all divers must be certified by **PADI** (Professional Association of Diving Instructors), **NAUI** (National Association of Underwater Instructors), or **SSI** (Scuba Schools International) before they can dive alone. A certification course runs $150-600 and usually entails written work and up to four practice dives. The one exception to this rule is that professional instructors can accompany non-certified divers on an introductory dive, called **Discover Scuba** or a **resort course.** This provides an excellent way to try diving before investing in a full course. It is possible to get certified in Puerto Rico, but this takes a significant portion of vacation time. Many travelers do the coursework at home, then get a **referral** to do the certification dives in Puerto Rico.

Puerto Rico has over 40 certified **dive shops** that send expeditions to countless sights. In choosing a dive shop, it is important to consider several criteria. Divers prone to seasickness may prefer large boats that remain more stable in the water. The majority of dives are done from boats, but some shops also do shore dives, where divers simply walk into the water—a bit difficult with cumbersome equipment and strong shore currents, but typically less expensive. It is also a good idea to investigate how the trips are organized. Some shops take divers and snorkelers out together, which means that divers get the most of the attention, leaving snorkelers to fend for themselves. Others have one divemaster for both certified and

Celebrating a Traditional Art in the Context of Modern Culture

Sometime in the first two weeks of December, *santeros* (artisans of wooden saints made of wood; *santos de palo*) congregate in the small mountain town of Orocovis, home to one of the most talented and prolific carving families of the island, the Avilés family. In fact, the festival is set up across the street from the family museum. There are at least three generations of carvers in the family, and the oldest living member, Don Ceferino Avilés, has been recognized by the Smithsonian as a master artisan. They serve as the focal point of this unique festival that brings together established artisans and beginners, and people come to show, see, and buy only one thing: carvings of saints.

Puerto Rico's tradition of saint carvings is very old, inherited from Spain as part of the Catholic legacy. Originally, 16th-century Spanish clergy used polychrome sculptures and paintings to educate and convert. It is unclear when individuals began to make carvings, though some families, like the Espada family, are known to have specialized in religious images during the 17th and 18th centuries. It was only during the 19th century that local carvers became firmly established.

Saints were originally carved for devotional reasons, and the carvings emphasize the personal attributes of the saints, such as the saint's faith, virtues, or power. These unique traits can include a miracle or important event related to the saint, the specific causes for which the saint is invoked, or an instrument used to martyrize the saint. Thus, Saint Francis is accompanied by birds or small animals (he is the patron saint of animals), Saint Barbara holds a sword (she was decapitated by one), and Saint John the Baptist is accompanied by a lamb and water (evoking his baptism of Jesus).

Initially, these small carvings were placed on a shelf or small niche in the bedroom or living area of the home. They were sold by the carvers who traveled through the countryside selling their wares and offering repair and paint services for saints in need. Because of the saints' power as intermediaries, the carvings became objects of devotion and veneration. Thus, it was common for owners to have the saint repainted once a year before the saint's day, or as a way of showing gratitude when favors were conceded. Today saints are kept for many reasons, not just devotion, and the art of carving has developed in many different directions.

The Orocovis festival offers a window into most recent developments of Puerto Rican culture and the many symbols of devotion that now appear around the island. With the beatification of Carlos Manuel Rodríguez, the first Puerto Rican candidate for sainthood, it is now common to see his image in suit and tie. Mother Theresa has recently become a favorite, as have representations of Jesus embracing the World Trade Towers in New York City. The carvings provide a medium for social and political expression as well, as evidenced by numerous representations of saints supporting the cause of peace and freedom for Vieques. It is worth noting the emergence of women carvers, who have become a stronger presence since the mid-1980s. In fact, there is a separate, all-female festival in the spring. Both women from established artisan families and newcomers have been able to establish their own style and interests.

Those who arrive at the festival early (around 7am) will see the hard-core collectors, who come to buy what they believe are the most valuable and unique pieces. (Collectors have been known to visit the Avilés family the day before the festival, "by mistake," in order to get first pick of the master carvers' pieces.) Both the speculators and the investors have inflated the prices of carvings, and it is now nearly impossible to find a $20 piece by one of the masters, as you could have several years ago. While this is good for the carvers in economic terms, it also has the negative effect of creating a gap between the saints and their most ardent devotees. Even those not interested in buying should try to arrive no later than mid-morning, as the pieces sell quickly.

Ironically, some of the best *santos de palo* are not found on the island, but in the United States. Teodoro Vidal, who held perhaps the largest and most valuable collection, donated it to the Smithsonian Institution in Washington D.C. But the saint carvings are only one part of the story, and there is much to be gained from watching the artisans show their most recent pieces and trade compliments and ideas. After all, they are themselves the intermediaries of our own devotion.

Camille Lizarribar has a PhD in Comparative Literature from Harvard University and a JD at Harvard Law. She has most recently returned to Puerto Rico to clerk for a Judge at the Federal District Court in San Juan.

resort divers, which means that the experienced divers will have to go to a more shallow site. Finally, scuba diving requires a lot of equipment and many shops have a hidden surcharge for **equipment rental.** Others do not rent equipment at all, so divers must purchase it. Most dives are done over **coral reefs,** but Puerto Rico has some unusual dive sites, including an **artificial reef** made out of tires and an enormous **sea wall.** For information about the island's dive sites, see **In The Sea,** p. 2.

If you plan to do a lot of snorkeling or diving in Puerto Rico, it may be a worthwhile investment to buy your own gear; otherwise, it costs about $10-15 per day to rent snorkel and fins.

SURFING

Puerto Rico ranks among the best surfing destinations in the world, and is certainly the best in the Caribbean. Ever since the **1968 World Championships** in Rincón, surfers from around the world, and particularly the US East Coast, have been descending upon the isle of enchantment to catch some world-class waves. **Rincón** continues to be the island's surfing paradise, with almost 20 breaks in a relatively small area, closely followed by Isabela's **Playa Jobos.** It is possible to surf almost anywhere along the north coast, but the southern, Caribbean coast does not have many waves. The prime **surfing season** runs from November to mid-April when a combination of low pressure and cold fronts creates excellent conditions. During the summer hurricane season (June-Nov.) waves tend to be more inconsistent, but still surfable, especially on the east coast. For current livecam images of surf in the Rincón area, check www.surfline.com. Private individuals in Luquillo, Dorado, Isabela, and Rincón teach lessons to surfers of all levels. Unlike many other surfing destinations, Puerto Rico has a fairly **local-dominated scene.** Visitors should respect the local hierarchy and be careful not to break into the line.

Surfers use one of two types of boards: **longboards** (traditional style of board that can range as long as 10-12 ft.) and **short boards** (less than 9 ft. in length). Although beginning surfers generally start off on longboards, most surfers use short boards as well, as they have better maneuverability and are better for riding larger waves. Surfboards have two to three fins, called **thrusters,** which provide even greater maneuverability. The addition of a **leash** improved both the safety of surfing and its style. Before leashes were added, surfers spent a lot of time swimming out to retrieve lost boards.

THEIR GAY IN THE SUN

Puerto Rico is quickly developing a reputation as one of the most gay-friendly destinations in the Caribbean. For 15 years running San Juan has dedicated the first full week in June to its gay community. Pride Week events include everything from billiard tournaments to art shows, but much of the action centers around the popular gay nightclub Eros, which hosts nightly, themed events including a foam party. While you're waiting for the evening festivities, check out the beach along C. Condado west near Wendy's in Condado, a popular gathering place for gay men.

But San Juan isn't the only place in Puerto Rico to celebrate *orgullo boricua.* While its celebration is considerably smaller than the capital's, the spirited west-coast town of Boquerón would probably win the prize for most enthusiasm per capita on the day of its Parada Orgullo Gay (Gay Pride Parade). Every year on the second Sunday in June, the tiny town nearly doubles in size and residents open their doors to wave rainbow flags at the passing parade. Five other small towns host similar events.

(For more information on these and other events, visit www.puertoricobreeze.com or www.orgulloboricua.com. Most events are free, but some clubs may have a cover charge for specific parties.)

FISHING

Both the ocean and the many lakes and reserves of Puerto Rico provide ample entertainment for fishermen. **Deep-sea fishing** is popular, but expensive, with half-day boat charters starting at $150 per person or $400 per boat. Fishermen frequently return with mahi mahi, tuna, mackerel, sailfish, dorado, and blue marlin. Most standing water in Puerto Rico is manmade, but the DRNA fills these with a variety of fish, including tilapia, catfish, sunfish, and large-mouth bass. Few charters supply equipment and almost nowhere on the island rents supplies (except some deep-sea charters), so fishermen should bring their own poles. Fishing licenses can be obtained from the Puerto Rican Port Authority.

BOATING

The largest **recreational ports** are in Fajardo and Salinas, while San Juan, Mayagüez, and Ponce have the primary **commercial ports.** Many boats in the Fajardo area (p. 164) take small groups out for day-long expeditions to nearby islands. **Salinas** (p. 218) is the best place to go if you're looking for passage on a boat through the Caribbean. Several companies scattered throughout the island **rent sailboats,** but usually require that renters have some sailing experience. **Kayaking** is a popular activity on many of the island's fresh-water reserves and in the bioluminescent bays in Fajardo and Vieques.

WINDSURFING

In recent years windsurfing has exploded in popularity in Puerto Rico. The island's largest windsurfing shop, **Velauno** (p. 135), rents equipment, teaches lessons, organizes events, and pretty much dominates the oceans around Punta las Marías in San Juan. Other popular windsurfing areas include La Parguera and Guánica. For more information and current wave reports check www.windsurfingpr.com.

HOLIDAYS AND FESTIVALS

Puerto Ricans love a good party; there is some kind of festival or event somewhere on the island nearly every week. The island has three primary types of celebration—patron saint festivals, harvest festivals, and national holidays. Almost every town celebrates at least one **patron saint festival** (see list below) with singing, dancing, rides, religious processions, concerts, and banquets of regional food spread out over 10 days. Typically held in the town square, these festivals are based on Catholic saints, but some incorporate elements of African culture as well. **Harvest festivals** are celebrated with similar festivities to commemorate the end of the harvest season. Despite the fact that agriculture has become increasingly unimportant in Puerto Rico's economy, many towns still host at least one harvest festival; see individual town write-ups. As for **national holidays,** Puerto Rico commemorates both US and Puerto Rican holidays. Because many of these holidays, such as Memorial Day and important birthdays, are celebrated on the nearest Monday, the island has a surplus of three-day weekends.

Finally, Puerto Rico also has a smattering of festivities that do not fall into specific categories. **San Juan** (p. 138) hosts several festivals, from cultural events (San Juan CinemaFest and Heineken Jazz Festival) to events that are just an excuse to party (Gallery Nights, Festival de la Calle San Sebastián). The island also has three major festivals that incorporate *vejigante* masks. Though far from Rio, Ponce's *carnaval* festival is still a major event. Loíza's *carnaval*, held in late July (p. 148), incorporates more African traditions, while Hatillo's **mask festival** (p. 271) in late December is based on the island's Spanish heritage. One of the island's most unique festivals is Aibonito's spectacular **Flower Festival,** a modern-day variation on the traditional harvest festival (p. 294).

COMMONWEALTH HOLIDAYS

DATE	HOLIDAY	NAME IN SPANISH
January 1	New Year's Day	Primer día del año nuevo
January 6	Epiphany/Three Kings' Day	Día de Reyes
January 11	María de Hostos's birthday	Día del Natalicio de Eugenio Maria de Hostos
January 16, 2006/January 15, 2007	Martin Luther King Jr. Day	Día de Martin Luther King Jr.
February 20, 2006/February 19, 2007	Presidents Day	Día de los Presidentes
March 22	Emancipation Day	Día de Abolición de Esclavitud
April 14, 2006/April 6, 2007	Good Friday	Viernes Santo
April 16	José de Diego's birthday	Día de José Diego
May 29, 2006/May 28, 2007	Memorial Day	Día de la Recordación
June 23	St. John the Baptist Day	Día de San Juan Bautista
July 4	US Independence Day	Día de la Independencia de los Estados Unidos
July 17	Luis Muñoz Riviera's birthday	Día del Natalicio de Luis Muñoz Riviera
July 25	Constitution Day	Día de la Constitución de Puerto Rico
July 27	José Celso Barbosa's birthday	Día del Natalicio de José Celso Barbosa
September 4, 2006/September 3, 2007	Labor Day	Día del Trabajo
October 9, 2006/October 8, 2007	Columbus Day	Día del Descubrimiento de América
November 11	Veteran's Day	Día del Veterano
November 19	Discovery of Puerto Rico Day	Día del Descubrimiento de Puerto Rico
November 23, 2006/November 22, 2007	Thanksgiving	Día de Acción de Gracias
December 25	Christmas Day	Día de la Navidad

PATRON SAINT FESTIVALS

DATE	PATRON SAINT	TOWN
January 9	La Sagrada Familia	Corozal
February 2	La Virgen de la Candelaria	Coamo, Manatí, Mayagüez
February 3	San Blas	Coamo, Guayama
March 17	San Patricio	Loíza
March 19	San José	Ciales, Gurabo, Luquillo
March 31	San Benito	Patillas
April 29	San Pedro Martín	Guaynabo
May 1	Apóstol San Felipe	Arecibo
May 3	La Santa Cruz	Bayamón, Trujillo Alto
May 30	San Fernando	Carolina
June 13	San Antonio de Padua	Barranquitas, Ceiba, Dorado, Guayama, Isabela
June 24	San Juan Bautista	Maricao, Orocovis, San Juan
July 16	Virgen del Carmen	Arroyo, Barceloneta, Cataño, Hatillo, Morovis
July 25	Santiago Apóstol	Aibonito, Fajardo, Guánica, Loíza
July 31	San Germán	San Germán
August 30	Santa Rosa de Lima	Rincón
September 8	Nuestra Señora de la Monserrate	Jayuya, Moca, Salinas
September 29	San Miguel Arcangel	Cabo Rojo, Naranjito, Utuado
October 2	Los Angles Custodios	Yabucoa

DATE	PATRON SAINT	TOWN
October 7	Nuestra Señora del Rosario	Naguabo, Vega Baja
October 12	La Virgen del Pilar	Río Piedras
November 4	San Carlos Borromeo	Aguadilla
December 8	La Inmaculada Concepción de María	Humacao, Vieques
December 12	Nuestra Señora de la Guadalupe	Ponce
December 28	Día de los Inocentes	Hatillo, Morovis

ADDITIONAL RESOURCES

HISTORY

The Taínos: Rise and Decline of the People Who Greeted Columbus. Irvin Rouse (Yale University Press, 1993). The most informed and accessible history of Puerto Rico's first major civilization from their migration to the Caribbean to the decline of the civilization.

Puerto Rico: A Political and Cultural History. Antonio Morales Carrión (W.W. Norton and Company, Inc., 1983). A bit dry and overly academic, but one of the few comprehensive histories of Puerto Rico available in English.

Puerto Rico: A Colonial Experiment. Raymond Carr (New York University Press, 1984). Though it can be difficult to find, this work by British historian Raymond Carr is one of the standard reads about Puerto Rico's complex relationship with the United States.

SCIENCE AND NATURE

A Guide to the Birds of Puerto Rico and the Virgin Islands. Herbert Raffaele, Cindy House, and John Wiessinger (Princeton University Press, 1989). This is hands-down the best book for bird-watchers traveling to Puerto Rico.

Where Dwarfs Reign: A Tropical Rain Forest in Puerto Rico. Katherine Robinson (University of Puerto Rico Press, 1997). A thorough look at the historical, geological, biological, and mineral aspects of El Yunque.

CULTURE

Puerto Rico, Borinquén Querida. Roger A. Labrucherie (Imágenes Press, 2001). A photojournalist's account of the culture, history, and natural wonders of the island, highlighted with spectacular photos.

Stories from Puerto Rico/Historias de Puerto Rico. Robert L. Muckley and Adela Martínez-Santiago (Passport Books, 1999). Eighteen traditional Puerto Rican folk tales with short historical contextualizations. The book is part of the Bilingual Books series and all stories appear in both English and Spanish.

Puerto Rico Mío: Four Decades of Change. Jack Delano, Arturo Carrion, and Sidney Mintz (Smithsonian Institution Press, 1990). This widely-acclaimed work combines Delano's photographs from 1941, with photos of the same places in 1981 to illustrate the change, consistency, and beauty of island life.

Boricuas: Influential Puerto Rican Writings. Robert Santiago (Ballantine Books, 1995). With 50 short stories, plays, poems, and essays, this anthology provides a solid introduction to Puerto Rican writings of the 19th and 20th centuries, as well as a glimpse into the island's culture and history.

Clemente! Kal Wagenheim and Wilfrid Sheed (Olmstead Press, 2001). Using narrative and interviews, Wagenheim and Sheed detail the life and career of Puerto Rico's most famous baseball legend, Roberto Clemente.

FICTION

Juan Bobo Goes To Work: A Puerto Rican Folk Tale. Marisa Montes (Harper Collins Juvenile Books, 2000). This short children's book relates the misadventures of Juan Bobo, a Puerto Rican version of Foolish Jack. The protagonist, a popular Puerto Rican folk character, has his own statue on one of Condado's plazas.

When I Was Puerto Rican. Esmeralda Santiago (Vintage Books, 1994). Santiago recalls her childhood growing up in the Puerto Rican countryside and her move to Brooklyn at age 13. One of the most popular novels about Puerto Rican life.

The Rum Diary: A Novel. Hunter S. Thompson (Scribner Paperback Fiction, 1999). Though Thompson's first novel falls far short of his dream to create the great Puerto Rican novel, it does provide an interesting glimpse at Condado in the 1950s. Plotless, but interesting.

LIFE AND TIMES

BEYOND TOURISM

A PHILOSOPHY FOR TRAVELERS

Let's Go believes that the connection between travelers and their destinations is an important one. We know that many travelers care passionately about the communities and environments they explore, but we also know that even conscientious tourists can inadvertently damage natural wonders and native communities. With this Beyond Tourism chapter, *Let's Go* hopes to promote a better understanding of Puerto Rico and enhance your experience there. You'll also find Beyond Tourism information throughout the book in the form of special "Giving Back" sidebar features that highlight regional Beyond Tourism opportunities.

There are several options for those who seek to participate in Beyond Tourism activities. Opportunities for **volunteerism** abound, both with local and international organizations. As a volunteer in Puerto Rico you can participate in projects from helping to research sustainable hardwood foresting techniques in Bosque Estatal Carite to tutoring elementary students at high risk for dropping out of school—either on a short-term basis or as the main component of your trip. Later in this chapter, we recommend organizations that can help you find the opportunities that best suit your interests. **Studying** can also be instructive, whether through direct enrollment in a local university or in an independent research project. Enrolling in a Spanish-language program is a popular option—most students immerse themselves in the Spanish language and Puerto Rican culture through a combination of classes and a homestay with a Puerto Rican family. Many programs meet for around 20hr. per week, leaving students plenty of free time to enjoy the island. There is also a limited number of programs in ecology and astrophysics. Some travelers structure their trips by the **work** that they can do along the way—either odd jobs as they go, or full-time stints in cities where they plan to stay for some time. *Let's Go* does not recommend working in Puerto Rico, because the island's longstanding high unemployment rates mean that travelers who work will take much-needed jobs away from locals.

BEYOND TOURISM HIGHLIGHTS

RESEARCH sustainable forestry techniques at **Las Casas de la Selva** (p. 85).

BUILD homes for **low-income Puerto Ricans** in San Juan (p. 87).

SPEAK with locals in Spanish after studying at a **language school** in Puerto Rico (p. 90).

TEACH communities about **environmental preservation** (p. 86).

 Start your search at ▨**www.beyondtourism.com,** Let's Go's brand-new search able database of alternatives to tourism, where you can find exciting feature articles and helpful program listings divided by country and program type.

VOLUNTEERING

Volunteering can be one of the most fulfilling experiences you have in life, especially if you combine it with the thrill of traveling in a new place. In Puerto Rico, many volunteers pitch in to help conserve the amazing flora and fauna on the island. In the last 50 years a concentrated effort to preserve Puerto Rico's

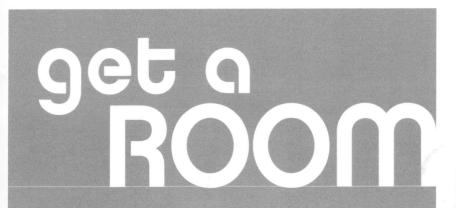

get a
ROOM

Crash at the best hotels and hostels
across the globe on any budget.

STA TRAVEL

www.statravel.com

(800) 777.0112

CST #1017560-40

natural resources has emerged. Now, several of the island's endangered species, such as the Puerto Rican parrot and the Leatherback sea turtle, are trying to make a comeback—with a little help. Volunteers can do everything from guarding turtle eggs during breeding season on the beaches of Culebra to rebuilding coral reefs in the seas surrounding the island. But ecological work isn't the only volunteer opportunity in Puerto Rico. Inner-city volunteer programs address issues such as educational shortfalls, poverty and housing shortages. Opportunities to teach school children, advocate for social justice, and promote community education abound.

Most people who volunteer in Puerto Rico do so on a short-term basis, at organizations that make use of drop-in or once-a-week volunteers. Most short-term opportunities are in environmental conservation. The best way to find opportunities that match up with your interests and schedule may be to check with **VolunteerMatch** (☎415-241-6855; www.volunteermatch.org) or **www.idealist.org,** which list volunteer openings with various organizations in Puerto Rico, though you are responsible for contacting the individual programs. Current listings include working in disaster relief services and volunteering at a community library.

Those looking for longer, more intensive volunteer opportunities usually choose to go through a parent organization that takes care of logistical details and often provides a group environment and support system—for a fee. There are two main types of organizations—religious and non-sectarian—although there are rarely restrictions on participation in either. Teaching and community-building activities generally require more training and a longer period of commitment.

WHY PAY MONEY TO VOLUNTEER?

Many volunteers are surprised to learn that some organizations require large fees or "donations." While this may seem ridiculous at first glance, such fees often keep the organization afloat, in addition to covering airfare, room, board, and administrative expenses for the volunteers. (Other organizations must rely on private donations and government subsidies.) If you're concerned about how a program spends its fees, request an annual report or finance account. A reputable organization will not refuse to inform you of how volunteer money is spent. Pay-to-volunteer programs might be a good idea for young travelers who are looking for more support and structure (such as pre-arranged transportation and housing), or anyone who would rather not deal with the uncertainty implicit in creating a volunteer experience from scratch.

ENVIRONMENTAL CONSERVATION

A precious 1% of Puerto Rico's virgin rainforest remained in the mid-20th century after the commonwealth's agricultural and industrial development. Underwater habitats such as coral reefs and shoreline mangroves also suffered as a result of industrial pollution and unsustainable development. Over the last 30 years, grassroots movements and activists such as Alexis Massol González—who was awarded the 2002 Goldman Environmental prize, the equivalent a Nobel Prize for environmentalists—have started to reverse this trend. Reforestation efforts have produced encouraging results. The island now faces the challenge of promoting economic development while simultaneously preserving its unique natural habitats. Volunteers are able to spend time working in Puerto Rico's beautiful outdoors environments with the goal of preserving them for generations to come.

Las Casas de la Selva, Rte. 184 Km 17.6 (☎839-7318; www.eyeontherainforest.org), in **Reserva Forestal Carite** (p. 290), outside of Patillas. This 1000-acre project is dedicated to the idea that rainforest can be preserved even as some of its resources are used for profit. Owned by the nonprofit Tropic Ventures and monitored by the Department of Natural Resources. Welcomes group and individual volunteers to stay a weekend or as long as a month to help with its many projects, from planting trees to building retaining walls to working in the nursery. Rustic accommodations are available for a small, negotiable fee. Food available at additional cost. For more information, see **Constructive Conservation, p. 300.**

Casa Pueblo, C. Rodulfo González 30, Adjuntas (☎829-4842; www.casapueblo.org). Founded in 1980 to campaign against environmentally destructive mining (see **In the People's House, p. 305**), this local nonprofit runs projects in environmental education, research, and advocacy. Volunteers accepted on a case-by-case basis and must provide their own accommodations and food.

Universidad de Puerto Rico Río Piedras Jardín Botánico, intersection of Hwy. 1 and Hwy. 3 (☎765-1845), Río Piedras, San Juan. Short-term volunteers to work as tour guides, gardeners, or teachers. No housing offered.

Earthwatch Institute, 3 Clock Tower Place Ste. 100, Box 75, Maynard, MA 01754, USA (☎800-776-0188; www.earthwatch.org). An international nonprofit organization that promotes the conservation of natural resources and cultural heritage around the world. Offers expeditions to Puerto Rico primarily dealing in flora and fauna preservation. Expeditions about $1000/week for one or two weeks. Membership $35 per year.

WILDLIFE CONSERVATION

A flash of brilliant red and green feathers, a series of squawks and squeaks—you've just witnessed the flight of one of 40 remaining endangered wild Puerto Rican parrots. Deforestation, coupled with agricultural development and industrialization, has destroyed Puerto Rican natural environments and their unique inhabitants—such as the Puerto Rican parrot—both on land and underwater. Through preservation efforts, animal populations are slowly recovering. With the help of dedicated scientists and volunteers, Puerto Rico's brilliant birds, tremendous turtles, and myriad marine life may be allowed to flourish for generations to come. Volunteering to help conserve Puerto Rican wildlife represents an opportunity to work with some of the rarest animals in the world.

US Fish & Wildlife Service (☎800-344-9453; www.fws.gov), has 3 offices around Puerto Rico.

Cabo Rojo office, Rte. 301 Km 5.1 (☎851-7258 ext. 35). Participates in the **Student Temporary Employment Program,** which pays full-time students to spend 1 year working and studying on the reserve. Housing available.

Vieques office, Rte. 200 Km 0.4 (☎741-2138; http://southeast.fws.gov/vieques). Accepts volunteers on an individual basis, but has no housing or structured program.

Culebra office, on Rte. 250 (☎742-0115). The best place to go if you want to work with turtles. Accepts individual volunteers and sometimes has housing available. Check www.volunteer.gov for information about projects around the island not associated with any particular office.

CORALations, P.O. Box 750, Culebra (☎787-556-6234; info@coralations.org). Focuses on coral reef preservation (see **Coral-ating Success, p. 199**). Volunteers can assist with beach clean-up, underwater coral farm development, and water quality studies. CORALations is in the process of developing accommodations for volunteers. Email for more details.

Vieques Conservation and Historical Trust, C. Flamboyán 138, Esperanza, Vieques(☎741-8850; www.vcht.com). Works to protect and preserve the natural resources of Vieques. Accepts volunteers on a case-by-case basis to help with various projects, including maintenance of the marine tank, animal collection from Vieques shores and coral reefs, feeding of animals, staffing of the gift shop and occasional fund-raisers. No housing. Contact Mark Martin for more information.

YOUTH AND COMMUNITY

Poorer than any US state but wealthier than any country in Latin America, Puerto Rico is still feeling the growing pains of economic development. An unemployment rate of around 11%, low education levels, and a housing shortage of approximately 100,000 dwellings are among the island's biggest economic and social challenges. Volunteers can impact Puerto Rico's future by teaching in struggling schools, working as community educators, or constructing affordable housing.

Vieques Humane Society, Rte. 200, Barrio Santa Maria, Vieques (☎741-0209; www.enchanted-isle.com/vhs/index.html; viequeshumansociety@hotmail.com). Educates communities about animal care and assists abandoned animals. Volunteers bathe, feed, and walk animals and sometimes assist in the clinic. Provides a shared room, bath, and kitchen in exchange for 20hr. per week of volunteering. Call at least a month in advance to check for housing availability.

Habitat for Humanity, 1357 Avenida Ashford, PMB 135, San Juan (☎640-5308; www.habitat.org). Builds houses around the world for low-income families. Puerto Rico does not have an established volunteer program, but the local chapter welcomes volunteers for a day or a year. They do not provide room and board, but they can sometimes arrange for a small stipend.

Puerto Rico Center for Social Concerns, P.O. Box 70171 PMB 152, San Juan (☎474-1912; www.prcfsc.org). Recent college graduates can volunteer for 1-2 years in various capacities, including teaching English, working with the homeless, and constructing homes. Airfare, housing, and stipend provided.

Americorps (www.americorps.org). Offers a variety of opportunities in Puerto Rico in education, conservation, and community-building for US citizens, nationals, or permanent legal residents ages 17+. Programs 10-12 months. Food and accommodations provided at no cost. Scholarships of $5000 for higher education available.

Museo del Niño, C. San Cristo 150, San Juan (☎722-3791; www.museodelninopr.org). Accepts university student volunteers in various capacities. Applications must be made in person at the museum.

STUDYING

Study abroad programs range from basic language and culture courses to college-level classes, often for credit. In order to choose a program that best fits your needs, research as much as you can before making your decision—determine costs and duration, as well as what kind of students participate in the program and what sort of accommodations are provided.

In programs that have large groups of students who speak the same language, there is a trade-off. You may feel more comfortable in the community, but you will not have the same opportunity to practice a foreign language or to befriend other international students. For accommodations, dorm life provides a better opportunity to mingle with fellow students, but there is less of a chance to experience the local scene. If you live with a family, there is a potential to build life-long friendships with natives and to experience day-to-day life in more depth, but conditions can vary greatly from family to family.

BEYOND TOURISM

VISA INFORMATION

Students enrolling in a program for less than 18hr. per week may be able to do so on a tourist visa. Students who wish to study more than that must apply for a F, M, of J visa. These can be obtained at the nearest US embassy or consulate and cost around $100. In order to obtain a visa, students must present a passport valid for more than 6 months, academic transcripts, standardized test scores, and proof of financial support. More information is available at www.travel.state.gov. **US citizens never need a visa to study in Puerto Rico.**

UNIVERSITIES

Most university-level study abroad programs are conducted in Spanish, although many programs offer classes in English and beginner- and lower-level language courses. Those relatively fluent in Spanish may find it cheaper to enroll directly in a university abroad, although getting college credit may be more difficult. You can search www.studyabroad.com for various semester-abroad programs that meet your criteria, including your desired location and focus of study. The following is a list of organizations that can help place students in university programs abroad, or have their own branch in Puerto Rico.

AMERICAN PROGRAMS

Several institutions based in the United States offer year-long, semester-long, and summer-long programs of study in Puerto Rico. Most of these center around Spanish-language studies. These programs do not have citizenship restrictions, but often have academic requirements. Most programs arrange accommodations for students either in university housing or at a homestay.

American Institute for Foreign Study, College Division, River Plaza, 9 West Broad St., Stamford, CT 06902, USA (☎800-727-2437; www.aifsabroad.com). Organizes a summer program in Puerto Rican culture and Spanish language for high school and college students at the University of Puerto Rico.

International Association for the Exchange of Students for Technical Experience (IAESTE), 10400 Little Patuxent Pkwy. Ste. 250, Columbia, MD 21044, USA (☎410-997-2200; www.aipt.org/subpages/iaeste_us/index.php). Offers 8- to 12-week internships in Puerto Rico for college students who have completed 2 years of technical study. $50 application fee.

National Astronomy and Ionosphere Center, 504 Spaces Sciences Bldg., Cornell University, Ithaca, NY 14853, USA (☎607-255-3735; www.naic.edu; jtm14@cornell.edu). Offers a 10-week research assistant program for 6-12 US citizens who are currently enrolled in an undergraduate program. Applications due early Feb. Housing and a stipend provided. 1-2 positions available for graduate students enrolled at US schools. Students need not be US citizens.

Two Worlds United Educational Foundation, 503 E. Jackson ST. Ste. 250, Tampa, FL 33602, USA (☎888-696-8808; www.twoworldsunited.com). Offers programs of various lengths for Spanish-language studies in Puerto Rico.

PUERTO RICAN UNIVERSITIES

If you are not a US citizen it may be more expensive to enroll directly in a Puerto Rican university, as funding for some programs is restricted to US citizens. A US visa may be difficult to obtain for citizens of countries outside of western Europe, Australia, and Canada. Most study abroad programs are based out of San Juan.

ANOTHER SIDE OF PARADISE
Volunteering at a Public Library in San Juan

Puerto Rico is indeed an enchanted island, but *puertorriqueños* manage to pull themselves away from their beautiful beaches and carry on normal lives beyond the coast. They go to school, debate local and international politics, and discuss news from around the world. As elsewhere, the world is becoming smaller thanks to the advances in technology and communication, the Internet, and Google. However, although in Puerto Rico the number of TVs per household outnumbers people, computers and other forms of information technology are still privileged commodities. Many people rely on libraries and paper resources for information. Unfortunately, libraries are scarce. Though universities and private schools have growing collections, from my own experience, these are often intimidating and hard to access, especially by those who lack the know-how of researching.

Yet there are a few libraries that are much less daunting and more user-friendly, perhaps because they are staffed by volunteers. During high school, I had the opportunity to work at one of these libraries. I came away from the experience with a new perspective on the community, a new appreciation for librarians, and the discovery that a little bit of volunteering can go a long way.

On Saturdays, during high school, I worked the morning shift at the San Juan Community Library. This is a relatively small library that obtains most of its resources from book donations and philanthropic funding. Despite its diminutive size, San Juan Community Library has a diverse collection of novels, reference books, magazines, and children's books. When I worked there, it also had a copier, four computers with Internet access, and even a digitalized library catalog—not bad for a community library entirely run by volunteers! The best part of it was that anyone could become a member at a very low cost and late fees were minimal (I believe only $0.25 per day).

As a librarian, I learned about the ins and outs of running a library, from cataloging and shelving books to maintaining databases and reordering supplies. The library held a children's reading hour on Saturdays, and I would read to the kids for about 30min. or until they became distracted. I also helped to run the library's reading contests for school-aged children, which challenged them to read a certain number of books in a short amount of time. Yet my most rewarding experiences came when I was able to help others use library resources. There is one particular incident that stands out, which I will always treasure in my memory. A teenage boy and his father from a nearby *barrio* came in search of information about dinosaurs for a school assignment. They didn't know where to start looking. After I helped them to perform various keyword searches and reference checks, we hit on enough information to complete his project, pictures and all. I distinctly remember how the boy's face lit up when we picked out which information would be most valuable. The father's pride showed in the twinkle in his eyes as he stood back and watched his son excitedly examine the pages in front of him. It was the most rewarding experience during my time as a volunteer, because I was able to introduce the boy to a whole new world of information.

The library served as a haven for a regular group of book-loving patrons. A neighborhood boy, who had an insatiable thirst for books, would show up every Saturday and ask if there had been any additions to the library. It was heart-warming to see someone with so much curiosity and love of literature. Another little girl would come in regularly to read the next installment of *The Baby-sitters Club*. She would check out four books at once, and have them read by the following Saturday. Her father said that she just devoured the books.

I had a great experience volunteering at the library and would have liked to have continued, mostly because the library is short-staffed, and thus has limited hours. I would love to see the library expand its hours and its size. If you find yourself on the island for an extended period of time, stop by and sign up to volunteer a couple of hours a week. The least you would gain would be a chance to meet the other volunteers; more likely, you would have the chance to open the world of books to someone who has yet to discover it.

For more information on how to help, contact Connie Estades, Head Librarian of the San Juan Community Library (787-789-4600). Both English- and Spanish-speakers are welcome.

María Pilar Barreto is a native of Guaynabo. She is currently pursuing an undergraduate degree in Latin American Studies at Harvard University. She hopes to enter a career in diplomacy or in any field where she can put her language skills to use.

Universidad de Puerto Rico, P.O. Box 364984, San Juan, 00936 (☎250-0000 ext. 3208 or 3202; www.upr.edu). The largest university system in Puerto Rico, with campuses in Aguadilla, Arecibo, Bayamón, Carolina, Cayey, Humacao, Mayagüez, Ponce, Río Piedras, and Utuado. The central Río Piedras campus alone has 23,000 students. Students must have at least an intermediate level of Spanish to enroll. Tuition for nonresident students $2470 per year. Some dormitories available.

InterAmerican University of Puerto Rico, C. Galileo Final, Urb. Jardines Metropolitanos, Río Piedras, San Juan; P.O. Box 363255, San Juan 00936 (☎766-1912; www.inter.edu). Campuses in Aguadilla, Arecibo, Barranquitas, Bayamón, Fajardo, Guayama, Ponce, San Germán, and San Juan. The original campus is in San Germán. With 38,000 students, this is the oldest and largest private university system in Puerto Rico. Most coursework is in Spanish, but the university offers a separate trimester program in English. Spanish immersion program available. Undergraduate tuition $120 per credit plus miscellaneous fees. Catalog available online in English. Many students live in dormitories on the San Germán campus.

Universidad del Sagrado Corazón, P.O. Box 12383, San Juan 00914 (☎728-1515; www.sagrado.edu), in the heart of Santurce. Known for its outstanding communications department, this university was established in 1880 and has a student population of 5000. Offers programs in humanities, communications, education, social sciences, business administration, and natural sciences. All classes are conducted in Spanish.

LANGUAGE SCHOOLS

Language schools can be independently run international or local organizations or divisions of foreign universities. They rarely offer college credit. They are a good alternative to university study if you desire a deeper focus on the language or a slightly less rigorous courseload. These programs are also good for younger high school students who might not feel comfortable with older students in a university program. A listing of Spanish language programs can be found at www.studyspanish.com/schools/agencies_2.html. Some worthwhile programs include:

AmeriSpan, P.O. Box 58129, Philadelphia, PA 19102, USA (☎800-879-6640, outside of US 215-751-1100; www.amerispan.com). Offers language programs for all levels in San Juan for anywhere from 1 week to 6 months. Price includes homestay with local family. Max. class size 6. Reserve at least 4 weeks in advance. $100 registration fee. 1 week $450, with meals $525; 4 weeks $1700/2000.

A2Z Languages, 5112 N. 40th St., ste. 103, Phoenix, AZ 85018, USA (☎800-496-4596; www.a2zlanguages.com). Offers language programs for all levels in San Juan. Price includes homestay. 1 week min. Max. class size 6. 1 week $430, with 2 meals per day $500; 4 weeks $1580/1860. Private lessons available at an additional cost.

Instituto Interdisciplinario y Multicultural, Domingo Marrero Navarro Building, María Rivera Room, 3rd fl., College of General Studies. University of Puerto Rico, Río Piedras (☎787-764-0000; http://generales.upr.clu.edu/INIM/inim_english.htm). Programs in Spanish language and culture. Some offer college credit. Tuition varies by program from $500-2200 for 3-week courses with meals, dorm housing, and transportation included.

Instituto Internacional Euskalduna, C. Navarro 56, Hato Rey, PR 00918 (☎787-281-8013; www.spanishinpuertorico.com). Spanish immersion classes for speakers of all levels. Classes 20hr. per week plus weekly excursions and cultural activities. Max. class size 6. Courses start at $300 per week. Homestays $150 per week, with meals $225.

LanguagesAbroad (In North America ☎800-219-9924, elsewhere 416-925-2112; www.languagesabroad.com). Spanish-language programs for students of all levels in San Juan. Classes 20hr. per week. Max. class size 6. Courses start at $300 per week. Homestays $150 per week, with meals $225.

Language Immersion Institute, JFT 214, State University of New York at New Paltz, 75 S. Manheim Blvd., New Paltz, NY 12561, USA (☎845-257-3500; www.newpaltz.edu/lii). 2-week summer language courses and some overseas courses in Spanish. Program fees are around $1000 for a 2-week course, not including accommodations.

Pan American Language Institute, PMB 295, P.O. Box 7891, Guaynabo, PR 00970 (☎787-793-4995, 787-782-0717, or toll-free 866-793-4995; www.panamericanlanguage.com). Offers individual lessons in Spanish on a flexible schedule. Housing not provided. 60 lessons start at $1680.

Spanish Abroad, Inc., 5112 N. 40th St., ste. 203, Phoenix, AZ 85018, USA (US and Canada ☎888-722-7623, UK 800-028-7706, elsewhere 602-778-6791; www.spanishabroad.com). Spanish immersion programs at the Instituto Internacional Spanish Language School in San Juan. Class 20hr. per week plus outings. Max. class size 6. Courses start at $270 per week. Homestays $125 per week, with meals $205.

ADDITIONAL RESOURCES

Alternatives to the Peace Corps: A Directory of Third World and U.S. Volunteer Opportunities, by Jennifer S. Willsea. Food First Books, 2003 ($10).

America's Guide to Volunteering and Community Service, by Blaustein. John Wiley & Sons, 2003 ($11).

Back Door Guide to Short-Term Job Adventures: Internships, Extraordinary Experiences, Seasonal Jobs, Volunteering, Working Abroad, by Michael Landes. Ten Speed Press, 2002 ($22).

Green Volunteers: The World Guide to Voluntary Work in Nature, by Ausenda and McCloskey. Universe, 2003 ($15).

How to Live Your Dream of Volunteering Overseas, by Collins, DeZerega, and Heckscher. Penguin Books, 2002 ($17).

International Directory of Voluntary Work, by Whetter and Pybus. Peterson's Guides and Vacation Work, 2000 ($16).

Invest Yourself: The Catalogue of Volunteer Opportunities, published by the Commission on Voluntary Service and Action (☎646-486-2446).

Live and Work Abroad: A Guide for Modern Nomads, by Francis and Callan. Vacation-Work Publications, 2001 ($16).

Vacation Work's International Directory of Voluntary Work, by Whetter and Pybus. Peterson's Guides, 2000 ($11).

Volunteer Vacations: Short-term Adventures That Will Benefit You and Others, by Cutchins and Geissinger. Chicago Review Press, 2003 ($18).

SAN JUAN

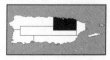

San Juan is not the most beautiful part of Puerto Rico, but it is the most vibrant, with over 25% of the island's population and 30,000 acres of land. This capital of the Caribbean defies classification: ritzy Isla Verde, working-class Santurce, and historic Old San Juan seem like different worlds, yet they are less than 7 mi. apart. The city's rich history and rapid progress are made vivid at sunset on the end of Paseo del Morro, as *sanjuaneros* stroll under the shadow of one of the oldest forts in the New World, in view the of enormous Bacardi factory across the bay.

For centuries, San Juan has been the center of attention on Puerto Rico. After Juan Ponce de León moved the island's capital from Caparra to San Juan in 1521, the Spanish constructed a giant wall around the city, considering it to be the only part of the island worth protecting. For the next 200 years San Juan served as a military base, evident today in the city's many fortresses. Old San Juan, where the Spanish capital once was, continues to be perceived as the heart of the city. Overflowing with history, culture, and charm, the old city has enough museums, galleries, and restaurants to satisfy any traveler. Sometimes it can seem like just another cruise stop, with every business competing to impress the one-day visitors, but a walk down the quiet streets of Calle Sol and Calle Luna proves that underneath the hype, the real old city continues to shine.

It wasn't until the 18th century that San Juan saw modernization, when economic reforms jump-started the city's growth. Working-class *sanjuaneros* migrated into Puerta de la Tierra, while the white minority settled in suburban Santurce. In the early 20th century the population of the city grew dramatically, producing a sprawling metropolitan area, and, in the 1950s, tourism hit the city. When the Cuban Revolution narrowed the choice of Caribbean travel destinations, Condado became the new hot spot. Today, Condado has become a center of gay culture, Hato Rey has emerged as an international financial powerhouse, and Río Piedras is the hub for university students and working-class vendors. Visitors who want rub elbows with locals, visit authentic markets, or check out city beaches should stop by these neighborhoods for a real taste of Puerto Rican life. *Sanjuaneros* have been known to go their entire lives without venturing outside the metropolitan area and it's easy to see why: everything you could ever want is here.

HIGHLIGHTS OF SAN JUAN

STEP BACK IN TIME on the cobblestone streets of **Old San Juan** (p. 119).

SHAKE YOUR BONBON with s*anjuaneros* at one of the city's hopping **discos** (p. 140).

GAZE at the impressive collection of art in Santurce's **Museo de Arte** (p. 132).

LOUNGE on the **white sand beaches** of Condado (p. 96), Ocean Park (p. 97), and Isla Verde (p. 97).

MUNCH on tropical fruits and fresh *batidas* in Río Piedras' **Plaza del Mercado,** San Juan's largest food market (p. 125).

✈ INTERCITY TRANSPORTATION

Flights: Aeropuerto Internacional Luis Muñoz Marín, on the eastern edge of San Juan in Isla Verde. Most major US airlines fly into San Juan (see **By Plane,** p. 28). **Iberia** is the main

European airline. Although more expensive than the bus, **taxis** are an affordable and very convenient way travel to and from the airport. Go to a marked "Ground Transportation" booth outside baggage claim and an English-speaking official will provide a set fare and a taxi. The cheaper (and much longer) way is by **bus.** Take bus B40 or C45 from the 2nd level in front of terminal C, then sit back and relax: the bus will complete its entire 45-60min. route before arriving in Isla Verde. From there, wait in front of the Isla Verde Mall for bus A5, which goes through Santurce and Puerta de la Tierra en route to Old San Juan. To get to the airport, take bus A5 to Isla Verde and get off at the end of Av. Isla Verde, in front of the orange cockfight arena (40min. from Old San Juan). Then switch to bus B40 or C45 (5min.). The airport is a 5min. **drive** from Isla Verde, 12min. from Condado, and 15min. from Old San Juan. The **Puerto Rico Tourism Company** tourist information office is outside the lower level of terminal C. (☎ 791-1014. Open daily 9am-8pm.) **Aeropuerto de Isla Grande** (☎ 729-8751), on the eastern edge of Puerta de la Tierra, hosts several smaller airlines flying primarily to Vieques, Culebra, and Santo Domingo. Taxis usually wait out front when flights come in; if they're not there, have the security guard call one. Open daily 6am-10pm.

Públicos: *Públicos* (shared vans) are Puerto Rico's only public form of intercity transportation. In San Juan, *públicos* congregate in **Río Piedras** and leave when full (approx. 6am-3pm, although a few may be available later). Arrive early for a faster departure. Drivers sit outside of the vans waiting for passengers; just tell any driver your destination and he'll point you in the right direction. The central **Terminal de Transportación Juan A. Palerm,** at the intersection of C. Arzuaga and C. Vallejo, near the market, houses *públicos* headed east to: **Fajardo** (1hr., $3.50) via **Luquillo** (45min., $3); and **Loíza** (30min., $1.75). Additional *públicos* leave from **Río Piedras's Plaza de Armas,** 1 block south of Paseo de Diego to: **Bayamón** (30min., $3); **Caguas** (30min., $2.50); **Guaynabo** (40min., $0.75); **Humacao** (45min.-1hr., $2.50); **Ponce** (1½hr., $10) via **Salinas** (1hr., $10). **Linea Boricua,** C. González 116 (☎ 765-1908), operates out of the Librería Norberto González parking lot. Walking downhill on C. González; the parking lot is on the right at the intersection with C. Jorge Romany. *Públicos* go to **San Sebastián** (1½-2hr., $12). **Linea Sultana,** C. Esteban González 898 (☎ 767-5205 or 765-9377), at Av. Universidad, sends vans to **Mayagüez** (3½hr., every 2hr. 7:30am-5:30pm, $12). **Linea DonQ,** C. Brumbaugh 102 (☎ 764-0540), sends *públicos* to **Ponce** (1½hr., 3-4 per day, $10).

Cars: All of the major American car rental companies have booths in the Luis Muñoz Marín International Airport. Some of the less-expensive companies are listed below. For a complete list see p. 32. Unless otherwise stated, all price quotes are for compact cars with unlimited mileage.

AAA Car Rental (☎ 791-1465 or 791-2609), in the Condominio Saint Tropez, Isla Verde. Nov. 24-May $35-45 per day; Apr.-Nov. 23 $35; special deals as low as $27 per day. As low as $695 per month. Ages 21-24 $10 per day surcharge. Open M-Sa 9am-6pm. AmEx/D/MC/V.

Charlie Car Rental (☎ 728-2418, toll-free 800-289-1227; www.charliecars.com), on Av. Isla Verde, across from the Borinquen Beach Inn, Isla Verde. High season $45-55 per day; low season $30-34. Ages 21-24 $10 per day surcharge. Open 24hr. AmEx/D/DC/MC/V.

Hertz, Av. Ashford 1365 (☎ 725-2027 or 800-654-3131; fax 725-5537), Condado. From $35 per day. Ages 21-24 $10 per day surcharge. Open daily 8am-noon and 1-5pm. AmEx/D/DC/MC/V.

▓ ORIENTATION

San Juan is conveniently divided into distinct neighborhoods, each with its own ambience and almost all of which are dominated by one major thoroughfare that holds the majority of the shops and services. The neighborhoods normally frequented by visitors are described below.

SAN JUAN

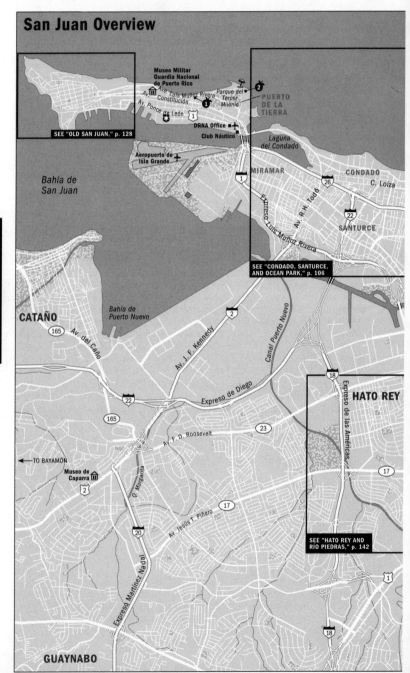

San Juan Overview

SEE "OLD SAN JUAN," p. 128

Museo Militar
Guardia Nacional
de Puerto Rico

Av. Luis Muñoz Rivera
Av. Constitución
Av. Ponce de León

Parque del
Tercer
Milenio

PUERTO
DE LA
TIERRA

DRNA Office
Club Náutico

Aeropuerto de
Isla Grande

Bahía de
San Juan

Laguna
del Condado

MIRAMAR

CONDADO

C. Loíza

Expreso Luis Muñoz Rivera

Av. R.H. Todd

SANTURCE

SEE "CONDADO, SANTURCE,
AND OCEAN PARK," p. 106

CATAÑO

Bahía de
Puerto Nuevo

Av. del Caño

Av. J. F. Kennedy

Canal Puerto Nuevo

Expreso de Diego

HATO REY

Expreso de las Américas

Av. F. D. Roosevelt

TO BAYAMÓN

Museo de
Caparra

Q. Margarita

Av. Jesús T. Piñero

Expreso Martínez Nadal

SEE "HATO REY AND
RÍO PIEDRAS," p. 142

GUAYNABO

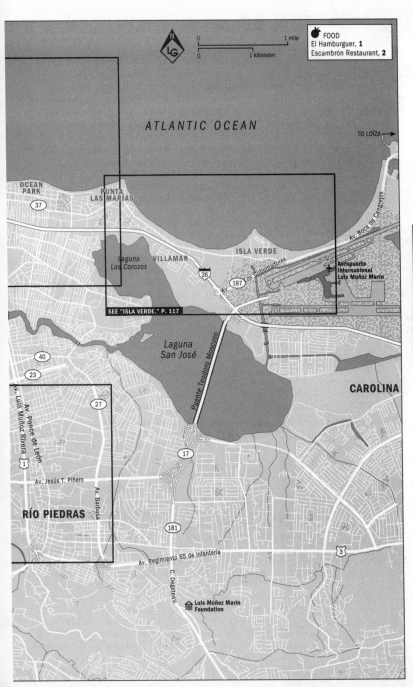

FOOD
El Hamburguer, 1
Escambrón Restaurant, 2

ATLANTIC OCEAN

TO LOÍZA →

OCEAN
PARK

37

PUNTA
LAS MARÍAS

Av. Boca de Cangrejos

VILLAMAR

ISLA VERDE

Laguna
Los Corozos

26

187

Av. Los Gobernadores

Aeropuerto
Internacional
Luis Muñoz Marín

SEE "ISLA VERDE," P. 117

Laguna
San José

Puente Teodoro Moscoso

CAROLINA

40

23

27

Av. Ponce de León

Av. Luis Muñoz Rivera

1

17

Av. Jesús T. Piñero

Av. Barbosa

RÍO PIEDRAS

181

3

Av. Regimiento 65 de Infantería

C. Degetau

Luis Muñoz Marín
Foundation

S A N   J U A N

ALL ABOARD

San Juan city planners are facing a difficult task: separating Puerto Ricans from their cars. Old wrecks lining the roadsides and driveways across the island attest to the fact that Puerto Ricans are attached to their vehicles. The island has 2.5 million cars for 3.9 million people, the highest vehicle density in the world. *Tapones,* or traffic jams, regularly bog down big cities and small mountain towns alike in clouds of dust and exhaust. The problem is most severe in San Juan, where the twice-daily rush hour can turn highways into parking lots.

In this climate, the June 2005 opening the new Tren Urbano (urban train) in San Juan is a gamble that even the US Department of Transportation calls "high-risk." In an effort to curb growing traffic and pollution problems, the city invested over $2 billion dollars in the project over ten years. Currently the lines go from Bayamón to Sagrado Corazón in San Juan, with stops in Río Piedras, and Hato Rey. Another fifteen years of expansion is planned and future stops will include Luis Muñoz Marín Airport, the eastern suburb of Carolina, and the town of Caguas.

(Visitors to San Juan can take advantage of this budget-friendly transportation option by inquiring about the latest stops and schedule information at the tourist office in Old San Juan, p. 99, or by calling ☎ 866-900-1284. The cost of a ride is $1.50.)

NEIGHBORHOOD SAFETY. Although San Juan is generally safe, visitors should avoid a few specific neighborhoods. **La Perla,** on the northern edge of Old San Juan between the cemetery and San Cristóbal, continues to be dangerous despite increased police surveillance. **Puerta de la Tierra** is fine during the day, but known to house drug dealers at night. In Santurce **Calle Loíza** and the surrounding areas should be avoided after dark. The neighborhood around Río Piedras's **Plaza del Mercado** also becomes a bit foreboding at night.

OLD SAN JUAN. Old San Juan is the tourist center of the city. From November to May, thousands of visitors disembark from cruise ships and find themselves in this neighborhood lined with cobblestone streets and antique buildings. Almost all of the capital's museums and sights are located in Old San Juan, and any visitor to the island should plan to spend at least a day or two here. The old city is easy to navigate on foot, and wandering through the small streets is half the fun. As a general rule, streets go downhill as they go south.

CONDADO. In the 1950s tourists flocked to Condado, the hottest beach destination south of Miami. There are still a few guesthouses from that era, but the big resort chains have now taken up most of the beachfront property. **Avenida Ashford,** a one-way street running parallel to the ocean, has all the restaurants and practical services. The increasingly residential **Calle Magdalena** runs parallel to Ashford, but traffic goes in the opposite direction. San Juan's gay district is within the square bordered by the Wendy's Restaurant to the west, C. Condado to the east, Av. Ashford to the south, and the ocean to the north.

MIRAMAR AND SANTURCE. Lying directly south of Condado and Ocean Park, Miramar and Santurce used to be the centers of San Juan's business community, but over the years the two neighborhoods have slowly deteriorated. Today Miramar is more of a residential neighborhood with a few hotels, while Santurce continues to house many of the city's smaller businesses and government agencies. Santurce in particular has many vacant storefronts and construction sites that should be avoided at night. **Avenida Ponce de León,** the major street that connects the two areas, is home to most of the restaurants, hotels, and services. **Avenida Fernández Juncos** is the street's parallel counterpart, with traffic running in the other direction. **Avenida José de Diego** and **Calle Roberto H. Todd** connect Santurce to Condado. By night, many of the city's major discos open in Santurce.

OCEAN PARK. Ocean Park proper is a gated community lying along the ocean between Condado and Isla Verde, but the term has come to include the surrounding streets as well. Most restaurants lie along **Avenida McLeary,** a continuation of Condado's Av. Ashford, but it's necessary to head into Santurce, Condado, or Isla Verde to find many services. Recently this quiet residential area has been invaded by young Puerto Ricans and North Americans in search of the perfect wave. However, it retains a calm, beachy atmosphere that the more touristy neighborhoods of Condado and Isla Verde and the highly urban Santurce cannot match.

ISLA VERDE. Although technically it's within the city limits of Carolina, most people consider Isla Verde to be part of San Juan. Isla Verde is home to the best beaches in the city, which are bordered by an endless row of resorts and time-share condominiums, along the busy **Avenida Isla Verde.** Beyond this street, a row of shops and stores follows before you reach the freeway. The major roads that cut through the neighborhood can make Isla Verde a difficult area to navigate on foot. Many establishments do not have addresses; instead, they are identified by the condo or building they reside in. If you get confused, ask a local; most have long since memorized the building names. Across the freeway lies tiny **Villamar. Punta las Marías,** the small peninsula dividing Ocean Park from Isla Verde, is home to fantastic restaurants of all stripes. Many surfers have set up camp in this area, and it's a good place to find water sports equipment. In this chapter, establishments in Punta de las Marías are listed under the Isla Verde header.

HATO REY. This is San Juan's business district; almost all of San Juan's major banks call Hato Rey home, and each has its own skyscraper to prove it. **Avenida Ponce de León** and **Avenida Luis Muñoz Rivera (Highway 1),** the two major north-south thoroughfares, hold most of the skyscrapers, while smaller businesses radiate outward. Av. Franklin D. Roosevelt (not to be confused with Av. Eleanor Roosevelt), a busy street with lots of restaurants, connects Av. Ponce de León to Expreso de las Américas and the big mall, Plaza las Américas. Hato Rey is difficult to navigate on foot, as many of the roads do not have sidewalks.

RÍO PIEDRAS. **Avenida Jesús Piñero (Route 17)** divides Hato Rey from Río Piedras, the most recent addition to San Juan. Río Piedras is the most Latin American part of the city, with a large produce and meat market, several *público* stations, Puerto Rico's largest university, and, on nearly every corner, lively *cafeterías* that turn into bars at night. Most visitors spend their time around the university and the market. This area can be a bit confusing, so a map is helpful. Av. Ponce de León and Av. Luis Muñoz Rivera (Hwy. 1) continue south through Río Piedras and connect to east-west Hwy. 3.

▐ LOCAL TRANSPORTATION

Subway: A new commuter rail now runs from Bayamón to Hato Rey (see **All Aboard,** p. 96). Tourists may be most interested in its stops in downtown Río Piedras and at the Universidad de Puerto Rico. Customer service ☎866-900-1284. $1.50; students, disabled, and ages 60-74 $0.75; 75+ free.

Buses: Metropolitan Bus Authority (☎250-6064) runs a comprehensive system throughout San Juan. The helpful A5 line leaves from **Covadonga station** in Old San Juan, follows Av. Ponce de León through Miramar, turns left on Av. José de Domingo, continues along C. Loíza and Av. Isla Verde, and finally ends in Iturregui (last bus 8:45pm). A6 goes from Río Piedras to Carolina. Route B21 leaves from Old San Juan, crosses Puerta de Tierra, follows Av. Ashford through Condado, and continues south to Hato Rey and Plaza Las Américas (last bus M-Sa 9pm, Su 7:45pm). B29 leaves from Río Piedras, heads through the University of Puerto Rico, and ends up in Guaynabo. B40 and C45 both run from Isla Verde to the airport. Metrobús M1 leaves from Old San Juan and passes through Santurce

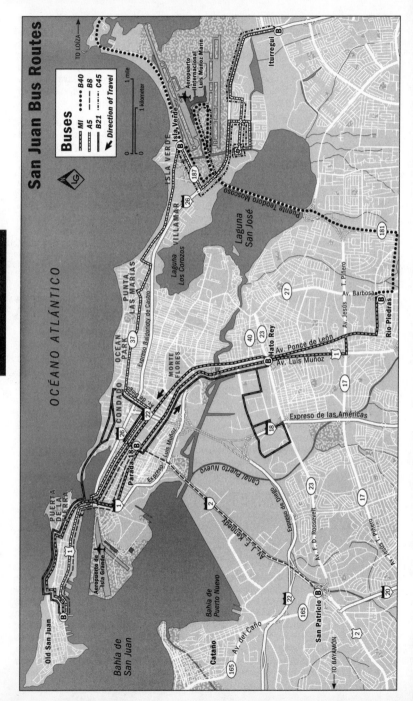

San Juan Bus Routes

Buses

- MI
- A5
- B21 ---- C45
- ---- B40
- ---- B8

→ *Direction of Travel*

0 ——— 1 mile
0 ——— 1 kilometer

OCÉANO ATLÁNTICO

TO LOÍZA →

Aeropuerto Internacional Luis Muñoz Marín

ISLA VERDE
Iturregui
187
26
VILLAMAR
Laguna Los Corozos
Puente Teodoro Moscoso
Laguna San José
181
PUNTA LAS MARIAS
OCEAN PARK
Expreso Baldorioty de Castro
37
27
CONDADO
40 23
Av. Jesús T. Piñero
Av. Barbosa
MONTE FLORES
Hato Rey
Av. Ponce de León
Río Piedras
Av. Luis Muñoz
1
26
22
Av. Luis Muñoz
Parada 18
17
18
Expreso de las Américas
OCÉANO ATLÁNTICO
PUERTA DE TIERRA
Aeropuerto de Isla Grande
1
2
Canal Puerto Nuevo
23
17
Old San Juan
Bahía de San Juan
Bahía de Puerto Nuevo
Expreso de Diego
Av. J. F. Kennedy
Av. F. D. Roosevelt
Av. Jesús T. Piñero
Cataño
165
Av. del Caño
22
165
San Patricio
2
20
TO BAYAMÓN →
SAN JUAN

and Hato Rey en route to Río Piedras (last bus 11:15pm). A map on the wall of the Covadonga station provides a complete route list. There are **2 main bus stations:** one in Old San Juan, near Pier 4, and another in Río Piedras, 2 blocks north of Paseo de Diego. Metrobuses come every 10min., "A" routes come every 15min., "B" routes come every 20min., and "C" routes come every 30min., but only Metrobuses regularly run on schedule. All buses run less frequently on Sundays. Buses stop at green signs that say "Parada" on them. When a bus passes, make sure the driver sees you or he may not stop. Metrobuses cost $0.50; all others cost $0.25. Exact change is required.

Taxis: Licensed taxis in San Juan are called **taxis turísticas** and are identifiable by the yellow lighthouse logo on the side. Fixed rates include: airport to Isla Verde $8, airport to Condado or Miramar $12, airport to Old San Juan $16, within Old San Juan $6, Old San Juan to Condado or Miramar $10, and Old San Juan to Isla Verde $16. Outside of these areas, all taxis should use a meter or you should agree on a price before leaving. In **Old San Juan,** taxis gather around the Plaza de Armas, outside the Sheraton Hotel near the pier, and behind the Teatro Tapia. Late at night try the latter two options. In **Condado** try one of the big hotels or just flag down a taxi along Av. Ashford. In **Santurce, Miramar, Ocean Park, Hato Rey,** and **Río Piedras,** taxis wait on the Plaza de Armas near the *públicos.* You can also call: Cooperativa Major Taxi Cabs (☎723-2460), Metro-Taxi Cab (☎725-2870), or Rochdale Radio Taxi (☎721-1900).

Trolleys: A **free trolley** *(trole)* passing all the major sites in Old San Juan departs regularly from the **Covadonga bus terminal** (daily 8am-10pm). Wait at any one of the marked trolley stops throughout the city (yellow signs that say "Parada" and have a picture of a trolley). The north route passes both forts and the museums along C. Norzagaray. The south route passes the Plaza de Armas and the piers.

Ferries: AcuaExpreso (☎729-8714) sends a ferry from Pier 2 in Old San Juan to **Cataño** (10min., every 30min. 6am-10pm, $0.50) and **Hato Rey** (15min., $0.75).

Bike Rental: Hot Dog Cycling, Av. Isla Verde 5916 (☎982-5344), Isla Verde, rents bikes ($15 per half-day, $25 per day). Open M-Sa 9am-6pm. MC/V.

▨ PRACTICAL INFORMATION

TOURIST AND FINANCIAL SERVICES

Tourist Offices: Puerto Rican Tourism Company (☎722-1709 or 724-4788), in the yellow house at C. Comercio and Pl. de la Dársena, near Pier 1, Old San Juan. Pick up your copy of *¡Qué Pasa!* magazine here. Free pamphlets and info. English spoken. Open M-W 9am-8pm, Th-F 8:30am-5pm, Sa-Su 9am-8pm. There is also a helpful **municipal tourist office** at C. Tetuán 250 (☎449-9174). Open M-Sa 8am-4pm.

Tours: Many big resort hotels, including the Sheraton in Old San Juan, open their tours to non-guests. Before booking, check to see if transportation and meals are included.

Rich Sunshine Tours (☎647-4545 or 647-4040; fax 745-4273). The garrulous Mr. Sunshine provides a wide spectrum of tours to the most popular destinations. To El Yunque (half-day $40, full day $60), Ponce ($60), Camuy Caves and Arecibo Observatory ($60), and the Bacardi factory ($35). Also offers kayaking in Fajardo's bioluminescent bay ($70), snorkeling trips ($77), and horseback riding ($75). Open daily 8am-3pm.

Atlantic San Juan Tours (☎593-9014; www.puertoricoexcursions.com). This smaller company offers fewer excursions than Rich Sunshine, but often at slightly better prices. To El Yunque (5½hr., $40), El Yunque and Luquillo Beach ($55), Old San Juan and the Bacardi factory ($43), and Camuy Caves and Arecibo Observatory ($70).

Eco Action Tours (☎791-7509 or 640-7385; ecoactiontours@yahoo.com). This 2-person company offers most of the tours found at larger companies, but much less formalized service. To El Yunque (half-day $35, full day $55) and Old San Juan and the Bacardi Factory ($35). Also offers kayaking in Fajardo's bioluminescent bay ($20 per hr.), 2hr. beach horseback rides ($35-45), snorkeling trips (half-day $45, full day $55), 2-tank dives ($95-150), rapelling in the Camuy caves ($75 per hr.), and power or sailboat rental ($195 for half-day). Admission and food not included. Transportation available at additional cost. MC/V.

Salty Dreams (☎717-6378 or 717-7259). Specializes in sailing and off-shore snorkeling trips. Full-day cruises $59. Sunset sails $45. Open daily summer 5:30-7:30pm; winter 5-7pm.

Madrid Tours (☎791-8777 ext. 1023), at the Hampton Inn, Isla Verde, offers tours to the following locations: Old San Juan and the Bacardi Factory (4½hr., M-F, $40); El Yunque (5hr., daily, $42); Ponce (7hr., Th, $60); and the Camuy Caves (7hr., W and F, $60). Prices do not include lunch or admission fees. They will pick you up from the closest major hotel. Tours only leave when enough people sign up. Reservations required. Open daily 8am-noon. MC/V.

Consulates: Britain, Av. Chardón 350 (☎758-9828), Hato Rey. Open M-F 9am-1pm and 2-5pm. **Canada,** Av. Ponce de León 273, Oficina 1350 (☎759-6629 or 250-0367), Hato Rey. Open by appointment.

Camping Permits: Departamento de Recursos Naturales y Ambientales, Parada 8 (☎724-3724), Miramar. Coming from Old San Juan on Av. Fernández Juncos, enter the parking lot before the Club Náutico and turn right. Provides camping permits and reservations for 9 designated camping areas (see **Camping, p. 42**). $5 per person. Open M-F 7:30am-4pm.

Banks and Currency Exchange: Banco Popular cashes AmEx Traveler's Cheques, exchanges currency, and gives MC/V cash advances (no commission). In **Old San Juan,** C. Tetuán 206 (☎725-2636). ATM out back. The 3rd fl. houses a gallery with changing exhibits about Puerto Rican culture. English and Spanish captions. Open M-F 8am-5pm, Sa 9am-1pm. In **Condado,** Av. Ashford 1060 (☎725-4197). ATM. Open M-F 8am-4pm, Sa 9am-1pm. In **Santurce** (☎725-5100), at Av. Ponce de León and de Diego. ATM. Open M-F 8am-4pm. In **Isla Verde,** Av. Isla Verde 4790 (☎726-5600). ATM. Open M-F 8am-6pm, Sa 9am-1pm. **BBVA Banco,** C. Arzuaga 112 (☎756-4638), at C. Monseñor Torres, **Río Piedras.** ATM. Open M-F 8:15am-4pm, Sa 8:30am-12:30pm.

Western Union: All **Pueblo** supermarkets (see **Supermarkets,** p. 101) have Western Union offices. Money sent to "San Juan" can be picked up at any location.

LOCAL SERVICES

English-Language Bookstores: BookShop, C. Cruz 201B (☎721-0863), near the Plaza de Armas, **Old San Juan,** has a wide variety of Spanish and English novels, as well as popular CDs and DVDs. Cafe sells sandwiches ($4-5) and smoothies ($3). Open M 9am-7pm, Tu-F 9am-6pm, Sa 10am-6:30pm, Su 11am-5pm. AmEx/D/MC/V. **By the Book,** Av. Ashford 1300 (☎724-4272), **Condado,** has a wide selection of English-language books and magazines. Also sells souvenir t-shirts and hats. Open M-Tu 10am-6pm, W-F 10am-7pm, Sa 9am-7pm, Su 9am-5pm. Another location at Av. Ponce de León 304, **Hato Rey.**

Language Classes: Berlitz, Av. Jesus Piñero 282 (☎753-2585 or 753-2586; centro.hato_rey@berlitz.com.mx), 2nd fl., Río Piedras, will give you private Spanish lessons and all you have to give them is an arm and a leg ($39 per 45min. lesson). Call ahead for an introductory interview and evaluation. Payment required for 10 lessons in advance. Open M-Th 8am-9pm, F 8am-6pm, Sa 8am-noon. AmEx/D/DC/MC/V.

Library: Biblioteca Carnegie, Av. Ponce de León 7 (☎722-4739 or 722-4753), Puerta de Tierra, in the large pink building. A full library and free Internet on 10 new computers (1hr. per day max.). Open M-Th 9am-5:15pm, F-Sa 9am-4:45pm. **Biblioteca José M. Lázaro,** at the Universidad de Puerto Rico (p. 126), is also open to the public.

Ticket Agencies: Ticket Center (☎792-5000; www.ticketcenterpr.com), on the 2nd fl. of Plaza las Américas (p. 136), near the food court. Sells tickets for most concerts and performances. Open M-W 9am-9pm, Th-Sa 9am-10pm, Su 11am-9pm. MC/V. **Ticketpop** (☎294-0001 or 866-994-0001; www.ticketpop.com), sells tickets for shows at the

Centro de Bellas Artes (p. 137) as well as other venues. Pick up tickets at the store Casa de los Tapes, at select movie theaters, or have them mailed to you on the island.

Markets: Plaza del Mercado (p. 115), Santurce, has a lively fruit and vegetable market. The Plaza del Mercado in Río Piedras **(p. 125)**, is even bigger, with more stands and a large food court.

Supermarkets: Pueblo has locations across San Juan. In **Old San Juan**, C. Cruz 201 (☎725-4839), on the Plaza de Armas. Also sells phone cards. Open M-Sa 6:30am-midnight, Su 8am-6pm. In **Condado** (☎725-1095), at the corner of C. de Diego and Wilson. Banco Popular branch inside. Open 24hr. In **Miramar**, Av. Ponce de León 670 (☎725-4479). Open M-Sa 6am-9pm, Su 11am-5pm. In **Isla Verde** (☎791-3366), in a large plaza on Av. Gobernadores near Embassy Suites. Open 24hr. All accept AmEx/MC/V.

Laundromats: La Lavandería, C. Sol 201 (☎717-8585), at C. Cruz, is the coolest laundromat in Puerto Rico. Friendly staff, modern art, funky music, a rack of magazines, and Art Deco furniture make doing laundry fun. Change available. Snacks $0.50-1.25. Wash $1.50; dry $0.25 per 5min. Open M 7am-9pm, Tu and Th 7am-8pm, F-Sa 7am-7pm, Su 8am-7pm. **Laundry Condado Cleaners**, C. Condado 63 (☎721-9254) will wash your clothes in 24hr. $2 per lb. Open M-F 7am-7pm, Sa 8am-5pm. **Coin Laundry**, Av. McLeary 1950 (☎726-5955), Ocean Park. Wash $1.75; dry $0.25 per 5min. Open daily 6am-9pm. **Isla Verde Laundromat**, (☎728-5990) at C. Emma and C. Rodriguez. Wash $2; dry $0.25 per 5min. Open M-Sa 7am-8pm, Su 8am-5pm.

Weather Conditions: ☎253-4586.

Publications: The San Juan Star, available at most newsstands, has been providing English-language news to the capital city for over 50 years ($0.45). The half-English, half-Spanish magazine **¡Qué Pasa!** is available at every tourism desk and provides info on accommodations, food, and outdoor activities for the entire island. The monthly publication **Mangrove**, found in most high-end restaurants and hotels, includes book reviews, entertainment news, and local interest stories. Occasionally articles are in English, but most appear in Spanish. **Agenda Noctámbulo** (www.agendanoctambulo.com), a small color brochure, gives the scoop on the hottest nightlife on the island, but it's all in Spanish.

EMERGENCY AND COMMUNICATIONS

Emergency: ☎911. **Fire:** ☎722-1120.

Police: Tourist police (☎726-7020). English spoken. Open 24hr. **State Police** (☎977-8310), on Fernández Juncos, Puerta de la Tierra. Open 24hr. **Municipal Police** (☎724-5170), in the Covadonga bus station, on C. Harding, Old San Juan. Open 24hr. In **Isla Verde**, Av. Isla Verde 5980 (☎728-4770). Open 24hr. In **Río Piedras**, C. Georgetti 50 (☎765-6439 or 274-1612), on the plaza. Open 24hr.

Rape Crisis Line: ☎877-641-2004.

Late-night Pharmacies: Puerto Rico Drug Co., C. San Francisco 157 (☎725-2202), on the Plaza de Armas, Old San Juan. Also has 1hr. photo developing. Open daily 7am-9pm. AmEx/D/DC/MC/V. **Walgreens** has several locations around the city: **in Santurce**, Av. Ashford 1130 (☎725-1510). Open 24hr. In **Ocean Park**, C. Loíza 1963, (☎728-0599) at C. Santa Cecilia. Open 24hr. AmEx/D/MC/V. In **Isla Verde**, Av. Isla Verde 5984 (☎982-0222). Open 24hr. AmEx/D/MC/V. In **Río Piedras**, Av. Muñoz Rivera 999 (☎294-0506). Open daily 7am-10pm. AmEx/D/MC/V.

Hospital: Ashford Presbyterian Community Hospital, Av. Ashford 1451 (☎721-2160), is the largest hospital in the tourist area. Ambulance service. Clinic open M-F 7am-7pm, Sa 7am-noon. Emergency room open 24hr. In an emergency, dial ☎911.

Internet Access: Internet is free at **Biblioteca Carnegie (p. 100)**, but the options below may be more convenient, depending on where you are in the city.

Ben & Jerry's (☎977-6882), at C. del Cristo and C. Sol, Old San Juan, has 2 computers. $3 for 15min. 1 scoop of ice cream $3. Open M-Th noon-10pm, F-Su noon-11pm.

SAN JUAN

CyberNet Café, Av. Ashford 1128 (☎724-4033), Condado. This techno-infused cafe also serves coffee ($1-2.50). $3 for 20min., $5 for 35min., $7 for 50min., $9 for 65min. Some computers have webcams. Fax service available. Coffee $1-2.50. Open M-Sa 9am-11pm, Su 10am-11pm. AmEx/MC/V. **Isla Verde** location (☎728-4195), Av. Isla Verde between Pizza City and Walgreens. Open M-Sa 9am-10:30pm, Su 10:30am-10pm. AmEx/MC/V.

Diner's Restaurant, C. Tetuán 311 (☎724-6276). This restaurant (see **Food,** p. 113) has the cheapest Internet in **Old San Juan** ($3 per 30min., $5 per hr.). Moneygram service and phone stations. Open M-W and Sa-Su 11am-10pm. AmEx/D/MC/V.

eMilio's, Av. Universidad 107 (☎759-5130), Río Piedras. $2 for 10min., $5 for 30min., $10 for 1hr. Open M-Sa 9am-9pm, Su noon-9pm. MC/V.

Postalinet, C. Loíza 1750 (☎726-5458), Santurce, near Ocean Park. $3 for 15min., $5 for 30min., $7 for 45min., $9 for 1hr. Also has a small cafe with sandwiches ($3-4) and coffee ($1). Open M-F 9am-6pm, Sa 9am-5pm. AmEx/MC/V.

UPS Store, Av. Ponce de León 1507 (☎723-0613), Santurce. Internet $3.50 for 20min., $10 for 1hr. Open M-F 9am-6pm, Sa 9am-1pm. AmEx/MC/V.

Post Offices: In **Old San Juan,** C. Fortaleza 153 (☎723-1277). Open M-F 7:30am-4:30pm, Sa 8am-noon. In **Condado,** C. Magdalena 1108 (☎723-8204). No General Delivery. Open M-F 8:30am-4pm, Sa 8:30am-noon. San Juan's largest post office is in **Hato Rey,** 585 Av. F.D. Roosevelt (☎622-1758 or 622-1759). General Delivery open M-F 5:30am-6pm, Sa 6am-2pm. Lobby mailing area open M-F 6am-10pm, Sa 8am-4pm. Bring ID to pick up mail. All post offices: AmEx/D/DC/MC/V.

Postal Codes: Old San Juan: 00901. **Puerta de Tierra:** 00902 or 00906. **Santurce:** 00907 or 00908. **C. Fernández Juncos:** 00909 or 00910. **Calle Loíza:** 00911 or 00914. **Hato Rey:** 00917 or 00919. **Río Piedras:** 00917 or 00919. P.O. Postal codes vary.

♫ ACCOMMODATIONS

ACCOMMODATIONS BY PRICE

UNDER $40 (❶)	
Guest House (104)	OSJ

$40-60 (❷)	
▨ The Caleta (103)	OSJ
Hotel Las Américas (105)	MI
Hotel de Diego (109)	RP
Hotel Metropol (105)	SA
Hotel Olimpio Court (108)	MI
▨ El Jibarito (104)	OSJ

$61-89(❸)	
Alelí by the Sea Guest House (105)	CO
Beach Buoy Inn (108)	OP
Borinquen Beach Inn (109)	IV
Casa del Caribe (105)	CO
▨ The Coqui Inn (109)	IV
Coral by the Sea (109)	IV
Embassy Guest House (104)	CO
L'Habitation Beach Guest House (108)	OP
Hotel El Portal (105)	CO
Mango Hotel (109)	IV

$61-89(❸), CONTD.	
El Prado Inn (105)	CO
Tres Palmas Guest House (108)	IV
Villa Verde Inn (109)	IV
▨ At Windchimes Inn (104)	CO

$90-130 (❹)	
El Canario Hotels (104)	CO
Empress Ocean Front Hotel (109)	IV
Hostería del Mar (108)	OP
Hotel El Consulado (104)	CO
Hotel Excelsior (108)	MI
Hotel Milano (104)	OSJ
Hotel La Playa (109)	IV
Hotel Plaza de Armas (104)	OSJ
▨ Hotel Villa del Sol (109)	IV
Número Uno Guest House (108)	OP
Tu Casa Hotel (108)	OP

OVER $130(❺)	
▨ The Gallery Inn (104)	OSJ

CO Condado **IV** Isla Verde **MI** Miramar **PT** Puerta de la Tierra **OP** Ocean Park **OSJ** Old San Juan **OP** Ocean Park **RP** Río Piedras **SA** Santurce

Accommodations in San Juan are quite expensive, but there are a few small, affordable guesthouses. In terms of ambience, safety, and proximity to cultural attractions, Old San Juan can't be beat. However, the closest beach is about 1 mi. down the highway in Puerta de la Tierra. For days of fun in the sun, head to Condado, Ocean Park, or Isla Verde. Condado is a very tourist-friendly beach area, with lots of restaurants and a beautiful promenade, but it does not have the nicest beach in town. Most accommodations in Ocean Park are on residential streets that offer peace and quiet, but little excitement. Isla Verde has the best beaches in the city, but accommodations generally offer less value and are sandwiched between huge resorts and condominiums. Furthermore, the entire neighborhood sits along a busy thoroughfare. Budget travelers who don't mind walking a few blocks to the beach may choose to stay in Santurce or Miramar, two neighborhoods inland from Condado where the accommodations offer much more bang for your buck. Remember that buses connect all neighborhoods and the longest commute (between Old San Juan and Isla Verde) takes less than an hour. Unless otherwise stated, all rooms below have private bathrooms. Most hotels have seasonal prices: "high season" (meaning higher prices) is generally November to May, and "low season" is generally June through October. However, many hotels have slight variations on these dates, which are noted wherever possible. Unless otherwise indicated, prices do not include the 9% Puerto Rico accommodations tax.

RENTAL AGENCIES

Several rental agencies offer short-term contracts specifically designed for travelers. Most of these are located in furnished condominiums along the beach, but make sure that you understand exactly what you are getting before you hand over your credit card number. Most have minimum stays of three days to one week, but some require monthly rentals. **The Caleta** (see **Old San Juan,** below) specializes in short-term rentals in Old San Juan.

ReMax (☎268-1241; www.remax-islaverde.com), on Av. Isla Verde, in the Marbella del Caribe strip mall, specializes in Isla Verde rentals. Check the website for photos. Utilities not included in monthly rates. Nov.-Apr. studios $1000-1500 per month; 1-bedroom $1200-2000; 2-bedroom $1500-3000; 3-bedroom $2800-3000. May-Oct. $750-1100/1000-2300/1500-2600/2300-2800. Weekly rates available. Open M-F 9am-6pm, Sa 9am-1pm. MC/V.

San Juan Vacations (☎726-0973 or 727-1591; fax 268-3604; www.sanjuanvacations.com), next to ReMax, Isla Verde. In the Marbella del Caribe strip mall. A smaller, but sometimes less expensive, selection of Isla Verde and Condado rentals. Prices vary widely from month-to-month depending on listings; all those quoted here approximate. Studios $750-1300; 1 bedroom $1000-1600; 2 bedroom $1300-2100. Open M-F 9am-5:30pm, Sa 9am-12:30pm. AmEx/MC/V.

Property Finders, Av. Isla Verde 5900 (☎728-1222 or 602-1800; fax 728-1235; www.propertyfinderspr.com), Isla Verde. Monthly apartment rentals in Isla Verde and around the island. Prices vary depending on listings. Studios $750-2000 per month; 1-bedroom $1000-2500; 2-bedroom $1500-3500. Open M-F 9am-4pm. AmEx/MC/V.

OLD SAN JUAN

▨ **The Caleta,** Caleta de las Monjas 11 (☎725-5347; www.thecaleta.com), on a quiet street near the ocean. By far Old San Juan's best deal for budget travelers. The penthouse "sunshine apartment" has bright orange walls and a balcony overlooking the water. Most rooms have cable TV and a portable A/C unit; all rooms have phone and kitchenette. Also rents 35 apartments around Old San Juan. Coin laundry. 3-night min. Reception around the corner at C. Clara Lair 151. Open M-F 10am-6pm, Sa-Su 11am-3pm. Check-out noon. Doubles and quads $210-700 per week; rentals $450-800 per week, $475-750 per month. MC/V. ❷

▨ **The Gallery Inn,** C. Norzagaray 204-206 (☎722-1808; fax 977-3929; www.thegallery-inn.com). Ring the bell at the unmarked gate and enter the courtyard filled with plants, trees, exotic birds, and original sculptures. Half working art gallery and half hotel. The seven working studios inside this 300-year-old building create art that fills the hotel's hallways, guest rooms, and several internal courtyards. The wine deck on the roof is the highest point in Old San Juan and offers views that have to be seen to be believed. If you ever splurge on one expensive hotel in your entire life, make it this one. All rooms $175-350. AmEx/MC/V. ❺

▨ **El Jibarito,** C. Sol 280 (☎725-8375). The owners of this popular restaurant (see **Food**, p. 111) also rent out a few guest rooms upstairs. The decor may be somewhat random, but rooms are a good value with a double bed, small kitchen, living area, A/C, and private bathroom. Rooms $60, weekly $350. AmEx/D/MC/V. Tax included. ❷

Hotel Plaza de Armas, C. San José 202 (☎722-9191; fax 725-3091; plazadear-mas@hotmail.com). This new and modern hotel has been stuffed into an old building; rooms tend to be small and not all have windows. Cable TV, phone, A/C, and hair dryer. Sinks are at the foot of the bed, next to the TV. Continental breakfast included. Dec. 16-Mar. singles $105; doubles $125; 2-person suites $160; 3-person suites with balcony $200. May-Dec. 15 $95/115/135/175. AmEx/D/MC/V. ❹

Hotel Milano, C. Fortaleza 307 (☎729-9050 or 877-729-9050; fax 722-3379; www.hotelmil-anopr.com). This traditional hotel might as well be an American chain. Rooms come with all the amenities—cable TV, telephone, A/C, small fridge—but little of the city's charm. Steps from restaurant row. 4 rooms have Internet connections. Rooftop restaurant. Breakfast included. Check-in 3pm. Check-out noon. Nov. 20-May singles $90; doubles $135. June-Nov. 19 $80/115. AmEx/MC/V. ❹

Guest House, C. Tanca 205 (☎722-5436). You get what you pay for at this inexpensive guesthouse. Larger rooms include both a queen and a twin bed, but smaller rooms seem like large closets. Call ahead, as the front gate is usually locked. No English. Rooms with 1 bed and fan $35; rooms with 2 beds and A/C $45. Tax included. Cash only. ❶

CONDADO

▨ **At Windchimes Inn,** Av. McLeary 1750 (☎727-4153; fax 728-0671), at C. Taft. This restored Spanish villa has the amenities of a resort with none of the pretension. Wicker furniture and glass tables grace bright rooms, with fun, beach-themed bathrooms. Friendly staff. All rooms have cable TV. Free wireless Internet in lobby, at bar, and in some rooms. Small pool with a jacuzzi bench. Fully stocked bar/restaurant by the pool. Parking $5 per night. Check-in 2-10pm. Dec. 1-May 30 singles $80-95; doubles $99-110; extra person $15. June 1-Nov. 30 $65/65-85/10. AmEx/D/MC/V. ❸

Embassy Guest House, C. Sea View 1126 (☎725-8284 or 724-7440; fax 725-2400; embas-syguesthouse@worldnet.att.net). With low prices and an unbeatable oceanfront location, it's easy to ignore the worn exterior and miniscule rooms at Embassy Guest House. When you've had enough sand, retreat to the small pool and tiny jacuzzi. All rooms have cable TV, fridge, and A/C. Continental breakfast included, except W. Dec.1-Apr. 30 doubles $65-125; extra person $15. May 1-Nov. 30 $45-95/10. AmEx/D/MC/V. ❸

Hotel El Consulado, Av. Ashford 1110 (☎289-9191; fax 723-8665). A subtle medieval theme, with a Spanish-tiled facade and Don Quixote sculptures in the lobby. Rooms are spacious and well-decorated. Some have balconies; all have A/C and cable TV. Continental breakfast included. Check-in noon. Check-out 3pm. Dec. 15-Apr. 15 1 queen bed $105; 2 beds $115. Apr. 16-Nov. 30 $85/95. AmEx/D/MC/V. ❹

El Canario Hotels (☎800-533-2649; www.canariohotels.com) has 3 locations in the Condado area. All have clean, bright rooms with cable TV, telephones, and A/C. Continental breakfast and newspaper included. Check-in 2pm. Check-out 11am. For all 3 locations extra person May 1-Dec. 15 $10, Dec. 16-Apr. 29 $15. A $3 energy charge is added to all room prices. AmEx/D/MC/V. ❹

El Canario Inn, Av. Ashford 1317 (☎722-3861; fax 722-0391). This self-dubbed bed and breakfast makes up for its plain rooms with its central location, beautiful yellow building, and tree-filled lobby and courtyard. The most charming of the Canarios. Dec. 16-Apr. 30 singles $105; doubles $119-134. May 1-Dec. 15 $75/85-95.

El Canario by the Sea, Av. Condado 4 (☎722-8640; fax 725-4921) is the only Canario located 10 steps from the beach. Rooms similar to those of the other Canarios, with sparse decor and small bathrooms. Dec. 16-Apr. 30 singles $105; doubles $119-134. May 1-Dec. 15 $75/85-95.

El Canario by the Lagoon, C. Clemenceau 4 (☎722-5058; fax 723-8590). The largest of the 3 locations, and the only one with an elevator, balconies, and free parking. 2 blocks from the ocean. Many rooms have views of the lagoon. Otherwise, rooms are similar to those of the other Canarios. Dec. 16-Apr. 30 singles $109-145; doubles $120-165. May 1-Dec. 15 $80/90.

Aleli by the Sea Guest House, C. Sea View 1125 (☎725-5313; fax 721-4744). Although its exterior has been worn by the salty ocean air, bright, recently renovated rooms and an oceanfront patio make Aleli one of Condado's better deals. 1 room handicapped-accessible. Cable TV and A/C. Common kitchen. Laundry $4. Free parking. Dec. 15-Apr. 15 doubles $65-100; Apr. 16-Dec. 14 $55-90; extra person $10. AmEx/D/MC/V. ❸

Casa del Caribe, C. Caribe 57 (☎722-7139; toll-free 888-722-7139; fax 723-2575; www.casadelcaribe.net). From the owners of At Windchimes Inn comes this slightly cheaper option. The hotel is clean and the management friendly, but it doesn't have the personality of its sister hotel. Small library. A/C, cable TV, and phone. 1½ blocks from the beach. Continental breakfast included. Parking $5. Dec. 15-May 15 doubles $75-125; extra person $15. May 15-Dec. 14 $55-65/10. AmEx/D/MC/V. ❸

El Prado Inn, C. Luchetti 1350 (☎728-5925, reservations 800-468-4221; fax 725-6978; www.elpradoinn.net), in a large white house at Av. Cervantes, off the hotel strip across from a park. Small pool. Phone, cable TV, A/C, and ceiling fan in every room. A vaguely African theme lends personality to otherwise standard rooms. Continental breakfast included. Parking. Aug. 1- Dec. 14 singles $69; doubles $79-119. Mar. 1-July 31 $89/95-129. Dec. 24-Jan. 2 $99/105-129; extra person $15. AmEx/MC/V. ❸

Hotel El Portal, Av. Condado 76 (☎721-9010; fax 724-3714; www.hotelelportal.com). Clean, standard rooms with superb A/C. The only drawback is the location, about 3 blocks from the beach. The hotel compensates with a rooftop terrace that boasts terrific views of the ocean and the city. All rooms have refrigerator, phone, and cable TV. Continental breakfast included. Rooftop sun deck. Dec. 16-Apr. 30 singles $85; doubles $95; triples $105. May 1-Dec. 15 $75/85/95. AmEx/MC/V. ❸

SANTURCE AND MIRAMAR

Hotel Las Américas, Av. Ponce de León 604 (☎977-0159; fax 268-7131), Miramar. While the ornate, mural-filled lobby of this 5-story hotel creates a regal ambience, the prices are not a king's ransom. Although some rooms have cable TV, microwave, and a small sitting room, others offer only the basic essentials. A great deal for couples. All rooms with A/C and phone. Parking. Check-out noon. Singles $60; doubles $61. AmEx/MC/V. ❷

Hotel Metropol, Av. Ponce de León 1661 (☎725-0525), at C. Bolívar, Santurce. A bit far from the beach, this hotel does not cater to the whim of the tourist. The fixtures are old, many rooms do not have TVs, the management speaks very little English, and it's not in the greatest of neighborhoods. But the rooms are large and clean, and the A/C is cold, making the hotel a decent bargain. Doubles $40-50. Monthly $400-500. ❷

S
A
N

J
U
A
N

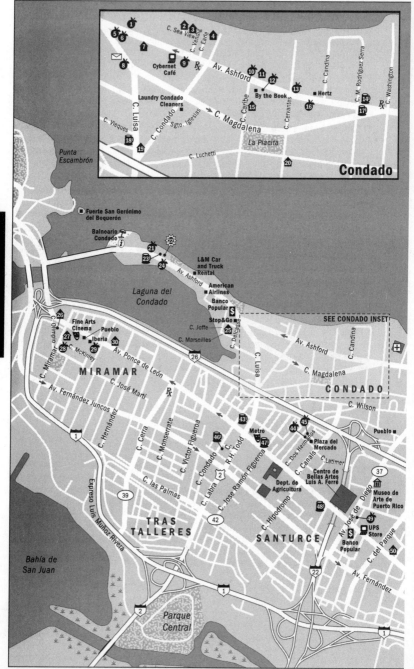

Condado, Ocean Park, Santurce, and Miramar

🏠 ACCOMMODATIONS
Alelí by the Sea Guest House, **2**
At Windchimes Inn, **35**
Beach Buoy Inn, **36**
El Canario by the Lagoon, **25**
El Canario by the Sea, **4**
El Canario Inn, **11**
Casa del Caribe, **15**
Embassy Guest House, **3**
L'Habitation Beach
    Guest House, **33**
Hostería del Mar, **34**
Hotel El Consulado, **7**
Hotel El Portal, **19**
Hotel Excelsior, **30**
Hotel Las Américas, **26**
Hotel Metropol, **50**
Hotel Olimpio Court, **27**
Numero Uno Guest House, **32**
El Prado Inn, **20**

Tres Palmas Guest House, **39**
Tu Casa Hotel, **38**

🍎 FOOD
Ajili-mójili, **24**
Bla Bla Coffeehouse, **49**
Café del Ángel, **6**
Casa Hilda's, **5**
Cherry Blossom, **10**
Cielito Lindo, **8**
Compay Cheo, **45**
Danny's International, **13**
Dunbar's, **41**
Kasalta Bakery, **42**
Latin Star Restaurant, **9**
Ocean Front Hacienda
    Don José, **21**
La Patisserie de France, **31**
Pinky's, **40**
Piu Bello Gelato, **12**
Pura Vida, **53**

Restaurant D'Arco, **28**
Restaurant Don Tello, **44**
Restaurant the Godfather #3, **1**
Tepe a Tepe, **29**
Uvva, **52**
Via Appia's Deli, **16**

🍸 NIGHTLIFE
Bliss, **18**
Cups, **51**
Eros, **47**
Habana Club, **43**
Junior's, **46**
Kalí's, **14**
El Teatro, **48**
La Terraza del Condado, **17**
Waikiki, **23**

☀ OUTDOOR RENTAL ACTIVITY
Ocean Sports, **22**
Tres Palmas, **37**

ATLANTIC OCEAN

0   400 yards
0   400 meters

Ashford Presbyterian
Community Hospital

Parque del Indio

OCEAN PARK

C. Italia
C. España
C. Cacique
C. McLeary

C. Atlantic
C. Santa Ana
C. Santa Ocuila

Coin Laundry
McLeary Mini-mart

Kings Court

Postalinet

Banco Popular

C. Santa Ana
C. del Río
C. Loiza

Park Blvd.
C. Laurel

Parque Barbosa

C. Taft

C. San Jorge
C. Diez de Andino
C. Julián Pesante
Av. Eduardo Conde
C. Aponte
C. Benítez Castaño
C. Manuel Corchado
C. Ismael Rivera

26

C. Tapia
C. Degetau
C. Ruiz Belvis
Gautier Benítez
C. Providencia
Av. Puerto Rico
C. Bartolomé Las Casas

Av. F. Díaz

Universidad del
Sagrado Corazón

Sala de Arte

Av. Ponce de León

Juncos

C. Rosales
C. Sagrado Corazón de Jesús

C. Tapia

Av. Eduardo Conde

Laguna
Los Corozos

35   25

Hotel Olimpio Court, Av. Miramar 603 (☎724-0600; fax 977-0655; hotelolimpio-court@hotmail.com), Miramar. Once you get past the dormitory-style hallways, Olimpio Court's very clean, very white rooms are more than satisfactory. All rooms have phone, cable TV, microwave, and A/C. Check-out noon. Singles $62; doubles $73; triples $82; quads $92. 50% discount for monthly stays. AmEx/MC/V. ❷

Hotel Excelsior, Av. Ponce de León 801 (☎721-7400, toll-free 800-289-4274), Miramar. The drab exterior hides a newly renovated marble-floored lobby and guest rooms filled with hardwood and plush blue carpets. Higher-priced rooms include kitchenettes. Rooms $109-145 in high season, $75-110 in low season. Price depends on amenities, not on number of people. AmEx/D/MC/V. ❹

OCEAN PARK

Hostería del Mar, C. Tapia 1 (☎727-3302, toll-free 877-727-3302; fax 268-0772; www.hosteriadelmarpr.com). Take one step into the spacious lobby with its oriental carpets and ocean views, and you may never leave. The lobby waterfall, wicker furniture, and oceanfront location—in addition to the standard A/C, phones, and cable TV—make it worthwhile. Check-in 4pm. Check-out noon. Nov. 15-May 15 doubles $94-264; extra person $25. May 16-Nov. 14 $69-209/15. Up to 2 children free. AmEx/D/MC/V. ❹

L'Habitation Beach Guest House, C. Italia 1957 (☎727-2499; fax 727-2599; www.habitationbeach.com). From the beachy, individually decorated rooms to the numerous rainbow flags to the kind staff, this gay-friendly hotel makes everyone feel at home. Great location between beach and town. All rooms have A/C and cable TV. Pets welcome. Coin laundry. Free use of beach chairs and towels. Continental breakfast included. Check-in 1pm. Check-out 11am. Dec. 15-Apr. 15 doubles $75-87; quads $96. Apr. 16-Dec. 14 $65-75/88; extra person $20. AmEx/D/MC/V. ❸

Número Uno Guest House, C. Santa Ana 1 (☎726-5010; fax 727-5482). Right on the beach (some of the restaurant's tables are on the sand), the immaculate white hotel manages to avoid the decay normally associated with an oceanside location. Spotless rooms include cable TV, A/C, private baths, and Internet. Common room with piano, books, and games; common balcony. Small pool. A 15% service charge pays for continental breakfast, beach towels, chairs, and umbrellas. Check-in 3pm. Check-out 11am. Dec.-Apr. singles $115-245; doubles $135-265. May-Nov. $75-185/95-185; extra person $20. AmEx/MC/V. ❹

Beach Buoy Inn, C. McLeary 1853 (☎728-8119; fax 268-0037). Although the rooms are in various states of renovation, a double room with 2 double beds is a great deal for 4 people who don't mind being a bit squished. Single rooms have fridges, double rooms have kitchenettes. All rooms with cable TV and A/C. Continental breakfast. Reception open 8am-10pm. Dec. 16-Apr. 30 singles $75; doubles $115; extra person $20. May 1-Dec. 15 $65/100/10. AmEx/MC/V. ❸

Tres Palmas Guest House, Park Blvd. 2212 (☎727-4617, toll-free 888-290-2076; fax 727-5434; www.trespalmasinn.com). Although it's a bit of a walk from Ocean Park, Tres Palmas compensates with a picturesque location across the street from the ocean. The view is especially good from the 2 rooftop jacuzzis. Rooms are small, clean, and well-decorated. Each has cable TV, a fridge, and a safe. Swimming pool. Continental breakfast included. Check-in 1pm. Check-out noon. Dec. 15-Apr. doubles $95-183; quads $130-144. May-Dec. 15 $84-149/111-121; extra person $15. AmEx/MC/V. ❸

Tu Casa Hotel, C. Cacique 2071 (☎727-5100; fax 982-3349). Someone clearly put a lot of care into the decoration of this hotel, with its aquatic-themed, hand-painted murals. Each room is decorated in its own style, and even the patio has carefully coordinated plants surrounding the pristine pool. 2 blocks from the beach. No children under 14. Check-in 3pm. Check-out noon. Winter 1 double bed $124-149; 2 double beds $195. Summer $99-175/175. AmEx/D/MC/V. ❹

ISLA VERDE

▨ **The Coqui Inn,** C. Uno 14 or 36 (☎ 726-4330, from the US 800-677-8860; fax 268-2415; www.coqui-inn.com), just past Villa Verde Inn, in Villamar. Consists of 2 identical adjacent hotels. Large rooms with A/C, cable TV, fridge, safe, and phone; some with kitchenette. Free wireless Internet in lobby and by pool. 1 computer free for guest use. Across the highway from the beach, but a pedestrian bridge is nearby. Continental breakfast included. Check-in 3pm. Check-out noon. Dec. 15-Apr. 30 singles $69; doubles $79, with kitchenette $89. May 1-Dec. 14 $75/85; extra person $15. AmEx/D/MC/V. ❸

▨ **Hotel Villa del Sol,** C. Rosa 4 (☎ 791-2600 or 791-1600; www.villadelsolpr.com), on a quiet road off the main street. This newly renovated, villa-style hotel is bright and charming, from the gorgeous pool to the suit of medieval armor in the lobby. Rooms are sparsely decorated, but quite large. 2nd fl. terrace. All rooms have A/C, fridge, and cable TV. Doubles $98; quads $109-150. Tax included. AmEx/D/MC/V. ❹

Borinquen Beach Inn, Av. Isla Verde 5451 (☎ 728-8400, toll-free 866-728-8400; fax 268-2411; www.borinquenbeachinn.com). Borinquen is a surprising find, located among the big resorts right on the beach. This, and the large rooms, make it a good value. Cable TV and A/C. Nice common kitchen for guest use. Check-in 2pm. Check-out noon. Dec. 1-Apr. 15 and June 15-Labor Day singles $70-95; doubles $85-95. Apr. 16-June 14 and Labor Day-Nov. 30 $56-76/68-76; extra person $10. AmEx/D/DC/MC/V. ❸

Mango Hotel, C. Uno 20 (☎ 726-4230, toll-free 800-777-1946; fax 728-2882; www.themangoinn.com), in Villamar. From Villa Verde Inn continue straight and take your first right on C. Uno. Rooms are clean and colorful, with basic amenities. Across the freeway from Isla Verde, but low prices help to make up for this. Check-in 1pm. Check-out noon. Nov. 9-Apr. 23 singles $70-75; doubles $80-85. Apr. 24-Nov. 8 $50-55/60-65; extra person $15. AmEx/D/MC/V. ❸

Hotel La Playa, C. Amapola 6 (☎ 791-1115 or 791-7298; fax 791-4650; www.hotellaplaya.com). Tucked away on a small peninsula, this family-run beach hotel offers clean rooms and a great location for surprisingly low prices. Steps from the beach. Basic TV and A/C. Check-in 2pm. Check-out noon. Dec. 14-Apr. 15 singles $90-105; doubles $100-115. Apr. 16-Dec. 13 $75-90/85-100; extra person $15. AmEx/MC/V. ❹

Villa Verde Inn, C. Marginal 37 (☎ 727-9457 or 728-5912, toll-free 1-866-476-7327; www.villaverdeinn.net), in Villamar. From Av. Isla Verde, cross the freeway bridge that lies next to Banco Popular (p. 100). Standard rooms come with a microwave and fridge, A/C, cable TV, phone, and a tiny balcony. A nice pool with a small jacuzzi. Friendly staff. Continental breakfast included. Check-in 3pm. Check-out noon. Dec. 15-Apr. 14 singles $64; doubles $74. Apr. 15-Dec. 14 $57/67; extra person $10. Discounts for stays over 2 days. AmEx/D/MC/V. ❸

Empress Oceanfront Hotel, C. Amapola 2 (☎ 791-3083, toll-free 1-800-678-0757; fax 791-1423). Empress has it all: a large pool with jacuzzi, a restaurant, bar, and club, and the ocean on 3 sides. The rooms are standard and the hallways can be a bit dank, but the ocean views from each room make up for this. A/C and cable TV. Check-in 2pm. Check-out noon. Dec.-Apr. 14 singles $128; doubles $148-168. Apr. 15-Nov. $108/128-148; extra person $20. AmEx/MC/V. ❹

Coral by the Sea, C. Rosa 2 (☎ 791-6868; fax 791-0092). The rich wood-paneled lobby gives way to dark hallways. Rooms with cable TV, phone, A/C, and tiny bathrooms. Check-in 1pm. Check-out noon. Winter doubles $76; quads $87. Summer $65/87. Tax included. AmEx/MC/V. ❸

RÍO PIEDRAS

Hotel de Diego, Paseo de Diego 207 (☎ 753-6008), at the end of the market, between C. William Jones and C. Padre Capuchino. You get what you pay for at this cheap hotel:

SAN JUAN

peeling paint, fuzzy TV, unreliable hot water, and tiny ants are part of the deal. But it's one of the only choices in Río Piedras, and a good option if you're planning to leave on an early-morning *público*. Check-out noon. All rooms $44, tax included. Cash only; payment at check-in. MC/V. ❷

⬙ FOOD

It's safe to assume that most restaurants have English menus, although some small *cafeterías* may cater exclusively to Spanish-speakers.

FOOD BY TYPE

AMERICAN AND BURGERS

El Hamburguer (113)	PT ❶
Danny's International (114)	CO ❷
Casa Hilda's Restaurant (113)	CO ❸
Ciao Mediterranean Café (118)	IV ❹
Dunbar's (115)	OP ❹
El Patio de Sam (112)	OSJ ❹

BAKERIES

Panadería Repostería España (118)	IV ❶
Das Pastellhaus (116)	IV ❷
Golden Bagel Bakery (118)	IV ❷
Kasalta Bakery (115)	OP ❷

CAFETERÍAS

Cafetería de la Rosa (119)	RP ❶
Country Health Food (119)	RP ❶
Cafetería Los Únicos (111)	OSJ ❷
Cafetería Mallorca (112)	OSJ ❷
Los Pinos (118)	IV ❷

CHINESE

Lin's (116)	IV ❸
Dragonfly (112)	OSJ ❹

CUBAN

Metropol (116)	IV ❸

FRENCH

La Patisserie de France (113)	CO ❶

INDIAN, JAPANESE, AND THAI

Dragonfly (112)	OSJ ❹
Royal Siam Thai Restaurant (118)	IV ❹
Tantra (111)	OSJ ❹
Cherry Blossom (114)	CO ❺
Shogun (118)	IV ❺

ITALIAN

Danny's International (114)	CO ❷
Via Appia's (114)	CO ❷
Restaurant the Godfather #2 (115)	SA ❸
Restaurant the Godfather #3 (114)	CO ❸
La Bella Piazza (113)	OSJ ❺
El Burén (113)	OSJ ❺

MEXICAN

Taquería Azteca (119)	RP ❶

MEXICAN, CONTD.

Cielito Lindo (114)	RP ❶
▨ Mango's Cafe (116)	IV ❸
Lupi's (112) and (118)	OSJ ❸ and IV ❸
Hacienda Don José (114)	CO ❸

MIDDLE EASTERN

Makarios (112)	OSJ ❹

PIZZA

Pizza City (118)	IV ❶
Das Pastellhaus (116)	IV ❷
Ferrari Gourmet (118)	IV ❷
Linda Sara (119)	RP ❷
Via Appia's (114)	CO ❸

PUERTO RICAN

Bohío Restaurant (118)	IV ❷
▨ El Jibarito (111)	OSJ ❷
Plaza del Mercado (115)	SA ❷
Café del Ángel (114)	CO ❸
Casa Dante (116)	IV ❸
Diner's Restaurant (113)	OSJ ❸
La Bombonera (111)	OSJ ❸
La Danza (112)	OSJ ❸
▨ Mi Casita (116)	IV ❸
Restaurant D'Arco (115)	MI ❸
Barrachina (112)	OSJ ❹
Latin Star Restaurant (114)	CO ❹
Mojito's (112)	OSJ ❹
Sonny's Terrace (119)	IV ❹
Ajili-mójili (114)	CO ❺
Uvva (116)	OP ❺

SANDWICHES AND CAFES

El Mesón Sandwiches (112)	OSJ ❶
▨ Bla Bla Coffeehouse (115)	SA ❷
▨ Guajanas Arte Cafe (119)	RP ❷
Piu Bello Gelato (114)	CO ❷
Pinky's (115)	OP ❷
▨ Tepe a Tepe (115)	MI ❷

SEAFOOD

Ostra Cosa (111)	OSJ ❹
Escambrón Restaurant (113)	PT ❺
Marisquería Atlántica (118)	IV ❺

SOUTH AMERICAN		VEGETARIAN	
▨ Arepas Y Mucho Más (111)	OSJ ❷	Restaurante Vegetariano Gopal (113)	OSJ ❷
Che's (116)	IV ❹	Hostería del Mar (108)	OP ❸
SPANISH		Pura Vida (116)	OP ❸
Divino Bocadito (112)	OSJ ❸	Cafe Berlin (113)	OSJ ❹

CO Condado **IV** Isla Verde **MI** Miramar **PT** Puerta de la Tierra **OP** Ocean Park **OSJ** Old San Juan **OP** Ocean Park **RP** Río Piedras **SA** Santurce

OLD SAN JUAN

Finding a good meal in Old San Juan is not difficult; it's finding an affordable meal that may prove problematic. Trendy restaurants along C. Recinto Sur and C. Fortaleza serve food from all over the world, with representatives hovering outside to compete for cruise passengers' dollars. Most restaurants near the docks theoretically close around midnight, but actually morph into hopping bars and stay open until the last customer leaves. The southern end of C. del Cristo, near the water, becomes a pedestrian walkway with a series of outdoor restaurants serving traditional Puerto Rican food during the day (entrees $8-18). For the penny-pinchers, cheaper food lies just off the beaten path, at a number of *cafeterías*. During the day several vendors set up around Plaza de la Dársena, near the tourist office.

▨ **El Jibarito,** C. Sol 280 (☎725-8375). Equally popular with locals and tourists, and famous city-wide for the best Puerto Rican food in San Juan. Appetizers $1.50-4. Most entrees $6-10. Open daily 10am-9pm. AmEx/D/MC/V. ❷

▨ **Arepas y Mucho Más,** C. San Francisco 351 (☎724-7776). As the name suggests, this small Venezuelan restaurant specializes in *arepas*, grilled corn dough patties served with meat and/or cheese ($4-5). *Arepas* are only about the size of an English muffin, so it's best to combine one with a delicious *cachapa* (sweet corn dough filled with cheese or meat; $5-7). Venezuelan paraphernalia plasters the primary-colored restaurant. *Batidas* (fruit shakes) $3. Open M-Sa 8am-8pm, Su 8am-6pm. MC/V. ❷

Cafetería Los Únicos, C. Tetuán 255 (☎977-0386). No frills, just the best *cafetería* in Old San Juan. Local office-workers grab a quick breakfast or lunch of typical Puerto Rican food while watching the flat-screen TVs in the busy restaurant. Breakfast $2-3. Sandwiches $2-5. Entree specials with 2 sides $5-6. Open M-F 5:30am-4pm. ❶

Ostra Cosa, C. del Cristo 154 (☎722-3672). This sophisticated restaurant provides a multi-sensory dining experience: you can listen to the romantic sounds of the tree-frogs, gaze at your companion by candlelight, feel the cool breeze sweep through the courtyard, and taste the scrumptious cuisine. All entrees (mostly seafood with some veggie and meat options) are rated on an aphrodisiac scale from one star (Oh!) to three stars (Ay Ay Ay!). The menu warns "We are not responsible for increments in passion. Please direct your claims to your partner." Ay ay ay! Appetizers $8-11. Entrees $14-22. Open M-Th and Su noon-10pm, F-Sa noon-11pm. AmEx/D/MC/V. ❹

La Bombonera, C. San Francisco 259 (☎722-0658). For over 100 years, this friendly soda fountain and restaurant has been serving the self-proclaimed "best coffee in town" ($1) to the local men who line the long bar and the many families who crowd into the red leather booths. Smartly dressed waiters bring a 1950s feel to this diner, which serves excellent *comida criolla* (most entrees $7-15) and a wide selection of pastries ($0.80). Entrees come with hot, fresh bread. Open daily 7:30am-8:30pm. D/MC/V. ❸

Tantra Restaurant and Bar, C. Fortaleza 356 (☎977-8141). Of all the touristy restaurants on Fortaleza and Recinto Sur, splurge on this one. Tantra presents an exoticized Indian experience, complete with cushions on the floor and hookahs at the bar. The

Tantra Mofongo ($12) with a "lust martini" ($7) will liven things up. Open M-Th and Su noon-11pm, F-Sa noon-midnight. Bar open Tu-Sa until 2am. AmEx/D/MC/V. ❹

El Mesón Sandwiches (☎721-5286), at C. San José and C. San Francisco. An exclusively *sanjuanero* crowd packs El Mesón at lunchtime for some of the quickest and best meals in the city, right on Pl. de Armas. Save on a combo meal (sandwich, fries, and a drink; $3-5) or choose from over 25 sandwiches ($2-5). Gigantic salads $6. Spanish only spoken, but the pictures of the sandwiches on the overhead menu will help you decide. Open M-Sa 6am-10pm, Su 7am-10pm. AmEx/MC/V. ❶

Divino Bocadito, C. Cruz 252 (☎977-0042). Exotic paper lanterns and brocade curtains make a meal in Divino Bocadito feel like a trip to Cádiz. The house specialty, Spanish *tapas* ($6-14), is a delectable prelude to passionate dancing on F nights (9pm). Flamenco show Sa 8pm. Open W-Th 6pm-midnight, F-Sa 6pm-1am, Su 6-11pm. Kitchen closes 45min. before restaurant. AmEx/MC/V. ❸

Mojito's, C. Recinto Sur 323 (☎723-7539). San Juan's high-flying business professionals come here for a power lunch at the classiest *comida criolla* establishment in town. The dark, bold hues of the tables match the bottles at the fully stocked wine bar. Entrees $10-23. Open daily 11am-10pm. AmEx/MC/V. ❹

Lupi's Mexican Grill & Sports Cantina, C. Recinto Sur 313 (☎722-1874). Autographed photos of athletes and conspicuous TVs give Lupi's the feel of an American sports bar. Sit on a cushioned, elevated seat against the wall and watch the game or crowd into a big booth with friends and slurp "Island Famous Margaritas" ($7-15). Typical Mexican entrees $9-20. Lunch $6-9. Happy hour daily 6-10pm. Karaoke F-Sa 10pm. Open M-Th 11am-10pm, F-Su 11am-2am. AmEx/MC/V. ❸

Dragonfly, C. Fortaleza 364 (☎977-3886). "Latinasian fusion" done right. Tourists and locals come in for the dark red walls, embroidered pillows on the chairs, and attentive waitstaff. The quesadilla spring rolls ($12) followed by the mint chocolate cream puff ($8) are an out-of-body experience. Also serves sushi. Most entrees $10-24. Open M-W 6pm-midnight, Th-Sa 6pm-1am. Kitchen closes 1hr. earlier. AmEx/MC/V. ❹

El Patio de Sam, C. San Sebastián 102 (☎723-1149 or 723-8802). Sam's wins praise for its convenient location, reasonable prices, and atmosphere friendly to families and large groups. Many a tourist has stopped here for a burger ($7) after visiting El Morro. The glass-covered dining area allows you to simultaneously enjoy the sun and the A/C. A semi-popular bar on weekend nights. Puerto Rican entrees $7-22. Cocktails $4.50-6. Open daily 11:30am-midnight. AmEx/MC/V. ❹

Makarios, C. Tetuán 361 (☎723-8653). Mediterranean cuisine from Greece, Italy, and the Middle East. The pizzas are the most authentic in the city, but the Arab influence is most prominent, with Arabic music videos on the flat-screen TVs, the smell of hookahs wafting from the bar, and belly dancing shows upstairs F-Sa 9pm. Personal pizzas $9-15. Entrees $9-23. Open M 6pm-midnight, Tu-Su 11am-midnight. AmEx/MC/V. ❹

Cafetería Mallorca, C. San Francisco 300 (☎724-4607), on Plaza Brau. Serves standard *comida criolla* at tables or a diner-style bar. The largely local crowd is drawn by the many pastries in the window and standard entrees like rice with pork sausages ($8). Menu varies daily. Most entrees $7-10. Open daily 7am-6pm. D/MC/V. ❷

Barrachina, C. Fortaleza 104 (☎721-5852). Why splurge on yet another tourist-oriented restaurant? Is it the charming, plant-filled courtyard or the fun-loving staff that occasionally breaks into salsa? The scrumptious *mofongo?* Of course not. It's the famous piña colada ($6), which supposedly originated here in 1963. Free samples. Entrees $14-23. Lunch $7-11. Open M-Tu and Th-Su 9:30am-11pm, W 9:30am-6pm. AmEx/D/MC/V. ❹

La Danza, C. Fortaleza 56 (☎723-1642), at C. del Cristo. This pleasant Puerto Rican restaurant is standard, except for its specials. At $25, the paella for 2, with 2 glasses of wine, fried plantains, garlic bread, and coffee, is a bargain. Or just sit outside and sip a Planter's Punch ($2). Most entrees $12-20. Open M-W and F-Su 11:30am-8pm. Kitchen closes at 7:30pm. AmEx/MC/V. ❸

Cafe Berlin, C. San Francisco 407 (☎722-5205). Quintessentially German, down to the dark wood and waitresses in lederhosen. Berlin combines a nice range of vegetarian options ($12-14) with an even nicer view overlooking Pl. Colón. Entrees $12-20. Breakfast $1-10. Open M-F 11am-10pm, Sa-Su 9am-10pm. AmEx/MC/V. ❹

Restaurante Vegetariano Gopal, C. Tetuán 201B (☎724-0229). This cavernous, sparsely decorated Indian restaurant is one of the few vegetarian-oriented eateries in Puerto Rico. The food is not outstanding, but it is quick, functional, and great for take-out. Small combo platters $6, large $8. Open M-F 11:30am-3pm. MC/V. ❷

La Bella Piazza, C. San Francisco 355 (☎721-0396). One of San Juan's best Italian restaurants, serving elegantly prepared pasta, meat, and fish. Although the food is delicious, it's nothing you can't find in any major city. Pastas $17-22. Meat dishes $19-28. Open M-Tu and Th-Su noon-2:30pm and 6:30-11pm. AmEx/D/MC/V. ❺

El Burén, C. del Cristo 103 (☎977-5023). Like several other tourist-oriented restaurants, El Burén offers Latin-fusion cuisine, this time called "cocina creativa internacional." This dimly lit restaurant features hardwood and modern art photographs, but little that could not be found elsewhere—and all this coolness comes at a price. Italian entrees $17-25. Open M-F 5:30-11:30pm, Sa-Su noon-11:30pm. AmEx/MC/V. ❺

Diner's Restaurant, C. Tetuán 311 (☎724-6276). Tucked away on a quiet side street, Diner's is more of a communication hub than a restaurant. Patrons sit alone and chat on the phone (each table is equipped with one) while eating. Brick walls, tall ceilings, modern lighting, a fully-stocked bar, and several Internet terminals contribute to the trendy atmosphere. Puerto Rican/international entrees $10-17. Internet $3 per 30min., $5 per hr. Open M-W and Sa-Su 11am-10pm. AmEx/D/MC/V. ❸

PUERTA DE TIERRA

El Hamburguer, Av. Muñoz Rivera 402 (☎721-4269), in front of the giant red headquarters of the PPD. Good, cheap, fast, and incredibly popular with locals. This shack is convenient to the beach and dishes out small, thick burgers ($2-4) and several varieties of tropical-flavored cheesecake. Watch them grill dozens of burgers at a time, then add your choice of fixings. Open M-Th and Su 11:30am-12:30am, F-Sa noon-3:30am. ❶

Escambrón Restaurant, (☎724-3344 or 722-4785; fax 724-1001; www.escambron.com), on the western end of Escambrón Beach. Within easy walking distance of the beach, the Radisson, and the Hilton, Escambrón is the best option for upscale beachfront dining. Savor the "Tipsy Lobster" (lobster flambéed with rum; $32) while looking out over its former home. Appetizers $4-8. Meat and poultry dishes $9-16. Seafood $13-32. ❺

CONDADO

Condado has restaurants that will satisfy almost every culinary craving. For those midnight munchies, **Stop & Go,** C. Magdalena 1102 (☎724-3106), a small convenience store, serves sandwiches ($3.50) 24hr. a day.

La Patisserie de France, Av. Ashford 1504 (☎728-5508). This busy bakery/restaurant is a popular lunch stop for Condado's businesspeople. Daily specials (breakfast $4, lunch and dinner $6) posted outside a week in advance. Sandwiches and wraps $5-9. Wide selection of French bread and desserts ($2.50-5). Open daily 7am-10pm. AmEx/MC/V. ❷

Casa Hilda's Restaurant, Av. Ashford 1104 (☎724-2147), offers a great variety of food, from pasta to steak to fish. More reasonable prices than most of Av. Ashford restaurants. Most entrees $11-20, $2 less at lunch. Open daily 10am-10pm. ❸

Danny's International, Av. Ashford 1351 (☎724-0501). Dishes out a variety of international entrees ($4-10), but the real reason to come is to try one of the 52 varieties of personal pizzas ($7-14). Most noteworthy is the *puertorriqueña,* a pizza with cheese, ground beef, and plantains. Outdoor and indoor seating. Beer $3-3.25. Open M-Th 7am-1am, F-Sa 7am-2am. AmEx/D/MC/V. ❷

Ajili-mójili, Av. Ashford 1006 (☎725-9195). Widely acknowledged as the best Puerto Rican restaurant in the city, Ajili-mójili receives rave reviews from everyone who tries the delectable cuisine. Huge windows with views of the lagoon and candlelit tables complete the ambience. No shorts or t-shirts. Lunches with drink and dessert $20. Dinner entrees $13-30. Open M-Th 11:45am-3pm and 6-10pm, F 11:45am-3pm and 6-11pm, Sa 6-11pm, Su 12:30am-4pm and 6-10pm. AmEx/D/MC/V. ❺

Restaurant the Godfather #3, Av. Ashford 1120 (☎722-3699). The Godfather has a surprisingly upscale interior, with dark wood and bold colors. Good, hearty American and Italian food. Breakfast $2-6. Entrees $7-20. Specials $4-12. Open 24hr. ❸

Café del Ángel, Av. Ashford 1106 (☎643-7594). This Caribbean-themed restaurant sticks to big, hearty portions of *comida criolla.* Seating on the patio or inside. Delicious hot bread with every meal. Stuffed *mofongo* $9-19. Island entrees $9-13. Open M and W-Su 11:30am-10pm. MC/V. ❸

Via Appia's Deli, Av. Ashford 1350 (☎725-8711). The walls are lined with liquor but it's the pizza that draws crowds. The relaxing street-side patio is a better choice for dining than the dark interior. Medium pizza $9-14. Italian entrees $8-16. Homemade *sangría* $4. Open M-Th and Su 11am-11pm, F-Sa 11am-midnight. AmEx/MC/V. ❸

Ocean Front Hacienda Don José, Av. Ashford 1025 (☎723-5959). This unabashed tourist trap is one of Condado's only oceanfront restaurants. Guests can sit on the back patio and look out on the water or on the front patio and look out on the street. Bar in between. Breakfast $3.50-6. Puerto Rican and Mexican entrees $11-19. Margaritas $3.75-5. Open daily 7am-11pm. MC/V. ❸

Cielito Lindo, C. Magdalena 1108 (☎723-5597). This surprisingly classy eatery transports you to Mexico and just begs you to try a margarita ($6). The restaurant is small, but an annex opens on weekend nights. Tasty Mexican enchiladas, burritos, and quesadillas $10-18. 2 Tacos $5. Open daily 11am-10pm. AmEx/MC/V. ❸

Piu Bello Gelato, Av. Ashford 1302 (☎977-2121). Yes it's a chain, but this immaculate, modern cafe draws tourists and college students with its yummy gelato ($2.50-4) in creative flavors and scrumptious sandwiches and wraps ($6-9). A huge assortment of enticing pastries and cakes ($4-5). Wireless Internet is available at the tables overlooking Av. Ashford. Vegetarian options. Open M-Th 8am-1am, F-Sa 8am-3am, Su 8am-2am. AmEx/D/MC/V. ❷

Cherry Blossom, Av. Ashford 1207 (☎723-7300). This upscale Japanese steakhouse seats guests at large tables where enthusiastic chefs cook meals in front of them. Bar and lounge upstairs. Dinner entrees $19-31. Early-bird specials $12-16, served 5:30-7pm. Open M-Th noon-3pm and 5:30-11:30pm, F noon-3pm and 5:30pm-midnight, Sa 5:30pm-midnight, Su 1-11:30pm. ❺

Latin Star Restaurant, Av. Ashford 1128 (☎724-8141). Serves Puerto Rican food and spaghetti around the clock. After a long night at the disco, nothing looks better than a big *mofongo* filled with crab ($16). Savor the A/C, or chill on a large outdoor patio covered with sports pictures. Bar inside. *Mofongo* $9-27. Entrees $5-26. Specials $6-12. Open 24hr. AmEx/MC/V. ❹

SANTURCE AND MIRAMAR

Countless indistinguishable restaurants along Av. Ponce de León serve inexpensive *comida criolla*, barbecue, and sandwiches to office workers. The few standouts are listed below.

🏛 **Tepe a Tepe,** Av. Ponce de León 762 (☎977-8373), Miramar. Set in an old mansion and its spacious, shady gardens, this restaurant serves exquisite sandwiches to trendy *sanjuaneros* who check their Palm Pilots while they wait to be served. "Black Forest Dream" (Black Forest ham and Gouda cheese on a kaiser roll; $6.50) goes well with a $2 homemade *sangría*. Sandwiches $6-8. Salads $4-8. Open M 11am-4pm, Tu-W 11am-5pm, Th 11am-10pm, F 11am-midnight, Sa 11am-9pm. MC/V. ❷

🏛 **Bla Bla Coffeehouse,** Av. de Diego 353 (☎724-8321; www.blablacoffeehouse.com). The friendly staff at this art-filled coffeehouse serve up wraps ($5-6) and burgers ($5-6), but the best deals are the daily specials ($6-9), which include a drink, salad, and dessert. Also serves the best *batidas* ($3.50) in the city, and that's saying a lot. Coffee $0.75-2.50. Breakfast $2-5. Open M-F 7:30am-4pm, Sa 8:30am-4pm. AmEx/MC/V. ❷

Cafe Restaurant Godfather #2, Av. Ponce de León Parada 23 (☎728-8303), Santurce. In the same family as the Godfather in Condado, but larger and brighter. One of the best *comida criolla* joints in Santurce, specializing in seafood. Breakfast specials $1.50 and up. Most lunch specials $4-13. Open daily 24hr. AmEx/MC/V. ❸

Restaurant D'Arco, C. Miramar 605 (☎724-7813), Miramar. This clean but unexceptional restaurant is a good place to get a Puerto Rican meal in Miramar. The sandwiches ($2-8), the breakfasts ($1-3), and the entree specials written on notecards at every table ($7-16) are the best deals. Open M-Sa 7am-9pm. AmEx/MC/V. ❸

Plaza del Mercado, 2 blocks north of Av. Ponce de León between C. Canals and C. Dos Hermanos. In the large yellow-and-brown building. A covered, well-organized **fruit and vegetable market** surrounded by clean restaurants serving *comida criolla* (entrees $6-11, seafood slightly more expensive; beer $1.25-2). Market open daily 6am-6pm. Most restaurants have a patio on the market square. Some of the best are:

Restaurant Don Tello, C. Dos Hermanos 180 (☎724-5752). Open M 11am-4pm, Tu 11am-9pm, W 11am-9pm, Th 11am-10pm, F 11am-11pm, Sa 11am-8pm, Su noon-5pm. AmEx/MC/V. ❷

Compay Cheo, C. Dos Hermanos 205 (☎724-2387). Open daily 11am-9pm. ❷

OCEAN PARK

A few good restaurants around Ocean Park cater to the beach crowd, but many only serve lunch. Dozens of *cafeterías* line C. Loíza, but that's not a good place to wander at night. What is the poor budget traveler to do for dinner? One solution is to head to Isla Verde or Condado, where good restaurants abound. Another is to just stock up on chips and drinks at the **McLeary Mini-Mart** on the corner of C. McLeary and C. Santa Ana and wait until morning. (Open daily 8am-8pm. MC/V.)

Pinky's, C. Maria Moczo 51 (☎727-3347), at C. McLeary. Where California meets San Juan you get Pinky's, a bright pink sandwich shop aimed at the North American crowd. The friendly staff will bring you a sandwich in the busy restaurant or deliver—even to the beach (delivery free; 11am-4pm). Hungry beachgoers may enjoy the house specialty, the "Surfer" ($6). Wraps and sandwiches $5-8. Breakfast $4-8. Limited free parking. Open M-W 7am-4pm, Th 7am-6:30pm, F-Sa 7am-8pm, Su 10am-4pm. MC/V. ❷

Dunbar's, C. McLeary 1956 (☎728-2920). This fun, friendly, popular English pub has been serving the Ocean Park community for 23 years, and the photos of satisfied customers that line the walls prove it. Offers a wide selection of American food, including Dunbar's famous potato skins ($6-9). By night, the restaurant becomes a lively pub. Entrees $12-23. Wraps and sandwiches $9-18. Beer $3-4. Happy hour daily 5-7pm. W sushi night (rolls $8-11). Open M-F 11:30am-last customer, Sa 5pm-last customer, Su 10am-last customer. AmEx/MC/V. ❹

Kasalta Bakery, C. McLeary 1966 (☎723-7340). People have been known to come to Kasalta for lunch, but they never leave without dessert. This incredible bakery boasts a

SAN JUAN

a huge variety of sweets, from flan to chocolate-covered strawberries. Desserts $1.25-1.50. Sandwiches $4.50-10. Open daily 5am-10pm. AmEx/D/MC/V. ❷

Pura Vida, C. McLeary 1853 (☎728-8119), in the Beach Buoy Inn. One of the few restaurants in San Juan that specializes in vegetarian cuisine. The best deal is the build-your-own wrap ($8), which allows you to choose three ingredients from a list including everything from pineapple to blue cheese. Vegetarian entrees $9-17. Non-vegetarian "nouvelle cuisine" $16-20. Open Tu-F 11:30am-9pm, Sa 8am-9pm, Su 8am-3pm. ❸

Uvva, C. Tapia 1 (☎727-3302 or 727-0631), in the Hostería del Mar guest house (**p. 108**). Wood decor and a breezy beach patio make this Mediterranean-Puerto Rican fusion restaurant Ocean Park's best choice for an upscale night out. Vegetarian options. Entrees $14-32. Sandwiches $10-18. Open daily 8am-10pm. AmEx/D/MC/V. ❺

ISLA VERDE

Most of the restaurants listed below provide at least a few parking spaces as well as free or inexpensive delivery within the Isla Verde area.

▨ **Mango's Cafe,** C. Laurel 2421 (☎727-9328), in Punta las Marías. It's a bit out of the way, but Mango's Caribbean cuisine is the best in Isla Verde and entrees are beautifully presented. Their specialty, the chicken breast stuffed with yucca ($12), is unbeatable. "Mexi burger" with chipotle sauce $8. Jerk chicken $12. Becomes a popular bar at night (beer $3-3.50). Open Tu 5-10pm, W-Sa 11am-2am. MC/V. ❸

▨ **Mi Casita** (☎791-1777), in La Plazoleta de Isla Verde. Dubs itself "the best local restaurant in town," and that may well be true, as it's filled with locals, who love the steak dishes. Steak and chicken entrees $8-15. *Mofongo* $10-19. Breakfast special $2.50. Open daily 7am-10:30pm. AmEx/MC/V. ❸

Casa Dante, Av. Isla Verde 39 (☎726-7310). Perhaps the most extensive selection of *mofongos* this side of Cuba: the crushed plantains are filled with everything from chicken soup to fajitas to filet mignon. Also options for those who don't live on *mofongos* alone. Entrees $8-23. Half-jar of *sangría* $14. Delivery $3. Open M-Th 11:30am-11pm, F-Sa 11:30am-midnight, Su 11:30am-10:30pm. AmEx/MC/V. ❸

Metropol (☎791-5585 or 791-4046; www.metropolpr.com), on the eastern edge of Av. Isla Verde, at the intersection with Av. Gobernadores. This slightly upscale restaurant offers an incredible array of Cuban food. Get the biggest bang for your buck by trying some of it all with the combo platter ($13). Or, try the cornish hen ($11), if you can ignore the fact that the restaurant is next to the cockfighting arena. Most specials $9-16. Seafood $14-36. Open daily 11:30am-10:45pm. AmEx/D/DC/MC/V. ❸

Che's, C. Caoba 35 (☎726-7202 or 268-7505). Widely acknowledged as the best Argentinean restaurant in town. Blue-and-white checkered tablecloths, bright red chairs, and many families make you feel right at home—if home serves tasty flank steak a la Argentina ($22). Meat entrees $16-27. Pastas $14-18. Wine $4.50, *sangría* $4.75. Open M-Th and Su 11am-11pm, F-Sa 11am-midnight. AmEx/D/DC/MC/V. ❹

Das Pastellhaus, C. Loíza 2482 (☎728-7106 or 728-7107). This large, modern cafe/bakery/pizzeria offers food for all occasions. Start the day with a homemade pastry ($1.50-2.50) or full breakfast ($4-6), then come back for lunch and sample one of the internationally themed sandwiches ($5.50-10). Finally, make one last stop for dinner and one of the specialty pizzas ($10-13), served with a white cream sauce instead of tomato sauce. Then just try to bypass the incredible desserts ($1.50-6.50). Open daily 7am-11pm. AmEx/D/MC/V. ❷

Lin's (☎791-6635), in La Plazoleta de Isla Verde. The creative, delicious food is what makes this Chinese restaurant worthwhile. Surprisingly classy for a strip mall. One interesting choice is "Butterfly Shrimp" (shrimp wrapped in bacon with special sauce) ($14). Chinese chicken and beef entrees $9-15. Lunch specials $5-7. Open M-Th and Su 11am-10pm, F-Sa 11am-11pm. AmEx/MC/V. ❸

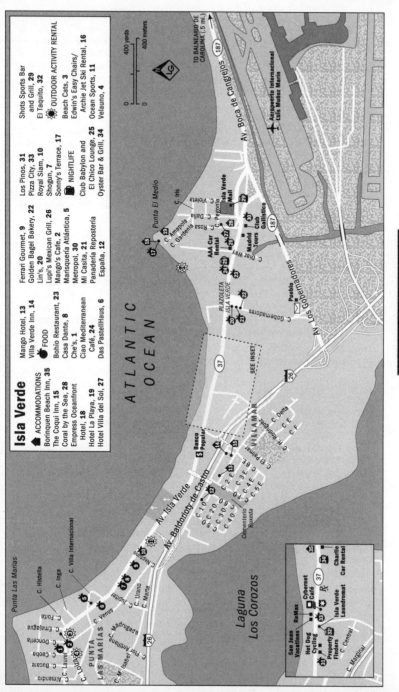

Isla Verde

⚓ **ACCOMMODATIONS**
Borinquen Beach Inn, **35**
The Coqui Inn, **15**
Coral by the Sea, **28**
Empress Oceanfront
  Hotel, **18**
Hotel La Playa, **19**
Hotel Villa del Sol, **27**

Mango Hotel, **13**
Villa Verde Inn, **14**

🍴 **FOOD**
Bohío Restaurant, **23**
Casa Dante, **8**
Che's, **1**
Ciao Mediterranean
  Café, **24**
Das PastellHaus, **6**

Ferrari Gourmet, **9**
Golden Bagel Bakery, **22**
Lin's, **20**
Lupi's Mexican Grill, **26**
Mango's Cafe, **2**
Marisquería Atlántica, **5**
Metropol, **30**
Mi Casita, **21**
Panadería Repostería
  España, **12**

Los Pinos, **31**
Pizza City, **33**
Royal Siam, **10**
Shogun, **7**
Sonny's Terrace, **17**

🌙 **NIGHTLIFE**
Club Babylon and
  El Chico Lounge, **25**
Oyster Bar & Grill, **34**

Shots Sports Bar
  and Grill, **29**
El Taquito, **32**

☀ **OUTDOOR ACTIVITY RENTAL**
Beach Cats, **3**
Edwin's Easy Chairs/
  Archie Jet Ski Rental, **16**
Ocean Sports, **11**
Velauno, **4**

SAN JUAN

ATLANTIC OCEAN

TO BALNEARIO DE CAROLINA (.5 mi.)

Ferrari Gourmet, Av. Isla Verde 51 (☎982-3115). This gourmet pizzeria creates a warm atmosphere. The extensive menu includes traditional pizzas and "specially for you" pizzas created by loyal customers. Small pizzas $6-11. Pitcher of *sangría* $20. Free delivery. Open M-Th 11:30am-10pm, F-Sa 11:30am-11pm, Su noon-10pm. AmEx/MC/V. ❷

Bohío Restaurant (☎253-5486), across from Hotel InterContinental. Nothing particularly special, but has an extensive variety of American, Italian, and Puerto Rican offerings. Entrees $7-19. Open daily 3-10:45pm. AmEx/MC/V. ❷

Lupi's Mexican Grill & Sports Cantina, Av. Isla Verde 6369 (☎253-1664). The Isla Verde version of this Old San Juan restaurant (p. 112) sports a larger space, a livelier evening crowd, and tons of sports memorabilia, much of it focusing on Yankees legend Ed Figueroa. Many sit outside and sip a post-beach beer ($2.75-3.75). Entrees $7-15. Live rock music F-Sa 11pm. Open daily 11am-4am. AmEx/MC/V. ❸

Pizza City (☎726-0356), at Av. Isla Verde and C. Diaz May, with the huge Medalla Light sign on the roof. Sometimes you just need a slice of pizza at 3am, and Pizza City exists to fulfill that need. This large, informal, open-air pizzeria is a good place to satiate post-clubbing munchies. Pizza slices $2-3. Sandwiches $1.50-6. Puerto Rican entrees $2-10. Beer $1.75-2.75. Open 24hr. ❶

Panadería Repostería España (☎727-3860 or 727-4517), on C. Marginal Av. Baldorioty de Castro, in Villamar; cross the bridge heading to El Patio Guest Lodge, and turn immediately left. This Spanish bakery is not very elaborate, but is always packed, and the sandwiches are as popular as the desserts. Also functions as a deli, selling cold cuts and meat. Cakes, pies, cheesecakes, pastries, and other temptations ($1-2). Sandwiches $5-7. Open daily 6am-10pm. AmEx/MC/V. ❶

Los Pinos (☎268-1259), on Av. Isla Verde between Banco Santander and 7-Eleven. The plastic-furnitured feel of a *cafetería* with slightly more expensive food. Popular bar with a pool table. Sandwiches $3-6. Entrees $8-15. *Mofongo* $9-15. Open 24hr. ❷

Ciao Mediterranean Café, Av. Isla Verde 5961 (☎797-6100 ext. 280), in the InterContinental Hotel. Walk across the lobby, leave through the back door, and continue past the pool to the restaurant on the beach. This Mediterranean cafe offers budget travelers a taste of luxury without the cost of a ritzy hotel room. Personal pizzas $14-18. Sandwiches, salads, and wraps $10-14. Open daily 11am-10pm. AmEx/MC/V. ❹

Royal Siam, Av. Isla Verde 65 (☎726-1167 or 726-1173). Although it may not look like much from the outside, the upscale Royal Siam is one of San Juan's few Thai restaurants. A large golden Buddha, carved statues, candlelit tables, and soft Thai classical music. Entrees $16-25. Lunch specials $14. Wine $6. Free delivery. Open Tu-Su 11am-11pm. AmEx/MC/V. ❹

Marisquería Atlántica, C. Loíza 2475 (☎728-5444 or 728-5662). Change out of your beach clothes—no shorts and t-shirts after 6pm in this elegant seafood restaurant. Waiters dress as sailors and sea life adorns the walls. Broiled prawns ($24) go well with a glass of wine ($4.50-7). The budget-minded can also visit the seafood store on the side, buy their own ingredients, and cook at home. Entrees $15-37. Open M-Th noon-10pm, F-Sa noon-11pm. Store open M-Sa 9am-8pm, Su 10am-3pm. AmEx/MC/V. ❺

Golden Bagel Bakery (☎791-2575), in La Plazoleta de Isla Verde. One of the few bagel stores on the island and surprisingly expensive. Bagels $1.75-5. Bagel sandwiches $5-10. Open M-F 6:30am-7pm, Sa 7am-7pm, Su 7am-2pm. MC/V. ❷

Shogun, Av. Isla Verde 35 (☎268-4622). Of the many Japanese restaurants in Isla Verde, Shogun provides the best sushi at reasonable prices. Standard options like tuna and California rolls and more glamorous designer rolls, such as the black dragon (eel, crab, avocado, and cucumber; $18). Flat-screen TVs play soothing videos of Japan in all corners of the restaurant. Sushi and maki rolls $6-8. Lunch specials $13-16. Entrees $17-24. Karaoke Th-Sa 9pm. Open M-F noon-11pm, Sa-Su 5pm-1am. AmEx/MC/V. ❺

Sonny's Terrace, C. Amapola 2 (☎791-3083), in the Empress Oceanfront Hotel. Visible from almost anywhere on the beach, Sonny's Terrace actually sits on a dock over the water at the end of a peninsula. Besides the superb location, Sonny's also boasts live music at night and great views of Isla Verde. The food pales in comparison to the ambience: the ribs ($10-17) are good, but the pasta ($10-19) is nothing special. Sandwiches $2-7. Live jazz Th 10pm. Live merengue and salsa F-Sa 10pm. Open daily 8am-11pm; bar open later. ❹

RÍO PIEDRAS

Av. Universidad, leading up to the Universidad de Puerto Rico, has a number of small, cheap restaurants that cater to students. Real bargains await at the back of Plaza del Mercado, where countless *cafeterías* dish out local fare.

▨ **Guajanas Arte Cafe,** C. Amalia Marín 4 (☎766-0497), located at the SW corner of UPR. Impressive student artwork lines the walls and complements brightly colored tables. Soothing, classy atmosphere. Free wireless internet. Puerto Rican lunch specials $5-8. *Batidas* $3.50. Open Aug.-May M-Sa 7am-4pm, June-July M-F 11am-3pm. MC/V. ❷

Linda Sara, Av. Universidad 111 (☎765-9908). This well-decorated restaurant with a serves 18 varieties of huge personal pizzas with delicious, garlicky crusts ($6-10). Calzones $8-10. Eat-in, carry-out, or free delivery. Open daily 11am-10pm. ❷

Country Health Food, C. Robles 53 (☎763-7056), between the market and the University. This small cafe/health food store offers a break from greasy fare with its three daily vegetarian entrees served *cafetería*-style. Huge combo platters with two sides and a salad $4-6. Delicious *batidas* $2. Open M-Sa 9am-3pm. AmEx/MC/V. ❶

Cafetería de la Rosa, C. Monseñor Torres 112 (☎274-1261). One of the cleanest *cafeterías* in the market area. Wooden tables, rather than the usual plastic ones. Entrees with sides $4-8. Sandwiches and burgers $2-4. Open M-Sa 6:30am-3pm. MC/V. ❶

Taquería Azteca, Av. Universidad 52 (☎763-0929). This typical Mexican joint attracts UPR students out for a cheap lunch. Complete with loud American pop music, shiny blue tables, and tasty Mexican staples, including nachos ($4-7), burritos ($4-6), and quesadillas ($3-5). Open M-Sa 11am-8pm. MC/V. ❶

> **SAN JUAN FOR POCKET CHANGE.** San Juan is home to expensive resorts for the rich and famous; fortunately for the rest of us, the city can be enjoyed on just dollars a day. Check into the **Guest House** (p. 104) in Old San Juan, before getting your dose of sun and sand at the city's **free public beaches** (p. 133). If you prefer the indoors, brush up on your history at **Museo Felisa Rincón Gautier** (p. 127) or **Museo de la Raíz Africana** (p. 130), both free. For some of San Juan's cheapest eats, swing by **El Mesón Sandwiches** (p. 118) in Old San Juan or **Plaza del Mercado** (p. 125) in Río Piedras.

⬡ SIGHTS

OLD SAN JUAN

CASTILLO SAN FELIPE DEL MORRO (EL MORRO). Most of San Juan has changed considerably over the last 500 years. However, when you walk up to the walls of El Morro, you are transported back to a time when Puerto Rico was largely uninhabited and pirates still posed a threat to colonists. The awe-inspiring six-level fortress, named after the patron saint of Spain's King Philip II, draws over two million visitors per year and became a UNESCO World Heritage Site in 1983.

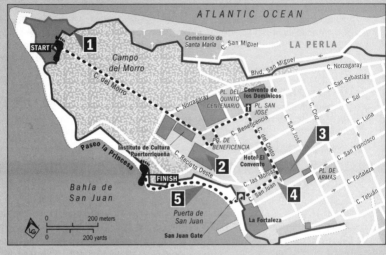

Puerto Rico's history is deeply rooted in the Spanish conquest of the island, which established its official language, dominant religion, and cultural traditions. Western Old San Juan can transport you back to the romance of an era when galleons and pirate vessels, rather than cruise ships, sailed into San Juan Port.

START: El Morro.
FINISH: Raíces.
DISTANCE: 1 mi.
DURATION: 4-5 hr.
BEST TIME TO GO: Early afternoon.

1 EL MORRO. Here you can spy the ocean through cannon embankments and understand how it must have felt to be stationed as lookout for invading Dutch and English vessels. Through binoculars, you can see across the bay to El Cañuelo, the small fort in the town of Cataño that provided crossfire with El Morro. If you look hard enough, you may even be able to see a pirate ship coming over the horizon. (See p. 119.)

2 MUSEO CASA BLANCA. The White House Museum was built in 1523 for the famous conquistador Juan Ponce de León, also the first Spanish governor of Puerto Rico. Although the museum is frequently closed, the gardens are the lushest in San Juan, with fountains and benches providing a welcome break form the heat. (See p. 131.)

3 CATEDRAL SAN JUAN BAUTISTA. Ponce de León is buried in this cathedral. In 1529, a few years after its construction, the cathedral also hosted the first ordination of a bishop in North America. Its ethereal beauty is captured in the many lit candles around the church and the side chapels containing reliquaries and portraits of saints. (See p. 123.)

4 OSTRA COSA. Take a break from the romance of the 16th century for a little romance of your own. At Ostra Cosa, diners can sit in the tree-filled courtyard and swoon to the sound of the tree frogs after ordering from the restaurant's menu of aphrodisiacs. (See p. 111.)

5 PASEO LA PRINCESA. As you pass through San Juan Gate, notice the thickness of the city walls, a point of defense in the colonial era. Turn left and walk down toward Raíces, a statue that was sculpted by a Spaniard to commemorate the 500th anniversary of the conquistadors' arrival here. It celebrates Puerto Rico's cultural heritage, past and present, and allows a great vantage point to once again look out over the ocean. (See p. 122.)

Construction of El Morro began in 1539, when the Spaniards realized that La Fortaleza was located too far inland to effectively prevent ships from entering the bay. El Morro originally consisted of one small tower, but as foreigners and pirates continued to besiege the island, the fortress continued to expand. El Morro's day of glory came in 1625 when Dutch soldiers attacked the fort by land and by sea. Stationed inside El Morro, Spaniard Don Juan de Haro and his army refused to surrender. Rumor has it that even the released prisoners chose to stay and help fight. The defenders were aided by the low profile of the fortress, which gave cannons a minimal surface area to aim at. Finally, over a month after their arrival, the Dutch left, burning the rest of San Juan on their way. Encouraged by their success, the Spaniards continued renovating the fort, and it wasn't officially "finished" until 1786. In 1876 they added a lighthouse to the sixth floor, which is now the oldest on the island and still in use. El Morro was put to the test once again in 1898 when the Americans bombarded the fort for 2½hr. before taking it, leaving 100 men dead. Then, during both World Wars, the US Army (now working from inside the fort) used it as a look-out post to protect the island. Finally in 1961 the military abandoned El Morro and donated it to the government. Today it is one of Puerto Rico's two US National Park protected areas (the other is **San Cristóbal,** down the road).

Visitors enter on the fourth floor, the Plaza Principal, which originally contained the prison, the chapel, and several cannon rooms. Today the prison room shows a 15min. video about the fort (shown in Spanish on the hr. and half-hr., in English on quarter-hr.) and several of the cannon rooms have become a museum with captions in English and Spanish. Look up and you will see three flags—the Puerto Rican flag, the US flag, and the old Spanish military flag, known as the Cross of Burgundy. The Artillery Ramp leads down to the Battery of Santa Bárbara on the second level, named after the patron saint of artillerymen, to whom the soldiers prayed for safety. *(C. Norzagaray 501. ☎ 729-6777; www.nps.gov/saju. Open daily 9am-5pm. $3, 65+ $2, ages 13-17 $1, 12 and under free. Combination ticket with San Cristóbal $5.)*

▨ CASTILLO DE SAN CRISTÓBAL. Frequently overlooked by tourists who visit El Morro and decide that one fort is enough, San Cristóbal is actually the larger of the two forts. After the Spaniards built El Morro to protect the bay, attacks by the British in 1598 and the Dutch in 1625 soon demonstrated that the city was still susceptible to assaults by land. Thus in 1634 they began constructing San Cristóbal about a half-mile down the road. The fort was not tested until 1797 when the British again tried, unsuccessfully, to take the city. Then, in 1898, Puerto Rico's involvement in the Spanish-American War was announced with a bang as a shot was fired from San Cristóbal. After the US won the war it took control of the fort, and in 1942 San Cristóbal was used as a WWII observation post.

Today the fort is open to visitors, who are given an English/Spanish pamphlet for a self-guided tour. Although less area is open to the public than at El Morro, San Cristóbal offers some unique features, such as a fully decorated replica of troops' quarters (including three-cornered hats above every bed), a military fife and drum soundboard, and old uniforms on mannequins (check out the hot pink stockings on one Spaniard). Visitors can also walk through the tunnels to the old dungeon, where a group of Spanish galleons are skillfully drawn on the wall. Archaeologists believe them to be the work of a mutinous captain awaiting execution. Beyond these additional attractions, San Cristóbal does have the same basic structure as El Morro, including cannon openings, historical exhibits, and splendid views of the city. The same 15min. video is shown at both forts. *(C. Norzagaray 501. ☎ 729-6777; www.nps.gov/saju. Open daily 9am-5pm. $3, 65+ $2, ages 13-17 $1, 12 and under free. Combination ticket with El Morro $5.)*

SAN JUAN

LA FORTALEZA. Reigning over the southwest corner of Old San Juan like a castle, La Fortaleza is the oldest **governor's residence** in the western hemisphere still used today. The Spanish originally began constructing the edifice in 1533 as a fort to protect San Juan, but after five years of work (and only one year shy of completion), they realized that the position of La Fortaleza would not allow them to see attackers entering the bay. Thus construction began on another fort, **El Morro** (see above), and La Fortaleza became the official residence of the governor. Over the years, the Neoclassical building has housed 124 governors appointed by the Spanish crown, 20 appointed by the US government, and eight elected by the people of Puerto Rico. The governor lives on the third floor of the mansion and works on the second. The flag out front waves only when the governor is on the island and flies at half-mast when he is away.

A free tour is the only way to see the mansion, but these are limited to the courtyard and never actually enter the house. If you lack time or interest, approach the building from C. Fortaleza for beautiful views of the facade. *(C. Fortaleza 1. Use the entrance at the end of C. Fortaleza. ☎721-7000 ext. 2211, 2323, or 2358; www.fortaleza.gobierno.pr. Tours 9:30am-3:30pm, free. Tours in English last 1hr.; in Spanish 30min. Check the poster outside the gate for the day's schedule.)*

PASEO LA PRINCESA. Extending from the San Juan gate to the piers, this wide promenade lined with trees, benches, and flowers provides a nice place for an evening stroll or a morning run. Start your walk on the western edge of the old city at the **San Juan Gate,** the symbolic entrance to the city through which visitors in the 18th and 19th centuries passed on their way to the Catedral San Juan Bautista to give thanks for a safe voyage. After you pass through the gate, follow Paseo de la Princesa to the left, where the path continues between the water and **La Muralla,** the original walls fortifying the city that took the Spaniards almost 150 years to build. Take a look at the thickness of the wall (20 ft. in places) as you pass through the gate. As the path turns away from the sea it approaches **Raíces,** a statue surrounded by a fountain. Possibly the most-photographed sight in Old San Juan, the statue, constructed in 1992 by Spanish sculptor Luis Antonio Sanguino, symbolizes Puerto Rico's cultural heritage. In front, a young man stands admiring the beauty around him, while in the back a young woman flanked by two dolphins welcomes visitors to the island. Images of a family and a *jíbaro* (traditional farmer) complete the sculpture. The ensuing broad promenade provides benches and a welcome respite from the sun. **La Princesa,** on the left, was constructed in 1837 as a prison. Today it is the central office of the Puerto Rico Tourism Company. Visitors may be more interested in the gallery inside that hosts a series of San Juan-themed temporary exhibits by local artists. There are no descriptions, but the front desk provides an English/Spanish information booklet. *(Open M-F 8am-4:30pm.)* Continue past the enclosed botanical gardens on your left to reach Plaza la Princesa, a brick rotunda centered on **Al Inmigrante,** a sculpture by Prat Ventos.

CEMENTERIO DE SANTA MARÍA MAGDALENA DE PAZZIS. Known simply as "the cemetery," this quiet plot of land may have the best views of any cemetery in the world, as it hovers precipitously between the old town walls, the low-income La Perla neighborhood, and the sea. Intricately carved, bright white headstones gleam in the morning light. Constructed in 1863, the cemetery has been the resting place for many of San Juan's most prominent citizens and is still used today. Visitors should exercise caution in the surrounding areas; avoid the cemetery and neighboring La Perla after dark. Solo travelers and women may want to avoid the area altogether. *(On the north side of the city between El Morro and Las Peñas. Walk down the street tunnel from C. Norzagaray. Open daily 8am-3pm.)*

CATEDRAL SAN JUAN BAUTISTA. Situated in the heart of the old city, the gorgeous San Juan Bautista is important for more than the fact that it houses the tomb of conquistador and former governor of Puerto Rico **Juan Ponce de León.** In 1529, the cathedral hosted the **first ordination of a bishop in North America,** while in 1984, it witnessed an event that it still celebrates: the visit of Pope John Paul II. The pope's visit is commemorated with displays of the actual vestments he used and in several larger-than-life pictures. Second in number only to those of Pope John Paul II, images of San Juan Bautista are found around the church—he appears in figurines on the outside facade, in the nave on the left-hand side of the interior, and in a stained glass window overlooking the main entrance. *(C. del Cristo 151-153. ☎/fax 722-0861; www.catedralsanjuan.com. Open M-F 8am-5pm, Sa 8am-3pm, Su 7am-2pm. Mass M-F 12:15pm, Sa 7pm, Su 9 and 11am. Free, although if you put $1 in any of the altars a candle lights up.)*

PARQUE DE LAS PALOMAS AND CAPILLA DEL SANTO CRISTO. A pigeon-hater's worst nightmare and many a child's greatest dream, Parque de las Palomas **(Pigeon Park)** is crawling with this urban bird. If you're into that sort of thing, buy some bird food from the vendor in the corner ($0.50) and soon birds will be crawling all over you, too. If you've seen Alfred Hitchcock's movie *The Birds* a few too many times, skip directly to the **Capilla del Santo Cristo,** the tiny chapel next to the park. Legend has it that the silver altar inside, dedicated to the Holy Christ of Miracles, was constructed in honor of Baltazar Montañez, who barely survived a horse-racing accident in the 1750s. The altar is built entirely out of silver, and the women outside sell silver charms to leave as offerings. Come on Tuesdays when the gate is open to get a closer look. *(At the south end of C. del Cristo. Chapel open Tu 11am-4pm. Free.)*

EL TEATRO ALEJANDRO TAPIA Y RIVERA. One of the largest theaters in Puerto Rico, the Tapia Theater serves as a monument of historical, architectural, and artistic interest. Governor Don Miguel de la Torre commissioned the building in 1824 as the first theater in San Juan, and the Tuscan-style Romantic edifice officially opened in 1836 as the Teatro Municipal (Municipal Theater). In 1937 the government renamed the theater after Alejandro Tapia y Rivera, one of Puerto Rico's most famous playwrights. The facade is beautiful, but it is the interior that really shines. The theater has 642 seats, but the third balcony and all of the booths are reserved for the governor and members of the municipal government—if they decide not to come, the seats remain empty. In order to see the inside, you'll have to buy a ticket for one of the weekend performances. For ticket information see **Entertainment,** p. 137. *(On the south side of Plaza Colón. Tickets ☎ 721-0180 or 723-2079, administration 721-0169. Office hours vary by performance.)*

PLAZA DE ARMAS. On most days Old San Juan's Plaza de Armas is just a large slab of concrete with a fountain, some benches, and a few kiosks. However, during holidays and special events (which tend to happen about once a week), the plaza fills with vendors hawking souvenirs, musicians playing traditional music, and hordes of people. The **Alcaldía** (Mayor's Office), on C. San Francisco on the plaza, is a Neoclassical building originally constructed in 1604 and restored in 1966-68 under the fashionable mayor Felisa Rincón. The mayor still works here, but visitors are free to visit the pleasant courtyard and **Sala San Juan Bautista,** which holds a small gallery of local artwork. A small tourist desk on the left-hand side of the lobby can answer questions. *(☎724-7171. Open M-F 8am-5pm.)*

PLAZAS. At the intersection of Caleta de las Monjas and C. Recinto Oeste, picturesque **Plazuela de la Rogativa** is a great place to snap a few photos and gaze out over the ocean. The statue in the middle of the plaza, La Rogativa, depicts the women and the bishop of San Juan tricking the English into believing that reinforcements are coming to protect the island, thus saving the city from the invaders. **Parque de Beneficencia** includes an impressive statue of Eugenio María de Hostos, "Citizen of America," behind the Museo de las Américas on Norazagaray. Otherwise, Beneficia is just a pleasant version of the standard mix of benches, lanterns, and concrete. **Plaza San José** seems to have a split personality. By day it's the typical plaza with a small outdoor dining area; at night it transforms into the hottest gathering place in town. On weekend nights and festivals Puerto Ricans flock to San José to meet, greet, wine, and dine. A heavy police presence testifies to the exuberance of the crowds. Nearby, **Plaza del Quinto Centenario** was constructed in 1992 to commemorate the 500 year anniversary of the discovery of America. The large totem pole in the middle, "Totem Telúrico," stands as a monument to the earth and the plenitude of America. The top level of the plaza supposedly represents the present while the lower level represents the past, and the stairs represent the connection between the two. The fountains in the ground intermittently spout water, causing delighted children shriek with pleasure. Drivers may be more interested in the **parking lot** underneath the plaza. Back in lower San Juan, off C. San Francisco, **Plaza Salvador Brau** is the place to find pigeons, families, school groups, and old men playing cards. The focus of the plaza is a statue of its namesake, Salvador Brau (1842-1912), a noted journalist, historian, and politician. **Plaza Cristóbal Colón,** north of Teatro Tapia between C. Fortaleza and C. San Francisco, plays host to a huge statue of Christopher Columbus, a five-tiered fountain, many benches, and even more tourists taking pictures.

IGLESIA SAN JOSÉ. Constructed in 1523, this large white building is the second-oldest church in the western hemisphere. Iglesia San José was closed for repairs in 2005, and it is unclear when it will reopen. *(On Plaza San José, at C. San Sebastián and C. del Cristo. Open M-F 7am-3pm. Mass Su noon.)*

PUERTA DE TIERRA

▧**EL CAPITOLIO.** San Juan's enormous capitol building is the home of the legislative branch of the government, with the Senate on the left (facing the building) and the House of Representatives on the right. It is easy to identify which branch anyone in the building works for based on their clothing—employees associated with the House wear green while Senate employees wear red. This may change, though, as a July 2005 vote approved a unicameral legislature for Puerto Rico. Architect Rafael Carmoega designed the building in an Italian Renaissance Neoclassical style, modeled after the US capitol in Washington, D.C., and it incorporates 22 different colors of marble. An interesting (and free!) tour shows off the entire building, including both the Senate and the House chambers. Even if one of the branches is in session, tours frequently enter the gallery and observe the proceedings. If you don't have time for a tour, it's worthwhile to enter the building and wander around. The main rotunda contains an original copy of Puerto Rico's constitution, a frieze (look at the top of the walls) depicting the history of the island from the Taínos to the time when Puerto Rico gained commonwealth status, four large mosaics (parts of which are covered in gold leaf), and the nine Greek muses on the ceiling rotunda. The third floor provides a better view of the mosaics and the muses. *(On Av. Muñoz Rivera, about ½ mi. from Old San Juan. ☎ 724-8979. Open M-F 8am-5pm. Free 45min. tours in English, Spanish, and French. If you are not going on a tour, you will need to show your identification and sign in.)*

CASA DE ESPAÑA. If you're in the area, Casa de España merits a stop for its beautiful Iberian architecture. Exquisite tiles cover the walls in the courtyard surrounding a fountain. The building was originally constructed in 1935 as a gentleman's club for the Spanish expat community, but today anyone is free to enter. *(Av. Ponce de León 9, between Carnegie Library and the Capitol. Open daily 9am-10pm.)*

FUERTE SAN GERÓNIMO DEL BOQUERÓN. Hidden behind the Hilton, this small 15th-century fort looks like a miniature version of San Cristóbal and played a similar role in protecting San Juan from foreign attacks. The fort has been closed since 1995 and the entire area is still under construction, though it is still possible to view the fort from outside. *(Enter the Hilton Caribe and follow signs to the San Cristóbal ballroom, then exit the glass doors behind the ballroom.)*

HATO REY AND RÍO PIEDRAS

▓ JARDÍN BOTÁNICO DE PUERTO RICO. Of San Juan's many attractive parks, the botanical garden in southern Río Piedras easily stands out as the best. The 175-acre Botanical Gardens contain two small lakes, an orchid garden, a bamboo forest, an herbarium with over 36,000 specimens of plants, countless paths, and most importantly, a place to escape the noise and commotion of the city. The park has several gardens devoted to specific themes, including a "Monet Garden, " which mimics the appearance of the French original. The visitors center provides a map of the premises, but it's equally enjoyable to just wander the well-marked paths and see what you stumble upon—it's easy to walk across the grounds in under an hour. The visitors center provides tours to large groups and individuals are welcome to join, but most are in Spanish. The University also welcomes volunteers who are interested in working in the gardens (see **It's Easy Being Green**). Call ahead for more information. *(Located directly south of the intersection of Hwy. 1 and Hwy. 3. From San Juan drive south on Av. Ponce de León to the end and follow signs. If you miss the sign (which can be hard to see), make a U-turn and look for the sign heading north on Hwy. 1. To reach the visitors center enter the park and travel uphill to the left just before the "Jardín Botánico" sign. If you are walking, exit downtown Río Piedras by heading south from the Plaza de Armas. From there, cross the bridge over the highway, turn left at the Texaco station, and walk 2 blocks. ☎ 767-1710 or 250-0000 ext. 6578. Gardens open daily 6am-6pm. Info center open M-F 7am-3:30pm. Tours M-F 8, 10am, 1pm; $25 for groups of up to 30. Admission free.)*

▓ PLAZA DEL MERCADO AND PASEO DE DIEGO. If the endless US chains stores have convinced you that Puerto Rico really is the 51st state, head to Río Piedras' Plaza del Mercado, the biggest market in San Juan, which offers a glimpse into daily life for many in Puerto Rico. This surprisingly well-organized, well-air-conditioned building contains stalls hawking everything from herbal medicines to fresh vegetables to even fresher meat, along with an overwhelming variety of bananas and plantains. In the

GIVING BACK

IT'S EASY BEING GREEN

Río Piedras's **Jardín Botánico** is an oasis of green amid the chaotic activity of San Juan. It is a quiet refuge for the public, where anyone can wander under the swaying palms trees or relax in the orchid garden. However, the garden serves other important purposes. For the students and faculty at the Universidad de Puerto Rico, it is a valuable research center. For members of the surrounding community, it is an education center that teaches adults' and children's classes in everything in from botany to flute-playing.

In order to support these activities, the botanical garden relies on an active volunteer corps. The volunteer program accepts new applicants year-round, and travelers can volunteer as much time as they wish, from a few hours for those who are just passing through to a more regular schedule for those who are planning to stay a few months in San Juan. Volunteers can choose their work from a number of different activities; options include helping out as a tour guide, a gardener, an administrator in the park office, or a teacher of one of the many classes. However they choose to support the gardens, volunteers will have the opportunity to spend hours in this leafy green haven.

(Call the volunteer cognition office at ☎ 765-1845 for more information.)

THE HIDDEN DEAL

CHEAP LEAVES

Books are essential for visitors who want to spend a long, lazy day lying on a perfect Puerto Rican beach, but in most of San Juan's neighborhoods, it is relatively difficult to find English-language books, especially inexpensive ones. What's the budget traveler to do?

Head on over to Río Piedras. This university neighborhood is a traveler's dream, with at least a dozen *librerías* (bookstores) within easy walking distance of one another. Many of them offer shelf after shelf of used English-language classics, which have been studied by Universidad de Puerto Rico (UPR) students in their English classes before being sold back to the bookstores. It is not unusual to find a Twain for $2 or Austen for $3. It is even possible to find contemporary popular fiction. Savvy travelers can snag a bargain on children's books left over from UPR English as a Second Language classes.

For rock-bottom prices, look for the $1 bargain tables in front of some stores. These mostly offer old magazines and textbooks but occasionally harbor a few stellar finds—for example, a hard-back *Anthology of English Literature* for a shockingly low $1.

(Bookstores can be found throughout Río Piedras, but they are most concentrated on Ave. Ponce de León between Ave. Gandara and the commuter train station. Most are open M-Sa 8am-6pm.)

back food court countless *cafeterías* serve up cheap *comida criolla* and fresh *batidas*. Near the entrance to the market is Paseo de Diego, a pedestrian street turned into an outdoor shopping mall. It features many American clothing chains and fast-food restaurants alongside a few *cafeterías* and warehouse-type stores selling very inexpensive clothing. *(Plaza del Mercado is located between C. José de Diego and C. Monseñor Torres. Open daily 6am-5:30pm. Paseo de Diego on C. José de Diego between Av. Ponce de León and C. William Jones. All stores close at 6pm, but the Paseo itself is always open.)*

UNIVERSIDAD DE PUERTO RICO. The largest university in Puerto Rico occupies a palm tree-filled campus in the heart of Río Piedras. Anyone who has wandered the streets of Río Piedras will appreciate the serenity of the grassy grounds, but the campus holds a number of interesting attractions in addition to its landscape. The **Museo de Historia, Antropología y Arte** (Museum of History, Anthropology, and Art) was in the process of renovation at the time of publication, but still offers a sampling of its collection into two small temporary rooms. The anthropology component has been reduced to a few Egyptian mummies, but the art section still has room for Francisco Oller's large painting, *El velorio*. *(Enter the University's main entrance, go to the top of the circular driveway, and turn left. ☎ 763-3939 or 764-0000 ext. 5852. Open M-Tu and F 9am-4pm, W-Th 9am-9pm. Free.)* Most of the university buildings are open to the public. The building directly opposite the main entrance on Av. Ponce de León has a colorful, intricately carved facade with a handsome seal dedicated to the American Republics for the Advancement of Learning. Facing the museum, turn right and head up the slight hill to **Biblioteca José M. Lázaro.** Anyone is welcome to explore the two floors and check out the books from the various collections. There are also several computers available for free internet use. *(Bring ID to check out books. Open M-Th 8am-midnight, F 8am-6pm, Sa 8am-5pm, Su 10am-10pm.)* Continue along the same road to the **Centro Universitario** (student center), where students gather to eat and hang out. A food court in the basement serves several varieties of fast food. On the first floor, to the right, through the sliding glass door, the **Oficina de Organizaciones Estudiantiles** (Office of Student Organizations) provides information about concerts, movies, and cultural events on campus. Public restrooms and an ATM are also located on the first floor. *(Campus at the intersection of Av. Ponce de León and C. Universidad. M: Universidad. Buses A3, A52, B4, B28, B29, C18, C31, and M1 pass in front. ☎ 764-1000.)*

LUIS MUÑOZ MARÍN FOUNDATION. If one figure stands out in Puerto Rican history, it has to be Luis Muñoz Marín, the island's first elected governor and the founder of the Partido Popular Democrático (p. 63). Thus it's not surprising that there's an entire foundation dedicated to studying Muñoz Marín and preserving the great man's legacy. In addition to providing ample fodder for academics, the Foundation also maintains the grounds and contents of the ex-governor's house and opens them to the public. Today visitors are welcome to come and explore; the house is closed, but anyone can peek through the windows at the furniture, decorations, and documents within. Muñoz Marín occupied the house with his second wife, Inés Muñoz Marín, from 1946-48 and 1964-80 (from 1948 to 1964 he lived in La Fortaleza). Two buildings out front hold Muñoz Marín's preserved office and a small gift shop. Car lovers will enjoy the garage, which contains Muñoz Marín's personal 1942 Packard, originally owned by US president Franklin D. Roosevelt. For true Muñoz Marín fanatics, this foundation also shows a 35min. video (in Spanish) about the man's life. *(Rte. 877 km 0.4. From San Juan take Hwy. 3 east, turn right onto Rte. 181, take the first left at the light, then a quick right; the house is on the left. ☎ 755-4506; www.munoz-marin.org. All info is in Spanish. Open M-F 8am-5pm. Tours 10am and 1pm, but call ahead. $2, under 12 and over 60 $1.)*

PARQUE LUIS MUÑOZ MARÍN. Situated on the border between Hato Rey and Río Piedras, Parque Luis Muñoz Marín offers an oasis of green amidst the sea of concrete. This sizable park is a great place to take a bike ride on a weekend afternoon, but if you're looking for real greenery and lots of shade, head to the Jardín Botánico. In addition to the large grassy fields, the park has playground equipment, picnic tables, and concrete **bike paths.** On weekends and holidays, or whenever the park is sufficiently crowded, a **train** tours the grassy expanse. *(Located south of Estadio Hiram Bithorn and west of Expreso las Américas. Enter on Av. Jesús Piñero. It is difficult to get to the park on foot—be prepared to walk along the edge of a busy 10-lane road. Bus B28 passes in front. ☎ 721-6121 or 763-0613 ext. 2247 or 2274. Train $1.50. Parking $2. Open W-Su 8am-5pm. Free.)*

🏛 MUSEUMS

OLD SAN JUAN

Old San Juan is easily the cultural capital of Puerto Rico. In addition to the numerous museums listed below, many streets, especially C. del Cristo and C. San José, are teeming with local art galleries. Your best bet is simply to wander around and explore. Most museums close on Mondays.

▥ MUSEO FELISA RINCÓN DE GAUTIER. This small museum is dedicated to preserving the memory of an extraordinary woman who devoted her life to achieving recognition of the rights of Puerto Rican women and improving the lives of the poor. Felisa Rincón de Gautier (1897-1994), who never even finished high school, served as the mayor of San Juan from 1946 to 1968, becoming the first female mayor of a major city in the western hemisphere. She also began the Head Start program for prekindergarten learning, which has spread throughout the US. The museum celebrates Rincón's accomplishments by displaying many of her honors and medals, including 11 honorary degrees from Puerto Rican and American universities and keys to 113 cities from Manila, Philippines to Gary, Indiana. Rincón's personal life is portrayed through dresses, fans, and photos with countless foreign dignitaries, including Lyndon B. Johnson and Eleanor Roosevelt. *(Caleta de San Juan 51. ☎ 723-1897. Open M-F 9am-4pm. Free tours in English and Spanish. Free admission.)*

Old San Juan

🏠 **ACCOMMODATIONS**

The Caleta, **17**
The Gallery Inn, **2**
Guest House, **29**
Hotel Milano, **30**
Hotel Plaza de Armas, **26**
El Jibarito, **16**

🍴 **FOOD**

Arepas y Mucho Más, **23**
Barrachina, **33**
La Bella Piazza, **24**
La Bombonera, **22**
El Burén, **15**
Cafe Berlin, **25**
Cafetería Los Únicos, **41**
Cafetería Mallorca, **28**
La Danza, **32**
Diner's Restaurant, **42**
Divino Bocadito, **37**
Dragonfly, **35**
Lupi's Mexican Grill and
    Sports Cantina, **44**
Makarios, **20**
El Mesón Sandwiches, **21**
Mojito's, **46**
Ostra Cosa, **43**
El Patio de Sam, **10**
Restaurante Vegetariano
    Gopal, **40**
Tantra Restaurant & Bar, **34**

🏛 **MUSEUMS**

The Butterfly People, **39**
Casa de Don Ramón
    Power y Giralt, **36**
Casa de la Familia
    Puertorriqueña
    del Siglo XIX & Museo
    de Farmacia, **31**
Casa Don Q Puerto Rico, **49**
Escuela de Artes
    Plásticas, **3**
Museo Casa Blanca, **8**
Museo de la Raíz Africana, **7**
Museo de las Américas, **4**
Museo del Niño, **18**
Museo de San Juan, **1**
Museo Felisa Rincón
    de Gautier, **19**
Museo Pablo Casals, **5**

🍺 **NIGHTLIFE**

Barú, **13**
Cafe Hijos de
    Borinquen, **12**
Cafe San Sebastián, **6**
Krugger's, **11**
Lazer, **38**
The Noise, **27**
Nono's, **9**
Oscar's Bar, **45**
The Pool Palace, **47**
Rumba, **14**
Señor Frog's, **48**

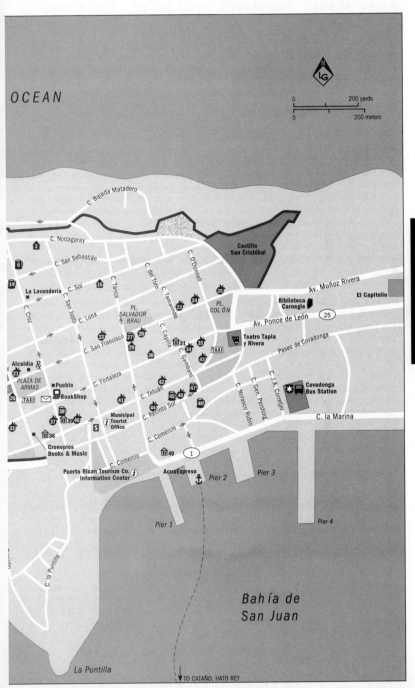

SAN JUAN

MUSEO DE LA RAÍZ AFRICANA. Starting with a description of African tribes, the Museum of African Roots progresses through the history of blacks in the Caribbean with a series of photos and artifacts, including real handcuffs and collars. A look inside the green swinging doors presents an eerily realistic portrayal of life on a slave ship, but the museum transcends the oppressive history of slavery to commemorate African contributions to Puerto Rican culture through displays on masks and music. *(On Plaza San José. ☎ 724-4294 or 724-4184; http://icp.gobierno.pr. Spanish signs only. Open Tu-Sa 8:30am-4:20pm. $2, under 12 or 60+ $1.)*

MUSEO DE LAS AMÉRICAS. Unlike most Old San Juan exhibits, this well-maintained museum extends beyond Puerto Rico and focuses on arts throughout the Americas in its two permanent and several temporary exhibits. The highlight of the 40,000 sq. ft. museum is a permanent exhibit on folk arts and handicrafts in the western hemisphere, including tools, toys, masks, and religious artifacts. A model of a Puerto Rican country chapel and a Mexican Day of the Dead altar are highlights of the display. The hodgepodge of items exemplifies the cultural variety found in the countries grouped together as Latin America. A second, smaller permanent exhibit on the western hemisphere's African heritage has captions only in Spanish, but the handcuffs and photos speak for themselves. The building itself is a display, as it was built in the 19th century and over the years has served as military barracks and hospitals. There is also a tourist information center inside the front lobby of the building. *(On Cuartel Ballajá, off C. Norzagaray, in the large green-and-yellow building. Enter the large courtyard and take the elevator or any staircase to the 2nd fl. ☎ 724-5052; www.prtc.net/~musame. Open Tu-Su 10am-4pm. Free.)*

MUSEO DEL NIÑO. If you are traveling with children, be sure to visit San Juan's fabulous, newly remodeled children's museum. The carefully thought-out museum has been designed to simultaneously educate and entertain. Friendly, informative tour guides lead groups or individuals through the eclectic assortment of displays, ranging from a giant ear in the health room (teaching children how to clean their ears) to a replica of a Puerto Rican town center (educating about Puerto Rican heritage) to a fully intact front half of a car (to teach children about car safety and wearing a seat belt). More interactive rooms allow children to make crafts out of recycled materials and practice brushing and flossing a giant set of teeth. There is also a room for children ages 1-3 that includes a firehouse. In July 2005, a third floor of the museum will open, featuring exhibits on hurricanes, butterflies, and caves. The museum also hosts special events on weekend afternoons; stop by for a three-month calendar. *(C. del Cristo 150. ☎ 722-3791; www.museodelninopr.org. Open Tu-Th 9am-3:30pm, F 9am-5pm, Sa-Su 12:30-5pm. Free English/Spanish guided tours. $4, under 15 $5. Additional $1 to use arts and crafts room. AmEx/MC/V.)*

MUSEO DE SAN JUAN. There are few exhibits in this museum, but what is there is well done. The main room presents the history of San Juan in floor-to-ceiling exhibits. The display in the second room changes regularly, but always focuses on some aspect of the capital. A recent temporary exhibit highlighted the city's Jewish population. Information in English is available in a supplementary packet. *(C. Norzagaray 150. ☎ 723-4317 or 724-1875. Open Tu-F 9am-4pm, Sa-Su 10am-4pm. Free.)*

CASA DON Q PUERTO RICO. Although not quite as famous internationally as Bacardi, Don Q is the best-selling rum on the island. This small museum explains the history of the rum and shows actual Don Q rum in the process of being distilled. While the historical information is nicely displayed with photos and English/Spanish captions, the highlight of the museum is the **free sample** of a Don Q rum drink at the end. *(On C. la Marina, across from Pier 1. ☎ 977-1721. Open Oct. 25-Apr. 30 F-Su 9am-6pm, M-W 11am-8pm; May 1-Oct. 24 M-F 9am-6pm. Free.)*

CASA DE LA FAMILIA PUERTORRIQUEÑA DEL SIGLO XIX AND MUSEO DE FARMACIA.
This two-story museum recreates the life of a wealthy resident of 19th-century
San Juan through two historical displays. Downstairs, the Pharmacy Museum
contains a pharmacy counter (including such remedies as ricin and Spanish fly)
and various other artifacts of early medicine, such as a model head with phreno-
logical information. Upstairs, the Museum of the 19th-century Puerto Rican
Family contains furniture from the 1870s. The chair with the hole in it served as
the bathroom on nights when the outhouse was just too far away. Perhaps the
most interesting object is the family portrait in the hall. Viewed from the front, it
simply looks like a large family with many Caucasian children. Viewed from the
side, however, a black child appears. According to the tour guide, this child was
the product of the father's affair with a slave, and he wanted to include her in the
family portrait. The museum merits a quick visit if you can understand the Spanish tour. *(C. Fortaleza 319. ☎ 977-2700. Open Tu-Sa 8:30am-4:20pm. Spanish tour
included if staff are available. Few captions in Spanish, none in English. Free.)*

THE BUTTERFLY PEOPLE. Since 1970, the Butterfly People have been accumulat-
ing butterflies from around the world and artistically assembling them by color in
display cases designed to prevent decay. Now in its second generation, this small
gallery/shop displays these floor-to-ceiling creations in a cheerful setting. *(C. Cruz
257. ☎ 723-2432. Artwork made from butterflies from $85. Open M-Sa 10am-6pm. Free.)*

MUSEO CASA BLANCA. The White House Museum was originally constructed in
1521 as the home of the first Spanish governor of Puerto Rico, **Juan Ponce de León.**
Unfortunately, a hurricane soon leveled the wooden edifice. Thus in 1523 the
Spaniards reconstructed the house as the first building made of stone on the
island. Ironically, Ponce de León never actually lived here, as he was off searching
for the Fountain of Youth, but the house remained in his family's possession for
the next 250 years. Casa Blanca also served as one of the few safe havens when
invaders attacked the city, and in 1898 it became the home of the Commander of
the US Army in Puerto Rico. Today the house has been redecorated in 16th-cen-
tury style in honor of Ponce de León. Although the interior was closed for construction as of 2005, the gardens out back—a jungle-like haven of trees and
fountains—are a beautiful place to rest on a hot day. *(C. San Sebastián 1. From C.
Norzagaray, turn down C. del Morro, pass Parque Beneficio, and enter the small gate on your
right. ☎ 725-1454. Open Tu-Sa 8:30am-4:20pm. Gardens free.)*

CASA DE DON RAMÓN POWER Y GIRALT. In the 18th century this building
housed Don Ramón Power y Giralt (1775-1813), an important Puerto Rican social
reformer who served as Puerto Rico's representative to the Spanish courts. Today,
this one-room museum has absolutely nothing to do with Don Ramón and instead
contains the office and museum of the **Conservation Trust of Puerto Rico,** an organization dedicated to preserving the island's natural resources. Their permanent
exhibition, **Ojo Isla,** uses a variety of media and interactive exhibits to explain
Puerto Rico's current environmental situation. The live colony of honeybees is
behind glass, but you can try your hand at a selection of traditional musical instruments. The captions are in Spanish, but the displays of animals and musical instruments speak for themselves. *(C. Tetuán 155. ☎ 722-5834. Open Tu-Sa 9am-5pm. Free.)*

ESCUELA DE ARTES PLÁSTICAS. The large white building across from El Morro
houses one of the largest fine arts schools in Puerto Rico. Originally constructed
as a mental hospital in 1861, the building was used to shelter soldiers wounded in
the 1863 war in the Dominican Republic before construction had even finished. In
1898 it became the US Army headquarters in San Juan until 1976 when it was converted into a school. Today visitors can wander in the tree-filled courtyard and
watch students work or head back to the small gallery of excellent student art. A

small food kiosk in the courtyard serves sandwiches ($2-4). *(On C. Norzagaray, across from El Morro. ☎ 725-8120. Open M-Sa 8am-5pm. Free.)*

MUSEO PABLO CASALS. Music lovers with some extra time in San Juan will appreciate this tiny museum devoted to Pablo Casals (1876-1973), one of Puerto Rico's most famous musicians (p. 73). Casals was born in Spain, but he moved to his mother's homeland of Puerto Rico at an early age. Here he played a role in the founding of the Puerto Rico Symphony Orchestra, the Casals Music Festival, and the Conservatory of Music. However, one step into the museum will remind you where Casals's musical interests began—with his cello. The museum doesn't contain much more than some photos, posters, and Casals's numerous diplomas, but the music room upstairs plays audiovisual recordings of Casals's performances and is a pleasant place to relax when it is not occupied by children receiving music lessons. *(C. San Sebastián 101. On Plaza San José. ☎ 723-9185. Open Tu-Sa 8:30am-4:20pm. $1, under 12 or 60+ $0.50.)*

PUERTA DE TIERRA

MUSEO MILITAR GUARDIA NACIONAL DE PUERTO RICO. Hidden amidst the government buildings on Puerta de Tierra, the Puerto Rico National Guard Museum presents a history of 20th-century American wars. Upstairs a large room focuses on American participation in WWII. Another room highlights the participation of the Puerto Rican Air National Guard in the various wars. The most interesting exhibits are the airplane fuselage and the uniforms from the different wars, including a WWII uniform for pregnant women. Portraits of heroic Puerto Rican soldiers and their stories line the walls. All captions are in English and Spanish. *(On C. General Esteves. From Old San Juan walk down Av. Luis Muñoz Rivera; the museum is on your right about 5min. after the capitol building. ☎ 289-1675. Open Tu-Sa 8:30am-3:30pm. Free.)*

SANTURCE

■ **MUSEO DE ARTE DE PUERTO RICO.** It may be an exaggeration to say that Puerto Rico's largest art museum is comparable to the great European museums, but in terms of quality of displays, presentation, and facilities, it does not lag far behind. The 13,000 sq. ft. Museum of Art, which stages a comprehensive display of Puerto Rican art from pre-colonial times to the present, is a must-see for anyone interested in the island's culture. All exhibits are described in English and Spanish.

The third floor contains the bulk of the permanent collection, a chronological display of Puerto Rican art. The North Wing starts with a display of pre-colonial and colonial art from throughout Latin America, then later becomes exclusively Puerto Rican. A large section is devoted to **José Campeche,** and another to the still-lifes of **Francisco Oller,** one of the first major artists to focus explicitly on Puerto Rican images. The South Wing moves into 20th-century art and introduces a few different types of media. The exhibits explain the Puerto Rican poster art of the mid-20th century and display several works by **Rafael Tufiño** and poster art pioneer Lorenzo Homar. The fourth floor houses a display of Puerto Rican art post-1970, including photography, ceramics, installation art, and works in a variety of other media that are arranged thematically rather than chronologically. The most interesting room is filled with leaf-covered barber's chairs, TVs playing Puerto Rican images, hubcaps on the walls, and a pool table in the center. Another gallery, entitled "None of the Above," discusses Puerto Rico's 1998 referendum on its political status, in which a majority of the respondents selected "none of the above," (a vote for the status quo in Puerto Rico's political relationship to the US) rejecting statehood, independence, and a new version of commonwealth status. This exhibit emphasizes the island's unique culture through film, sculpture, and modern art.

Behind the museum a five-acre **sculpture garden** houses countless sculptures, beautiful flora, and a large screen for special events. The first-floor **education center** provides child and adult classes on subjects from yoga to art and holds a rotating exhibit of local student work. The center also accepts volunteers to work at the museum. The second-floor **Galería activARTE** is a children's gallery that contains computer programs, games for visitors to create their own artwork, and child-friendly introductions to various media. Finally, the museum's **400-seat Raúl Juliá Theater** hosts regular events, including orchestra concerts, dance performances, and plays. The theater curtain is created out of the world's largest piece of **mundillo** lace; see the museum's website for more information on special events. (*Av. de Diego 299. Buses A5 and B21 have stops here. ☎977-6777 ext. 2230; www.mapr.org. Open Tu and Th-Sa 10am-5pm, W 10am-8pm, Su 11am-6pm. Tours Tu-Su 10:30am and 1:30pm. Students $6, under 12 and 60+ $3, 75+ free. Entrance free W after 2pm.*)

SALA DE ARTE. The Sala de Arte is a small but worthwhile museum that focuses on student photography. High schoolers, students at the Universidad del Sagrado Corazón, and that school's alumni contribute images of daily life in San Juan. The Sala also houses temporary exhibits which focus on some aspect of Latino culture. (*In the Edificio Barat on the campus of the Universidad del Sagrado Corazón. From Av. Ponce de León, turn north on C. Rosales and enter the university campus at the end of the street. The museum is on the 2nd fl. of the large blue building on the left. ☎727-5249; www.museocontemporaneopr.org. Open M-F 8am-noon and 1-5pm, Sa 9am-noon and 1-5pm. Free.*)

◪ BEACHES

As a general rule, the beaches get better as you go farther east. Few beaches in the San Juan area have amenities or public bathrooms. **Do not swim near Old San Juan—** although small sandy beaches do appear during low tide, the bay is quite polluted.

PUERTA DE TIERRA

Encompassing Parque Escobar, Estadio Sixto Escobar, and Balneario Escambrón, the extensive **Parque del Tercer Milenio** boasts the closest beach to Old San Juan— several swimming areas with calm, shallow water inside a manmade reef. Some easy **snorkeling** can be done in the reef that surrounds the swimming area, especially in the morning before the crowds arrive. The eastern beaches tend to be nicer than the western beaches, which progressively have less and less sand area. Parque del Tercer Milenio has many amenities, including restrooms, snack bars, trash cans, and signs identifying the current water quality. The park also includes several picnic tables, an area for barbecuing, a well-lit walkway, a bit of grass, a playground, and a large parking lot. **Lifeguards** are on duty during the high season 8am-6pm, low season 8:30am-5pm. (At the western end of Puerta de Tierra, near Av. Muñoz Rivera. Parking $3. Handicapped access at Pier 9.)

CONDADO

Almost every perpendicular street in Condado ends at the beach, which is fairly empty on weekdays and crowded on weekends. While this is far from being the nicest beach on the island, it is clean and the location is unbeatable. Because this is the city's gay district, many gay men frequent the beaches around the end of C. Condado. The official public beach, **Balneario Playa de Condado,** is relatively small and is located at the far western edge of Condado near the bridge to Puerta de la Tierra. A line of rocks protects the bay here, creating a lagoon of shallow, wave-free water, a contrast to the crashing waves outside the swimming area. The beach also has lifeguards (daily 8:30am-5pm), outdoor showers, and beach chairs (M-Tu and Th-Su $4 per day). Be forewarned—there are few public bathrooms in the area and many restaurants along Av. Ashford only let customers use their facilities.

OCEAN PARK

Condado may have the reputation, but Ocean Park can deliver. The shores of this posh suburb boast nicer sand, less trash, and better waves for swimming. However, Ocean Park's beaches have few amenities and may often be filled with teenagers playing loud *reggaetón*.

ISLA VERDE

Isla Verde has the best beaches in San Juan. Although it is hard to access the western beaches, a few tiny paths squeeze between the row of condominiums. The eastern side of Isla Verde has long, beautiful beaches that are most easily reached by turning toward the water at the Isla Verde Mall, then taking C. Dalia to C. Amapola to the end. Near the San Juan Hotel, **Edwin's Easy Chairs** rents for $3 a day. Directly in front of the hotel, **Archie Jet Ski Rental** rents jet skis (singles $50 for 30min., doubles $60). The far eastern edge, in front of the airport and the Ritz Carlton, is farther away from the amenities and shops, but consequently has fewer people, smoother sand, and a more picturesque landscape.

BALNEARIO DE CAROLINA

The best public beach in the San Juan metro area lies beyond Isla Verde in the city of Carolina. On weekends this enormous *balneario* is packed with Puerto Ricans who want to enjoy the long stretch of white sand and crashing waves. But come on a weekday, and the beach is one of the least crowded in the area. Facilities include covered benches, a playground, bathrooms, fire pits, vendors, trash cans, and lifeguards. (Rte. 187, past the Ritz Carlton about 1 mi. past Isla Verde. ☎791-2410. Open daily May-Sept. 8am-6pm; Oct.-Apr. Tu-Su 8:30am-5pm. Cars $3, vans $4.)

OUTDOOR ACTIVITIES

WATER SPORTS

DIVING AND SNORKELING

Ocean Sports, Av. Ashford 1035 (☎723-8513 or 268-2329; www.osdivers.com), Condado, specializes in advanced diving but offers water sports equipment rental and lessons. Snorkeling gear rental half-day $20, full day $30. Kayak rental $20/40. Boogie boards $10/15. Half-day diving trips in San Juan $75-95; full-day trips to the Fajardo area $115-150; half-day shore dives $65-75. Once a month they lead trips to more exotic dive sites, such as Isla Mona, La Parguera, or St. Thomas (2-tank dive $100-150, equipment $25). 4-day NAUI/SSI certification course $350. Ocean Sports also offers rebreather dives, Nitrox and advanced Nitrox drives, and Normoxic Trimix diver training. Wide selection of wetsuits. Open M-Sa 10am-7pm. AmEx/D/MC/V. Additional location at Av. Isla Verde 77 (☎268-2329 or 791-3483). Open M-Sa 9am-6pm.

La Casa del Buzo, Av. Jesús Piñero 293 (☎758-2710; fax 753-3528; www.lacasadelbuzo.com), Río Piedras. Possibly the cheapest PADI certification courses in San Juan. 4-week course includes evening classroom instruction twice a week, and 4 weekend dives ($150 per person). Open M-Sa 9am-6pm. AmEx/MC/V.

Scuba Dogs, C. 5 #D-4, Prado Alto (☎783-6377 or 399-5755; scuba-dogs@yunque.net), Guaynabo. Has a big pool for SCUBA training. They also offer excursions every weekend to dive sites around the island. These trips vary from 1-3 days and cost $150 and up. In Sept. they organize a huge beach clean-up in which anyone can participate. Call ahead. MC/V.

SURFING, SAILING, AND WINDSURFING

Reefs lining the coast of San Juan create several good surfing spots, and any surfboard rental company listed below can provide the full scoop. Many people surf off Parque del Tercer Milenio, in Puerta de Tierra, but local surf shops recommend that beginners head to Pine Grove, near the Ritz Carlton in Isla Verde.

Tres Palmas, C. McLeary 1911 (☎728-3377), Ocean Park, rents longboards ($40 per 24hr.) and fun boards ($35). Open M-Th 10am-6pm, F-Sa 10am-7pm, Su 11am-5pm. AmEx/D/MC/V.

Beach Cats, C. Loíza 2434 (☎727-0883), Punta Las Marías, teaches catamaran sailing lessons ($450 per 8hr., including all equipment). It also sells kayaks, windsurfers, Hobie Cats, sunfish, kite surfing equipment, and surfboards. Also repair surfboards. Open M-Sa 10am-6pm. AmEx/MC/V.

Velauno, C. Loíza 2430 (☎728-8716), Punta Las Marías, rents surfboards ($35 for the first day, $25 per additional day; $120 per week) and windsurfers ($75 per day, $225 per week). They also teach classes in surfing ($50 per hr.), windsurfing ($150 for a 4hr. beginning class), and kite surfing ($150 per class for a series of 3 2hr. classes). Open M-Th 10am-7pm, F-Sa 11am-7pm. MC/V.

FISHING

Mike Benítez Marine Services, Av. Fernández Juncos 480 (☎723-2292 or 724-6265; fax 725-4344), Miramar. In the Club Náutico. Sends a 45 ft. air-conditioned boat on daily deep-sea fishing trips. In winter fish for mahi mahi, sailfish, and tuna; in summer, blue marlin. Half-day (4hr.) $175 per person, min. 2 people. Private charter for up to 6 people, half-day $525, full day $900. All equipment and sodas included. Open daily 7:30am-6pm. AmEx/MC/V.

DRY LAND ADVENTURES

Aventuras Tierra Adentro, Av. Jesus Piñero 268-A (☎766-0470), Río Piedras. Specializes in rock climbing and rapelling in the Río Camuy caves (p. 269). Experienced guides lead full-day trips to Ángeles Cave, and canyoning trips to El Yunque. No experience necessary—all expeditions begin with a short lesson. $150 per person includes all supplies except food. Open Tu-Sa 10am-6pm. AmEx/MC/V.

🎴 ENTERTAINMENT

CASINOS

Gambling is a popular activity in San Juan, but unless you stick to the five-cent slot machines it can quickly eat up your budget. Almost all the large chain hotels have sizable casinos. For a night of betting, hit up the glamorous row in **Isla Verde**—the Wyndham El San Juan, the InterContinental, the Embassy Suites, and the Ritz Carlton. On Av. Ashford in **Condado** the Radisson Ambassador Plaza, the Diamond Palace Hotel, and the San Juan Marriott provide places to bet. Old San Juan's only place to gamble is the **Sheraton Old San Juan,** by the piers. The general dress code at casinos prohibits jeans and t-shirts; the legal gambling age is 18.

SAN JUAN

CINEMA

Most of the movie theaters are located away from the primary tourist districts. **Metro,** Av. Ponce de León 1255, Santurce, screens three American films. (☎721-5903. $5.50, under 10 $3.50.) **Plaza las Américas** (see **Shopping,** p. 139) has two large movie theaters. On the third floor, **Plaza Theaters** is the cheaper of the two. (☎758-3929. Nine movies with Spanish subtitles. $5.50, children and seniors $3.50. MC/V.) One floor down, **Caribbean Cinemas** has a slightly larger selection. (☎767-4775. 11 movies with Spanish subtitles. $6, ages 2-10 $3.50, seniors $4.) The **Fine Arts Cinema,** Av. Ponce de León 654, shows three American films in English, sometimes with Spanish subtitles. (☎721-4288. $5.50, children $3.50, 60+ $4. W women $3.50.)

PARTICIPATORY SPORTS

San Juan's premier outdoor sports area, Parque Central, has exceptional sports facilities. The large well-manicured park holds 20 tennis courts, four racquetball courts, a playground, several large fields, a well-lit stadium, a series of jogging paths, a track, a cafeteria, public restrooms, and telephones. Covered benches provide a shady place for parents to sit while their children play. Parque Central is open to the public, but it is almost impossible to reach without a car. It can also be quite busy on evenings and weekends when San Juan families head out after work, so if you want to play tennis during these peak hours it's best to stop by in the morning and reserve a court (in person; telephone reservations not accepted). The tennis shop sometimes offers free beginning tennis lessons—all you need to bring is a new set of tennis balls. Call ahead for more information. The park is located in Santurce. Drive south on C. Roberto H. Todd until it turns into a highway, then look for signs. Or from Puerta de la Tierra take Hwy. 1 south to the Parque Central exit. (☎722-1646. Open M-F 6am-9pm, Sa 6am-7pm, Su 6am-5pm. Parking $1. Tennis courts $3, after 6pm $4. Racquetball courts $8 per hr.)

Parque Barbosa, next to Ocean Park, also offers a plethora of athletic facilities. Named after notable politician José Celso Barbosa (1857-1921), the park includes three basketball courts (one of which is covered), half- and full-length soccer fields, a track, a baseball field, and three tennis courts. Unfortunately, the tennis courts are really the only part of the park that is well maintained. A 24hr. police station is on the premises. (Directly east of Ocean Park, next to the ocean. Police ☎726-7020. Free parking. Track lights on all night.)

There are a few good areas for **running** in San Juan, if you can bear the heat. **Paseo de la Princesa,** along the western edge of Old San Juan (p. 122) hosts several joggers at dawn and dusk when it is a bit cooler. A nice track passes through Parque del Tercer Milenio in Puerta de la Tierra (p. 133).

SPECTATOR SPORTS

BASEBALL. Puerto Rico has an active professional baseball league, and most of the action takes place in San Juan. From the end of October until the beginning of January, the Santurce Cangrejeros and the San Juan Senadores play about three times per week at **Estadio Hiram Bithorn.** Tickets and schedules are available at the stadium box office on game days. (South of Av. F.D. Roosevelt and west of Expreso Las Américas, across from Plaza las Américas. Enter from Av. F.D. Roosevelt. ☎294-1480. Cangrejeros ☎772-9573. Senadores ☎269-3531. Box office open from 9am on the day of the game. Most games 8pm, Su 4pm. $5-7, children $2.50. MC/V.)

BASKETBALL. From April to June, professional basketball descends on Puerto Rico. The Santurce Cangrejeros play most of their home games at the Coliseo de Puerto Rico. (Tickets are available at ☎294-0001 or www.ticketpop.com.)

COCKFIGHTS. The **Club Gallístico,** at the intersection of Av. Isla Verde and Av. Los Gobernadores in Isla Verde, is the only **cockfighting arena** in Puerto Rico open to tourists. While Gallístico is a tourist attraction, it is also a working arena, and the crowd is largely local. Betting is a rather informal affair; only those in the first three rows can easily place bets, and they bet by yelling out "azul" or "blanco" (the color on their desired cock's ankle) and then a number of dollars. Bets are mentally recorded by a few men working the gambling operation, but these men are not officially labeled. After the fight, bettors pay up or get paid. If you would like to bet, it is best to make friends with someone in the first three rows and have him bet for you. Each fight lasts 15min. or until one of the roosters is knocked down; one session can include up to 40 fights. Waitresses serve beer, ice cream, and (interestingly enough) fried chicken. Come on Saturday for a rambunctious experience. Women are welcome, but will be something of a curiosity. (Av. Isla Verde 6600. ☎ 791-6005. Ringside seats $12, men general admission $10, women free. Fights Tu 4pm, Sa 2:30pm, sometimes Th 2:30pm. Buy tickets at the door. Office open M-F 8:30am-3pm.)

THEATER AND MUSIC

San Juan's premier fine arts center, the **Centro de Bellas Artes Luis A. Ferré** in Santurce, created in 1981, holds a variety of different performances, from dance shows to symphony orchestra concerts to theater to stand-up comedy. The center has four theaters: the Antonio Paoli seats 2000 people, the Carlos Mavrichal seats 210, the René Márques seats 760, and the Sylvia Rexach seats 200. Twice a month the Puerto Rican symphony orchestra performs here, and in January the center hosts the **Casals Festival** (see **Festivals,** p. 138). For tickets, check **Ticketpop** online (see **Ticket Agencies,** p. 100) or visit the box office. Often, you can simply show up at the box office on the night of the show and buy tickets. (On Av. Ponce de León, west of the intersection with C. de Diego. ☎ 620-4444; www.cba.gobierno.pr. Shows F-Su $20-60, ages 60-74 50% off, 75+ free. Wheelchair accessible. Ticket office open M-Th 10am-6pm, F-Su 10am-the show begins. MC/V.)

Teatro Tapia (p. 123), on Plaza Colón in Old San Juan, has theater performances or musicals every weekend. Shows rotate every 2-3 weeks, but most are in Spanish. (☎ 721-0180 or 723-2079. Shows F-Su $25-30. Ticket office hours vary. MC/V.) The small **Corralón de San Juan,** C. San José 109, Old San Juan, occasionally hosts student performances, but the schedule is erratic.

FROM THE ROAD

COCKFIGHTS: THE REAL DEAL

As the two roosters were lowered from the ceiling in their glass boxes, shouts of "¡Cincuenta azul!" and "¡Doscientos blanco!" filled the air. As soon as they hit the ground, ring workers began to goad them on, waving a stuffed rooster at each, and then showing them each other. I'd heard rumors the *gallos* (roosters) were fitted with spurs on their claws, and that it was very bloody as they fought to the death. Signs warned that visitors wearing sleeveless shirts should not sit in the first two rows: was that the bloody "splash zone?" I was apprehensive, but also curious to experience what is proclaimed on many bumper stickers to be the island's "national sport."

In the end, the cockfight was much less gory than I thought it would be. The birds pecked at each other for awhile, and, although feathers flew, there was little blood. The fight ended like a boxing match, when one of the roosters could not get up after a specified period of time. Then the bets were paid off, and a new pair of roosters were lowered into the ring for the next fight.

Although Puerto Rico's cockfights have become controversial in the recent decades, witnessing a fight in San Juan's Club Gallístico represents a unique opportunity to meet the men who continue to make their living raising, training, and fighting cocks.

—Lauren Truesdell

Many of the biggest acts touring the US also make a stop at San Juan's **Coliseo Roberto Clemente.** Over the last few years, the 10,000-seat theater has seen concerts by Jennifer Lopez and *reggaetón* superstar Vico C; special events such as the Miss Universe Pageant, National Salsa Day, and Disney on Ice; and sporting events from basketball to volleyball. To buy tickets or find information about coming events, check **Ticket Center** (see **Ticket Agencies,** p. 100), in Plaza las Américas or online. (Located in Hato Rey, south of Av. F.D. Roosevelt, west of Expreso las Américas. ☎754-7422. Parking $1, during events $2.)

❋ FESTIVALS

San Juan hosts more festivals, and more outlandish festivals, than any other city on the island. Most are held in Old San Juan and the hordes of visitors can create horrendous traffic jams; if you go, take the bus or park in one of the several parking garages on the eastern edge of town. Some of the largest events are listed below. For more information about any festival, or exact dates, contact the Puerto Rican Tourism Company (see **Tourist Offices,** p. 99).

FESTIVAL DE LA CALLE SAN SEBASTIÁN. By day this is one of the biggest *artesanía* festivals on the island, and hundreds of artisans exhibit their wares in the Cuartel de la Ballajá (the same building as the Museo de las Américas). As dark falls the government shuts down C. San Sebastián for an incredible party attended by thousands of drunken revelers. *(A full week in mid-Jan., though the party gets going on the weekend. Old San Juan.)*

GALLERY NIGHTS. The premise is that galleries stay open late to show new exhibitions and host special events. However, many young people skip the galleries and head straight to C. San Sebastián, which becomes an enormous street party lasting until the wee hours of the morning. This has caused many galleries to avoid participating altogether and Gallery Nights is now focused mostly on drinking. Although the entire area is abuzz with energy, the Plaza de Armas, C. del Cristo, and Plaza San José tend to be the centers of activity. *(1st Tu of the month Feb.-May and Aug.-Dec. Exhibitions 7-9pm. Old San Juan.)*

HEINEKEN JAZZ FESTIVAL. This is Puerto Rico's largest jazz festival, drawing acts such as Manhattan Transfer and Eddie Palmieri. The event focuses on Latin jazz, but features musicians from all over the world to play under the Caribbean skies. *(Th-Su in May or June 8-10pm. Anfiteatro Tito Puente in the Parque Luis Muñoz Marín. www.prheinekenjazz.com. 1-day ticket $23, 4-day tickets $65; available from Ticketpop, p. 100.)*

LA FERIA DE ARTESANÍA. Vendors selling everything from soap to handmade *guiros* pack Old San Juan's Paseo la Princesa in one of the island's largest craft fairs. Orchestras, folkloric dancers, and big-name salsa acts like El Gran Combo de Puerto Rico put on free shows on the western end of the Paseo and in the Plaza de la Dársena. *(1st weekend in June. 7-10pm. Paseo la Princesa, Old San Juan. ☎721-2400.)*

CASALS FESTIVAL. Created by Spanish composer Pablo Casals (p. 73), this two-week festival consists of a series of classical music performances by the Puerto Rican Symphony Orchestra and visiting musicians. Posters from past Casals Festivals are on display in the Casals Museum in Old San Juan. *(Dates vary widely, but the festival is always held in the spring. In the Centro de Bellas Artes Luis A. Ferré (p. 137), Santurce. ☎721-7727; www.festcasalspr.gobierno.pr.)*

FESTIVAL SAN JUAN BAUTISTA. San Juan's patron saint festival is the island's largest party, hands down. In addition to the traditional art, music, and food, this unusual festival includes bonfires and parties on the beach. To bring luck for the following year, hundreds of *sanjuaneros* walk backwards into the ocean. *(The week preceding June 24. Old San Juan and Isla Verde.)*

QUE VIVE LA SALSA. This salsa exhibition and convention features dancers from around the world and classes for visitors of every skill level. *(Last weekend in July. Sheraton, Old San Juan. ☎ 791-1000. 10am-7pm.)*

CINEMAFEST DE PUERTO RICO. This internationally renowned film festival draws producers, directors, and actors from around the world; however, only films relating to the Caribbean are allowed to compete for prizes. Over 100 films are shown. *(Held over 1 week in Nov. Screenings at various locations around the island, but primarily in San Juan.)*

BACARDI FERIA DE ARTESANÍA. The Bacardi Corporation hosts yet another enormous artisans festival. Every December over 100,000 people venture out to Cataño to check out local arts and crafts, dance to live salsa and merengue, and, of course, sample their favorite rum. The drinks aren't free, but all proceeds go to charity. *(1st 2 weekends in Dec. Bacardi Factory (p. 145), Cataño.)*

LELOLAI FESTIVAL. This continual event is less of a festival and more of a series of shows and performances, including salsa lessons, tropical music, and rumba performances, designed by the Puerto Rican Tourism Company to highlight Puerto Rico's multicultural heritage. Some of the events are free, but others require the "Puerto Rico is Fun" card, available for purchase at over 50 island hotels. *(6 nights per week. Primarily in San Juan, but shows held throughout the island. ☎ 800-866-7827 or 723-3136; lelolai@prtourism.com.)*

◻ SHOPPING

Paseo de Diego, in Río Piedras (p. 125), is a pedestrian boulevard lined with clothing stores and fast-food restaurants. The clothing stores run the gamut from American chains like Foot Locker to bargain-basement wholesalers. **Old San Juan** is a great place to shop for hokey Puerto Rican souvenirs, designer clothing, some quality artwork, and expensive jewelry. It's also a great place to wander and browse. C. Fortaleza has an abundance of souvenir and clothing shops, while C. San Francisco has many jewelry shops. The area near the **Plaza de Armas** teems with expensive clothing stores like Coach and Ralph Lauren. C. del Cristo and C. San José are the best places to find original (and expensive) Puerto Rican modern art. In **Condado,** Puerto Rican Handmade Crafts, Gallery Av. Ashford 1035, has a large collection of *vejigante* masks ($25-125), as well as other souvenirs made by the shop owners. Each item sold comes with a brief history and introduction to the meaning of the craft. (☎ 724-3840. Open M-Sa 10:30am-9pm, Su 10:30am-6pm. Sometimes stays open later on weekends. AmEx/MC/V.)

More generic shopping awaits in Hato Rey, at **Plaza las Américas,** the largest shopping mall in the Caribbean. This three-story extravaganza has over 300 stores, two movie theaters, a food court, a ticket center, a fountain, a multi-story Old Navy, and everything else you could want in a mall. (Av. F.D. Roosevelt 525, in Hato Rey. Take Expreso Las Américas to the Av. F. D. Roosevelt exit. The B21 bus route goes around the mall. ☎ 767-5202. Open M-Sa 9am-9pm, Su 11am-5pm.)

◖ NIGHTLIFE

Check out the local publication *Agenda* (www.agendanoctambulo.com) for more information on the latest nightlife happenings (see **Publications,** p. 101).

> **■ NIGHTCLUB SECURITY** Many San Juan nightclubs have tighter security than the airport. To save time and hassles, do not bring pocket knives, pens, or any potentially hazardous object when you go out, and prepare to be frisked.

SAN JUAN

OLD SAN JUAN

In terms of bars and restaurants, Old San Juan has the trendiest nightlife in the capital. A few bars and clubs are scattered throughout the southern half of the city, but C. San Sebastián around **Pl. San José** is consistently the nucleus of activity. On weekend nights **Paseo de la Princesa** is crowded with vendors and young couples. Two companies also send out weekend night cruises from the dock in front of Plaza de la Dársena that become lively dance parties ($12 per person).

■ **Rumba,** C. San Sebastián 130 (☎725-4407). The Latin club you've always been looking for. Rumba packs in a crowd of all ages, races, and nationalities to dance the night away. Sip a drink up front or push your way to the back where live bands play charanga, salsa, and rumba (F-Sa 11pm). Beer $3.50. Open Tu-Su 8pm-3am. AmEx/MC/V.

■ **Lazer,** C. Cruz 251 (☎725-7581; www.clublazer.com). The many levels, hidden corners, and smoke machines combine to make Lazer one hot nighttime destination for young *sanjuancros*, who get down on the two big dance floors to hip-hop and techno or chill out on the palm-filled rooftop terrace. Mixed drinks $5-7. Ladies' Night Sa, with free wine for the women before midnight (women free, men cover $20). Other nights cover $5-10. Open W-Sa 11pm-3am.

Barú, C. San Sebastián 150 (☎977-7107). The place to go for a more mature night out. On weeknights and before 10pm, an older crowd sips *mojitos* under elegant yellow and purple lights. Later in the night and on weekends, twentysomethings make Barú C. San Sebastián's latest hot spot. Dress to impress; no jeans. Wine $7. Mixed drinks $6-10. Open M-F 5pm-midnight, Sa-Su 5pm-1am. AmEx/D/MC/V.

Señor Frog's (☎977-4142), on C. Comercio. Every night is a party at this flashy Mexican chain where drinks are sold in "yard" (really about 1½ ft. long) bottles. Señor Frog arrived in San Juan in early 2003 and instantly became the hottest venue in town for tennis-skirt-clad cruise passengers and vacationers who heed the restaurant's sign: "If the music is too loud...you're too old." This hasn't stopped the over-30 men who make up a decent part of the crowd before midnight. Beer $3-3.50. Mixed drinks $6. Yards $7.50-20. Good live rock and pop nightly at 9pm. Open daily 11am-2am or last customer. AmEx/D/MC/V.

Krugger's, San José 52 (☎723-2475), half a block down from C. San Sebastián; enter under the sign and turn left through the green doors. Everybody needs a karaoke fix from time to time, and Krugger's is one of San Juan's most popular bars because of its weekend mix of deejayed dance music and karaoke (11pm). Beer $1-3. Mixed drinks $1-5. Open Th-Sa 7:30pm-3:30am; in summer also open W. AmEx/D/MC/V.

Cafe Hijos de Borinquen, C. San José 51 (☎723-8126), at C. San Sebastián. Crowds of tipsy Puerto Ricans pack this bar on weekends. Push your way in, grab a beer ($2-3.50), and just try to make conversation over the shouts and the loud Latin dance music. Although it looks like a bar, it functions as a dance club for local teenagers. Mixed drinks $3.50-6. Happy hour 10pm-1am. Open Th-Sa 8pm-last customer. MC/V.

Cafe San Sebastián, C. San Sebastián 153 (☎725-3998), at Plaza del Mercado. A laid-back crowd heads to San Sebastián to relax on wicker furniture and enjoy the breeze coming through the large open doors while listening to good salsa music. San Juan's best chill-out bar. Beer $2.50-3.50. Mixed drinks $3.50-7.50. Claims to be open Tu-Su 8pm-3:30am, but will open late or close early if there are no patrons.

The Pool Palace, C. Recinto Sur 330 (☎725-8487). Cooler than you, or at least it thinks it is. Past the metal detector and two brawny security guards, lies the huge, chic, uber-hip zone of the Pool Palace. Two huge bars and a stage flank the cavernous room filled with 12 pool tables, several flat-screen TVs, and rich leather furniture. Still new and clean from its recent opening, the Pool Palace exudes a hip vibe. Happy hour 4-8pm. W karaoke night ($500 prize for winner). 23+. Open daily 10am-4:30am.

Nono's, C. San Sebastián 109 (☎725-7819), at C. Fortaleza, is a good place to drink. And drink. And drink. A relatively sedate crowd settles down at the bar with a drink in hand, buys cigars out of the vending machine ($3-13), and whiles the night away as the breeze comes through the many open doors. Beer $4-5. Mixed drinks $4-8. Open daily noon-4am. AmEx/MC/V.

The Noise, C. Tanca 203 (☎724-3426). Pumping out floor-shaking rap and *reggaetón,* The Noise packs in crowds of college-aged Puerto Ricans who disappear into the depths of this long, narrow club. It pulls out all the stops in an attempt to be cool—smoke machines, neon lights, and balloon sculptures on the ceiling. Beer $5. Mixed drinks $6. 18+. Cover $20. Open F-Sa midnight-last customer.

Oscar's Bar, C. Recinto Sur 321 (☎724-7255). Past the giant fish in the tank at the entrance is a cavernous bar filled with red Budweiser lamps. With 4 pool tables, mirrors on the walls, and countless TVs, this hole-in-the-wall doesn't seem to fit in with its trendy, touristy neighbors, but it's that local quality that makes it a good place to relax with friends and a beer ($3.50). Open daily noon-last customer. AmEx/MC/V.

CONDADO

Condado has a relatively mellow nightlife scene, primarily limited to a few low-key bars. Most of the local crowd heads to the open-air restaurant patios—Via Appia's is lively every night of the week. Tourists generally stick to the hotel nightclubs and casinos, of which there are many lining Av. Ashford.

▨ La Terraza del Condado (☎723-2770), at the eastern intersection of Av. Ashford and C. Magdalena. Young locals sip beer ($4) and margaritas ($5) in this plant-filled, open-air bar. Blue lights and chrome furniture create a space-age ambience. AmEx/D/MC/V.

Kali's, Av. Ashford 1407 (☎721-5104). Named after the Hindu god of destruction, this trendy lounge is decked out in a South Asian theme. Sweep aside the gauzy curtain to find dark maroon walls, candlelit nooks, huge black leather couches, and a flat-screen TV. Hookah bar. Appetizers $7-12. Beer $3-4. Mixed drinks $5-7. Open Tu-Sa 8pm-last customer. Kitchen closes 3am. AmEx/D/MC/V.

Waikiki, Av. Ashford 1025 (☎977-2267). A huge crowd of Condado's twentysomething glitterati fill up this new upscale bar/restaurant every night of the week, sipping wine (bottles $21-30) on the retro oceanfront patio or in the wine-cellarish interior. Those who stay out too late can also come back for breakfast ($2-5). Open daily 8am-last customer. MC/V.

SANTURCE

Santurce is home to San Juan's most outlandish and popular discos. However, with its many empty storefronts and construction sites, it is dangerous at night. The popular **Habana Club,** C. Condado 303 (☎722-1919), is a salsa mecca. Enter from C. Todd next to Stargate, across the street from Burger King. (Lessons Th-F 8pm. Live salsa F-Sa. Age restrictions and cover may apply.) At **Plaza del Mercado** (p. 115), young *puertorriqueños* ride into the plaza on their motorcycles Th-Sa and the place becomes completely packed. Locals hang out on the patios of the small restaurants and mingle in the streets, while salsa blares from every direction. Other clubs in the area include **Bliss,** C. Luisa 66, at C. Vieques, and **El Teatro,** C. Ponce de León 1420.

ISLA VERDE

The rich and famous (and the wannabe rich and famous) flock to Isla Verde after dark to party with the best of them. The dress code is slightly more elegant in this area—t-shirts, sandals, and other beachware are generally not allowed.

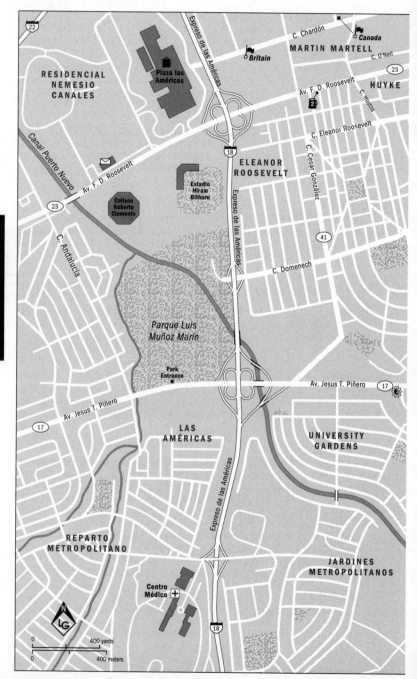

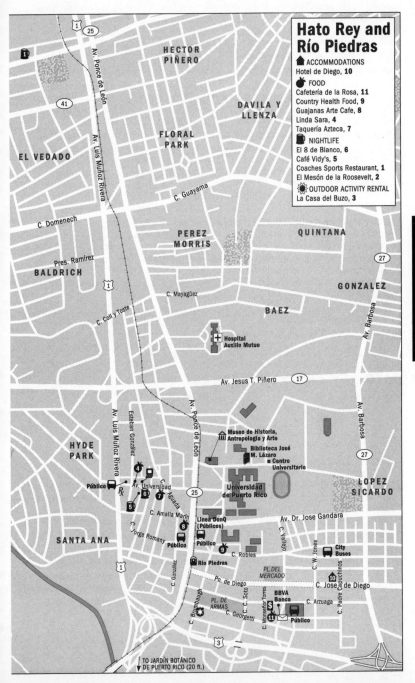

Hato Rey and Río Piedras

ACCOMMODATIONS
Hotel de Diego, **10**

FOOD
Cafetería de la Rosa, **11**
Country Health Food, **9**
Guajanas Arte Cafe, **8**
Linda Sara, **4**
Taquería Azteca, **7**

NIGHTLIFE
El 8 de Blanco, **6**
Café Vidy's, **5**
Coaches Sports Restaurant, **1**
El Mesón de la Roosevelt, **2**

OUTDOOR ACTIVITY RENTAL
La Casa del Buzo, **3**

SAN JUAN

HECTOR PIÑERO

DAVILA Y LLENZA

FLORAL PARK

EL VEDADO

Av. Ponce de León

Av. Luis Muñoz Rivera

C. Guayama

C. Domenech

Pres. Ramírez

BALDRICH

PEREZ MORRIS

QUINTANA

GONZALEZ

C. Coll y Toste

C. Mayagüez

BAEZ

Av. Barbosa

Hospital Auxilio Mutuo

Av. Jesus T. Piñero

Av. Ponce de León

Av. Barbosa

Museo de Historia, Antropología y Arte

Biblioteca José M. Lázaro

Centro Universitario

HYDE PARK

Av. Luis Muñoz Rivera

Esteban González

Av. Universidad

Universidad de Puerto Rico

LOPEZ SICARDO

Público

C. Aguada

C. Amalia Marín

Av. Dr. Jose Gandara

C. Jorge Romany

SANTA ANA

Linea DonQ (Públicos)

Público

C. Robles

C. Vallejo

City Buses

Río Piedras

PL. DEL MERCADO

C. W. Jones

Po. de Diego

C. Jose de Diego

C. Padre Capuchinos

C. Brumbaugh

PL. DE ARMAS

C. Georgetti

C. Soto

C. Monseñor Torres

BBVA Banco

C. Arzuaga

Público

TO JARDÍN BOTÁNICO DE PUERTO RICO (20 ft.)

Lupi's (p. 118) becomes a popular nightlife venue; a predominantly male crowd congregates by the bar and couples sip drinks on the outdoor terrace. **Sonny's Terrace** (p. 119) has all the makings of a successful bar (live music, ample space, good location), but nobody seems to be catching on, making it a good place to relax and get away from the crowds.

> **Shots Sports Bar & Grill** (☎253-1443), in Isla Verde Mall. This huge, dark-wood pub defies Isla Verde's glamour and pretension. A young, local crowd relaxes at the big wooden bar or grinds on the dance floor. Puerto Rican boxing decor. Beer $3-4. Happy hour daily 5-8pm, Red Dog 2 for $3. Live salsa Th 11pm. Live Spanish rock F-Sa 11pm. 21+. Cover $5 after 10pm. Open daily 9:30pm-4:30am. AmEx/D/MC/V.
>
> **Oyster Bar & Grill** (☎726-2161), on Av. Isla Verde, across from the Marbella Caribe building. This New Orleans-themed bar is one hot place to party, with the younger crowd grinding to pop music on the dance floor and kicking back at tables hidden in nooks and crannies. The most alcohol-filled house specialty drinks you'll find anywhere. Beer $4. Mixed drinks $5 and up. 21+. Beer and wings 2 for 1 Tu 9-11pm. $10 open bar on selected drinks W 7-11pm. Live rock F-Sa. Cover after 10:30pm W $3, Th-F $5. Open M-Tu 11am-2am, W 11am-4am, Th 11am-5am, F-Sa 11am-5:30am. Kitchen closes 3am.
>
> **Club Babylon,** Av. Isla Verde 6063 (☎791-2781 or 791-1000 ext. 1657; www.babylonpr.com), in the Wyndham El San Juan Hotel. Located in Isla Verde's fanciest hotel, this opulent club hosts over 1000 people on a busy night. Although the velvet ropes may seem pretentious, the drink specials are a steal. Hip-hop Th-F, trance Sa. Beer $4. Mixed drinks $4-7. Drinks with special liquor of the night 2 for $5. College night Th. Happy hour 10pm-midnight, beer $3. Th 18+, F 21+, Sa 23+. Cover Th and Sa $10, F $12. Open Th-Sa 10pm-4am. AmEx/MC/V.
>
> **El Taquito,** Av. Isla Verde 5940 (☎726-5050), across from Pizza City. This new but cheap bar/restaurant allows you to sip margaritas ($5; half-gallon $20) or their fruit frappe concoctions ($4.50) while watching TV and noshing on Tex-Mex staples like tacos ($1.50). If you stay out too late, don't worry: they serve big breakfast specials, too. Beer starts at $1. Open 24hr. AmEx/MC/V.

HATO REY AND RÍO PIEDRAS

> ◪ **El 8 de Blanco** (☎751-5208), at Av. Universidad and C. Consuelo Carbo, Río Piedras. Located 2 blocks from UPR, El 8 de Blanco is the classic student bar, with cheap beer, loud music, video games, pool tables, and even a dominoes table. The place fills up early, every night of the week. Beer $1-3. Mixed drinks $3-4. Happy hour daily 6-8pm. 18+. Open M-Sa 2pm-4am, Su 5pm-last customer. MC/V.
>
> **Coaches Sport Restaurant,** Av. F.D. Roosevelt 137 (☎758-3598), Hato Rey. Huge American-style sports bar with pool tables, many TVs, and large bar. Football helmets on the wall keep track of the week's NFL matchups. Packed on big game nights. Entrees $6-16. Beer $3-3.50. Mixed drinks $3-5. Happy hour daily 5pm-7pm, with half-price chicken wings and drinks. Live Spanish rock Tu-Sa when there's not a big game on. Open M-W 11am-midnight, Th-F 11am-3am, Sa 6pm-4am. AmEx/D/DC/MC/V.
>
> **Café Vidy's,** Av. Universidad 104 (☎767-3062), Río Piedras. You can hang out with the locals and drink a Medalla on the streetside patio at just about any time of day. Also a popular *cafetería* serving Puerto Rican food (entrees $4-7). Beer $1-4. Happy hour daily 9-11pm. Karaoke W 9pm. Open daily 11am-last customer. MC/V.
>
> **El Mesón de la Roosevelt,** Av. F.D. Roosevelt 300 (☎767-3721), Hato Rey. Two bars, one in the pub-like front section and the other in the back restaurant. Sandwiches ($1.25-9) are popular during the day; cheap beer ($2.50-3.50) is the drink of choice

when the bar starts hopping at night. The crowd is mostly post-college. Open 24hr. AmEx/D/MC/V.

GAY AND LESBIAN NIGHTLIFE

For the latest information on gay nightlife and events, check out *Puerto Rico Breeze*, the capital's gay and lesbian newspaper, available at stores in Condado's gay district, free in some hotels and restaurants, or online at www.puertorico-breeze.com. **Eros,** Av. Ponce de León 1257, in Santurce, plays house, progressive, and techno music, with some hip-hop thrown in. (☎787-722-1131; www.erosthe-club.com. Happy hour Th-Su until midnight. W urban pop, free before 11pm. Th college nights, free with student ID. F 80s and 90s, free entrance until midnight. Su hip-hop, R&B, *reggaetón*.) **Junior's,** C. Condado 615, is one of San Juan's less pretentious gay discos. This small club with the feel of a cozy, private party plays an unremarkable mix of salsa, reggae, and pop. That feeling is enhanced by the fact that to enter, you must approach the door and wait to be buzzed in. (☎723-9477. Beer $3. Mixed drinks $54. 21+. Open daily 8pm-last customer. Cash only.) **Steamworks,** C. Luna 205, Old San Juan, is a popular gay destination, with a gym, whirlpool, and a steam room. All men 21+ welcome, but they must first become a member and agree to the club rules. (☎725-4993; www.steamworksonline.com. 6-month membership $6. Lockers $7 per visit. AmEx/D/MC/V.)

◪ DAYTRIPS FROM SAN JUAN

CATAÑO

Public Transportation: *From Pier 2 in Old San Juan take the AquaExpreso ferry (10min.; every 30min. 6am-10pm; $0.50) to Cataño. To get to the Bacardi factory, walk outside, turn right, and walk to the large green parking garage where públicos wait inside ($2 per person for 4 or more people or $6 alone).* **Driving:** *Take Rte. 165 from San Juan and turn right after the John Deere factory; if you see the huge Bacardi sign, you've gone too far.*

Rum's the word that most visitors have in mind as they head across the bay to Cataño, home of the **Bacardi Rum Factory.** Although Bacardi originated in Cuba and now has factories in Mexico and the Bahamas, the Cataño factory is the world's largest producer of Bacardi rum and one of the largest companies on the island. All of this combines to make the Bacardi Factory one hot attraction for families, couples, and those looking for a free drink.

Tours, which last 1-1½hr., are offered every 15min., alternating between English and Spanish. Upon arrival, visitors receive **two free drink tickets.** Many *sanjuaneros* have been known to come for the free drinks and then leave before the tour. However, Bacardi fanatics may find that the tour provides an interesting explanation of the rum-making process and the company's history. The tour begins with a tram ride to the new Visitors Center, where guests watch an amusing film—suspiciously like a long Bacardi commercial—telling the story of "the king of rums and the rum of kings." Next, audioguides allow visitors to explore a re-created antique distillery room (ca. 1900) and another room devoted to the Bacardi family. Guests are also given the chance to smell the various Bacardi products at different stages in the fermentation process. Then, visitors are taken to a high-tech room playing hot Bacardi commercials. Here they are allowed to dance and tape 10-second video clips to email home. Finally, another tram passes the working distillery and bottling plant before heading back to the start of the tour and the requisite Bacardi store.

Few visitors make it past the Bacardi Factory, but Cataño has more to it than rum. Just down the road, **Isla de Cabras** used to be an island with its own leper colony, but has long since morphed into a grassy peninsula with picnic tables and some superb views of Old San Juan. And unlike the bustling capital, Isla de Cabras is quite peaceful, making it an ideal spot for a picnic. The island also houses **El Cañuelo,** a Spanish fort built in the 1500s to create crossfire with El Morro. The fort looks like a mini version of El Morro, and no one is allowed to enter, so there's really not much more than what you see from across the bay from binoculars atop El Morro. Unfortunately, public transportation to Isla de Cabras is difficult. A taxi from the Bacardi factory costs at least $6 each way, so the island is only worth a visit if you have a car. From Rte. 165, drive past the Bacardi factory, turn right on Rte. 870, and continue to the end. (Open daily 8:30am-5:30pm. $2 per car.)

CERRO GORDO

Public Transportation: Take a público out of Río Piedras to Vega Baja ($3), where occasional públicos traveling to Cerro Gordo from Vega Baja will let you off at the beach ($0.75). On weekdays, during daylight hours, you may be able to catch a passing público back to Vega Baja from the beach. *Driving:* From Hwy. 22 exit at Rte. 693 and drive west, then turn right onto Rte. 6690 at the sign pointing to the beach. Follow this road all the way to its end, then turn right; the beach is on your right.

The beaches of San Juan simply cannot compare to those found around the rest of the island. While the public beach in Luquillo basks in the glory of the unofficial title of "the most beautiful beach in Puerto Rico," **Balneario Cerro Gordo** has a lot to

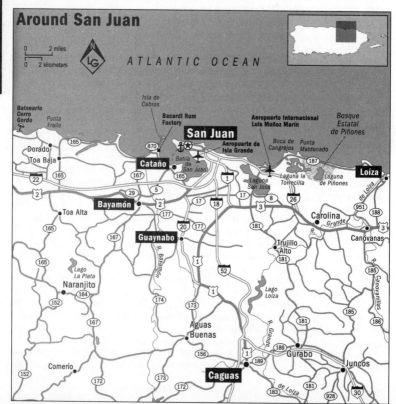

offer travelers who are looking for shorter excursion to sublime sands. T'
Rican government has invested $3.4 million into remodeling this **public** *i*
ating first-rate facilities in an already first-rate environment. The *bal?*
rently boasts tiny waves of crystal clear water, a palm tree-lined beacl
of the picturesque village of Cerro Gordo. The beach and the town make ..
daytrip from San Juan or a requisite stop on any tour of the island. (☎ 883-2736.
Lifeguards, picnic tables, food stands, and public showers. Parking $3. Open daily
8:30am-6pm.) If you work up an appetite lounging on the beach, the cheapest eats
in the area come from the various beach kiosks, but for a heartier meal you can
stroll to **El Batey del Indio ❸**, on Rte. 690, one block up the road away from the
ocean. The small, casually refined restaurant specializes in *mofongos* and seafood. (☎ 883-7312. Entrees $7.50-22. Open Th-Su noon-10pm. MC/V.)

If you decide to extend your daytrip a little, Cerro Gordo has a nice **campground ❶** in the woodsy area up the hill on the eastern edge of the beach. Some
sites have ocean views, but there is little privacy. Guards control access, but it's
still wise to keep valuables out of sight. Call the beach for reservations, especially from June to August. ($13 per person.)

BOSQUE ESTATAL DE PIÑONES

*Public Transportation: San Juan city bus B40 travels from the Isla Verde bus stop, in front
of the Cockfight Arena, along Av. Boca de Cangrejos to the eastern edge of Piñones. **Driving:** From Isla Verde, Rte. 187 runs though the forest. **Biking:** By far the best way to experience Piñones is by bicycle. Bike path open daily 6am-6pm.*

Although physically separated by less than 1 mi., wild and rugged Piñones State
Forest and ritzy Isla Verde could not be more different. Where Isla Verde has
upscale "authentic" Puerto Rican restaurants, Piñones has food stands with open
flames frying African-influenced Puerto Rican foods. Isla Verde's population of
wealthy Puerto Ricans and expats contrasts with Piñones' relatively poor community. In Piñones, the sunburnt tourists of Isla Verde are missing and the beaches
are deserted. Travelers who want to experience a more traditional Puerto Rico,
but don't have time to stray far from San Juan, should head straight for this area.

Coming from San Juan along Rte. 187 visitors will first pass **Boca de Cangrejos**,
a small peninsula filled with restaurants and food shacks. An offshore reef
makes this a bad area to swim, but a great place to stop for a snack. Keep
going—it's not until around Km 9 that you will find the nearly deserted **beaches**
with pristine sand and rows of palm trees. Drivers can pull off on any one of the
sandy roads leading to the ocean and relax. Piñones is also a popular **surfing**
spot; local surf shops can point out the best breaks.

Lying on the beach is nice, but the best way to experience Piñones is by riding
along the **Paseo Piñones bike path.** A combination of paved trails and wooden
bridges, the path weaves through the forest providing incomparable views of the
flora, the small communities of houses, and the beach. A fabulous daytrip from
San Juan can be spent riding along the path, swimming for an hour or two at a
deserted beach, then stopping for a snack at a food kiosk on the way home. It is
possible to rent a bicycle at any shop in the city (see **Bike Rental**, p. 99), and then
ride along the road to the reach the path. To avoid riding down busy streets in
the urban section, rent a bike at **El Pulpo Loco**, located on the water behind Soleil
in the second cluster of restaurants, right on the bike path. (☎ 791-8382. Bikes $5
per hr., $20 per day. Open daily 10am-6pm. AmEx/MC/V.)

Farther inland, the forest also encompasses **Laguna de Piñones** and **Laguna la Tor-
recilla**. These two lakes are quite swampy and can emit a powerful smell, but it is
possible to **kayak** on them. To reach the lake, drive to Km 9 and turn right at the
sign pointing toward Bosque Estatal de Piñones. Continue all the way down the
road to the parking lot and the kayak launch. **Tortuga Kayak** in San Juan (p. 134)
leads 3hr. tours for $50 per person.

FESTIVAL DE SANTIAGO APÓSTOL OR THE CARNAVAL DE LOÍZA

Nowhere on the island is Puerto Rico's rich African heritage more evident than the small northeastern town of Loíza during its annual carnaval festival, celebrated every year over five days at the end of July. This lively party combines the island's Catholic and African traditions with a religious ceremony, parades, food, and intricate costumes. After dark the entire town settles down to participate in the interactive *bomba* song and dance (p. 73). The carnaval festival originated in 15th-century Spain, as the Spaniards reenacted the defeat of the Moors, and it has remained faithful to its roots. In Loíza participants dress up either as finely dressed *caballeros* (Spanish gentleman) or brightly colored *vejigantes* (representations of the Spanish Moors). Though they are supposedly the villains, *vejigantes* have become renowned because for their beautiful *vejigante* masks (see **Arts and Crafts,** p. 69). The distinct Loíza-style masks are made out of painted coconut shells with several thin circular horns protruding. In recent years the Loíza carnaval has attracted an increasing number of tourists, but it remains a local and authentic festival, with many *puertorriqueño participants*.

(For more information and exact dates contact the San Juan office of tourism ☎ 722-1709.)

Piñones is filled with dozens of small food shacks. The best and the cheapest option is to grab some fried chicken or a *batida* from one of these vendors and head to the beach. Those looking for more refined dining options can usually find one in each of the restaurant clusters. In addition to renting bikes, **El Pulpo Loco ❸** (see above) doubles as a clean restaurant with palm-covered picnic tables and tasty Puerto Rican seafood. Specialties include red snapper and octopus, but the menu offers less adventurous options such as beef and chicken. (Entrees $8-18. Open M-Th and Su 10am-11pm, F-Sa 10am-2am. AmEx/MC/V.) **The Reef Bar and Grill ❸,** in the first inlet of restaurants directly after the bridge coming from San Juan, has the best view in Piñones, with crystal clear water breaking on the reef in the foreground and the San Juan skyline in the distance. The menu includes seafood entrees as well as chicken and beef. (☎791-1374. Sandwiches and burgers $5-7. Entrees $7-13. Beer $2.75-3. Open M-Th and Su 10am-11pm, F-Sa 10am-2am. MC/V.) Piñones also has an impressive **nightlife scene.** Many restaurants, including both of the above, double as bars, but the hot spot is **Soleil.** Located in front of El Pulpo Loco in the second inlet, the two-story restaurant has live salsa and Spanish rock on weekend nights. One of the most modern-looking bars in the park, it boasts a gorgeous ocean view from the patio (☎ 253-1033; fax 791-2299; www.soleilbeachclub.com. House specialty mixed drinks $5.50-6. Appetizers $7-9. Open M-Th and Su 11am-11pm, F-Sa 11am-2am. AmEx/D/MC/V.)

LOÍZA

Public Transportation: *Públicos go from Río Piedras (p. 93) to Loíza (30-75min., M-Sa 5am-3pm, $1.75). From the público terminal in Loíza face the grassy area, turn left, and walk 3 blocks to the plaza.* ***Driving:*** *Take Rte. 187 east through the Piñones Forest. After you cross the large bridge over Río Grande de Loíza follow signs into the town center.*

The small town of Loíza has a culture that reflects Puerto Rico's African heritage more than anywhere else on the island, but unfortunately its tourism infrastructure is undeveloped. However, all faults disappear during the last week in July, when the town's annual carnaval festival is celebrated. This is really the only motivation to visit Loíza; during the rest of the year, it is a sleepy town with a few small attractions. Three miles south of town on Rte. 187, the **Estudio de Arte Samuel Lind** is one of the best working art galleries in the San Juan metro area. The studio/gallery/home of Loíza's premier artist houses a collection of colorful paintings and big bronze sculptures, both finished and in-progress. Lind's work is largely inspired by the people and culture of Loíza; anywhere you go in the town,

you will come across his work. Some small reproductions go for as little as $25, and hand-pressed prints run around $150-200. However, Lind welcomes people who just come to look, as he is eager to teach about the town's African culture. Drive toward Río Grande and look for the small sign pointing to the studio, then turn left onto the small road; it's the third house on the left. Or take a *público* to Río Grande and ask to be let off at the studio. (☎876-1494. Open daily 10am-6pm, when Lind is home. MC/V.) Across the street, the **Ayala Souvenir Shop** displays *vejigante* masks crafted by Raúl Ayala, a second-generation Loíza mask artist. The masks ($20-500) are all for sale, from the small, ornamental ones to the head-sized masks used in festivals. (☎876-1130. Open daily 11am-6pm.) Loíza's only sight is **La Iglesia de San Patricio**, the large yellow-orange church on the plaza. Registered as a National Historic Sight, the attractive church is unfortunately closed most of the time. But the plaza itself is a shady and relaxing stop, with a fountain and a large tile mosaic focusing on the town's African heritage. **Yawa's Café ❶**, C. Espíritu Santo 20, on the plaza, is a *cafetería*-style restaurant, and one of the few places to eat in the town center. Hamburgers ($2), sandwiches ($1.50-3), and breakfast combos ($1-2.50) characterize their standard fare. (☎886-6084. Open M-F 7am-1pm.)

CAGUAS

Public Transportation: Públicos *make the trip from Río Piedras to Caguas (35min., $2.50). From Caguas públicos travel to Cayey (30min., $1.25), Gurabo (20min., $0.70), and Río Piedras (35min., $2.50).* **Driving:** *Take Hwy. 1 south out of San Juan, then exit onto Hwy. 52 (toll $0.70) and follow the signs to Caguas Centro (30-45min., depending on traffic).*

Although few foreign visitors make it to Caguas, the city makes a great daytrip from San Juan. Caguas has opened five small but informative ▨**museums** highlighting various aspects of island culture. Although all exhibits are in Spanish, many tour guides speak English and are more than happy to show you around. (All museums open Tu-Sa 8am-noon and 1-4pm. Free). **Casa del Trovador**, C. Tapia 18 (☎744-8833 ext. 1843), is devoted to Puerto Rico's traditional island musicians, the **trovadores.** Found primarily in the central mountains, these musicians sing a popular rhythm called the *décima.* The museum explains the *trovador* through photos, musical instruments, and a full costume, while *trovador* music plays in the background. The special exhibit on female *trovadores* is particularly interesting. On Saturdays, the museum offers free music lessons for children in traditional *cuatro* and guitar. The **Museo del Tabaco,** C. Betances 87 (☎744-2960), contains artifacts and several display boards about the history of tobacco and its importance in Caguas, a major tobacco producer in the 19th century. Today the city's tobacco farms are gone, but the art of cigar-making lives on the second half of the museum, where several elderly *cagüeños* spend 4hr. each day making cigars by hand. Many were employed in the tobacco industry in their younger years; working in the museum allows them to preserve their *artesanía* while earning some extra cash. Visitors can watch them work from behind glass and even buy the finished products afterward (cigars $4 for 25). At the corner of C. Ruiz Belvis and C. Padial the **Museo de Arte de Caguas** upholds Puerto Rico's tradition of impressive art collections

Caguas

🍴 FOOD
Kam Ying, 1
RexCream, 6

🏛 MUSEUMS
Casa del Trovador, 2
Casa Rosada Abelardo Díaz Alfaro, 3
Centro Musical Criollo José
    Ignacio Quintón, 5
Museo de Arte de Caguas, 4
Museo del Tabaco, 7

C. Dr. Goyco
C. Baldorioty
C. Corchado
C. Celis Aguilera
Av. Muñoz Rivera
Av. Baldorioty
C. Tapia
Público
C. Tamire
C. Ruiz Belvis
C. Ruiz Belvis
PL. PALMER
C. Padial
Av. Mercado
C. Betances
C. G. Benítez
C. Acosta
C. Jiménez Sicardó
C. Vizcarrondo

0   100 yards
0   100 meters

with an exhibit of primarily local work. Visitors will recognize the scene in Alejandro de Jesús's "Jugadores de Dominó" as a familiar sight in any San Juan street. Make sure you don't miss the huge mural hidden behind the side wall.

Continue down C. Ruiz Belvis to reach the **Centro Musical Criollo José Ignacio Quintón** (☎744-4110 or 744-4075), at the corner of C. Intendente Ramírez. The bright yellow First Baptist Church of Caguas was converted into a museum in 1995, and it now features displays showing how traditional Puerto Rican instruments are made and the history of various musical styles on the island. The museum becomes more engaging when local groups perform inside; call ahead or ask at the tourist office for more information. Finally, head half a block down C. Intendente Ramírez to **Casa Rosada Abelardo Díaz Alfaro,** C. Intendente Ramírez 12 (☎286-7640), former home of **Carlos Manuel "Charlie" Rodríguez,** a native *cagüeño* who was beatified by the Pope and continues to be Puerto Rico's highest-ranking Catholic. The first floor is a reconstruction of a 19th-century home, but the second floor is devoted exclusively to Rodríguez, with an explanation of his life, pictures of his beatification, and a bone held in a reliquary. There is also an altar in the museum that many Puerto Ricans visit to pray for Rodríguez's intercession. The helpful tourist office plans to open additional museums in the near future. For the latest information, head to the large **Oficina de Turismo,** on Pl. Palmer next to the Alcaldía. (☎744-8833 ext. 2906. Open M-Sa 8am-noon and 1-4pm.)

While upper-end restaurants are located outside of the city center, budget travelers can find several good, affordable eateries within walking distance. **Kam Ying ❶,** C. Acosta 22, serves Chinese food with a Puerto Rican twist. Everything comes with french fries and most patrons order fried chicken. (☎743-3838. Huge entrees with shrimp, rice, and french fries $4-7. Open daily 10:30am-11pm. MC/V.) Travelers with a sweet tooth should not miss a trip to the popular **RexCream ❶,** C. Muñoz Rivera 45, which serves the best ice cream in town. Most flavors are Caribbean fruits, like *acerola* (West Indian cherry) and *parcha* (passion fruit). (Ice cream $1.10-2. Open daily 9am-10pm.)

GUAYNABO

Public Transportation: Take Metrobús II from Parada 18 in Santurce. Driving: Take Rte. 2 south; after the intersection with Rte. 20 look for the museum on the right, immediately after the Caparra housing development.

The only real attraction of this large suburb is the **Museo de Caparra,** located at the sight of Ponce de León's first home and the island's original capital. In 1937 archaeologists excavating the area found artifacts from the time of Ponce de León's inhabitation, but there was no venue to display them. Consequently the government opened this one-room museum to hold the old coins, broken shreds of pottery, and 16th-century weapons and armor. The most interesting object is a letter from de León to the Spanish king notifying him of the explorer's discovery of Florida. In front of the museum, the ruins of Ponce de León's home are still visible, while artists' reconstructions are inside. Most visitors will be able to get their Ponce de León fix with a stop by Museo Casa Blanca in Old San Juan (p. 131); only die-hard de León buffs need to make the trek out to Guaynabo. (☎781-4795. All displays in Spanish only. Open Tu-Sa 8am-noon and 1-4pm. Free.)

BAYAMÓN

Public Transportation: The sparkling new Urban Train travels from Ha3to Rey and Río Piedras to Bayamón ($1.50). Driving: From San Juan take Rte. 2 (J.F.K. Expressway) all the way into Bayamón. When you see the immense City Hall hanging over the center of the road, turn right and park in a garage near the central plaza or in the ample on-street parking.

The dense population and many shopping malls of Bayamón just don't match up with most tourists' dreams of tropical paradise. However, one sight that does cap-

Countless visitors come to San Juan, lie on the beach for a week, and never discover the treasures of inland Puerto Rico. For those who want to experience just a little bit more, but who don't have time to venture very far inland, this scenic drive offers a glimpse of Puerto Rico's incredible natural and cultural diversity. From the towering office buildings of Hato Rey to the towering peaks of the Cordillera Central, from the traditional devotion of Trujillo Alto to the traditional roadside snacks of Piñones, this road trip highlights the island's variety in a great one-day excursion from Puerto Rico's capital.

TIME: 5-7hr.

DISTANCE: 50mi.

BEST TIME TO GO: Dec.-Mar., or when no rain is expected.

Travelers should take note that the times given are highly variable estimates, dependent on traffic and weather conditions. The trip travels along narrow, winding mountain roads, which become perilous after dark. Make sure to leave early and allow plenty of time for your trip. From San Juan, take Hwy. 1 south through the business district of Hato Rey. After passing through the city, take Hwy. 3 heading east toward Carolina. This is far from the most picturesque part of the journey, but it does provide insight into San Juan's problems with urban sprawl and traffic congestion. Stay on Hwy. 3 for about 1 mi., then turn right and head south on Rte. 181, a pleasant tree-lined street that leads to the suburb of Trujillo Alto.

1. LA GRUTA DE LOURDES. After passing the intersection with Rte. 850, take the next exit to the right and head up the hill on the middle street; then turn right at the sign for La Gruta de Lourdes. This small place of worship was created in 1925 as a replica of the sanctuary in Lourdes, France where, according to tradition, three girls saw the apparition of the Virgin Mary in 1858. Continue to the top of the hill to visit a 12-pew chapel with a small but beautiful altar. A path out back passes a large church and several beautiful statues depicting various biblical scenes. The lush grounds that surround the church make a nice escape from the road. (Church open daily 7am-10pm.) After taking a look around, continue on Rte. 181, bearing to the right at the intersection, after which the highway turns into a small road without lane lines. You will cross **Río Grande de Loíza,** one of the largest rivers in Puerto Rico, before turning onto Rte. 851.

2. EMBALSE RÍO GRANDE DE LOÍZA. Tiny Rte. 851 continues to ascend through the mountains providing excellent views before it eventually descends into more tropical vegetation. When you reach a small village, turn onto Rte. 941 for panoramic views of the 422-hectare **Lago Loíza,** constructed by the government in 1954 to provide water for the metropolitan area. It is difficult to actually reach the lake, as most side roads lead to private, gated residences. Here, you've finally escaped the traffic of San Juan. The village of Jaguas has a couple of small mini-markets if you need to make a stop. Soon the surroundings flatten out and the road passes through idyllic arches of trees and vegetation. Continue past the end of the lake.

3. GURABO. Rte. 941 leads straight into the village of Gurabo. Gurabo is known as the city of the stairs, and it's easy to see why—streets leading toward the mountain all end in steep steps heading up the hill. Hike all the way up for a great view of the city and the surrounding valley. There's not much else to Gurabo, but the newly remodeled Plaza de Recreo is a pleasant place to sit and relax. The **Departamento de Arte y Cultura,** on C. Santiago, across from the church, supposedly has a small gallery of local artwork on the second floor, but opening hours are sporadic. (☎737-8416. Theoretically open M-F 8am-4pm.) If you're starving, or looking for a dirt-cheap meal, there are a few inexpensive *comida criolla* and pizza joints along C. Santiago. If you're looking for a more sophisticated meal, hop back in the car and drive east toward Juncos.

4. EL TENEDOR. To leave Gurabo, head east on the street C. Anuz Rivera, perpendicular to C. Santiago next to the plaza, turn right at the stoplight, and hop on Hwy. 30 east. Those in a hurry can skip to **5.** Otherwise, take the second exit at **Juncos Centro,** and follow the road toward the building with the tall brick chimney, **El Tenedor 5.** Formerly a rum distillery, the stately edifice now holds one of the best restaurants on the island, where well-dressed wait-

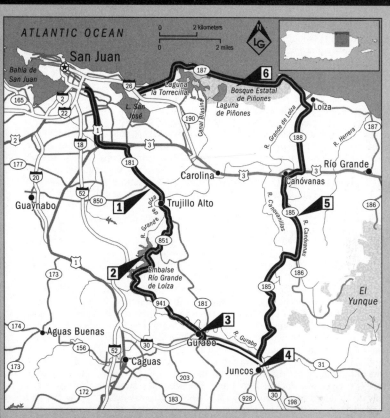

ers bring every customer wine glasses full of water, buttered bread, and steak or seafood entrees. *Sanjuaneros* have been known to drive all the way out here for a meal. The entrees are a bit heavy for lunch, but after such a long drive you deserve a hearty 8 oz. steak, and at only $16, it's quite a deal. (C. Emelia Príncipe 1. ☎734-6573. Entrees $9-19. Open M-Th and Su 11am-9pm, F-Sa 11am-10pm. AmEx/MC/V.) To leave El Tenedor, go to the intersection with Hwy. 30, but take Rte. 952, then turn right on Rte. 185.

5. FINAL DESCENT. To continue the scenic route, head north on the small, winding Rte. 185, which leads through more mountains, villages, and grassy fields. (If you want the more direct route home, take Hwy. 30 west to Hwy. 52, which will lead right back to San Juan.) After about 15 mi., head east on the large Hwy. 3 for about 1 mi., then exit onto Rte. 188 north. Now you're back at a lower elevation, and the vegetation is much more wild and tropical. If you're up for another stop, Rte. 951 leads to the small town of Loíza, with its historical church and fascinating African culture (p. 135). Otherwise, continue on Rte. 188 then take a left onto Rte. 187 west.

6. BOSQUE ESTATAL DE PIÑONES. Rte. 187 leads through the incredible wilderness of Piñones State Forest (p. 147). Wrapping along the Atlantic Coast, the scenery here is as stunning as the mountain regions you just left, but in a more stereotypically Caribbean way. If your stomach has any room left, grab a snack at one of the many roadside kiosks and eat while watching waves crash over the reefs. Or, if it's still before sunset, stop at one of the deserted beaches for a quick swim. Then it's back onto Rte. 187, which will take you straight back to San Juan.

tivate visitors (mostly Puerto Rican schoolchildren) is the **Luis A. Ferré Parque de las Ciencias** (Science Park). This educational theme park contains over 10 museums, a trolley, a planetarium, a 500-seat amphitheater, a panoramic elevator, a zoo, a mock town square, and an artificial lake with paddleboats. Though definitely geared toward a pre-adolescent audience, the museums are interesting for visitors of all ages. The **Museo de Transportación** contains a collection of historical cars, including a 1907 Ford Model N and a Batmobile. The somewhat politically incorrect **Museo de Ciencias Naturales** commemorates the safaris of Puerto Rican Ventura Barnés and holds about 100 stuffed heads of African animals, from zebras to warthogs. Rifles, stools made from elephant feet, and tables held up by ivory tusks are also on display. The **Museo de Reproducciones Artísticas** contains reproductions of famous artwork from around the world, as well as some original work by lesser-known artists. The central Anfiteatro Tito Rodríguez frequently has shows that teach children, interestingly, through *reggaetón* songs. With the largest concentration of museums outside Old San Juan, Parque de las Ciencias merits a visit. (On Rte. 167, about ½ mi. from central Bayamón. The highway is a difficult place to walk; instead, drive or take a taxi from in front of the *público* station. The park is visible by the US spaceships towering over the entrance. (☎ 740-6868 or 740-6871. Open W-F 9am-4pm, Sa-Su 10am-6pm. Ticket sales stop 1½hr. before closing time. Parking $1. Admission $5, ages 2-12 $3, ages 65-74 $2.50, 75+ free. Trolley $1. Planetarium $3, children $2. Paddle boats $3 per person.)

Although Bayamón is largely residential, the government has restored a historical downtown area and opened three interesting museums near the plaza behind the mayor's office. The ▓ **Museo Francisco Oller** has a slightly misleading name, as it only holds five works by Oller, who was born in Bayamón. Nonetheless it houses a respectable collection of artwork by artists and sculptors such as Tomás Batista and Juan Santos. The many sculptures, made of everything from jade to lava rock, are well-preserved and depict various subjects including fish and famous Puerto Ricans. Upstairs, the museum crams a substantial body of incredible work by contemporary Puerto Rican artists into a relatively small space. The helpful guides are eager to talk about the art and answer questions. (C. Degetau 15, at C. Maseo. ☎787-0620. Open M-F 8:30am-4pm. Free.) Next door, the **Museo Archivo Bayamón** is neatly divided into two sections. The first floor details the history of the city and its astounding growth through pictures, city models, and maps. The second floor is devoted to plaques, newspaper clippings, and other memorabilia from Bayamón's former mayor, Ramón Luis Rivera, who controlled the city for 24 years before his son's election in 2000. Rivera's suit from his first inauguration sits at his desk, arranged as if he were working. The historian is usually willing to explain anything you ever wanted to know about Bayamón. (C. Degetau 14. ☎785-6010. If the door is locked at either the Museo Archivo or the Museo Oller, go to the other one and ask them to open it. Open M-F 8:30am-4pm. Free.) The most unique of the museums is undoubtedly the two-story, excessively pink **Museo de Muñecas** (Doll Museum), C. Degetau 45, which contains an incredible collection of international dolls—including African, Chinese, and Russian nesting varieties—displayed in several fully decorated bedrooms. (Open M-F 8:30am-4pm. Free.)

The rustic wooden sign at **Nino's Café ❷** beckons passersby to come enjoy steaming plates of *comida criolla*. At night, the cafe turns into a hopping bar filled with couches, pool tables, cheap drinks (piña coladas $2.50), and live music. (On Rte. 167. From C. Degetau, walk uphill past the plaza, turn left on C. Dr. Veves, and continue down to Rte. 167. Turn right and walk 5min.; Nino's is just after the Universidad Metropolitano on the left. Entrees $5-19. Open M-Sa 9am-2am.)

NORTHEAST

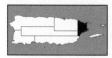

Northeast Puerto Rico has several extraordinary natural attractions within a relatively small area, making it easy for visitors to take a daytrip from San Juan to explore the island's great outdoors. This is the most stereotypically tropical area of Puerto Rico, filled with lush forest and turquoise waters. Playa Luquillo and Balneario Seven Seas are beautiful palm-tree-lined crescents of sand good for both swimming and sunbathing. La Cordillera, an archipelago of islands off Fajardo, looks like a series of desert oases in the midst of the deep blue Caribbean. At night, Fajardo's bay glows with natural luminescence. However, the highlight of the northeast lies inland. The tropical rainforest of El Yunque, the largest protected area on the island, inspires pride in residents and awe in visitors. You can "see" El Yunque in one day, and even summit El Yunque mountain in about 2hr., but camping offers visitors the opportunity for more quality time in the forest. The only downside to visiting this region is the heavy traffic on Hwy. 3 from San Juan, but, with that behind you, prepare to be astounded by unparalleled natural beauty.

HIGHLIGHTS OF NORTHEAST PUERTO RICO

DISCOVER the 24 mi. of hiking trails, 2 waterfalls, and countless mountain peaks of the only tropical forest in the US, **El Yunque** (p. 155).

SNORKEL, DIVE, SWIM, OR TAN on an excursion to La Cordillera, the archipelago of islands off **Fajardo** (p. 169).

MONKEY-WATCH from the deck of a boat near the infamous **Cayo Santiago** (p. 172).

EL YUNQUE

Occupying over 28,000 acres of land, the Caribbean National Forest, commonly referred to as "El Yunque," is one of the island's greatest treasures. El Yunque is the only tropical rainforest in the US Forest Service, and the largest protected land area in Puerto Rico. With four different types of forest, over 200 native species of trees, several varieties of mammals, and countless insects, El Yunque is one of the best places to experience the real natural landscape of Puerto Rico. The narrow Rte. 191 cuts through the forest, providing access to the park for the over 1 million annual visitors. On busy afternoons, it can seem like a good portion of them are right behind you on the path. Longer, more difficult trails offer more seclusion and often better views.

TRANSPORTATION

Because there is no public transportation to El Yunque, most visitors come either with a tour group or by car. **Renting a car** is the best option, as it's cheapest and allows you to hike the trails at your own pace. It only takes a little over an hour to drive to the park from the capital. From San Juan take Hwy. 26 east to Hwy. 3. About 4 mi. past Río Grande turn right on the small Rte. 191 and follow signs up the hill. Alternatively, from Isla Verde take Rte. 187 east through Piñones until it intersects Hwy. 3. This small road takes about 10min. longer (depending on traffic), but offers scenic ocean views. Although the park is easily navigable without a guide, those who can't rent a car may want to book a **tour** from San Juan (p. 99).

EL YUNQUE AT A GLANCE

AREA: 28,000 acres.

CLIMATE: Tropical. Rainy season is May-June and Oct.-Nov., but showers occur year-round.

HIGHLIGHTS: Hiking over 24 mi. of trails, swimming in pristine waterfalls.

FEATURES: Tropical forest, diverse flora, 2 waterfalls, Yokahú Tower.

GATEWAYS: Fajardo (p. 164), Luquillo (p. 161), and San Juan (p. 92).

CAMPING: Free at select areas throughout the park, but not in developed picnic areas. A permit from the park office is required (see below).

FEES: $3 to enter El Portal Visitors Center; free to enter the park.

⚜ 🛈 ORIENTATION AND PRACTICAL INFORMATION

Although El Yunque occupies almost 25% of the land area of northeast Puerto Rico, most tourist activities occur around **Route 191,** which leads past the tourist centers and the trailheads.

Visitors Centers: El Portal Visitors Center Rte. 191 Km 4.0 (☎888-1880; www.southern-region.fs.fed.us/caribbean), is the first stop for most visitors. The well-maintained, attractive center offers a 12min. movie (in Spanish on the hr. and half-hour, in English on the quarter-hour), gift shop, snack bar (smoothies $4, sandwiches and wraps $5), and small museum with interactive exhibits. The friendly staff distributes brochures with rudimentary maps and lots of information. Bathrooms, pay phones, and snack machines. Entrance $3, ages 5-12 and seniors $1.50, under 4 free. Open daily 9am-5pm.

Palo Colorado Information Center, Rte. 191 Km 11.8, has a souvenir shop, the same maps as El Portal, and a park ranger who can answer questions. Free to enter. Park tours (see below) also leave from here. Open daily 9am-5pm.

Maps: Campers and serious hikers should definitely purchase the National Geographic map available at both visitors centers ($10); day visitors should be able to navigate with the visitors center brochure and the map in this book.

Hours: The gate at Coca Falls is open daily 7:30am-6pm.

Supplies: All visitors should bring insect repellent, water, food, a swimsuit, and sturdy hiking shoes.

Tours: Many companies in **San Juan** offer excursions to El Yunque (p. 99). A National Forest Service ranger leads 1hr. English/Spanish tours from the Palo Colorado Information Center along the Caimitillo and Baño de Oro trails (every hr. 11:30am-3:30pm; $5, children under 12 and seniors $3). Tours are offered regularly Dec. 15-May 15 and sporadically the rest of the year—call ahead.

❗ WARNINGS. The National Park Service warns that all visitors should watch out for **flash floods,** especially during the rainy season. If it starts to rain heavily, head away from streams, to higher ground, or toward the road. Visitors should also be aware of the threat of **mongoose attacks.** Mongeese look like light-colored skunks, and most mongeese who approach humans are infected with **rabies**—avoid any contact.

🏕 CAMPING

To **camp ❶** in El Yunque you must get a **free permit,** available in the park. From Monday to Friday, permits are available at the **Catalina Service Center,** Rte. 191 Km 4.4, directly after El Portal Visitors Center. (Open M-F 8am-4:30pm.) On weekends and holidays, permits can be found at the **Palo Colorado Information Center** (p. 156). Permits are good only for the day they are distributed. Park rangers also hand out a map designating permissible camping areas. There are no facilities in the park, so campers should plan to take out everything that they bring in (including trash). There are no hotels along the northern section of Rte. 191, but upscale options await near **Naguabo** (p. 170) and on the western edge of the park, near Río Grande. **Fajardo** (p. 164), with its large selection of hotels, is only a 15min. drive away.

🍴 FOOD

There are no food stands along the hiking paths, so many families come with picnics. **Covered picnic tables** at Caimitillo, Palo Colorado, and Quebrada Grande have running water and grills. Palo Colorado, at the head of La Mina trail, is the most popular area, and fills up with families and parties every day around lunchtime. For those who don't want to cook their own food, there are several options inside the park. **El Bosque Encantado ❶**, Rte. 191 Km 7.2, serves up delicious *batidas* ($4), freshly fried tacos ($2), and other snacks. (Usually open 9am-6pm.) Just down the road, **La Muralla ❶**, Rte. 191 Km 7.3, serves similar fare. (Shishkebabs $1.75. Usually open 9am-6pm.) For slightly healthier fare, try **Yuquiyú Delights ❶**, Rte. 191 Km 11.4. (Sandwiches $4.50. Smoothies $4. Open daily 9am-5pm.)

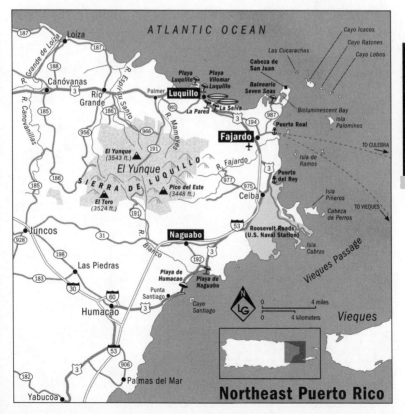

Northeast Puerto Rico

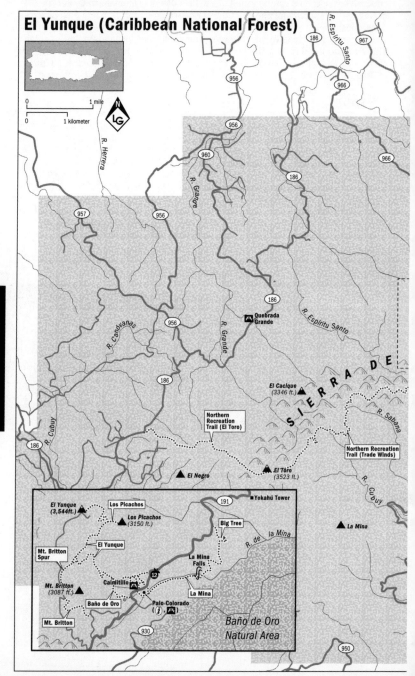

El Yunque (Caribbean National Forest)

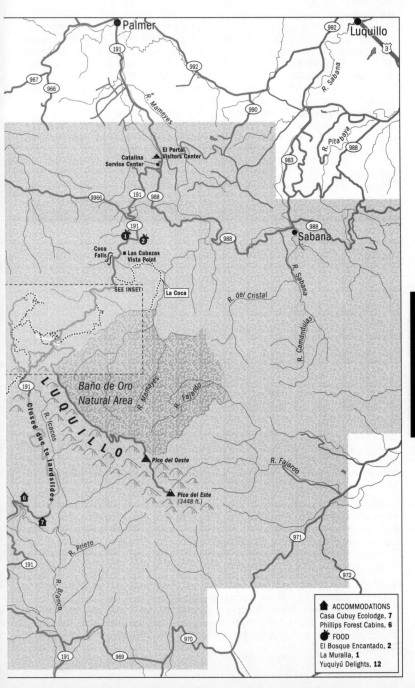

NORTHEAST

ACCOMMODATIONS
Casa Cubuy Ecolodge, **7**
Phillips Forest Cabins, **6**

FOOD
El Bosque Encantado, **2**
La Muralla, **1**
Yuquiyú Delights, **12**

◉ SIGHTS

Heading up Rte. 191 the first major sight is **Coca Falls,** Km 8.1. There is not much more to see than the view of the waterfall from the road. **Yokahú Tower** appears on the left at Km 8. Built in the 1930s, the tower provides spectacular views of the mountains of El Yunque, Luquillo, and far-off Fajardo. **La Mina Falls,** accessible via a 25-35min. walk along Big Tree Trail or La Mina Trail, is undoubtedly the most popular destination in El Yunque. On weekend afternoons it can seem like every family in San Juan (and every tour group of North Americans) has journeyed out to the falls to picnic on the rocks and swim in the small lagoon. The sight merits its popularity, but if you come early in the morning, you may have the place to yourself. In any case, bring a swimsuit and join in the merriment.

◙ HIKING

TRAILS	DURATION (ONE-WAY)	DIFFICULTY	LENGTH	ALTITUDE
La Coca	1hr.	Moderate-Difficult	1¾ mi.	820-1476 ft.
Big Tree	35min.	Moderate	¾ mi.	1833-1667 ft.
La Mina	25min.	Easy-Moderate	¾ mi.	2132-1640 ft.
Baño de Oro	20min.	Moderate	¼ mi.	2132-2362 ft.
El Yunque	2hr.	Moderate-Difficult	2½ mi.	2067-3445 ft.
Los Picachos	5min.	Moderate	¼ mi.	2952-3051 ft.
Mt. Britton Spur	10min.	Easy	¼ mi.	2788-2952 ft.
Mt. Britton	40min.	Moderate	½ mi.	2493-3087 ft.
National Recreation Trail	7hr.	Difficult	6¼ mi.	2533-3578 ft.

LA COCA. Most visitors ignore the first trail on the way up Rte. 191, which makes it the ideal path to experience the forest in blissful solitude and see a secluded waterfall. The path descends from the trailhead, making the uphill return trip extremely challenging. This is one of the more rugged hikes, with dirt trails and small streams that you must cross without the aid of a bridge. The steep inclines get quite muddy, so do not try this hike in the rain.

BIG TREE. As one of two hikes that lead to La Mina Falls, Big Tree is one of the most popular hikes in El Yunque. Almost the entire path is paved and the steepest inclines have stairs, but the rocks can get slippery. Even with the stairs, the inclines can be difficult. Informative signs along the path provide educational facts about the surrounding lush *tabonuco* forest.

LA MINA. This hike is essentially the second half of the Big Tree Trail, and an alternative route to La Mina Falls. La Mina receives slightly larger crowds than Big Tree and is completely paved, but it runs alongside Río de la Mina, allowing hikers to take a quick dip along the way down. La Mina is slightly easier than Big Tree. It is possible to walk down one trail and up the other, but you will have to walk 1.5km along Rte. 191 to return.

BAÑO DE ORO. This short trail across from Palo Colorado is one of the park's hidden treasures. Baño de Oro is easy enough to be accessible to most visitors, but retains the naturalism of the longer trails and is much less crowded than La Mina or Big Tree. It also makes a good warm-up for those attempting to ascend El Yunque. Be aware that you may have to cross small streams without a bridge if there has been rain recently.

EL YUNQUE. This aptly named path travels from Rte. 191 all the way to the peak of El Yunque mountain, offering a challenging trek that can be completed in an afternoon. The path passes over countless tiny waterfalls and through several cloud forests on the way up. This route is much less traveled than any of the shorter trails, and it is unlikely that you will encounter any other hikers until you reach the summit. Several turn-offs (Mt. Britton Spur, Los Picachos) allow tired hikers to choose an alternative ending along the way, but those who continue all the way up with be rewarded with a feeling of accomplishment and an amazing view. When you reach the road at the end of the trail, turn left and go past the many satellites dishes, all the way up to the El Yunque tower for the best views. On a clear day you can see all the way out to St. Thomas, and even if it's foggy, the haze shrouding the surrounding mountains looks mysterious and beautiful.

LOS PICACHOS. A small turn-off about 30min. from the peak of El Yunque, Los Picachos provides an alternate ending for hikers who can't make it to the top of the mountain, or a quick stopover for those who want to see views unobstructed by the electronic equipment that mars the peak of El Yunque. The short, rocky trail ends in 59 steep steps, which make for a tough finale.

MT. BRITTON SPUR. Mt. Britton Spur is an easy pebble path connecting El Yunque to Mt. Britton. To make a full loop, head up El Yunque (perhaps via Baño de Oro), cross over on Mt. Britton Spur, then head down Mt. Britton. At the end you will have to walk a mile or so down the road to get back to your car. Mt. Britton has a steep incline that can get very slippery, so it is easier to ascend El Yunque, then descend Mt. Britton, rather than vice versa. If you're coming off Mt. Britton Spur, walk downhill on the road to reach Mt. Britton (walking uphill will get you to the Mt. Britton Tower lookout point).

MT. BRITTON. Rugged hikers may be disappointed that the entire Mt. Britton trail is paved and it ends with a short walk along the road. However, the trail is shorter than El Yunque and offers great views of the forest as well as a quick route to another observation tower with views of Fajardo, Luquillo, San Juan, and the Spanish Virgin Islands. For this reason, Mt. Britton is quite popular with foreign tourists. The steep path gets extremely slippery when wet—proceed with caution.

NATIONAL RECREATION TRAIL. Consisting of El Toro Trail and Trade Winds, the National Recreation Trail, the longest trail in El Yunque, follows the mountain peaks from Rte. 191 to Rte. 186. The highlight of the path is the summit of El Toro, the tallest mountain in El Yunque. Along the way, the path passes through all four types of forest present in the park: *tabonuco, palo colorado,* palm, and dwarf. Only experienced hikers should attempt this hike, as they must battle mud, overgrown plants, steep hills, and isolation.

LUQUILLO

Many visitors to Luquillo never see the town: they come for the beach, spend a day lounging in the sun, then return to San Juan. In comparison to San Juan, Luquillo Beach is undoubtedly paradise; it is lined with palm trees, has ample amenities, and during weekdays in the winter offers solitude that visitors to Isla Verde can only dream about. Don't be misled—Luquillo does not have the best beach on the island, just the best developed swimming beach close to San Juan. Those with only a short time on the island may find this small town to be the perfect escape.

TRANSPORTATION. Públicos traveling between San Juan and Fajardo will let passengers off at **Luquillo** (45min., $3). To get back, sit on a bench on Hwy. 3

beneath the pedestrian bridge the connects Luquillo and Brisas del Mar, and flag down a passing *público*. If you choose this option, remember that *públicos* primarily run M-Sa 6:30am-5pm. Driving from San Juan (45min.-1¼hr., depending on traffic), head down Hwy. 3 and get off at Rte. 193, when signs point to Luquillo. If you want to travel between the main beach and the center of town, a car is very helpful—walking along the beach is not possible without doing some wading, and your other choice is to walk along Rte. 193.

■ ⁊ ORIENTATION AND PRACTICAL INFORMATION. Most of the city is located along **Route 193,** which becomes **C. Fernández García** as it passes by the main plaza. The parallel street C. 14 de Julio holds most of the city government buildings, including the post office, police station, and town hall. La Pared beach is directly in front of the town square, and is distinguished by its white wall and big waves. La Pared is almost deserted most of the time. To the west of it is Vilomar Luquillo, a slightly more popular but still fairly isolated beach. To reach Playa Luquillo from town, take Rte. 193 to its western end.

Banco Popular, on Hwy. 193, is right at the main town entrance. (☎889-2610. ATM. Open M-F 8am-4pm, Sa 9am-1pm.) **La Selva,** C. Fernández Garcia 250, two blocks off the plaza away from the beach, rents **surfboards** ($20 per day), **boogie boards** ($10 per day), and **snorkels** ($10 per day) to travelers. The surfing crowd hangs around out front. (☎889-6205. Surfing lessons $25 per hr. Open M-Sa 9am-5pm, Su 9am-3pm. AmEx/MC/V.) **Amigo,** across Hwy. 3 in Brisas del Mar, sells groceries and offers Moneygram (a money transfer service; ☎889-1919. ATM inside. Open M-Sa 7am-10pm, Su 11am-5pm. MC/V.) The **police station,** C. 14 de Julio 158, is visible from the plaza, next to the Alcaldía. (☎889-2020 or 889-5500. Open 24hr.) The **post office,** C. 14 de Julio 160, is next to the police station. (☎889-3170. Open M-F 8am-4:30pm, Sa 8am-noon.) **Postal Code:** 00773.

⌐⌐ ACCOMMODATIONS AND FOOD. Considering its popularity, Luquillo has surprisingly few accommodations options. Unless you are looking for a long-term stay or wish to camp, you should consider finding accommodations in Fajardo or San Juan and commuting to the beach. Those looking for rentals should consult the rental agencies listed in San Juan, all of which have many listings in various price ranges (❸ to ❺) for Luquillo. **Camping** at **Balneario La Monserrate** ❶ is usually like attending a big, family-oriented party. The beach has a large grass camping area with concrete picnic tables, gazebos, and grills scattered throughout. (☎889-5871. Call ahead. $13, with electricity $17.)

Most of the food in Luquillo comes straight from the sea and can be found at the famous **food kiosks** that line Hwy. 3 at the western edge of Playa Luquillo. Over 60 kiosks, ranging from full restaurants to grill stands, serve traditional food (full lunches $3-5) and fried *empanadillas* stuffed with just about anything ($1-2). Hours vary with the size of the crowd, but when the beach is open, chances are a few food kiosks will be also. In town, **Erik's Gyros & Deli** ❶, C. Fernández García 352, three blocks south of the plaza, provides typical Puerto Rican lunch choices, plus many Greek alternatives. (☎889-0615. Gyros $3.50-4.50. Puerto Rican sandwiches $1.50-6. Open W-Sa 7am-8pm, Su 7am-3pm. MC/V.) For a slightly fancier meal, try **The Brass Cactus** ❸, on Rte. 193 just west of Playa Azul. With US license plates lining the walls, fake cacti on the bar, a big TV tuned to ESPN, and sizzling steaks, the Brass Cactus provides visitors from the States with a little taste of home. (☎889-5735. Burgers $7-8. Big steaks $18-23. Open M-Th and Su 11am-midnight, F-Sa 11am-1am. Kitchen closes 1hr. earlier. MC/V.) The conventional **La Exquisita Bakery** ❶, Av. Jesús Piñero 1, on the plaza, serves up big sandwiches and a small selection of pastries. (☎633-5554. Breakfast $2.25-3. Sandwiches $1.50-4. Pastries $0.75. $10 min. Open M-Tu 6am-7pm, W-Su 6am-9pm. MC/V.) Next door, **Victor's Place Seafood ❹**, Av. Jesús T. Piñero 2, offers excellent but slightly expensive food in a sea-themed environment that's not too stuffy for beachgoers. (☎889-5705. Beef and chicken entrees $10-15. Seafood entrees $12-26. Open Tu-F 11am-10pm, Sa-Su noon-10pm. MC/V.)

◪◪ **BEACHES AND OUTDOOR ACTIVITIES.** The crescent-shaped **Playa Luquillo,** or more properly **Balneario La Monserrate,** is the city's primary attraction and one of the most beautiful public beaches on the island. As a public *balneario*, Playa Luquillo has lifeguards, picnic tables, souvenir shops, bathrooms, showers, food kiosks, and lawn chair ($4 per day) and umbrella ($8 per day) rental. However, it is also one of the most popular beaches on the island, and on weekends in the summer it can become packed with Puerto Ricans. Still, anyone who comes to Luquillo prepared to deal with the crowds should enjoy this picturesque setting. To reach the beach, take Rte. 193 all the way to the west. (☎889-5871. Parking $2, minivans $3. Open daily 8:30am-5:30pm.)

Playa Luquillo is also home to the remarkable ◪**Mar Sin Barreras** (Sea Without Barriers), **the island's only handicapped-accessible beach** (☎889-4329). The idea originated when 14-year-old Rosimar Hernández wrote a letter to then-governor Pedro Rosselló, pointing out that people in wheelchairs, including herself, could not enjoy the natural attractions of Puerto Rico. Today Hernández's dream has become a reality. *Mar Sin Barreras* has incredible facilities—including a ramp to the water, a clubhouse, and showers—all specifically designed to help handicapped people and elderly citizens enjoy the water.

East of Balneario la Monserrate, but not contiguous with it, **Playa Vilomar Luquillo** has better sand, slightly larger waves, and usually much smaller crowds. However, it is not a public beach and thus lacks the facilities of Monserrate. Luquillo is also a popular destination for **surfers.** The next beach to the east, **La Pared,** in front of the central plaza, has good waves and a sandy bottom ideal for beginners. The surfing extends for about 2 mi. to the east and just gets better. Try **La Selva,** another surfer favorite farther to the east with both sand and reef bottom, or just walk along the beach until you find a break that suits your fancy.

Just outside of town, **Hacienda Carabalí** offers **horseback rides** over the foothills of El Yunque along the Río Mameyes. From Luquillo take Hwy. 3 west, turn left on Rte. 992, take the first right up the hill, and go through the second gate. (☎889-5820. 1hr. rides need no reservation; $30, ages 3-12 $20. 2hr. rides must be reserved in advance; daily 10am, 12:30, 2:30pm; $60/40. Am/Ex/MC/V.)

◪◪ **SIGHTS AND FESTIVALS.** The attractive **Centro de Arte y Cultura** (Center for Art and Culture), Hwy. 3 Km 38.4, is located across Hwy. 3 away from the beach. The complex has great facilities, with an exhibition hall, a 550-seat theater, and an open-air amphitheater, but not much to put inside. The most remarkable exhibits usually come from *luquillense* Tomás Batista. (☎633-1096 or 221-8326. Open M-F 8am-4:30pm. Free. Performances usually around $20-25, children $8-10.)

In addition to the Luquillo's patron saint festival (held on the week preceding March 19), the city also celebrates an annual **Festival de Platos Típicos** or the Festival of Traditional Foods (the last weekend in Nov.). The festival brings music, *artesanía*, and feasts of delicious Puerto Rican food to the Plaza de Recreo.

◪ **NIGHTLIFE.** Luquillo's nightlife scene is small and bar-oriented. Most expats and visitors down a couple of beers at **The Brass Cactus** (see **Food,** p. 163). Across

NORTHEAST

the street **El Flamboyán** hosts a friendly and local crowd, who come for the pool tables, cheap beer (Medalla $1.25-1.50), and semi-outdoor picnic tables. (☎889-2928. Happy hour Sa 10pm-1am. Open M-Th and Su 8am-midnight, F-Sa 8am-2am.) The bars at the food kiosks also attract a number of locals in the evening.

FAJARDO

Most travelers simply zip through Fajardo on their way to Vieques and Culebra and never see the real city. But Fajardo and its surrounding area deserve a closer look. In the hills above the city sits Las Croabas, a traditional fishing village that seems stuck in time. To the north, the Las Cabezas de San Juan nature reserve offers visitors a tour through the region's ecosystems and a glimpse of restored 19th-century lighthouses. The reserve's Laguna Grande bay is one of the few places in the world to see the incredible phenomenon of bioluminescence. Closer to the city lies Villa Marina, a busy port full of seafood restaurants and yachtsmen ready to take you on a snorkeling excursion. Even the congested downtown area is full of excellent Puerto Rican *cafeterías*, and its beautiful, newly-renovated town square and mayor's office may be a sign of better things to come.

▇ TRANSPORTATION

It is almost impossible to get around Fajardo without a car. Getting to one sight should be no problem, but visiting multiple destinations on public transportation will be frustrating and time-consuming.

Flights: Fajardo's tiny airport (☎863-1011) sends even tinier planes to Culebra, San Juan, St. Croix, St. Thomas, and Vieques. Most airlines sell tickets by phone or at the airport. Reserve in advance or the flight may not leave. To reach the airport, take the main entrance to central Fajardo, then follow signs. Parking $8.50 per 24hr.

Airlines:

Air Flamenco (☎801-8256) flies to **Culebra** (7am, noon, 5:45pm; $25, round-trip $45). If someone wants to fly to San Juan the 3:30pm flight from Culebra will stop in Fajardo ($40). MC/V.

Isla Nena (☎877-812-5144) flies to **Culebra** (15min.; 1-2 per day; $30, round-trip $60) and **Vieques** (8min.; on demand only; $25, round-trip $50). Open daily 6am-6pm. MC/V.

Vieques Air Link (☎860-2290) sends flights on demand 6am-6pm. To: **Culebra** (6 per day; $26, round-trip $56), **St. Croix** (2 per day; $80, round-trip $155), and **Vieques** (10 per day; $21, round-trip $40). AmEx/MC/V.

Públicos: *Públicos* are based out of the **Terminal de Transportación Pública Fajardo,** on C. Valera between Banco Popular and the Plaza de Armas. To: **Ceiba** (10min., $0.85); **Humacao** (45min., $2.45); **Las Croabas** (5min., $0.65-75); **Luquillo** (15min., $0.70); **San Juan** (1hr., $3.50). If you take a público from San Juan to the ferry terminal, ask the driver to go all the way to the port.

Taxis: *Públicos* are the only vehicles that function as taxis in Fajardo. If you go to the *público* terminal early in the day and ask around, you can find one heading to any major sight. Otherwise, they can be flagged down on Rte. 194 or 195.

Ferries: The **Puerto Rican Port Authority** (☎863-0705 or 863-4560) runs ferries from Puerto Real to the Spanish Virgin Islands. To get to Puerto Real from central Fajardo take C. Celis Aguilera (parallel to C. Muñoz Rivera) away from the plaza, then turn right on Rte. 195 (1 mi.). To avoid the traffic downtown, from Hwy. 3 take the 2nd Fajardo exit onto Av. Conquistador, then turn right onto Rte. 194, then turn left on Rte. 195.

Long-term **parking** $5 per day. *Públicos* from Fajardo go to the port ($1) and are usually waiting when a boat comes in. **Travel With Padin taxi service** takes passengers from the San Juan airport to the ferry terminal ($60 for 2 people, $65 for 4 people). Call for reservations (☎644-3091).

Passenger ferries go to **Culebra** (70min.; daily 9am, 3, 7pm; $2.25, ages 3-11 and 60-74 $1, 75+ free) and **Vieques** (1hr.; M-F 9:30am, 1, 4:30, 8pm; Sa-Su 9am, 3, 6pm; $2, ages 3-11 and 60-74 $1, 75+ free). **Cargo ferries** take a few cars to **Culebra** (M-Tu and Th 4am and 4:30pm; W and F 4, 9:30am, 4:30pm; $26.50) and **Vieques** (M-F 4, 9:30am, 4:30pm; $26). Reservations are required for cars and should be made far in advance. For passenger ferries, show up at least 1hr. in advance. When possible, buy round-trip tickets. Reservation office open M-F 8-11am and 1-3pm.

Car Rental: L&M Car Rental, Hwy. 3 Km 43.7 (☎860-6868). Compact cars $35-49 per day. Insurance $20. 25+. Open M-F 7am-6pm, Sa-Su 8am-5pm. AmEx/D/DC/MC/V. If you're desperate, there are a few small independent car rental companies near the ferry terminal. Try **World Car Rental,** C. Unión 466 (☎860-4808 or 863-9696), entrance on C. Cometa. Compact cars $33-35 per day. Insurance $12. 21+. Open daily 7:30am-7pm. MC/V.

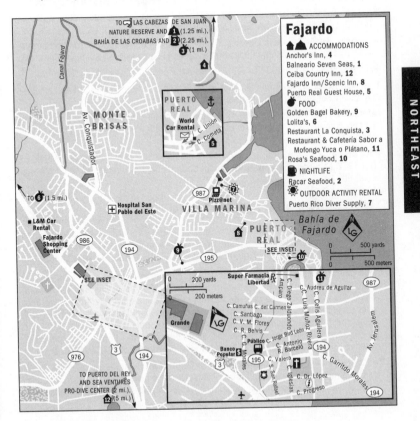

⚡ 🔢 ORIENTATION AND PRACTICAL INFORMATION

Fajardo is difficult to navigate without a car. **Highway 3** connects the city to Luquillo and eventually San Juan, and most of Fajardo is located to the east, between the highway and the sea. The first exit off Hwy. 3 goes to **Route 194**, which travels parallel to Hwy. 3 and passes the center before intersecting Hwy. 3 again. The second major exit leads to Av. Conquistador, which goes to the Wyndham hotel. The third and most prominent exit deposits visitors on **Route 195**, which passes the plaza then continues to the **ferry dock**. **Route 987** originates from Rte. 195, passes **Villa Marina** (a major port with a shopping center), intersects Av. Conquistador, and leads to the beach, the nature reserve, and Las Croabas.

Banks: Banco Popular (☎863-0101), on C. Garlinda Morales at the corner with C. Valero. ATM. Open M-F 8am-45pm, Sa 8:30am-noon.

Laundromat: Wash n' Post, C. 2 #100 (☎863-1995), in the Santa Isidra Shopping Center in Villa Marina. Wash $1.50; dry $0.25 per 5min. Change available. Wash-and-fold service $0.75 per lb., min. $6. Fax 1st page $2, additional pages $1. Also **Western Union,** FedEx, and US Postal Service. Open M-Sa 8am-8pm, Su 10am-5pm. MC/V.

Supermarkets: Grande (☎863-3420), on Hwy. 3, just east of the intersection with Rte. 195. Open M-Sa 8am-10pm, Su 11am-5pm. AmEx/MC/V.

Pharmacy: Super Farmacia Libertad, C. Muñoz Rivera 206 (☎863-0810). Pharmaceuticals and a wide selection of housewares. Open M-Sa 8am-9pm, Su 11am-5pm.

Police: ☎863-2020 or 863-2042. Across from the *público* station. Open 24hr.

Hospital: Hospital San Pablo del Este (☎863-0505), on Rte. 194 just off Av. Conquistador. The largest hospital in eastern Puerto Rico. 24hr. emergency room.

Internet Access: Pizz@net (☎860-4230), in Villa Marina. Internet $3 for 30min., $5 per hr. Lunch combo with huge personal pizza and soda $5. ATM. Open daily 11am-11pm. MC/V.

Post Office: In Puerto Real, C. Unión 477 (☎863-1827). General Delivery available. Open M-F 7am-5pm, Sa 7am-noon. **Postal Code:** In Central Fajardo: 00738. In Puerto Real: 00740.

🏠 📷 ACCOMMODATIONS AND CAMPING

Fajardo's claim to fame as a tourist destination may be its attractive accommodations. The city is home to several small guesthouses and inns that offer incredible, amenity-filled rooms for a fraction of what you'd pay in a more touristy town.

▨ **Ceiba Country Inn,** Rte. 977 Km 1.2 (☎885-0471; prinn@juno.com), 5 mi. from Fajardo in Ceiba. When you exit Hwy. 53, turn right toward the mountains (not left toward Ceiba). On a clear day you can see St. Thomas from this quiet mountain lodge. The indoor-outdoor patio/library is a great place to curl up with a book or pull something out of the chest of board games. Large, sparkling-clean rooms include phone, A/C, and fridge, as well as wicker furniture and enormous showers. Continental breakfast included. Singles $65; doubles $75; triples $85; quads $95. AmEx/D/MC/V. ❸

▨ **Puerto Real Guest House,** C. Cometa 476 (☎863-0018). Homey is an understatement for this small guesthouse—the lobby is actually someone's living room. Rooms are clean. Amazing amenities for the price: A/C, cable TV, and small fridge. 1 double bed $40; 2 double beds $60. Tax included. Cash only. ❷

▨ **Fajardo Inn,** Parcelas Beltrán 52 (☎860-6000; www.fajardoinn.com), off Rte. 195; look for signs pointing uphill to the Inn. With a big, white building, grand palm-lined entrance road, and perfectly manicured grounds, the Fajardo Inn looks like an expensive resort—but with guesthouse prices. Large, spotless pool. All rooms with A/C and cable TV; some with kitchenettes. 2 restaurants and a bar. Doubles $85-100; extra person $10. Suites $110-250. AmEx/MC/V. ❸

▨ **Anchor's Inn,** Rte. 987 Km 2.6 (☎863-7200; frenchman@libertypr.net). A happy medium between the rustic guesthouses and the expensive hotels, this nautically themed inn offers enormous rooms with clean bathrooms, comfy beds, cable TV, and A/C at reasonable prices. The inn also houses an upscale seafood restaurant. 1 queen bed $60; 2 queens $72; 3 queens $95. Tax included. AmEx/MC/V. ❸

Scenic Inn, Parcelas Beltrán 52 (☎860-6000; www.fajardoinn.com), on the same property as the **Fajardo Inn** (above) and under the same management. Rooms are smaller and not as glamorous. Doubles $60; extra person $10. ❷

Balneario Seven Seas (☎863-8180), off Rte. 987 (see **Beaches,** p. 168) has an RV park and a large field for tents. The beach and the tent area are close together, so be prepared for neighboring beachgoers during the day. $10 per tent. ❶

◪ FOOD

Fajardo has good seafood restaurants in Las Croabas and along Rte. 978, but they are expensive. The city center is filled with countless small *cafeterías* where you can find filling Puerto Rican lunches for under $5, but most close at 2pm.

Rosa's Seafood, C. Tablazo 536 (☎809-863-0213). Heading into Puerto Real, take a right at the last turn-off before the big archway; it's at the end of the street, on the right. Widely acknowledged as the best seafood restaurant in Puerto Real, Rosa's seems like an oasis of class. Enjoy fresh seafood—including shrimp and lobster—on white tablecloths in this big, 2-story house. Seafood entrees $14-25. Small selection of non-seafood entrees $8.50-20. Open M-Tu and Th-Su 11am-10pm. AmEx/MC/V. ❹

Restaurant & Cafetería Sabor a Mofongo Yuca o Plátano, labeled "Sam 2" on the sign, C. Unión 60 (☎860-2212). One the nicest *cafeterías* in Fajardo and one of the only ones that stays open for dinner. Puerto Rican entrees ($4.50-7.25) are huge and delicious. Green-and-white tile tables and wicker chairs add a touch of class. Breakfast, which curiously includes cheeseburgers, $1-3. Sandwiches $1.35-3.50. Open M-F 6am-7:30pm, Sa 6am-3:30pm. MC/V. ❷

Lolita's, Hwy. 3 Km 41.3 (☎889-0250), is technically in Luquillo, but it's closer to Fajardo and a welcome change from seafood. The popular Mexican restaurant serves up all the favorites, from tacos to enchiladas to fajitas. Breezy, tiled tables by the windows. Dinner entrees $6-18. Burritos $2-7. Margaritas $6. Open M, W-Th, Su 11am-10pm; F-Sa 11am-midnight. AmEx/MC/V. ❸

Golden Bagel Bakery, C. Unión 171 (☎860-8987), is a little out of place in Fajardo. Even the food seems more east coast US than east coast Puerto Rico, with a variety of sandwiches on bagels, croissants, and wraps ($3.50-6), and big American breakfasts ($2.50-5). But don't worry—you can still get your entrees served with rice and beans. The cheerful, modern interior is a lovely place to enjoy a casual lunch. Soups and salads $3.25-6.50. Open M-Sa 6am-6:30pm, Su 6am-2:30pm. Cash only. ❶

Restaurant La Conquista, Rte. 987 Km 4.8 (☎801-1938), a short walk up from the beach. This is one of the best seafood restaurants along Rte. 987, and the wooden rafters and crimson carpeting class things up a bit. As usual, quality seafood is not cheap, but the reason to come is the Su all-you-can-eat seafood buffet, featuring several kinds of fish, lobster, shrimp, and octopus (Su noon-6pm; $20). Entrees $15-22. Open daily noon-midnight. MC/V. ❹

SIGHTS

LAS CABEZAS DE SAN JUAN NATURE RESERVE. This 316-acre nature reserve is by far the most interesting land attraction in Fajardo. The reserve contains **seven different ecological zones**—coral reef, Thalassia bed, sandy beach, rocky beach, mangrove forest, lagoon, and dry forest—in addition to over 40 species of fish, 84 species of birds, and several species of mammals. Most visitors will at the very least see tiny fiddler crab and huge iguanas. Although Hurricanes Hugo (1989) and George (1998) destroyed over 80% of the reserve, it has recovered quickly and seems to be thriving again.

The privately run Conservation Trust of Puerto Rico maintains the reserve and offers 2hr. guided tours through all seven ecosystems, including a tram ride through the dry forest, a 30min. stroll along a boardwalk over the mangroves, a stop at a rocky point overlooking the ocean, and a visit to the small lighthouse museum. The **lighthouse,** which has been in continuous operation since 1882, affords views of La Cordillera, Culebra, and St. Thomas from its upper story. The only other way to see the reserve is to take a **kayak trip** through Laguna Grande, the bioluminescent bay that occupies over 100 acres of the park. The Conservation Trust does not offer kayak tours, but it is possible to arrange your own rental (see **Kayaking,** p. 170). *(Off Rte. 987 just past Seven Seas beach (p. 168). M-F ☎ 722-5882, Sa-Su ☎ 860-2560; www.fideicomiso.org. **Reservations required**—call at least a week in advance. Tours W-Su Spanish 9:30, 10, 10:30am, 2pm; English 2pm. $7, under 11 $4. AmEx/MC/V; $25 min.)*

BAHÍA DE LAS CROABAS. Despite its proximity to commercialized Fajardo, Las Croabas retains the feel of a small fishing village. Here local fishermen still head out every morning to catch the sea creatures that fuel the restaurants along Rte. 987. All of the action takes place in the morning, but in the afternoon the bay becomes a serene place to walk along the boardwalk or relax at one of the seafood restaurants. If you come early (before 6am), it may be possible to negotiate with one of the fishermen for an inexpensive trip to the islands. *(At the end of Rte. 987. Públicos from central Fajardo (10min.) cost $0.65-0.75.)*

⛱ BEACHES

On a sunny day Fajardo's public beach, **Balneario Seven Seas,** Rte. 987 Km 5, glistens as one of the best on the mainland; the water really does look like it has seven different colors. However, when the climate is less cooperative, Seven Seas looks dreary and the pine needles and trash become more obvious. There is good **snorkeling** on the far right side. While this is a nice beach, much more stunning stretches of sand are a $2 ferry ride away on Vieques or Culebra. (☎ 863-8180. Trash cans and several shelters. Lifeguards daily 9am-5pm. Parking $3. Open 24hr.)

🏄 WATER SPORTS

Most visitors to Fajardo head straight toward the sea and the archipelago that extends from the eastern tip of Puerto Rico to the Spanish Virgin Islands. These beautiful tropical islands, and their surrounding coral reefs, provide opportunities for snorkeling, diving, fishing, swimming, or just relaxing. The most popular islands are Cayo Icacos, Cayo Lobos, and Isla Palominos, although the latter is owned by the Wyndham Resort and theoretically closed to outside visitors. Charters usually have their own favorite spots and they will take you wherever the weather looks good and the crowds are relatively small.

BOATING

Fajardo has two enormous marinas, Villa Marina and Puerto del Rey (about 2 mi. to the south). Many of the boats anchored here offer charter expeditions to La Cordillera with snorkeling, swimming, and sunbathing. Some boats are listed below; check a recent issue of *¡Qué Pasa!* (p. 101) for the most current offerings. Most boat owners operate out of their homes—call in advance to make a reservation.

Caribbean School of Aquatics (☎383-5700). Captain Greg Korwek offers snorkeling trips on the Fun Cat (includes all supplies, lunch, and transportation from San Juan; $79, without transportation $65) and diving trips on the Island Safari (includes 2 dives, transportation from San Juan, and picnic lunch; $139). The mast of the boat reads "Sail-Dive-Party," and that's exactly what you'll do. AmEx/D/MC/V.

Erin Go Bragh (☎860-4401; www.egbc.net), Puerto del Rey dock #1204. This 50 ft. sailboat travels to the 2 islands. Trips include barbecue lunch, snacks, open bar, fishing poles, and snorkel gear. 6 person max. Trips (10am-5pm) $85 per person, 2-person min. Sunset cruises (5-7pm) $75, 4-person min. Dinner cruises (5-9pm) $85, 4-person min. Also offers overnight charters to Vieques and Culebra; call for info.

Getaway (☎860-7327), a 32 ft. catamaran in Villa Marina. Trips (10am-3:30pm) include soda, lunch, and a piña colada for $55 cash per person, $60 on a credit card. Sunset cruise $45 per person. MC/V.

Traveler (☎863-2821), a 50 ft. catamaran (with a waterslide) operating out of Villa Marina. Trips (10am-3:30pm) include snorkeling equipment, lunch, and an all-you-can-eat salad bar. $55 cash per person, $59 on a credit card, ages 5-12 $35. Also offers a sunset cruise for the same prices. MC/V.

Salty Dog (☎717-6378 or 717-7259; www.saltydreams.com), in Villa Marina. Sails to Cayo Icacos and Palomino Island. Trips include lunch, drinks, and snorkel equipment. $59 per person.

Ventajero 4 (☎645-9129; www.sailpuertorico.com). 52 ft. sloop at Puerto del Rey dock #1267, holds up to 6 people. Trips (7am-5pm) include beer, snorkeling equipment, and a full Puerto Rican lunch. 4 person min. $85 per person. MC/V.

FROM THE ROAD

BEHIND THE WHEEL

In order to visit most of the sights of the northeastern Puerto Rico, travelers will need to use a car. But driving on the island can be a terrifying experience. Puerto Rican drivers, used to the madness and mayhem, have little patience for newcomers. Above all, avoid driving in San Juan—Old San Juan is very walkable and Hwy. 26 skirts the slow streets of Condado, Santurce, and Ocean Park. For driving on the rest of the island, maintain the following.

A good set of shocks: In many places roads have been dug up, but not repaved, leaving irregular patches of dirt on the highway that your car will not appreciate. For a fantastic example of this, check out Rte. 987 in Fajardo.

An excellent CD collection: On an island with 2.5 million cars for 4 million people, severe traffic jams are simply part of the daily routine. Sit back, enjoy the tunes, and remember patience is a virtue; no matter how many times you honk the horn, you'll probably be in the car for a while.

A sense of humor, with a dash of daring: You'll need this when whipping down narrow roads (here's looking at you Rte. 187 between Loíza and Río Grande) or crossing 6 lanes of rush-hour traffic (Expreso de Diego, of course) or squeezing out of a parking space after being boxed in on either side (just about everywhere).

—Lauren Truesdell

DIVING

Puerto Rico Diver Supply, A-E6 Santa Isidra III (☎863-4300; www.prdiversupply.com), in front of Villa Marina, sends their 36 ft. boat on regular expeditions to La Cordillera (2-tank dive $75, 1-tank dive $50, snorkeling $50) and the Spanish Virgin Islands (2-tank dive $95). Discover Scuba 1-tank dive $95. Snorkeling trip $50. Also rents snorkeling and diving equipment. Open daily 8am-5pm. AmEx/D/MC/V.

Sea Ventures Dive Centers (☎863-3483 or 800-739-3483; www.divepuertorico.com), at Puerto del Rey. Sends out 2-tank dives every morning ($89, with gear $99), but the location changes daily due to weather and visibility conditions. Discover Scuba package $150. Transportation from San Juan round-trip $2 per person. 1-week PADI certification course $450. Open daily 7:30am-12:30pm, later if an afternoon dive is scheduled. AmEx/MC/V.

KAYAKING

Fajardo has one of Puerto Rico's most amazing **bioluminescent bays** (see **Feet on Fire,** p. 187). All tours are done through private companies.

Yókahu Kayak (☎604-7375). 1½-2hr. Tours $35 per person. MC/V.

Eco Action Tours (☎791-7509 or 640-7385), has a 2hr. program that takes kayaks ($40 per person) into the bioluminescent bay. Large snack and piña colada at the end. Transportation from San Juan available. MC/V.

❀ FESTIVALS

Every Presidents' Day weekend (mid-Feb.), from Friday to Monday, Puerto del Rey hosts the Caribbean's largest in-water **boat exhibition,** with local music and an incredible display of boats and boat merchandise. (For more information, call ☎860-1000 ext. 4214. Tickets $10 per person.)

◧ NIGHTLIFE

Despite its size, Fajardo has no real nightlife scene. A few restaurants along Rte. 987 double as bars and stay open late on weekend nights. **Racar Seafood,** Rte. 987 Km 6.7, next to Las Croabas, has live music from 7pm to midnight on Saturday nights. (Beer $1.50-2. Open M-F and Su 8am-around 9:30pm, Sa 8am-midnight). For a more lively scene, head to the active **Marina Liquor Store,** in Villa Marina. A motley collection of yachters and Puerto Rican men gather at this liquor/convenience/cigar store to sit at outdoor tables and drink their purchases. Come on Friday or Saturday night for live Latin music. (☎860-8112. Beers $1 and up. Mixed drinks $2-4. Open W-Th 8am-midnight, F-Sa 8am-2am. MC/V.)

NAGUABO

Life passes a little bit slower in Naguabo. South of tourist-oriented Fajardo, residents sit on their porches watching the traffic go by. The town itself has no real attractions, but the vistas from Playa Naguabo, trips to Monkey Island, and several attractive accommodations nearby make this little town a good place to relax.

◧◧ ◨ ORIENTATION AND PRACTICAL INFORMATION

Naguabo is located just off Hwy. 53, along Rte. 31. From Rte. 31, turn down **C. Garzot,** at the **Econo supermarket,** to reach the town plaza. C. Muñoz Rivera runs perpendicular to C. Garzot along the plaza; C. Goyco is on the other side of the plaza.

Públicos leave from **Terminal de Carros Públicos Salvador Clara Cotto,** next to the plaza across C. Garzot, for: **Fajardo** (20min., $1.65); **Humacao** (20min., $1.40); and **Playa Naguabo** (15min., $0.70). **Banco Popular,** C. Garzot 19, at the corner with C. Muñoz Rivera, has an ATM in front. (☎874-2880. Open M-F 8am-4pm, Sa 9am-1pm.) **Econo,** on Rte. 31 at the corner with C. Garzot, sells groceries. (☎874-3720. Open M-Th 7am-8pm, F-Sa 7am-9pm, Su 11am-5pm. MC/V.) To reach the **police station** from Rte. 31, head down C. Garzot, turn right on C. Muñoz Rivera, and continue three blocks. (☎874-2020. Open 24hr.) The **hospital,** Centro de Salud Familiar, Rte. 31 Km 4, just west of the city at the intersection with Rte. 192, has a 24hr. emergency room. (☎874-2837, emergency room ☎874-3152. Clinic open M-F 7:30am-4pm.) The **post office,** Rte. 31 #100, lies across from the Econo supermarket. (☎874-3115. Open M-F 7am-5pm, Sa 7am-1pm.) **Postal Code:** 00718.

ACCOMMODATIONS AND FOOD

For many, ▨**Casa Cubuy Ecolodge** ❹ is the only reason to venture out to Naguabo. From Naguabo, go west on Rte. 31, then turn right on Rte. 191, and head all the way up, almost to the end of the road; about 20min. This American-run B&B perches on the edge of Rte. 191, 1500 ft. above sea level, and is the only accommodation inside the El Yunque forest. With a small library, trails surrounding the property, and spectacular rainforest views from every room, the tranquil lodge is the ideal spot to get away from it all. Beautiful rooms are tastefully decorated with wooden furniture and comfy mattresses. It's worth it to pay for one of the rooms with an entire window wall and a private balcony over the forest. (☎874-6221; www.casacubuy.com. No phones or TVs. Dinner $18-20. Doubles $90-115; extra person $25. AmEx/MC/V.) **Phillips Forest Cabins** ❶, Rte. 191 Km 24.2, actually has just one operating cabin about ¼ mi. off the road, deep in the forest, with cold water and a double bed. A two-bedroom house is slightly more refined with two full beds and hot water, while four campsites create the most rustic (and cheapest) accommodations of all. (☎874-2138; www.rainforestsafari.com. Turn left off Rte. 191 about 15min. up the road, immediately before El Bambú restaurant. Cabin $35 for the 1st 2 nights, $25 for each additional night; extra cot $5. House $35; extra person $15. Campsites $15.) The best restaurants serve fresh seafood in Playa Naguabo or Punta Santiago. Within city limits, busy and centrally located **Joe's Pizza Place** ❶, C. Muñoz Rivera, on the plaza, offers big slices of mouth-watering pizza, even for breakfast. (☎874-1519. Large pizza $10-15. Calzones $3-5. Open daily 8am-midnight. Cash only.)

DAYTRIPS FROM NAGUABO

PLAYA NAGUABO

Public Transportation: A público runs from Naguabo to the beach ($0.70). Públicos between Humacao ($1.40) and Fajardo ($1.65) also stop at Playa Naguabo. Driving: From Hwy. 53, take Exit 18 onto Rte. 31. Turn left, then go south on Hwy. 3 toward Humacao to Playa Naguabo (Km 66).

The serene bay at Playa Naguabo provides a terrific escape. Technically called **Playa Húcares,** this bay doesn't have a beach, but an attractive boardwalk overlooks the brownish water, Cayo Santiago, and, in the distance, Vieques. At the southern end of the bay, two large pink turn-of-the-century houses, both on the list of National Historic Sights, provide an interesting lesson in development. One house has been kept up and is now the most attractive residence in the area. The other, **El Castillo Villa del Mar,** was built at the same time, but it has fallen into such a state of decay that it now looks like the set of a horror movie. Playa Naguabo has several restaurants with a good view and equally good food. The $4 lunch special at **Bar-Restaurante Vinny ❶**, at the northern end of the beach, is an excellent deal with rice, beans, beverage, and either pork chops or chicken. Add on a side of *amarillos* for just $0.25. (☎874-7664. Beer $1.25-2. Open daily 8am-10pm. MC/V.) If you're looking for something without plastic tables, the air-conditioned **Restaurante Griselle Seafood ❸**, where Hwy. 3 hits the playa, serves live lobsters right out of the tank for $22 per lb. (☎874-1533. Entrees $7-25. Open M-Tu, Th, Su 11am-8pm; F-Sa 11am-midnight. D/MC/V.)

CAYO SANTIAGO

*The island is only accessible via private tour. Contact **Frank López** (see below).*

A tiny island uninhabited by humans is certainly not unique in Puerto Rico. But one inhabited solely by their primate cousins is a rarity, making Cayo Santiago one of the most unusual attractions in the northeast. In 1938 the University of Puerto Rico and Columbia University in New York City teamed up to create a new research area—they took 500 Indian rhesus monkeys, isolated them on 38-acre Cayo Santiago, and **Monkey Island** was born. The monkeys thrived in their new environment and today over 1200 primates frolic on the tropical shores. Only scientists and researchers are allowed on the island, but visitors can take a boat close to the island and watch the monkeys from afar. An abandoned 1944 boat wreck just off the shore and a small reef on the other side of the island makes this a great place for snorkeling, and unlike other islands near Fajardo, Cayo Santiago is usually isolated. Amiable Captain Frank López leads 2-2½ hr. excursions from Playa Naguabo to Monkey Island on his boat, **La Paseadora.** For only $25 per person, Lopez offers the opportunity to fish, kayak, snorkel, and swim. This is a very different experience than the Fajardo boat trips—come with expectations of a friendly face, lively music, and personal attention, and you'll have a great time. (You can look for López's boat at the northern end of Playa Naguabo on Sa-Su, but calling ahead is advisable. ☎850-7881. 6 person max. Limited equipment provided. Cash only.)

VIEQUES

The first thing that comes to mind when most people think of Vieques is the US Navy base on the island, which was protested vocally by locals. But as of May 1, 2003, the Navy left Vieques, closing one chapter of history and leaving *viequenses* with the prize that they had long been fighting for: their beautiful island. Once again, the only sounds heard on the island are the chirps of *coquís* and the crows of roosters—a marked contrast from the recent past, when it was common to hear the sounds of bombs falling less than 10 mi. away. But even Vieques's tumultuous history is not as remarkable as the island's natural beauty. Often referred to as La Isla Nena (the little girl island), Vieques is covered with lush tropical forests and surrounded by crystalline seas that rival any in the Caribbean. The entire island feels a bit untamed—palm trees are scattered amidst gnarled jungle vegetation, bumpy dirt roads crisscross the land, and herds of wild horses wander through the forest as if they owned it. On the south coast, the island has two bioluminescent bays that are among the best in the world.

With fewer than 10,000 residents, Vieques is just large enough to contain two small settlements. Isabel II (Isabel Segunda), the largest city, feels like any small Puerto Rican town, complete with a plaza, a busy main strip, and, when the ferry arrives, a bit of traffic congestion. The ferry terminal, the fort, most local services, and several of the best restaurants are located in Isabel II. Esperanza, on the south side of the island, is more tourist-oriented and has a large population of US expats. This primarily residential neighborhood becomes increasingly commercialized as you head toward the water. The street running parallel to the sea, called Calle Flamboyán, the Malecón, or simply "the strip," is almost completely lined with guesthouses, restaurants, gift shops, tour operators, and English speakers.

Like much of Puerto Rico, Vieques has its share of issues. With the Navy gone, the island must figure out how to deal with one of the highest unemployment rates in the US, a budding tourism industry, and the allocation of hundreds of acres of valuable land. Locals have organized nonprofit organizations to deal with these issues and to protect the island for future generations. But *viequenses* know that even if the island's future is a bit unsure, in many respects, they live in paradise.

HIGHLIGHTS OF VIEQUES

MAKE WATER GLOW in the world's most vibrant **bioluminescent bay** (p. 187).

LOUNGE on the white sands of **Sun Bay** (p. 186).

BRUSH UP on Vieques's fascinating history, including the controversial US Navy presence, at **Fortín de Conde de Marisol** (p. 183).

◨ INTER-ISLAND TRANSPORTATION

Flights: Aeropuerto Antonio Rivera Rodríguez (☎741-8358 or 741-0415), on Rte. 200, may be the most attractive airport in Puerto Rico. The following airlines sell tickets over the phone or at their airport desks. Reserve at least 24hr. in advance, even farther ahead during high season and holidays. A *público* waiting on Rte. 200 when flights come in will take visitors anywhere on the island (see **Públicos**, p. 176). Open 24hr.

Air Sunshine (☎741-7900, toll-free 888-879-8900; www.airsunshine.com) flies to: **San Juan International** (25min.; 4 per day; $75, round-trip $150). Open daily 8am-6pm. AmEx/MC/V.

Isla Nena (☎741-1505, toll-free 877-812-5144) flies on demand to: **Culebra** (8min.; $26, round-trip $58); **Fajardo** (8min.; $25, round-trip $50); and **San Juan International** (20min.; $80, round-trip $150). Open daily 7am-6:30pm. MC/V.

M&N Aviation (☎741-3911, toll-free 877-622-5566) flies to: **Fajardo** (7min.; 1-2 per day; $30, round-trip $50); **San Juan Isla Grande** (19min.; 3 per day; $55, round-trip $100) and **San Juan International** (20min.; 2 per day; $80, round-trip $150). Open daily 6am-7pm. AmEx/MC/V.

Vieques Air Link (☎741-8331, toll-free 888-901-9247) flies to: **Fajardo** (10min.; on demand; $21, round-trip $40); **San Juan International** (30min.; 3 per day; $76, round-trip $153); **San Juan Isla Grande** (30min.; 3-4 per day; $45, round-trip $86); **St. Croix, USVI** (30min.; 2 per day; $67, round-trip $133). Open M-Sa 7:30am-5pm. AmEx/MC/V. Or stop by their **reservations office**, C. Antonio Mellado 258. Open M-F 7:30am-4:30pm.

Ferries: Puerto Rican Port Authority (☎741-4761 or 741-0233, in Fajardo 863-0705, 863-0852, or 863-4560) operates ferries between **Vieques** and **Fajardo.** In addition to the routes below, a ferry runs between **Vieques** and **Culebra** (W only; leaves Vieques 7:30am and 2:30pm, returns from Culebra 9am and 3:30pm; round-trip $4). No reservations are accepted for passengers, so show up at least 1hr. in advance. Reservations are required to take a car onboard and should be made several months in advance to snag one of the few spots. Ticket office open daily 8-11am and 1-3pm. MC/V

FERRIES	FAJARDO-VIEQUES	VIEQUES-FAJARDO	PRICE
PASSENGER	M-F 9:30am, 1, 4:30, 8pm; Sa-Su 9am, 3, 6pm	M-F 6:30, 11am, 3, 6pm; Sa-Su 7am, 1, 4:30pm	$2
CARGO	M-F 4, 9:30am, 4:30pm	M-F 6am, 6pm	$15; round-trip $26.50

■ ORIENTATION

Measuring 20 mi. by 4½ mi., Vieques looks like a mini, elongated version of Puerto Rico. As of July 2005, both the eastern and western thirds of the island, former US Navy lands, are controlled by the US Fish and Wildlife Service. Most of the area is open to the public as a natural reserve, although certain areas containing unexploded bombs or other hazardous materials remain closed (these areas are clearly marked and cordoned off). Most people arrive in Isabel II, the island's largest town and home of the ferry dock. The dock is also the home base for *públicos*, which congregate there by the dozen when a ferry is scheduled to arrive. If you are driving your own car and wish to leave Isabel II, take a right at the ferry dock, then take a left on C. Benítez Guzmán, then a right just past the plaza to reach Rte. 200 and leave town. The fastest route between Isabel II and Esperanza is Rte. 997; however, for a much more scenic route drive west on Rte. 200, then south along Rte. 995, one of the most beautiful roads on the island. Then turn left on Rte. 201 and right on Rte. 996, which leads straight into Esperanza. Coming into Esperanza on Rte. 996, veer left as you hit La Tienda Verde and the road will reach the ocean and become **"the strip,"** home to many of the town's hotels.

■ LOCAL TRANSPORTATION

Unless you plan to stick exclusively to one of the towns, it is very time-consuming and almost impossible to get around Vieques without a car. *Públicos* run between Isabel II and Esperanza but rarely head to any beaches except Sun Bay, and there may be as long as a 1hr. wait, even if you call ahead.

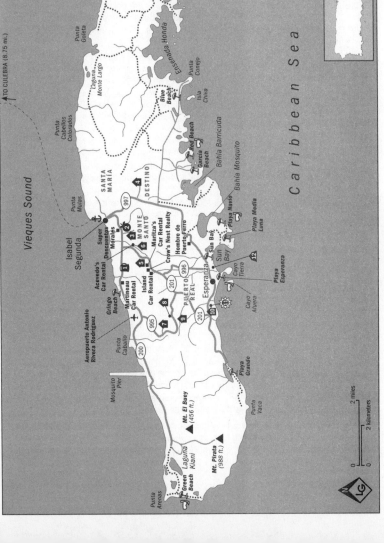

Vieques

ACCOMMODATIONS
Abreeze, 4
Adventures Inn, 3
Balneario Sun Bay, 12
Cabañas Playa Grande, 6
The Crow's Nest, 5
La Finca Caribe, 7
Great Escape B&B Inn, 9
Hacienda Tamarindo, 10
Hix Island House, 8

FOOD
Bayaonda, 2

OUTDOOR ACTIVITY RENTAL
Island Adventures, 11

NIGHTLIFE
M Bar, 1

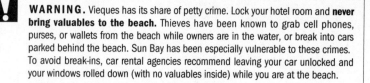

WARNING. Vieques has its share of petty crime. Lock your hotel room and **never bring valuables to the beach.** Thieves have been known to grab cell phones, purses, or wallets from the beach while owners are in the water, or break into cars parked behind the beach. Sun Bay has been especially vulnerable to these crimes. To avoid break-ins, car rental agencies recommend leaving your car unlocked and your windows rolled down (with no valuables inside) while you are at the beach.

Car Rental: Several small companies rent Jeeps and SUVs, but there are no major chains. Make reservations far in advance during high season (Dec.-May) as it's not uncommon for every car on the island to be booked. Even during low season, call a few days ahead. Most of the former Navy roads are unpaved, extremely bumpy, and rife with water-filled potholes; these should not be attempted without four-wheel drive. Even the island's paved roads can be challenging, as many are only one lane wide but have traffic going in both directions. There are two **gas stations** around Rte. 200 Km 1.5. The third station is at the intersection of Rte. 200 and Rte. 997. Usually, only one of these stations is open at any given time.

Island Car Rental, Rte. 201 Km 1.1 (☎741-1666), provides drop-off service. Jeeps $55, SUVs $65, minivans $75. Discounts for 5 or more days. Insurance $10 per day. Driver's license required; no min. age. $500 deposit required. Open daily 8am-5pm. AmEx/MC/V.

Martineau Car Rental, Rte. 200 Km 3.2 (☎741-0087), across from the Wyndham resort. Rents shiny new Jeeps ($60-70 per day). Insurance $12 per day. 25+. Ages 21-24 $5 per day surcharge. They also rent bikes ($25 per 24hr.). Pick-up and drop-off available. Credit card required. Open daily 8am-6pm. AmEx/MC/V.

Maritza's Car Rental, Rte. 201 Km 1 (☎741-0078). Rents Jeeps for $40-60 per day. Insurance $12 per day. 25+. No pick-up, but they will drop off cars at any hotel. Open daily 8am-5pm. AmEx/MC/V.

Acevedo's Car Rental, Rte. 201 Km 0.4 (☎741-4380), in the Cabañas Playa Grande complex. Rents 3 types of Jeeps ($45-60). 21+. No pick-up or delivery. Open M-Sa 9am-6pm, Su 10am-noon. AmEx/MC/V.

Steve's Car Rental (☎741-8135, cell 319-8524), by the ferry dock, rents several types of off-road vehicles and vans ($40-70 per day). No pick-up, but the car will be waiting when you arrive at your hotel or guesthouse. 18+. MC/V.

Acacia Car Rental (☎741-1856). The owners of Acacia Apartments also rent 4 Jeeps (in winter $65 per day, in summer $50). Driver's license required; no min. age. Rentals come with an orientation. No pick-up. MC/V.

Públicos: Shared vans travel the island, usually circulating between the airport, the **ferry terminal** in Isabel II, and **the strip** in Esperanza. If you flag down a *público,* it will usually take you anywhere on the island. Passengers traveling alone may have to pay the fare of 3 passengers. When ferries arrive, all of the operating *públicos* will be at the dock, then about 30min. later most will end up on the strip in Esperanza; plan your schedule accordingly. Transport anywhere on the major roads should cost about $3 per person; transport to the beaches on former Navy lands runs $5 or more; extra luggage costs $0.50 per item. Keep in mind, especially if you want to go to the more remote beaches, that *públicos* may not be around to pick you up, so have some numbers handy and be prepared to wait. *Público* drivers include: **Ana** (☎741-2318, cell 313-0599), **Ángel** (☎741-1370, cell 484-7896), **Eric** (☎741-0448), **Fernando** (cell ☎605-4100), **Henry** (☎741-8621, cell 380-1866), **Ismael** (☎741-0095), and **Jorge** (☎741-2116).

Bike Rental: La Dulce Vida (www.bikevieques.com) rents 15- to 27-speed mountain bikes ($25-35 per day including helmet, lock, and delivery). The owner also leads half-day bike tours around the western end of the island ($65 per person including snacks and water). New 2-day bike/kayak/snorkel tours $75-120 per person. Reservations required. MC/V.

▓ PRACTICAL INFORMATION

Unless otherwise stated, all services are located in Isabel II.

Tourist Office: Puerto Rico Tourism Company, C. Carlos LeBrun 449 (☎ 741-0800), on the corner of the plaza. Helpful staff offers maps, magazines, and brochures. Open daily 8am-5pm. Island tourism websites include www.vieques-island.com and www.isla-vieques.com.

ISLAND INFO. Several publications and websites provide information about Vieques in English. Take a look at the following:

www.enchanted-isle.com. Almost every tourist service on the island has a link on this comprehensive site. Resident expat Judy writes *What's Happenin'!*, which lists many island events, including unscheduled closings of establishments and special nights at bars and restaurants.

www.vieques-events.com. On the first of every month this helpful newsletter appears on the web with a calendar of current events, articles about recent happenings, and a small classifieds section. Almost every tourist-related business on the island carries a hard copy.

www.elenas-vieques.com. A longtime expat and owner of Blue Heron Kayak, Elena has compiled a personal website with information about Vieques.

Bank: Banco Popular, C. Muñoz Rivera 115 (☎ 741-2071). ATM. Open M-F 8am-3pm.

Supermarkets:

Super Descuentos Morales, Rte. 200 Km 1.3 (☎ 741-6701). The largest grocery store on Vieques. Open M-Sa 6:30am-7pm, Su 6:30am-noon. MC/V. Another location at C. Baldorioty de Castro 15.

La Tienda Verde, C. Robles 273 (☎ 741-8711), Rte. 996, at the entrance to Esperanza. A centrally located, glorified minimart. Open daily 9am-9pm. MC/V.

Colmado El Molino, on C. Antonio Mellado next to El Patio, in Isabel II. Small store with basic groceries. Open later than other grocery stores. Open M-Sa 7am-11pm, Su 10am-11pm.

Colmado Lydia (☎ 741-8678), on C. Almendro in Esperanza. This small grocery store is close to the strip. Open M-Sa 7:30am-6pm, Su 7:30am-noon. Cash only.

Laundromat: Familia Ríos, C. Benítez Castaño 1 (☎ 438-1846). Self-serve washers $2.50-5. Dryers $0.60 per 10min. Wash-and-fold $1.75 per lb.; available by 4pm if in by 10am. Change unnecessary; uses declining-balance cards. Detergent included. Open Tu-W and F-Su 7am-5pm.

Police: Rte. 200 Km 0.2, at Rte. 997 (☎ 741-2020 or 741-2121). Open 24hr.

Pharmacy: Isla Nena Pharmacy (☎ 741-1906), on C. Muñoz Rivera. Open M-Sa 8am-6pm. AmEx/MC/V.

Hospital: Centro de Salud Familiar, Rte. 997 Km 0.4 (☎ 741-0392, emergency room 741-2151). Clinic open M-F 7am-4:30pm. Emergency room open 24hr.

Library: Biblioteca Pública de Vieques José Gautier Benítez (☎ 741-2706), at the corner of C. Baldorioty de Castro and C. Benítez Guzmán. Small selection of mostly reference books, but has free public **Internet** use. Open M-F 8am-4:30pm.

Internet Access: Museo de Esperanza, C. Flamboyán 138 (☎ 741-8850), Esperanza, allows travelers to use their computer ($3 for 30min.). Open Tu-Su 11am-4pm.

Post Office: C. Muñoz Rivera 97 (☎ 741-3891). General Delivery mail to: General Delivery, Vieques, PR 00765. Open M-F 8am-4:30pm, Sa 8am-noon. **Postal Code:** 00765.

VIEQUES

ISLAND TIME. All hours and prices in Vieques are subject to change. Hours change with the season, and owners (and *público* drivers) frequently close down shop in the middle of the day for lunch. Even restaurant service is slow: where could you possibly be going in a hurry? To avoid frustration, make plans with a grain of salt and retain a sense of flexibility.

ACCOMMODATIONS AND CAMPING

Vieques has excellent accommodations for travelers of all budgets. If you want to be in the middle of local action, stay in Isabel II; if you want to join the expat crowd and be close to the beaches, try Esperanza. If you just want to get away from it all, try one of the accommodations in the middle of the island, but you will need a car. Many hotels do not allow children; generally, the more expensive an accommodation is, the less likely it is to allow children.

REALTORS

The realtors below, along with several others, offer short-term vacation rentals around the island. Prices are for weekly rentals and are taxed at the rate of 7%.

Rainbow Realty, C. Flamboyán 62 (☎/fax 741-4312; www.enchanted-isle.com/rainbow), in Esperanza right next to the Tiki Hut. Most rentals have washer and dryer, some have pool and A/C. 1 week min. Nov.-Apr. $650-4000; May-Oct. $450-3000. Open in winter daily 9am-5pm; in summer Tu, Th, Sa 9am-3pm and W, F 9am-noon. MC/V with 5% surcharge; personal checks preferred.

Crow's Nest Realty, Rte. 201 Km 1 (☎741-0033 or 1-888-484-7837; fax 741-1294; www.crowsnestvieques.com). 1 week min. Rentals $1000-4000. AmEx/MC/V.

Connections Real Estate, C. Muñoz Rivera 117 (☎741-0023; fax 741-2022; www.vieques-realtor.com), in Isabel II. 1 week min. 50% deposit. Houses vary in size; most rent for $300-1200. Open Oct.-May M-F 10am-5pm, Sa-Su by appointment; June-Sept. W-F 10am-5pm and by appointment. Credit card deposit required; payment only by cash or check.

ISABEL II

▨ **Casa de Amistad,** C. Benítez Castaño 27 (☎741-3758; www.casadeamistad.com), in the heart of Isabel II. The helpful and enthusiastic owners have created an affordable, attractive guesthouse. 7 artistically decorated rooms with A/C and wicker furniture. Rooftop deck. Tiny pool. Common area with TV. Common kitchen and dining room. Beach towels ($2), snorkel equipment ($10), Internet ($3 per 30min.), and bar. Free use of coolers and beach chairs. Doubles $60-70; quads $80-90. MC/V. ❷

Hotel Vieques Ocean View, C. Plinio Peterson 571 (☎741-3696). Standard budget hotel—except for the balconies and pool that look out over the ocean. Convenient to town. All rooms have A/C and TV; most have fridge. Doubles $66-78; quads $99; 6-person rooms $119; 8-person rooms $143. AmEx/MC/V. ❸

El Seagate, (☎741-4661), on the hill above the fort. With the fort's entrance at your back, take the left fork and continue to bear left. The guesthouse is lovingly cared for, and all guests receive the owner's personal attention. All rooms have ceiling fan; some have a full kitchen. A few dogs run around. Free wireless Internet. Pets welcome. Large book exchange. Pool. Doubles $45; quads $80. MC/V. ❷

Tropical Guest House, C. Progreso 41 (☎741-2449). Leaving Isabel II on Rte. 200 take the first left after El Patio restaurant, then take the left fork and then the right fork; the hotel is on your left. The walls are bare and the blankets thin, but the price is right. All rooms have A/C and TV. Singles $50; doubles $60; quads and quints with kitchen $75. Tax included. No credit cards. ❷

ESPERANZA

Trade Winds Guest House, C. Flamboyán 107 (☎741-8666; fax 741-2964; www.enchanted-isle.com/tradewinds). Cozy guesthouse and great location make this a good value. Colorful rooms with bright, Caribbean-themed wall murals. Some rooms share an ocean-view patio. All rooms have fridges, reading lights, and ceiling fans. Free use of beach towels. Check-out 11am. Check-in 2pm. Singles $60-70; doubles $70-80; extra person $15. AmEx/MC/V. ❷

Bananas Guest House, C. Flamboyán 142 (☎741-8700; fax 741-0790; www.bananasguesthouse.com). An elegant wood cabin just across the street from the beach. Friendly backpacker atmosphere. Lively restaurant. Check-in noon. Check-out 11am. Doubles with fan $55, A/C, fridge, and porch $75-85; extra person $15. MC/V. ❷

Pablo's Guest House, C. Piños 217 (☎741-8917). The cheapest option on the island, but a 10min. walk from the fun of the strip. Incredibly clean rooms are located on the 2nd fl. of Pablo's home. 4 identical rooms contain a full bed and a twin bed. All rooms include hot water and fridge. Triples $40, with A/C $55. Cash only. ❷

Ted's Guest House, C. Húcar 103 (☎741-2225; www.vieques-island.com/rentals/ted), ½ block from the strip in the big coral-and-blue house. Though they are located on the 2nd fl. of the owner's home,

Isabel Segunda

🏠 **ACCOMMODATIONS**
¡Bravo!, **1**
Casa de Amistad, **6**
Hotel Vieques Ocean View, **4**
El Seagate, **13**
Tropical Guest House, **12**

🍴 **FOOD**
Mucho Gusto, **9**
Panadería y Respostería Lydia, **5**

El Patio Bar and Restaurant, **10**
Richard's Cafe, **14**
Scoops Cafe, **7**
Shaunaa's Restaurant, **11**
La Taverna Española, **8**
Wai Nam Seafood Restaurant, **3**

🌙 **NIGHTLIFE**
Al's Mar Azul, **2**

these 3 immaculate apartments look professional. All come with a full kitchen, A/C, TV, and a kitchen table. Common balcony. 2-night min. Doubles $80; 2-bedroom quads $125. Tax included. No credit cards. ❸

Amapola Guest House, C. Flamboyán 144 (☎741-1382). Enter through the corridor between Bananas and Bilí, on the strip. Amapola can best be described as colorful,

VIEQUES

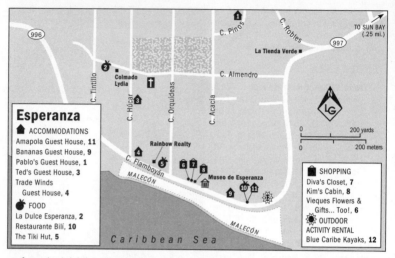

Esperanza

🏠 ACCOMMODATIONS
Amapola Guest House, **11**
Bananas Guest House, **9**
Pablo's Guest House, **1**
Ted's Guest House, **3**
Trade Winds
  Guest House, **4**
🍎 FOOD
La Dulce Esperanza, **2**
Restaurante Bilí, **10**
The Tiki Hut, **5**

🛍 SHOPPING
Diva's Closet, **7**
Kim's Cabin, **8**
Vieques Flowers &
  Gifts... Too!, **6**
☀ OUTDOOR
ACTIVITY RENTAL
Blue Caribe Kayaks, **12**

from the brightly painted exterior to the parakeets in the courtyard. Excellent location. All rooms have A/C and wicker furniture, and free morning coffee. Quads come with a well-equipped kitchen. Doubles $75-95; quads $125. AmEx/MC/V. ❸

AROUND VIEQUES

Abreeze, Rte. 997 Km 1.6 (☎741-1856; www.vieques-island.com/rentals/abreeze). The owners of Acacia Car Rental rent out 2 apartments in their beautiful yellow house. With 3½ acres of land on the top of a hill with nearly panoramic views, this house feels like a Caribbean country estate. Rooms include kitchens, private patios, phones, games, barbecues, and free Internet. All guests can use pool, beach towels and chairs, coolers, washer, and dryer. 1 week min. 2-person studio Nov.-May $1050 per week, June-Oct. $850; 4-person apartment $1250/1050. MC/V. ❹

The Crow's Nest, Rte. 201 Km 1 (☎741-0033 or 1-888-VIEQUES/1-888-843-7837; fax 741-1294; www.crowsnestvieques.com). On 5 acres of land just off busy Rte. 201, the hotel looks like an expensive resort from the outside, with a pool, poolside restaurant, and newly painted yellow-and-white exterior. Inside, the rooms are aging a bit, but very large. A/C, satellite TV, phone, and patio. Most with full kitchen. Internet $4 for 20min. No children under 12. Continental breakfast included. Reception 8am-7pm. Doubles Dec. 20-May 1 $85-111; May 2-Dec. 19 $80-95; extra person $15. AmEx/MC/V. ❸

La Finca Caribe, Rte. 995 Km 2.2 (☎741-0495; fax 741-3584; www.lafinca.com). If you enjoyed summer camp as a kid, try this rustic wooden hotel hidden on a farm in the middle of Vieques. The tin-roofed house strives for tranquility and simplicity; most rooms share bathrooms and guests use outdoor solar-heated showers. All rooms have a loft bed. Friendly conversation ensues in the common kitchen area/lounge. Pool. Book exchange. Doubles mid-Nov. to mid-May $80; mid-May to mid-Nov. $60. Large cabins $1000/750 per week. 4% credit card fee. AmEx/MC/V. ❸

Adventures Inn, Rte. 200 Km 1.5 (☎741-1564). Turn left off Rte. 200 across from the 3rd gas station. Big turquoise house in the middle of a residential neighborhood. Rooms are comfortable yet unremarkable. $25 fee for maid service. All rooms have A/C. Continental breakfast included. Doubles $80; extra person $20. AmEx/MC/V. ❸

Cabañas Playa Grande, Rte. 201 Km 0.4 (☎ 741-4380). Like a government-run *centro vacacional*, Playa Grande has 2 options: well-equipped, clean apartments with A/C, TV, VCR, and fully stocked kitchen, or rustic cabins with nothing but mattresses and a tiny fridge. All rooms sleep up to 5 people, which makes the apartments a very good deal, though the grounds are less than inspiring. Cabins $75; apartments $110. Tax included. AmEx/MC/V. ❸

Balneario Sun Bay (☎ 741-8198), on Rte. 997, ¼ mi. east of Esperanza, is essentially a large field next to the beach. Nothing compares to falling asleep to the sound of waves crashing on the shore 20 ft. away from your tent. Relatively popular; crowded during major holidays. Facilities include trash cans, picnic tables, fire pits, surprisingly nice bathrooms, showers, and a water fountain. The only downside is that the area has virtually no shade. Parking $2 if you enter Tu-Su 8:30am-5pm. $10 per tent. ❶

THE SKY'S THE LIMIT
Vieques has several beautiful high-end guesthouses spread throughout the island.

¡Bravo!, C. North Shore 1 (☎ 741-1128; www.bravobeachhotel.com). The new ¡Bravo! made Condé Nast's Hot List, and it's easy to see why: DVDs and Playstations in every room, outdoor rooftop massages, modern furniture with clean lines, Frette sheets, and floor-to-ceiling windows with spectacular ocean views. Watch the sunset from the pool just feet from the ocean. All standard amenities including free use of beach chairs and towels, continental breakfast, fridge with minibar, and 300-channel satellite TV. Worth the splurge for rooms with the ocean view. Restaurant becomes tapas and wine bar at night. Reception 8am-5pm. Check-in by 3pm. Check-out noon. Doubles Easter-Thanksgiving $99-175, Thanksgiving-Easter $99-190; villa (sleeps 4) $375/425. ❹

Hacienda Tamarindo, Rte. 996 Km 4.5 (☎ 741-8525; fax 741-3215; www.haciendatamarindo.com). Great views and beautiful rooms make this one of Vieques's best small accommodations. Each room is adorned with murals and antiques. Gorgeous common library and lounge. Big pool. A/C and ceiling fans. No children under 15. Bar. American breakfast included. Reception 8am-6pm. Check-out 8:30-11am. Nov. 16-May 4 singles $160-190; doubles $170-275. May 5-Nov. 15 $125-160/135-225; extra person $35. 10% service charge not included. AmEx/D/MC/V. ❺

Hix Island House, Rte. 995 Km 1.2 (☎ 741-2302; fax 741-2797; www.hixislandhouse.com). Hix Island House may be the most unique accommodation in Puerto Rico. 3 concrete buildings contain breezy rooms that manage to be private even though they have only 3 walls. Fully stocked kitchen, breakfast supplies, table, semi-outdoor shower, homemade bread, and mosquito nets for the bed. Concrete pool fits ingeniously into the landscape. You'll either love it or you'll hate it; not everyone wants to live in a work of art. No children under 13. Doubles Nov. 20-Apr. 30 $220-295, 3 night min.; May-Nov. 19 $160-210, 2 night min. AmEx/MC/V. ❺

Great Escape Bed & Breakfast Inn (☎ 741-2927; www.enchanted-isle.com/greatescape), on Rte. 201 between Rte. 995 and Rte. 996. Follow signs to the side road, then drive up it and turn right onto the dirt road after the pink concrete fence. Located on 3.8 acres of land in farm country, the Great Escape offers fresh air, tranquility, and great mountain views. In spite of the cheesiness (a trellis labeled the "Love Nest," and a latrine covered in mirrors that form the shape of Mickey Mouse), the 10 rooms are nice, with wrought-iron beds and private balconies. Pool. Continental breakfast included. Dec.-Apr. doubles $150; May-Nov. $125; extra person $25. Apartments $200-400. Tax included. Cash only. ❺

VIEQUES

◨ FOOD

Keep your ATM card handy; with the food prices on Vieques as high as they are, you may be making frequent withdrawals. Several American expats have opened delicious but expensive restaurants. However, it is easy to find high-quality, filling eats at one of the *comida criolla* joints in Isabel II.

ISABEL II

▨ **Shaunaa's Restaurant** (☎ 741-1434), on C. Antonio Mellado. Vieques's best *cafetería*. Extremely popular with locals; if you want to eat in, it'll be tough to find a seat. A budget traveler's dream. Huge lunch platters with a choice of meat, rice, plantains, and beans $6. Open M-F 11am-3pm. MC/V. ❶

▨ **Panadería y Repostería Lydia** (☎ 741-8679), at C. Plinio Peterson and Benítez Guzmán. Simple sandwiches on delicious, freshly baked bread. Huge pastries ($0.50-1, including the very Puerto Rican pineapple-and-cheese danish). No seating area inside, but there are 2 plastic tables out front. A great bargain. Sandwiches $1.50-2.50. 1 lb. fresh bread $1.25. Pastries served M-F. Open M-F 5am-2pm, Sa 5am-noon. Cash only. ❶

El Patio Bar and Restaurant (☎ 741-6381), on C. Antonio G. Mellado. This relaxed, local favorite serves food similar to Shaunaa's. At El Patio, you'll find a slightly nicer atmosphere and more menu choices, but smaller portions. Lunch special 11am-2pm $5. Typical seafood, chicken, and meat entrees $5-15. Beer $1-2. Mixed drinks $2-3. Open daily 10:30am-6:30pm. MC/V. ❷

Scoops Cafe, C. Benítez Guzmán 53 (☎ 741-5555). Vieques's only ice cream parlor offers tasty traditional flavors as well as the local favorite pineapple-coconut (one scoop $3, two scoops $4.50). Also serves delicious and popular brick-oven pizza (slices $2-2.50). Open daily 11am-11pm. ❶

Mucho Gusto, C. Muñoz Rivera 121 (☎ 741-3300). A little classier than the average *comida criolla* eatery. Lots of local art on the walls, but plastic furniture. Octopus salad with *tostones* $12.50. Burgers $6.50. Entrees $8.50-18.50. Open in winter daily 11am-last customer; in summer Tu-W 11am-11pm, Th 11am-3am, F 11am-last customer, Sa 4:30pm-last customer. ❸

La Taverna Española (☎ 741-1175), at the corner of C. Carlos LeBrun and C. Benítez Castaño. The decor is a bit tacky and the food overpriced at this Spanish restaurant, but the reason to come is the *sangría*, the best you've ever had (glass $3, pitcher $11). Entrees $15-25. Open M-Sa 5-10pm. MC/V. ❹

Richard's Cafe (☎ 741-5242), at the intersection of Rte. 997 and Rte. 200. Popular with families. Skip the unremarkable Puerto Rican cuisine ($4-19) and just grab a big burger ($4-5). *Mofongo* $13-19. Open daily 11am-11pm. AmEx/MC/V. ❸

Wai Nam Seafood Restaurant, C. Plinio Peterson 571 (☎ 741-0622), under Hotel Ocean Front. Like any good Puerto Rico town, Isabel II must have the requisite Chinese/seafood/fried chicken restaurant, where all the entrees are served with french fries. However, this may be the only one with a fantastic sea view. Chinese entrees $3-17. Open M-Th and Su 10am-9:30pm, F-Sa 10am-10:30pm. MC/V. ❷

ESPERANZA

▨ **The Tiki Hut,** C. Flamboyán 62 (☎ 741-4992; www.tikihutvieques.com). A rare combination of deliciousness and affordability in a convenient location. This simple outdoor stand serves made-to-order sandwiches and salads for lunch with friendly service. Full breakfast served all day $4.50-7.50. Sandwiches and wraps $6.50-7.50. House specialty ginger iced tea $1.50. Open daily 7am-2pm. MC/V. ❶

Trade Winds, C. Flamboyán 107 (☎741-8666; fax 741-2964). Soft music plays while you sit in a big wooden chair, gaze out over the water, and dine on some of the best food on the strip. Resort-type food with an island twist. Chicken, bacon, and veggie wrap with passion fruit sauce $8.50. Breakfast $4.50-7. Lunch $5-8.50. Dinner $13-28. Open M and W-Su 8am-2pm and 6-9:30pm, Tu 6-9:30pm. AmEx/MC/V. ❸

La Dulce Esperanza (☎741-7085), on C. Almendro. Located just off the strip, but feels worlds away. One of the few affordable yet appetizing restaurants in Esperanza. Serves breakfast subs (6 in. $2-3; 12 in. $4-5.50), dinner pizza (slices $2-2.50; large pizzas $13-17), and pastries all day long ($1). Take your food to go and catch a baseball game down the street. Open daily 7-11am and 5-9pm. Cash only. ❶

Bananas, C. Flamboyán 142 (☎741-8700), at the guesthouse of the same name. Cheap eats and a lively bar attract the crowds. ½ lb. sandwiches and salads ($6-9) are a good deal. Beer $1.75-3. Frozen drinks $5-6.50. M after 5pm Medalla $1. Occasional live music. Restaurant open daily 11am-9:30pm. Bar open M-Th and Su until 1am, F-Sa until 2am. MC/V. ❸

Restaurante Bilí, C. Flamboyán 144 (☎741-1382). This new restaurant by the water serves high-class Caribbean treats, including the unique mahi mahi with plantain chutney ($20). Entrees $17-30. Appetizers $6-12. Open W-Su noon-11pm. AmEx/MC/V. ❸

AROUND VIEQUES

Bayaonda ❹, Rte. 200 Km 1.5 (741-0312). Vieques's hippest restaurant. Though it's 20 ft. from the main road, Bayaonda maintains an aura of isolation with an intimate dining area surrounded by trees. The food, defined as Artisan Caribbean, is pricey but deliciously complex. Diners can start with the "Trilogy of Iberian Cod" ($11), then try one of the entrees like spice-dusted game hen with coconut curry sauce ($17). Several vegetarian and vegan options. (Entrees $17-23. Open M and F-Su 6-10pm. MC/V.)

🅖 SIGHTS

Unlike Culebra, Vieques does have a fair share of cultural sights. It's worth an afternoon of missed beach time to check out the island's major museums.

FORTÍN CONDE DE MIRASOL. Vieques's most impressive sight was constructed in the 1840s as the last Spanish fort in the New World. It then entered a long period of neglect and disrepair until the Puerto Rican Institute of Culture restored the fort and installed a museum inside. The majority of the museum is devoted to standard displays of pre-Hispanic archaeological artifacts, histories of various European groups on Vieques, and tools used by early *viequenses*. But the museum also hosts rotating exhibits of local artwork, much of which has focused on the US Navy presence. A recent exhibit entitled "En Concreto (Gráfica Urbana)," a photography display by Rafael Trelles, contemplated the religious and urban consequences of the US Navy's previous presence on Vieques. The criticism of the US often voiced in the Fortín exhibitions is complicated by the fact that the US government partially funds the museum. The fort merits a visit for both its architecture and its well-thought-out displays. Although almost all of the signs are in Spanish only, bilingual tour guides are happy to show visitors around. (*Rte. 989 Km 0.5. Follow signs to the Fuerte neighborhood. ☎741-1717; www.icp.gobierno.pr. Open W-Su 8:30am-4:20pm. $2, under 12 and 60+ free.*)

PAZ PARA VIEQUES?

As far back as most *viequenses* can remember, islanders have clashed with the US government over the US Navy presence on the island. And even though the bombing range that formerly occupied 2/3 of the island was closed in 2003, the controversy over land use continues.

The US began appropriating land on Vieques for naval training in the 1940s and by 1949, the Navy controlled 72% of the island. In the early 1960s US President John F. Kennedy proposed taking over the rest of Vieques and moving all of its residents to the main island of Puerto Rico, but repercussions from the Cuban Revolution thwarted this plan. As early as 1964 locals spoke out against the Navy's plans for expansion, but the Navy argued that Vieques's combination of jungle and ocean environments made it an invaluable training site.

Minor protests continued throughout the 1980s, but in 1999 Vieques erupted. On April 19 two live bombs accidentally hit an observation post, killing resident patrol guard David Sanes Rodríguez. Vieques made international news as hundreds of Puerto Ricans camped out on Navy land, preventing military exercises from taking place. In 2000 Sila M. Calderón was elected governor largely because of her promise to get the Navy out of Vieques. Protests continued, and in 2000 and

FARO PUNTA MULAS. From the ferry, the view of the Punta Mulas lighthouse crowning the hill is quite stunning. From the lighthouse itself, it is no less so: the 360-degree views—the ocean on one side and mountains on the other, and Culebra in the distance—are about as good as it gets. The lighthouse was built by the Spaniards in 1895-96, but it was partially destroyed when the Americans attacked, and was finally restored in 1992. *(On Calle A, uphill from the ferry dock. ☎741-0060. Free 15min. Spanish/English tour. Open daily 8am-4:30pm. Free.)*

MUSEO DE ESPERANZA. The Vieques Conservation and Historical Trust has established a small museum in Esperanza to display artifacts and educate the public about their work. The front area focuses primarily on Taíno artifacts recovered from the island, as well as artifacts from the era of Spanish conquest. Unfortunately, the exhibits are displayed in old, dark cases. The real reason to visit the museum is for the small **aquarium** in the back. The Trust collects animals from the waters surrounding Vieques, then displays them in tanks for a few weeks before returning them to the sea and catching new ones. The workers sometimes even let visitors hold and touch the creatures. Previous displays have included starfish, sea urchins, lobsters, and frog fish, which are camouflaged to look like sponges. *(C. Flamboyán 138, Esperanza. ☎741-8850 or 741-2844; www.vcht.com. Also has a book exchange. Open Tu-Su 11am-4pm. Free.)*

🔲 SHOPPING

Vieques does not share Culebra's wealth of yuppie boutiques, but there are a few good places to get some local art or a classy souvenir.

Diva's Closet, C. Flamboyán 134 (☎741-7595; divasclosetpr@aol.com). This new store caters to the under-30 crowd with hip clothing. Also carries bathing suits, flip-flops, and beachy jewelry. Open daily 10am-5pm. MC/V.

Vieques Flowers & Gifts...Too!, C. Flamboyán 134, Esperanza (☎741-4197). Manages to stuff a complete flower store and many locally made handicrafts into its small space. Open daily 10am-4pm. AmEx/MC/V.

Kim's Cabin, C. Flamboyán 136, Esperanza (☎741-3145) sells women's clothing, local art, and high-quality jewelry. Open daily 9:30am-5pm. MC/V.

Luna Loca Art Gallery, (☎741-0264), on C. Antonio Mellado across from El Patio, Isabel II. Has its fair share of cheesy tchotchkes and tie-dyed women's wear, but also offers some quality local artwork. The owner makes attractive Vieques magnets ($3.50). Open M-Sa 9am-5pm, Su 10am-4pm. MC/V.

NIGHTLIFE

Vieques may be a major tourist area, but its nightlife scene is laid-back, surprisingly local, and oriented toward an older crowd.

Al's Mar Azul, C. Plinio Peterson 577, (☎741-3400) in Isabel II. Some tourists and all the local characters stop by daily to shoot pool and hang out on the wooden patio overlooking the water. Don't miss the annual **Spam Cook-Off,** held in May. This one-of-a-kind celebration features competitions for best entree, appetizer, and sculpture, and at the end everyone eats the winning entries. Beer $1.50-3.25. Mixed drinks $2.50-5. Pool tables. Occasional live music. Sa karaoke 9pm-1am. 18+ after 9pm and to use pool tables. Happy hour daily 5-7pm. Open M-Th and Su 11am-1am, F-Sa 11am-2:30am. Closed Tu Mar.-Nov. MC/V.

M Bar, Rte. 200 Km 3.0 (☎741-4000; www.m-bar.com), is on the cutting edge of cool, with a minimalist, semi-outdoor lounge in which guests relax on pillow-covered couches and sip *mojitos* ($8) or a selection off the lengthy wine list. Also serves Caribbean-fusion and steakhouse cuisine, specializing in make-your-own pasta dishes ($10-15). As of press time, M Bar was located at the address above, but planned to move to C. Antonio Mellado, next to Uva, in Isabel II. Open Tu-Su 6-10pm.

Restaurante Bilí, C. Flamboyán 144 (☎741-1382), located along the popular tourist strip in Esperanza. The specialty martinis ($7) are the reason to come. Beer $2-3. Frozen drinks $5-6. Open daily 11am-11pm. AmEx/MC/V.

BEACHES

Spectacular beaches ring the island of Vieques. The southern Caribbean coast tends to be slightly more appealing than the northern Atlantic coast, but really, who's complaining? Major spots are listed below, but the best strategy is to take a map of the dirt roads and just start driving. Make sure you take a truck or an SUV, as many roads are bumpy and require four-wheel drive. On the former Navy lands, especially on the eastern half of the island, just about any dirt road will take you to your own tiny private beach, so even if you make a wrong turn (very easy to do on the unmarked roads), you should still end up somewhere special.

in 2001 over 150 people were arrested on charges of civil disobedience in relation to the naval presence. Finally, the US Navy left the western half of the island and turned the land over to the US Fish and Wildlife Service. But *viequenses* were not satisfied and protests continued. In June 2001, President George W. Bush announced that the Navy would leave the eastern third of the island as well. A huge celebration on ensued, but the problems were far from being resolved.

Although most of the former Navy land, including all the major beaches, is open for public use, some roads are still closed off due to the possibility that unexploded ordnance (UXO) is still buried there. The slogan, *"Paz Para Vieques"* (Peace for Vieques) is still visible on yard signs and bumper stickers. Among the populace, there is a bitter divide over what should be done with the former Navy lands. Some want US government agencies to leave and turn over the land to the Puerto Rican government for preservation. Others argue that if the commonwealth government owns the land, it will not be as well-preserved as if the federal government were in control. Still others believe that the land should be privatized for commercial development. The controversy surrounding the US government's presence on Vieques is largely a reflection of the eternal Puerto Rican question: how should this "Free Associated State" relate to the larger US?

BALNEARIO SUN BAY. At Vieques's only public beach, medium-sized waves of crystal clear water hit an enormous crescent of white sand lined with palm trees. And on weekday mornings, you can have this sumptuous stretch of sand to yourself, although it is Vieques's most popular beach. Snorkelers may want to head to Navío, as the water is clearer there. Like most public *balnearios*, Sun Bay contains picnic tables, fire pits, a huge parking area, a drinking fountain, trash cans, lifeguards during daylight hours, bathrooms, and a camping area. (*On Rte. 997, ¼ mi. east of Esperanza. ☎ 741-8198. Parking $2; minivans $3. Fee covers Balneario Sun Bay, Playa Media Luna, and Playa Navío. Open Tu-Su 8:30am-5pm; the gates are always open, but during these hours you have to pay to park and lifeguards patrol the beach.*)

PLAYA MEDIA LUNA. Located directly east of Sun Bay, Half Moon Beach is part of the *balneario* complex, but it is physically separated and feels worlds away. This quiet bay has soft waves and perfectly turquoise water that stays shallow a long way out, making it a popular place for kids to play. The only facilities are trash cans and a couple of covered picnic tables. (*Enter the Sun Bay complex, then drive east on the dirt road for about ½ mi. 4WD required.*)

■ **PLAYA NAVÍO.** The third member of the Sun Bay *balneario* complex, Navío feels a bit more isolated than its western neighbors. This small bay is less protected by cliffs and thus waves pound directly against the shore, creating large waves great for boogie boarders but dangerous for small children. Due to the its rough access roads, Navío is usually nearly deserted and feels like a private beach. This is the Sun Bay complex's best **snorkeling site,** due to the depth and clarity of the water. (*Continue ½ mi. past Playa Media Luna on the bumpy dirt road. 4WD required.*)

■ **GREEN BEACH.** Green Beach actually consists of a series of small, disconnected sandy areas running south from Punta Arenas. The gentle waves lap against the palm-lined beach, making for enjoyable swimming and picturesque sunsets. Mainland Puerto Rico is visible in the distance. Green Beach is also known for some of the **best snorkeling** on Vieques, in the shallow-water reef at the south end of the beach. And the trek to get out to the beach, through jungly forest, is half the fun. (*Take Rte. 200 west into the old Navy base, then continue onto the dirt road. Veer right at the fork, and cross 2 bridges. The road forms a T at the end—go left for snorkeling and right for Punta Arenas. Facilities include trash cans and 1 covered picnic table. 4WD required.*)

■ **RED, BLUE, AND GARCÍA BEACHES.** These three popular, incredibly beautiful beaches can be accessed on the former Navy lands. Red Beach has the island's second-best **snorkeling,** which can be found by swimming out to the small island about 100 yd. offshore, on the right-hand side of the beach. All three offer perfect white sands and bright blue waters, although Blue Beach is by far the largest. Some have covered picnic tables. (*Take Rte. 997 to the Camp García gate, then follow the dirt road east. 4WD required for Blue and García Beaches, strongly recommended for Red Beach.*)

GRINGO BEACH. Located between the airport and the Wyndham Martineau Bay resort, this aptly-named, narrow stretch of sand provides a place to rest in the sun if you don't mind the sound of traffic and the stares of passersby. Although it is nowhere near being the best beach on the island, the reason to visit is its accessibility—it is one of the few that can be reach via a paved road. (*Rte. 200 Km 3.8. Park on the side of the road.*)

PLAYA GRANDE. For a bit more privacy, head to Playa Grande. This long, narrow beach has coarse sand and no facilities but it is almost always deserted. This is the place to sit on a rock, watch the tide roll in, and let your mind drift. The water has big waves and gets deep quickly, so this is not the best place for swimming. *(Drive west on Rte. 996 past Esperanza to Rte. 201, continue to the end of the road and turn left. Park in the circle of pavement.)*

🚩 OUTDOOR ACTIVITIES

BIOLUMINESCENT BAY
Nowhere on Puerto Rico does the water shine like it does in Bahía Mosquito. This large bay on the south coast of Vieques is the most impressive example of dinoflagellitic bioluminescence anywhere in the world. When you jump in the bay, it looks like you are on fire; when you float, it looks as though you have thousands of glowing sprinkles all over your body. Local organizations and the Department of Fish and Wildlife are working to preserve the bay's magic by reducing artificial light pollution and educating locals about the bay's value, but Mosquito Bay continues to be threatened. Barracuda Bay, the next inlet to the east, is also bioluminescent, but most tours don't head out that far. **Island Adventures** (below) and several kayak operations (see **Boating**, below) offer bio bay tours, but individuals can also just drive east on the rough Sun Bay road and jump in the water. While cheap, this option means that you miss the guided tour and the opportunity to take a boat across the bay. Only choose this option if you have four-wheel drive, and drive cautiously over the bumpy dirt road in the dark.

- 🏞 **Blue Caribe Kayaks** (☎ 741-2522), on C. Flamboyán in Esperanza. Offers 2hr. kayak tours of the bioluminescent bay with a chance to swim ($30) and 2½hr. kayaking/snorkeling trips around Cayo Afuera ($30). Single kayak rental $10 per hr., doubles $15. Open daily 9am-5pm. MC/V.

- **Island Adventures,** Rte. 996 Km 4.5 (☎ 741-0720; www.biobay.com). Run by the Bio Bay Conservation Group, Island Adventures leads 1½hr. tours through the bio bay. First, groups listen to an informative talk, then they take a bus to the bay for the electric boat tour and swimming. Call ahead for reservations. Trips almost every night, except during a full moon. $23, under 12 $12. MC/V.

- **Aqua Frenzy Kayaks** (☎ 741-0913) rents double kayaks ($15 for the 1st hr., $10 per hr. thereafter, or $405 per day). Allows renters to take the kayaks overnight, and provides information about kayaking in the bio bay. Also offers bio bay tours ($25-35 per person), snorkeling tours ($50 per person), and 3hr. tours of Vieques ($45 per person). Kayak drop-off available.

THE BIG SPLURGE

FEET ON FIRE

At 7pm, you begin paddling out into the bay in your kayak. Nothing unusual happens. You wonder: isn't this a bioluminescent bay? Why isn't it glowing? You follow your group leader out to the middle of the bay. He asks who would like to go first. A bit unsure, you volunteer. When you jump in the water, your entire body lights up. The people still in their kayaks look on in amazement. All you can think is, *This is so weird.* As you swim through the water, you realize that every stroke you take, every time you move your hands or feet, it looks as if they are leaving a trail of glowing fire through the water. When you stay relatively still, it looks as if someone has poured thousands of tiny glowing sprinkles on your body. You can see glowing streaks caused by fish swimming below you and a ray, the predator of the bay, flapping its ghostly fluorescent-yellow wings. The bioluminescence is caused by tiny dinoflagellates in the water. They are supported by the mangrove trees surrounding the bay, which deposit large quantities of vitamin B-12, a major dinoflagellate nutrient. When the dinoflagellates sense a predator (or in this case, a human body) in the water, they light up to warn their companions of the danger.

*Several companies operate bioluminescent bay tours in Vieques. The best of the bunch is **Blue Caribe Kayak,** which charges $30 for a 2hr. trip.*

BOATING
Marauder Sailing Charters, C. Flamboyán 136 (☎435-4858), is run by the owners of Kim's Cabin. Their specialty is a full-day sail on their 34 ft. yacht, with swimming, snorkeling, lunch, and open bar included ($95 per person).

DIVING AND SNORKELING
Like Culebra and Fajardo, the area around Vieques is flush with good, relatively shallow diving opportunities. However, the island does not have a scuba shop, so you can only dive here with a charter from the mainland. Vieques also has some great snorkeling, but the best areas are accessible only by boat. The best place to snorkel from land is **Green Beach** (p. 186), followed closely by **Red Beach's Mosquito Pier** (p. 186). At Red Beach, good snorkeling can be found under the pier and the four pylons just off the side. In **Esperanza,** the small dock in front of Playa Esperanza attracts a few fish. **Cayo Afuera,** the island in front of the strip, has good reefs, but it's quite a swim.

HORSEBACK RIDES
Penny Miller at **El Seagate** (p. 178) leads horseback rides through the mountains, the beach, and Isabel II. (☎741-4661 or 667-2805. Reservations requested. 2hr. ride $50 per person, group rates available. MC/V.)

▓ FESTIVALS

The island of Vieques celebrates two annual festivals. The weekend after Easter, the Institute of Puerto Rican Culture hosts a **cultural festival** at the Fort with local artwork and music. (Call ☎741-1717 for more info.) Vieques's **festivales patronales** are celebrated during the third weekend in July in the Sun Bay area. Contact the tourist office (☎741-0800) for exact dates.

CULEBRA

If you came to Puerto Rico in search of a picture-perfect beach, look no further than Culebra. The island easily has the most beautiful beaches in Puerto Rico and, due to its crystalline water, is also home to several superb snorkeling spots. What makes this prime tourist destination unique is the small-town charm it has retained. With just over 2000 inhabitants, this is an island where neighbors stop to chat with each other and the ferry arrival is the big event of the day. Because nearly everyone is employed in the tourist industry, Culebrans are friendly to travelers: from helping change a flat tire to reminding you to wear sunscreen, they go out of their way to make sure you enjoy their island. Tiny Culebra has few cultural attractions, and the dry vegetation is more like that of the Virgin Islands than tropical eastern Puerto Rico, but the beaches alone are reason enough to visit.

Culebra has not always been such a haven of tranquility. In 1901, two years after winning the Spanish-American war, the US government established military bases on Culebra, forcing residents to resettle in the area now known as Dewey. In 1975, after years of using the island as a bombing range, the military moved all exercises to Vieques, but Americans continued to flock to Culebra. The island now houses a significant expat population, composed of Americans who came on vacation and never left. During holidays such as Christmas and *Semana Santa* the island's population can increase by as much as 15,000, as Puerto Ricans head east on their own vacations. In recent years, some locals have complained that a younger generation more interested in rowdy beach antics than peace and quiet has discovered Culebra. But for the majority of the year—and anywhere outside of the road between the ferry landing and Playa Flamenco—Culebra continues at the slow pace to which it is accustomed, where nobody has anything to do but go to the beach.

HIGHLIGHTS OF CULEBRA

ESCAPE THE CROWDS with an adventurous hike down to the wild waves at isolated **Playa Resaca** (p. 199).

JOIN THE CROWDS at stunning **Playa Flamenco** (p. 197).

DIVE IN at one of Puerto Rico's best snorkeling sites, **Playa Carlos Rosario** (p. 198).

TAKE A RIDE to the cays of **Isla Peña** or **Culebrita**, with their pristine beaches and prime snorkeling (p. 198).

✈ INTER-ISLAND TRANSPORTATION

Flights: Aeropuerto Benjamín Rivera Noriega (☎ 742-0022), 21 mi. north of town at the intersection of Rte. 250 and Rte. 251. A 15min. walk or a $2 taxi ride. All of the airlines flying out of Culebra use tiny 6- to 8-seat planes and leave on demand. For reservations call or stop by the airport at least 1-2 days in advance. During major holidays reserve a few weeks in advance. Airport open daily 6am-6pm.

Air Flamenco (☎ 742-1040, reservations 724-6464) flies to **Fajardo** (15min.; 4 per day; $25, round-trip $44) and **San Juan Isla Grande** (30min.; 2 per day; $48, round-trip $92). Open M-F 8am-5pm. MC/V.

Isla Nena (☎ 863-4447) flies to **Fajardo** (15min.; 1-2 per day; $30, round-trip $60) and **San Juan International** (30min.; 4 per day; $70, round-trip $130). Open daily 6am-6pm. MC/V.

Vieques Air Link (☎742-0254, reservations 1-888-901-9247) flies to **Fajardo** (15min.; 3 per day; $26, round-trip $50) and **San Juan Isla Grande** (30min.; 2 per day; $51, round-trip $92). Open M-F 7:30am-4:45pm. AmEx/MC/V.

Ferries: The **Puerto Rican Port Authority** (☎742-3161) runs ferries between Culebra and Fajardo. In addition to the routes below, a passenger ferry goes between Culebra and Vieques (W only; leaves Vieques 7:30am and 2:30pm, returns from Culebra 9am and 3:30pm; round-trip $4). There is an additional charge for beach equipment, including tents ($2) and sleeping bags ($1). Reservations required for cars, but not accepted for passengers. Car reservations should be made several months in advance to secure one of the few spots. Passengers should arrive 1hr. in advance. Reservation office open daily 8-11am and 1-3pm. MC/V.

FERRIES	FAJARDO-CULEBRA	CULEBRA-FAJARDO	PRICE
PASSENGER	M-F 9:30am, 3pm Sa-Su 9am, 2:30, 6:30pm	M-F 6:30, 11:30am Sa-Su 6:30, 11am, 4:30pm	$2.25
CARGO	M-F 3:30am, 4pm W and F 10am	M-F 7am, 6pm W and F 1pm	$15; round-trip $26.50

◼ ORIENTATION

Culebra lies 17 mi. east of Puerto Rico and 12 mi. west of St. Thomas. Measuring 7 mi. in length and 3½ mi. in width, the island is tiny, and seems even smaller because almost all attractions are concentrated on the eastern side. The ferry arrives at the only town, **Dewey,** which is located on the southwest corner. From Dewey **Route 251** heads north past the airport to Playa Flamenco. **Route 250** goes east, past Fish and Wildlife and the turn-offs for Playa Resaca and Brava, before finally ending up at Playa Zoni. The only other real road, **Calle Fulladoza,** heads south from town along Ensenada Honda to Punta Soldado. When people refer to

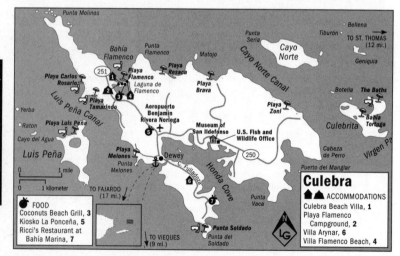

Dewey's "main road" or "calle principal", they are usually talking about **Calle Pedro Márquez,** which originates at the ferry terminal and continues through town. **Calle Escudero** connects the airport with Dewey and is home to several accommodations and food establishments.

▣ LOCAL TRANSPORTATION

Culebra's diminutive size makes it very easy to get around. Travelers staying in Dewey or Playa Flamenco can get by using only public transportation, but will be relatively stranded after dark. Those who want to explore the island and get to any beach other than Flamenco or Carlos Rosario should rent a Jeep. Don't bring a rental car to Culebra; just rent a new one when you arrive. In theory biking seems like a good option, but the combination of hilly roads and hot afternoon sun can tire even the most athletic travelers.

> **! CAR TROUBLE.** Culebra police are extraordinarily vigilant about parking violations. Do not park in front of a fire hydrant, along a yellow curb, in a handicapped area, in a public vehicle spot, or along any curve in the road. Also, many streets are one-way or only allow parking on one side of the street, but are not marked as such. As a rule, do not do anything unless other cars are doing it.

Públicos: Carros públicos, or shared taxi vans, run from the ferry terminal past the airport to **Playa Flamenco,** stopping at **Culebra Beach Villa.** Any trip between these points should cost $2-3. For an additional fee, vans will go almost anywhere on the island. During the day it is easy to hail down a *público* along Rte. 251; at night, or from a different location, try one of these: **Kiko's Transportation Services** (☎514-0453), **Willy's Taxi** (☎742-3537), **Rubén Taxi** (☎405-1209), **José** (☎363-2183), **Samuel** (☎504-6678), **Iván** (☎405-8447), **Luis** (☎223-3428), or **Adriano** (☎590-1575).

Car Rental: Several companies rent Jeeps and other off-road vehicles, but during major holidays you should reserve at least a month in advance. Most companies require drivers to be at least 25, but some do not rigidly enforce this requirement. The age and condition of vehicles varies greatly and the condition of the car should be reflected in the rental price. Almost all companies offer airport/ferry pick-up service and weekly discounts.

LIKE A BIRD

You could take the ferry from Fajardo to Vieques or Culebra for a measely $2. But shelling out for a 10min. plane ride between island and mainland is well worth the $20 splurge. Instead of spending an hour rocking back and forth on a boat, you can fly over the most beautiful part of the Caribbean, looking down on the dozens of tiny cays and perfect turquoise water. Planes fly low enough that you can clearly see the landscape below, down to the individual trees on tiny islands.

The ride is spectacular from any seat, but the secret to the best flight is to request the copilot's seat. The companies that run these 6- to 10-passenger planes sometimes allow one person to sit right up front next to the pilot. This vantage point opens up a 270-degree view for lucky passengers, who are encouraged to take pictures as they fly—not to mention the thrill that comes from sitting in the front seat of a plane.

Flights head out to the offshore islands on **Vieques Air Link** (☎888-901-9247) and **Isla Nena** (☎877-812-5144). One-way tickets run $20-30 and should be reserved ahead of time, although single passengers can often find last-minute spots, even during holiday weekends. Keep in mind that since the planes are quite small, passengers are routinely asked to state their weight upon boarding and are limited to 25 lb. of luggage. Enjoy the ride!

Carlos Jeep Rental (☎742-3514 or 613-7049), on Rte. 250 at Vacation Property Realty. One of Culebra's more professional operations. $50-65 per day. Also rents car seats ($3 per day). $5 per day discount for weekly rentals. 25+. Open daily 8am-5pm. AmEx/MC/V.

Jerry's Jeep Rental (☎742-0587), on Rte. 251 across from the airport. When you pick up the Jeep Jerry spends 30min. explaining a map of Culebra. $45-60 per day. $5 per day discount with weekly rental. 25+. Open daily 8:30am-5pm, but can make arrangements for later arrivals. AmEx/MC/V.

Dick and Cathie Rentals (☎742-0062) rents VW Things. Standard transmission only. No pick-up service. $45 per day. 21+. No office; call ahead. No credit cards.

Willy's Jeep Rental (☎742-3537), on Rte. 250. $40-45 per day. 25+. Open daily 8am-5pm. AmEx/MC/V.

Bike Rental: Culebra Bike Shop (☎742-2209), on C. Fulladoza, rents 24-speed mountain bikes ($20 per 24hr., $100 per week), boogie boards ($8 per day), and snorkel equipment ($12 per 24hr.). Open daily 9am-5pm. MC/V. **Dick and Cathie Rentals** (☎742-0062) delivers bikes ($15 per day). No credit cards. Reservations recommended.

Scooter Rental: JM Rentals (☎742-0521; www.scooterspr.com), on Rte. 251 across from the airport, in the same office as Thrifty Car Rental. 150 cc scooters for $45-50 per day, including 2 helmets. Open M-Sa 8:30am-6pm, Su 9am-5pm. AmEx/D/MC/V.

⁊ PRACTICAL INFORMATION

Tourist Office: The **municipal tourist office** is a small desk on the semi-outdoor patio of the big building that you see immediately when you get off the ferry. Has standard Puerto Rico tourism booklets. Open M-F 8am-4:30pm, but frequently unattended. Culebra also has several very good tourism websites. Check out www.culebra-island.com, www.islaculebra.com, and www.culebra.org.

Bank: Banco Popular (☎742-3572), across from the ferry terminal at the corner of C. Pedro Márquez, is the only bank on the island. ATM. Open M-F 8:30am-3:30pm.

Publications: The Culebra Calendar (www.theculebracalendar.com), an invaluable monthly island publication, lists local events, advertisements, a tide table, a ferry schedule, classified ads, letters to the editors, and articles on current Culebra issues. It's a bit difficult to find; Cafe Isola usually has a copy.

Supermarkets:

Superette Mayra, C. Escudero 118 (☎742-3888), is Culebra's largest grocery store. Good selection of over-the-counter pharmaceuticals. Open M-Sa 9am-6:30pm. MC/V.

Colmado Milka (☎742-2253), across the bridge and to the right, is Culebra's 2nd-largest grocery store. Has a small butcher shop and some fresh fruits and veggies. Open M-Sa 7am-7pm, Su 7am-1pm. MC/V.

Isla del Sol Minimarket (☎742-0886), on a side street off Rte. 251. Turn left immediately after Jerry's Jeep Rental and follow the signs. A small selection of groceries and fresh hot bread. Open daily 6am-7pm. MC/V.

Laundry: There are no laundromats on Culebra, but **Dick and Cathie Rentals** (☎742-0062) provides wash, dry, and fold service ($1.25 per lb.). Call ahead. Cash only.

Police: ☎742-3501. On C. Fulladoza, about ¼ mi. past Dinghy Dock. Open 24hr.

Pharmacy: Culebra has no real pharmacies. The **hospital** (below) has a pharmacy with prescription drugs only. **Superette Mayra** (see **Supermarkets,** above) has a decent selection of over-the-counter remedies such as Dramamine for the ferry ride. Bring your own tampons, contact lens supplies, condoms, and any other hard-to-find supplies.

Medical Services: Hospital de Culebra (☎742-3511 or 742-0001, ambulance service 742-0208) at the end of C. William Font, in the building marked "recetas" (prescriptions) at the top of the hill. Small health clinic. Emergency room 24hr. Clinic open M-F 7am-4:30pm.

Internet Access: eXcétera, (☎ 742-0844; fax 742-0826), on C. Escudero between Culebra Gift Shop and the corner with C. Pedro Márquez, offers Internet ($5 per 15min., $15 per hr.), **fax service,** a long-distance telephone station, Western Union, and a 24hr. ATM. Open M-F 9am-5pm, Sa 9am-1pm; closed Sa in summer. MC/V.

Post Office: C. Pedro Márquez 26 (☎ 742-3862). General Delivery available. Open M-F 8am-4:30pm, Sa 8am-noon. **Postal Code:** 00775.

ACCOMMODATIONS AND CAMPING

Culebra may play host to a plethora of visitors, but most of the accommodations are either lackluster or severely overpriced. An attractive room here will cost at least $90 per night, and summer offers little relief from high prices, as the island is then populated with Puerto Rican vacationers. Most accommodations offer discounts for stays over a week or during low season (Aug.-Oct.).

REALTORS

The following realtors rent properties around the island equipped with linens, towels, and a kitchen. Check out the houses online, then call for rates and availability.

Vacation Planners, (☎ 742-3112, toll-free 866-285-3272; fax 742-1060; www.allvacationreservations.com), across from the ferry under Hotel Kokomo. Most properties have A/C, some have TVs. Free pick-up. Check-in 3pm. Check-out 11am. $400-500 per night. 15% weekly discount. Open M-Sa 9am-noon and 2-5pm, Su 3-5pm. MC/V.

Culebra Island Realty (☎ 742-0052; www.culebraislandrealty.com), at the intersection of C. Romero and Escudero. Rents a wide range of homes and assists in car rental. Free pick-up. 1-week min. 50% deposit required. 2- to 6-person homes $800-2600 per week. Hours are sporadic; call ahead. Checks only.

DEWEY

Villa Fulladoza (☎ 742-3576 or 742-3828), on C. Fulladoza. A combination of low prices and large rooms makes this waterside guesthouse a good deal. Sparkling, brightly colored rooms come with a kitchen, fan, balcony, and ocean view. Room price varies by size. Spacious common patio filled with mango trees. Private dock. Book exchange. Check-in 2:30pm. Check-out 10am. $10 surcharge for 1-night stay. Doubles $65-80; weekly $420-525; extra child (in larger rooms only) $10. MC/V. ❸

Mamacita's, C. Castelar 64-66 (☎ 742-0090; fax 742-0301; www.mamacitaspr.com). Feels like a fun European hostel painted in Caribbean colors. A popular place to be at all hours of the day. All rooms come with microwave, fridge, A/C, satellite TV, and DVD players. Check-in 2pm. Check-out 11am. Doubles $85-95; 2-person suites with kitchen $125; extra person $15. MC/V. ❸

Casa Ensenada Guest House, C. Escudero 142 (☎ 742-3559; www.casaensenada.com). 3 hand-decorated rooms in the owners' home. All rooms come with 13 in. satellite TV, VCR, A/C, microwave, fridge, full utensils, and a guest info packet. Library. Common waterfront patio with picnic table and grill. Free use of kayak; $50 discount on 1st-day motorboat rentals. Check-out 10am. $20 surcharge for 1 night stay. Doubles Nov. 25-Apr. 30 $115-170; May 1-Sept. 4 $95-140; Sept. 5-Nov. 24 $75-110; extra person $20. 7th night free. MC/V. ❸

Casita Linda (☎ 742-0360 or 403-5292; www.culebra-sanjuan.com), the brightly colored house on the right after you cross the bridge. This small 3-room guesthouse was clearly a labor of love. The friendly owners have hand-decorated every room with flowers, and unique furniture. All rooms have a full kitchen, a balcony or patio with canal views, a TV, and a VCR with videos. Some rooms have fold-out futons for beds. No office and the owners can be hard to reach; call ahead. Quad $100; 6-person suite $150; 8-person house $250. Tax included. MC/V. ❹

Palmetto Guest House, C. Manuel Vásquez 128 (☎742-0257), in a residential neighborhood north of town. 4 simple rooms come with a fridge. Common kitchen, living room, TV, VCR, and movie collection. 10min. walk from town. Call ahead; the friendly owner is rarely home. Free pick-up and drop-off. $20 surcharge for 1-night stay. Doubles $65, with semi-private kitchen $85. MC/V. ❸

Villa Boheme, C. Fulladoza 368 (☎742-3508 or 370-4949; www.villaboheme.com), has great grounds; a large wall surrounds several buildings and a common patio area with several hammocks, right on the bay. The rooms themselves are very colorful, with a fun aquatic theme. Fully equipped communal kitchen with DirecTV. Also offers kayak rentals ($8 per hr.). Check-in noon. Check-out 10:30am. 2-night min. on weekends; 3-night min. on holiday weekends. Doubles $104-137; quads $141-148; 6-person rooms $148. Tax included. AmEx/MC/V. ❹

Hotel Kokomo (☎742-3112 or 866-285-3272; www.allvacationreservations.com), across from the ferry dock. The great location and clean rooms with A/C make this hotel a good value. Top-floor suites are huge and have great ocean views. Office is in Vacation Planners (p. 193). Check-out 11am. Doubles $40, with bath $60; triples $80; 4-to 6-person apartments with kitchen $125-150. MC/V. ❷

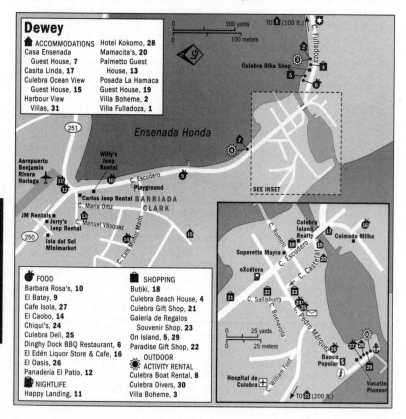

Dewey

▲ ACCOMMODATIONS
Casa Ensenada
  Guest House, **7**
Casita Linda, **17**
Culebra Ocean View
  Guest House, **15**
Harbour View
  Villas, **31**
Hotel Kokomo, **28**
Mamacita's, **20**
Palmetto Guest
  House, **13**
Posada La Hamaca
  Guest House, **19**
Villa Boheme, **2**
Villa Fulladoza, **1**

Ensenada Honda

251

Aeropuerto
Benjamín
Rivera
Noriega

Willy's Jeep Rental

C. Escudero
Playground

Carlos Jeep Rental BARRIADA
C. Maria Ortiz   CLARK

JM Rentals
Jerry's   C. Manuel Vásquez
Jeep Rental

250 Isla del Sol
     Minimarket

Culebra Bike Shop

SEE INSET

C. Romero
Culebra
Island
Realty
C. Escudero
Superette Mayra
eXcétera

Colmado Milka

C. Sallisbury

C. Buenavista

C. Castelar

Hospital de
Culebra

C. William Font

C. Pedro Márquez

Banco
Popular

Vacation
Planner

TO **31** (200 ft.)

🍴 FOOD
Barbara Rosa's, **10**
El Batey, **9**
Cafe Isola, **27**
El Caobo, **14**
Chiqui's, **24**
Culebra Deli, **25**
Dinghy Dock BBQ Restaurant, **16**
El Edén Liquor Store & Cafe, **16**
El Oasis, **26**
Panadería El Patio, **12**

🍸 NIGHTLIFE
Happy Landing, **11**

🛍 SHOPPING
Butiki, **18**
Culebra Beach House, **4**
Culebra Gift Shop, **21**
Galería de Regalos
  Souvenir Shop, **23**
On Island, **5, 29**
Paradise Gift Shop, **22**

☀ OUTDOOR
ACTIVITY RENTAL
Culebra Boat Rental, **8**
Culebra Divers, **30**
Villa Boheme, **3**

Posada La Hamaca Guest House, C. Castelar 68 (☎742-3516 or 435-0028; fax 742-0181; www.posada.com). Small hotel-style rooms are acceptable but a bit dreary, and Mamacita's next door is a lot more fun. A/C and ceiling fans. Book exchange. Snorkel gear $10 for 24hr. Free use of beach towels. Check-in 2pm. Check-out 10am. $10 surcharge for 1-night stay. Doubles $80-98; quads $129; 8-person room $173; extra person $11. Tax included. MC/V. ❸

Harbour View Villas (☎742-3855 or 742-3171; www.culebrahotel.com), 1½ mi. west of town en route to Playa Melones. Look for the "Bienvenidos" sign and the 3 A-frame houses on the hill. Ambiance that blurs the line between classy and rustic. Quiet location with great views, but far from beaches and town. 1- and 2-bedroom suites have A/C in the bedroom and some sort of kitchen and hot water. Villas are houses with kitchens, but they lack A/C. No office. Free pick-up and drop-off. Suites: doubles in winter $125, in summer $100; quads $175/150. Villas: doubles $175/125; quads $225/175; extra person $25/20. Cash only. ❹

Culebra Ocean View Guest House, C. María Ortíz 201 (☎360-9807 or 309-4301; www.culebraoceanview.com), high in the hills above Dewey. Radiant rooms are well-kept and have new furnishings. Popular with Puerto Rican tourists. Common balcony. Fridge, A/C, TV. Check-in 1pm. Check-out 11am. Doubles $74-94; quads $104-124; extra person $15. MC/V. ❸

NORTH OF DEWEY

▨ **Culebra Beach Villa** (☎742-0517, reservations 754-6236; fax 742-0319; www.culebrabeachrental.com), on the dirt road off Rte. 251 just before Playa Flamenco. This is the largest hotel on the beautiful sands of Playa Flamenco. Enough said. A 3-story wooden hotel faces the beach, and several boldly painted bungalows hide in back. This is the place to be at Playa Flamenco, with a popular bar out front and barbecues in the back. All rooms are clean and include A/C, TV, and a full kitchen. Book exchange. Reception 10am-1pm and 2-7pm. Check-in 3pm. Check-out 11am. Doubles $136; quads $180; 6-person apartment $250; 8-person $300. Tax included. MC/V. ❺

Villa Flamenco Beach (☎742-0023; www.culebra-island.com). Villa Flamenco Beach also boasts direct access to Playa Flamenco. With only 6 rooms, Flamenco feels much more personal than its neighbor. Neat and functional rooms. Airy front studios have big windows, balconies, and an ocean view. All rooms have kitchenettes; only doubles have A/C. Doubles $110-125; 4-person apartments $130. MC/V. ❹

Playa Flamenco Campground (☎742-7000), at Playa Flamenco. Located just 20 ft. from the beach, this campground is easily the best in Puerto Rico. Unfortunately, it's also the most crowded; during high season (Apr.-Sept.) hundreds of people squeeze into the big field. It can get rowdy and liquor-oriented in Area C, but Areas D and E tend to be quieter and more suitable for families. Toilets, outdoor showers, potable water, a bike rack, trash cans, and picnic tables. Reservations recommended during high season. Check-out 4pm. Office open 6am-7pm. $20 per tent; up to 6 people. Cash only. ❶

SOUTH OF DEWEY

Quiet C. Fulladoza receives little traffic and the accommodations on the hill offer tranquility and beautiful bay views. Unfortunately, there are no sandy beaches and it's quite a walk to town; if you're staying here, it's a good idea to splurge on a car.

Villa Arynar (☎742-3145; www.arynar.com), on C. Fulladoza. The American couple running Culebra's only B&B welcomes guests as part of the family. Everyone sits down to breakfast together. Complimentary use of snorkel gear, beach towels and chairs, umbrellas, and coolers. Shared bathroom. 1 rental car ($40 per day). Free pick-up. Private pier. Adults only. 5-night min. Open Nov.15-May 15. Doubles $100. MC/V. ❹

♦ FOOD

Food in Culebra tends to be expensive. Luckily many accommodations offer kitchen facilities; it's more affordable to cook at home (see **Supermarkets,** p. 192).

DEWEY

Cafe Isola (☎742-0203), across from the ferry dock, under Hotel Kokomo. This trendy cafe seems to represent the changing times in Culebra. Lanterns hanging from the ceiling bathe this hip coffee-and-sandwich shop in soft colored light. Delicious food is both reasonably priced and relatively healthy. Pitas $5. Salads, sandwiches, and hamburgers $4-10. Coffee $0.50-3. Beer $1.50-6. Open M, W, F 11am-8pm (tapas served after 5:30pm), Tu and Th 11am-3pm. MC/V. ❶

El Oasis (☎742-3175; eloasispr@aol.com), on C. Pedro Márquez. It's difficult to walk past El Oasis at night; if the smell doesn't draw you in, the raucous crowd certainly will. This is the best pizzeria on Culebra and the bartenders welcome everyone like an old friend. Indulge on pizza or sample one of the salads with homemade dressing such as guava vinaigrette. Homemade desserts, including piña colada cheesecake ($2.75). Limited pasta entrees $7-10. Medium pizza $10-19; by the slice $1.50, toppings $0.25 each. Open M and Th-Su 6-10pm; may stay open later F-Sa. Cash only. ❷

Barbara Rosa's, C. Escudero 189 (☎397-1923). Chef Barbara Rosa used to work at Club Seabourne, then decided to open her own restaurant with the perfect budget dining formula: a relaxed vibe, counter service (no tip), and BYOB. The result is a group of picnic tables around a trailer serving simple but delicious entrees, most of which are Puerto Rican takes on international cuisine. Gets buggy at night. Lunch sandwiches $4-6; lunch entrees $6-12. Dinner $6-19. Open Tu-Sa 11:30am-9pm. Cash only. ❸

El Edén Liquor Store and Cafe (☎742-0509). Turn left on the road just past Colmado Milka and follow the signs. Surprisingly hip, given its name and location. Construct your own sandwich ($6.50) by choosing among various meats, breads, cheeses, and toppings. All sandwiches are on fresh homemade bread, and desserts are also homemade ($3.50). Also a deli and liquor store. Open M-Sa 9am-6pm, Su 9am-2pm. MC/V. ❶

Dinghy Dock BBQ Restaurant (☎742-0233), on C. Fulladoza. Dinghies actually dock beside your table as you enjoy tasty Puerto Rican, American, and Mexican food at this relaxed and colorful expat favorite. Big breakfasts $5-10. Puerto Rican lunch special $7. Sandwiches, grill foods, and Mexican entrees $5-14. Open daily 8am-5pm and 6:30-9pm. Bar open noon-11pm. MC/V. ❸

Chiqui's, on C. Pedro Márquez near the post office. One of the few places in town with fresh ice cream. 1-topping sundaes are ludicrously cheap ($1.25). Also serves piraguas (flavored shaved ice; $1) and packaged snacks. Open daily approx. 11am-10pm. ❶

Mamacita's, C. Castelar 64-66 (☎742-0090). This popular establishment serves typical beach entrees for lunch ($6.50-8.50), but is better known for its relatively upscale dinners, which include local seafood, steaks, and 1 veggie option ($12-22). Open daily 8am-2:30pm and 6-9pm. MC/V. ❸

El Batey, Rte. 250 Km 1.1 (☎742-3828), ½ mi. north of town, looks like a local joint but serves mostly foreigners. Choose between a fun, aquatically-decorated interior and a patio with harbor view. Appetizers $5-5.50. Meaty sandwiches $5.50-7.50. Burgers $6-6.50. Dinner $8-15. Open W-Su noon-6pm. Bar open until 2am. Cash only. ❸

Ricci's Restaurant at Bahía Marina (☎742-0535). Drive south on C. Fulladoza; near the end, turn left up the steep hill. This new restaurant is one of the nicer places on the island, but has a surprisingly relaxed atmosphere. Incredible views of the entire island. Seafood $17-40. Steak, pork, and chicken entrees $14-19. Open tentatively W-Su 6-10pm, with possible plans to begin serving lunch. ❹

Panadería El Patio (☎742-0374), at the end of the airport runway. A typical Puerto Rican sandwich shop. The restaurant has an outdoor seating area, but the sandwiches ($2.75-3.75) taste even better as a beach picnic. Serves sandwiches until 11:30am, then serves as a small convenience store. Open daily 5:30am-7pm. Cash only. ❶

El Caobo (☎742-0505), on C. Luis Muñoz Marín. The linoleum floor, plastic tablecloths, handwritten menu, and abundant fans create a rustic charm. Big plates of genuine Puerto Rican food; however, more expensive than you might expect from the atmosphere. Entrees $8-20. Open M-Th 11am-6pm, F-Sa 11am-8pm. Cash only. ❸

Culebra Deli, C. Pedro Márquez 26 (☎742-3277). This hole-in-the-wall *cafetería* dishes out fast, cheap Puerto Rican food, such as fried chicken drumsticks ($1) and *empanadillas* ($1). Open M-Sa 5:30am-2pm. Cash only. ❶

OUTSIDE OF TOWN

Coconuts Beach Grill, in front of Culebra Beach Villa (p. 195), is nothing more than an outdoor bar and grill, but it's the only sit-down eatery near the beach. Tasty beach entrees like burgers ($6-7) and meat and seafood platters ($12-20). Also has a wide variety of frozen mixed drinks ($4.50). Open W-Su noon-8pm. Cash only. ❸

Kiosko La Ponceña, Rte. 251 Km 5.5 (☎608-7964). This little roadside kiosk makes an excellent stop between town and Playa Flamenco. The menu changes daily, but always includes typical Puerto Rican rice, beans, meat, and fish ($6-8). Homemade desserts $1.50. Delivers to Dewey or Playa Flamenco. Open M-Sa 11am-10pm. Cash only. ❷

◪ BEACHES

The water around the island is a translucent aqua that looks unmistakably Caribbean and invites swimmers to float beneath the sun for hours. While popular Playa Flamenco is amazing, it is worthwhile to venture out to other, less populated beaches, especially if you have a car. Regardless of where you travel, don't search for palm tree-lined beaches. Culebra has a very dry landscape and there are only a few scattered palms; shade-lovers should grab a spot early.

BEACHES	ACCESSIBILITY FROM DEWEY	CROWDS	ACTIVITIES	FACILITIES
Flamenco	8min. drive	Large	Swimming, snorkeling, boogie boarding	Bathrooms, picnic tables, trash cans, outdoor showers, grills, lifeguards
Carlos Rosario	25min. walk from Flamenco	Medium	Swimming, snorkeling	None
Culebrita	25min. boat ride	Small-Med.	Snorkeling, swimming, turtle-watching	None
Luis Peña	15min. boat ride	Small-Med.	Snorkeling, swimming	None
Zoni	15min. drive	Small-Med.	Swimming, boogie boarding	None
Brava	15min. drive plus 20min. hike	Small	Boogie boarding, turtle-watching	None
Resaca	15min. drive plus 30min. hike	Small	Boogie boarding, turtle watching	None
Punta Soldado	15min. drive	Small-Med.	Snorkeling	None
Melones	15min. walk	Medium	Swimming	Trash cans

▧ PLAYA FLAMENCO. In comparison to this exquisite beach, every *balneario* on the mainland looks like a dirty swimming pool. Numerous media outlets, including the Travel Channel, have listed Flamenco among the best beaches in the world— with good reason. Playa Flamenco is Culebra's largest, most popu-

CULEBRA

lar, and most accessible beach. It is also the only beach on the island with facilities, including bathrooms, picnic tables, lifeguards and a campground. Because of these factors, and because Flamenco looks like it was created to be on a postcard, the beach can get crowded, especially on holidays when thousands of Puerto Ricans descend. Luckily Flamenco is huge and there's more than enough room for everyone. Flamenco also offers a few decent **snorkeling** opportunities. Facing the water, walk all the way to the left past the abandoned tanks (remnants of the US Navy's stint on Culebra) to the jetty, where you'll find a small reef. Alternatively, walk all the way to the right, just past the second rock jetty for another small reef. Near the parking lot, there is a tourist information kiosk (open daily 10am-2pm) that distributes copious amounts of literature. *(Drive north on Rte. 251 until the road ends. A público from Dewey costs $2-3. Públicos line up at a special stand in the parking lot, so it should not be difficult to catch one going back to Dewey.)*

■**PLAYA CARLOS ROSARIO.** Culebra's premier snorkeling beach requires a bit of effort to access, and therefore tends to have far smaller crowds than Flamenco. The crescent-shaped beach has coral on the right and boulders on the left, a sandy passageway in the center, and the clearest ocean water you've ever seen. Enter the water in the middle, then swim about 15-30 ft. in either direction to find amazing schools of blue tang, sergeant majors, and the occasional barracuda. Don't forget to bring water and a snack, as Carlos Rosario has no facilities. *(From the Playa Flamenco parking lot, walk 25min. on the dirt path over the hill. Carlos Rosario is the second beach; Playa Tamarindo, a popular kayakers' gateway to Luis Peña, is the first.)*

■**CULEBRITA.** If you're looking for a deserted island, and Culebra doesn't quite do the trick, continue east to the tiny island of Culebrita. With adequate hiking, fabulous snorkeling, gorgeous beaches, and a lighthouse, Culebra's little sister easily merits a day of exploration. Most water taxis drop passengers at the pier on the west side of the island. This beach has great **snorkeling**, but the snorkeling is best done in the numerous tide pools and in the coral reefs that surround much of the island. Continue along the marked trail for 10min. to reach **Bahía Tortuga,** the biggest and best beach on Culebrita. Few people make it out here during the week, so it's not uncommon to share the brilliant waters only with the other people on your boat. Culebrita is a protected wildlife refuge, and this is another popular turtle breeding ground. From the pier a different trail leads 15-20min. uphill to the lighthouse. This relic of the Spanish occupation was condemned in 2003, but conservation groups are working to have it restored. The peninsula on northeast Culebrita known as **The Baths** also has some great snorkeling, although the water can sometimes be a bit rough as it crashes against the rocks. Culebrita is worth the transportation costs, but avoid the little island on weekends and holidays, when it turns into a zoo of private boats. *(From Dewey water taxis (p. 201) take 25min. to reach Culebrita and cost $40. No facilities.)*

■**LUIS PEÑA.** For yet another quasi-deserted Caribbean beach with white sand, blue water, and lots of fish, head out to Luis Peña, a short 15min. water taxi ride from Dewey. On weekdays the long, narrow beaches surrounding the island are almost always empty and the water is as calm as a lake. The snorkeling is superb all the way around the little island, especially in the channel facing Culebra. The best beach is Luis Peña beach, located on the north side of the island. Like Culebrita, Luis Peña is a designated wildlife refuge, and there are several marked nature walks on the island. *(15min. water taxi ride from Dewey ($25; p. 201) or a short kayak ride from Playa Tamarindo. No facilities.)*

■**PLAYA ZONI.** Not many people make it out to the eastern side of the island, but those who do will be rewarded with acres of undeveloped land at Culebra's second-most-popular swimming beach, Playa Zoni. It seems impossible, but the water here tends to be an even more impressive color than the water at Flamenco. The waves are a bit bigger, too, making for some excellent boogie boarding. There are no facilities, and crowds are generally rather small. The long, narrow, sandy beach is lined with palm trees and affords views of numerous tiny cays, the Culebrita lighthouse and, in the distance, St. Thomas. *(Take Rte. 250 all the way east to the end.)*

PLAYA BRAVA AND PLAYA RESACA. It's just you and the turtles at these two bays on Culebra's northern coast. Visitors rarely make the long, hot trek out to these secluded beaches, but those who do will be rewarded with long stretches of beautiful tan sand and azure water. Both Brava and Resaca have strong waves that create conditions bad for swimming but decent for surfing and boogie boarding. There are reefs on both sides of Resaca's bay, but the water is generally much too rough to snorkel. From March to August leatherback turtles lay their eggs on Resaca and Brava, as you will see from the numerous marked turtle nesting sites; never stay at these beaches after dark and if you see tracks during the day, try not to disturb them. *(To reach Playa Brava drive east on Rte. 250, continue past the cemetery, and turn left on the road just after the house with the "1905" sign. Park at the end of the pavement, then follow the dirt road for 20min., veering right at the fork. To reach Playa Resaca drive east on Rte. 250 and turn left on the road directly after the airport. Drive all the way to the top, stopping at the landing just before the radio tower. Follow the narrow trail through the brush and mangroves for 30min. until you reach the beach. Call Fish and Wildlife (☎742-0115) before attempting the difficult hike, because if it hasn't been marked recently you will get lost.)*

PUNTA SOLDADO. Located on the southern tip of Culebra, the coral beach at Punta Soldado has excellent snorkeling; the best site is on the left-hand side of the beach, but reefs line the entire shore. However, if you just want to lie in the sand, it's best that you go elsewhere, as the beach is covered in rocks and coral. *(Drive all the way down C. Fulladoza, and down the dirt road until the end.)*

PLAYA MELONES. Melones's claim to fame is that it is the most easily accessible beach from Dewey. The rocky, coral-laden location on the Luis Peña Channel makes for decent snorkeling, but the water is not as clear as it is on Carlos Rosario. There are few shady areas and no facilities, so come prepared with lots of sunscreen. The best snorkeling is on the right side of the beach. Swim all the way north, past the peninsula, and you'll end up at Playa Tamarindo, another good snorkeling beach and the kayakers' gateway to

GIVING BACK

CORAL-ATING SUCCESS

The growth of most coral is measured in fractions of an inch per year, a pace that cannot keep up with destructive forces such as pollution and damage from irresponsible diving. Culebra's coral reefs are endangered, and their demise poses a double threat for the area. Aside from their environmental importance, the reefs attract divers who are needed to support the local economy.

One small nonprofit organization has begun several programs to help increase the amount of coral in the seas surrounding Culebra. CORALations works with the US Department of Natural and Environmental Resources and the Department of Fish and Wildlife to maximize its few resources. It also welcomes travelers of all ages to help in its volunteer programs.

CORALations' underwater coral farm propagates corals that can later be returned to the sea and experiments to determine which types of coral are most resistant to harsh conditions; the hardiest coral are then returned to the sea to repopulate the reefs. Certified divers can volunteer to monitor sea grass populations. However, as a small organization, CORALations is willing to tailor programs to volunteer interests and abilities. Even small children can participate: for example, they can count the number of sea urchins in a given coral farm tank.

(For more information or to volunteer, contact Mary Ann at CORALations at ☎877-772-6725.)

Luis Peña. *(From town walk uphill past the tourist office, veer left, and continue walking for 15min. Melones is the second beach at the end of the road.)*

👁 🌼 SIGHTS AND FESTIVALS

Apart from the condemned lighthouse on Culebrita, Culebra does not have many sights. However, the Culebra Foundation has been working to preserve the island's history by renovating abandoned buildings and promoting island culture. The first fruit of this project is the **Museum of San Ildefonso,** Rte. 250 Km 4, just behind the DRNA office. Located in a 1905 US Navy magazine, the museum contains historical pictures and some pre-Taíno artifacts. The Foundation plans to add an art museum and more historical markers. (In the building with the "1905" sign, next to the water. Open daily M-F 8am-noon and 1-3pm, Sa-Su on request. Free.) Culebra does not celebrate *fiestas patronales*, but Dewey hosts a large **artisans festival** every year over a weekend in late July. For information contact the tourist office (☎742-3116 ext. 441 or 442).

🛶 OUTDOOR ACTIVITIES

BOATING

Culebra Boat Rental (☎742-3559 or 866-210-0709; www.culebraboatrental.com), at Casa Ensenada Guest House (p. 193), rents 4 16-18 ft. motorboats ($160-215 for the 1st day, $110-165 per additional day; $500 deposit; 25+) and a 14 ft. Sunfish sailboat ($100 per day, $65 per additional day; $200 deposit; 15+). All come equipped with emergency supplies. Discounts for guests and multi-day rentals. Call ahead. Limited fishing equipment for sale. Boats available 7am-6pm. MC/V.

Ocean Safari Kayaks (☎379-1973) rents single kayaks for $40 per day (8hr.) and tandem kayaks for $60, including a free lesson and info on the water conditions. Most people go from Playa Tamarindo to Luis Peña. Free pick-up and delivery.

Villa Boheme, C. Fulladoza 368 (☎742-3508 or 370-4949; www.villaboheme.com), rents single and double kayaks ($8 per hr., min. 3hr.) and windsurfers ($25 per hr.). $45 for a 1hr. beginning windsurfing lesson. AmEx/MC/V.

Buenadonga (☎235-7099) offers sailboat charters along the Culebran coast ($100 per person per day, $60 per half-day) and sailing lessons ($20 per hr.). Reservation with deposit required. Cash only.

DIVING AND SNORKELING

Over 50 attractive dive sights surround Culebra and its cays. Conditions here are very similar to those in Fajardo, with visibility around 30-80 ft. and plenty of shallow dives for beginners, making this a great place to get certified. Many beaches around Culebra have amazing snorkeling (see **Beaches,** p. 197).

Culebra Divers, C. Pedro Márquez 4 (☎742-0803; www.culebradivers.com), across from the ferry terminal, has two 26 in. boats that make dive trips in the morning (1-tank dive $60, 2-tank dive $85, equipment rental $55) and 3hr. snorkel trips in the afternoon ($45, ages 6-12 $30; min. 2 people). 1-tank night dive $70. 1-dive first-time instruction package $90. NAUI Scuba Diver certification $550. During high season reserve up to 1 month in advance. All trips include beverages. Snorkel rental $12.50 for the 1st day (back by 9am the next day), $10 for additional days. High season open daily 9am-noon and 2-5:30pm. Low season call for hours. MC/V.

HIKING

While most of Culebra's land is privately held, the US Fish & Wildlife Service protects over 1500 acres of the island, including all of the off-shore cays (except Cayo Norte), the majority of the Flamenco Peninsula, a large section of land around Playa Resaca, and all of the wetlands and mangroves. The trail down to Playa Resaca (see p. 199) is more than just a beach path; this intense 30min. hike descends Culebra's tallest hill. You must crawl over boulders and find your way through a mangrove grove before reaching the beach. The trail to Playa Brava is also quite an adventure, although it is somewhat less strenuous. Another path leads across Culebrita from the boat landing to Bahía Tortuga. The friendly staff at the US Fish and Wildlife Service is happy to answer questions about hikes, beaches, or the turtle-watching program. (Drive east on Rte. 250 and look for the sign just after the cemetery. ☎742-0115; www.fws.gov. Open M-F 7am-4pm.)

SURFING

Culebra's surf can't compete with the mainland's northern coast, but if you have your own board there are a few waves to be found. It's best to hit the beach from May to July, the beginning of hurricane season, when heavier winds create larger waves. Locals recommend **Carlos Rosario, Punta Soldado,** and **Zoni** as some of the best surfing beaches. Almost all of the beaches along the northern coast occasionally have big waves that are great for boogie boarding.

WATER TAXIS

Small motor boats take visitors on daytrips primarily to Luis Peña and Culebrita, but also to other parts of Culebra. All certified boat captains charge $25 round-trip to Luis Peña and $40 to Culebrita. Trips do not leave every day; call ahead.

Cayo Norte Water Taxi (☎742-0169; kidcayopr@aol.com). Offers trips to all islands surrounding Culebra, including Cayo Norte, Culebrita, Luis Peña, Carlos Rosario, St. Thomas, and Vieques. Call for rates.

Tanamá (☎501-0011 or 397-7494). Culebra's only glass-bottom boat. Tanamá does a 2hr. harbor cruise ($30), a ½ mi. cruise over the reefs ($25), a 2-5hr. snorkeling trip ($40; equipment not included), and other trips upon request. Also sails to Culebrita ($40) and Luis Peña ($25). Typically leaves from Dinghy Dock. Cash only.

Culebra Water Taxi (☎360-9807) leaves from Mamacita's (p. 193). 1hr. tour of the bay $20. Fully equipped snorkeling trip to Luis Peña with lunch, kayaks, snorkel equipment, and beverages $45. Also drops off at Culebrita ($40) and Luis Peña ($25). Cash only.

⌂ SHOPPING

Over the past few years Culebra has experienced an influx of trendy little gift shops.

Paradise Gift Shop, C. Sallisburry 110 (☎742-3569), has an excellent selection of locally made items, from artwork to jewelry to books by local authors. Free book exchange. Open M-Tu and Th-Su 9am-6pm. MC/V.

Butiki (☎913-481-8367; www.shopbutiki.com), on C. Romero, next to Superette Mayra. Colorful handicrafts and local art, mostly made by the owner. Also a wide selection of women's islandwear. Open M and Th-Su 9am-1pm and 3-6pm.

Culebra Gift Shop (☎742-0566), on C. Escudero near the corner with C. Sallisburry, sells the usual mix of clothes, Culebra-themed knickknacks, and local art. The biggest souvenir shop on the island. Open daily 9am-6pm. AmEx/D/MC/V.

CULEBRA

Culebra Beach House, C. Fulladoza 372 (☎742-0602). Sells various beach supplies, as well as local art and a few books and videos. Open M and W-Su 9am-5pm. MC/V.

On Island, C. Pedro Márquez 4 (☎742-0439), at the ferry landing. The typical mix of tchotchkes and jewelry, with some new agey women's clothing to make it unique. Open daily 10am-noon and 1-5pm-ish. MC/V. Also at C. Fulladoza 372 (☎742-0704), above Dinghy Dock. Same approx. hours.

Galería de Regalos Souvenir Shop (☎742-2294), on C. Pedro Márquez, has a small room with Culebra t-shirts and some women's clothing and another room full of knick-knacks and souvenirs. The only souvenir shop on the main road, so it's often packed. Open daily 9:30am-6pm, sometimes later. AmEx/MC/V.

▣ NIGHTLIFE

Don't come to Culebra for its nightlife. On weeknights the loudest sound is the song of crickets and even on weekends most of the more popular bars shut down by 11pm. During summer weekends and holidays the biggest party may be at Flamenco's campground.

▨ **Mamacita's,** C. Castelar 64-66 (☎742-0090). On weekend nights Mamacita's is hugely popular with foreigners and young locals. The trendy tropical bar is straight out of a travel brochure. Come on Sa when conga drummers shake the place up (9-11pm). House mixed drinks include the Iguana Colada ($6). Beer $2.50-3. Happy hour daily 3-6pm. 18+. Bar open M-Th and Su 8am-10pm, F-Sa 8am-11pm. MC/V.

El Oasis (☎742-3175), on C. Pedro Márquez. A long bar dominates the front of this popular pizzeria (p. 196). Join the locals and watch TV with a bottle of Medalla or chat with the friendly bartenders. Beer $1.50-3. Mixed drinks $3.50-7. Happy hour daily 6-7pm with $0.50 beers. Open M, Th, Su 6-10pm; F-Sa 6-11pm. Cash only.

El Batey, Rte. 250 Km 1.1 (☎742-3828), a 5min. walk from town. The only place on the island to bust a move—or stay out past 11pm. This local favorite dominates the nightlife scene with a large dance floor and cheap beer. But don't expect glamour and glitz; the walls are decorated with giant fake fish. Beer $1.50-2. Mixed drinks start at $3. Open as a club F-Sa 10pm-2am. Cash only.

Happy Landing, at the end of the airport strip. When even El Batey gets too touristy, there's always Happy Landing, Culebra's own dive. Locals gather here for the cheapest beer in town. Just about the one place on Culebra you'll hear only Spanish. Jukebox, electronic slot machines, and 2 pool tables. Medalla $1.25. Heineken $1.50. Open daily 9am-midnight. Cash only.

SOUTHEAST

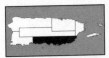

In southeast Puerto Rico, the mountains abruptly give way to miles of flat land reaching to the ocean; this was sugar country, and years of crops transformed the landscape from dry forest to empty plains. After sugar stopped being profitable, the region turned to manufacturing, producing the endless factories that line Rte. 3. This is also, officially, the Caribbean, but beaches are generally better on the northern, Atlantic coast. West of Patillas, palm-tree-lined beaches with tiny waves make for postcard-perfect sunsets, but are not great for swimming or sunning—the one exception may be the those along Rte. 901. For a really good beach you'll have to take a trip to Isla Caja de Muertos, off Ponce, or travel farther west. Ponce is the undisputed capital—and star—of southern Puerto Rico. Ponce's 19th-century architecture, rich history, and myriad museums make a trip over the mountains worthwhile for the city alone. However, apart from this pearl, southeast Puerto Rico does not have much to attract tourists. But maybe that's just the reason to come. In this languid area, you can escape the congestion of San Juan, soak in the hot springs of Coamo, and enjoy the beautiful scenery from the beach.

HIGHLIGHTS OF SOUTHEAST PUERTO RICO

TRY OUT TURN-OF-THE-CENTURY LIFE at the spectacular museums, houses, and sights in dignified **Ponce** (below).

BECOME A BEACH BUM at any one of the many idyllic accommodations along **Route 901** (p. 223).

WASH AWAY YOUR WORRIES in the hot springs of **Coamo** (p. 218).

PONCE

Elegant, proud, and steeped in tradition, Ponce is one of the most attractive cities in Puerto Rico. In many ways the city still lives in the 19th century: ornate turn-of-the-century buildings line the streets and locals seem to have a sense of hospitality from a different era. Ponce first found fame in 1511, when the city's namesake, Juan Ponce de León, finally defeated the Taínos there. Far from the Spanish government in San Juan, the city thrived as a port for contraband goods. But in the early 1700s *ponceños* transferred their resources into more legitimate businesses and the city became an exporter of tobacco, coffee, and rum. By the mid-19th century Ponce had the largest concentration of sugar cane on the island. When sugar diminished in importance the city began producing other goods, including metal, iron, and textiles. Throughout early their history *ponceños* remained fiercely independent—when the Americans took over in 1898, Ponce still had its own currency.

But the city hit its prime at the turn of the century and by 1950, Ponce was in need of revitalization. Most of the big factories created by Operation Bootstrap landed in the north, and Ponce continued to subsist on cement and textiles—not exactly quick money-makers. However, with substantial government investment, Ponce has gradually become a cultural center: this is Old San Juan minus the tourist kitsch, plus a couple of suburban comforts. The municipal government and the Institute of Culture maintain several good museums, and nearby Hacienda Buena

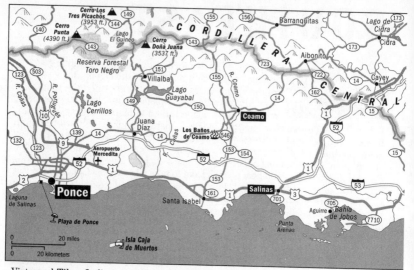

Vista and Tibes Indigenous Ceremonial Park are among the most interesting historical sights on the island. However, the heart of Ponce continues to be the charming plaza, filled with historic buildings. Standing on a balcony overlooking the busy city center can transport you back to Ponce's glory days.

✈ INTERCITY TRANSPORTATION

Flights: Aeropuerto Mercedita (☎848-2822), 4 mi. east of town. From the plaza take Rte. 1 (C. Cristina) east to Rte. 5506. Hwy. 52 also passes by the airport. A taxi from the city center should run $6-7. Only one airline flies out of Ponce: **Cape Air** (☎844-2020 or 253-1121) goes to Aeropuerto Luis Muñoz Marín in **San Juan** (20min.; 5 per day; $93, round-trip $137). Open daily 6am-7pm.

Públicos: Ponce's *público* terminal is 3 blocks north of the plaza at C. Unión and C. Vives. More popular routes run approx. 6am-5pm. *Públicos* head to: **Adjuntas** (45min., $2); **Coamo** (30min., $2.50); **Guayama** (1hr., $5); **Mayagüez** (1hr., $6); **Parque Ceremonial Indígena Tibes** (15min., $6); **Playa Ponce** (5min., $0.75); **Salinas** (45min., $3); **San Germán** (45min., $5); **Utuado** (1½hr., $5); **Yauco** (25min., $2.75). 2 companies go to **San Juan** (45min.-2hr., $10) including: **Linea DonQ** (☎842-1222 or 764-0540); and **Linea Universitaria** (☎844-6010 or 765-1634).

Cars: Several car rental companies operate out of the airport. All prices are for the smallest compact cars available. Some of the cheapest are listed below.

Dollar Rent-A-Car, Rte. 1 Km 124.7 (☎843-6970 or 843-6940), at the intersection with Rte. 578. They are planning to move to Ponce Bypass next to Wendy's. $31-40 per day, with insurance $37-45. Ages 21-24 $35 per day surcharge. AmEx/D/DC/MC/V. Open M-Sa 8am-5pm.

L&M Car Rental (☎841-2482), in the airport. $27 per day, with insurance $40. Ages 21-24 $5 per day surcharge and insurance required. AmEx/D/DC/MC/V.

Payless Car Rental, Av. Hostos 1124 (☎842-9393 or 1-800-PAYLESS), on Rte. 10 between Av. las Américas and Rte. 2. $35-55 per day, with insurance $37-60. Ages 21-24 $5 per day surcharge. Open M-F 7:30am-6pm, Sa 8am-5pm. AmEx/D/DC/MC/V.

Thrifty (☎290-2525), in the airport. $35 per day, with insurance $50. Ages 21-24 $7 per day surcharge. Open daily 4am-5pm. AmEx/D/DC/MC/V.

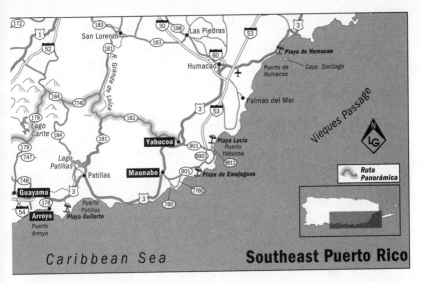

Southeast Puerto Rico

ORIENTATION

Don't be intimidated by Ponce's size; the city is rather easy to navigate once you get your bearings. The vast majority of sights cluster around the compact city center and **Plaza las Delicias,** making it feasible to get around on foot or by public transportation. Rte. 1, 10, and 14 lead toward the city center. Just south of the center, **Route 163 (Avenida las Américas)** is a large tree-lined street that serves as a convenient landmark. **Highway 2,** also referred to as the **Ponce Bypass,** originates just east of the city, skirts around the edges, and continues toward the western half of the island. If you are just passing through, Hwy. 52 avoids the center entirely and deposits travelers on Rte. 2 west of the city. Rte. 12 connects the city center to the **port** area, the boardwalk, and the beach. *Ponceños* do their shopping at the malls along Rte. 1 and 2.

LOCAL TRANSPORTATION

Taxis: Ponce Taxi (☎ 840-0088 or 842-3370), on C. Méndez Vigo, just south of C. Villa. Open daily 4am-midnight. **Coop Taxi del Sur,** C. Concordia 22 (☎ 848-8248 or 848-8249), has cabs at its office and at the intersection of C. Estrella and C. Salud. Open daily 4am-midnight. **Victory Taxi** waits on C. Vives at the intersection with C. Atocha. Open daily 6am-6pm. Most taxis charge $1 plus $0.10 for each third of a mile, $3 min.

Trolleys: The city of Ponce operates 4 **free tourist trolley** routes that take visitors from the plaza to various sites around the city. Each complete route takes about 1½-2¼hr. depending on demand and traffic. The north, east, and west routes depart from in front of Farmacia El Amal, on the plaza (daily 8:30am-5pm). The **north route** goes to the Cruceta del Vigia and the Castillo Serallés. The **east route** passes Hotel Meliá, Ponce High School, and Museo "Pancho" Coímbre. The **west route** passes the Museo de la Música, the Museo de la Historia, Casa Weichers Villaronga, and Panteón Nacional Román Baldorioty de Castro. The **south route** (daily 9am-6pm) looks more like a train and leaves from the Alcaldía and passes the university en route to **La Guancha.**

Parking: A free municipal lot is located under Parque Dora Colón Clavell. The entrance is on C. Concordia between C. Jobos and C. Ferrocarril; the exit is on C. Marina.

🔃 PRACTICAL INFORMATION

Tourist Offices: The **municipal tourist office** (☎284-3338; www.visitponce.com), on C. Cristina across from the entrance to Hotel Meliá, has a friendly, English-speaking staff that distributes maps and brochures. Open daily 8am-5:15pm. A helpful **tourist information computer terminal** is located on Pl. Delicias in front of the Parque de Bombas. Users can select different sights and museums from its menu to learn about their history and hours. In Spanish and English.

Camping Permits: DRNA (☎723-1373 or 844-4660), on the 2nd fl. of the building across from Pier 5, near the turn-off to La Guancha. Look for the American and Puerto Rican flags; the building is poorly labeled. Provides camping permits ($4, children $2). Open M-F 7:30am-4pm.

Banks: Numerous banks line Plaza las Delicias. **Banco Popular,** C. Marina 9205 (☎843-8000), has an ATM on Paseo Arias to the left of the bank. Open M-F 8am-4pm.

Supermarket: Pueblo (☎844-7488), in Centro Comercial Santa María, at the corner of C. Ferrocarril and C. Muñoz Rivera. **Western Union.** Open M-Th 6am-10pm, F-Sa 6am-midnight, Su 11am-5pm. AmEx/MC/V.

Publications: La Perla del Sur, Ponce's largest newspaper, comes out every W and can be found in restaurants and hotels or online at www.periodicolaperla.com. Free.

Police: Av. Hostos 1242 (☎848-7090 or 284-4040), at Rte. 10 and Av. las Américas. Open 24hr.

Pharmacy: Walgreens, Rte. 2 Km 225 (☎812-5978), west of Ponce, just past the intersection with Rte. 2R. Open 24hr. AmEx/D/MC/V.

Hospital: Hospital Dr. Pila (☎848-5600, emergency room ext. 127 or 124), on Av. las Américas, across from the police station. Emergency room open 24hr.

Internet Access: Archivo Municipal, C. Marina 9215 (☎843-1422), on Pl. Las Delicias next to Banco Santander, has **free** Internet access. No games or chat rooms. Open M-F 8am-8pm, Sa 9:30am-6pm. **Universidad Interamericana,** on the 1st fl. of Plaza del Caribe (p. 214), near Sears Homelife, offers Internet access. $4 per hr. Open M-Sa 9am-9pm, Su 11am-5pm.

Post Office: C. Atocha 93 (☎842-2997). General Delivery. Open M-F 7:30am-4:30pm, Sa 7:30am-noon. **Postal Code:** 00717.

🛏 ACCOMMODATIONS

The only reason to pass up the convenient location and cheap rates of the plaza hotels, which are nicely positioned for sightseeing, is to take advantage of the El Tuque recreation complex.

▨ **Fox Delicias Hotel,** C. Isabel 6963 (☎290-5050; fax 259-6413; www.foxdeliciashotel.com), on the plaza. Quite possibly the best accommodations bargain in Puerto Rico. With an incredible location, a beautiful mosaic facade, 4 in-house restaurants, room service, valet parking, and even a beauty salon, this brand-new hotel has all the trappings of a fine resort for a shockingly low price. Rooms are large and immaculately clean, with hardwood furniture, A/C, and cable TV. Check-in 3pm. Check-out noon. Doubles $65-69; quads $109-119; extra person $20. AmEx/MC/V. ❸

▨ **Hotel Bélgica,** C. Villa 122C (☎/fax 844-3255; www.hotelbelgica.com), is an amazing deal. Right off the plaza in the middle of the historic district, this hotel brings Ponce's old-world charm to budget travelers. Rooms with A/C and clean, modern bathrooms. Check-out noon. Doubles $50, with TV $65; quads with TV $75. Tax included. MC/V. ❷

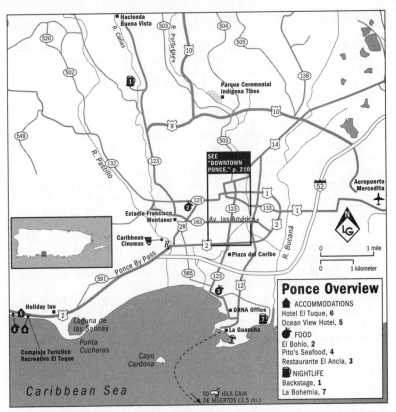

Ponce Overview

🏠 **ACCOMMODATIONS**
Hotel El Tuque, **6**
Ocean View Hotel, **5**

🍴 **FOOD**
El Bohío, **2**
Pito's Seafood, **4**
Restaurante El Ancla, **3**

🎵 **NIGHTLIFE**
Backstage, **1**
La Bohemia, **7**

Hotel Meliá, C. Cristina 75 (☎842-0260 or 800-448-8355; fax 841-3602; www.hotelmeliapr.com). Like most of Ponce, Hotel Meliá has a keen sense of its own history—it opened in 1915 and is still under family management, even sporting its own coat of arms. Beautiful high-ceilinged lobby and 2nd-fl. outdoor hallways overlooking the Plaza las Delicias. Rooms have cable TV with HBO, A/C, and telephone. Free Internet in business center. Continental breakfast on rooftop patio included. Singles $85-110; doubles $100-120. AmEx/MC/V. ❸

Hotel El Tuque, Ponce Bypass 3330 (☎290-2000; fax 290-2002; www.eltuque.com), at Rte. 2 Km 220.1. This race car-themed, chain-style hotel is part of the El Tuque entertainment complex (see **Sights,** p. 211). During the winter this is a peaceful retreat away from the city, but in summer the place fills up with families headed to the water park. Cable TV, A/C, free Internet connection, and telephone. Large, clean rooms. Lively courtyard with pool, jacuzzi, hammock pavilion, and poolside restaurant. A video arcade and convenience store inside. Continental breakfast included. Check-in 3pm. Check-out noon. Doubles $85-105; extra person $10. AmEx/MC/V. ❸

Ocean View Hotel, Rte. 2 Km 218.7 (☎844-9207), is far from downtown, but inexpensive and right on the ocean. The rooms, though a bit small and dim, are surprisingly full of amenities: A/C and cable TV, and most have kitchenettes. Rooms in back have ocean views. Tiny pool. Triples $60; weekly $350; monthly $1200. AmEx/MC/V. ❷

🔲 FOOD

🔳 **El Bohío,** Rte. 2R #627 (☎844-7825), near the intersection with C. Villa. *Comida criolla* goes gourmet at this excellent restaurant. Laid-back, local atmosphere. The grilled chicken in asparagus sauce ($12) is especially tasty. Entrees $9-13. Open M-Th and Su 11am-9pm, F-Sa 11am-10pm. AmEx/D/DC/MC/V. ❸

Pizza's Heaven, C. Concordia 8023 (☎844-0448; fax 844-3836). It may not look like much from the outside, but this is the best Italian eatery in town. The interior keeps it casual with chairs made from rum barrels. Tasty, cheesy personal pizzas $4-5.50. Vegetarian lasagna $9. Entrees $8-18. Open Tu-Th 11am-10pm, F 11am-11pm, Sa noon-11pm, Su noon-10pm. AmEx/MC/V. ❸

Rincón Argentino, C. Isabel 34 (☎284-1762 or 608-7668), entrance on C. Salud. Where the locals go for a romantic night out. Diners choose between the intimate interior and the softly lit, relaxed outdoor patio. Carefully prepared meat, seafood, and pasta options are delicious, and the artistically presented desserts are well worth the splurge. Entrees $10-20. Wine $4.50. Open M-W noon-10pm, Th noon-11pm, F-Sa noon-midnight, Su noon-9pm. MC/V. ❸

Café Paris, C. Isabel (☎840-1010), on the plaza, is remarkably hip considering that it's half of a jewelry store. Indulge in a rich chocolate drink ($1-3) or fruity house cocktail ($3-6) on 2nd-story balcony, which overlooks the plaza.The best gourmet coffee in town ($1-5). Sandwiches $2.50-5. Lunch special with sandwich, drink, and soup $5. Open M-Sa 8am-6pm, Su 9am-5:30pm. ❶

King's Cream, C. Marina 9322 (☎843-8520). Stocked with Puerto Rican flavors, like *tamarindo* and *parcha*, which are whipped through a mixer and served up soft. Refreshingly low prices. Ice cream $1.10-1.60. *Batidas* $1.70-2. Open daily 9am-11:45pm. ❶

El Fenix Panadería & Repostería, C. Unión 110, across from the *público* station. The scrumptious smell that emanates from this simple bakery every morning draws people from blocks away for fresh bread and pastries. A great place to escape the tourists for a cheap lunch. Sandwiches $1-4. Breakfast $0.60-2.25; oatmeal $1. Open M-F 6am-4pm, Sa 7am-3pm. Cash only. ❶

Tompy's (☎840-1965), at C. Isabel and C. Mayor, looks like a standard Puerto Rican *cafetería*, but its meaty sandwiches, convenient location, and late hours set it apart. Breakfast $1-3. Sandwiches $4.50. Open M-Sa 7am-midnight. MC/V. ❶

El Sabor, C. Isabel 6963 (☎290-5050), in the Fox Delicias Hotel. A cafetería in the atrium of the spectacular Fox Delicias Hotel (see **Accommodations,** above). Serves great daily lunch specials including a Puerto Rican entree, 2 sides, and a drink ($4.50). Open daily 11am-2pm. AmEx/MC/V.

Restaurante El Ancla, Av. Hostos 805 (☎840-2450 or 840-2454), at the end of the street overlooking the water. For high-quality seafood, look no further. This elegant *mesón gastronómico* naturally has a nautical theme, with subtle sea-inspired artwork and a long menu of seafood options. Of course, quality doesn't come cheap. Entrees $14-30. Extensive wine list sold by the bottle. Live Bohemian music F-Sa 7pm, Su noon. Open M-Th and Su 11am-10pm, F-Sa 11am-midnight. AmEx/D/DC/MC/V. ❹

Naturismo Health Food, Av. las Américas 2223D (☎284-1300), in a health food store. The menu at this vegetarian restaurant changes daily but usually includes rice, beans, *tostones*, and vegetables. Large, pleasant dining room. Lunch $5.50. Drinks $1.50-2. Open M-F 10:30am-2:30pm. AmEx/MC/V. ❶

Pito's Seafood, Hwy. 2 Km 218.7 (☎841-4977; fax 259-8328). Large patio over the sea and seafood with a Puerto Rican twist. Entrees $13-32. Delicious house martinis

$7. Cigar room with extensive menu. Live music Sa-Su. Open M-Th and Su 11am-11pm, F-Sa 11am-midnight. AmEx/MC/V. ❹

Lupita's Mexican Restaurant, C. Isabel 60 (☎848-8808), is open late, close to the center of town, and reasonably priced. The highlight is the beautiful central atrium; eat there to avoid the crowds, which typically gather in the bar area to watch TV. Typical Mexican entrees like burritos and fajitas $6-14. Margaritas $5. Open M-Sa 11am-last customer. AmEx/D/MC/V. ❸

🄰 SIGHTS

▦ PLAZAS LAS DELICIAS. With an enormous fountain, a stately church, and one of the funkiest museums in Puerto Rico, Ponce's legendary central plaza provides hours of entertainment. The first stop is the **Parque de Bombas,** the bright red-and-black structure on the northern side of the plaza. Featured on dozens of postcards, calendars, and tourist brochures, this unique museum serves as the unofficial symbol of Ponce and a monument to the city's long history. Three years after a fire nearly destroyed the city in 1820, Ponce officials created Puerto Rico's first firefighter corps, and in 1883 the fire department moved to an Arabic Pavilion on the main plaza. Fast-forward over 100 years and the city government transformed the same building into a monument to honor the many fire officials who have protected the city from countless disasters. Today the small museum contains old fire equipment, a timeline of firefighting, and portraits of famous firefighters. The highlight is the old fire engine, whose bell you can ring and siren you can sound. Even so, the monument is most prized by tourists as a great photo opportunity. (☎284-3338. Open daily 9am-6pm. Free.) You can't miss the enormous **Catedral de Nuestra Señora de Guadalupe,** behind the Parque de Bombas. The largest cathedral in Ponce was built in 1836 on the sight of the city's first church, constructed in 1670. There aren't many surprises inside, but the stained-glass windows and golden altar are striking. This is a functioning Catholic church, so do not enter if you're wearing shorts. (☎842-0134. Open M-F 6am-1pm, Sa-Su 6am-12:30pm and 3-8pm.) Across the street, the exquisite **Casa Armstrong Poventud** was built in 1899 as a residence and most recently housed the offices of the Institute of Puerto Rican Culture. The house is currently under construction and it may eventually become another museum. On the southern border of the plaza sits the beautiful **Casa Alcaldía** (City Hall).

NO WORK, ALL PLAY

PONCE'S FAT TUESDAY

Ponce's biggest shebang is its elaborate carnaval, one last party in the days prior to the sacrifices of Lent. The celebration combines Puerto Rico's Spanish, African, and Taíno heritages. Masqueraders (referred to as *vejigantes*) dress up in brightly colored costumes and ornate, handmade masks made from wood or coconut shells. They represent the "good" characters, who are supposed to scare away the evil ones by dancing to *bomba* and *plena* folk songs. The primary character is **King Momo,** a local who dresses up in an enormous doll costume. Throughout the week people try to guess the identity of the *Rey Momo* and the winner receives a monetary reward. While it's no Rio de Janiero, Ponce's carnaval offers a whole week of festive fun. Each day has its own unique activity. Unless otherwise stated, all events take place in the plaza at 7:30pm.

Day 1 (W): Masquerade Dance. Everyone shows off their costumes.

Day 2 (Th): Entrance of King Momo: Celebrated with a parade.

Day 3 (F): Crowning of the Infant Queen. Parade again.

Day 4 (Sa): Crowning of the Queen. Another parade.

Day 5 (Su): Grand Carnaval. You guessed it: a parade. Starts a 1pm.

Day 6 (M): Carnaval Grand Dance. A big party with live music.

Day 7 (Tu): Burial of the Sardine. Funeral, parade, and party!

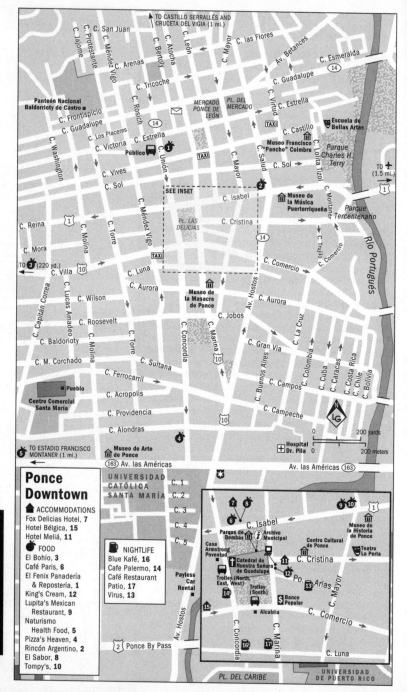

TO CASTILLO SERRALLÉS AND
CRUCETA DEL VIGIA (1 mi.)

C. San Juan
C. Méndez Vigo
C. Protestante
C. Jalone
C. Atocha
C. León
C. Bertoly
C. las Flores
C. Mayor
Av. Betances
C. Esmeralda
14
C. Arenas
C. Guadalupe
C. Tricoche
C. Estrella
C. Virtud
Panteón Nacional
Baldorrioty de Castro ■
C. Frontispicio
C. Rosich
MERCADO
PONCE DE
LEÓN
PL. DEL
MERCADO
TAXI
C. Castillo
Escuela de
Bellas Artes
C. Guadalupe
C. Los Placeres
C. Victoria
C. Estrella
Museo Francisco
"Pancho" Coímbre
Parque
Charles H.
Terry
C. Washington
Público
C. Unión
C. Sol
TO ✚
(1.5 mi.)
1
TAXI
C. Vives
C. Mayor
C. Salud
C. Montaner
C. Sol
SEE INSET
2
Museo de
la Música
Puertorriqueña
C. Reina
1
C. Isabel
Parque
Tercentenario
C. Mora
C. Molina
C. Torre
C. Méndez Vigo
PL. LAS
DELICIAS
C. Cristina
14
Río Portugués
TO 3 (220 yd.)
TAXI
C. Comercio
C. Trujilo
C. Comercio
C. Villa
10
C. Luna
C. Capitán Correa
C. Lucas Amadeo
C. Wilson
C. Aurora
Museo de
la Masacre
de Ponce
Av. Hostos
C. Aurora
C. La Cruz
C. Roosevelt
C. Jobos
C. Baldorioty
C. Torre
C. Molina
C. Concordia
C. Marina
C. Gran Via
C. Colombia
C. Cuba
C. Caracas
C. Costa Rica
C. Chile
C. Bolivia
C. M. Corchado
C. Sultana
10
C. Buenos Aires
C. Campos
N
LG
■ Pueblo
C. Ferrocarril
Centro Comercial
Santa María
C. Acropolis
C. Providencia
C. Campeche
0   200 yards
TO ESTADIO FRANCISCO
MONTANER (1 mi.)
5
C. Alondras
4
Museo de Arte
de Ponce
163 Av. las Américas
Hospital
Dr. Pila
0   200 meters
Av. las Américas 163

UNIVERSIDAD
CATÓLICA
SANTA MARÍA
C. 1
C. 2
C. 3
C. 4
C. 5

Ponce Downtown

🏠 ACCOMMODATIONS
Fox Delicias Hotel, **7**
Hotel Bélgica, **15**
Hotel Meliá, **11**

🍅 FOOD
El Bohío, **3**
Café Paris, **6**
El Fenix Panadería
  & Repostería, **1**
King's Cream, **12**
Lupita's Mexican
  Restaurant, **9**
Naturismo
  Health Food, **5**
Pizza's Heaven, **4**
Rincón Argentino, **2**
El Sabor, **8**
Tompy's, **10**

🍺 NIGHTLIFE
Blue Kafé, **16**
Cafe Palermo, **14**
Café Restaurant
  Patio, **17**
Virus, **13**

Payless
Car
Rental

2 Ponce By Pass

INSET:
7 8
9 10
1
6
Museo de
la Historia
de Ponce
Parque de
Bombas
Archivo
Municipal
C. Isabel
Casa
Armstrong
Poventud
Centro Cultural
de Ponce
Teatro
La Perla
Catedral de
Nuestra Señora
de Guadalupe
11 C. Cristina
12
Po. Arias
13
Trolley (North,
East, West)
Trolley
(South)
Banco
Popular
14
15
Alcaldía
16 17
C. Comercio
C. Marina
C. Concordia
Av. Hostos
C. Luna

PL. DEL CARIBE
UNIVERSIDAD
DE PUERTO RICO

SOUTHEAST

Built in 1490, the building used to be a jail and was the site of the island's last lynchings. Today, it does not have much of general interest other than a pretty facade. (☎ 284-4141. Open M-F 8am-4:30pm.)

CASTILLO SERRALLÉS. It may have been over a century since Puerto Rico was ruled by a monarch, but the island definitely has its own royalty. One such dynasty is the Serrallés family, the original producers of Don Q rum, and their house reigns over Ponce like the castle it was designed to be. The family immigrated to Puerto Rico from Spain in the mid-18th century and by 1890 their Hacienda Mercedita produced over 4000 acres of rum-making sugar cane. In 1930 the family started construction on a Spanish Revival house overlooking Ponce, but the elaborate structure took over four years to complete. This is one of the most beautiful homes on the island that is open to the public, and almost all of the original furniture has been preserved. The only way to visit the interior is with a 1¼hr. guided tour, which starts with a 15min. film, continues through the many elegant rooms, and passes through a display on the rum production process. The highlight of the tour is the formal dining room, with hand-carved ceilings in three kinds of wood and crystal imported from France and Italy. The tour ends at a gift shop selling the Serrallés family's many brands, including Captain Morgan rum. The large, manicured gardens are also open to the public, providing an excellent place to wander after the tour. (El Vigil 17. Just downhill from the Cruceta del Vigia, p. 211. ☎ 259-1774 or 259-1775. Open Tu-Th 9:30am-5pm, F-Su 9:30am-5:30pm. Free English/Spanish tours. Combo ticket with Cruceta la Vigia $9; ages 3-15, 60+, and students with ID $4. AmEx/D/DC/MC/V.)

LA GUANCHA. Despite its lack of sandy beaches, Ponce makes good use of its coastal location with La Guancha, an elaborate boardwalk filled with food kiosks. By day this is a pleasant, quiet place to walk (on weekdays it can be entirely empty), but come weekend nights the boardwalk overlooking the harbor is packed. Thousands of *ponceños* of all ages come out of the woodwork to enjoy a cool drink and look out at the yachts in port. (From the plaza head south on Av. Hostos, turn left on Rte. 2, then turn right onto Rte. 12 and follow signs. Kiosk hours vary, although at least a couple are usually open during the day and everything is open on weekend nights.)

COMPLEJO TURÍSTICO RECREATIVO EL TUQUE. There's no better place in Puerto Rico to relive your childhood than El Tuque, 4 mi. west of Ponce. The highlight is the **Speed & Splash Water Park,** with several water slides, a wave pool, and a lazy river. (At the El Tuque Hotel, see **Accommodations,** p. 206). Open Apr.-May and Aug.-Sept. F-Su 10am-6pm; June-July daily 10am-6pm. $13, under 12 $10. AmEx/MC/V.) In the same complex, the **Ponce International Speedway Park** offers a ¼ mi. drag strip, 1½ mi. raceway, and ½ mi. go-kart track, open to any group that wants to race; call ahead for information about upcoming races. (☎ 290-2000. Open mid-Jan. to Nov. Races usually Th and Sa. $10, children and hotel guests free. Cash only.)

CRUCETA DEL VIGIA. This popular monument can be seen towering overhead from every point in the city. The original Vigia cross was built on this spot (233 ft. above sea level) in 1801 to mark the spot where guards sat to watch ships entering the harbor. If the ship was an enemy to the Spanish crown, they would alert the authorities. If it was an ally, they would alert local traders to come fetch their goods. The current cross was built in 1984 to honor these faithful guards. A glass elevator leads to the observation tower, which has the best views in the city and an interactive English/Spanish directory pointing out the dozens of visible landmarks. (On Vigia Hill. From the plaza drive down C. Cristina, turn left on C. Salud, turn left on C. Guadalupe, and turn right on C. Bertoly, which leads all the way up the hill. The north trolley takes visitors up the hill. ☎ 259-3816. Open Tu-Su 9:30am-5pm. Combo ticket with Castillo Serrallés $9, 3-15, 60+, and students with ID $4.)

TEATRO LA PERLA. Designed in 1941 in imitation of the original 1864 theater that was destroyed in an earthquake, La Perla has a large balcony and 1047 velvet seats. The beautiful Neoclassical building is regularly open to the public, and the lobby has a small museum commemorating past shows. By far the best way to experience the theater, though, is by attending one of the many musical and theatrical performances. *(Corner of C. Mayor and C. Cristina. ☎843-4322, box office ☎843-4080. Theater open M-F 8am-noon and 1-4:15pm, box office open M-Sa 10am-4pm. Performances late Aug. to early July F-Su. Tickets $20-35. Student discounts available occasionally.)*

PANTEÓN NACIONAL ROMÁN BALDORIOTY DE CASTRO. In 1843 the city of Ponce constructed a Catholic cemetery at what was then the edge of the city. For over 70 years Ponce's most prominent citizens were buried here, including Román Baldorioty de Castro, an instrumental figure in securing emancipation for Puerto Rico's slaves, and members of the Serraillés family (see **Castillo Serraillés,** above). The cemetery closed in 1918 for health reasons, and has been severely vandalized over the years, but in 1991 the government reopened the area, began renovations, and even buried famous tenor **Antonio Paoli** and former governor **Roberto Sánchez Vilella** here. The graves of the famous people are beautifully wrought in marble, but the older graves are in disrepair. *(At C. Simón de la Torre and C. Frontispicio. The west trolley route stops here for 30min. ☎841-8347. Open W-Su 8:30am-5pm. Free.)*

MARKETS. Ponce has two traditional markets within walking distance of the plaza. The **Plaza del Mercado,** in a 1970s-style building, has stands for everything you'd expect to see in a Puerto Rican market, including *cafeterías,* lottery stands, salted fish, and thousands of plantains. *(Between C. Salud, C. Mayor, C. Estrella, and C. Guadalupe. Open M-Sa 6am-6pm, Su 6am-noon.)* Next door, the smaller **Mercado Juan Ponce de León** has a more eclectic collection of kiosks, where you can get your sewing done, watch a cobbler at work, buy hand-rolled cigars, or sample a tasty *batida.* In both markets about half of the storefronts are empty. *(Between C. León, C. Mayor, C. Estrella, and C. Guadalupe. Most kiosks open M-Sa 9am-3pm.)*

🏛 MUSEUMS

■ MUSEO DE ARTE DE PONCE. While San Juan's new art museum consists primarily of Latin American and Puerto Rican works, the Ponce museum focuses almost exclusively on European art and has been called the premier European art museum in the Caribbean. The two-story building includes rooms for the Spanish School, the Dutch School, the British School, and several Italian schools. Some of the more famous artists include El Greco, Peter Paul Rubens, Charles Le Brun, and Edward Coely Burne-Jones. Of course, the museum also has a room dedicated to Latin American artists, including Francisco Oller, José Campeche, and Tomás Batista, as well as temporary exhibitions of modern work. A small sculpture courtyard with a reflecting pool provides a pleasant place to wander. From the outside, the building, designed by Edward Durell Stone, a student of Frank Lloyd Wright, looks unexceptional, but the interior is exquisitely designed to display art, with unusual window and lighting schemes. All captions are in Spanish and English. *(Av. las Américas 2325. ☎848-0505 or 840-1510; www.museoarteponce.org. Open daily 10am-5pm. $5, students with ID $1.25, children under 12 $2.50, clergy or handicapped free.)*

MUSEO DE LA HISTORIA DE PONCE. It is only appropriate that a city with so much local pride should also have a museum dedicated exclusively to its history. The Ponce History Museum uses a combination of artifacts, descriptive signs, and hundreds of photos to describe every aspect of the city, with separate rooms dedicated to subjects such as health, education, and even the native birds. The most unique exhibit has to be the photo montage of the "personajes" of Plaza las Delicias, including homeless people and local celebrities like "Juana la loca" (Juana the madwoman). All captions are in Spanish, but employees may offer English tours on request, which can be very helpful in navigating the many materials. *(C. Isabel 53, at C. Mayor. ☎844-7071. Open M and W-F 10am-5pm, Sa-Su 10am-6pm. Free.)*

MUSEO DE LA MÚSICA PUERTORRIQUEÑA. The Institute of Culture filled this museum with musical instruments and artwork that tell the story of Puerto Rican music, from the Taínos to salsa. Two rooms focus on *bomba y plena*, (see **Music**, p. 72), the latter of which is said to have originated in Ponce and continues to play an important role in the city's culture. Exhibits include many different types of guitars, from an 18th-century *bordonúa* to a Hawaiian steel guitar from the 1930s. Tours are excellent, and guides may even let you play some of the instruments. All captions are in Spanish but guides speak English. *(C. Isabel, at C. Salud. ☎848-7016. Open W-Su 8:30am-4:30pm. Free English/Spanish tour. Free.)*

MUSEO FRANCISCO "PANCHO" COIMBRE. Named after one of Ponce's all-time greatest baseball players, this one-room museum honors *ponceño* athletes in all sports. There are a few interesting pieces of memorabilia, including a uniform from Ponce's short-lived women's baseball team and a baseball bat that was the only object to survive the house fire that killed Coimbre. Ask for a tour; the endless rows of photos have little meaning without one. *(On C. Lolita Tizol, near C. Castillo. ☎843-6553. Open M and W-Su 8:30am-4:30pm. Free.)*

MUSEO DE LA MASACRE DE PONCE. In 1937 nineteen Puerto Rican Nationalist demonstrators were killed by police forces in Ponce. For a long time afterwards the government denied any responsibility and schools did not teach students about the controversial event. In an effort to remedy this situation, the Puerto Rican Cultural Institute opened a small museum to promote awareness of the tragedy and prevent something similar from happening again. The museum contains informative timelines and posters, but few actual artifacts. The most interesting are the 1930s-era government cards listing laborers who were suspected to be dangerously revolutionary. Although most captions are in Spanish, there are a few English explanations and the English-speaking guides are happy to answer any questions. *(C. Marina at C. Aurora. ☎844-9722; masacredeponce@hotmail.com. Open Tu-Su 8:30am-4:320pm. Free English/Spanish tour. Free.)*

CENTRO CULTURAL DE PONCE. This bright pink Neoclassical building is sometimes home to temporary art exhibits. Although they vary in form and medium, they usually explore the theme of blending European and American cultures. *(C. Cristina 70. ☎844-2540. Open M-F 8am-1pm. Free.)*

🎵 ENTERTAINMENT

BEACHES
Beaches are not Ponce's strong point, but the city has created one acceptable beach area in the La Guancha area just east of the boardwalk. The imported sand barely covers a concrete surface and the water doesn't get much more than two feet deep, but *ponceños* fill the beach on hot weekend days. Bathrooms, playground equipment, parking, a beach volleyball court, and food kiosks appease the masses. For a better beach, catch the boat to **Isla Caja de Muertos** (p. 215).

CINEMA
Caribbean Cinemas has two locations in Ponce. The first, in **Ponce Towne Center** (☎843-2602), Rte. 2 Km 225, behind Big K-mart, has 10 theaters. The **Plaza del Car-**

ibe Mall location (☎844-6704), at the intersection of Rte. 2 and Rte. 123, has six. Both play Hollywood films. ($5.50, ages 2-10 $3, 65+ $3.50. W women $3.)

CONCERTS

Founded in 1883 as the Firefighter's Corps Band, the **Municipal Band of Ponce** has been entertaining locals for well over a century. Today the group sounds like a professional symphony orchestra and performs lively classical music every Sunday at Parque Dora Colón Clavell (8pm).

FESTIVALS

Ponce's big shebang is undoubtedly carnaval (see **Ponce's Fat Tuesday,** p. 209). However, the following festivals have also been known to bring out the crowds. The city's **patron saint festival,** held on the six days around December 12 in La Guancha, includes mariachi-filled processions, traditional music, *artesanía*, and carnival rides. On December 12 a huge public breakfast is served on the boardwalk around 3am to celebrate the end of a long night out on the town. During a three-day weekend in mid-March the city hosts a **Feria Artesanal.** Over 100 artists set up booths on the south side of the plaza for this enormous artisan festival with music and parties.

SHOPPING

Ponce's best shopping awaits on the pedestrian **Paseo Atocha,** just north of Plaza las Delicias. This three-block market spills onto the streets and houses the predictable combination of American footwear chains, Puerto Rican discount stores, and independent kiosks hawking baseball caps. This busy shopping experience is most active on weekdays from 9am to 5pm. For more stereotypical American shopping try **Plaza del Caribe,** the largest mall in the Ponce area. Here you can stock up on favorites from the Gap, Sears, and Foot Locker. There is also a large, intricately carved carousel and a food court. (At the intersection of Rte. 2 and Rte. 123. ☎840-8989. Open M-Sa 9am-9pm, Su 11am-5pm.)

SPORTS

The **Leones de Ponce** (Ponce Lions), Ponce's professional baseball team, play from November to January at **Estadio Francisco Montaner,** near the intersection of Av. las Américas and the Rte. 2 spur. Games are held every day except Monday. Purchase tickets at the stadium box office. (☎848-0050. $6, children and seniors $5.)

THEATER

La Perla (see **Sights,** p. 212), is the city's primary venue for theater. Ponce's **Escuela de Bellas Artes,** on C. Lolita Tizol at C. Castillo, holds occasional student ballet and theater performances. Contact the school or check La Perla del Sur for info. (☎848-9156. Most performances during the school year. Admission $5.)

◗ NIGHTLIFE

Ponce is home to variety of nightlife hot spots, including clubs blasting *reggaetón*, quiet corner bars, and a popular boardwalk filled with night owls of all ages. The best place to enjoy a drink, live music, and even livelier Puerto Rican company, is ▨**La Guancha,** the seaside boardwalk south of town. On weekend nights kiosks blast music and couples, families, and teenagers wander the street. Mixed drinks run $2.50-6, beer $1-2. Sandwiches, pizza, and empanadillas are also served. Gamblers can head to one of the city's two **casinos,** at the **Ponce Hilton,** just off Rte. 124 (see **La Bohemia,** below; open daily 8am-4am), or the **Holiday Inn,** Ponce Bypass 3315 (☎844-1200), about 2 mi. west of town down Hwy. 2, which is open 24hr.

PLAZA LAS DELICIAS

Blue Kafé, C. Luna 70, at C. Concordia. Half popular disco and half popular bar, Blue Kafé is where Ponce's young and beautiful go for a loud night out. The exuberant crowd spills into the street, and big signs on the walls list nightly drink specials, including $1.25 Bacardi all day Tu. Club cover occasionally $5-10. Open M-Sa 5pm-3am. MC/V.

Virus, C. Arias, off the plaza between Banco Popular and Banco Santander. Ponce's newest and hottest club pumps out *reggaetón* to crowds of twentysomething men in basketball jerseys and scantily clad women. Like San Juan's hottest clubs, but much cheaper. Very tight security. Rum punch $1 Th. Beer $2-3. Mixed drinks $4-5. Cover Th $3, F-Sa $5. 18+. Open Th-Sa 10pm-3am. Cash only.

Café Restaurant Patio, C. Luna 35 (☎848-3178), at C. Marina. Located in the center of the action on the hip (and loud) C. Luna, this café keeps things laid-back with a young professional crowd and chill vibe. Killer happy hour (10pm-1am) specials change by the day, including Medalla $1 Th and Dewar's and Bacardi each $1.50 Sa. Beer $2-3. Live Spanish rock Th and Sa. 18+ after 10pm. Open M 7:30am-3pm, Tu-Su 7:30am-3am. AmEx/D/MC/V.

Cafe Palermo, C. Unión 3 (☎812-3873), on the plaza, is popular with tourists who enjoy the convenient location and pleasant outdoor tables. A nice spot for post-dinner drinks and friendly conversation. Beers $2-3. Mixed drinks $3-5. Open Tu-Sa 6pm-3am. MC/V.

OUTSIDE THE PLAZA

☒ Backstage (☎448-8112), off Rte. 123, north of the city. Follow directions to Hacienda Buena Vista (p. 216), but after you pass the huge Cemento Ponce factory, drive about 1 mi farther. Turn left at the Esso station and drive up the hill about 1 mi.; Backstage is up a hill on the left at the white gate. Hidden high in the hills above Ponce, this popular, warehouse-like disco features flashing lights, smoke machines, and Ponce's hippest club kids. This is a gay club, and many fashionable young men do strut their stuff, but everyone is welcome. Drag Show Sa 2:30am. Mixed drinks $3-6. 18+. Cover F $3, Sa $6. Open F-Sa 11pm-last customer. AmEx/MC/V.

La Bohemia (☎259-7676 ext. 5121), in the Ponce Hilton. Take Rte. 12 toward La Guancha, then turn left after the Texaco station and drive about 1½ mi. down the road. A slightly older crowd hits up this luxurious retreat on weekend nights. It's two-thirds classy, with candlelit tables and a live salsa band, and one-third sporty, with a big-screen TV showing athletic events. Large dance floor for when the salsa party gets going. Don Q drinks $3 Sa-Su 7-9pm. Beers $4.50-5. Mixed drinks $6-8. Live salsa music 10pm Th-Sa. 18+. Open Th-Sa 8:30pm-last customer.

▶ DAYTRIPS FROM PONCE

ISLA CAJA DE MUERTOS

Island Ventures (☎842-8546) offer trips out to Isla Caja de Muertos. However, they rarely answer their phone, so leave a message and they should call you back. The only other means of accessing the island is to ask fishermen around the docks for a ride.

Isla Caja de Muertos (Coffin Island), a 500-acre island with subtropical dry forest surrounded by a few nice beaches, provides one of those relaxing escapes that you imagine before traveling to the Caribbean. The secret behind Caja de Muertos's magic is the limited means of transportation; in an attempt to minimize human influence and protect the island's rare animal population, the DRNA mandates that only private boats carrying fewer than 150 people can visit the island. Consequently, from May to December hawksbill turtles are able to lay their eggs on the eastern side of the island without human interference. And nobody is

A PIRATE'S TALE

With a name like **Isla Caja de Muertos** (Coffin Island), it seems inevitable that this small piece of land should have an exceptional history. Over the years the island has served as the hideout for several pirates, including notables such as Sir Frances Drake and the local menace Roberto Cofresí. Originally from the Cabo Rojo area, Cofresí supposedly traveled the southern shores on a 60 ft. schooner, burning Spanish ships and stealing the treasure. Although some historians claim that Cofresí was a sort of Puerto Rican Robin Hood, sharing his plunder with the poor, legend has it that he divided his treasure in two and buried half on the north side of Coffin Island and the other half in the cave to the south. In 1954, after one of these caves collapsed, excavators discovered a human skeleton inside, still chained to the wall.

Of course, eager visitors have searched for the treasure, but with no success. Then again, many locals have stories about cousins or friends who mysteriously disappeared during an expedition to Caja de Muertos. Maybe they got a little bit too close to the pile of gold? No one knows for sure, but an aura of mystery continues to shroud the island today. As for the name, well, that's no mystery at all. An 18th-century French writer called the island "Cofre A'morr" (Coffin Island) because from a distance the island looks a little like a large coffin.

For information on how to plan your own getaway to the mysterious Isla Caja de Muertos, see p. 215.

allowed on the southern tip of the island, which serves as a protected bird sanctuary.

Caja de Muertos' main attractions are the quiet beaches, small strips of sand that stay relatively empty, and gentle, clear waters that make for excellent **snorkeling. Scuba divers** can explore a 40 ft. wall just offshore, and on a good day the visibility can be as extensive as 100 ft. Back on land, the DRNA maintains bathrooms and covered picnic tables. Caja de Muertos is large enough that it also offers activities beyond the beach. An easy **30min. hike** leads through the shrubs and cacti and up the hill to a 19th-century **lighthouse.** Because the US Coast Guard operates the lighthouse today, visitors cannot enter, but they can enjoy the astounding view from the top. A small cave on the island has **Taíno petroglyphs** inside, but there is no trail. The resident DRNA employee sometimes offers guided tours.

HACIENDA BUENA VISTA

*No **public transportation** goes to Buena Vista. It may be possible to have a público heading to Adjuntas drop you off, but getting a ride back will be almost impossible. **Driving:** Drive west on Av. las Américas (Rte. 163) past the Museo de Arte, then turn right on Rte. 2R. Then turn left onto Rte. 123 and continue until Km 16.8 (30min.).*

This restored fruit, corn flour, and coffee plantation is one of the best-preserved farm houses on the island and one of Ponce's must-see attractions. Back in 1821 Salvador de Vives arrived in Ponce and began looking for land to buy. Unfortunately, he couldn't afford the prime real estate by the sea, which was used to grow sugar cane, so instead in 1833 he purchased 500 acres in the mountains just north of the city. Initially the land was used as a fruit farm, then it became a corn flour factory; however, by 1872, when the third generation of the Vives family took over, the plantation was used almost exclusively to grow Arabic coffee. The frequent changes in production mean that a variety of equipment can still be found on the grounds. Most interesting is the 1121 ft. canal system that the Vives family used to extract water from Río Canas, power the machinery, and return the water to the river without polluting or damaging the ecosystem. The farm continued to be used until the 1950s when it was divided between local farmers.

Since 1984 the site has been managed by the Conservation Trust of Puerto Rico, a private organization that strives to preserve the island's natural resources while educating the public, and both goals are well accomplished here. The only way to visit the plantation is through a 1½hr. guided tour that includes a beautiful walk along the canals through the subtropical forest, a visit to the restored and refurnished house, and fascinating demonstrations of the plantation's still-functioning machinery. In October, the *hacienda* has a celebration of coffee, including a tasting of coffee grown on site; call for more information. (Rte. 123 Km 16.8. ☎ 722-5882, weekends 284-7020; www.fideicomiso.org. **Reservations required.** Call at least one week in advance. Tours F-Su Spanish 8:30, 10:30am, 1:30, 3:30pm; English by request only 1:30pm. $7, ages 5-11 and 65+ $4, under 5 free.)

PARQUE CEREMONIAL INDÍGENA TIBES

Public Transportation: Públicos to Tibes leave from the main station on C. Unión *(15min., $6).* **Driving:** From central Ponce, drive down C. Cristina, turn left on C. Salud, then turn left on C. Guadalupe and right on C. Mayor, which turns into Rte. 503. Alternatively, drive north on Hwy. 10, then exit at the Tibes sign onto Rte. 503.

Tibes is the largest known indigenous center on the island. Technically this is not a Taíno site, as it was constructed between AD 600 and 1200, during the reign of the pre-Taínos and Igneris, but many of the customs were continued and Tibes is the best place on the island to learn about the area's indigenous peoples. The sight was uncovered in 1975 when Hurricane Eloise flooded the banks of the Río Portugués, allowing a surprised Puerto Rican farmer to discover several Taíno artifacts. The city expropriated the land and upon excavation unearthed 12 structures, including seven *batey* courts, lots of pottery, and 187 sets of human remains (see **Taíno Terms**). The presence of multiple structures leads archaeologists to believe that this was one of the largest ceremonial sites in the Caribbean.

The small museum introduces visitors to the various aspects of the Taíno and pre-Taíno cultures, displaying most of the pottery found on the site. A 25min. film illustrates many aspects of indigenous life, from warfare to recreation, through reenactment. Finally, during the 1hr. tour, guides lead visitors through the subtropical forest, explaining the indigenous peoples' uses of each type of tree. Then the tour heads past a replica of a Taíno village, and finally to several *batey* courts. The site does not boast an overwhelming quantity of artifacts, but as a whole the complex provides a thorough introduction to Puerto Rico's indigenous culture. On several days during the year (usually Oct. 12, Nov. 19, and Apr. 30) employees don indigenous dress and recreate Taíno ceremonies; call ahead for more information. (Rte. 503 Km 2.8. ☎ 840-2255 or 840-5685; www.ponce.inter.edu/tibes/tibes.html. Open Tu-Su 9am-4pm. Visits with guided tours only; free English/Spanish guided tours every hr., usually on the hr. $2, ages 6-12 and 60+ $1, under 6 free.)

THE LOCAL STORY

TAÍNO TERMS

Today, the only traces of the Taínos, who lived in Puerto Rico from 600 AD to 1600 AD, are stone walls, ancient tools and mysterious drawings, but this group of people once ruled all of the island. When you visit the archaeological sites dedicated to the Taínos and try to decipher to broken stones and remaining petroglyphs, the following terms may help you understand the artifacts you see.

Batey: A traditional Taíno ball game that was used as both a sport and a religious ritual. Two teams of between 10 and 30 men tried to keep a 3-5 lb. ball made of tree fiber in the air; the first team to drop the ball lost. The court used for the game is also called a *batey.*

Bohío: A circular hut made of straw and wood that served as home for Taínos. *Caciques* (chiefs) lived in rectangular huts.

Cemís: Stone icons shaped like a cone with bulbs on either side of the base that served as a Taíno object of worship. The shape combines elements of male and female reproductive parts and of the mountains, in an expression of the fertility of the earth.

Caguana: A woman traditionally associated with fertility, also known as the Women of Caguana.

Boríkén: This word roughly translates as "land of the lords." Puerto Ricans still refer to their island by the Spanish variant: *Borinquén.*

COAMO

Public Transportation: Públicos between Ponce and Coamo will drop passengers off at the intersection of Rte. 546 and Rte. 153, 1 mi. from the baths ($2.50). They may go all the way to the end if arranged in advance ($5). *Driving:* From Ponce take Hwy. 52 east to Exit 76, then drive north on Rte. 153 to Rte. 546. The baths are at the end.

Puerto Rico has plenty of opportunities to de-stress, but few compare to the **hot springs** just outside of Coamo. With temperatures reaching 109°F, the baths are like all-natural, communal jacuzzis—without the bubbles. These are reportedly the oldest thermal baths in the New World, and as early as 1847 a hotel at the baths allowed rich Puerto Ricans to access the soothing waters. Today, two **public baths** just behind the hotel are free to the public. These look like Old World baths, with small brick- and-concrete-lined pools and little waterfalls. Park at the end of Rte. 546, then walk past the gate and down the dirt path. To satiate the post-bath munchies, try **La Cava Grill House ❺**, Rte. 153 Km 11.2. The incredible steak and seafood are worth the splurge. (☎803-3277 or 825-4843. Entrees $15-26. All-you-can-eat buffet F-Sa 4-11pm, Su 11am-10pm; $19. Open M-Th 11am-11pm, F-Sa 11am-2am. MC/V.) If the lure of the hot springs tempts you to extend your daytrip to an overnight stay, **Hotel Baños de Coamo ❸**, at the end of Rte. 546, offers a more modern take on the baths, with a swimming pool fed by hot springs. The attractive *parador* looks and feels like a ski lodge plopped down in the middle of a tropical forest. Rooms are large and wood-paneled, and have cable TV, phone, and A/C. (☎825-2186 or 825-2239; fax 825-4739). Pool, restaurant, game room, and souvenir shop. Check-in 3pm. Check-out 1pm. Singles $86; doubles $91; extra person $10; 2 children under 12 free. Tax included. AmEx/D/MC/V.)

SALINAS

On the surface, Salinas looks like any other city in south-central Puerto Rico, with traffic-crowded streets and a town square surrounded by *cafeterías*. But just south of town is Playa Salinas, one of the island's largest ports and the best for wandering island-hoppers to find passage on vessels traveling throughout the western hemisphere. The activity centers around Marina de Salinas & Posada El Náutico, a hotel complex with a bulletin board that travelers use to coordinate rides. Playa Salinas also offers scrumptious seafood, some boating opportunities, and a funky international charm rarely found in small Puerto Rican towns.

▦ TRANSPORTATION. Two of Puerto Rico's major thoroughfares, Rte. 1 and Rte. 3, meet in downtown Salinas. From San Juan take Hwy. 52 south to the final intersection with Rte. 1; this road becomes **C. Muñoz Rivera**. **Públicos** travel to **Guayama** (30min., $1.55) and **Playa Salinas** (5min., $0.45). To reach the plaza from the *público* station, turn left onto C. Amadeo and walk one block.

▦▦ ORIENTATION AND PRACTICAL INFORMATION. The convergence of **Route 1** and **Route 3** is Salinas's main street; off the central plaza, Rte. 1 is called C. Amadeo, and to the east, Rte. 3 becomes C. Barbosa. C. Muñoz Rivera runs perpendicular to this street along the plaza. To reach **Playa Salinas** drive west on **Rte. 1**, then turn south on **Rte. 701**, which follows the bay. All of the services are located near the town center, about 1 mi. north of Playa Salinas. **Banco Popular,** C. Muñoz Rivera 1, on the plaza, has two ATMs. (☎824-3075. Open M-F 8am-4pm.) **Grande supermarket,** on Rte. 7701 across from the post office, has **MoneyGram** service. (☎824-1400. Open M-Sa 7am-9pm, Su 12-5pm. AmEx/MC/V.) The **police station,** C. Muñoz Rivera 500, is ¼ mi. north of the plaza. (☎824-2020. Open 24hr.) **Sur**

Med Medical Center, C. Colón Pacheco 8, lies east of
town off Rte. 3, behind the Esso Station. (☎824-1100
or 824-1199. 24hr. emergency room. Open 24hr.) Also
has a well-stocked **pharmacy** inside (Open M-Sa 8am-
11pm, Su noon-8pm.) The **post office,** Rte. 7701 #100,
off Rte. 701 near the intersection with Rte. 1, has
General Delivery. (☎824-2485. Open M-F 8am-
4:30pm, Sa 8am-noon.) **Postal Code:** 00751.

**▐▐ ACCOMMODATIONS AND FOOD. Marina de
Salinas ❸,** C. Chapin G-9, on Rte. 701, is both a bustling sailors' port and the best hotel in Salinas. Colorful rooms with nautical paintings have A/C, cable
TV, wicker furniture, and nice showers. Spacious
suites come with a full kitchenette. The hotel also
has laundry facilities, a restaurant, a book
exchange, a small pool, a waterfront snack bar, and
a playground area. (On Rte. 701 past the seafood
restaurants. ☎752-8484 or 824-3185; fax 768-7676.
Check-in 2pm. Check-out 1pm. Doubles $77; quads
$88-99; suites $110-150; extra person $15; children
under 11 free. AmEx/D/DC/MC/V.) Across the bay,
Puerta La Bahía ❸ has a similar design, but lacks the
facilities and the aesthetic touch. Aluminum-doored
rooms don't aim to charm, but they do come with
TV, A/C, and private baths. (From Rte. 701 drive to
Marina de Salinas, turn left at the gate, then continue around the bay, always veering right. ☎824-
7117. Pool. 1 double bed $84; 2 beds $150. Tax
included. There is also an **RV area.** AmEx/MC/V.)

Food options tend to clump together in Salinas.
C. Muñoz Rivera and C. Amadeo, near the plaza,
have several inexpensive *comida criolla* lunch
options. The seafood restaurants near Playa Salinas,
along Rte. 701, are somewhat more expensive, but
offer fresh surf 'n' turf on patios overlooking the
water. Both of the hotels have nice restaurants, but
they can't beat **El Balcón del Capitán ❸,** C. A 54, on
Rte. 701. The restaurant's bright orange balcony
sits directly over the water, providing incomparable views and a cool sea breeze. El Balcón specializes in seafood flavored with the local favorite,
mojo isleño, a tomato-based sauce. (☎824-6210.
Entrees $7-27. Tropical drinks $5. Open daily
11:30am-10pm. AmEx/MC/V.)

▟ OUTDOOR ACTIVITIES. The many off-shore
islands provide ample opportunity for nautical
exploration. **Marina de Salinas & Posada El Náutico**
rents **kayaks** and **bikes** ($15 per hr., $40 per day). Or
just forget the kayak and hop on **La Paseadora,** a fun-
filled, music-blasting boat that takes groups on

THE HIDDEN DEAL

GOLFIN' IN PARADISE

On the majority of the island,
golf is a sport reserved for the
wealthy, and green fees can
climbs high as $200 per round.
But all of this changes in little
Aguirre, where the local golf club
hails from a different era. This
18-hole course was built back
when Aguirre was a bustling
sugar town, and the rich North
American executives needed
some way to relax and amuse
themselves while the profits
rolled in.

Over time sugar stopped making the big bucks, the mainland-
ers disappeared, and Aguirre
entered a slow state of decay.
However, the golf club continues
to thrive, one of the few lively
areas in this quasi-ghost town.
Best of all, the prices too seem
frozen in time; you can get a
green fee as low as $10. At this
price, even amateurs may be
tempted to pass a few hours on
the neatly cut grass.

Green fees are $10 from
Tuesday through Friday and $18
on weekends and holidays. Golf
carts are an additional $12 per
nine holes, though this cost can
be divided between two people
sharing one cart. The pro shop
also rents equipment for $10 per
person per day.

*(Rte. 705 Km 1.6. From Rte. 3
turn south onto Rte. 705 and veer
right when the road splits. ☎853-
4052. Open Tu-Su 7am-6pm and M
if it is a holiday. Am/Ex/MC/V.)*

tours of the bay ($3, children $2) or drops people off at a nearby island ($5, children $3). The boat leaves every weekend; for more info contact Ity Jiménez (☎824-2649) or wait on the dock next to El Balcón del Capitán (see **Food,** above) in the morning. Playa Salinas's only swimming area is at **Polita's Beach,** Rte. 701 Km 2.1. Sadly, there is no sand, just a large wooden platform. (☎824-4184. Open Sa-Su and holidays 9am-dusk.)

GUAYAMA

Once the center of Puerto Rico's sugar industry, today Guayama is a busy business hub congested with traffic. Nevertheless, several attractions await the handful of visitors who make their way out here: in addition to the town square that hearkens back to the sugar cane glory days, Guayama is close to several natural attractions, from beaches to a butterfly sanctuary. If you can find a parking space, Guayama is a surprisingly pleasant place to visit.

▐ TRANSPORTATION

Rte. 3 leads directly into downtown Guayama. **Públicos** leave from the station at the corner of C. Ashford and C. Enrique González for: **Patillas** (30min., $0.90) via **Arroyo** (10min., $0.60); **Ponce** (45min., $4.35); **San Juan** (1½hr., $7) via **Caguas** (45min., $7); and **Salinas** (30min., $1.55). Most *públicos* leave in the morning or early afternoon. From the *público* station exit onto C. Ashford, turn left, walk two blocks, and turn left again to reach the plaza. **Hertz,** in Molino Inn Hotel (see **Accommodations,** below), rents compact cars starting at $39 per day. (☎866-6417. 21+. Under 25 surcharge $10 per day. Open M-Sa 9am-5pm. AmEx/D/MC/V.)

▰▱ ORIENTATION AND PRACTICAL INFORMATION

The commercial area of Guayama is near the intersection of Rte. 3 and Hwy. 54. **Route 3** leads past the **plaza,** but it can get a bit confusing and road signs are sporadic. The tall church steeple on the plaza is visible from far away and serves as a handy landmark if you get lost. Coming from the east, Rte. 3 becomes **Calle Ashford,** a major thoroughfare that runs parallel to C. Santiago Palmer, which passes the plaza. Drive past the church, then turn left on C. Vicente Pales, then left again on C. Martínez, going around the plaza, to stay on Rte. 3. C. Derkes forms the southern border of the plaza. **Plaza Guayama Mall,** Rte. 3 Km 135.2, east of town, has many shops and services, including a six-screen movie theater.

Banks: Banco Popular (☎866-0288), in front of Plaza Guayama Mall, has an ATM. Open M-F 8am-4pm, Sa 8am-3pm, Su 11am-3pm.

Camping Permits: The **DRNA** office, Rte. 3 Km 144.5 (☎864-8903 or 723-3073; fax 864-1147), west of town, issues camping permits ($4). Allow 3-4 days for processing. Open M-F 7:30am-noon and 1-4pm.

Supermarkets: Pueblo Xtra (☎866-1225), next to Plaza Guayama Mall. **Western Union.** Open M-Sa 6am-midnight, Su 11am-5pm. AmEx/MC/V.

Police: ☎866-2020. Located on Av. José Torre, behind the hospital. Open 24hr.

Hospital: Hospital Episcopal Cristo Redentor, Hwy. 54 Km 2.7 (☎864-4300). Clinic open M-F 8am-4pm. Emergency room open 24hr.

Internet Access: Postland, in the Plaza Guayama Mall, has 3 fast computers. Internet $2.50 per 15min., $7.50 per hr. Also has UPS, FedEx, and **Western Union** services. Open M-Sa 9am-6pm. MC/V.

Post Office: C. Ashford 151 (☎864-1150), several blocks east of the plaza. General Delivery available. Open M-F 7:30am-4:30pm, Sa 7:30am-noon. **Postal Code:** 00784.

ACCOMMODATIONS

Hotel Brandemar (☎864-5124), at the end of Rte. 748. From Guayama drive east on Hwy. 54 to Km 5.7, then turn right on Rte. 748; the reception is in the restaurant. Located in a quiet neighborhood near the water, this affordable hotel has everything travelers need, including private bath, TV, A/C, and a huge swimming pool. However, mosquitoes and ants have been known to invade. Doubles $54-64; triples $75; quad with kitchenette $95. Tax included. AmEx/D/MC/V. ❷

Molino Inn Hotel, Hwy. 54 Km 2.1 (☎866-1515; www.molinoinn.net), is the only hotel within city limits. Clean, chain hotel-style rooms include A/C, phone, cable TV, and a balcony overlooking the courtyard and the large, narrow pool. As the hotel is located on a busy highway, it's worth asking for a room in the back. Check-in 3pm. Check-out noon. Nov. 15-Feb. 14 and May 15-Aug. 14 doubles M-Th and Su $101, F-Sa and holidays $106. Feb. 15-May 14 and Aug. 15-Nov. 14 $95/101; extra person $10. Tax included. AmEx/MC/V. ❹

FOOD

Fine dining is sparse in Guayama; however, several restaurants in the *barrio* of **Pozuelo,** at the end of Rte. 7710, off Rte. 3, west of town serve fresh seafood near the water. The city center is filled with *panaderías* serving up hearty sandwiches.

La Casa de Los Pastelillos, Rte. 7710 Km 3.8 (☎864-5171), in Pozuelo. Serves dozens of different types of *pastelillos* (fried dough; $2-5), filled with everything from pizza to shark. You may need more than one to fill up. The highlight of this creative restaurant is the laid-back atmosphere; chow down on the large deck or lie in a hammock right on the beach. Bar with live music on some weekend nights. Happy hour M-Sa 4-8pm (beer $1-2). Open daily 11am-8pm. ❶

Supreme Bakery (☎866-8175 or 864-7501), at C. Derkes and C. Hostos. This *panadería* deserves its popularity, dishing out loaded baked potatoes ($3-5) and even bigger grilled sandwiches (most $2.50-4) to the local crowds. Great baked goods $0.50-2. Breakfast $2-4. Open daily 6am-9:30pm. MC/V. ❶

El Suarito (☎864-1820), across from Supreme Bakery. This big, semi-outdoor building is another local lunch favorite, serving breakfast ($1-4), sandwiches ($1-6), and Puerto Rican entrees ($4-8). Open M-Sa 8am-3pm. MC/V. ❶

Cafetería Vegetariana, C. Hostos 46 (☎864-5471), at C. Enrique Gonzalez, a few blocks south of the plaza in the back of Natural Health Food. The only vegetarian restaurant you'll ever see that features salami sandwiches. Also traditional veggie choices like tofu. Sandwiches $1.50-3.25. *Batidas* $2.50. Open M-F 9am-1:30pm. MC/V. ❶

SIGHTS

MUSEUMS. The cultural tour of Guayama begins on the plaza at **Museo Casa Cautiño.** Built in 1887 by a *guayamés* architect, this magnificent house has been restored to its former glory and decorated with much of the original artwork and furniture, including magnificent chandeliers and sculptures. A walk inside provides insight into the life of Guayama's wealthy sugar families. (*C. Vicente Pales 1, on the plaza.* ☎864-9083. Open Tu-Sa 9am-4:30pm, Su 10:30am-4pm. Free.) Housed in a Classical 1927 Superior Tribunal building, Guayama's **Centro de Bellas Artes** displays a

SOUTHEAST

variety of paintings, sculptures, and prints by professional Puerto Rican artists and incredibly talented art students. One room holds Taíno artifacts, but all the explanatory signs are in Spanish. *(Rte. 3 Km 138, west of the plaza. ☎864-7765. Open Tu-Su 10am-4:30pm. Free.)* The quirky **Pabellón de la Fama Deporte Guayamés** (Pavilion of Guayaman Sports Fame) details local sports accomplishments through photos, newspaper clippings, and memorabilia. A surprising number of track stars are represented, and who knew that a *guayamés* had played for the Yankees? *(C. Ashford 22, at C. Derkes. ☎866-0676. Open M-F 8am-noon and 1-4:30pm, Sa 9am-noon and 1-4:30pm.)*

RESERVA NATURAL MARIPOSARIO LAS LIMAS. The first butterfly sanctuary in Puerto Rico hides high in the hills, about 5 mi. north of Guayama. Created by an environmentally-minded Puerto Rican couple, the 198-acre, semi-tropical reserve has received support from several government facilities, including the DRNA, but still retains the personal feel of a private enterprise. A 1¼hr. guided walk leads visitors from a small museum filled with hundreds of butterfly specimens, past ponds filled with shrimp, turtles, and fish, and into the woods, where guides point out the various species of plants and animals. Of course, there is time for a stop at the small butterfly cage, and a cafeteria and gift shop await at the end. *(From Guayama take Rte. 15 north to Rte. 179. After about 2 mi., turn onto Rte. 747 and make a right at Km 0.7 where signs lead to the forest. ☎864-6037 or 866-6756. Open Th-Su 10am-3pm. Mostly Spanish, but guides speak some English. Mandatory tour $3. Reservations recommended.)*

ARROYO

When the sugar boom came to an end and Guayama developed as an industrial town, little Arroyo lagged behind. The result is a much smaller, and much more charming, oceanside town where the main attraction is walking down the boardwalk watching the boats dock. Surprisingly, though, the city also has several worthwhile cultural attractions. Arroyo's **Tren del Sur,** Rte. 3 Km 130.9, the only operating train left in Puerto Rico, rekindles the atmosphere of the sugar era on a 1hr. ride through sugar fields and past plantation ruins. (Theoretically open Sa-Su and some holidays 9am-4pm. $3, under 12 $2.) Employees at Arroyo's castle-like **tourist office,** in the same parking lot as Tren del Sur, distribute pamphlets about the town and can answer questions. (☎271-1574. Open M-F 8am-3pm.) Arroyo's colorful and beautifully carved old customs house has been converted into the **Museo de la Antigua Aduana,** C. Morse 65, but it was under construction at the time of publication. (South of the plaza. ☎839-8096. Open W-Su 9am-4pm.) The charming **boardwalk** at the end of C. Morse is lined with palm trees on one side and seafood restaurants on the other.

The most popular part of Arroyo is not the town itself, but rather **Centro Vacacional Guilarte,** the best beach between Yabucoa and Guánica. This enormous government-run vacation center doesn't have too much sand, but makes up for that with scattered palm trees, lush vegetation, and incredible sunsets. Here, families picnic in the grass and children play in the shallow water. Facilities include outdoor showers, bathrooms, trash cans, picnic tables, and lifeguards during daylight hours. A few kiosks sell *empanadillas* and beer. The accommodations options at this large complex fit any budget. An enormous grassy **camping area ❶** at the far eastern edge of the complex has trash cans and a bathroom. The tiny cement **cabañas ❸** provide a roof over your head, in addition to two cramped bedrooms that hold up to six people. The rooms are less than comfortable, but *cabaña* guests also have access to the large, clean **pool,** as well as **beach volleyball courts.** For a more relaxed sleeping experience, head straight to the **villas ❹,** which are similar to the *cabañas* but have been newly renovated and include A/C and hot water. (Rte. 3 Km 128.4 to 129.6, east of Arroyo. The western entrance leads to the *villas;* the eastern entrance leads to the *cabañas,* the camping area, the public beach, and the office. ☎839-3565. Office open daily 8am-4:30pm. Entrance to complex $3 per car. Camping $10 per tent. *Cabañas* $66; *villas* $109. Tax included. AmEx/D/MC/V.) Arroyo's best restaurants line the **boardwalk**, where several serve seafood on patios overlooking the water. For a cheaper option, **Panadería and Repostería La Familia ❶**, on C. Morse, two blocks south of the plaza, serves pizza (slices $1.25-1.75), sandwiches ($1.25-4.50), a daily lunch special ($3), and of course, pastries. (☎271-5162. Open daily 7am-9pm. MC/V.)

Públicos between Patillas and Guayama stop in Arroyo along C. Morse; flag down a van and ask which direction it's going (15min., $0.50). If you're going to Centro Vacacional Guilarte, ask the driver to drop you off at the intersection, then walk 1 mi. down to the beach. It's about a 2 mi. walk back into town.

ROUTE 901

Following the southeast corner of the island through the heart of sugar country, Rte. 901 is the tail end of Puerto Rico's Ruta Panorámica. Here, it seems that the crest of every hill open on yet another gorgeous ocean vista. Several enterprising Puerto Ricans have capitalized on the road's ideal location by building attractive accommodations and appetizing seafood restaurants. There is not really much to do, but foreigners and Puerto Ricans alike make the trek out to this corner of the island to relax on a hammock with a book, bake in the sun, or just watch the waves. Yabucoa, at the northern end of the road, serves as the starting point for the scenic Ruta Panorámica (p. 290), and anyone embarking upon this journey should take one last glance at the ocean from Rte. 901 before heading into the mountains.

▐ TRANSPORTATION. From San Juan take Hwy. 52 south to Caguas, get on Rte. 1 temporarily to catch the exit for Hwy. 30 east, then exit onto Hwy. 53 south. At the end of Hwy. 53 turn right to reach Yabucoa or turn left for Rte. 901. Rte. 901 is easiest to navigate by car; however, **públicos** do go from Yabucoa to **Humacao** (20min., $1.20) and **Maunabo** (20-25min., $1). From Yabucoa's *público* station, walk uphill and turn right on C. Cristóbal Colón to reach the plaza and the taxi stand. **Taxis** travel to **Playa Lucía** ($6), **Maunabo** ($15), and everywhere in between. (☎266-4047. Open 6am-6pm.) If you do plan to reach a hotel by public transportation, either bring your own food or head to an all-inclusive—the mountain roads are not suited to walking and food establishments are not spread over the area.

THE HIDDEN DEAL

THE GARDEN OF EATIN'

Most country *paradores* or guesthouses offer suites with kitchenettes, making it easy for travelers to buy their own groceries, cook at home, and beat restaurant prices. But there are other great ways to eat on the cheap.

If you stop by any of Puerto Rico's "Panadería y Repostería" eateries (bakeries and confectioners) for lunch, you'll gain a fresh appreciation for Puerto Rico's hidden deals. A half-pound loaf of fresh-baked bread—filled to the brim with ham, cheese, and eggs—costs about $2 at most of these eateries. In fact, it might be wise to bring a friend to share your sandwich. If you can find room for dessert, indulge in sweet treats such as donuts, flan, *tres leches* cakes, or guava-and-cheese croissants (a ridiculously low $0.50-2).

For something fresher than the bakeries can offer, just hop in your car. As you drive around the island, you'll notice the fruits of centuries of tropical farming hanging from the trees along the road, on the grounds of university campuses, and in public parks. Mangos, coffee, and bananas grow in abundance. While it might be a bit much to pick, dry, roast, and grind your own coffee beans, grabbing an almost-ripe mango from a public tree and letting it ripen in your car isn't that hard. In the end, you're left with a free, healthy supplement to lunch. Just be sure you don't pick fruit from someone's private property.

▣ ❼ ORIENTATION AND PRACTICAL INFORMATION.

Rte. 901 follows the southeast coast of the island between Yabucoa and Maunabo; however, the scenic route continues south past Maunabo along Rte. 3 all the way to Patillas. If you get lost just follow the numerous signs to the *parador*. Coming into Yabucoa, when you reach the concrete island, turn right onto **C. Cristóbal Colón** (also called Rte. 9910) to reach the plaza, or continue straight onto Rte. 182 (also called C. Catalina Morales) for most government buildings and the beginning of the Ruta Panorámica. All of the services listed below are in Yabucoa. **Banco Popular,** on Rte. 9914 1 mi. south of town, has one walk-up ATM and several drive-thrus. (☎893-2620. Open M-F 8am-4pm, Sa 9am-1pm.) **Yabucoa Municipal Library,** on C. Catalina Morales, past the post office, houses the city's small **Casa de la Cultura** and its collection of Yabucoan artifacts that range from pre-Taíno ceramics of 250 BC to dishes made of squash shells from the 1940s. (☎893-5520 or 893-3385. Open when school is in session M-Th 8am-7pm, F 8am-4:30pm; in summer M-F 8am-4:30pm.) **Supermercado del Este,** on Rte. 901, just south of Yabucoa in the plaza labeled "La Reina," has groceries. (☎893-4340. Open M-Sa 7am-6pm, Su 11am-5pm. MC/V.) **60 Minute Cleaners,** C. Cristóbal Colón 67, has self-serve washers ($1.25) and dryers ($0.50). (☎893-2855. Open M-Sa 7:30am-5pm.) The **police station,** C. Catalina Morales 102 (☎893-2020), is open 24hr. **Farmacia Feliciano** is next to Supermercado del Este. (☎893-6709. Open M-F 7:30am-9pm, Sa 8am-9pm. AmEx/D/MC/V.) Yabucoa's small **hospital** is across from the supermarket. (☎893-7100. 24hr. emergency room.) **PostNet,** on Rte. 901, about half a mile south of town, across from the stadium, has **Internet access.** (☎893-0520. $5 per hr. Also has UPS and FedEx service. Open M-F 8:30am-1:30pm and 2-5pm.) The **post office** is at C. Catalina Morales 100. (☎893-2135. No General Delivery. Open M-F 7:30am-4:30pm.) **Postal Code:** 00767.

⌂ ACCOMMODATIONS.

The inviting accommodations along this scenic route are one of the region's major draws. Like the region itself, most are relatively quiet and will frown upon groups of drunk teenagers. **Playa Emajaguas Guest House ❷,** Rte. 901 Km 12.5, combines a great location overlooking the beach with excellent prices. Behind a field off the road, this two-story guest house comes with a pool table, tennis court, pool, picnic tables, and a path down to Playa Emajaguas (see **Beaches,** below). The downside is that this small guest house is a bit messy and beginning to show its age. (1½ mi. north of Maunabo. ☎861-6023. TV, A/C, and fridge. In summer small rooms $60; apartments $80. Rest of the year $50/70. Cash only.) The **Caribe Playa Beach Resort ❹,** Rte. 3 Km 112.1, south of Maunabo, exudes a resort-like professionalism rarely found in the Rte. 901 area. This relaxing hotel right on the beach enhances the striking location with numerous hammocks and beach chairs, a barbecue, beachside pool, and jacuzzi. The cheapest rooms are clean and brightly colored, but it's worth it to spring for the ocean-view rooms, where $20 extra buys you a much larger room (and a larger bed), fridge, cable TV, phone, shared balcony, and of course, an ocean view. (☎839-6339; www.caribe-playa.com. Standard doubles $95, ocean view $115. AmEx/MC/V.) A parrot greets guests at **Parador Palmas de Lucía ❺,** at Rte. 901 and Rte. 9911, about 5 mi. southeast of Yabucoa. As one of the island's premier *paradores*, this elegant hotel surrounds a large pool area. Large carpeted rooms are clean and tasteful, and the hotel is just steps away from the fun Playa Lucía. (☎893-4423; www.palmasdelucia.com. Cable TV, A/C, and phone. Only offers all-inclusive packages. 2 nights $319 for 2 people, $395 for 3 people, $490 for 4 people. Tax included. AmEx/MC/V.)

❐ FOOD.

Several restaurants along Rte. 901 are upscale eateries offering spectacular views and equally amazing seafood entrees. Many more are cheap kiosks hawking *pinchos* to beachgoers, but they too have the spectacular views. If you happen to be near Yabucoa, **Doredmar Restaurant ❸,** on Rte. 3 just south of the intersection with Rte. 901, is one of the few standouts. A small back patio surrounded by vegetation is a great location to enjoy fresh steak and seafood. (☎893-3837. Meat entrees $6-12. Seafood $13-25. Open daily 11am-midnight. MC/V.) The well-marked **Los Bohíos Restaurant ❹,** on Playa Maunabo, provides a refreshing change from the dozens of kiosks and offers seafood and meat in a beachside, semi-outdoor environment. Bohíos keeps it classy—you may not want to come straight from the beach. (☎861-2545. Seafood entrees $12-22. *Mofongo* $11-22. Open W-Th 11am-3pm, F-Su 11am-7:30pm. AmEx/MC/V.)

◪ **BEACHES.** Rte. 901 is lined with beaches, but many are rocky and have minimal shore area. Just below the guesthouse of the same name, palm-lined **Playa de Emajaguas** has an unusually wide stretch of smooth sand, few rocks, medium-sized waves, and remarkably small crowds. Unfortunately, there are no facilities, but this is still one of the best sites for lounging and swimming in the clearest water on Rte. 901. Another attractive beach is **Playa Lucía,** located just past Parador Palmas de Lucía (see **Accommodations,** above). The long beach lined with palm trees is often filled with guests from the *parador.* A few food kiosks open when the beach is crowded.

The only sight in this area is actually located on a beach; the **Punta Tuna Lighthouse,** just outside of Maunabo, is visible from both Playa Maunabo and Playa Larga. Built by the Spanish in the late 1800s, the lighthouse is now operated by the US Coast Guard and closed to the public. For the best views, head down to the secluded **Playa Larga.** Coming south on Rte. 9011 turn toward the ocean on Rte. 7760, pass Villa del Faro, and take the first left going downhill at the mailboxes. You will have to find somewhere on Rte. 7760 to park your car, as the street that leads to the beach does not allow parking. When you get to the closed gate, walk down the short path to the beach. There can be a lot of seaweed on the sand, but it is a small price to pay for this rare solitude.

Traveling south, the next beach area is **Playa Maunabo,** which is popular with young people and has a bit more sand. Its big waves are good for boogie boarding and facilities include grills and bathrooms. To reach the beach, continue down Rte. 760 and follow signs to Restaurant Los Bohíos.

SOUTHWEST

Forget those images of lush palm tree-lined beaches; here, the landscape is dramatic and dry, and the coastline alternates between striking cliffs, stretches of uninterrupted sand, and rocky ports. Inland lies the cactus forest of Bosque Estatal de Guánica, and, just offshore, hundreds of mangrove-filled islands invite exploration. Southwest Puerto Rico feels so different from San Juan that the Spaniards gave the region its own capital in 1514. Nowadays, college towns attract young people while the beaches draw families and partygoers from around the island. The fruits of the sea make up the southwest's extensive culinary offerings, enticing visitors and Puerto Ricans alike. Summer weekends can be very crowded, but during the week and particularly in the off-season, travelers can have a dramatic cliff top or a quiet beach all to themselves. Casual hiking, kayaking, diving, and snorkeling in state forests and protected waters attract active visitors, but the greatest natural wonders are found on protected Isla Mona, nearly 50 mi. offshore. Cultural offerings are not lacking either. The region's long colonial history has resulted in architecture to rival anything in Old San Juan, and legends of pirates, nuns, smugglers, and town fathers speak to 500 years of contested ownership.

HIGHLIGHTS OF SOUTHWEST PUERTO RICO

REVEL in the many delights of **Guánica's** superb dry forest (see below).

GET IN TOUCH WITH YOUR WILD SIDE on **Isla Mona,** land of enormous iguanas, gorgeous beaches, and the best diving in Puerto Rico (p. 248).

ESCAPE TO THE END OF THE EARTH at the **Cabo Rojo Lighthouse,** where breathtaking cliffs produce some of the most dramatic scenery in Puerto Rico (p. 243).

SAVOR the seafood and other culinary delights of small-town **Joyuda** (p. 253).

BOSQUE ESTATAL DE GUÁNICA

Cactus-covered cliffs give way to the gently lapping waves of Caribbean beaches in Bosque Estatal de Guánica. This dry forest contains such a unique diversity of plant and animal life, including the largest variety of birds on the island, that it was named a United Nations Biosphere Reserve in 1981. This is Puerto Rico's paradise for outdoor pursuits, as it has some of the best hiking and water sports on the island. With over 20 mi. of trails, two islands just offshore, and half a dozen beaches, it's not unusual to see visitors lacing up their hiking boots, taking a kayak off the roof rack, unpacking snorkel gear, or just wandering off with a picnic.

▐ TRANSPORTATION

From Hwy. 2, turn south onto Rte. 116. The first important left is Rte. 334, which leads to the forest info center. The next left, onto Rte. 333, leads to most of the beaches, the accommodations, and the ferry dock. At the next intersection, Rte. 116R leads to Guánica's center. Inquire at the tourist office about *públicos;* road construction in the town center means drop-off and pick-up points are in flux.

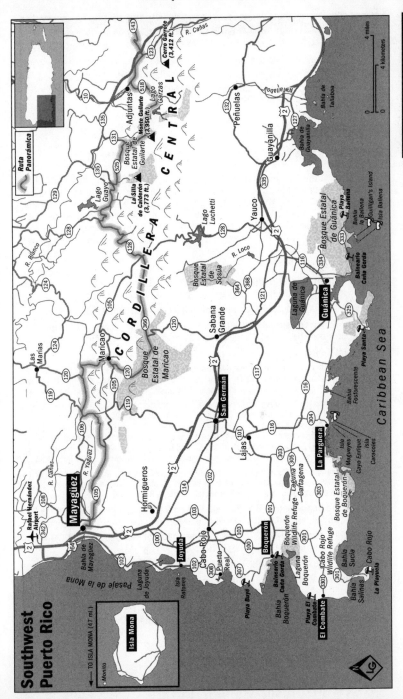

Southwest
Puerto Rico

Caribbean Sea

Isla Mona

← TO ISLA MONA (47 mi.)
• Monito

Ruta Panorámica

AT A GLANCE	
AREA: 9876 acres.	**GATEWAYS:** Guánica, Ponce (p. 203).
CLIMATE: Hot and dry. Average temperature 79°F. Little variation.	**CAMPING:** Unfortunately, there is no camping in or near Guánica.
HIGHLIGHTS: Hiking through dramatic landscapes, water sports, bird-watching.	**FEES:** None.
FEATURES: Rare dry limestone scrub, incredible Caribbean coastline.	

ORIENTATION AND PRACTICAL INFORMATION

Bosque Estatal de Guánica is divided into two sections. The larger eastern half contains the hiking trails, the two most popular beaches, and the two off-shore islands. Playa Santa and the surrounding sights lie adjacent to the undeveloped western section. In between, the small town of Guánica is a good place to stock up on supplies, but ongoing construction makes it difficult to get around or find visitor information. Rte. 116R deposits drivers on Calle 25 de Julio, which passes the plaza and veers left before intersecting with Rte. 333. C. 39 de Marzo intersects 25 de Julio just past the plaza.

Visitors Center: The **DRNA info center** (☎821-5706), at the end of Rte. 334, provides extensive info about the trails (in Spanish). Open daily 8:30am-4:30pm.

Hours: The DRNA parking area (and thus most trails) is open daily 8:30am-4:30pm.

Supplies: Sunscreen and water are the most important items you will need in Guánica; many paths don't have shade. Bring at least 35 oz. of water per person per hr. of hiking.

Equipment Rental:

Dive Copamarina, in Copamarina Beach Resort (see **Scuba Diving**, p. 232), rents tennis rackets ($5 per hr.), kayaks (singles $12 for 1st hr., doubles $20), snorkel gear ($10 for 3hr.), water tricycles ($15 per hr.), Barracuda paddleboats ($20 per hr.) and Hobie Cats ($40 per hr.).

Pino's Boats and Water Fun (☎821-6864 or 484-8083), a trailer on the beach at Playa Santa, rents jet skis ($40-45 per 30min.), kayaks (singles $12 per hr., doubles $20), paddleboats (2-person $12 per hr., 4-person $20), and lounge chairs ($5 per day). The owner also offers 40min. motorboat ecotours through the mangroves with narration of the ecological role of features along the way ($5 per person), 20min. banana boat rides ($6), and jet ski tours ($45) of the mangroves. Open Sa-Su and most weekdays; hours depending on crowds but usually between 11am-5pm. MC/V.

Island Divers is a full-service dive shop with equipment ($15) for rent, lessons available, and a boat and divemaster available for dives at La Parguera's famous Wall and other dive sites. Limited scuba equipment is available at **San Jacinto Boats & Restaurant** (p. 230).

Bank: Banco Santander, C. S.S. Rodriguez 63 (☎821-2700 or 821-2283), at the corner of C. 25 de Julio. ATM. Open M-F 8:30am-4pm.

Supermarket: Econo (☎821-2789), at the intersection of Rte. 116 and 116R. Open M-Sa 7am-8pm, Su 11am-5pm. AmEx/D/DC/MC/V.

Police: C. 13 de Marzo 51 (☎821-2020). Open 24hr.

Hospital: From Rte. 116 drive down C. 25 de Julio and turn right after the plaza, turn right at the end of the street, then take the first left. The emergency room (☎821-1481) is open 24hr.

Post Office: C. 13 de Marzo 39 (☎821-2645). No General Delivery. Open M-F 8am-4:30pm, Sa 8am-noon. **Postal Code:** 00653.

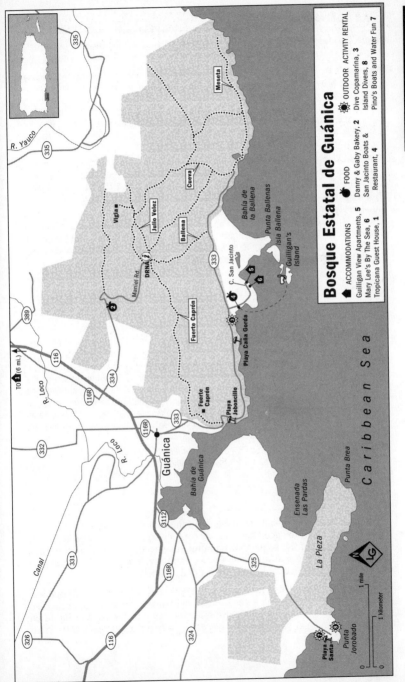

Bosque Estatal de Guánica

▲ ACCOMMODATIONS
Guilligan View Apartments, 5
Mary Lee's By The Sea, 6
Tropicana Guest House, 1

● FOOD
Danny & Gaby Bakery, 2
San Jacinto Boats &
Restaurant, 4

☀ OUTDOOR ACTIVITY RENTAL
Dive Copamarina, 3
Island Divers, 8
Pino's Boats and Water Fun 7

Caribbean Sea

▐ ACCOMMODATIONS

Bosque Estatal de Guánica has no camping, and most guesthouses are fairly expensive. Nearby Guayanilla and La Parguera have more affordable options.

■ **Mary Lee's By The Sea,** C. San Jacinto 25 (☎821-3600; www.maryleesbythesea.com). US expat Mary Lee has put great care into the decoration of each room. Haitian grass rugs, brightly colored curtains, and lots of seaside knick-knacks create a charmingly tropical effect. All rooms include a kitchenette, A/C, and access to a deck with a barbecue. Trips to Guilligan's Island $5 per person. Kayak rental single $10 per hr., doubles $15. Laundry. Check-in 3pm. Check-out noon. Singles $80-100; doubles $120; quads $130-140; 6-person rooms $140-250; extra person $10. MC/V. ❸

Guilligan View Apartments, C. San Jacinto 27 (☎821-0972 or 821-4901). Clean, colorfully decorated rooms with a view of the mangrove islands. Pool table and common yard in back. Full kitchens. Kayak rental $35 per day. Doubles $75; quads $100. ❸

Tropicana Guest House, Rte. 127 Km 8 (☎835-3382), about 8 mi. east of Guánica in Guayanilla, on the 2nd fl. of a *panadería*. From Hwy. 2 take Exit 207, then go east on Rte. 127 and turn in at the sign for Panadería Grande 2. Indoor tiled hallway leads to dark wooden doors with elegant brass knockers. A bit far from the sea, but the combination of ambience and price is a rare find. Cable TV, A/C, fridge, and microwave. Breakfast included. Doubles $55; quads $65. MC/V. ❷

▐ FOOD

Most lodgings have full kitchens, so the best budget option is to stock up on groceries and cook for yourself.

■ **San Jacinto Boats & Restaurant** (☎821-4941), on C. San Jacinto. Turn right just past the Copamarina tennis courts and look for the large parking lot on the right. This bayside restaurant wears many hats: by day it sells ferry tickets ($5), rents scuba equipment ($15), and serves inexpensive *comida criolla* lunches ($6); but by night it opens up as one of Guánica's best seafood restaurants (entrees $18-23). The midday dining area consists of a few outdoor picnic tables, but the nighttime atmosphere is much better, as the intimate interior has been designed to resemble a ship's hull. Also delivers lunches to Islas Guilligan and Ballena ($5). Outside open daily 9:30am-6pm; inside open M-F 3-10pm, Sa-Su noon-10pm. MC/V. ❹

Danny & Gaby Bakery (☎821-5373), on the right side of Rte. 334. A small convenience store with a pastry cabinet and a few tables. A good place to stock up on picnic supplies, snacks, or water. Sandwiches $1.25-3. Open daily 6am-9:30pm. MC/V. ❶

▐ HIKING

Unlike most reserves, Guánica's trails are long and frequently loop between sights, making it easy to spend a whole day (or longer) hiking through the forest. However, because of the somewhat monotonous vegetation, many of the trails look similar. The DRNA Information Center can provide personalized trail suggestions. Some of the more popular hikes are listed below.

■ **CAMINO BALLENA.** This 1 mi. gravel trail is possibly the best path in Guánica. Not only does it pass through some of the most wild desert scenery, but it also conveniently leads from the information center down to the road at Bahía La Ballena. Along the way you'll pass Guayacán Centenario, a 100-year-old tree that rises proudly above the lowland vegetation. The marked, northern trailhead is next to the DRNA visitors center. The southern trailhead is not marked, but is easily identifiable by the large blue gate on Rte. 333.

VEREDA MESETA. Meseta is the only trail in Guánica that borders the ocean. The path departs from the Puerto Ballena parking lot, then continues west along the coastline, and the view remains consistently incredible. At the beginning there are several good beaches just off the path, but farther east sand gives way to steep oceanside cliffs. The flat trail also makes a good mountain biking path; unfortunately, there are no nearby rental options. The trail continues for over 2 mi. and is one of the most isolated paths in the forest; bring a friend, cell phone, or inform the rangers that you're heading there.

CAMINO JULIO VELEZ/CAMINO LOS GRANADOS. This 2 mi. circular route leaves from the information center and provides a nice introduction to the forest. Reserve workers recommend this path because it is well-marked, relatively short (only 1hr. round-trip) and a great place to see many of the forest's birds; over 40 bird species have been identified in this area. A detour at the eastern edge of the circle leads to La Vigia, a look-out with incredible views of the forest.

FUERTE CAPRÓN. One of the forest's longer trails leads southwest from the info center along a gravel path toward a small fort. Don't be misled by the word "fort"—this is a tiny observation tower built by the Civilian Conservation Corps in the 1930s on the site of a former Spanish fort. The path does not pass through particularly dramatic vegetation, but it does have great views of the city of Guánica and the bay. The 2½ mi. trail undulates up and down small hills and eventually intersects Rte. 333 at Km 3.2. Coming from the south, park in the small turn-off at Km 3.2 and take the narrow path headed toward the old water tower.

CAMINO CUEVA. This unmarked path leads uphill from the Punta Ballena swimming area parking lot to the intersection with Camino Llúberas, offering an alternate return from Camino Ballena. The trail is clear, but lacks adequate signage. To enter from the south, step over the short wire gate next to the turquoise gate at the parking lot entrance, then continue uphill. No sign marks the intersection with Camino Llúberas, but keep veering to the left and eventually you'll reach Camino Julio Velez. Supposedly there are caves off this trail, but they're nearly impossible to find without a guide; ask at the DRNA office for help arranging a guided tour.

◢ BEACHES

Guánica's coastline alternates between steep cliffs and sandy beaches, and the water can be everything from large, rough waves to tiny, shallow pools. There are several nice public beaches, but the most rewarding experience may be to explore until you find your own quiet stretch of sand.

THE ISLANDS. If you've ever wanted to visit **Guilligan's Island,** here's your chance. A 10min. motorboat ride takes you to the tiny mangrove-covered island where a few small beaches hide amidst the trees. There's not much sand, so arrive by 11am on weekends to get a spot. The water here is shallow and clear, making for some nice **snorkeling.** Guilligan's Island has an outhouse, a DRNA office, and covered picnic tables, but nearby **Isla Ballena** is a different story. Ballena is less crowded and has a long sandy isthmus good for lounging but has no facilities. *(Ferries travel from Restaurant San Jacinto (see Food, p. 230) to Guilligan's Island and Isla Ballena. Tu-F every hr., Sa-Su every 30min. 9am-5pm; $5 round-trip. Open Tu-Su 9am-5pm.)*

PLAYA SANTA. From Guánica, follow Rte. 116 west, turn off onto Rte. 3112, turn south onto Rte. 325, continue to the end, turn left at the T, and take the first right to the parking area. Playa Santa is at the doorstep of a *centro vacacional* for state employees, but is open to the public and offers good swimming. Public facilities were under construction at the time of publication. Rental from **Pino's Boats and Water Fun** is available (see **Equipment Rental,** p. 228).

BALNEARIO CAÑA GORDA. Situated right next door to the Copamarina Beach Resort, this long, white sand beach lined with dry forest trees has some excellent sunning areas. This popular beach has all the amenities of a *balneario,* including lifeguards, showers, bathrooms, chair rental ($4 per day with ID), covered picnic tables, a cafe, and a mini-market. *(Rte. 333 Km 6. ☎821-5676. Open daily Sept.-May 8am-5pm; June-Aug. 7am-6pm.)*

BAHÍA LA BALLENA. This long patch of sand provides ample space for sunbathing, and the water is deep enough for swimming. However, the only facilities are trash cans, and the area can get relatively crowded. *(At the end of Rte. 333.)*

■**PLAYA JOBONCILLO.** For true privacy, head down the steep dirt road to this beautiful blue bay surrounded by rocky cliffs on either side. A few picnic tables and some very old outhouses reveal that others enjoy this beach, but during weekdays it can provide an oasis of picturesque solitude. *(Rte. 333 Km 3.1.)*

🐟 SCUBA DIVING

Island Scuba, C-2 Principal, is a full-service dive shop at Playa Santa with equipment for rent ($15), its own boat, and divemaster. Two-tank dives to La Parguera's famous Wall (p. 237) and other sites ($75 per person) include boat, gear, and oxygen for six people. Prices higher for smaller groups. Follow the directions to Playa Santa, but continue a block past the parking lot; the shop is on the right. **Dive Copamarina,** in the **Copamarina Beach Resort,** Rte. 333 Km 6.5, offers 2-tank dives to The Wall. (☎821-0505, toll-free 800-981-4676; www.copamarina.com. 2-tank dive $85, equipment $10 more. 3-day certification course $450, advance registration required. Discover Scuba package $150. Open daily 9am-5pm. AmEx/MC/V.)

LA PARGUERA

Puerto Ricans know that this small town makes an excellent destination for a long-weekend getaway. Just offshore, several mangrove islands and calm, shallow water create a paradise for boaters and water-lovers. Most foreigners come to La Parguera to see the phosphorescent bay, frequently touted as the best in Puerto Rico. Don't be confused—this is not La Parguera's principal attraction and although it is the cheapest place to see the glowing water, both Fajardo and Vieques have better bioluminescent bays. Father out to sea, The Wall, a 20 mi. long coral reef cliff, attracts serious scuba divers from around the island. On weekends and holidays the small neighborhood takes on the feel of an oceanside carnival, with crowds of people wandering the streets, munching on *pinchos,* and looking for a cheap Medalla beer.

▐ TRANSPORTATION

Coming from the east, drive west on Hwy. 2, then turn toward Guánica on Rte. 116 and continue west to the intersection with Rte. 304, which leads south into town. From the west, take Rte. 2 to Rte. 100, then turn left on Rte. 101. Con-

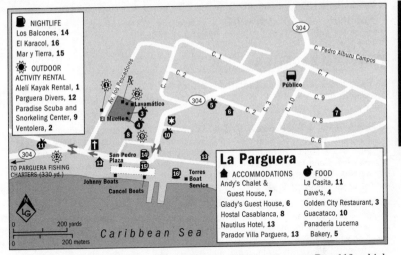

NIGHTLIFE
Los Balcones, **14**
El Karacol, **16**
Mar y Tierra, **15**

OUTDOOR ACTIVITY RENTAL
Alelí Kayak Rental, **1**
Parguera Divers, **12**
Paradise Scuba and Snorkeling Center, **9**
Ventolera, **2**

La Parguera

ACCOMMODATIONS
Andy's Chalet & Guest House, **7**
Glady's Guest House, **6**
Hostal Casablanca, **8**
Nautilus Hotel, **13**
Parador Villa Parguera, **13**

FOOD
La Casita, **11**
Dave's, **4**
Golden City Restaurant, **3**
Guacataco, **10**
Panadería Lucerna Bakery, **5**

TO PARGUERA FISHING CHARTERS (330 yd.)

Johnny Boats

Cancel Boats

San Pedro Plaza

Torres Boat Service

Caribbean Sea

0   200 yards
0   200 meters

SOUTHWEST

tinue on Rte. 303, then Rte. 305, and finally take a right onto Rte. 116, which leads to Rte. 304, which leads to La Parguera. (It's much easier than it sounds.) Occasional **públicos** pick up travelers from the brightly painted bench just north of town on Rte. 304 and take them to **Lajas** ($1), but this service is very sporadic. From Lajas *públicos* continue to San Germán.

ORIENTATION AND PRACTICAL INFORMATION

Many of the streets in the tiny town of La Parguera do not have names. Luckily, almost nothing is more than a short walk away from the central wharf area. Rte. 304 leads straight into town and becomes the main thoroughfare. After the church turn right on Av. los Pescadores to find the Centro Commercial **El Muelle,** a small shopping center filled with many traveler-friendly amenities.

ATMs: La Parguera has no banks, but there are ATMs in the **supermarket** (see below) and in front of **Panadería Lucerna Bakery** (p. 235).

Equipment Rental: Ventoera (☎808-0396 or 505-4541), in El Muelle, rent 12-17 ft. sailboats ($125 per day) and kayaks (singles $10 per hr., doubles $15). Also offers lessons in sailing ($35 per hr.; 8hr. to complete course), windsurfing (8hr. course $275) and kite surfing ($55 per hr.). All equipment included. Open Tu-Sa 9am-8pm, Su 9am-5pm. Summers also open M 9am-8pm. AmEx/MC/V.

English-Language Books: A **free book exchange** in the corner of El Muelle next to the Ventolera has a large selection of English-language books.

Supermarket: Supermercados Selectos (☎899-6065), in El Muelle, carries several English-language magazines. Open M-Sa 7am-10pm, Su 7am-8pm. AmEx/MC/V.

Laundromat: Lavamático (☎899-4844), on the left side of El Muelle. Wash $1; dry $1. No detergent. Change available in the supermarket. Open M-Sa 7am-9:30pm, Su 7am-7:30pm.

Pharmacy: Farmacia San Pedro (☎899-8719), in El Muelle. Open M-Sa 8am-9pm, Su 8am-8pm. AmEx/MC/V. Photocopies $0.10.

Police: (☎899-2250 or 899-2020). On Rte. 304, across from Guacataco. Open 24hr.

Post Office: The small postal service in El Muelle (☎899-6075) has General Delivery. Open M-F 8am-noon and 1-3:30pm. **Postal Code:** 00667.

ACCOMMODATIONS

La Parguera offers a pick of relatively affordable accommodations, from quasi-oceanside resorts to rustic guesthouses. Call ahead as many places don't staff their reception areas 24hr.

Andy's Chalet & Guest House, C. 8 #133 (☎899-0000). Entering the town from Rte. 304, turn left on C. 7, then right on C. 8. This residential guesthouse offers the best price in the region for standard rooms with TV and A/C. Common 2nd-fl. patio with microwave and fridge. No 24hr. reception; call ahead for reservations. Singles $40; doubles $55; triples $65; quads $71; 2-room apartments with kitchen $80-95. Tax included. AmEx/MC/V. ❷

Nautilus Hotel (☎899-4565 or 899-4004; fax 899-5337), near the boat parking lot. Glistening rooms with TV and A/C are just as nice as those at the *paradores* at a fraction of the price. Private balconies look out on the parking lot. Reception in the gift shop 3 doors down. Pool and jacuzzi. Doubles Sept. 16-June 14 M-Th $50, F-Sa $70. June 15-Sept. 15 $70/80. Tax included. AmEx/MC/V. ❷

Parador Villa Parguera (☎899-7777 or 899-3975), on Rte. 304. The exceptional oceanside setting makes it a popular wedding destination. Beautiful poolside grass patio and courtyard waterfall. Pristine rooms. A/C, phone, TV, and private balcony. Check-in 3pm. Check-out noon. Doubles M-F and Su $97-107, Sa $107-120. AmEx/D/MC/V. ❹

Glady's Guest House, C. 2 #42B (☎899-4678), near the intersection with Rte. 304. Exudes professionalism and maintains tidy rooms just steps from the town center. A/C, TV. Doubles $60; triples $65; 4-person apartment $75. Tax included. AmEx/MC/V. ❷

Hostal Casablanca (☎899-4250), on Rte. 304, is certainly in the middle of the action. You can see the best part of the hotel from out front—a beautiful swimming pool and a large, breezy patio. A/C. Check-out noon. Doubles F-Sa $85, M-Th and Su $65; quads $118/97; extra person $17. Tax included. AmEx/MC/V. ❷

FOOD

La Parguera is the place to come for seafood, but also offers visitors the choice of American, Chinese, and Mexican cuisine.

La Casita (☎899-1681), on Rte. 304 at the western edge of town. This big family-friendly restaurants fills up on weekend nights with Puerto Ricans who know that they don't have to go to one of the fancy 5-star restaurants to get the freshest seafood in town. Entrees $10-25. House wine $5.50. Open Tu-Th 11am-10pm, F-Sa 11am-10pm, Su 11am-9pm. AmEx/MC/V. ❹

Dave's (☎899-6065), in El Muelle. This utterly American beach bar serves hamburgers, sandwiches, pizza, and ice cream along with some local meat dishes. The food is well-prepared, if not particularly unique to La Parguera. Pleasant outdoor deck, pool table inside. Occasional pool tournaments and live music. Lunch $4-6. Dinner $7-14. Beer $1.25-2. Open M-Th 7am-9:30 pm, F-Sa 11:30am-1am. ❷

Guacataco, Rte. 304 Km 3.2 (☎808-0303). This local lunch favorite has tiled tables on an outdoor patio. Choose from over 30 varieties of flavorful burritos, quesadillas, and tacos. Wheat and spinach tortillas. Entrees $2-6, but it may take more than 1 to fill up.

Open M and W-Th 11am-9pm, F-Sa 11am-11pm, Su 11am-10pm. MC/V. ❶

Panadería Lucerna Bakery (☎899-7637), at the intersection of Rte. 304 and C. 2. This tiny bakery is a good place to go for a hearty island breakfast, or a big, tasty muffin. No menu, but the friendly staff will whip up just about any breakfast food. Also serves sandwiches. Everything under $5. Open M-W 7am-9pm, Th-Su 7am-midnight. MC/V. ❶

Golden City Restaurant (☎899-5644), in El Muelle, has the ambience of a strip mall eatery, but it's hard to argue with the standard Chinese-American favorites at affordable prices. Combos $4-6. Open M-W 11am-10pm, Th 11am-10:30pm, F-Sa 11am-11pm, Su 11am-10:30pm. Cash only. ❶

OUTDOOR ACTIVITIES

La Parguera is one of the most popular boating destinations in Puerto Rico and during school vacations, the area becomes packed. Boating companies offer tours of the mangrove channels, nearby mangrove islands, and the bioluminescent bay at night, as well as motorboat rentals. The calm waters of this area provides excellent opportunities for beginners to try their hand at windsurfing, kite surfing, sailing, or kayaking (see **Equipment rental,** p. 233). Dense mangrove forests lining the coast mean that there is not much sandy beach, but plenty of marine life for snorkelers and divers. Also, huge off-shore reefs are home to fascinating sea creatures.

BOATING

Most Puerto Rican boaters head to **the mangrove canals** *(los canales manglares)* just west of the main docks, where they anchor their boats and jump in the shallow water. On busy days, a floating store sells *pinchos* and other Puerto Rican snacks to revelers. To get away from the hubbub, it's possible to hire a boat and visit the relatively isolated and very pretty **Cayo Enrique.** Farther south, **Isla Mata Gatas** is the most distant island accessible by small motorboat, the only island with a dock, and supposedly the best area for **snorkeling.** The small island has bathrooms, picnic tables, and trash cans, but as a result it's quite over-visited; you might be happier parking your boat offshore and exploring the shallow waters. (Open June-Sept. Tu-Su 9am-5pm; Oct.-May Th-Su 9am-5pm. If M is a holiday, open M and closed Tu. $1 per person.) **Caracoles Tierra** has a bit of land in the middle where people have been known to **camp,** but none of the boating services or kayak rentals provide

ON THE MENU

HERE'S TO INDEPENDENCE!

Over the centuries, the Puerto Rican independence movement (first directed against the Spanish government, later against US control) has produced small-scale revolutions in the mountain towns, a political party in San Juan, and, in laid-back La Parguera, a signature drink. **Coño Sangría,** a *sangría* created 23 years ago at **El Karacol** (p. 237), is made from a traditional blend of fresh fruit juices and (cheap) Argentine Trapoche label red wine. The name of the drink comes from the *independentistas'* battle cry, "¡Coño Despierta, Boricua!" (loosely translated: Darn it, wake up Puerto Rico!), which was turned into a song by musician Andrés Jiménez. While independence hasn't yet passed in a referendum, the whole island seems to agree that El Karacol is doing something right: 90,000 cups of Coño Sangría are sold each year.

Bar owner Carlos "Cuco" Belaval, who family has operated El Karacol for 39 years, wouldn't give away the secret of his recipe to *Let's Go,* but adventurous travelers can attempt their own freedom *sangría* by getting creative with the following basics:

1 L. red wine
1 orange slice
4 sliced peaches
5 spoonfuls of sugar
2 lemon slices
Juice from 2 oranges

drop-off/pick-up service or allow overnight rental. On the way out to any of the islands you'll pass **Isla Magueyes,** an island managed by the University of Puerto Rico marine sciences department. You have to get special permission from the Mayagüez campus to visit, but if you take one of the smaller boat tours, the guide may hop out and open the gate so that the huge iguanas (used for research) can come out on the dock.

> **THE REAL DEAL.** La Parguera's bioluminescent bay is the attraction that draws most of the town's visitors, but pollution in the bay has damaged the dinoflagellate population, taking some of the sparkle from the water. For the same price any of the boat companies on the dock should be willing to take a small motorboat (6-8 people) away from the bay to surrounding canals—and to brighter waters. Just make sure your group is large enough to fill the boat.

The **Bahía Fosforescente (Phosphorescent Bay)** is the attraction that draws most visitors to the water off La Parguera. This all-natural water light show is produced by bioluminescent dinoflagellates, which light up like small sparks in the water when it is stirred. The nighttime trip to the bay takes about 20min. each way, and while most companies only stay for 5-10min., smaller boats allow more flexibility and sometimes a chance to swim in the bay. The best option might be to find enough people to charter a small (6- to 8-person) boat and ask the boatman to take you to a bioluminescent spot away from the main bay, which is crowded and not necessarily any better than some of the closer mangrove canals.

Theoretically, most of the boat companies at La Parguera's main dock are open every day. On busy weekends in the summer this may be true, but on slower weekdays it may be difficult to find anyone at all; ask around at any of the shops on the dock and someone should be able to track down a boatman. At least one company opens every night for trips to the phosphorescent bay from 7:30pm until people stop showing up. All companies charge $5-6 per person for the 1hr. trip, but there are slight variations in the service. Trips only leave if and when enough customers come.

Cancel Boats (☎899-5891 or 899-2972). 150-passenger glass-bottom boat takes day-trips through the mangrove channels to see Isla Mata Gata and the coral reefs (Sa 3:30pm, Su 2 and 5pm) and night trips to the phosphorescent bay for only $5 per person (Sept. to late Dec. and early Jan. to Mar. Sa-Su 7:30pm; Mar.-Sept. and late Dec. to early Jan. daily 7:30pm). Smaller motorboats lead private tours throughout the day ($25 for 1-5 people or $5 per person with up to 10 people). MC/V.

Johnny Boats (☎299-2212) is the only company that lets you swim in the phosphorescent bay. Daytime tours of the mangroves in small motorboats are $5 per person with at least 5 people. Motorboat rental for licensed boaters or those born before July 1971 ($20 for the 1st hr., $15 for the 2nd hr.).

Alelí Kayak Rental (☎899-6086 or 390-6086) has a spot at the main dock, as well as a repair shop across the street from El Muelle. They rent kayaks (singles $10 per hr., $30 per half-day, $50 per day; doubles $15/40/60) and lead 2-4hr. guided ecotours through the mangrove channels ($50 per person). Open daily 10am-5pm. Call ahead, as owner also operates the occasional chartered catamaran tour ($700 per day) and the shop may not be open during posted hours.

Torres Boat Service (☎396-2089), rents small motor boats ($25 per hr. for 4 people, $25 for 5-7) and offers 40min. guided tours of the bay on a larger boat ($5 per person). June-Aug. open daily 9am-6pm and 7:30pm-last customer; Sept.-May open Sa-Su only.

DIVING AND SNORKELING

Many of the dive operators in San Juan actually head to La Parguera when they want to do some serious diving—that's how good it is here. The big attraction is **The Wall** *(La Pared)*, a 20 mi. coral reef cliff that starts at 60 ft. and drops down to over 150 ft. Visibility tends to be 60-100 ft. and divers have reported seeing sea turtles, manatees, and even dolphins. But beware; The Wall is 6 mi. offshore in open sea, and the voyage tends to be rough. Even those who don't normally get seasick may consider taking anti-nausea medications. Snorkelers can hire a boat (see **Boating**, p. 235) or guide (see below) to take them out to one of the nearby, fertile mangrove islands for shallow-water snorkeling.

Paradise Scuba & Snorkeling Center (☎899-7611; paradisescubapr@yahoo.com), next to Hostal Casa Blanca. Several opportunities include: daytime snorkeling trips to 3 areas (3hr., 10am, $35), a sunset snorkeling trip that includes a swim in the phosphorescent bay (4hr., 4pm, $50), a 2-tank dive to The Wall ($70, with equipment rental $80), a 1-tank night dive ($50), and a Discover Scuba package with 1 pool lesson and 2 open-water dives ($125). Private PADI certification course $350, 3-week group course $200 per person. Snorkeling trips include all equipment and a snack. Also rents kayaks ($10 per hr., doubles $15 per hr.). Open daily 9am-9pm. AmEx/MC/V.

Parguera Divers (☎899-4171; www.pargueradivers.com), in el Muelle with a stand in the Parador Posada Porlamar parking lot. Daily trips to The Wall on a 30 ft. Island Hopper. 2-tank dive $70, equipment rental $15; wet suit not included. 1-tank night dive $45, equipment $10. 4-day PADI & NAUI open-water certification courses $350. 3hr. snorkeling trips $25. Open most days 9am-6pm. MC/V. Accepts traveler's checks.

FISHING

The ocean around La Parguera is considered to be one of the most productive fishing areas in Puerto Rico. **Parguera Fishing Charters** (☎899-4698 or 382-4698; http://hometown.aol.com/mareja) provides visitors with the opportunity to head out to open waters, at least 6 mi. offshore, and catch exotic fish such as barracuda, mahi mahi, blue marlin, dorado, and tuna on a 31 ft. Bertram Sportfisherman. (1-4 people half-day $450, full day $750; additional person (up to 6 total) $25/50. Equipment included. MC/V.)

FLYING

Experiencing the southwestern corner of the island and Caribbean's clear, shallow waters from the air provides a new perspective on the coastal environment. Several local aircraft owners give aerial tours of the coastline. ($35 per passenger, one passenger at a time). Call Willy Millayes (☎319-7772 or 659-3405) or Micky Rivera (☎448-7629) for more information. The private airfield is on the right-hand side of Rte. 305, past the agricultural airfield, just before the intersection with Rte. 303.

◪ NIGHTLIFE

La Parguera knows how to party. On weekends and holidays the many bars along main street are packed until 1am in the summer when the local law requires that they shut down. On Saturday nights the restaurant at Parador Villa Parguera (p. 234) hosts an elaborate live music/dance/Spanish comedy show that attracts a fair number of older visitors ($35 includes dinner and show).

▨ **El Karacol** (☎899-5582), in front of the docks. For over 36 years this classy bar and *cafetería* has been serving up the house specialty, *Coño Sangría* in a signature cup ($4.50), and Spanish and Puerto Rican cooking ($5-15) for the hungry dockside crowds. Arcade room. Open June-Aug. M-Th and Su 11am-11pm, F-Sa 11am-1am; Sept.-May M-Th and Su 11am-11pm, F-Sa 11am-midnight. MC/V.

Los Balcones (☎899-2145), across from the plaza. Attracts a rambunctious college crowd, especially on Sa nights when live music packs the place. Pool tables ($0.50) and the dance floor draw a loyal crowd. Beer $2-2.50. Happy hour Sa 7pm-midnight. Live Spanish rock F-Sa 10pm. 18+. Open June-Aug. M-W 5pm-midnight, F-Sa 5am-1am; Sept.-May M-W and F-Sa 5pm-midnight. MC/V.

Mar y Tierra (☎899-4627), on Rte. 304. Young male Puerto Ricans practice their game at the 4 pool tables ($0.50) at this popular sports bar. In back, the *cafetería* attracts an entirely different crowd—families who enjoy hot *empanadillas* with their beer ($1-2.25). Piña colada $4. Open June-Aug. M-Th 5pm-midnight, F-Sa 6pm-1am; Sept.-May M-Th 5pm-midnight, F-Sa 6pm-midnight. MC/V.

SAN GERMÁN

As one of the oldest settlements on the island and home to the island's oldest chapel, San Germán is steeped in Puerto Rican history. The delicate architecture of many homes still echoes the city's cultural heritage, and the presence of the Universidad Interamericana gives San Germán a college-town feel outside of the historic center. Travelers come here for a break from the beach and an opportunity to absorb the culture of what was once the western capital of the island. Nightlife and accommodations are limited, but San Germán makes a good day trip.

⌐ TRANSPORTATION

From Hwy. 2 exit onto Rte. 122, then turn right onto C. Luna. Coming from Boquerón, La Parguera, or anywhere southwest of the city, follow Rte. 101 all the way into the old center of town. *Públicos* connect San Germán to: **Cabo Rojo** (20min., $1.75); **Lajas** (20min., $1); **Mayagüez** (30min., $2.80); **Sabana Grande** (15min., $1.30). The *público* station is near the intersection of C. Luna and Rte. 122; turn right and walk up C. Luna to reach the historical center.

✦ 🛈 ORIENTATION AND PRACTICAL INFORMATION

San Germán's busy main street used to be called **Calle Luna,** but the government recently changed the name to Av. Universidad Interamericana. Like most *sangermeños, Let's Go* still refers to the street as C. Luna. The two plazas sit a couple of short blocks north of C. Luna. Many services are available around the western end of C. Luna, with the fast-food restaurants and the university, or the eastern end of C. Luna, where Rte. 122 leads to a shopping plaza and Hwy. 2.

Tourist Office: Oficina de Turismo should be in the Alcaldía on the main plaza by late 2005 (☎892-3790). Offers guided tours by appointment.

Bank: Western Bank, C. Luna 170 (☎892-1207). Exchanges traveler's checks, but not foreign currency. Drive-thru ATM. Open M-F 7:30am-5pm, Sa 8:30-11:30am.

Supermarket: Mr. Special Supermercado, Rte. 102 Km 32.9 (☎892-1098), past the intersection with Rte. 122. Open daily M-Sa 6:30am-9pm, Su 11am-5pm. AmEx/MC/V.

Laundromat: Emmsue Wash & Dry, Rte. 102 Km 34 (☎892-5252), behind Panadería La Marqueta, 1½ mi. east of town. Wash $1.50; Dry $0.25 per 4min. Change available. Open daily 5am-9pm.

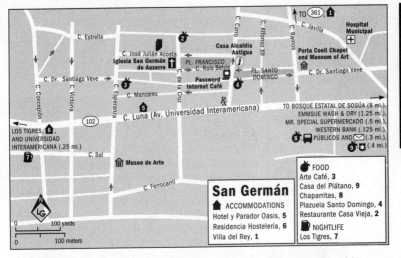

Police: On C. Casto Perez, behind the *público* terminal (☎892-2020). Open 24hr.

Late-Night Pharmacy: Walgreens (☎892-1170), at the corner of C. Luna and C. Carro. Open M-Sa 7am-10pm, Su 9am-6pm. AmEx/D/MC/V.

Hospital: Hospital Municipal, C. Javilla 8, (☎892-5300), just behind the Porta Coeli chapel. 24hr. emergency room.

Internet Access: Biblioteca Pública, C. Acosta 11 (☎892-6820), on Plaza Quiñones. Free Internet access. Open June-July M-F 8am-5pm, Sa 8am-1pm and 2-4:30pm. Aug.-May M-Th 8am-8:30pm, F 8am-6pm, Sa 8am-1pm and 2-4:30pm. **Smart Technology Internet Cafe,** C. Ruiz Belvis 9 (☎892-3177), at C. Carro, charges $3 per 30min. Open M-F 9am-6pm, Sa 9am-3pm.

Post Office: C. Luna 181 (☎892-1313), near the intersection with Rte. 122. No General Delivery. Open M-F 7:30am-4pm, Sa 8am-noon. **Postal Code:** 00683.

🏠 ACCOMMODATIONS

San Germán's accommodations are relatively budget friendly, but don't come looking for first-class rooms.

Residencia Hostelería (☎264-1912 ext. 7300 or 7301). Continue on C. Luna to the university's 2nd entrance, then enter the blue building to the left of the track field. Your dream come true or your worst nightmare, depending on how you feel about living in an all-male dorm (men and women both welcome). The university rents several clean dorm rooms with a small living room in the front, a bedroom in the back, and 2 dorm-style showers in the middle. You must reserve in advance M-F 8am-noon and 1-5pm. Rooms without sheets: singles $22; doubles $27; triples $33; quads $38. With sheets: $27/33/38/49. TV, A/C, and sheets: $49/59/65/75. Larger rooms available. Tax included. AmEx/MC/V if you check in M-F 8am-5pm. ❶

Hotel y Parador Oasis, C. Luna 72 (☎892-1175). All the amenities are here—pool, cable TV, A/C. Prime location makes this a good base for exploring downtown.

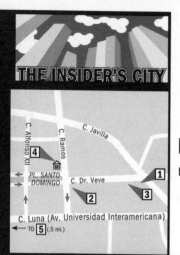

HISTORIC HOUSES OF SAN GERMÁN

Although the city is full of interesting old buildings, the following are ideally positioned for a stroll.

1. Casa Jaime Acosta y Forés **(1918),** C. Dr. Veve 70, grabs your attention with its bright-yellow, Art Nouveau exterior.

2. Casa de los Ponce de León o Lola Rodriguez de Tió **(1870),** C. Dr. Veve 13, once served as the holiday home for famous poet and political activist Rodriguez de Tió.

3. Casa de Los Kindy **(19th century),** C. Dr. Veve 64, stands out with polychrome stained-glass windows.

4. Casa Morales **(1915),** was built in Queen Anne Victorian style and remains one of the city's best-maintained houses.

5. Museo de Arte **(19th century)** (p. 241) is the only historic house in town that allows visitors inside. Continue south on C. Ramos, west on C. Luna, and south on C. Esperanza.

Check-out noon. Singles $61-63; doubles $68-70; extra person $10. Tax included. MC/V. ❸

Villa del Rey, Rte. 361 Km 0.8 (☎642-2627 or 264-2542), just across Hwy. 2 from town. The newest hotel in San Germán. Bright, tile-floored rooms. Modern amenities, but not the historic charm of traditional *paradores.* Cafeteria (lunch buffet $6) and pool. TV, A/C, fridge on request. Doubles $82; quads $92. MC/V.

🍴 FOOD

🍽 **Casa del Plátano,** C. Oriente 174 (☎892-2633), across from the post office. Uses island-grown bananas with sandwich toppings to create banana sandwiches ($4). That's right, no bread. Open M-Sa 6:30am-8pm. ❶

Plazuela Santo Domingo, C. Carro 13 (☎318-1539), at C. Dr. Veve. One of the best eateries in town. Workers on their lunch break come for the clean interior, friendly staff, and heaping piles of *comida criolla.* Vegetarian options. Lunch buffet $3.50. Open M-F 11am-2:30pm, Th-Sa 11am-10pm. MC/V. ❷

Chaparritas, C. Luna 171 (☎892-1078). Successfully combines classy decor, quality food, and affordable prices. This brightly colored restaurant serves a variety of meat-heavy Mexican entrees ($11-15). Beer $3. Open W-Tu 11:30am-3pm and 6-9pm, F 11:30am-3pm and 6-10pm, Sa 6-10pm, Su 3-8pm. MC/V. ❸

Restaurante Casa Vieja (☎264-3954), on the corner of C. de la Cruz and C. Estrella. Occupies a traditional Spanish building, spilling out from the ground floor into a shady courtyard. Like the local artwork on the walls, the menu is constantly changing, but in general it sticks to Caribbean-Spanish fusion. Entrees $12-20. Open W-Th 5-10pm, F noon-11pm, Sa 5-11pm. Bar open W-Th 5pm-midnight, F noon-2am, Sa 5pm-2am. ❹

Arte Café, C. Dr. Veve 19b (☎892-6727). Brings a touch of university life to downtown San Germán. Students relax in this European-style cafe and enjoy a variety of coffees and baked goods. Sandwiches $2-4. Open M-F 9am-10pm, Sa 5-10pm. ❶

👁 SIGHTS

Apart from the two exceptional churches, most of San Germán's "sights" are actually private residences with exquisite architecture. Many are close to the main plazas—**Plaza Francisco Quiñones,** a quiet tree-lined plaza overshadowed by the enormous modern church, and **Plazuela Santo Domingo,** a slightly more active plaza just to the east. The most interesting way to sightsee may be to just wander the streets, where a pleasant surprise awaits around every corner. Some of the more historically significant houses are described below.

PORTA COELI CHAPEL AND MUSEUM OF RELIGIOUS ART. This modest structure on the southern edge of Plazuela Santo Domingo, known as "The Gate to Heaven," is the oldest chapel in Puerto Rico, and the second-oldest religious building (only Iglesia San José in Old San Juan is older). The building was constructed in 1606 as a convent, but over time it slowly deteriorated and by 1866 only the chapel remained. Finally, in 1949 the Puerto Rican Institute of Culture took control of the Porta Coeli and restored it to a recognizable shape, though only the columns, walls, and stairwell remain from the original. The chapel is no longer used for services, but it now houses a small museum of religious art. This collection of paintings and large *santos* are worth the visit and entering the chapel is one of the best ways to get in touch with San Germán's extensive history. *(At C. Ramos and C. Dr. Veve. ☎892-5845. Open W-Su 8:30am-noon and 1-4:30pm. $1, under 12 free.)*

IGLESIA SAN GERMÁN DE AUXERRE. Austere Porta Coeli may have satisfied the needs of the sisters in the convent, but church fathers spared no expense in building the impressive Neoclassical Iglesia San Germán to monumental standards. The church closes for most of the day, but it's worthwhile to stop by just before mass (or attend mass) in order to see the elegant interior, with its tall ceilings, numerous chandeliers, colorful stained-glass windows, and creative paint job. Dress nicely (slacks and a collared short), as this is a working church. *(☎892-1027. Office on C. José Julian Acosta open M-F 8-11am and 1-3pm, Sa 8-11am. Church open for mass M-Sa 7am and 7:30pm; Su 7:30, 8:30, 10am, 7:30pm.)*

MUSEO DE ARTE Y CASA DE ESTUDIO ALFREDO RAMÍREZ DE ARELLANO Y ROSELL. On the way back from a walking tour through San Germán's historic district, you may want to stop by this turn-of the-century home that now holds a small art museum. The collection contains oils with both Catholic and Taíno subjects. This is a rare opportunity to enter one of San Germán's historic homes. *(C. Esperanza 7. ☎892-8870. Open W-Su 10am-noon and 1-3pm. Free.)*

UNIVERSIDAD INTERAMERICANA. You can't miss the presence of the Interamerican University in San Germán. Founded in 1912 as the Instituto Politécnico de San Germán, this is now the largest private university in Puerto Rico. The attractive campus on the western edge of town, off C. Luna, is a pleasant place to wander and absorb the hustle of student activity. The campus grounds include the only round chapel in Puerto Rico.

▧ NIGHTLIFE

Considering the size of the university, San Germán has a remarkably tame nightlife scene, as most students head to Mayagüez or La Parguera for their nights out. ▧**Los Tigres,** C. Luna 6, at the main university entrance, is the student hangout. All day long, college kids shoot pool in the small wooden house or chill on the porch with a beer, taking advantage of daily happy hour specials. This is the place to bond with the younger crowd. *(☎264-5504. Happy hour daily generally 8pm-midnight, beer $1-1.50. Live music Th. Open Sept.-May M-W 11am-1am, Th-Sa 11am-2am; June-Aug. M-W 4pm-1am, Th-Sa 4pm-2am. MC/V.)*

BOSQUE ESTATAL DE SOSÚA

Just 40min. east of San Germán, the 3341-acre Bosque Estatal de Sosúa provides an excellent taste of the Puerto Rican countryside for those vacationing on the southwest coast and a refreshing return to nature for anyone overwhelmed by city life. Sitting on the border between the mountainous rainforests and the coastal dry forests, Sosúa is the only state forest with both dry and humid forests, which contributes to a diversity of over 150 species of trees. More peaceful than impressive, this forest has trails for hiking and one for mountain biking.

This is one of the island's more isolated forest reserves, and unlike most of the forests along the Ruta Panorámica, Sosúa does not have a thoroughfare bisecting the forest. Instead, visitors must drive east on Rte. 102 through Sabana Grande, then follow Rte. 368 past Rte. 365 to Km 2.1, where they'll turn left at the DRNA sign and continue on the small road for 15-20min. to reach the forest center. The DRNA office is located at the end of the road in a valley next to a large and attractive picnic area. (☎487-4890. Open M-F 7am-3:30pm, Sa-Su 9am-5pm.) There are lots of covered **picnic tables** (although many don't have benches), fire pits, bathrooms, and even a snack machine. Two **hiking trails** leave from the same trailhead, marked "Vereda al Río" between the DRNA office and the visitors center. One heads uphill into mountainous country and the other follows the Río Loco; both are at least 2 mi. long. More compelling is the rigorous **mountain bike trail**, which narrows to single track on its 3 mi. loop. You must bring your own bike, but rangers can show you a hand-drawn map of the trail.

The DRNA has been building three **camping areas** ❶ at Sosúa for years now, adding cabins to the first, and expanding water and bathroom facilities at the other two. For more info on when the campsites will open, contact the DRNA. (See **Camping**, p. 42. Tents $4 per person.)

EL COMBATE

If the diminutive nature of many of Puerto Rico's beaches has gotten you down, perk up and try El Combate on for size. El Combate's beach is one of the longest on the island; its white sand extends for miles in either direction. During weekdays this tiny *barrio* feels like a ghost town, but during holidays and summer vacations it fills up with Puerto Ricans. There's not much to do here but lie on the beach and drink beer, but that's exactly what most people come for.

Almost every house in town becomes some sort of vacation rental, and countless signs advertise rooms for rent. However, snagging this sort of rental can be difficult because few owners live near their properties or answer their phones. For more traditional accommodations, try **Combate Beach Hotel** ❸, Rte. 3301 Km 2.7, a real hotel with clean, spacious rooms with TV, fridge, and A/C. The hotel's biggest assets are the pool, jacuzzi, and direct beach access. Locals place the hotel's seafood restaurant among the best in town. (☎254-2358; fax 851-2134. June-Aug. doubles $88; quads $100, with kitchen $125. Sept.-May $69/90/115. MC/V.) On the northern edge of town, directly across C. 1 from the beach, friendly **Apartamentos Kenny** ❸ is El Combate's best value for groups. The small, one-bedroom apartments manage to accommodate a double bed, a set of bunkbeds, a satellite TV, a kitchen area with stove and fridge, a small kitchen table, bedroom A/C, and up to six people—although two must sleep on a small fold-out couch. (☎254-0002 or 509-8833. Check-in 4pm. Check-out 3pm. Easter-Labor Day $105; Labor Day-Easter $90. No credit cards.) Although ⚑**Annie's Place** ❸, offers six guest rooms with A/C, cable TV, and kitchenettes ($65-110), it shines as El Combate's best seafood **restaurant** ❸. Auspiciously located at the turn in the road, this is the place to sit over the ocean enjoying *mofongo* filled with fresh seafood, and watch the sunset. In the evening, the front half of the restaurant comes to life as a bar and *empanadilla* stand. (☎254-2553. Entrees $7-23. Beer $1.50-2. Open M-Th 10:30am-9pm, F-Sa 10:30am-1am, Su 10:30am-9pm. MC/V.)

CABO ROJO SCENIC DRIVE

If you don't like suspense, stop reading now and skip down to **3** because the Cabo Rojo lighthouse and its spectacular surroundings are the highlight of this roadtrip. However, if you have a bit more time on your hands, meandering down Rte. 301 to the tip of Punta Jagüey, through the flat plains and dry vegetation, is a pleasant way to see the region's fascinating topography en route to the southwestern point on the island.

1. REFUGIO DE VIDA SILVESTRE CABO ROJO. The Cabo Rojo Wildlife Refuge (Km 5.1) offers 587 acres of subtropical dry forest managed by the US Fish & Wildlife Service. A small museum in the headquarters explains the area's flora and fauna (English/Spanish captions) and a decent 1½ mi. interpretive trail provides a real life introduction to the nature you just read about. (☎851-7258 ext. 35. Open M-F 7:30am-4pm.)

2. CABO ROJO SALT FLATS. The landscape becomes progressively flatter as you continue south to Puerto Rico's largest salt production facilities. The scenery alone is impressive, but this area is also the Caribbean's most important meeting point for migratory shore birds, with over 125 species of birds stopping here. The new observation tower (Km 11.1) affords panoramic views, and the opportunity to spot Cape May Warblers, Prairie Warblers, and Common Yellowthroat Merlin.

DISTANCE: 10mi.

DURATION: 2-5hr.

WHEN TO GO: Year-round. The beach is more crowded June to August and the restaurant closes Monday through Wednesday.

3. CABO ROJO LIGHTHOUSE. From the salt flats, continue south on Rte. 301 all the way to the end—after it becomes a bumpy dirt road, after you're sure that you've gone too far, after you feel like you're in the middle of nowhere. The Cabo Rojo Lighthouse will appear like a beacon. Park at the metal gate and continue on foot up the hill to this Neoclassical structure, built by the Spanish in 1881. The lighthouse is impressive, but it pales in comparison to the truly incredible views from its base. Standing on a limestone cliff 200 ft. over the crystal waters of the Caribbean crashing below is one of the most amazing experiences in Puerto Rico.

4. PLAYUELA. Anyone who explores the lighthouse area will eventually stumble upon La Playuela, the beautiful beach just east of the point. Continue on the dirt road left of the path to the lighthouse on foot to reach it. This long white sand bay has some of the best swimming in Puerto Rico, as the clear, turquoise water hits the beach in a gentle, shallow arc. There are no facilities, but the remote location also means that there are fewer people than you will find at other nearby beaches.

5. PARADOR BAHÍA SALINAS BEACH HOTEL. If you're ready to splurge, stop for lunch than **Agua al Cuello Restaurant ❹**, Rte. 301 Km 11.5. This *mesón gastronómico* scores big points for its elegant wooden balcony over the calm water. Live music Sa helps create an atmosphere of relaxation in which to enjoy the artsy seafood dishes. (☎254-1212. Entrees $15-30. Open Th-Su 11am-9pm, sometimes M-W 5-9pm. AmEx/MC/V.) If the atmosphere has you sufficiently bewitched, this is also a beautiful place to spend the night. The award-winning **Parador Bahía Salinas ❹** is one of the island's premier *paradores*, with two pools, an oceanside location, an all-natural mineral water jacuzzi (using saltwater from the way), and a relaxed, and tropical atmosphere. Birds warbling in cages around the shady grounds. (☎254-1212; www.bahiasalinas.net. Continental breakfast included. Check-in 3pm. Check-out noon. Doubles M-W and Su $90-125; Th-Sa $180 with breakfast, lunch, and dinner for 2 included during these days. Extra person $22 including meals. Tax included. AmEx/MC/V.)

El Combate sits at the end of Rte. 3301. Turn left at the Combate Hotel sign to reach the beach parking lot and the better, southern half of the beach. Or continue straight on Rte. 3301 to enter town, which extends north on four parallel streets: C. 1 is closest to the water, C. 2 is the next inland, etc. *Públicos* occasionally journey out from Cabo Rojo, but service is sporadic.

BOQUERÓN

Boquerón has an attractive public beach. Clear, shallow water laps on the long *balneario* of white sand lined by a grassy park with palm trees and a picnicking area. By day, the quiet beach attracts families; by night, the tiny two-road town comes alive, closing down its streets to traffic so that people can roam freely. Boquerón is geared more toward Puerto Ricans than foreigners and the entire town feels prepackaged for tourist consumption, but if you don't mind the family crowds, Boquerón is a great place to just *relajar*.

◼ TRANSPORTATION

Coming from the east (Ponce, San Germán, Lajas, and La Parguera), take Rte. 101 west straight into town. From Mayagüez and San Juan, take Hwy. 2 to Rte. 100, which travels south and intersects with Rte. 101 just outside Boquerón. **Públicos** come from **Cabo Rojo** (the city) and drive through **Boquerón** on weekdays and some Saturdays, but have no designated stops (5min., $1.75). From Cabo Rojo, *públicos* continue to **Mayagüez** (15-20min., $2).

◼ ◼ ORIENTATION AND PRACTICAL INFORMATION

The main street, **Route 101,** becomes Calle Muñoz Rivera as it enters town, then turns north along the coast and changes names again, to Calle José de Diego. **Route 307** splits off Rte. 101 to become the town's other road, Calle Estación, then heads north toward Joyuda. Boquerón is tiny, and if you want to find most practical necessities you'll have to head into Cabo Rojo, or even better, Mayagüez.

Tourist Office: Puerto Rican Tourism Company, Rte. 100 Km 13.7 (☎851-7070), 1 mi. north of town. Open daily 8am-noon and 1-4:30pm.

ATM: Boquerón has an ATM located at the liquor store on the left as you enter town from the intersection of Rte. 100 and Rte. 101 and another across the street from Super Colmado Rodriquez. Nearby Cabo Rojo has several banks.

Equipment Rental: Boquerón Kayak Rental, C. de Diego 15 (☎255-1849), rents single kayaks ($10 per hr., $40 per day), double kayaks ($15/65), 5-person pedal boats ($15 for the first 2 people, $5 for each additional person), and surfbikes (a combination surfboard and bike; $15 per hr.). They also give 15min. banana boat rides ($5 per person). If the office is closed, call. Summer open daily 10am-5pm; Labor Day-Easter open F-Sa 10am-6pm. Cash only.

Supermarket: Super Colmado Rodriguez, C. Muñoz Rivera 46 (☎851-2100), has limited groceries. Open M-Sa 6am-6:30pm, Su 6am-noon. MC/V.

Laundromat: Adamaris Apartments, on C. de Diego. Wash $1; dry $0.25 per 7min. Open daily 7am-7pm.

Police: In the Centro Vacacional, past the reception office (851-1122). Open 24hr.

Internet Access: Boquerón Travel Agency, C. Muñoz Rivera 60 (☎851-4751; fax 254-2144) offers 1 computer with Internet access ($6 per hr.) and **fax** service. Open M-F 9am-5pm, Sa 9am-noon.

Post Office: Rte. 101 Km 18.3 (☎851-3848). Open M-F 7:30am-4pm, Sa 8am-noon. **Postal Code:** 00622.

ACCOMMODATIONS

Boquerón does not lack for accommodations, but many of the rooms are actually 1- to 2-bedroom apartments designed to be affordable for large groups (see **Vacation Rentals,** p. 40). Prices go up considerably during the summer, which generally begins during *Semana Santa* (the week of Easter) and ends on Labor Day, in the beginning of September.

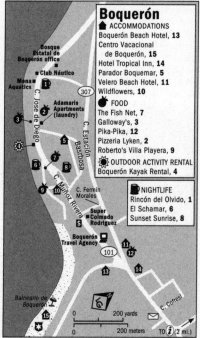

Boquerón

♠ ACCOMMODATIONS
Boquerón Beach Hotel, 13
Centro Vacacional
  de Boquerón, 15
Hotel Tropical Inn, 14
Parador Boquemar, 5
Velero Beach Hotel, 11
Wildflowers, 10

● FOOD
The Fish Net, 7
Galloway's, 3
Pika-Pika, 12
Pizzeria Lyken, 2
Roberto's Villa Playera, 9

☀ OUTDOOR ACTIVITY RENTAL
Boquerón Kayak Rental, 4

■ NIGHTLIFE
Rincón del Olvido, 1
El Schamar, 6
Sunset Sunrise, 8

■ **Centro Vacacional de Boquerón** (☎851-1900). Coming into town on Rte. 101, turn left at the sign for the beach and continue to the end. This enormous vacation complex resembles most other *centros vacaciona-les*, except for the fact that it is remarkably well maintained, and *cabañas* have ideal beachfront locations. If you go for a *villa*, request one of the newer units at the south end of the beach. Check-out 1pm. *Cabañas* $66; *villas* $109. Tax included. AmEx/MC/V. ❷

Boquerón Beach Hotel (☎851-7110; fax 851-7110; www.boqueronbeachho-tel.com), at the turn-off to the beach. One of Boquerón's more professional accommodations. An inviting blend of old Spanish tile floors, French wrought-iron work, and modern rooms. All rooms have TV, A/C, and fridge. Near the beach. Large pool area. Parking. Check-in 1pm. Check-out noon. Mar. to mid-Sept. doubles $88-109; quads $120-148. Mid-Sept. to Feb. $60-77/89-99. Tax included. MC/V. ❹

Wildflowers, C. Muñoz Rivera 13 (☎851-1793 or 851-8874). This Victorian house exudes charm. Rooms have been carefully decorated with dark wood furniture and coordinated linens, but also include practical benefits like TV, A/C, and fridge. All rooms fit 4 people; smaller rooms have 1 full and 1 bunk bed, larger rooms have 2 beds, though one may be a fold-out sofa. Call ahead. Parking. Check-in 1pm. Check-out noon. June-Aug. small rooms $100; large rooms $125. Sept.-May $75/95. MC/V. ❹

Velero Beach Hotel, Rte. 307 Km 9.3 (☎255-1000; www.velerobeachhotel.com). Clean, large rooms. A/C, cable TV, and VCR. Balcony on request. Parking. Check-out noon. Summer doubles $100; quads $195. Winter $65/85. AmEx/MC/V. ❸

SAN JUAN BAUTISTA: BACK TO THE FUTURE

The eve of the festival of Puerto Rico's Patron Saint, San Juan Bautista, is a eventful night across the island. At the stroke of midnight, Puerto Ricans walk backward toward the ocean. The agile can also choose to backflip toward the sea, but the correct number of backflips is disputed: is it 12 for the months of the year or seven for good luck? However you get to the water, it is generally agreed that you must fall in backward three times. The waters are thought to be blessed with special powers on this night and immersion in them is supposed to bring good luck for coming year.

However, the ladies on Puerto Rico's west coast have teamed up with San Juan Bautista not just for good luck, but for a detailed glimpse into their futures. Some women swirl water and egg white in a glass, which, according to tradition, will show a woman the face of her future husband. Because a pretty face isn't everything, thorough women will also tuck three beans under their pillows. One is peeled, one is half-peeled, and the other is left unpeeled. The bean the woman pulls out form under her pillow in the morning reveals her husband-to-be's financial status: a peeled bean means a poor man, half-peeled suggests a man of moderate means, and an intact bean means she's hit the jackpot.

(Festival de San Juan Bautista is celebrated June 24th each year.)

Hotel Tropical Inn, Rte. 101 Km 18.7 (☎851-0284), across the street from the road to the beach. One of the cheapest places in town. TV and A/C. May-Sept. 15 doubles $55; quads $80. Sept. 16-Apr. $45/65. AmEx/MC/V. ❷

Parador Boquemar (☎851-2158, toll-free 888-634-4343; www.boquemar.com), just off C. de Diego. You can't miss this pink building rising above town. Lacks the elegance of other *paradores*, but modern rooms come with phone, A/C, and a small TV. Check-in 4pm. Check-out noon. Doubles $70-95; quads $120-125; extra person $16, 2 children under 12 free. AmEx/MC/V. ❸

🍴 FOOD

Boquerón is the only place in Puerto Rico where you'll find multiple vendors selling fresh oysters (*ostiones;* about $3-4 per dozen) and clams (*almejas;* about $8 per dozen). Visitors can stop by a cart, peel apart the shells, and dump hot sauce onto the succulent centers. While the cheapest option is cobbling together a meal from the various stands along C. de Diego, the restaurants below provide quality food for the particularly hungry.

The Fish Net and **Roberto's Villa Playera** (☎254-3163), both on C. de Diego. Roberto had such success with his first seafood restaurant that he opened another one right across the street. These 2 restaurants share the undisputed title of best seafood in town, as well as a menu and similar nautical decor, although only Villa Playera has a view of the canal out back. Entrees $10-18. Fish Net open W-Th and Su 11am-9pm, F-Sa 11am-9:30pm. Villa Playera open M-Tu and F-Su 11am-8pm. AmEx/MC/V. ❸

Pika-Pika, C. Estación 224 (☎851-2440), is expensive, but delicious. A variety of meat options are served with rice, beans, and tortillas. Don't miss the incredible *tres leches* for dessert ($4). Entrees $13-24. Margaritas $5.50. Open W-Th 5-10pm, F-Sa 12-11pm Su 12-10pm. AmEx/MC/V. ❹

Galloway's (☎254-3302), next to Club Náutico. Americans, this is your home away from home. Galloway's caters to the foreign crowd with an English menu, US TV, and rows of US license plates lining the ceiling. The oceanfront dining room is a great place to watch the sunset. *Comida criolla* with a few American faves $6-26. Lunch specials from $4. Open M-Tu, Th, Su 11am-noon, F-Sa 11am-1am. AmEx/MC/V. ❸

Pizzeria Lyken (☎851-6335), on C. de Diego. Offers an alternative to the endless seafood—pizza, obviously—but never fear, they also serve a full spread of seafood entrees, as well as seafood pizza. Windchimes liven up the outdoor seating area. Entrees $10-20. Small pizza $7-10. Open Th-Sa 11am-10pm. Bar open until midnight. AmEx/MC/V.

OUTDOOR ACTIVITIES

The 4773-acre **Bosque Estatal de Boquerón,** Rte. 101 Km 1.1, reserve encompasses the mangroves west of La Parguera (p. 235), the salt flats in Cabo Rojo (p. 243), the Boquerón Wildlife Refuge near the intersection of Rte. 101 and 301, and Joyuda's Isla Ratones (p. 259), and protects over 120 species of birds. Unfortunately, the DRNA now limits guests to a boardwalk outside the office. Keep an eye out for the fiddler crabs crawling in the shallow waters beneath it, but don't expect to see much else. (☎851-4795. Open daily 7:30am-4pm.) Back in town, the forest's main office, just past Club Náutico, can tell you whether any new hiking trails have opened up. (☎851-7260. Open M-F 7:30am-3:30pm.)

BEACHES AND WATER SPORTS

The **public balneario,** Rte. 101 Km 18.8, is the only show in town, and it's stunning. Like most beaches run by the Compañía de Parques Nacionales, it contains picnic tables, showers, bathrooms, a cafeteria, and lifeguards. The beach attracts crowds, but there is generally enough sand to go around. (Open daily June-July 8am-6pm; Aug.-May 8am-5pm. Parking $3. Showers $1, children $0.50.) **Mona Aquatics,** C. de Diego 59, next to the Club Náutico, has a 42 ft. boat. The PADI- and YMCA-certified owner leads diving expeditions (2-tank dive $65; 1-tank night dive $40), but does not rent equipment. (☎851-2185; fax 254-0604. MC/V.)

NIGHTLIFE

Boquerón draws large crowds on weekend nights. The plaza in front of El Shamar closes down to traffic after 6pm and people gather around tables to play dominoes, beers in hand. Students and younger adults gather farther north, near the Club Náutico. The entire town resembles a street party and it's almost impossible to miss the hot spots. **It is illegal to drink out of a bottle on the streets in Boquerón, so get a plastic cup or a can from any bar.**

> **Rincón del Olvido,** across from Club Náutico. This outdoor kiosk proves that you don't need fancy decor and gimmicks to reel in the crowds. Students and young people park their cars around the bar and use it meeting place. Beer $1.25-2. Mixed drinks $3. Open W-Th 2pm-midnight, F-Sa 10am-1am, Su 10am-9pm. Cash only.

> **El Schamar,** C. de Diego 1 (☎851-0542). With a plaza overlooking the ocean, tasty *empanadillas,* and a location right in the center of town, this bar has a lot going for it. Add a pool table and $1 Medalla beers, and it's no wonder that it's consistently packed. Beer $1-2. Mixed drinks $2-6. Open daily 11am-midnight. Cash only.

> **Sunset Sunrise,** C. Barbosa 65 (☎255-1478), on the main square. This little hole-in-the-wall is a popular gathering spot for a demure crowd that grabs a drink then sits on the tables out front playing dominos. Beer $1-2. Mixed drinks $2-4. Open M-Th and Su 10am-midnight, F-Sa 10am-1am.

> **Galloway's** (☎254-3302), on C. de Diego (see **Food,** p. 246). The countdown to St. Patrick's Day hangs on a wall at this popular Irish pub. The bar provides a relatively quiet place to relax and make some new friends, with a fantastic view of the sunset

over the water. Parking. Beer $2.50. Mixed drinks $3.75-5. Appetizers $3-7. Open M-Tu, Th, Su 11am-midnight; F-Sa 11am-1am. AmEx/MC/V.

ISLA MONA

Cynics who claim that Puerto Rico is too developed for adventure have clearly never heard of Isla Mona. Touted as "the Galápagos of the Caribbean," Isla Mona offers one of the best excursions into the Caribbean's untamed wilderness. At almost 13,000 acres, the island is twice as large as Culebra, but remains completely uninhabited except for a few researchers. Nature still reigns on this protected reserve, as enormous iguanas, thousands of hermit crabs, and non-native goats and pigs roam the island. Visitors arriving by sea may be surprised by the flatness of the island, which looks like a large pancake sitting on the water. Closer still, it becomes apparent that the edge of the island is actually composed of cavernous limestone cliffs. Strips of bright white sand emerge along the water, which shines an incredible clear blue. While most people stay near the beaches or venture inland on short hikes, a trip to Mona could include exploring the extensive cave network, hiking through the dry scrub forest, diving and snorkeling at the flourishing reefs, or lounging on the exquisite beaches. In addition to adventure,

Isla Mona

Monito

ATLANTIC OCEAN

TO PUERTO RICO (47 mi.)

TO DOMINICAN REPUBLIC (37 mi.)

Cabo Noroeste

Cabo Norte

Cueva El Gato

Cueva El Toro

Cabo Barrio Nuevo

Cueva El Capitán

Camino de los Cabros

Bajura Empalme

Vereda de las Antenas

El Corral de los Indios

Playa Sardinera

Vereda los Caobos

Taíno Ball Court

Vereda Corral

Camino de los Cactos

Cueva Negra

Camino de la Bajura de los Cereos

Cueva del Centro

Vereda Cueva del Centro

Cueva Lirio

Punta Arenas

Cueva Carita

Cabo Este

Camino del Faro

Cueva La Escalera

Playa de las Mujeres

Camino del Diablo

Playa del Carabinero

Camino del Infierno

Cueva del Pájaro

Cueva de Doña Geña

Playa Pájaro

Cueva Los Ingleses

Punta Los Ingleses

Playa Uvero

Punta Caigo o no Caigo

0   1 mile

0   1 kilometer

Caribbean Ocean

Mona offers almost absolute tranquility. The only sounds are the waves crashing on the beach and the quiet rustling of the hermit crabs. Most charters head to the island for three or four days; this taste of Mona is just enough time for adventurous visitors to get hooked and begin planning the next trip.

AT A GLANCE

AREA: 12,800 acres.

CLIMATE: Semi-arid subtropical. Year-round temperatures 80-90° F.

HIGHLIGHTS: Climbing through caves, diving in 120 ft. visibility, swimming through aquamarine water, hiking with endemic animals.

FEATURES: Wildlife, caves, Taíno petroglyphs, spectacular beaches, coral reefs, ruins of a lighthouse.

GATEWAYS: Boquerón (p. 244), Joyuda (p. 253), Rincón (p. 280), San Juan (p. 99).

CAMPING: Permitted at Playa Sardinera and Playa Pájaro with a DRNA permit ($10 per person).

FEES: Boat passage alone costs $135-400. Most charters charge more for food, equipment, tour services, and snorkeling or diving.

⌐ TRANSPORTATION

It takes a bit of tenacity to reach Isla Mona. The small airstrip is currently closed, so anyone who doesn't have a private boat will have to find passage on a Puerto Rican charter. If you have a group of at least six people, or a lot of money, the easiest option is to arrange a trip with one of the operators below. However, the ordinary traveler will have to join a pre-existing group that is still accepting additional passengers; this requires a lot of advance notice and flexible travel dates. Dive shops travel to Mona most regularly, though they don't always land on the island, to avoid DRNA permit hassles. Individuals or small groups attempting to go to Mona should first call the charter below to inquire about expeditions planned during the time period they're interested in going. If that is unsuccessful, try the dive shop in Rincón, which may be planning a trip. Finally, try calling the various dive shops based away from the west coast that make one or two trips to Mona per year. All prices listed below are round-trip.

> **A ROUGH JOURNEY.** Getting to Mona requires taking a relatively small boat 50 mi. across open seas; if you have ever been **seasick**, or are worried about seasickness, it's wise to plan ahead. Some boat captains recommend that potentially queasy travelers take **Dramamine** the night before the boat ride. For a more natural cure, **ginger tea** has been known to ease seasickness.

 Tourmarine Adventures, Rte. 102 Km 14.1 (☎375-2625; tourmarine@yahoo.com), Joyuda (p. 259), sends charters to Isla Mona. Headed by Captain Elick Hernández, who has a 34 ft. boat. 10 person min. One-day passage $135 per person. AmEx/MC/V.

Oceans Unlimited, on Rte. 115 Km 11.9 (☎823-2340; fax 823-2370; www.oceans-unlimited.com), Rincón (p. 280). Dive shop with a 6 ft. boat. 6 person min. 3-day, 6-dive trip $550 per person; 1-day, 3-tank trip $175 per person. Equipment included.

Scuba Dogs, C. 5 #D-4, Prado Alto (☎783-6377 or 399-5755; scuba-dogs@yunque.net), Guaynabo. Has a big pool for SCUBA training. They also offer excursions every weekend to dive sites around the island, occasionally including Mona. These trips vary from 1-3 days and cost $150 and up. Call ahead. MC/V.

THE MONA PASSAGE

The uninhabited nature of Isla Mona and its proximity to the mainland have long made it an access point for those who would sneak into Puerto Rico. During colonial times, the island was a boon to smugglers, pirates, and foreign governments intent on hounding Spanish settlements on Puerto Rico's west coast. It is even rumored that the infamous Captain Kidd hid out on the island briefly and stashed treasure there in 1699. Today, Mona's location approximately halfway between the Dominican Republic and the Puerto Rican mainland has made it a lightning rod for an invasion of a different sort. As many as 2000 illegal immigrants from the Dominican Republic and as far away as Cuba are caught each year by the US Coast guard attempting to cross the Mona Channel. The seas in this area are made dangerous by the presence of the undersea Puerto Rican Trench, the second deepest in the world. The trench produces strong waves and rough sailing on the ocean's surface, making for a desperate crossing that often lasts four days. Many immigrants leave the Dominican Republic in rickety handmade boats called *yolas*, and it is unknown how many never complete their journey. However, the prospect of a back-door entry into Puerto Rico and the US and a chance to experience prosperity seen nowhere else in the Caribbean continues to attract hopeful immigrants.

Ocean Sports, Av. Ashford 1035 (☎ 723-8513; www.osdivers.com), San Juan (p. 99). Makes 1-day trips to dive at Isla Mona for $85 not including equipment or tanks. NAUI certified. 2-tank dive $75, equipment rental $25. Open M-Sa 10am-7pm. AmEx/D/MC/V.

Arecibo Dive Shop, Av. Miramar 868/Hwy. 2 Km 78 (☎/fax 880-3483), Arecibo (p. 266). 8 person min. 3-day, 4-dive trip $275. Includes food and DRNA permit. You must have your own snorkeling gear. Open M-Sa 10am-6:30pm. Cash only.

ORIENTATION AND PRACTICAL INFORMATION

Located 47 mi. west of Puerto Rico and 37 mi. east of the Dominican Republic, Isla Mona sits roughly in the middle of nowhere. Most visitors arrive at **Playa Sardinera,** home of the main dock, the DRNA offices, and one Mona's most beautiful beaches. From Sardinera marked trails lead to **Playa Pájaro** (the other camping area), the lighthouse, the airport, and several caves. Little **Monito,** 3 mi. northwest of Mona, is a 160-acre limestone rock; according to the DRNA it is officially closed.

> **WHEN TO GO.** The DRNA prohibits camping on weekdays during goat- and pig-hunting season (Dec.-Apr. M-Th). During school vacations Puerto Ricans with private boats significantly decrease the serenity of Mona.

Visitors Center: The DRNA office next to Playa Sardinera is often open during the day.

Maps: Theoretically the DRNA provides a map of hiking trails, but it frequently runs out of copies. However, it's also possible to get maps at the DRNA office in Mayagüez.

Supplies: There are **absolutely no supplies on Mona.** You must bring everything that you might want on the island, including **food, drinking water** and **toilet paper.** In addition to the typical supplies don't forget mosquito repellent, long pants, sneakers if you plan to do any hiking, trash bags (to take your trash out when you leave), and a flashlight.

CAMPING AND FOOD

If you're looking for the Ritz, head back to San Juan. On Mona the only option is to camp at the two official beachfront camping areas. **Playa Sardinera ❶,** on the west coast, is the larger of the two and has two rustic cold-water showers and two flush toilets. For more seclusion head to **Playa Pájaro ❶**, on the southeast coast. This beautiful beach has a dock and room for 30 campers, but no facilities. Visitors looking for isolation and the "real" Mona tend to head here.

Isla Mona also has no food apart from fresh fish (bring your own pole) and **no potable water** (consult with tour operators about how much you should bring). Many tour groups provide food and a cook, but if not, travelers must be entirely self-sufficient. Furthermore, the DRNA does not allow open-flame fires.

> **ALCOHOL.** Alcoholic drinks are not permitted on Isla Mona due to the risk of death from dehydration and inebriation.

🐾 OUTDOOR ACTIVITIES

It's best to decide what activities you're interested in before heading to Mona in order to procure the necessary supplies. Obviously divers should invest in a dive trip, but everyone should bring snorkeling equipment. Visitors planning to explore the caves need a good flashlight, and those seeking further adventures should look for a tour group with a knowledg.eable guide. The DRNA office in Mayagüez (p. 256) can help to arrange a tour with the biologists living on the island.

BEACHES
Isla Mona has over 5 mi. of beautiful beaches and the most popular activity may be lying in the sand. **Playa Sardinera** is a long white beach with relatively calm water protected by an offshore reef. The pine trees lining the sand drop some needles, and there are occasionally bothersome sand flies, but these two small inconveniences do not tarnish Sardinera's beauty. This is also the only beach with facilities, including bathrooms, picnic tables, and showers. The other camping area, **Playa Pájaro**, looks similar, but has more palm trees, rocks, and seaweed. Although these are the two most frequented beaches, all of the sand on Mona is a bright white color that far outshines the mainland beaches, and yes, the water maintains that incredible blue color all the way around the island. Other beaches include: **Playa Mujeres,** along the airport's shoreline, **Playa del Uvero,** past the airport near the southernmost tip of the island, and **Playa Brava**, past the airport on the way to the lighthouse.

DIVING AND SNORKELING
Isla Mona has the best diving in Puerto Rico, with visibility regularly reaching 150-180 ft. Reefs nearly surround the island and many organisms grow underwater on the island's steep cliffs, creating almost limitless dive opportunities. Because the island is undeveloped and has no erosion damage, the reefs around Isla Mona are remarkably healthy and home to corals that are hard to find on the main island. More advanced divers head to one of Mona's most spectacular sights, a sea wall surrounding the island that starts at 50-60 ft., descends to 150 ft., then drops again. Due to potentially strong currents and profound depths, Mona divers should choose their sites carefully according to their experience and dive conditions.

CAVE EXPLORATION
Mona has over 150 acres of limestone caves that vary greatly in terms of size (heights range 3-30 ft.) and accessibility. Only experienced cavers should attempt to navigate the caves without a guide. DRNA employees occasionally accompany interested visitors to various caves, but don't count on this. Some tour groups and

boat captains also lead visitors through the caves; check before departing to see if your trip includes any cave exploration. **Cueva Negra** and **Cueva Carita**, near Playa Sardinera, are some of the most easily accessible caves. There are more spectacular caves on the southeastern shore, near Playa Pájaro, but these can be difficult to find. Visitors with a guide should not miss **Cueva del Agua**, which includes a crawl through a tiny passage to reach a pitch-black pool of water.

HIKING

Over 10 trails wind through Isla Mona, but not all are regularly maintained. The most frequented path is a dirt access road traveling south from Playa Sardinera to: Cueva Negra (33 ft., 2min.); Playa Mujeres (1 mi., 20min.); Cueva Carita (½ mi., 15min.); the airport (¾ mi., 20min.); Playa Carabinero (2 mi., 40min.); Playa del Uvero (3¼ mi., 1¼hr.); Playa Pájaro (6mi., 3hr.); and the lighthouse (8mi., 4hr.). A second, more rustic path leaves Playa Sardinera and heads east straight up the cliff where it breaks off into two paths; one continues east across the island and the other continues north along the cliff. The eastern branch, called Camino de los Cabros, leads past the Taíno site known as Bajura Empalme. Another trail, known as the Bajura de los Ceresos, branches southward from this one past the Taíno ball court before reaching the Playa Uvero area. On the east coast, the Vereda Cueva del Centro leads from the lighthouse trail to the Cueva del Centro. Before undertaking any hikes, check in with the DRNA to ensure that they are still open and let them know your plans. Remember that water is not available on the island and you may require much more water than usual when hiking in the heat.

> **! TROUBLE IN PARADISE.** The flat terrain makes it very easy to get lost when hiking on Isla Mona, and every couple of years visitors die from dehydration after losing their way on the featureless plateau. Watch out also for deep limestone holes and plants with sharp spines. Wear long pants and don't touch anything that you cannot identify.

▓ FLORA AND FAUNA

Isla Mona's wildlife is fascinating. The small island houses 700 species of animals, 58 of which are endemic to the island and 75 of which have never been found on the Puerto Rican mainland. By far the most famous is the **Mona Iguana**, a gargantuan 4 ft. reptile found nowhere else in the world. These stunning creatures frequently emerge from their burrowed nests to observe new campers. Visitors will also be greeted by piles of crawling **hermit crabs**, crustaceans that migrate to the sea during early August to breed. The only amphibian on Mona is the unique **Mona coquí**, which has a song slightly different from its Puerto Rican relative. Unlike the mainland, Mona also has a significant number of creepy crawlies. Watch out for the 52 species of spiders and the three species of scorpions. Luckily the 3 ft. **Isla Mona Boa**, yet another endemic species, generally only comes out at night and is not harmful to humans. This curious creature is one of the only snakes that gives birth to developed offspring and does not lay eggs. **Bird-watchers** will enjoy looking for the 100 species of birds found on Mona. Only two, the yellow-shouldered blackbird and the ground dove, are native to the island. The **goats** and **pigs** that were left behind after earlier attempts to farm the island roam freely as wild animals. Every year, the two animals are hunted from December to April Monday through Thursday, closing the island to camping. There are over 270 species of **fish** around Mona, including dolphins, silky sharks, nurse sharks, barracudas, flying fish, moray eels, and, during the winter months, humpback whales. From May to October the endangered **hawksbill turtle** nests on the shores of Mona. The **loggerhead sea turtle** also swims in the waters around Mona; if you see a turtle, leave it alone, as human interference is one important cause of the species's decline.

Mona's flora cannot match the diversity of its fauna, but the island does contain four endemic plant species. The vegetation is a combination of eastern Hispaniola and southwestern Puerto Rico, and most of the island consists of **dry plateau forest** filled with white cedar, cactus, and posionwood. Most of the coastal forest consists of princewood and oysterwood, although there are a few acres of mangroves.

JOYUDA

This 3 mi. strip of coastal road contains more seafood restaurants than any other place in Puerto Rico, and *mayagüezanos* regularly drive down to sample the fresh delicacies and watch the sunset. The town has few beaches, but **Isla Ratones,** about ½ mi. offshore, has a small sandy beach. A ferry runs out to the island from Rte. 102 Km 13.7, next to Island View Restaurant. (☎851-7708. Open Tu-Su 9am-5pm. $5 round-trip.) For a much longer trip out to sea, check in with **Tourmarine Adventures,** Rte. 102 Km 14.1. Captain Elick Hernández charters his 34 ft. boat for the 3hr. trip to Isla Mona ($135 per person; min. 10 people) or for more local sightseeing. He is very flexible, but you must either have a group or pay for the entire boat. Common trips include: a 2-tank dive at the offshore cliffs ($40 without equipment), a 5-6hr. whale-watching trip in the Mona Passage (Feb.-Mar.; $65 per person), or local snorkeling ($35 with equipment). Call ahead to see if you can join another group. (☎375-2625; www.tourmarinepr.com. Cash only.)

Joyuda has an extraordinary number of hotels considering the area's limited attractions. Several small hotels and guesthouses are tucked between larger, pricier offerings. Little **Hotel Costa de Oro Inn ❷,** Rte. 102 Km 14.7, is a modern building with a friendly guesthouse feel and immaculate rooms that live up to the standards of a much larger hotel. A pool fills the courtyard. (☎851-5010. A/C and cable TV. Check-in 2pm. Check-out noon. Sept.-May doubles $45; quads $60. June-Aug. doubles $60; quads $85; extra person $15. MC/V.) Beyond the rows of modern, commercial hotels sits **Tony's Restaurant and Hotel ❷,** Rte. 102 Km 10.9. The bright blue rooms surround a parking lot, with a pool in the back. (☎851-2500. TV, A/C; quads have fridges. Doubles $50; quads $70.) Portraits of Tony's musician friends hang on the walls of the upscale **restaurant ❹.** (Entrees $15-25.)

Choosing a restaurant in Joyuda is like picking a bar in San Juan; there are just too many good options. Most of the seafood is fresh and almost all restaurants serve crab, mahi mahi, red snapper, lobster, shrimp, conch, trunk fish, and octopus. The only real variety is in location and atmosphere. **Mao's Seafood House ❸,** Rte. 102 Km 13.8, is one of the friendlier places along this stretch of road, owned and operated by a lifelong Joyuda resident. All the standard seafood dishes and a casual atmosphere combine with a view of Isla Ratones for a pleasant dining experience. (☎255-1801. Appetizers $3-8. Entrees $13-20. Open Tu-Su 11:30am-11pm.) The Puerto Rican Tourism Company selected **Tino's Restaurant ❹,** Rte. 102 Km 13.6, as their Joyuda *mesón gastronómico.* Although it does not look out over the water, Tino's offers a touch of class and specialty seafood-filled *mofongos.* (☎851-2976. Entrees $8-26. Open W-Su 11am-10pm. AmEx/MC/V.)

MAYAGÜEZ

The self-proclaimed capital of the west coast has few attractions but ample spirit. With over 100,000 inhabitants, Mayagüez is one of the island's major metropolitan areas, yet unlike many smaller cities it has not yet developed a tourist infrastructure. Like Ponce, this city has some beautiful turn-of-the-century houses, but most have fallen into a state of decay. Mayagüez has a deep port, but for now it is used primarily for industrial purposes, with cruise ship stops planned in the next few years. Although the city is less of a destination than a stopover on a tour of the west coast, the active university district's bars do provide ample entertainment for an evening visit. Construction in preparation for the Juegos Centroamericanos y del Caribe in 2010 indicates that Mayagüez does have potential to become a more attractive tourist destination.

▐▀ TRANSPORTATION

Flights: Aeropuerto Eugenio María de Hostos (☎832-3390), 4 mi. north of town on Rte. 342, just off Hwy. 2, has 1 airline: **Cape Air** (834-2870) sends flights to **San Juan** (1 per day, one-way $114). A taxi into Mayagüez costs about $7 (plus luggage), though you may have to call (see **Taxis**, p. 254).

Públicos: The *público* terminal is located at the end of C. Pablo Maiz, near Parque de los Proceros. *Públicos* head to: **Aguadilla** (30-40min., $3); **Añasco** (10-15min., $2); **Cabo Rojo** (15-20min., $2); **Ponce** (80-90min., $5-6); **Rincón** (20min., $2). **Linea Sultana** (☎832-1041 or 832-2502) sends vans to **San Juan** (3-3½hr.; 5, 7, 9, 11am, 1, 3, 5pm; $12). Call ahead and they'll pick you up from your hotel.

Ferries: Ferries del Caribe (☎832-4800 or 832-4905), north of town. From Hwy. 2 turn left at Km 152.2 on Rte. 102 and follow the signs. A taxi costs about $6. An enormous 1000-passenger ferry travels between **Santo Domingo, Dominican Republic** (12hr.; M, W, F 8pm) and Puerto Rico (Tu, Th, Sa 8pm). Prices vary depending on cabin size: general one-way ticket (no cabin) $182, round-trip $189; suites (shared 4-person rooms) round-trip $208 per person; single cabins (essentially a hotel room) round-trip $295; double cabins round-trip $237 per person; quads $208 per person. The boat has airplane-style seats for those who do not purchase a bed. To purchase a one-way ticket you must have an airplane ticket or some other proof of departure from the Dominican Republic. Cars round-trip $182; vans, minivans, and pickups $212; motorcycles $112; bikes $20. You must reserve at least 1 day in advance or there is a $10 fee. The ferry terminal does not have parking, but a local man named Willy allows people to park at his house for $5 per day (☎831-0835). Arrive 2hr. early. Terminal office open Tu, Th, Sa 8am-5pm; M, W, F 8am-8pm; Su noon-4pm. MC/V.

Cars: The car rental companies below operate out of the airport. All prices are for the smallest compact cars available. Rates rise during Christmas, Easter, and summer.

Avis (☎833-7070). $44 per day. 25+. Open daily 7am-9:30pm. AmEx/D/DC/MC/V.

Budget (☎832-4570). $44 per day, with insurance $53. 21+. Under 25 surcharge $10 per day. Open daily 8-9pm. AmEx/D/MC/V.

Thrifty (☎834-1590). $52 per day. 21+. Under 25 surcharge $10 per day. Open daily 8am-noon and 1-5pm. AmEx/D/DC/MC/V.

Taxis: White Taxi Cab, C. de Diego 18 (☎832-1154), at C. Peral. Open daily 6:30am-midnight. **City Taxi** (☎265-1992) leaves from the *público* station. Open daily 6:30am-11pm. **Western Taxi** (☎832-0562), at C. del Río and C. McKinley. Open daily 6am-midnight.

SOUTHWEST

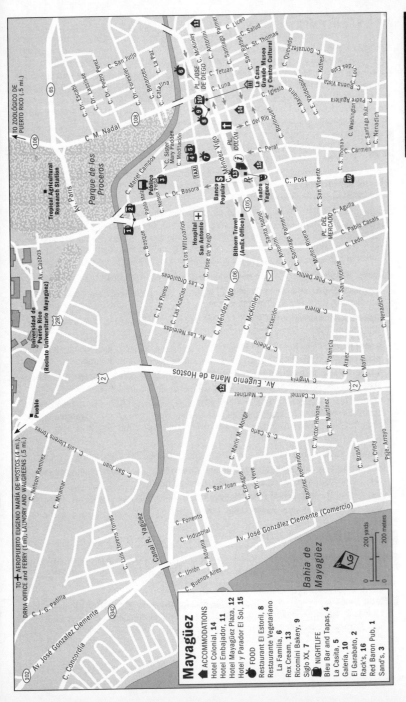

TO ZOOLÓGICO DE
PUERTO RICO (.5 mi.)

TO † AEROPUERTO EUGENIO MARÍA DE HOSTOS (4 mi.),
DRNA OFFICE and FERRY (1 mi.), LAUNDRY AND WALGREENS (.5 mi.)

Universidad de
Puerto Rico
(Recinto Universitario Mayagüez)

Pueblo

Parque de los
Proceres

Tropical Agricultural
Research Station

Hospital
San Antonio

Bithorn Travel
(AmEx Office)

Banco
Popular

Teatro
Yagüez

La Casa
Grande Museo
y Centro Cultural

PL. JOSÉ
DE DIEGO

PL. DEL
MERCADO

Canal R. Yagüez

Av. Eugenio María de Hostos

Av. José González Clemente (Comercio)

Bahía de
Mayagüez

200 yards
200 meters

Mayagüez

⚑ ACCOMMODATIONS
Hotel Colonial, 14
Hotel Embajador, 11
Hotel Mayagüez Plaza, 12
Hotel y Parador El Sol, 15

♦ FOOD
Restaurant El Estoril, 8
Restaurante Vegetariano
La Familia, 6
Rex Cream, 13
Ricomini Bakery, 9
Siglo XX, 7

▮ NIGHTLIFE
Bleu Bar and Tapas, 4
La Casita, 5
Galería, 10
El Garabato, 2
Rack's, 16
Red Baron Pub, 1
Sand's, 3

ORIENTATION AND PRACTICAL INFORMATION

Mayagüez has a relatively small, walkable city center on the eastern side of Hwy. 2. To reach the city center from Hwy. 2, exit toward C. McKinley or C. Post. This is one of the few cities in Puerto Rico where most hotels and restaurants do congregate around the plaza. **Calle Post,** also called Hwy. 2R, leads north from Plaza Colón to the university area. **Mayagüez Town Center,** located at the intersection of C. Post and Hwy. 2, just north of the center, holds some convenient services and a food court.

> **!** After dark, stick to the well-lit streets on and around Plaza Colón, or the university area at the northern end of C. Post.

Tours: AdvenTours (☎831-6447) offers walking tours of downtown Mayagüez (3hr., M-Tu, $18). 2 person min. Cash only.

Camping Permits: The **Departamento de Recursos Naturales** (DRNA; ☎833-3700 or 833-4703), north on Hwy. 2. Exit toward the east at Km 150.2, then follow signs; the office is at the end of Alturas de Mayagüez shopping center. Issues permits to camp ($4 per person) and visit Isla Mona ($10 per person), but you must first call the San Juan office to check availability and make a reservation. Open M-F 7:30am-noon and 1-4pm.

Banks: Banco Popular, C. Méndez Vigo 9 (☎832-0475). ATM. Open M-F 8am-4pm.

American Express: Bithorn Travel, C. Méndez Vigo 8 (☎834-3300; www.bithorntravel.com). Open M-F 8:30am-5pm.

Supermarket: Pueblo (☎834-8720), on the 1st fl. of the Mayagüez Town Center. **Western Union.** Open M-Sa 6am-midnight, Su 11am-5pm. AmEx/MC/V.

Laundromat: Across Rte. 2 from Walgreens, around the corner in a shopping plaza is a nondescript facility. Wash $1; dry $0.25 for 7min. Open daily until 10pm.

Police: Policía de Puerto Rico (☎832-9699), about 2 mi. south of town on Av. Corazones, 1059. Turn left at Denny's. Open 24hr.

Pharmacies: Farmacia Yaguez, C. Ramos Antonini 5 (☎832-5060), at C. Basora, near the plaza, has a basic selection. Open M-Sa 8am-9pm. AmEx/MC/V. **Walgreens,** Av. Hostos 2097 (☎805-4005), just north of town at Hwy. 2 Km 152.7, is open 24hr. AmEx/D/DC/MC/V.

Hospital: Hospital San Antonio, C. Post 18 Norte (☎834-0056). 24hr. emergency room.

Internet Access: The **Biblioteca Municipal,** C. McKinley 14, between the Alcaldía and the Teatro Yaguez (☎834-8585 ext. 440), has free Internet.

Post Office: C. McKinley 60 Oeste (☎265-3133). General Delivery available. Open M-F 7am-5pm, Sa 7am-1pm. **Postal Code:** 00681.

▐ ACCOMMODATIONS

This is one of the most affordable places to stay in Puerto Rico, and you can expect to get quite a bang for your buck. Still, hotels are frequently filled almost to capacity. Most include continental breakfast.

▨ **Hotel Colonial,** C. Iglesia 14 Sur (☎/fax 833-2150). One of the best values on the island. This colonial building has most of the traditional amenities—A/C, TV, parking—and throws in tall ceilings and 24hr. reception. A real bargain. Continental breakfast. Parking. Check-in 1pm. Check-out noon. Singles M-Th $32, F-Sa $43; doubles $43-54/

54-65; quads $97/108; extra person $11. Tax included. MC/V. ❶

Hotel Mayagüez Plaza, C. Méndez Vigo 70 Este (☎832-9191). The nicest hotel downtown. Tropical bedspreads brighten up clean, airy rooms with glistening bathrooms. Ideally located right behind the church. Cable TV, A/C, phone, small swimming pool. Continental breakfast included. Parking. Check-in 3pm. 1 king bed $93; 2 full beds $104. Tax included. AmEx/D/DC/MC/V. ❹

Hotel y Parador El Sol, C. Santiago Palmer 9 Este (☎834-0303), suffers from a lack of space, despite the fact that this 5-story building is one of Mayagüez's tallest, and has all the formality of a big-city hotel. Tiny rooms still manage to fit in a phone, A/C, cable TV, and a small fridge. Clean and well-maintained. A small pool is tucked into the courtyard. Restaurant. Continental breakfast. Parking. Singles $75; doubles $86; extra person $11. Tax included. AmEx/MC/V. ❸

Hotel Embajador, C. Antonini 111 (☎833-3340), is bringing a cosmopolitan feel to Mayagüez with its modern art and slick new nightclub El Chapas. Rooms have artwork above the bed, along with cable TV, A/C, and carpeting. Singles $60; doubles $71. ❷

🔲 FOOD

Mayagüez has a number of attractive dining options around the plaza, and fast food abounds in the malls surrounding town.

🔳 Ricomini Bakery/Brazo Gitano, C. Méndez Vigo 101 (☎833-1444), takes the cake (and the flan, and the *quesito*, and the *arroz con dulce*) as the best bakery/cafe/eatery in town. This clean, airy cafe swarms with activity during the lunch hour when it seems like everyone in Mayagüez stops by. Delicious food, efficient service, immaculate setting. Hot *comida criolla* $4.50 per lb. Breakfast $2.50-3. Sandwiches $3.50-5. Pastries $0.30-1.50. Open daily 6am-midnight. AmEx/MC/V. ❶

Restaurant Siglo XX, C. Peral 9 Norte, (☎265-2094). A popular *cafetería*-style lunch place, with hot sandwiches and heavier fare available. Upstairs seating with dark wood furniture and railings. Entrees $8-13. Open M-Sa 6am-8:30pm. ❷

Restaurant El Estoril, C. Méndez Vigo 100 Este (☎834-2288). The owners claim this is "The Best in the West" and they're not far off. First-rate Portuguese food in a first-class setting, with fountains in the corner, porcelain plates decorating the wall, and a huge wine rack.

IN RECENT NEWS

LET THE GAMES BEGIN

Mayagüez recently earned the honor of hosting the **Juegos Deportivos Centroamericanos y del Caribe de 2010** (Games of Central America and the Caribbean 2010). Although they are still a long way off, the games are already changing the face and character of the city. Mayagüez has budgeted $68 million for construction to prepare for the event, including new sports facilities and improved tourist facilities. The city is reinventing itself as the symbolic port of entry for west-coast Puerto Rico. The port itself is being renovated and brought up to the code of international cruise line standards in an effort to attract some of the bustling cruise traffic away from Old San Juan to this sleepy coast. Although the sporting events of the games will be held along the entire west coast, Mayagüez will serve as the center of festivities. In preparation, the town plaza is under construction, as is the **Teatro Yagüez** downtown.

Today, all the changes in Mayagüez mean that travelers must navigate a maze of one-way streets and closed-off avenues in the downtown area, which can become quite a headache. But for future visitors, increased tourist infrastructure will likely mean better transportation options, livelier nightlife, and more tourist-friendly venues in the years to come.

Lunch buffet $10. Entrees $12-30. Open June-July Tu-F 11:30-10pm, Sa 5-10pm. Aug.-May M-F 11am-10:30pm, Sa 5-11pm. AmEx/MC/V. ❸

Rex Cream, C. McKinley 17 (☎832-2121). This ice cream stand is so popular that there are two locations around the corner from each other, one on C. McKinley and one on C. Mendez Vigo. Open M-Th 10am-10pm, F-Sa 10am-11pm, Su 11am-11pm. MC/V. ❶

Restaurante Vegetariano La Familia, C. de Diego 151 Este (☎833-7571). Clean, spacious, and super friendly, not to mention one of the few vegetarian options in Puerto Rico. A full buffet serves a variety of vegetarian entrees, usually including several kinds of rice, a tofu dish, and fresh salad. Mix and match your favorites. $6 for a filling meal. Open M-F 11am-3pm. Cash only. ❶

👁 SIGHTS

ZOOLÓGICO DE PUERTO RICO. If you're still lamenting the fact that Puerto Rico is not home to any large mammals, you may enjoy a visit to Puerto Rico's largest zoo. Managed by the Compañia de Parques Nacionales, the zoo contains a wide selection of animals divided into "African Forest" and "African Savannah" groups, which boils down to a typical selection of monkeys, zebras, lions, camels, caimans, and hippopotami. All things considered, this is a laudable effort by the CPN and by far the most interesting attraction in Mayagüez. *(Take Rte. 108 north past the university, then turn right at the sign for the zoo. Don't attempt to walk, as the road is narrow and cars drive fast. Taxis about $4. ☎834-8110. Open W-Su 8:30am-4pm. Parking $2, vans $3. Admission $6, ages 11-17 and 60-74 $4, ages 5-10 $2, under 5 and 75+ free. MC/V.)*

TROPICAL AGRICULTURE RESEARCH STATION. Ecologists and botanists may drool over this 127-acre agricultural center where the US Department of Agriculture breeds plant species suitable to the South Atlantic. For less scientifically-inclined visitors, the station is a de facto botanical garden and a wonderful place to walk. A self-guided tour leads past over 70 labeled plant species native to the island. *(Between Rte. 108 and Rte. 2R. ☎831-3435. Open M-F 7am-noon and 1-4pm. Free.)*

RECINTO UNIVERSITARIO MAYAGÜEZ (RUM). Any university with the acronym RUM has to be something interesting, and Mayagüez's branch of the University of Puerto Rico does not disappoint. NASA and other government agencies have been known to recruit engineering students from this primarily science-focused division of UPR. The attractive palm-filled campus is one of the more picturesque in Puerto Rico. Enter the gate across from Mayagüez Town Center and follow the broad Av. Palmeras to reach the main university plaza, the general library, and the student center. *(North of the city at the intersection of C. Post and Hwy. 2.)*

TEATRO YAGUEZ. Mayagüez has one of the most attractive public theaters in Puerto Rico. In 1976 the municipal government bought a historic church and converted it into the city's grandiose theater, complete with enormous chandeliers and two balconies. Unfortunately, restoration keeps it under wraps; the 900-seat theater has been undergoing renovation since 2003. *(Behind the Alcaldía between C. McKinley and C. Antonini.)*

🎵 NIGHTLIFE

University students dominate Mayagüez's nightlife, which heats up on Wednesday and Thursday, then dies down over the weekend when everyone heads to the beach. If drinking with college kids is not your cup of tea, **Sand's** (below) has more of a young-professional feel, and several malls on Rte. 2 have movie theaters.

El Garabato, C. Post 102 Norte (☎834-2524). A university pub where students gather throughout the day and night to grab a beer, play some dominos, and chat. Daily happy hour specials with various $1 beers. Open M-Sa 3pm-1:30am. AmEx/MC/V.

Red Baron Pub, C. Post 102 Norte (☎805-1580), upstairs from El Garabato. Once they've gotten good and toasted downstairs, RUM students head up to this steamy pub to dance the night away. Beer $1-2. Karaoke Tu. A live DJ plays *reggaetón*, rock, and hip-hop W-Sa. Occasional live Spanish rock. Open Tu-Th 6pm-last customer, F-Sa 9pm-last customer. Cash only.

La Casita, C. de Diego 65 (☎805-1505). True to its name, located in a little house. Reggae, rock, and *reggaetón* give the cheerful twenty-something crowd something to nod their heads to while drinking at the bar. Beer $2.25-2.50. Mixed drinks $3-5. Daily happy hour specials $1.25-1.50. Cover bands Th-Sa 11pm. Open M-F 5pm-1:30am, Sa-Su 8pm-1:30am. MC/V.

Bleu Bar and Tapas, C. de Diego 63 (☎831-1446). One of the largest dance floors in town lit, of course, in blue. The polished metal doors and trimmings make it feel industrial and hip, so hip that the 2nd fl. is VIP-only. Beer $2.50. Mixed drinks $4. Tapas $3-8. DJ W. Live music Th-Sa. Sa cover $4. Open W-F 6pm-1:30am, Sa 8pm-1:30am.

Rack's, C. Post 167 Sur (☎265-4726). A spacious, trendy new pool hall and across town from the university. The crowd is young and the music loud. One of the few non-smoking establishments in Mayagüez. Tu ladies' night and karaoke. F-Sa models serve drinks. Beer $2.50. Mixed drinks $4. Pool $0.75. Open M-Sa 6pm-3am.

Galería, adjoining the elegant El Estoril, has a changing display of local artwork. Warm yellow walls produce an intimate feel at this art-gallery-turned-dance-party. Mixed drinks $3-6. Live rock or jazz F. No cover. Open W-Sa 10pm-last customer.

Sand's, C. Peral 36 (☎831-5587). Packed with *mayagüezanos* young enough to enjoy F night karaoke but old enough to afford the pricey drinks. Dance floor with mirrors and flashing colored lights. Appetizers $6-20. Beer $2.75-3.25. Mixed drinks $3.75-6. W 7-11pm cover $10, includes limited open bar. 21+. Open M-Tu and Su 11am-11pm, W 11am-1am, Th 11am-2am, F-Sa 11am-3am. AmEx/MC/V.

NORTHWEST

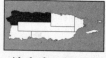

West of San Juan, the terrain becomes more rugged, the locals more laid back, and somewhere between the volcanic surfing beaches of the north coast and the dramatic *mogotes* of the inland mountains you realize that you have arrived in western Puerto Rico. The Atlantic Ocean pounds the coast with the heaviest waves on the island, creating ideal surfing territory, while the limestone cliffs and sinkholes known as karst create a rugged, otherworldly atmosphere.

Most travelers leave San Juan and head east, but the wilder country of the northwest has attractions to rival any others. Just south of Arecibo, the Camuy Caves and Arecibo Observatory (containing the world's largest radio telescope) are two of the most impressive sights on the island and make an excellent daytrip from San Juan. Farther west, Isabela and Rincón have some of the best surfing in the Caribbean, but even non-surfers will be enamored with the beautiful terrain, the friendly atmosphere, and the comfortable accommodations. However, strong waves make beautiful beaches less than ideal for swimming, and the region is also one of the most developed on the island, meaning that overpopulation, huge factories, and heavy traffic may mar an otherwise pleasant journey. Indeed, some city centers on the north coast—Manatí, Arecibo, Aguadilla—should be avoided entirely if possible. Fortunately, Hwy. 22 skirts most of the heavy traffic and deposits travelers in Arecibo within an hour and a half. The adventurous can explore the region more extensively by bypassing the main highways and taking small, one-lane roads along the northern coast or through inland karst country.

HIGHLIGHTS OF NORTHWEST PUERTO RICO

HANG TEN, OR JUST HANG OUT in **Rincón**, Puerto Rico's favorite expat haunt and home of some of the world's best surfing and nightlife (p. 280).

TRAVEL TO ANOTHER PLANET by exploring the underground world at the **Camuy Caves** (p. 269) or the **Arecibo Observatory** (p. 268).

GET UP CLOSE AND PERSONAL with karst country by hiking in **Bosque Estatal de Guajataca** (p. 278) or mountain biking in **Bosque Estatal de Cambalache** (p. 262).

START THE WEEKEND EARLY at **Jobos' relaxed surfer beaches** with the young Puerto Rican crowd and bass-bumpin' *reggaetón* (p. 272).

MANATÍ

A practical town sprawled along Hwy. 2, Manatí serves as a convenient roadside source of necessities, but isn't really a destination in its own right. Fast-food joints and big-box retailers have taken over the town itself. Farther afield several interesting natural attractions, including rugged surfing beaches and lakes full of caimans, provide incentive to venture out to this area.

⬛ TRANSPORTATION. Manatí centers on Hwy. 2, but it is much faster to travel via Hwy. 22, despite the intermittent tolls ($0.50-0.70), then exit onto Rte. 149, and turn right at the intersection with Hwy. 2. *Públicos* traveling between Parada 18 in Santurce and Arecibo will stop in **Manatí**, or anywhere along Hwy. 2. To catch a *público*, sit at a green bench along Hwy. 2 and flag one down. However, it is almost impossible to reach most sights via public transportation, and there really is nothing to do in Manatí proper.

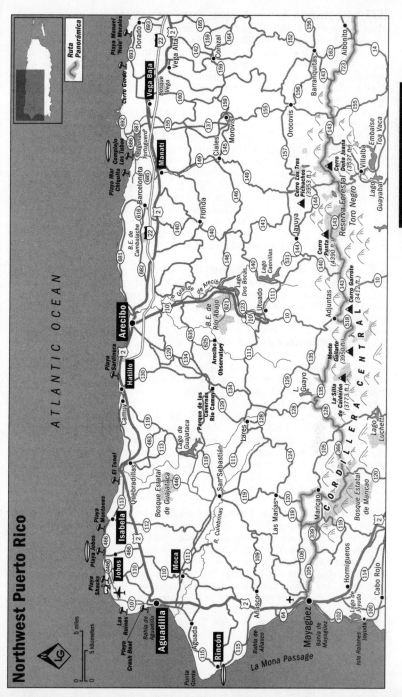

NORTHWEST

Northwest Puerto Rico

ATLANTIC OCEAN

Ruta Panorámica

⌗ ⁊ ORIENTATION AND PRACTICAL INFORMATION. Notwithstanding a lack of addresses, Manatí is very easy to navigate. Just drive along Hwy. 2 and eventually you'll find everything. Barceloneta lies to the west and Vega Baja lies to the east. Most sights are located to the north, between Hwy. 2 and the ocean. Traveling west to east along the ocean, Rte. 686, Rte. 692, and Rte. 691 provide superb views and access to numerous beaches. **Banco Popular,** at Hwy. 2 and C. Vendig in the Bella Maria Shopping Center, has an **ATM.** (☎854-2030. Open M-F 8am-4pm, Sa 9am-1pm.) **Grande,** on Hwy. 2 in the same shopping center as Banco Popular, is a good place to stock up on groceries. (☎884-7273. Open M-Sa 7am-10pm, Su 11am-5pm. AmEx/MC/V.) They also have **Moneygram** money transfer service. The **police station** (☎854-2020 or 854-2011), just up the road from the intersection of Hwy. 2 and Rte. 149, is open 24hr. **Walgreens,** at the intersection of Hwy. 2 and Rte. 149, in Manatí Plaza, parcels out pharmaceuticals 24hr. a day. (☎884-0545. AmEx/D/MC/V.) The enormous sign at **Hospital Alejandro Otero Lopez** is visible from Hwy. 2, but the building is set back from the road one block along Rte. 668. (☎623-3700. 24hr. emergency room.) In Barceloneta, **Vkcafe** has touch-screen computers with **free Internet** (see **Nightlife,** p. 278). The **post office,** C. Eliot Velez 29, across from the Burger King west of Rte. 668, set back from Hwy. 2, does not have General Delivery. (☎854-2296. Open M-F 8am-4:30pm, Sa 8am-noon.) **Postal Code:** 00674.

⌗ ⁊ ACCOMMODATIONS AND CAMPING. There are not many accommodations in the Manatí area. **Motel La Roca ❷,** just off Hwy. 2 near Barceloneta, rents some rooms by the night and others by the hour (see **A Room Without a View,** p. 263). The former come with TV, A/C, and music dials on the walls. Not all rooms have windows. (From Hwy. 2, turn south on Rte. 663. ☎881-0483. 1 double bed $50; 2 double beds $60. Cash only.) The best option is to ⛺camp at **Bosque Estatal de Cambalache ❶** (see **Sights,** below). The large La Rosa area holds up to 30 people and has covered picnic tables, trash cans, showers, and toilets (when the water is turned on). You must have a DRNA permit ($4 per person) and a reservation to camp here (see **Camping,** p. 42). Call ahead to insure that the gate is left open for your arrival.

⌗ FOOD. Puerto Ricans usually dine at the fast-food restaurants lining Hwy. 2, More unique sit-down eateries are hidden along the marginal roads of Hwy. 2, including the hopping ⛱**Wine Gallery and Diego Restaurant ❹,** C. B3 Marginal, off of Hwy. 2. An outdoor balcony and indoor bar attract chatty young professionals, who enjoy *comida criolla* and international dishes for $11-23. (☎884-0109. Beer $2. Wine bottles from $20. Live music Sa. Karaoke Th. Open Tu 10am-8pm, W 10am-11pm, Th-Sa 10am-2am.)

⌗ SIGHTS. ⛱**Bosque Estatal de Cambalache** provides a welcome retreat from the development along Hwy. 2. At slightly under 1000 acres, this humid subtropical forest is large enough to provide a full day of activity, but small enough to be manageable; for visitors staying in San Juan, this is a convenient day-long introduction to karst country. Over 4 mi. of well-marked, beginner-friendly hiking trails wind through the forest, including an interpretive trail with signs, and a **mountain biking path.** Unfortunately, San Juan (p. 92) is the closest place to rent bikes. The picnic area contains covered tables and playground equipment. From Hwy. 22, take the exit immediately after the Arecibo tollbooth, then go north on Rte. 683. Turn right on Rte. 682 and look for the large sign on the right. To get to the forest **office,** take a right as soon as you enter the premises, directly before the welcome sign. (☎881-1004. Open M-F 8am-4:30pm.)

The Department of Natural Resources has classified **Laguna Tortuguero** as the only natural lake in Puerto Rico. And it's full of a reptile species similar to a crocodile, called a **caiman**. In the mid-1970s many Puerto Ricans began purchasing the South American animals as pets; however, they soon discovered that caimans are cranky little critters that rapidly outgrow fish tanks, so they ditched the animals in the lake. Unfortunately, the introduction of a new species disrupted the existing ecosystem. The Department of Natural Resources attempted an eradication program in the early 1980s, but to no avail. Now both parties have accepted peaceful coexistence. The caimans only come out at night, so most visitors remain blissfully oblivious to their presence. The curious, or masochistic, can obtain a special permit from the office in Manatí to visit after nightfall and attempt to see one of the animals. During the day the peaceful lake is a great place to fish, kayak, or just sit with a picnic and enjoy the scenery. A 5min. walk uphill from the parking lot leads to great views of the lake and the ocean. From Hwy. 22 take Exit 41, turn right on Hwy. 2, then left on Rte. 687, and look for the second big sign on the left. The Manatí office (☎884-2587) is open W-F 8am-4pm and Sa-Su 6am-6pm.

North of Manatí, **Reserva Natural Hacienda la Esperanza** has the potential to be a regional attraction. This 19th-century sugar cane plantation occupies over 2200 acres with six different ecosystems, from mangroves to coral reefs, much of it preserved as it was 100 years ago. The Conservation Trust of Puerto Rico has big plans to renovate the house and open the area to the public; unfortunately, it may not be finished until well after 2006. For now the area offers solitude and a nice view along the beach. From Manatí head north on Rte. 685, then turn left on Rte. 616, continue past the town, and pass through the empty fields, until you see the reserve sign on the left. To reach the beach at Punta Manatí, continue on the road through a tiny neighborhood to the Fideicomiso gate (open weekends and holidays to vehicles, always open to foot traffic) and continue on the dirt road through the dense mangroves to the sandy beach.

◪ **BEACHES.** The rugged beaches lining the northwest coast rival Piñones in terms of solitude, surfing potential, and sheer beauty. The best way to find your own private spot is to drive along the

THE HIDDEN DEAL

A ROOM WITHOUT A VIEW

Pull into any of the self-dubbed "motels" along Hwy. 2 and you may be in for a surprise. You'll find no reception office and you may notice that the rooms don't have any windows overlooking the parking area. Hourly and overnight prices posted on placards inside each room's private garage. After you park in the garage, be sure to close the door after you—this is the signal for the attendant to approach the room. You'll be expected to pay cash through a small, private window below eye-level and the attendant will ask if you want to the room for 8hr. or for the whole night. Catching on yet? When you turn away from the exchange window, you may be greeted by three reflections of yourself in full-length mirrors that line the room. Dials on the wall are tuned to mood music. For an extra $10, you can get a room with a *"yakusi"* (jacuzzi).

Puerto Rican motels are distinguished from other accommodations by their short-term bookings and ultra-private rooms, designed strictly for indoor pursuits. A great deal for budget-travelers, they are characterized by a high level of cleanliness and courteous staff. See for yourself at **Motel La Roca,** (☎881-0483), Rte. 663 south off of Hwy. 2 (8hr. $25-30) or **Bosque Verde Motel,** Rte. 2 Km 107.2 (☎872-5377), east of Isabel (8hr. $25-30; suites $60).

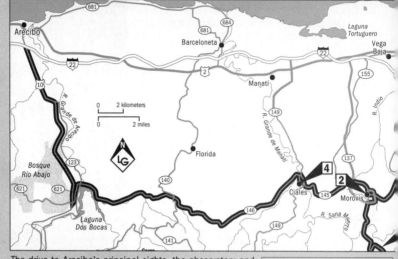

The drive to Arecibo's principal sights, the observatory and nearby Camuy Caves, leads past the steep limestone sinkholes and looming *mogotes* of karst country (p. 269). However, the fastest route from San Juan entails a substantial drive along a series freeways, on which you will speed through the beautiful countryside. For a more leisurely and scenic route, try this series of backroads that twists and turns through the spectacular land-scape of northern Puerto Rico, from verdant farmlands to the

TIME: 3-4hr.

DISTANCE: 55mi.

BEST TIME TO GO: Dec.-June, or when it's not raining.

heart of karst country. The drive is more interesting than most of the man-made sights along the way, but these serve as nice breaks during the long trip. Because the route runs parallel to Hwy. 2 and Hwy. 22, it is easy to head back north at any time and zip on to Arecibo. Otherwise, sit back and enjoy the ride through some of Puerto Rico's most dramatic countryside.

The drive begins just past Manatí. From San Juan, take Hwy. 22 west, then take Exit 22 north onto Rte. 165. Turn onto Hwy. 2 and drive west to take Rte. 142 toward Corozal. Drive south past the bright orange trees, then turn right (west) on Rte. 818 and continue past the residential neighborhood to Km 2.5.

1 CENTRO HISTÓRICO TURÍSTICO DEL CIBUCO (HISTORICAL TOURIST CENTER). Nestled in the middle of a valley with steep karst cliffs and wide vistas, this tourist center offers a sampling of various Puerto Rican cultural attractions on the grounds of an old sugar plantation. The guided visit begins at the plantation's old home, **Casa Museo Aurora.** Although it was built in the 1930s, the museum has been redecorated with 19th century furniture and a mishmash of historical artifacts. Next stop is the small **Museo de la Caña de Azucar** (Museum of Sugar Cane), which explains the history of sugar cane in Spanish. Tours then travel back through time about 500 years as visitors hop on a tram to see **Taíno petroglyphs.** A wooden walkway skirts the original petroglyphs by 3 ft., but the museum has constructed a replica that visitors can inspect up close. Next stop is a small mock sugar mill where visitors can sample the sickeningly sweet sugar milk. Last stop is the **Artificial Lake.** With a maximum depth of 30 ft., the lake is large enough to support wildlife and visitors can borrow a paddle boat or just stand at the edge and watch the turtles swim below. In mid-July the center hosts an **artisans festival.** The complex is designed for groups (primarily Puerto Rican schoolchildren) and visits require a guided tour. However, when it's not busy, guides are happy to accommodate individual visitors.

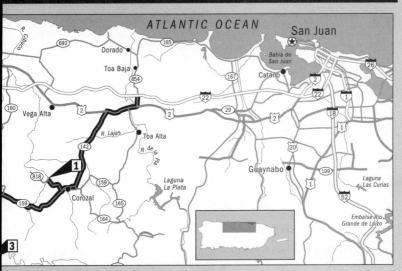

The center may not be very accessible to non-Spanish speakers. (Rte. 818 Km 2.5. ☎859-8079 or 859-0213. Open Th-Su and most holidays 9am-5pm. $5, ages 1-12 $3, 60-74 $2.50, over 75 free.) If you plan to visit during October, don't miss Corozal's **Festival del Plátano,** which features artisans, music, and lots of plantain-based foods in the city plaza. After leaving the complex, turn left and backtrack on Rte. 818 to Rte. 159, then head west toward Morovis.

2 MOROVIS. Upon reaching Morovis, turn left onto Rte. 137, then turn right at Rte. 155 which leads right into town. Despite the fact that Morovis serves as the production center for much of Puerto Rico's *artesanía* (artesanal work), including traditional musical instruments such as *cuatros* and *tiples,* there is almost no tourist infrastructure. The **Alcaldía** public relations office on the plaza provides a list of the names, phone numbers, and specialties of current artisans. Open M-F 9am-4:30pm.

3 CASA BAVARIA. The Dutch may have been turned back at the walls of Old San Juan, but the Germans seem to have left their mark on the island at this charming Bavarian beer garden. The drive up to **Casa Bavaria ❸** is stunning; as you enter Morovis turn left onto Rte. 137, then left again onto Rte. 155, and continue for about 20min. to Km 38.3. Around Km 41 look left to see a waterfall cascading down the mountain across the valley. At the Casa, join bikers and tourists at long wooden tables overlooking the valley, the perfect location to enjoy schnitzel, bratwurst, and Lowenbräu. During the third weekend of October Casa Bavaria springs to life with its own Puerto Rican version of **Oktoberfest.** (Rte. 155 Km 38.3. ☎862-7818. www.casa-bavaria.com. Puerto Rican and German entrees $8-16. German beer after 3pm $2.50. Sa live jazz *criollo* music. Open Th and Su noon-8pm, F-Sa noon-10pm. Bar open until 2am. MC/V.) Take Rte. 155 back to Rte. 137, then turn right onto Rte. 137, then right again onto Rte. 155 (avoiding town) then turn onto Rte. 145, which leads to Ciales.

4 CIALES. From Morovis it's a straight shot to Hwy. 22 and a speedy return to Arecibo. However, if you're looking for a break, try Ciales, which offers beautiful views and a miniscule coffee museum. (At C. Santiago Palmer and C. Hernández Usera, on Rte. 149 one block past the plaza. ☎871-3439. Open by appointment. $2, university students $1.50, secondary students $1, under 12 free.) From Ciales, continue west on Rte. 146 to reach **Lago Dos Bocas** (p. 270). Watch out for the several sharp turns in the road, which aren't particularly well-marked. From Dos Bocas it's a quick 20min. drive down to the town of Arecibo and Hwy. 2.

oceanside highway and pull off on any dirt road. Unfortunately the coast is rocky in places, creating superb vistas, but not the best swimming conditions. The westernmost beach in the Manatí area, Playa Mar Chiquita, at the end of Rte. 648, is also one of the more popular—several cars can usually be found watching the waves crash through a small rock isthmus. From Rte. 686, turn north at Manatí Office Supply and drive over the hill. (No facilities.) Surfers recommend ◙ Complejo Los Tubos, just down the hill on Rte. 686, which has a more developed beach area with a gated parking lot, lifeguards, covered picnic tables, and bathrooms. An offshore reef creates decent surfing conditions for intermediate and advanced surfers, but swimmers should be aware of the rip current. (Open W-F 8am-4pm, Sa-Su 9am-5pm.)

◙ **NIGHTLIFE.** Manatí's nightlife scene is not exactly robust. In addition to the **Wine Gallery** (see **Food**, above) the bar/restaurant/Internet cafe **Vkcafe**, Hwy. 2 Km 56.4, has become popular with the young professional crowd. After work, hordes of twentysomethings head to this trendy yellow bar for appetizers ($4-10), a drink, and good rock music. (☎846-0404. Beer $2-3. Mixed drinks $5. Live 1-man band Th 6pm. Live Spanish rock F 8pm. Live 80s music Sa 10pm. Open M-Tu 11am-4pm, W-Sa 11am-midnight. AmEx/MC/V.)

◙ **DAYTRIP FROM MANATÍ: VEGA BAJA.** Vega Baja is the real beginning of the west. Here, you can leave your cares behind, grab a surfboard, and head to **Balneario Puerto Nuevo**, the most party-friendly beach this side of Arecibo. Bob Marley blasts from car stereos and laid-back Puerto Ricans of all ages park on the sand and watch the waves with a couple of beers. In the background, food kiosks serve refreshments throughout the night. As a public *balneario*, Vega Baja has a small recreation area with covered picnic tables, showers, and bathrooms, but it is set back from the ocean, leaving plenty of room to party after dark. Despite strong rip tides, the sea is a full of **surfers, snorkelers, swimmers,** and **jetskiers** during the day. For great views and even better surfing, continue east to the end of Rte. 691 to reach **Cibuco,** an advanced, shallow break over a reef. (At the intersection of Rte. 686 and 692. ☎855-4744. Lifeguards during the day. Recreation area open M-F 8am-5pm, Sa-Su 8am-6pm.) To get to Vega Baja from Manatí, drive east to the intersection of Rte. 686 and Rte. 692.

ARECIBO

Although the town itself offers little to attract visitors, the impressive sights just outside of Arecibo make it the hidden treasure of Puerto Rico's travel destinations. The star attractions are the Arecibo Observatory, which contains the world's largest single telescope, and, a little further afield, the neighboring Camuy Caves, the world's third-largest cave system. Traveling to these two parks also means a trip through the stunning karst country of the north coast, and the views may inspire you to spend more time exploring nearby lakes and natural reserves. To avoid the traffic and endless chain stores of Hwy. 2, consider taking the **Karst Country Scenic Drive** (p. 264) to reach Arecibo's backcountry treasures.

▐ TRANSPORTATION

Driving to Arecibo is the only way to see the sights without battling irregular *públicos* and spending extensive amounts of time in the city. From San Juan, take Hwy. 22 west, then exit onto Rte. 129 and go north to reach the town and the lighthouse or south to reach the other attractions. From the **Terminal Sur** *públicos* go to: **Manatí** (1hr., $2.50); **San Juan** (2-3hr., $7-10); and **Utuado** (30min.,

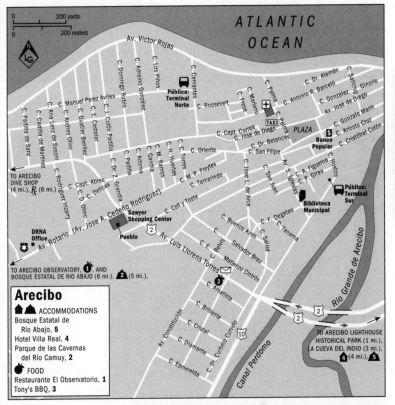

Arecibo

🔺🔺 ACCOMMODATIONS
Bosque Estatal de
  Río Abajo, **5**
Hotel Villa Real, **4**
Parque de las Cavernas
  del Río Camuy, **2**

🍴 FOOD
Restaurante El Observatorio, **1**
Tony's BBQ, **3**

$2.50). However, most vans leave before 8am. The **Terminal Norte** sends *públicos* to: **Camuy** (10-25min., $1.25); **Hatillo** (15-25min., $1.25); and **Quebradillas** (30-45min., $2.50). To reach the observatory or caves, negotiate with a *público* driver to see if he will drop you off and come pick you up later. Even better, head down C. José de Diego to **Arecibo Taxi Cab,** on the plaza, where taxis can take you to the observatory ($15) or the Camuy Caves ($20) and pick you up later. (☎878-2929. Open 4am-9pm daily.) Another option is **Diego Taxi Cab** (☎878-1050).

🔲 🔢 ORIENTATION AND PRACTICAL INFORMATION

Arecibo's city center sits between Hwy. 2 and the Atlantic Ocean. The major sights lie about 30min. south of Arecibo proper just off Rte. 129. Av. Rotario holds most of the government offices and connects Hwy. 2 to Rte. 129. It is entirely possible for a physically fit person explore the city of Arecibo on foot.

Bank: Banco Popular, Av. Gonzalez Marín 67 (☎878-8500), on the plaza. ATM. Open M-F 8am-4pm. Numerous other banks line Hwy. 2.

Camping Permits: The **DRNA** office (☎878-9048) is in Centro Govermental building A, behind the police headquarters on Av. Rotario. Reserve 2 weeks in advance. Open M-F 7:30am-noon and 1-4pm.

Supermarket: Pueblo (☎878-1975), in the shopping center at Hwy. 2 and Av. Rotario. **Western Union.** Open M-Sa 6am-midnight, Su 11am-5pm. AmEx/D/DC/MC/V.

Police: Av. Hostos 300 (☎878-2020). Open 24hr.

Pharmacy: Walgreens, Hwy. 2 Km 81.8 (☎880-0290), across from Plaza del Norte mall, in Hatillo. Open 24hr. AmEx/D/MC/V.

Hospital: Hospital Metropolitano Dr. Susoni (☎650-1830), on the plaza, has a 24hr. emergency room.

Post Office: Hwy. 2 Km 75.8 (☎878-1246). No General Delivery. Open M-F 7:30am-4:30pm, Sa 7:30am-noon. **Postal Code:** 00612.

ACCOMMODATIONS AND CAMPING

Arecibo has very few accommodations. There are some camping options farther south, but if you're looking for an actual hotel, try nearby Hatillo (p. 271) or Utuado (p. 304).

Hotel Villa Real, Hwy. 2 Km 67.2 (☎881-4134 or 881-8277; fax 881-1992), about 4 mi. east of Arecibo. Designed for businessmen on the go, this roadside hotel has all the necessities but few perks. On our visit, the hot water was not working. Rooms with A/C, fridge, phone, and TV. Pool. Coin laundry. $25 key deposit. Check-in 3pm. Check-out noon. 1 queen bed $66; 2 queen beds $77; suites $87-98. Tax included. AmEx/MC/V. ❸

Parque de las Cavernas del Río Camuy (☎898-3100), 20min. south of Arecibo (p. 269). The CPN allows visitors to camp at this tourist attraction. Campers pitch their tents in the picnic area, but the site does have bathrooms, showers, and a 24hr. guard. Reservations required. $5 per person. AmEx/MC/V. ❶

Bosque Estatal de Río Abajo, on Rte. 621. From Hwy. 2 take Hwy. 10 south, then turn right onto Rte. 6612, which soon intersects Rte. 621. A beautiful creekside camping area in the middle of karst country. Includes trash cans, water spigots, bathrooms, rustic showers, fire pits, and picnic tables. 1 marked trail. Office open M-F 7am-noon and 1-3:30pm, Sa-Su 8:30am-12:30pm and 1:30-5:30pm. Must have a permit ($4) and a reservation from the DRNA (p. 267). ❶

FOOD

When asked to recommend a good restaurant, most *arecibeños* generally appear stumped and eventually start mentioning the chain restaurants in Plaza del Norte, on Hwy. 2 in Hatillo. There are establishments near every attraction, but nothing outstanding. The cheapest options are usually roadside *panaderías* (bakeries) offering sandwiches and supplies for making your own meals.

Tony's BBQ, Hwy. 2 Km 75.8 (☎881-2871), across from the post office, is very popular. Although Tony's seems like just another fast food joint in Arecibo, its lunches are exceptionally filling. Combos $5-6. Open daily 9:30am-10pm. Cash only. ❶

Restaurante El Observatorio, Rte. 625 Km 1.1 (☎880-3813), just outside the observatory. Clearly geared toward passing tourists, with a souvenir shop, pictures of the observatory, and signed pictures from SETI on the walls. Standard seafood and *comida criolla.* Medalla $2.50. Entrees $10-17. Open W-Su 11am-5pm. AmEx/MC/V. ❸

SIGHTS

OBSERVATORIO DE ARECIBO. Known as "El Radar" to Puerto Ricans, the Arecibo Observatory is the largest single telescope in the world, and has the unique capability of both sending and receiving signals from a similar sender up to 1500 light years away. The observatory was built in the late 1960s about 6 mi. south of Arecibo because the site fits two specific requirements: it is close to the equator, thereby providing observers with access to most of the sky, and the karstic geography provides a natural sinkhole for the enormous reflector. Since then the observatory has served as a work station for scientists from around the world, including the 1993 Nobel Prize winners Joseph Taylor and Russell Hulse. One of the more well-known projects at Arecibo involves SETI, the **Search for Extra Terrestrial Intelligence,** a project in which the public can take part by downloading a screensaver that processes data and sends it back to astronomers at http://seti.berkeley.edu. The project looks for radio signals sent our way from outer space, either on purpose or accidentally. So far the project has been fruitless, but scientists promise to keep the world updated. The observatory has also served as the site of several less scientific projects, including the filming of four movies (*Contact, Goldeneye 007, Survivor, Dream Team*) and an episode of *The X-Files*. The observatory is run by Cornell University's National Atmosphere and Ionosphere Center.

Visits begins at the two-story **museum,** where all exhibits are explained in English and Spanish. The lower level has several interactive displays designed to introduce astronomy to curious visitors. Upstairs, signs describe the different projects undertaken at the observatory. When it's playing, a 20min. movie explains how the telescope operates. Finally, head out to the viewing platform and see the main attraction, the telescope itself. Not nearly as white or solid as it appears in the movies, the dish, 1000 ft. in diameter, is actually made out of tens of thousands of perforated aluminum quadrangles that collect the grayish grime of their jungle surroundings. Hanging 450 ft. above the reflector, the receiver (looking like an enormous golfball) houses 11 different instruments for collecting data from the dish, and intrepid astronomers and technicians can sometimes be seen walking the long catwalk out to the receiver. The sight is especially impressive when the entire platform rotates. *(From Arecibo take Rte. 129 south, turn left on Rte. 134, continue east on Rte. 635, and finally turn right onto Rte. 625. You can take a público from Terminal del Norte in Arecibo headed to the barrio of Esperanza, but there will be a surcharge. Or take a taxi from Arecibo ($15). ☎878-2612; www.naic.edu. Open W-F noon-4pm, Sa-Su and holidays 9am-4pm. $4, ages 5-12 and 65+ $2, under 5 free. AmEx/D/MC/V.)*

PARQUE DE LAS CAVERNAS DEL RÍO CAMUY. The Camuy Cave Park is one of Puerto Rico's most extraordinary and accessible natural attractions. For millions of years the Río Camuy has been slowly eroding away the soft karstic limestone to create the third-largest cave system in the world. In 1958 scientists discovered this unique phenomenon, and in the 1980s the site opened to the public. Today Puerto Rico's National Parks Company operates 250 acres of the incredible terrain as a tourist attraction where visitors can walk on a paved path through one of the enormous caves amidst slowly dripping water and hundreds of sleeping bats. Most visitors come to Camuy in the morning, then continue to the observatory in the afternoon. Consequently, the park is often quite crowded before noon; arrive in the early afternoon to avoid a long wait for the tour.

The tour starts with a 20min. film that covers a brief history of the park. Afterward, tour groups of up to 50 people board trolleys that lead to the main attraction, **Cueva Clara.** At 170 ft. in height, Clara awes even big-cave veterans. Tour groups follow a winding path through the artistically lit cave past a series of stalactites and stalagmites, as mist rises eerily around them. At the Palma Sinkhole visitors can look down at the river rushing 150 ft. below. Groups then reboard the trolley to head to **Tres Pueblos Sinkhole,** an enormous 400 ft. hole located at the intersection of Lares, Camuy, and Hatillo, where visitors can imagine exploring off-limits caves visible from the vantage point. The last stop, **Spiral Sinkhole,** is the most recent addition to the park. A 205-step wooden staircase leads to a platform looking into a huge ravine. Finally, it's back on the trolley for a stop at the cafeteria, the gift shop, and the picnic area.

Most visitors will be satisfied with a tour through the park, but the truly adventurous may try a guided expedition into the caves. **Tanamá Expediciones,** in nearby Utuado, leads intense hiking/tubing trips into the caves but does not offer rapelling (p. 305). In San Juan, **Aventuras Tierra Adentro** specializes in 1-day rapelling trips (p. 99). *(Rte. 129 Km 18.9. 20min. from Arecibo. ☎898-3100; www.geocities.com/espeleodatos. Open W-Su and holidays 8am-3:30. Parking $3. Tickets $10, ages 4-12 $7, ages 60-74 $5, under 4 and 75+ free. AmEx/MC/V.)*

ARECIBO LIGHTHOUSE HISTORICAL PARK. Arecibo's attractive lighthouse is one of the few in Puerto Rico that has been developed and opened to the public. The historical park around the lighthouse has the feel of a theme park, with models of a Taíno village, Christopher Columbus's three ships, a pirate ship, and a slave hut, complete with recorded African music. The entire assortment is just as tacky as it sounds, but two wooden platforms afford great ocean views that almost compensate for the kitsch. The lighthouse has a small nautical museum with assorted maritime artifacts and no explanations. You can climb up the stairs, but the US Coast Guard still uses the top of the lighthouse. *(Take Hwy. 2 to Rte. 681, then turn left on Rte. 655. ☎880-7250. Parking $2. Open M-F 9am-6pm, Sa-Su 10am-7pm. Adults $9, children and seniors $7. MC/V.)*

LA CUEVA DEL INDIO (INDIAN'S CAVE). This attraction is less a cave and more a wild limestone cavern that the ocean has carved out over the years. Leave your car in the dirt parking area, then climb out over the lunar-like landscape to the rock steps that lead down into the cave. The petroglyphs on the wall were supposedly created by the Taínos over 500 years ago, but the crashing ocean may be more impressive. Wear good shoes and watch your step, as holes in the limestone lead down to the ocean over 20 ft. below. The owners of the parking lot can sometimes be prevailed upon to give an unofficial tour with the history of the cave in return for a tip. *(2 mi. past the lighthouse on Rte. 681, turn left at the red "Aceso a la Cueva" on the left, just past the Esso station. Parking $1. Admission $0.50.)*

🐚 BEACHES AND WATER SPORTS

Arecibo's most popular **beach** for both surfers and swimmers is **Poza del Obispo,** just east of the lighthouse. On the western edge of the beach, a small protected inlet provides a good place to swim. **Surfers** head east, where the surf gets progressively more impressive. Unfortunately the beach offers neither shade nor facilities. (From Hwy. 2 turn north on Rte. 681 and continue past the lighthouse.) If you continue down Rte. 681, several turn-offs mark additional popular surf breaks. To reach the public Balneario Morillo, follow directions to the Arecibo Lighthouse (see **Sights,** above); the beach is on the left, across from the parking lot.

Arecibo Dive Shop, Av. Miramar 868, at Hwy. 2 Km 78, leads excursions to local destinations, such as a sunken barge, underwater mountains, and the Cueva del Indio, as well as more distant destinations, such as Isla Desecheo and Isla Mona. They also offer PADI certification courses. (☎/fax 880-3483. 3- to 4- person min. Dives range anywhere from $45 shore dives to $280 for a Mona trip. Equipment rental $30. You must have your own snorkel gear. Group open-water PADI certification $150. Open M-Sa 9am-7pm. Cash only.)

LAGO DOS BOCAS

After a long day of driving around Arecibo, visitors may welcome the tranquility of Lago Dos Bocas. Surrounded by steep limestone cliffs and lush mountain vegetation, this calm lake in the hills of karst country offers opportunities for several activities. Dos Bocas is a popular fishing lake, but no fishing equipment rental is available. **Locura Arecibeña** rents **kayaks** from the main ferry dock. (☎878-1809. Call ahead. Single $15 per hr., double $25.) Perhaps the most relaxing way to explore is by riding the **free government ferry** that makes a trip around the lake every hour. The ferry brings visitors to several restaurants, or you can just enjoy the 40min. loop. (☎879-1838. Ferries leave M-F 6:30, 8:30, 10, 11am, noon, 3, 5pm; Sa-Su every hour 6:30am-3pm. Office open daily 7am-3pm.)

Located on 132 acres of land, the relatively new **Rancho Marina Restaurant** ❸ and **camping** ❶ stands out as one of the lake's superior food and accommodation combos. Large wooden platforms over the water provide a picturesque setting from which to enjoy delicious *comida criolla*. The friendly owners also allow travelers to camp on the manicured grounds or stay in one of the renovated cabins. The rustic cabins were under renovation as of July 2005, but can accommodate up to six people and have ceiling fans, kitchenettes, and cold water. The ranch also rents kayaks ($10 per hr.) and plans to build one trail. (Ask the ferry to drop you off here. Also accessible by car from Rte. 146 Km 7.6, but you must have 4WD and call for directions. ☎894-8034 or 630-2750; www.ranchomarina.com. Entrees $10-15. Camping $25 per tent. *Cabaña* prices not established at time of publication; call ahead. Open Sa-Su 10am-7pm. MC/V.)

To get to Lago Dos Bocas, drive south on Rte. 10, then turn left at the sign and take Rte. 621 east to Rte. 123 south. You can't miss the dock at Km 67.1.

HATILLO

Hatillo's shopping plazas and eateries may seem a little generic, but the town is redeemed as a travel destination by its mask festival and attractive beaches. Also, its cheap accommodations make for a convenient base from which to explore the sights around Arecibo. Hatillo's annual ◪**Festival de las Máscaras** (Mask Festival), held on December 28, is the island's third-largest mask exhibition. Inspired by a traditional festival in the Canary Islands, this popular celebration includes parades, music, and colorful costumes, as participants dress up to reenact the Biblical tale of King Herod. The rest of the year, Hatillo is a quiet town with two attractive beaches. **Playa Sardinera**, Hwy. 2 Km 84.6, at Centro Vacacional Luis Muñoz Marín, is one of the best north coast beaches for young children. Several large boulders shelter a calm, shallow wading area perfect for the

THE LOCAL STORY

LUNAR LANDSCAPE

The first thing most visitors to Puerto Rico's north coast notice are the bizarre formations in the countryside, which look like something out a modernist painting. A geological formation, known as karst, produces steeply eroded cliff sides, sinkholes, underground rivers, and *mogotes*—dramatic hills that form around holes where underground caverns have collapsed. Karst is a kind of limestone that forms when carbon-dioxide-carrying water (which is mildly acidic) slowly dissolves the stone, carving out eye-catching rock formations.

The word karst comes from a region in the former Yugoslavia that contains such formations, but also describes several regions around the world, including Puerto Rico's north coast, Vieques, Isla Mona, and Cabo Rojo. The area traversed by the Karst Country Scenic Drive (p. 264) is so important as a watershed that the US Congress recently passed a bill authorizing the purchase of land to protect Puerto Rican water supplies and the unique environment.

Many of the attractions in this region exist thanks to the karstic geology. The Arecibo Observatory (p. 268) is nestled in a natural sinkhole and erosion produced the enormous Camuy Cave system (p. 269). Explorers can see karst up close on a tour (p. 305) through the caverns of the Tanamá River.

young 'uns. Older visitors can head past the boulders where big waves pound the beach, though the entire area is a bit rocky. Just west, in the actual town of Hatillo, wild **Playa Marina** makes an ideal destination for sunbathing or long beach walks. As you continue west the sand gets smoother and the big waves make for perfect boogie boarding. (From Hwy. 2 turn north onto Rte. 119 and continue to downtown Hatillo. Turn north again at Rte. 130. No facilities.)

Centro Vacacional Luis Muñoz Marín ❸, Hwy. 2 Km 84.6, marked by a sign for Punta Maracayo Resort, offers a bit more entertainment than typical government-run beach *cabañas*. The complex contains two pools, a waterslide, children's play area, and a wooden walkway. Best of all, the entire complex sits in front of Playa Sardinera (above). The six-person *cabañas* far outshine other vacation centers; the clean buildings have bright yellow walls, A/C, cable TV, full kitchens, and balconies. Don't forget to request an ocean view; it's the same price. The grassy **camping/RV area ❷** offers water spigots, indoor bathrooms, and cold-water showers. (☎820-0274; fax 820-9116. Cafeteria and picnic tables. Office open M-F 8am-4:30pm, Sa-Su 8:30am-5pm. Non-guest entrance $3, with waterslide $5. Check-in 3pm. Check-out 2pm. Camping $50 per tent for a 3-day weekend; $70 for a 4-day holiday weekend; $20 for an additional night. 6-person cabins with A/C $250/290/60; 6-person cabins without A/C $220/255/40. Tax included. MC/V.) There is little to complain about at **Parador El Buen Cafe ❹**, Hwy. 2 Km 84, just west of Arecibo. The roadside *parador* feels institutional, but the big, clean rooms contain cable TV, fridge, A/C, and phone. The friendly staff adds a touch of life to the business-like hotel. (☎898-3484; fax 898-1000; www.elbuencafe.com. Pool. Check-in 3pm. Check-out noon. Doubles $90-105; extra person $15. AmEx/MC/V.)

The waterfront **Baja Beach Restaurant ❸**, Rte. 119 Km 1.9, has the best views in town. Unsurprisingly, Baja Beach serves the usual combo of burgers, sandwiches, Puerto Rican food, and seafood, with a few pasta dishes thrown in for variety. (☎820-8773. Beer $2.50-3. Entrees $5-20. Open W-Th noon-midnight, F-Sa noon-2am, Su noon-midnight. AmEx/MC/V.) For quick eats head to **Cafetería El Buen Cafe ❸**. Locals flock to the large diner for inexpensive Puerto Rican breakfasts and lunches. (☎898-3495. Breakfast $2.75-5. Sandwiches $1.75-5. Entrees $5-26. Open daily 5:30am-10pm. AmEx/MC/V.)

NORTHWEST CORNER

This remote corner of the island remains relatively undiscovered, but fully equipped for an ocean getaway. When the surf is poor in Rincón, surfers in the know head to the Jobos coastal area, where northern winds reliably kick up big waves year-round. Even non-surfers will be impressed by sight of lonely cliffs overgrown with tropical vegetation and fierce Atlantic waves pounding on crescent beaches. The road between Isabela and Jobos winds through miles of uninterrupted natural landscape—a real change from the malls and factories of that typify the north coast. Although the beach is the main attraction here, inland adventures await: horseback riding, the Ramey golf course, and a water park near Aguadilla offer alternative entertainment. Jobos makes a convenient base from which to explore this area, just a short drive from the practical necessities of Isabela, the attractions of Ramey, and the transportation hub of Aguadilla. Outside of Jobos, establishments are sprawled along the highways between Isbela and Aguadilla, making travel by car the only way to go.

▐ TRANSPORTATION

Aguadilla's airport is the only direct link from the US to the west coast of Puerto Rico. **Aeropuerto Rafael Hernández** is located on the former Ramey Air Force Base; go north of town on Rte. 107, then turn right after passing the white spherical radar station on the left. **Continental Airlines** (☎800-525-0280) flies direct to Newark, US (4hr.; daily 9:25am; round-trip $250-350). **JetBlue** has direct service from JFK Airport, New York City, US (4 hr.; twice daily; round-trip $250). Numerous **car rental** agencies operate out of the airport; the most affordable are generally **Budget** (☎890-1110; $30-43 per day, insurance $15; ages 21-22 surcharge $10 per day, ages 23-24 surcharge $6; open daily 4am-6pm; AmEx/D/MC/V) and **L&M** (☎890-3010; $33-46 per day, insurance $13-20; 23-24 surcharge $5 per day; open daily 8am-5pm; AmEx/D/DC/MC/V).

The **público** hubs in the area are Aguadilla and Isabela. The terminal in Aguadilla offers service to: **Isabela** (25-30min., $1.75); **Mayagüez** (30-45min., $3); **Moca** (15min., $1.25); **Ramey Base** (30min., $1.30). **Choferes Unidos** (☎891-5653 or 630-5725) travels from Aguadilla to San Juan (2-3hr.; 7 per day between 4am and noon; $10, with reservation $15). Public transportation from Isabela offers more limited destinations. *Públicos* to **Aguadilla** leave from Av. Augustín Ramos Calero at the intersection of Rte. 113 and Rte. 112 and those to the **Jobos area** leave from the small concrete pavilion two blocks east of the plaza, across from Econo supermarket (15min., $0.60).

✦🛈 ORIENTATION AND PRACTICAL INFORMATION

Almost all of area's tourist activity takes place along the coast. Although distinct beaches have their own names, most locals refer to the entire north coastal stretch as **Jobos.** The majority of hotels and restaurants are located at the intersection of Rte. 466 and Rte. 4466, near Playa Jobos proper. Once you get to Playa Jobos it's easy to walk between beaches, restaurants, and most accommodations. The practical services most convenient to this area are located in Isabela, 5mi. west of Jobos. Bosque Estatal de Guajataca, also part of Isabela's jurisdiction, lies another 7 mi. inland, south of Hwy. 2, on Rte. 446. Coming from the east on Hwy. 2, turn north at Rte. 112 to reach the Isbela area. If you want to go straight to Jobos continue through town onto Rte. 466, which leads to the beach. To head toward Aguadilla, take Rte. 466 west until it turns into Rte. 4466. Then take Rte. 110 south and continue to Rte. 107, which connects to **Route 111,** Aguadilla's main road. Aguadilla's city center is located on a narrow strip of land between Hwy. 2 and the ocean. All area accommodations and sights lie north of the center.

Tourist Office: Puerto Rican Tourism Company, in the Ramey airport, provides *¡Que Pasa!* and information about the area. (☎890-3315. Open M-Sa 8am-4:30pm.)

Bank: Banco Santander, C. Barbosa 19 (☎872-2050), on the plaza in Isabela, has an ATM. Open M-F 8:30 am-4pm.

Equipment Rental: 🏄**Playa Brava Longboards and Coffee House,** Rte. 110 Km 9.8 between Isabela and Aguadilla, serves coffee and Puerto Rican-style soup and sandwiches ($2.50-4) in addition to renting ($20) and selling boards. The welcoming owner provides advice on local conditions and breaks, and 1½hr. lessons for $40. Internet $3 for 30min. Open daily 9am-7pm. **Hang Loose Surf Shop,** Rte. 4466 Km 1.1 (☎872-2490) near Isabela, rents surf and boogie boards ($25 per day), sells gear, and offers lessons ($45 per hr. including board). Upstairs, local surf legend Werner Vega makes and repairs longboards. Open Tu-Sa 10am-5pm. AmEx/MC/V. **Pelicano Surfboards and Surf Shop,** Rte. 4466 Km 1.2 (☎872-7311) near Isabela, carries a similar selection and rents boards for $20-25 a day. Open M-Sa 10:30-5:30. MC/V.

Supermarkets: Econo, C. Barbosa 4 (☎872-4033), in Isabela, a few blocks west of the plaza. Open M-Sa 6:30am-9:30pm, Su 11am-5pm. AmEx/MC/V. **SuperCoop,** Rte. 107 Km 3 (☎882-1425). Open M-Sa 7am-9pm, Su 11am-5pm. MC/V.

Laundromat: Laundromat El Familiar, Av. Juan Hernández Ortiz, just before the police station, in the new Plaza del Mercado in Isabela. Wash $1; dry $1. No change available. Open daily 7am-6pm.

Police: Av. Hernández Ortiz 3201 (☎872-2020 or 872-3001) in Isabela. From the plaza, go south on Rte. 112, take the first left, and continue for about ¼ mi. Open 24hr.

Pharmacy: Super Farmacia Rebecca, C. Barbosa 51 in Isabela (☎872-2410); facing the Catholic church on the plaza, head down the right-hand street. Open M-Sa 8am-9pm, Su 9am-9pm. AmEx/D/DC/MC/V.

Hospital: Centro Isabelino de Medicina Avanzada (☎830-2705 or 830-2747), 1½ mi. south of Isabela on Rte. 112. Clinic open M-F 7am-3pm. Emergency room open 24hr.

Internet Access: Post 2 Go, Rte. 107 Km 2.8 (☎997-4190), north of Aguadilla, has Internet service. $4.50 for 30min. or $8 per hr. Open M-Sa 8am-6pm. MC/V.

Post Office: C. Jesus Piñero 5 (☎872-2284), in Isabela, behind the *público* station. No General Delivery. Open M-F 8am-4:30pm, Sa 8am-noon. **Postal Code:** 00662 near Isabela and 00603 near Aguadilla.

ACCOMMODATIONS

The most unique and budget-friendly accommodations are situated in the Jobos area. Nearer to Aguadilla, more upscale options await.

NEAR JOBOS

▨ **Ocean Front Hotel,** Rte. 4466 Km 0.1 (☎872-0444; www.oceanfrontpr.com). Someone should tell the owners of the Ocean Front Hotel that bright ocean view rooms with TV, coffee maker, A/C, and private balconies are supposed to be expensive. A great deal during the week. Restaurant. Check-out noon. Doubles M-Th and Su $60-70, F-Sa $90-100; extra person $25. AmEx/MC/V. ❷

▨ **La Torre Guest House,** Rte. 466 Km 7.2 (☎872-7439), ¼ mi. from the beach near the intersection of Rtes. 4466 and 466. This friendly guesthouse/pizzeria is located on the 1st fl. of the owner's home. Popular surfer hangout. Standard rooms are clean and include TV and A/C. Doubles $55, with kitchen (no dishes) $65; quads $80-90. Prices rise on weekends. Tax included. Cash only. ❷

Pelican Reef Apartments (☎872-6518 or 895-0876), at the intersection of Rte. 466 and Rte. 4466, is actually a small apartment complex with a few nightly rentals. The concrete hotel-style building was not built with aesthetics in mind, but it does overlook the ocean. Clean, comfortable rooms include TV, A/C, stove, and fridge. Doubles $125; extra person $20. Tax included. Cash only. ❹

Costa Dorada Beach Resort, (☎872-7255, US toll-free 800-981-5693; fax 872-7595; www.costadoradabeach.com), on Rte. 466 between Jobos and Isabela. Standard beach resort. 3-story buildings surround a dry grassy courtyard filled with palm trees, a bar, and a big pool. Rooms include telephone, TV, fridge, and courtyard balcony. Beach access. Doubles $122; villas with kitchen $195; extra person $20. AmEx/D/MC/V. ❸

RAMEY AREA

Ramey Guest House, Loop 102 #16-17 (☎890-4208 or 431-2939; www.rameyguesthouse.com). From Rte. 107, the owner's well-marked house is past the golf course, across the street from a shopping center. 4 full houses provide all the conveniences of home, from a laundromat to a coffee maker. The original Air Force decor remains. A/C and TV. 2-bedroom house $75; 3-bedroom $95; 4-bedroom $115. AmEx/MC/V. ❸

NEAR AGUADILLA

Hotel Villa Forín, Rte. 107 Km 2.1 (☎882-8341 or toll-free 877-723-6746), maintains the aura of a professional hotel, but with reasonable prices. All rooms have A/C and cable television; some have cooking facilities. Small pool. Check-in 2pm. Check-out noon. Doubles $64; quads $70. Tax included. AmEx/MC/V. ❸

Hotel Cielo Mar, Av. Montemar 84 (☎882-5959 or 882-5960; fax 882-5577; www.cielomar.com), sits high up on a hill overlooking the ocean. Turn uphill at Rte. 111 Km 1.3, then follow signs. Almost every room boasts views of the water and the spectacular sunset from a private balcony. Rooms with plenty of space, carpeted floors, A/C, TV, VCR, and phone. Pool. All-inclusive packages available. Doubles $80; quads $85-95; extra person $15; up to 2 children free. Also home to **Restaurant Terramar,** with a patio overlooking the ocean. Entrees $11-25. Open M-Th and Su 7am-10pm, F-Sa 7am-midnight. AmEx/MC/V. ❸

▐ FOOD

Inexpensive *cafeterías* and fast food abound on the highways in the city centers of this corner of Puerto Rico. Some of the more unique eateries, which can be found in the Jobos area, are listed here.

Ocean Front Restaurant, Rte. 4466 Km 0.1 (☎872-3339), in the hotel of the same name, is Jobos' premier seafood restaurant. Over 13 years this restaurant has perfected its recipe for the best salmon on this side of the island. Decorated with tiny lights and lush plants, the interior dining room is one of the classier areas of town. Relaxed outdoor patio. Entrees $12-20. Wine $4. Live guitar music nightly. Open W-Th and Su 11:30am-10pm, F-Sa 11:30am-midnight. AmEx/MC/V. ❸

Happy Belly's (☎872-6566), on Rte. 466, just east of Rte. 4466, is your stereotypical oceanfront tourist bar. The wooden patio overlooking the water is a perfect place to enjoy shrimp *mofongo* ($15) with a lively crowd. Sandwiches $6-7. Entrees $10-19. Open M-Tu 11am-10:30pm, W-Su 11am-2am. AmEx/MC/V. ❸

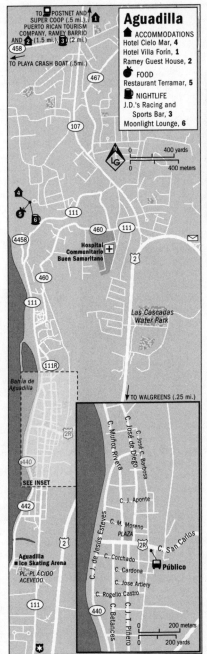

Aguadilla

🏠 ACCOMMODATIONS
Hotel Cielo Mar, **4**
Hotel Villa Forín, **1**
Ramey Guest House, **2**

🍎 FOOD
Restaurant Terramar, **5**

🍷 NIGHTLIFE
J.D.'s Racing and Sports Bar, **3**
Moonlight Lounge, **6**

NORTHWEST

GIVING BACK

A DAY AT THE BEACH

Puerto Rico may be known as the "Isla Encantadora" (the enchanting isle), but it has a less-than-enchanting problem with litter. Public beaches are often marred by heaps of garbage, sometimes just feet from garbage cans provided by costal authorities. Playa Jobos and Playa Mar Chiquita stand out as particularly trash-covered. Snorkelers here may see a glint of light from the bottom of a colorful reef only to be disappointed when they find a crushed beer can. Sunbathers must choose their sand carefully to avoid the waste of their fellow beach-goers.

After a holiday weekend, dozens of DRNA clean-up crews hit the beaches to pick up the trash. If you're looking for a way to help keep Puerto Rico beautiful for future travelers, volunteering with the DRNA clean-up effort may be the perfect way to pitch in and log some hours at the beach. The crews are generally made up of a DRNA employee leading a volunteer student group, making it easy for solo travelers to join in with little advance notice.

Call one of the region DRNA offices in Aguadilla (☎882-5893), Arecibo (☎878-9048), Mayagüez (☎833-3700) or Ponce (☎723-1373) to join other volunteers in the effort to combat litter. This is a great opportunity to get to know Puerto Rico's beaches and the people who maintain them for the enjoyment of travelers and locals alike.

Sonia Rican Restaurant (☎872-0808), on Rte. 466, at the Playa Jobos parking lot, benefits greatly from its beachfront location. Essentially just a very long bar, Sonia Rican serves up affordable seafood and well-prepared Puerto Rican cuisine. Sit inside for great views of the surf. After dark a quiet crowd comes to enjoy drinks at the bar. Beer $1.50-2. Entrees $6-26. Open W-Su 11am-2am, M-Tu 11am-9pm. AmEx/MC/V. ❸

Restaurante Sonido del Mar, Rte. 466 Km 5.6 (☎872-5766), along Playa Jobos. Serves typical seafood entrees ($7-16) and beers ($3) but is distinguished from its neighbors by its pool tables and energetic patrons, some of whom have created beer-can sun visors. Open Tu-Th and Su 11am-10pm, F-Sa 11am-2am. ❸

Cano's Trattoria Italiana, Hwy. 2 Km 111 (☎830-9154), about 5 mi. east of Jobos. Cano serves up large portions in gracefully decorated Italian surroundings. The menu includes pizza, foccaccia, pasta, calzones, meat, and more. Blue checked table cloths liven up the friendly interior. Outdoor seating available. Wine list. Entrees $7-23. Open M-W 11am-10pm, Th and Su 11am-11pm, F-Sa 11am-midnight. AmEx/MC/V. ❸

🏖 BEACHES AND SURFING

PLAYA JOBOS BAY. Second only to Rincón, this is the island's surfing mecca and the site of the 1989 World Surfing Championships. Waves almost always pound the coast, especially when there is a north shore wind. Even Rincón's surfing crowd comes here in the summer when the waves are weak elsewhere. On the eastern edge of the beach, in front of the sand parking area, a protected bay provides a calm, shallow area for swimmers. Because of its popularity with surfers and sunbathers, the eastern edge of Playa Jobos can get crowded and filled with trash at times. *(At the intersection of Rte. 4466 and Rte. 466.)*

EAST OF JOBOS. The road to the east of the popular Jobos Bay is a largely undeveloped green jewel of a coastline. Surfers use these beaches to avoid crowded Jobos when the waves are up. First is the sandy, close-breaking surf break known as **Golondrinas,** which attracts intermediate surfers. Past that is **Middles,** a more advanced break requiring an entry over rocks, which is one of the shallower breaks in the area. Last is the grimly named **Sal Si Puedes** (Get Out If You Can), which provides a rare leviathan break across rocky reefs.

PLAYA SHACKS. This bay looks similar to Jobos, but has a few more rocks and no parking area, and thus remains significantly less crowded. Shacks is known as the best **snorkeling and diving area** near Isabela. The consistent waves make Shacks one of the best wind and kite surfing beaches on the island. Even without all the diversions, Shacks provides a nice place to lie on the beach. *(Follow directions to Tropical Trail Rides, Rte. 4466 Km 1.8. Park just past the bridge and continue to the end of the road on foot. No facilities.)*

LAS RUÍNAS. Named for the ruins of several Air Force buildings, Las Ruínas provides a relatively quiet and scenic beach. The first turn-off leads to a parking lot alongside this white sand beach at the edge of a dramatic cliff. Continue along the bumpy dirt road to find big waves popular with surfers, and beautiful vistas popular with young couples. *(Drive north on Rte. 107 into Base Ramey, turn left on the unmarked road that goes through the golf course, and continue to the end. No facilities.)*

PLAYA CRASH BOAT. This Aguadillan beach is known for its good swimming; old concrete piers provide a place to jump off of into the water. Unfortunately, local crowds can get quite large, especially on weekends during the summer. The beach has bathrooms, but only the most desperate would consider using them. Shaded picnic tables make a great lunch spot. *(From Hwy. 2 turn west onto Rte. 107, then follow Rte. 458 to the left-hand turn-off for the beach.)*

PLAYA MONTONES. This small, calm beach occasionally produces big surfing waves in the winter, but is usually relatively deserted. There are no facilities, but there is a long bay and lots of sand. The water is deep, but gets shallower as you head east. *(Drive east on Rte. 466 to Km 10.2, then turn left toward Villas del Mar Hau and continue to the end of the road.)*

📷 WATER SPORTS AND OUTDOOR ACTIVITIES

Playa Shacks is the area's best **snorkeling** beach and one of the few places on the island where **shore diving** is feasible and worthwhile. ◪**La Cueva Submarina,** Rte. 466 Km 6.3, in the Jobos area, leads two shore dives every day (9:30am and 1:30pm; 1-tank dive $45 including equipment; extra tank $20). They also offer Nitrox dives ($65), guided snorkeling trips ($25), Discover Scuba packages ($55), and 4-day open-water certification courses ($250, including equipment) Cave dives are arranged upon request for advanced divers only. (☎/fax 872-1390; lacuevasubmarina.com. Open daily 8am-5pm. AmEx/MC/V.) **Aquatica Adventures,** Rte. 110 Km 10, is a full-service dive shop that offers shore dives in Isabel and Aguadilla ($50; private certification courses for $325, less for groups), bike tours (around $50 for 2-3hr.), surf lessons, and guided snorkeling tours. (☎890-6071; aquatica@caribe.net. Open M-Sa 9am-5:30pm, Su 9am-3pm. AmEx/MC/V.)

This area also features several unusual (and affordable) options for adventures on land. The popular **Las Cascadas Water Park,** Hwy. 2 Km 126.5 is built into a hillside near Aguadilla and contains several waterslides and a large wave pool. (☎819-1030. Open late Mar. to May Sa-Su 10am-5pm; June-Sept. daily 10am-5pm. $16, ages 4-12 $14, ages 55-74 $8, under 3 and over 75 free. MC/V.) Eighteen-hole **Punta Borinquen Golf Club,** between the airport and the sea, boasts palm trees, distant ocean views, and reasonable prices. (Enter the former Ramey Base on Rte. 107 and turn left at the golf club entrance. ☎890-2987. Green fees M-F $18, Sa-Su $20; golf cart $30, required on weekends. Club rental $10. Open M-F 7am-dusk, Sa-Su 6:30am-dusk. AmEx/MC/V.) **Tropical Trail Rides,** Rte. 4466 Km 1.8, can be reached by taking the driveway for the Villa Montañas between Rte. 110 and Playa Jobos. This American-run operation leads 2hr. rides along beautiful Jobos coastline, through the almond forests, and then back along the cliff caves. (☎872-9256;

www.tropicaltrailrides.com. Rides leave daily at 9am and 4pm. $40 per person. Reservations required. Open daily 7:30am-6:30pm. AmEx/D/MC/V.)

📧 NIGHTLIFE

Most locals head to the beach for their evening fun, but a variety of exciting options await visitors who are interested a livelier night out.

Happy Belly's Sports Bar & Grill (☎872-6566), on Rte. 466, just east of Rte. 4466 near Jobos. As the night goes on this popular restaurant morphs into a relaxed beach bar with a primarily tourist crowd. Balcony over the beach. Beer $3. Mixed drinks $5-6. Live DJ W and F-Sa. Karaoke Th. No cover. Open daily 11am-midnight. AmEx/MC/V.

Mi Casita Tropical (☎872-5510), next door to Happy Belly's. On busy nights young travelers chill on the oceanfront balcony. On slow nights, a local crowd congregates around the bar. Beer $2.50. Mixed drinks $2.50-5. Karaoke W. No cover. Open W-Su noon-3am. AmEx/MC/V.

Aguadilla Ice Skating Arena, Rte. 442 Km 4.2 (☎819-5555), south of Aguadilla. Popular with locals. Indoor rink offers dance music and a light show in the evenings. Couples night W has 2-for-1-tickets. Student night Th, half-price with ID. Open daily 9:30am-11pm. Before 5:30 $10 per hr., 5:30-11pm $13 per hr., including skates.

J.D.'s Racing and Sports Bar, Rte. 110 Km 10.8, east of Aguadilla. A popular *reggaetón* nightclub with checkered flags, a huge dance floor, and a bar with wheels at either end. Young locals looking for weekend action fill the parking lot with their own hot rides. Beer $2-3. Mixed drinks $4-5. Live DJ F-Sa. Cover $5 when there is live music, $3 otherwise. Open Th-Sa 8pm-2am. AmEx/MC/V.

Moonlight Lounge, at Hotel Cielo Mar in Aguadilla (see **Accommodations,** p. 274). This elegant establishment remains true to its Latin roots with salsa, merengue, and Spanish ballads at 5pm. Ocean view. 80s night Sa 5-9pm, then live tropical music at 9pm. Beer $3. 21+. Open M-Th and Su 7am-10pm, F-Sa 7am-1am. AmEx/MC/V.

🎢 DAYTRIPS FROM THE JOBOS AREA

BOSQUE ESTATAL DE GUAJATACA

*No **public transportation** goes to the Bosque de Guajataca. **Driving:** To reach Guajataca from Hwy. 2 drive east to Rte. 446, then follow Rte. 446 south all the way into the forest.)*

As if having some of the island's most beautiful shoreline weren't enough, the municipality of Isabela also contains the 2300 acres of Bosque Estatal de Guajataca, one of the island's prime examples of karst country. Despite its diminutive size, this subtropical forest is one of the more clearly organized on the island, with a cave, several picnic areas, and an abundance of 📍**well-marked trails.** Unlike almost all other trails in Puerto Rico, these narrow dirt paths were originally constructed as trails (not access roads) and they have not yet been paved over, providing one of the best hiking experiences on the island. First stop by the **visitors center,** 5 mi. down Rte. 446 in the middle of the forest, where rangers distribute maps and info about which trails are open. (☎872-1045. Open daily 8am-5pm.) The most popular, with good reason, is the 1½ mi. **interpretive trail,** which starts at the visitors center and loops past 14 marked points of interest, including an observation tower. **Trail #1** (2.55km) starts on the interpretive trail, then breaks off to lead to **Cueva del Viento,** where wooden stairs lead down into a dark cave filled with stalactites and stalagmites. Bring a flashlight to explore the 180 ft. cave, and make sure the rangers know you're inside. The DRNA maintains several small **picnic areas** along Rte. 446 near the visitors center. The first has a bathroom, but continue south for more serene and spacious eating areas. The Guajataca **camping area** was under construction at the time of publication; contact the office to see if it has opened.

LAGO DE GUAJATACA

*No **public transportation** goes to Lago de Guajataca. **Driving**: From Hwy. 2 drive east to Rte. 446, then follow Rte. 446 south to Rte. 457. Take Rte. 457 to Rte. 119.*

The 3.6 sq. mi. Lago de Guajataca has some of Puerto Rico's best fishing. Located in the heart of karst country, but less than 30min. from Hwy. 2, Guajataca is also a pleasant place to experience Puerto Rico's serene countryside. The best destination for daytrippers is the **DRNA visitors center**, Rte. 119 Km 22. This office lends out bamboo fishing poles (bring your own bait; they recommend corn kernels) and provides a dock, full bathrooms with shower, and a grassy picnic area. During holidays the area gets crowded, but on weekdays it is the perfect place to relax with a fishing pole and a cool drink. Swimming is prohibited; kayaking is allowed, but nobody near the lake rents kayaks. (☎896-7640. Open Tu-Su 6am-6pm.)

If the serenity of the lake seduces you, check out **Nino's Camping ❶**, Rte. 119 Km 22.1, with a lakeside camping area, three small cabins, and a clean pool. The pleasant tent area includes water spigots, a bathroom, a cold-water shower, and an electric lightbulb. The cabins look like *centro vacacional cabañas*, with linoleum floors and rooms stuffed with lots of beds. All cabins have a balcony with a hammock, a full kitchen, a TV, and fans, but only one has A/C. Bring your own sheets and utensils. No guard, but the owner's family lives on the premises. (☎896-9016 or 349-5074. $25 per tent per night. 4- to 7-person cabin M-Th and Su $75, F-Sa $175-200, holiday weekends F-Su $225-$250; 12-person cabin $75/300. Cash only.)

MOCA

*Public Transportation: Públicos make the short trip from Aguadilla to Moca (15min., $1.25). **Driving**: From Aguadilla, continue south on Rte. 111 past Hwy. 2, and follow the road as it turns east. Turn right just before the pedestrian bridge to reach the town center.*

The small town of Moca is the island's center for the production of *mundillo*, an intricate type of lace originally imported from Spain and now famous in Puerto Rico. Many *mocanos*, especially women, spend hours hand-weaving the fine lace that adorns shirts, towels, and, most frequently, beautiful baby clothes. *Mundillo* is considered to be one of Puerto Rico's premier handicrafts (see **Arts**, p. 68). Just walking through town demonstrates the importance of the art, as several houses advertise *mundillo* where women weave and sell from the comfort of their own living rooms. To read the history of the town's relationship with *mundillo* and to see framed copies of newspaper articles about local *mocanos*, visit the **Museo de Mundillo**, C. Barbosa 237. Facing the church on the plaza, take the first right-hand street and the museum appears on the left. At the museum, local artisans spend several days a week teaching their art to the next generation and are always willing to talk to visitors about their work. (☎877-3815. Open W-Su 9am-5pm.) Local Augusto Hernández has written a several-hundred-page book called *Historia y Desarrollo del Mundillo Mocano* (History and Development of Moca Mundillo; $17) that is sometimes available at the museum. For the inside scoop on the *mundillo* scene, stop for a chat with **Ada Hernández**, who seems to know every *mundillo* artisan in town. She is more than happy to give visitors a grand tour, or take them to individual artisans' houses to buy the lace. Facing the Alcaldía, turn left and walk down the side street known as C. Miranda. Ada lives at number 126. (☎877-3800. For English, call her brother Benito at 487-7924.) **Artesanía Leonides**, C. Blanco E. Chico 185, the only real *mundillo* store in town, sells a variety of products, but focuses primarily on elaborate baby dresses. (☎877-4092. Open M-Sa 10am-6pm, Su 10am-5:30pm. MC/V.) The best time to visit Moca is during the annual three-day **Festival de Mundillo,** when the town's artisans gather on the main plaza to display and sell their wares. The festival was recently moved from June to November, but it is unclear whether it will be held then in future years; for more information, call the museum.

RINCÓN

Most surfers already know about Rincón; the city lept into the spotlight as the host of the 1968 World Surfing Championships. Waves here can get as high as 25 ft., and at least 15 breaks lie within close proximity to town, making this the best surfing area in Puerto Rico and the Caribbean. But Rincón is a lot more than a big wave. This beautiful area remains largely undeveloped, with a series of tiny roads winding through tropical forest down to pristine beaches. Travelers who want a real taste of Puerto Rican culture may disappointed, as English language and American culture predominate, but the robust US expat community welcomes visitors with open arms. Life in Rincón is essentially one relaxed party, and even non-surfers find it easy to join right in. First-rate diving, snorkeling, and whale-watching conditions ensure that there is no lack of activities, even in the summer when the waves are flat.

▐ TRANSPORTATION

Take Hwy. 2 to Rte. 115, which eventually leads through the town of Rincón. To reach Puntas, and most of the beaches and guesthouses, turn off on Rte. 413, a small road that follows the arc of the coastline. Very few **públicos** come to Rincón from other cities, but you can occasionally find transport from the terminal to **Aguadilla** (20min., $2) and **Mayagüez** (20min., $1.75). More frequent *públicos* follow Rte. 413 to **Puntas** (15min., $0.50). Most long-distance *públicos* leave by 7am. A **free trolley** travels between the post office north of town on Rte. 115 and the factories south of town, but travels on an irregular schedule (daily between 10am and 3pm. Wait at by of the trolley signs.) There are no taxis in Rincón, but the town center is walkable. **Angelo's Car Rental,** Rte. 115 Km 12.3, rents cars and will pick up customers from the Aguadilla and Mayagüez airports, or any guesthouse. (☎823-3438. 25+. Cash rentals $40 for the first day, $35 each additional day; $500 deposit. Credit card rentals $43/38. Open M-Sa 8am-noon and 1pm-5pm. MC/V.)

▐ ORIENTATION AND PRACTICAL INFORMATION

Even veteran travelers may initially find themselves a bit lost in Rincón. With only about 10 streets, the town itself is reasonably straightforward, but most of the action takes place in the surrounding hills. From the town center continue north on Rte. 115 to the intersection with **Route 413,** which follows the coastline. After about ½ mi. you'll reach a turn-off to the Black Eagle Marina, marked by a huge sign for Taíno Divers. Another ½ mi. down the road, a sign points left to **"the lighthouse road."** North of the lighthouse you are officially in **Puntas.** Five steep roads lead downhill to the beach, but only three intersect with Rte. 413. The westernmost road, at Km 3.3, passes the dead-end Nuclear Vista Rd. and leads to the flat road lining the beaches, known as **"Beach Rd."** The next road to the east has a sign labeling it as Vista Linda Rd. The next road connecting Rte. 413 to Beach Rd. doesn't appear to have a name, but runs past the Rincón Surf and Board to Casa Isleña. The easternmost road has a sign labeling it Alfonso Arzmendi. The **Estella** neighborhood, about 14 numbered streets south of town near the intersection with Rte. 429, contains several condos on Playa Corcéga.

Tourist Office: Rincón Municipal Tourist Office (☎823-5024), at the end of C. Nueva, behind the police station, has limited literature. The English-speaking staff can

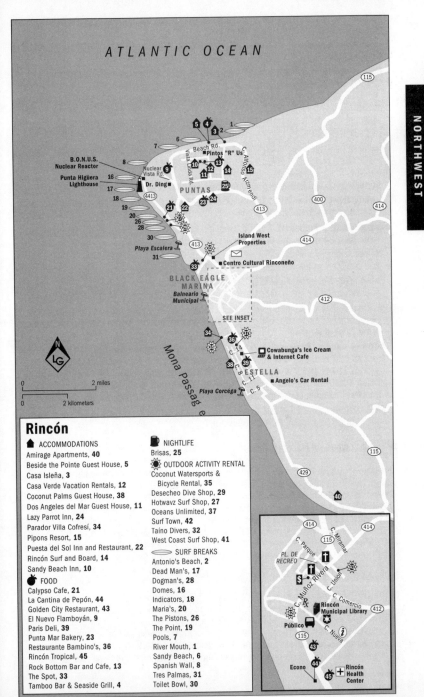

ATLANTIC OCEAN

Rincón

ACCOMMODATIONS
Amirage Apartments, **40**
Beside the Pointe Guest House, **5**
Casa Isleña, **3**
Casa Verde Vacation Rentals, **12**
Coconut Palms Guest House, **38**
Dos Angeles del Mar Guest House, **11**
Lazy Parrot Inn, **24**
Parador Villa Cofresí, **34**
Pipons Resort, **15**
Puesta del Sol Inn and Restaurant, **22**
Rincón Surf and Board, **14**
Sandy Beach Inn, **10**

FOOD
Calypso Cafe, **21**
La Cantina de Pepón, **44**
Golden City Restaurant, **43**
El Nuevo Flamboyán, **9**
Paris Deli, **39**
Punta Mar Bakery, **23**
Restaurante Bambino's, **36**
Rincón Tropical, **45**
Rock Bottom Bar and Cafe, **13**
The Spot, **33**
Tamboo Bar & Seaside Grill, **4**

NIGHTLIFE
Brisas, **25**

OUTDOOR ACTIVITY RENTAL
Coconut Watersports &
  Bicycle Rental, **35**
Desecheo Dive Shop, **29**
Hotwavz Surf Shop, **27**
Oceans Unlimited, **37**
Surf Town, **42**
Taíno Divers, **32**
West Coast Surf Shop, **41**

SURF BREAKS
Antonio's Beach, **2**
Dead Man's, **17**
Dogman's, **28**
Domes, **16**
Indicators, **18**
Maria's, **20**
The Pistons, **26**
The Point, **19**
Pools, **7**
River Mouth, **1**
Sandy Beach, **6**
Spanish Wall, **8**
Tres Palmas, **31**
Toilet Bowl, **30**

answer some questions, but does not currently hand out maps or other information. Open M-F 8am-4:30pm.

Bank: Western Bank, C. Munoz Rivera 18. ATM. ☎823-1280. M-F 7:30am-5pm, Sa 8:30-11:30am.

Equipment Rental: Coconut Watersports & Bicycle Rental (☎309-9328 or 823-2450), at Parador Villa Cofresí (p. 284), rents kayaks (singles $10 per hr., doubles $15), 3-person pedal boats ($20 per hr.), inflatable tubes ($5 per day), boogie boards ($5 per day), beach umbrellas ($5 per day), snorkel gear ($10 per day), and bikes ($5 per hr.). They also offer banana boat rides (20min., $10). Open Sa-Su during daylight hours, M-F by phone only.

Publications: The Rincón Cultural Center (see **Sights,** p. 285) publishes the bi-monthly newsletter, *Juntos,* available at the cultural center. This seemingly random collection of articles, poems, and photos perfectly exemplifies Rincón's quirky charm.

English-Language Bookstore: See **Internet Access,** below.

Supermarket: Econo, Rte. 115 Km 13.2 (☎823-2470), south of town. Open M-Sa 7am-9pm, Su 11am-5pm. AmEx/MC/V.

Laundromat: A **laundromat** in the shopping center across the street from Bambino's is open daily 8am-7pm. Wash $1; dry $0.25 for 5min.

Police: At the end of C. Nueva (☎823-2020 or 823-2021), in town. Open 24hr. A second station is at the intersection of Rte. 115 and 414.

Late-Night Pharmacy: Farmacia del Pueblo, C. Muñoz Rivera 33 (☎823-2540), has a relatively large selection. Open M-Sa 8am-9pm, Su 8am-6pm. AmEx/D/MC/V.

Medical Services: Rincón Health Center, Rte. 115 Km 13.6, across from the Econo (☎823-0909), is open 24 hr., not to be confused with the daytime-only clinic by the same name downtown.

Internet Access: ■**Cowabunga's Ice Cream and Internet Cafe,** Rte. 115 Km 11.6 (☎823-5225). Offers Internet service ($1 per 15min.). Sells used English books ($4) and ice cream ($2). Rents surf boards, beach toys, and snorkeling gear. Open daily 11am-10:30pm. **Rincón Public Library** (☎823-9075), on C. Nueva, has computers with **free,** medium-speed Internet access. Open M-F 8am-5:30pm and 6:30-9pm.

Post Office: Rte. 115 #100 (☎823-2625), has General Delivery. Open M-F 8am-4:30pm, Sa 8am-noon. **Postal code:** 00677.

▌ ACCOMMODATIONS

Outside of San Juan, Rincón has the best selection of accommodations on the island. Several American-run guesthouses cater to both surfers and plain ol' vacationers. If you want to jump into the surfer scene, hang out with Americans all day, and drink lots of beer, head to Puntas. For more Puerto Rican accommodations, try the area south of town, where a few nice hotels hide in quiet residential neighborhoods. **Island West Properties ❹,** Rte. 413 Km 0.7, rents condos, beach houses, and villas throughout Rincón for $150-550. (☎823-2323; fax 823-3254; www.islandwest.com. 3 night min. 50% deposit required. Open M-F 9am-3pm. MC/V.)

PUNTAS

■ **Rincón Surf and Board** (☎823-0610; fax 823-6440; www.surfandboard.com). Take Rte. 413 out of downtown towards Puntas and take the second intersection, marked by a small sign for the Surf and Board. Bear right at the next intersection and the guest house will appear on the right. With inexpensive dorm rooms and an on-site surf school (p. 286), it's no wonder that this has become the prime surfer hangout. This guesthouse sits on stilts 70 ft. above a jungle canopy, creating a unique tropical atmosphere.

The facade is under renovation, but attractive private rooms have handmade mosaics, a private library, and cable TV. Dorms have a common room with cable TV. The only downsides are the voracious mosquitoes and the neighborhood's frequent power outages. Quiet time starts at 10pm. Small pool. 20min. walk from the beach. Private rooms include continental breakfast in the winter. 4-bed coed dorms $20 per person; doubles $60; 2-person suites with kitchen $90; extra person $10. 3-bedroom house $185. $5-10 discount Apr. to mid-Nov. MC/V. ❶

Dos Angeles del Mar Guest House (☎431-6057; www.dosangelesdelmar.com), up the street from Casa Verde. This 3-story house glows with an aesthetic charm unavailable at most other guesthouses in the area. 5 spotless rooms with microwave, fridge, TV, A/C, wicker beds, daily maid service, and ocean views. The friendly owners have also installed a backyard pool with a poolside, handicapped-accessible room. Doubles $69-89; quads $109. MC/V. ❸

Sandy Beach Inn (☎823-1146), on C. Vista Linda, uphill from Casa Verde, offers Rincón's most affordable private accommodations. Clean rooms with TV, A/C, and fridge. 4min. walk to the beach. Great view from the restaurant. Singles $55-65; doubles $65-87; 4-person apartment with kitchen $109. Tax included. AmEx/MC/V. ❷

Casa Verde Vacation Rentals (☎605-5351) on Beach Rd., has become one of the most hopping surfer hangouts, primarily due to its ideal location (1min. from Sandy Beach) and its well-stocked bar. Modern suites all include a kitchen, A/C in 1 room, and a TV. Doubles $60; 2-bedroom apartment $129; 3-bedroom house $200. MC/V. ❸

Lazy Parrot Inn, Rte. 413 Km 4.1 uphill from the beach and conveniently next door to Punta Mar Bakery (☎823-5654; www.lazyparrot.com). This brightly painted guesthouse is filled with parrot images. Elegant rooms with TV, A/C, and fridge, overlook the forest heights of Puntas. Sunny restaurant area for continental breakfasts (included), lunch (11am-3pm), and dinner (5:30-10pm). Doubles $85-95; quads $125-135. ❸

Beside the Pointe Guest House (☎/fax 823-8550; toll-free 888-823-8550; www.besidethepointe.com), on Beach Rd. This guesthouse boasts a great location right on Sandy Beach, and a popular restaurant/bar (see **Tamboo Bar**, p. 284). 8 brightly painted rooms with murals on the wall have lots of character. Cable TV, fridge, and A/C. Dec. 15-Apr. 24 doubles $90-150; quads $120; 2- to 6-person apartments with kitchen $125-180. Apr. 25-Dec. 14 $70-120/100/110-150. MC/V. ❹

Casa Isleña, Rte. 413 interior, Km 4.8 (☎823-1525, toll-free 888-289-7750; www.casa-islena.com). Gorgeous 6-room *hacienda* right on the beach. Big, spacious rooms with Mexican tiles offer incomparable ocean views. All rooms have A/C, cable TV, and daily maid service; most have fridges, and 2 have private balconies. Big patio, swimming pool, direct beach access, and restaurant (p. 284). Doubles $115-165; extra person $15. AmEx/MC/V. ❹

Pipons Resort (☎/fax 823-7154 or 823-5106; www.piponsresort.com), on Bummer Hill, ¼ mi. from beach. 6 spacious luxury apartments in a huge white house overlooking Antonio's Beach. Every room has a private balcony, an ocean view, A/C, kitchen, TV, and wicker furniture. The 5th and 6th guests have to sleep on couches. Doubles $100-115; quads $125-165; MC/V. ❹

SOUTH OF TOWN

Amirage Apartments, Rte. 429 Km 4 (☎/fax 823-6454; www.proceanfront.com), is the ultimate spot for tranquility. An expat couple has constructed their dream home, a beautiful white villa overlooking the water, and luckily they've opted to share it. 3 gorgeous rooms with tasteful murals feel just like home, down to the bathrobe waiting in the closet. Common courtyard contains a lush garden and a jacuzzi. Want more? All rooms have cable TV, A/C, balcony, and kitchen. Free kayak and snorkel equipment use. The one fault is the rocky beach, but it's a short kayak trip to sandier stretches. 2-person suite $125; 4- to 6-person suites $150. Cash only. ❹

Parador Villa Cofresí, Rte. 115 Km 12 (☎823-2450; fax 823-1770; www.villacofresi.com), feels like a beachside resort, but at a fraction of the price. As soon as you enter the spacious open-air lobby, your vacation may start to look like it needs an extension. Big pool area, bar, and 3 pool tables are right on the beach and are enormously popular with large family groups, who get discounts. Cable TV, A/C, and fridge. Check-in 3pm. Check-out noon. Doubles $105-125; 2-bedroom apartments $140-155; extra person $15; 2 children under 15 free. AmEx/D/MC/V. ❹

Coconut Palms Guest House, C. 8 #2734 (☎823-0147; www.coconutpalmsinn.com). A low-key beach villa in a quiet residential neighborhood. Natural courtyard garden with birds and a jacuzzi. Board games, used-book library, kitchenette, and cable TV. Right on Playa Córcega. Studios $100; apartments $125; extra person $10. MC/V. ❹

🔆 FOOD

Rincón offers a smorgasbord of dining options designed to satiate the healthy surfer appetite. Most of the food options are heavily American-influenced and almost all Puntas restaurants have a vegetarian option.

THE SURF BREAK (PUNTAS, LIGHTHOUSE AREA, THE MARINA)

🎏 **The Spot** (☎823-3510), at Black Eagle Marina. When you tire of burgers, sandwiches, and beach grub, head to The Spot for a satisfying gourmet meal. The owner brings in a rotating series of chefs from the US to cook up elegant fusion cuisine found nowhere else in Rincón. A house has been converted into a relaxed, welcoming, tropical restaurant; try the back patio at sunset. Entrees $12-27. Happy hour 4-7pm. Open Oct.-May noon-midnight; June-Aug. Th-Su noon-10pm. AmEx/MC/V. ❹

El Nuevo Flamboyán, on the southernmost road, manages to serve Puerto Rican cuisine and still be a foreign favorite. This simple eatery offers candlelit dinner in a small house hanging over the cliff in prime sunset-viewing position. Brush up on your Puerto Rican history with the patriotic posters on the wall. Entrees $10-17. Happy hour daily 5-10pm. Open daily 5-9pm. Bar open later. Cash only. ❸

Tamboo Bar & Seaside Grill (☎823-8550), at Beside the Pointe Guest House (p. 283). In addition to being a popular bar (all day long), Tamboo serves a variety of grill items, including fish, burgers, chicken, and wraps, on the big patio. Good lunch spot. Entrees $9-18. Sandwiches $6-9. Open M-Th and Su noon-midnight, F-Sa noon-2am. MC/V. ❸

Rock Bottom Bar and Cafe, (☎605-5351) next door to Casa Verde, sits on an upstairs deck with retired surfboards from locals mounted on the beams and roof. Restaurant serves burgers and other American food ($4-12) from 11am-9pm. ❷

Punta Mar Bakery, Rte. 413 Km 4.1 (☎823-2455). This standard *panadería* is one of the cheapest eateries in Puntas. Grab a quick breakfast ($2) or sandwich ($2-3) on the go. Very limited indoor and outdoor seating. Also sells some toiletries and groceries. No written menu. Open daily 6am-10pm. AmEx/MC/V. ❶

Casa Isleña (p. 283), on Beach Rd., serves up breakfast and lunch on its poolside courtyard. Enjoy an elegant lunch with the walnut pineapple chicken salad ($7.25). Breakfast $4-6.25. Lunch $5-13. Open W-Su 7am-3pm. AmEx/MC/V. ❷

Calypso Cafe (☎823-1626), on the road to the lighthouse, stands out for its prime location overlooking María's Beach. Use the outdoor patio to watch either the sunset or the surfers below. Popular lunch spot for surfers. Caribbean grilled seafood $3-12. Open in winter 11am-2am; summer noon-last customer. MC/V. ❷

THE REAL WORLD (TOWN, SOUTH OF TOWN)

Rincón Tropical, Rte. 115 Km 12.4 (☎823-2017), south of town. To experience real Puerto Rican culture, forgo the American-run places in Puntas and try out a more tropical Rincón. Reasonably priced seafood and *comida criolla* at a clean outdoor restaurant. $4 lunch special M-F. Entrees $6-19. Open daily 11am-10pm. AmEx/MC/V. ❸

Paris Deli, Rte. 115 Km 11.3 (☎823-7641), south of town, won't quite take you back to Paris, but this is one of Puerto Rico's few French delis. Not surprisingly, a largely foreign crowd comes for the gourmet lunch sandwiches and fresh baked goods. Entrees $3.75-5. Open M, Tu, Th 8am-6pm, F-Sa 8am-9pm, Su 8am-3pm. Cash only. ❶

Restaurante Bambino's, Rte. 115 Km 12 (☎823-3744). A friendly Italian restaurant with well-priced sit-down meals. Italian and *comida criolla* entrees $11-19. Lunch buffet M-F $7. Open M-Th and Su 11am-10pm, F-Sa 11am-11pm. AmEx/MC/V. ❸

Golden City Restaurant, C. Muñoz Rivera 57/Rte. 115 (☎823-5829). Good, cheap Chinese food. The generic City serves the cheapest Hunan Beef ($6), and *comida criolla* ($4.75), in town. Entrees $4-7.25. Open Tu-Su 11am-10pm. Cash only. ❶

La Cantina de Pepón, Rte. 115 Km 11.6 (☎823-0554), fills with locals in search of $2 beers and Mexican food ($5 lunch special). On the weekends, crowds party out front, on a mechanical bull. Entrees $7-10. Beer $2. Open Th-Tu 11am-midnight. ❶

👁 SIGHTS

Nobody comes to Rincón for its sights, but there are a couple of attractions.

PUNTA HIGÜERA LIGHTHOUSE. Rincón's lighthouse is both newer and less dramatic than others on the island. The original 1892 lighthouse was destroyed in 1918 and rebuilt in 1921 (then again in 1922). A fire severely damaged the structure in the 1930s but, undeterred, officials rebuilt the lighthouse in 1993 to commemorate the 500th anniversary of Columbus's landing on the island. You cannot enter the lighthouse, but the manicured park, with benches, grass, and trees, is a popular and pleasant place to walk and watch the surfers below. Sometimes a Puerto Rican couple offers horse-and-carriage rides around the lighthouse and over to María's Beach, a particularly romantic trip at sunset. *(At the end of the lighthouse road.)*

B.O.N.U.S. NUCLEAR REACTOR. Of all the contraptions the US has bestowed upon Puerto Rico, this may be worst. The large green dome just past the lighthouse was built in 1964 as the first nuclear energy plant in Latin America, but quickly closed later that year. There have been plans to turn the plant into a nuclear museum, but only school groups receive tours. *(Just past the lighthouse.)*

CENTRO CULTURAL RINCONEÑO. This eclectic museum seems to house everything that nobody could find a home for elsewhere in Rincón. The two rooms contain local artwork, Taíno artifacts, *vejigante* masks, and assorted antiques. *(Rte. 413 Km 0.3. ☎823-5120. Open Tu and Th 9:30am-2:30pm, Sa-Su 9am-2pm. Free.)*

MIRADOR DE AÑASCO. Rte. 115 just north of the Rincón Beach Resort. A concrete tower located just where the land rises toward Rincón, with a view back toward Mayagüez over the water. *(Open daily 6am-7pm. Free.)*

🌊 RIDING THE WAVES

Rincón is the premier surfing spot in the Caribbean, and one of the top surfing destinations in the world. Below is a list of the various surfing spots and services, but this is just a brief summary of a rapidly changing industry. Conditions change daily, surfing instructors come and go, and prime surfing weather may surface unexpectedly. To get the scoop, head to happy hour at Calypso and make some new friends.

SURF SHOPS AND LESSONS

■ **Surf Town,** C. Muñoz Rivera 40 (☎823-2515), in town, sells surfboards and surf gear. The friendly and knowledgeable staff answers questions about the area and will sketch a map for newcomers. Open daily 9am-5pm. AmEx/MC/V.

Rincón Surf and Board (p. 282) is the only surf school in town. Full-day lessons for all levels (9am-4pm $89, 2 days $169) include transportation and equipment. The shop also rents surfboards ($20 per day), boogie boards ($13 per day), snorkel gear ($12 per day), and beach supplies. Discounts for guests. MC/V.

West Coast Surf Shop, C. Muñoz Rivera 2E (☎823-3935; www.westcoastsurf.com), in town. Rents surfboards ($25 for 24hr.) and boogie boards ($15 for 24hr.). They also arrange surfing lessons ($35-50 per hr. per student, depending on the instructor) and sell a wide selection of surf gear and clothing. Open M-Sa 9am-6pm, Su 10am-5pm. AmEx/MC/V.

Hotwavz Surf Shop (☎823-3942), on the lighthouse road below Calypso (p. 284), rents surf and boogie boards ($8 for the 1st hr., $2 per additional hr.; $15 per day; $20 per 24hr.). Also provides info about surfing lessons. Sells original t-shirts and accessories. Open Oct.-May daily 11am-6pm, June-Aug. F-Su 11am-6pm. MC/V.

Desecheo Dive Shop (☎823-2672 or 823-0390), on the lighthouse road, rents surfboards ($25 per day), boogie boards, and snorkeling equipment ($10 per half-day, $15 per day). Open daily 9am-7pm. AmEx/MC/V.

SURFBOARD REPAIRS

Dr. Ding (☎823-6082), on Nuclear Vista Rd., repairs boards and makes new ones. Open daily; call ahead for an appointment.

Ocean Tribe (☎242-7985 or 242-7978), upstairs from Brisas on Rte. 413 and the road to Rincón Surf and Board, repairs and makes boards.

SURF BEACHES

From south to north, the principal surfing beaches in Rincón are listed below. Remember that winter and summer conditions differ dramatically. For instance, the best snorkeling spot in the calmer summer months is The Stairs, which is right next to the strongest surf break in the winter, Tres Palmas.

■ **Sandy Beach.** Come early in the morning to beat the crowds. A sandy bottom makes this a good place for beginners.

Tres Palmas. The best surfing spot in the Caribbean. Waves sometimes up to 25 ft. during winter and beyond break about ¾ mi. out. Experienced surfers only.

Toilet Bowl. The surf at this corner of Dogman's will pull you under like a toilet bowl would.

Dogman's. A shallow beach with fast, well-formed waves. Better for more advanced surfers. A local favorite.

María's. A popular break right underneath Calypso Cafe (p. 284). The waves break relatively close to the shore here, so you won't have to paddle out much. Attracts the biggest crowds, but not very beginner-friendly. **The Point** is the beginning of María's, and is only distinguished from it when the surf is low. When María's is big, a wave can run from here through Dogman's. **The Pistons** is a portion of María's named after the shipwreck engine pistons that remain lodged in the water. The prominent pistons can be dangerous if you get caught up in them; experienced surfers only should surf here.

Indicators. Located under the lighthouse, this break is rocky, shallow, has stinging sea urchins, and only attracts locals.

Dead Man's. No, it's not folklore, this beach was actually named after the dead bodies that have washed up here. This is an advanced break right against a perilous cliff.

Domes. One of the most popular and consistent breaks in the Rincón area. Can get extremely crowded, as it is beginner-friendly. Located in front of the nuclear reactor.

Spanish Wall. A shallow break that requires walking from the Domes parking lot along an old wall. Popular with local bodyboarders.

Pools. Right-hand waves break quickly across this shallow, uncrowded spot at the turn in Rte. 413, marked by Pools Guest House.

Antonio's Beach (aka Parking Lots). Located in front of the parking lot at Casa Isleña. Best surfed in the morning. Beginner-friendly.

River Mouth. The most difficult to access of the Rincón breaks. Two sandy breaks formed by the sand bars at a river's mouth. Requires walking east along the shore from Parking Lots.

OUTDOOR ACTIVITIES

BEACHES
In spite of the ample coastline, many of the beaches near Rincón are too rough or inaccessible for swimming during the winter. However, a few patches of white sand and calmer waters invite more tame recreation. A couple of miles south of town **Playa Córcega** has the best swimming beaches near Rincón and remains refreshingly empty. Drive south on Rte. 429 to the area around Km 1, then turn west, park near the condos, and walk between buildings to the beach. The *balneario municipal* **(public beach)** has both gentle Caribbean waves and larger Atlantic waves. Half of the beach has almost eroded away, but the other half is still a nice place for swimming. Facilities include trash cans, a playground, parking, and bathrooms that occasionally work. To reach the beach, take the road marked *balneario* just south of town, past Surf Town surf shop (p. 286).

FISHING
Captain José Alfonso of **Makaira Fishing Charters** leads fishing charters on his 32 ft. boat (half-day $450, full day $700). He also charters whale-watching and sunset cruises upon request. (☎823-4391 or 299-7374; makaira@caribe.net. Price includes refreshments, gear, and tackle. 25% deposit required for reservations. MC/V.)

THE LOCAL STORY

SURF'S UP

Amateur surfers-turned-instructors Vance Berry and Eric Wheaton explain life in Rincón to *Let's Go.*

On becoming surf instructors:
VB: We started coming to Puerto Rico a couple years ago and ended up at Rincón Surf and Board as guests last Christmas. They must have like us, because they asked us for our number.

EW: They asked us to take first aid and CPR classes. Vance spoke Spanish and I could drive heavy machinery.

On the seasons:
VB: In the summer we check Parking Lots and the other Rincón breaks in the morning and, if they're good, we'll surf them and then bring our clients down to surf. Otherwise it's Jobos.

On going out:
VB: We go to Calypso like everyone else.

EW: On the way out, we do the "brush 'n' go" by walking under the palm fronds and letting it comb our hair for us.

On Puerto Rico vs. The World:
EW: We're from Florida, but we've also surfed at Kauai, and I've surfed Costa Rica and the Bahamas. My most scary wave was here in Puerto Rico in the winter.

On their ride:
VB: We bought the surfmobile for $340 from this guy we met at a bar. He called it a "luxury automobile." It's got heated seats from the exhaust leaking in.

EW: On the drive from San Juan I couldn't touch the floor with my feet it got so hot.

HORSEBACK RIDING

It is illegal to ride horses on beaches in Rincón. However, **Pintos "R" Us,** next to Casa Verde (p. 283), leads rides along the Domes trail through fields and woods during the day (2hr., $40) and beach rides (2hr., $50) after dark. (☎598-8614. Cash or traveler's checks.)

SNORKELING AND DIVING

Some of Puerto Rico's best diving and snorkeling waits just 14 mi. from Rincón around rocky, deserted **Isla Desecheo.** With thriving reefs, visibility consistently over 100 ft., and ample fish species, this ranks among the best diving spots in Puerto Rico. The DRNA prohibits visitors from camping on the island, but Rincón's two superb dive shops take visitors out to dive and snorkel near the shore. If you don't want to head out on a boat, **Playa Escalera** is the best snorkeling beach in Rincón; it can be accessed by a dirt road from Rte. 413 labeled "Playa Escalera" on a whale-shaped sign.

Oceans Unlimited, Rte. 115 Km 11.9 (☎823-2340; fax 823-2370; www.oceans-unlimited.com). Takes their 46 ft. boat on regular trips to Desecheo and the Cabo Rojo wall (8am-3:30pm; 2-tank dive $99, snorkeling $50, 2-tank Discover Scuba package $125). Shorter trips go to the Mayagüez reefs (8am-12:30pm; 2-tank dive $65, snorkeling $45). Full-day expeditions include snorkeling equipment and lunch; scuba equipment rental $20. Half-day expeditions include a snack. Also offers 2hr. BYOB sunset cruises ($25), whale-watching cruises (Jan.-Mar.; $25), and PADI dive certification (3-day open-water diver course $400). Also goes to Isla Mona and offers Nitrox diving. Boat leaves from Puerto Real, near Cabo Rojo. Open daily 9am-6pm. MC/V.

Taíno Divers, Rte. 413 Km 1 (☎823-6429; www.tainodivers.com), in Black Eagle Marina. Their 34 ft. boat goes to Desecheo almost daily (2-tank dive $99, snorkeling $55). Shorter, less frequent trips go to reefs around Rincón (2-tank dive $75, snorkeling $35). All trips include lunch and beverages. Scuba equipment rental $20. 2hr. whale-watching and sunset cruises $25. 1-tank Discover Scuba package $125. Open-water certification $450. Open daily 10am-6pm. MC/V.

WHALE WATCHING

As if there weren't already enough to do, Rincón also has a prime location to watch the humpback whales migrate through the deep waters of the Mona passage every winter. From January to April, it is quite common to see the massive creatures spurting water, or even jumping, from most area businesses. The lighthouse park is prime observation area, and both **Oceans Unlimited** and **Taíno Divers** (see **Snorkeling and Scuba Diving,** above) offer excursions to give you a closer look.

🔊 NIGHTLIFE

It's tough to surf at night, so Rincón has a hopping nightlife scene in winter, the height of surfing season. Because most partiers are on vacation, weeknights can be as exciting as weekends. Even nightlife is a bit of a misnomer, as it's quite common to find people chilling with a Medalla beer at 11am. Cheers to the surfing life.

Puesta del Sol Inn and Restaurant, Rte. 413 Km 2.8 (☎823-2787). One of the few places to get your groove on in Puntas. The night starts off slow, with a few people playing pool ($0.50) downstairs or sipping drinks ($2.50-4) at the bar, then crescendos to a 2-story dance party with fluorescent lights and loud rock/pop/*reggaetón* music. Puerto Rican and foreign crowd. F-Su live music 11pm. $3 cover for monthly music show only. Open noon-2am daily. MC/V.

Tamboo Bar & Seaside Grill (☎823-8550), at Beside the Pointe Guest House (p. 283). Don't worry, be happy; everyone's knows everyone here. Surfers and surf-lovers sit on the large wooden patio watching people try their luck at Sandy Beach. Happy hour daily 7-9pm. Beer $2-3. Mixed drinks $4-6. Open Th-Tu 11am-last customer. MC/V.

Brisas, at the intersection of Rte. 413 with the road to Rincón Surf and Board, below Ocean Tribe. Expat waiters and waitresses from Rock Bottom and Tamboo end the night here with local friends. Pool tables dominate the dim red room. Surfing slideshows W and live music weekends during the winter. Beer $2-3. Mixed drinks $3-4. Open Tu, W, Su 7pm-midnight; Th-Sa 7pm-2am. Cash only.

Calypso Cafe (p. 284), on the road to the lighthouse. Every day surfers, locals, and wanderers gather at this tropical outdoor bar to watch the sun drop down over María's Beach and enjoy happy hour specials (5-7pm; rum punch $2). Live music Sa 10pm. Beer and mixed rum drinks $2.75-3. Open daily 11am-last customer. MC/V.

Rock Bottom Bar and Cafe (☎605-5351), adjoining Casa Verde Vacation Rentals (p. 283), is an upstairs surfer bar replete with dozens of broken and graffitied boards, candles, and open-air seating. Beer $1.50. Piña coladas $5. Open 5pm-midnight.

LA RUTA PANORÁMICA

The Central Mountains are the heartland of the island, both geographically and culturally. In the home of the *jíbaro*, or mountain farmer, boys still trot their Spanish mounts along mountain lanes. For over 100 miles the series of the roads known as La Ruta Panorámica (The Panoramic Route) twists through this region—ascending mountains, descending into valleys, and offering easy access to luscious expanses of jungle. Sudden vistas of forested peaks appear around the bends of the road and former-coffee-plantations-turned-*paradores* overlook quiet valleys. You can go miles without seeing a fast food restaurant, the stars are visible at night, and locals tend to respond to you in Spanish. Lodging is generally divided between upscale hotels and camping, meaning that travel here can be either extremely cheap or comfortably classy, depending on your preference.

Still, in some ways, the Ruta Panorámica is less than idyllic. Trash, including quite a few abandoned cars, litters the roads, and stray or abandoned dogs bark out their turf as cars drive by. Mountain towns under constant construction still suffer from traffic jams on weekends and holidays. The winding mountain roads range from narrow to tiny, with frequent washouts, and Puerto Ricans accustomed to the area feel no need to go slow. It's best to avoid driving on the Ruta Panorámica at night or during an afternoon rainstorm, and to honk your horn as you drive around blind curves. For those who can accept its imperfections, a drive through the island's mountains is an incomparable way to experience the remnants of pre-industrial Puerto Rico.

HIGHLIGHTS OF LA RUTA PANORÁMICA

VOLUNTEER in forest conservation at **Las Casas de La Selva** (p. 292).

DESCEND into the depths of the **Cañón de San Cristóbal** near Aibonito (p. 294).

ASCEND the island's highest peak at **Reserva Forestal Toro Negro** (p. 298).

UNCOVER the secrets of Taíno culture amidst the numerous *batey* fields at Utuado's **Parque Indígena Caguana** (p. 305).

RESERVA FORESTAL CARITE

Carite's proximity to the capital makes it one of the most visited nature reserves on the island. During summer months, hundreds of *sanjuaneros* trek over the hills to picnic in the cool subtropical forest or feast on the tasty *lechón* (roast pig) at one of the area's famous *lechoneras* (the best examples of these roadside grills/dance halls are on Rte. 184 along Km 27-8). Inside the forest, most Puerto Ricans relax at picnic tables and swimming holes at one of the three recreation areas. Visitors can explore the reserve under the guidance of the knowledgeable staff at the privately run Casas de la Selva (see **Accommodations and Camping,** below), but it is not feasible to hike alone deep in the forest as there are few marked trails; the DRNA has not been able to maintain established trails in the face of hurricane damage and funding shortages. From September to May the reserve sees few visitors and makes an excellent place to camp on a trip across the island.

▐ TRANSPORTATION

The only way to reach Bosque Estatal Carite is by car. From San Juan or Ponce take Hwy. 52 south to Exit 32, then hop on Rte. 184 southbound. Drivers should be aware that Puerto Rican drivers often use the whole road when taking tight mountain turns and may pose a threat to traffic in the opposite lane.

AT A GLANCE

AREA: 6680 acres.

CLIMATE: Humid and cool. Average temp. 72°F. Dry months Jan.-Mar.; wet May-Oct.

HIGHLIGHTS: Wading in streams, dining on *lechón*, driving through lush forest.

FEATURES: Charco Azul Area.

GATEWAYS: Cayey, San Juan (p. 92).

CAMPING: The park has camping areas at Charco Azul and Guavate. Campers must obtain a DRNA permit ($4) in advance (see below). Private camping at Casas de la Selva ($10, reservations required, see below).

FEES: None.

✴ 🛈 ORIENTATION AND PRACTICAL INFORMATION

Rte. 184 runs directly through the forest and contains most of the forest's points of interest. The DRNA office is located in the northwest corner near Cayey. To reach the popular Charco Azul Recreation Area, follow Rte. 184 southeast to Km 16.6. The Ruta Panorámica follows Rte. 179 out of the forest toward Lago Carite, which is located near a separate section of forest southwest of the main reserve.

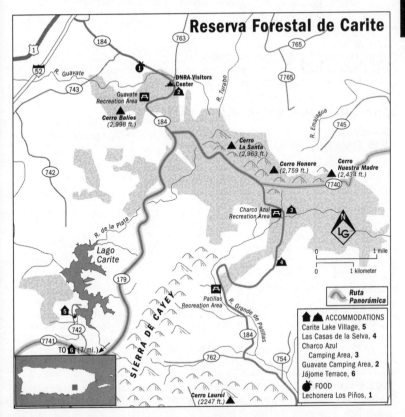

Reserva Forestal de Carite

ACCOMMODATIONS
Carite Lake Village, 5
Las Casas de la Selva, 4
Charco Azul Camping Area, 3
Guavate Camping Area, 2
Jájome Terrace, 6

🍴 FOOD
Lechonera Los Piños, 1

LA RUTA PANORÁMICA

La Ruta Panorámica

Visitors Center: The DRNA office, Rte. 184 Km 27.5 (☎747-4545 or 747-4510), at the northwest corner of the park. Open M-F 7am-3:30pm.

Hours: Charco Azul Recreation Area open daily 9am-5pm. **Guavate Recreation Area** open M-F 9am-4:30pm, Sa-Su 8am-5pm.

Supplies: All visitors should bring mosquito repellent, bottled water, and any food they may want. There are no supplies in the park.

🏠 🏕 ACCOMMODATIONS AND CAMPING

The unique lodging options in and around Bosque Estatal Carite are sharply divided between upscale lodges and camping sites.

▨ **Las Casas de la Selva,** Rte. 184 Km 17.6 (☎839-7318), 1 mi. past Charco Azul. This 1000-acre private reserve opened over 25 years ago in an effort to promote reforestation and protect the surrounding forest. Rents rustic rooms with private bath and a mosquito bed-net. Campers can set up tents either under a shelter near the lodge or in the middle of the forest among the crooning *coquís*. Renting a tent gets you access to the kitchen and bathroom. Las Casas are quieter and further from the road than nearby Charco Azul campsites and visitors will likely get to meet volunteers working on ecological projects or volunteer themselves (see **Constructive Conservation,** p. 300). Meals and guided hikes available at reasonable prices. Limited modem Internet connection. Reservations required or the gate will be closed. Tent space $10; dome tent rental with 2 air mattresses $40. Room with private bath $50. Tax included. Cash only. ❶

Jájome Terrace, Rte. 15 Km 18.6 (☎738-4016), where Rte. 741 and Rte. 15 meet, near the town of Jájome. Well-decorated, quiet rooms, a popular restaurant, and a remarkable view extending all the way to the Caribbean. All 10 beautiful rooms have views of the mountains, the town of Salinas, or the sea. There are no TVs or phones, just ample room for relaxation in the garden and wicker chairs. Popular restaurant open W-Th 11am-6pm, F-Sa 11am-10pm, Su 11am-8pm. Downstairs double with A/C $100; upstairs quads $125. Tax included. AmEx/MC/V. ❹

Carite Lake Village (☎763-2950). From San Juan follow directions to Carite, then take Rte. 184 to Rte. 179 to Rte. 742 Km 2. The huge Carite Lake Village looks a bit like a

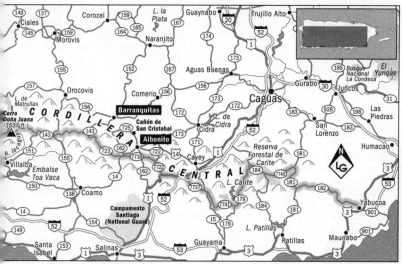

misplaced Alpine retreat, with over 50 peach-and-white steep-roofed villas surrounding Lago Carite. The undecorated, concrete 2-story villas come with bathroom, a full kitchen, a living room, and 3 upstairs bedrooms. Restaurant, swimming pool, basketball court, playground, and boat ramp round out the gated vacation community. Reservations required. Villas M-Th and Su $75, F-Sa $82. MC/V. ❸

Charco Azul Camping Area, Rte. 184 Km 16.6, on the east side of the road, across from the day-use picnic area. Popular with families for its accessibility and the swimming hole 10min. up an asphalt walkway. Bathrooms (bring your own toilet paper), trash cans, and fire pits. Reservations and a DRNA permit ($4) required (p. 292). ❶

Guavate Camping Area, Rte. 184 Km 27.3 2, just south of the visitors center with parking across the road. Walk through the green wood entryway to the tentsites. Hillside camping area right next to a stream and the roadside; easy access to a peaceful and scenic spot. Bathrooms (bring your own toilet paper), covered picnic tables, and an outdoor shower. Reservations and a DRNA permit ($4) required (p. 292). ❶

🍴 FOOD

What could make *sanjuaneros* leave their homes at 3am and drive to Puerto Rico's central mountains? Roast pig, of course. *Lechón*, as it's called, is a staple in Puerto Rico. On Rte. 184, just north of the DRNA visitors center, curious visitors can choose from a long row of *lechoneras*, where whole pigs roast in the windows. Most of the open-air *cafeterías* open only for the weekend crowds, but local favorite **Lechonera Los Piños ❶**, Rte. 184 Km 27.7, opens daily at 4am to lines of hungry customers. A full meal with *lechón*, rice, side, and drink goes for $7. Live music on weekends competes with the live music from every other *lechonero* on the block, contributing to the festive atmosphere. A pool table and bar in back provide the entertainment for smaller crowds after dark. (☎286-1917 or 489-7578. Live traditional music Sa 3pm. Live merengue Su 2pm. Open daily 4am-8pm. Bar open until 10pm. AmEx/MC/V.)

The DRNA maintains several **recreation areas** throughout the park. The best are at **Charco Azul,** across the road from the campground, where a dozen covered picnic tables are spread throughout a large area surrounded by the river. (Facilities include pit toilets, trash cans, and picnic tables.) The largest picnic area, **Área Recreativa Guavate,** on Rte. 184 about 1 mi. south of the visitors center, has countless picnic tables. (Facilities include fire pits, trash cans, water, and bathrooms.) Beverages of various kinds are sold at **Área Recreativa Patillas,** at the southern extremity of the Bosque. Local José keeps a family-friendly bar there, known as the **Teak Bar ❷,** and recognizable by the sign "Vegas' Place." A friendly crowd of locals sip beers in manmade swimming holes in the slow-moving river next to the road. The Teak Bar does not have regular hours or a phone number, but José lives upstairs and opens up most afternoons.

◪ HIKING

Serious hikers should head to **Las Casas de la Selva** (p. 292), where the managers can provide information about hikes or guides for longer treks into the forest, including the rugged 6hr. journey through Hero Valley. Only experienced hikers should attempt this trek, on which 60 ft. precipices lead down to a boulder-filled river. Hikes can be tailored to the visitor's experience level.

The DRNA maintains the **Vereda Charco Azul** trail (8min.), a short paved path that follows a creek through beautiful forest surroundings. The path ends in a little pond good for wading. In the summer this trail can become overcrowded with families but in the winter it offers a serene glimpse of the nature reserve. Longer trails are not well maintained by the DRNA due to continual hurricane damage and understaffing. Check with the DRNA office for current conditions.

AIBONITO

¡Ay, bonito! (Oh, pretty!) exclaimed the Spaniard upon seeing this mountain hamlet. Or so the legend goes. More likely the town's name came from the native Taíno word Atibonicu, meaning "River of the Night," but the Spanish expression is still applicable today. With scenic vistas, roadside *cafeterías*, and cool mountain air, it's no wonder that Aibonito is the vacation home of choice for *sanjuaneros*. The town center pays homage to its Spanish roots with plaza built in the tradition of a small Spanish town and a historic church. Every June the town celebrates the Flower Festival (p. 296), one of the largest such festivals in the world. For hikers, Aibonito serves as a trailhead for expeditions into the Cañón de San Cristóbal.

 TRANSPORTATION. From San Juan take Hwy. 52 to Cayey, then take Rte. 1 south to Rte. 7722. From Rte. 7722, turn right on Rte. 722 or Rte. 162, both of which lead directly into town. **Públicos** (☎735-1375) from Aibonito go to: **Barranquitas** (25min., $2); **Cayey** (30min., $2); and **Coamo** (30min., $2). Supposedly **taxis** (☎735-7144) gather across from the Alcaldía, but it might be faster to call.

 ORIENTATION AND PRACTICAL INFORMATION. Most routes from out of town retain their numerical signage in town, but local streets can be harder to identify, and many run one-way. The main street, **Route 14** (C. San José), runs one block north of the plaza and is usually clogged with traffic. From the Ruta Panorámica, **Route 162** goes directly into the city center, passes the plaza, and then intersects Rte. 14. Rte. 725 and Rte. 726 originate at Rte. 14 and then head north towards Barranquitas. Rte. 722 intersects with Rte. 14 just east of the city center. The city center is walkable, but most sights lie outside of town. The Alcaldía (☎735-8181) on the main plaza has some tourist and historical information. **Banco Popular** is at the intersection of Rte. 14 and Rte. 722. (☎735-3681 or

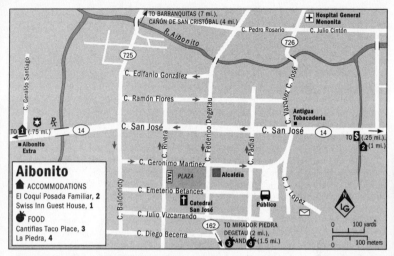

Aibonito

▲ ACCOMMODATIONS
El Coquí Posada Familiar, **2**
Swiss Inn Guest House, **1**

🍴 FOOD
Cantiflas Taco Place, **3**
La Piedra, **4**

735-6191. ATM. Open M-F 8am-4pm, Sa 8:30am-1pm.) For groceries try **Aibonito Extra,** C. San José 96. (Rte. 14 Km 50.3. ☎735-7979. Open M-Sa 7am-9pm, Su 11am-5pm. MC/V.) The **police station** (☎735-2020 or 735-2111), C. San José 53 (Rte. 14 Km 50.2), is open 24hr. Next door **Farmacia Unity,** C. San José 51, sells pharmaceuticals. (☎735-4747 or 735-2241. Open daily 8am-9pm. AmEx/MC/V.) The largest medical center in the area is **Hospital General Menonita,** Rte. 726 Km 0.5. (☎735-8001 or 735-8002. 24hr. emergency room. Open daily 10am-8pm.) The **post office,** C. Ignacio Lopez 20, does not have General Delivery. (☎735-4071. Open M-F 8am-4:30pm, Sa 8am-noon.) **Postal Code:** 00705.

🛏 **ACCOMMODATIONS.** Aibonito is one of the few mountain towns that has accommodations within walking distance of the plaza. The best deal is the **Swiss Inn Guest House ❷,** Rte. 14 Km 49.3, west of the plaza, just before the cemetery. Don't be misled by the "for sale" sign out front—just buzz at the bottom of the right-hand stairs and the friendly owner will let you in. Guests may encounter the occasional ant, and the vented doors don't block sound from the common area, but this is still a great bargain. (☎735-8500. Common fridge, TV, and microwave. $50, during the Flower Festival $75 for 1 night or $40 per night for the week. AmEx/MC/V.) For chain motel-like uniformity, try **El Coquí Posada Familiar ❸,** Rte. 722 Km 7.3. All rooms include private bath, cable TV, telephone, kitchenette with microwave, and a balcony overlooking a parking lot. The hotel is located on the second floor of a shopping center, so if nobody is at the second-floor reception, ask at the first-floor pharmacy. (Check-in 1pm. Check-out 11am. 1 double bed $7; 2 double beds $86. Tax included. AmEx/MC/V.)

🍴 **FOOD** A few days in the central mountains can leave you desperate for something besides *comida criolla,* the only option for miles on end. While cheap local and fast-food places are found near the town center, Aibonito's most distinctive eateries line the Ruta Panorámica. Locals recommend **La Piedra ❹,** Rte. 7718 Km 0.7. The fresh seafood and expansive mountaintop views produce a rare dining experience. The friendly owner also coordinates tours of Cañón de

San Cristóbal. (☎735-1034. Entrees $7-25. Su buffet $14. Open W-Th 11am-6pm, F-Sa 11am-10pm, Su 11am-8pm. D/DC/MC/V.) **Cantiflas Taco Place ❷,** at Rte. 722 and Rte. 162, on the Ruta Panorámica, provides a Mexican twist to the roadside menu. Their specialty is fajitas, but everything on the menu is fast, tasty, and less than $11. (☎738-8870. Karaoke F. Live dance music Sa 3pm. Open M-W 11am-10pm, Th 11am-midnight, F-Sa 11am-1am, Su 11am-10pm.)

◙ **SIGHTS** Complete with steep cliffs, waterfalls, and several ecological zones, the impressive 5½ mi. **▨Cañón de San Cristóbal** is the jewel of Puerto Rico's central mountains. Located between Aibonito and Barranquitas, the canyon was used for years as the local garbage dump. In the early 1970s local citizens protested this state of affairs, and in 1974, the Association of Environmental Control ordered that the canyon be protected. Now, the private Fideicomiso de Conservación de Puerto Rico (Conservation Trust of Puerto Rico) has acquired control of the area, reforesting it and using it for research purposes. The best way to experience the canyon is by hiking into the basin. However, locals warn that nobody should attempt the descent into the canyon without a guide, as several visitors have been killed hiking into the canyon alone. The Fideicomiso recommends going with Dr. Samuel A. Oliveras Ortiz (☎857-2094 or 647-3402), a Barranquitas geographer and historian who offers tours tailored to each participant's interests and abilities ($30 per person). For information about other local guides contact Joe at La Piedra restaurant (see **Food,** above) who is rumored to arrange helicopter tours of the canyon in addition to weekly hikes. At least one trek usually leaves every weekend, unless it rains, in which case it is too dangerous to enter the canyon.

Private property surrounds most of the canyon, but non-hikers can still catch glimpses of its waterfalls and forbidding cliffs. From Aibonito take Rte. 725 to approximately Km 5.5, then turn right down any of the roads leading downhill before the intersection with Rte. 162. If you tell locals that you're interested in seeing the canyon, most should be able to point out the best viewing spot. If your Spanish is rusty, a good view of the canyon is available from the Fideicomiso office in **Barranquitas** (p. 296).

The **Mirador Piedra Degetau,** Rte. 7718 Km 0.7, is worth a stop. The lookout tower has great views of the island—on a clear day you can see San Juan, El Yunque, the Caribbean, and the Atlantic. (Covered picnic tables and bathrooms. Open W-Su 9am-6pm. When M is a public holiday open Th-M 9am-6pm. Free.)

▧ **FESTIVALS.** Aibonito blossoms during the last 10 days of June, during the annual **Festival de las Flores (Flower Festival).** Locals display their home-grown flowers, farmers compete for the prizes of best garden and best plant, vendors hawk food, and musicians perform traditional mountain tunes. (For more information call ☎735-4070, or try the mayor's office at ☎735-8181.)

BARRANQUITAS

Barranquitas is a typical mountain town, perched on the edge of steep hill in the forest. The recently renovated plaza's wrought-iron benches, gazebo, and fountains set a stylish tone for the birthplace of Luis Muñoz Rivera—politician, journalist, and ostensibly the most important man in island history (see **History,** p. 59). His home is preserved here as a museum, and the town center's other attractions also tend towards the historical. Similar in size to Aibonito, Barranquitas also offers access to the Cañón de San Cristóbal.

▣ **TRANSPORTATION.** From the west, continue on Rte. 143 after it leaves the Ruta Panorámica, then turn left on Rte. 162. Coming from Aibonito, skip the Ruta Pan-

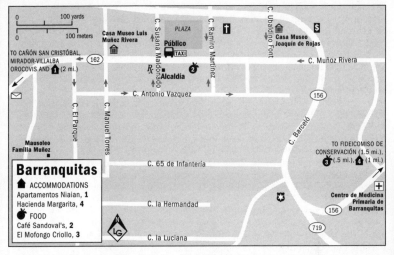

LA RUTA PANORÁMICA

Barranquitas

🏠 ACCOMMODATIONS
Apartamentos Niaian, 1
Hacienda Margarita, 4

🍴 FOOD
Café Sandoval's, 2
El Mofongo Criollo, 3

orámica altogether and take Rte. 14 to Rte. 162. Alternatively, coming from the east on the Ruta Panorámica, turn right on Rte. 143, then take a left onto Rte. 162, which leads into town. **Taxis** (☎857-0508) and the occasional **público** congregate around the plaza in front of the Alcaldía, but there is no regular public transportation to surrounding towns. A taxi to Aibonito, which has regular *públicos*, costs about $15.

🔌🚹 **ORIENTATION AND PRACTICAL INFORMATION.** Coming into town, Rte. 162 becomes **Calle Muñoz Rivera**, the main street, which passes the Alcaldía and the plaza before intersecting **Route 156**, which leads east. Remember that going downhill will always lead east. Continue east along Rte. 156 to find a large supermarket, fast food, and suburbs. **Casa Museo Joaquín de Rojas**, on C. Ubaldino Font, behind the church, does double duty as a tourist office and a small museum. The staff answers questions and distributes maps. (☎857-2065. Open M-F 8am-4:30pm with a break for lunch.) **Banco Santander,** Rte. 156 Km 16 (C. Barceló 60), 1½ blocks downhill from the plaza, exchanges AmEx Traveler's Cheques and has an ATM. (☎857-2355. Open M-F 8:30am-4pm.) The **police station,** Ave. Villa Universitaria 2 (☎857-2020 or 857-4400), down the hill at the intersection of Rte. 156 and Rte. 719, is open 24hr. **Farmacia del Pueblo,** C. Muñoz Rivera 27, is across the street from the Alcaldía. (☎857-3035. Open M-Sa 7:30am-6pm. MC/V.) The **Centro de Medicina Primaria de Barranquitas,** Rte. 156 Km 16.4, about ¼ mi. downhill from the police station, is the main hospital. (☎857-5923. Open M-F 6am-4:30pm. Emergency room open 24hr.) Free **Internet** is available at the sleek, modern **Biblioteca Municipal** on C. Susana Maldonado, across the plaza from the church. (☎857-6661. Open M-Th 8am-8:30pm, F 8am-4:30pm.) Head uphill to find the post office, C. Muñoz Rivera 41. (☎857-3020. General Delivery. Open M-F 8am-4:30pm, Sa 8am-2pm.) **Postal Code:** 00794.

📱📟 **ACCOMMODATIONS AND FOOD.** The beautiful **Hacienda Margarita ❸**, about 15min. from town, is the more scenic of the two accommodations in the area. The peaceful mountain retreat sits on the very edge of a hill, offering incredible views of the valley below. Rooms come with TV and A/C and all are sparkling clean. (Head east on Rte. 156 past the Shell Station, then turn left on Rte. 152.

Drive all the way up the hill, then at Km 1.7, turn right directly before the wooden restaurant. Passing all the driveways, take your first left at a fork, then take another left just before a sign for the hotel. Continue to the end of the residential road, following the signs. (☎857-4949. Check-in noon and check-out noon. 1 double bed $65; 2 double beds $75, whirlpool room $85. MC/V.) **Apartamentos Niaian ❶**, at Km 57.0 on Rte. 143 west of town, are conveniently located for travelers on their way west to Bosque Estatal de Toro Negro but are not well-signed. Look for the blue highway sign with a white bed just before the yellow building. Brightly lit rooms and kitchenettes make this a pleasant place to stay. (☎857-8955. $30 for 8hr., $60 per day.) Of the many inexpensive *cafeterías* surrounding the plaza, **Café Sandoval's ❶**, C. Muñoz Rivera 34, is the most welcoming. It serves a variety of breakfast and lunch foods—from burritos to sandwiches to pizza to ice cream. (☎857-3475. Entrees $1-6. Breakfast $1-3. Open M-Sa 6:30am-4pm.) Outside of town, just before the turn for Hacienda Margarita, is a good example of the roadside *cafeterías*, **El Mofongo Criollo ❶**, serving local seafood dishes for $6-15. It also has a bar, jukebox, and TV. (☎857-0480. Open Tu-Th 9am-5pm, F-Su 9am-midnight.)

◨ **SIGHTS.** Luis Muñoz Rivera, famous for negotiating Puerto Rican autonomy from Spain just before the US invaded in 1898 (see **History**, p. 59), dominates the town's cultural attractions. The **Mausoleo Familia Muñoz**, on C. El Parque, contains quiet courtyard and monuments to the Muñoz clan. Inside, a small exhibit contains biographical information, as well as an impressive mural depicting Muñoz Rivera's life. If the building is closed, ask someone in the office on the left side of the building to open it. (Open M-F 8am-3:30pm. Free.) Down C. Muñoz Rivera towards the plaza is the Casa Museo Luis Muñoz Rivera, where Muñoz Rivera's birthplace has been reconstructed with much of the original furniture. (☎857-0230. Open Tu-Sa 8:30am-4:30pm. $1.)

Tours of ◨**Cañón de San Cristóbal** leave from neighboring **Aibonito** (p. 294), but the best views are found in Barranquitas at the office of the **Fideicomiso de Conservación** (Conservation Trust); head east on Rte. 156, then turn right at Km 17.7. Continue to the end of the street, turn left on Calle A, and drive to the end. The office, which provides brochures on the canyon and the Fideicomiso, is on the right just after the road becomes a narrow one-lane path. (☎857-3511. Open M-F 1-3:45pm.)

On the road from Barranquitas to Bosque Forestal Toro Negro, another government-constructed viewpoint rivals **Mirador Degetau** for the best view of the ocean. **Mirador Villalba-Orocovis**, Rte. 143 Km 39.3, makes a nice stop for those driving the Ruta Panorámica. The viewpoint has covered picnic tables, bathrooms, a play area, a basketball court, a small restaurant, and of course the panoramic view—on a clear day it is possible to see the Caribbean, the Atlantic, Ponce, Embalse Toa Vaca, and the islands off the southern coast. (☎867-6111. Open W-Su 9am-6pm, when M is a holiday open Th-M 9am-6pm. Free.)

RESERVA FORESTAL TORO NEGRO

Toro Negro marks the high point of the island—literally. The reserve encompasses Cerro Punta (4930 ft.), the highest mountain in Puerto Rico, and some of the most impressive views on the Ruta Panorámica. Most visitors stick to the popular Área Recreativa Doña Juana, which contains several short trails, a large, stream-fed swimming pool, and a public campground. Island-spanning views and solitude reward visitors who make their way to the less-developed western half of the forest.

◨ **TRANSPORTATION**

You must drive if you want to visit Reserva Forestal Toro Negro. From San Juan take Hwy. 22 to Barceloneta, then take Rte. 140 south past Florida to Rte. 141.

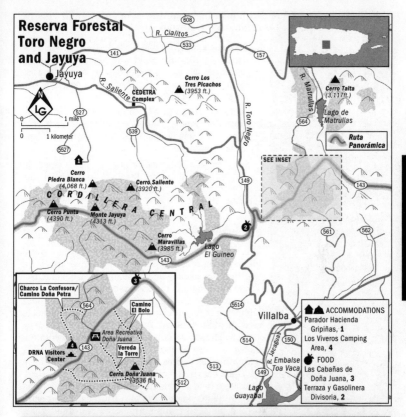

Reserva Forestal Toro Negro and Jayuya

AT A GLANCE

AREA: 6945 acres.

CLIMATE: Cool and moist. Averages 67-75°F. Rainy season Apr.-Dec.

HIGHLIGHTS: Summitting Cerro Punta, reveling in views of the distant Caribbean.

FEATURES: Waterfalls, acres of isolated palm forest, the island's tallest peak.

GATEWAYS: The Ruta Panorámica, Jayuya, Adjuntas, Ponce (p. 203).

CAMPING: Public camping at Los Viveros camping area. Campers must obtain a DRNA permit ($4) in advance (p. 300).

FEES: $1 to enter Area Recreativa Doña Juana, under 10 free.

Turn left on Rte. 144 in Jayuya and right on Rte. 149, which will run into Rte. 143. From Ponce, take Hwy. 123 north then exit onto Rte. 143 and drive east.

ORIENTATION AND PRACTICAL INFORMATION

Almost all sights lie along **Route 143,** which runs directly through the forest as the Ruta Panorámica. The only other important road, **Route 149,** overlaps briefly with Rte. 143 just west of the Doña Juana Recreation Area and runs north-south between Manatí and Juana Diaz. Toro Negro is Puerto Rico's most remote reserve,

GIVING BACK

CONSTRUCTIVE
CONSERVATION

Puerto Rico's much-needed economic development often comes at the expense of its unique natural resources. The Tropic Ventures Foundation, through its research station at the private rainforest reserve called **Las Casas de la Selva**, is working to prove that economic growth and environmental conservation need not always be at odds. Adjoining the government-run Reserva Forestal de Carite, the reserve is run entirely by volunteers who pay their own lodging expenses. Part of a large network of similar operations in unique biospheres around the world, Las Casas' goal is to develop eco-friendly forestry methods as an economically viable alternative to slash-and-burn logging and monoculture farming. Volunteers test out a forestry technique studied by the British Institute of Ecotechniques that involves planting and harvesting limited stands of valuable hardwood trees. The hope is that this method of utilizing Puerto Rico's natural wood resources will prove to be profitable while having a low impact on the surrounding forest.

(Las Casas de la Selva is located at Rte. 184 Km 15.9, Patillas. ☎839-7318. Volunteers pay $10 per day for their tent platform lodgings and have the opportunity to take part in ongoing research projects. To get involved, check out the website at www.eyeontheforest.co or call to reserve a campsite.)

with only the small towns of Jayuya and Villalba nearby.

Visitors Center: The **DRNA** office, Rte. 143 Km 32.4 (☎867-3040), west of Área Recreativa Doña Juana, distributes info and a hand-drawn trail map. Open daily 8am-4pm. Guards at the police office next door can help when the DRNA office is unattended.

Hours: Área Recreativa Doña Juana is open daily 9am-5pm. The pool is theoretically open Apr.-Sept., but more consistently open June-Aug., Sa-Su and holidays 9am-5pm.

Supplies: All visitors should bring mosquito repellent, bottled water, and food. There are no supplies in the park; the only "restaurant" open regularly doubles as a gas station.

▚ CAMPING

There are no hotels around Toro Negro, but several locals along Rte. 149 north of the forest advertise guesthouses, usually only available for weekend use. These are generally rustic, two-bedroom cabins with enough room for large families. Most include a kitchen, a bathroom, and several beds, but no sheets or dishes. Visitors will find more options in nearby Jayuya. The most economical and idyllic accommodation in Toro Negro is a campground. The DRNA maintains **Los Viveros camping area ❶,** Rte. 143 Km 32.5, just east of the office down a short paved road. This large field surrounded by Doña Juana Creek has covered picnic tables, fire pits, trash cans, and bathrooms. Several trails start here. You must get a DRNA permit ($4) in advance (p. 300).

◲ FOOD

The best option in Toro Negro is to bring your own food and picnic. Almost all of the rental cabins have kitchens and **Área Recreativa Doña Juana** has an attractive picnic area with fire pits, running water, and 10 covered tables. There are also a couple of *comida criolla* options. Despite its name, **Las Cabañas de Doña Juana ❶,** Rte. 143 Km 30.5, is actually a restaurant specializing in charcoal-grilled meats. The "cabañas" are covered concrete picnic tables that allow guests to be one with the surrounding mountains. (☎867-3981. Everything on the menu under $6. Open Sa-Su and holidays 8am-6pm; summer also open F.) If Las Cabañas is closed, try **Terraza y Gasolinera Divisoria ❶,** at the intersection of Rte. 143 and Rte. 149. The foods hibernating in glass cases will probably not make your mouth water, but we all have to eat. (☎847-1073. Meals under $5. Open daily 7am-8pm. MC/V.)

◎ SIGHTS

On the eastern side of the reserve **Doña Juana Waterfall,** Rte. 149 Km 41.5, cascades 120 ft. over a rocky cliff just next to the road. This is a great photo spot and one of the most accessible, impressive waterfalls on the island. Nearby, at the Área Recreativa Dona Juana, Rte. 143 Km 33, clever engineering has turned the a simple swimming hole into serious business. A stream-fed concrete **pool** divided in sections of different depths attracts the crowds. (Changing rooms, showers, lifeguards, and bathrooms. Open Apr.-Sept. Sa-Su 9am-5pm. $1, under 10 free.)

The western portion of Toro Negro has not been developed for tourism, but that just means you'll have the best views on the island to yourself. West of the intersection with Rte. 149, Rte. 143 continues ascending until it follows the ridge of Puerto Rico's tallest peaks. Almost all of the mountains have radio towers, which means that they also have roads leading to the top. Traveling east to west you first past Cerro Maravillas (3880 ft.) at the intersection of Rte. 143 and Rte. 577. Although it is by no means the tallest, this peak is well known as the site of one of the most infamous murders in Puerto Rican history (see **The Watergate of Puerto Rico,** p. 61). Two small white crosses still mark the gravesite. Continue past two more radio-towered mountaintops to reach the road up to **Cerro Punta, the tallest mountain in Puerto Rico.** The mountain is distinguishable by the gravel area at the base and the steep paved road winding up the side. Get to the observation platform early, before the clouds roll in, and you'll be rewarded with the best view on the island. While signs at some of the radio stations seem to warn visitors off, the local DRNA rangers will say that it is legal to visit the summits, and the workers there are friendly, if a bit surprised to see visitors.

◎ HIKING

Some of the longer and more popular trails are listed below; for a complete list, visit the DRNA office. These trails are often old unpaved roads, so they are accessible to hikers of most abilities.

CAMINO EL BOLO. At 2¾ mi., this is the longest trail in Toro Negro, and viewpoints are perfect for a picnic lunch. The trail begins across the street from the visitors center; walk through the parking lot and continue on the rocky road leading uphill. After about 15min. you reach a flat grassy path along the ridge of the mountain with great views to the south. When you come to the paved road, turn left to continue along the path. Vereda La Torre crosses this trail and leads uphill to another viewpoint. El Bolo ends farther east on Rte. 143. It is possible to make a circle by coming back along the road, but given the blind turns and narrow roads, it's easier to return via the same path.

VEREDA LA TORRE. Because the trailhead is located at the Doña Juana Recreation Area, and because it leads up to an observation tower with stellar views, Vereda La Torre is the most popular trail in Toro Negro. From the picnic tables follow the grass path uphill past valleys full of ferns and palm trees. The 2 mi. trail gets slightly rougher as you progress, but the path is always easy to follow. After 20min. the trail comes to what looks like an old service road, which is actually Camino El Bolo. Turn left and walk about 5min. past the short stretch of concrete to reach the second half of La Torre, which leads to the observation tower.

CHARCO LA CONFESORA/CAMINO DOÑA PETRA. From Los Viveros, take the paved road below the campsites. When you reach a bridge, turn right and follow the red mud trail through tropical vegetation and rows of orange trees. Eventually Camino Doña Petra (1 mi.) leads back to Rte. 143, though it's quite a walk back along the road.

JAYUYA

Located at the foothills of Cerro Punta, 30min. off the Ruta Panorámica, this town merits a visit for its collection of Taíno sights, from impressive petroglyphs to a small museum designed as a *cemí*, a Taíno religious icon. Historically, Jayuya was the site of a revolution against American control. In 1950, a group of *nacionalistas* led a rebellion that produced in the independent republic of Jayuya—for three days. Today the town offers a quiet place to spend the night at the spiritual home of the Taínos, surrounded by the island's highest mountains.

E TRANSPORTATION. Coming from the Ruta Panorámica, detour north on Rte. 140 between Toro Negro and Adjuntas, then take Rte. 144 straight into town. From San Juan, take Rte. 123/Hwy. 10 to Utuado, then follow Rte. 111 to Rte. 144. **Públicos** in Jayuya leave from the parking lot next to Mueblería Doris between C. Figueros and C. Guillermo, just off the plaza. They head to **Ponce** ($4) very early in the morning—ask locals the night before for scheduled times. No public transportation goes to the major sights outside of town.

■ ⑦ ORIENTATION AND PRACTICAL INFORMATION. Coming into town, Rte. 144 deposits you on C. Figueros; then you will have to veer right onto C. Guillermo. **Calle Guillermo, Calle Figueros,** and **Calle Barceló,** the three main streets in town, run parallel to each other and the latter two border the plaza. Most of the major sights are on Rte. 144 as it continues south out of town. **Banco Popular,** C. Guillermo Esteves 84, has an ATM. (☎828-4120. Open M-F 8am-4pm.) To reach the **police station,** C. Cementerio 1, from the plaza, walk down C. Barceló, turn right after the Alcaldía, and walk uphill. (☎828-2020 or 828-3600. Open 24hr.) Across the street, the **hospital,** C. Cementerio 2, has a 24hr. emergency room. (☎828-3290 or 828-0905. Open M-F 8am-4:30pm.) The university **library** on C. Figueras across the plaza from the church offers free **Internet** access (☎828-2824 ext. 1759. Open M-F 7:30am-9pm Sa 8am-noon). The **post office,** C. Barceló 15, has General Delivery. (☎828-3010. Open M-F 7:30am-4:30pm, Sa 7:30am-11:30pm.) **Postal Code:** 00664.

⑥ ⑥ ACCOMMODATIONS AND FOOD. The recently opened ◪**Hospedería Coabey ❷,** Rte. 144 Km 8, strikes a happy medium between price and comfort. Cool rooms on the lower level are a stone's throw from a private swimming hole in the river. (☎828-2836. TV, mini-fridge. Double $50.) **Parador Hacienda Gripiñas ❹,** on Rte. 527, was originally a 19th-century coffee plantation and still retains the charm of an old country house, with wooden porches and hammocks overlooking an incredible mountain landscape. Carpeted rooms have cable TV and A/C. Room prices include dinner and breakfast at the hotel restaurant, making this a good deal for midweek travelers. (Take Rte. 144 east to Rte. 527, then follow the green signs. ☎828-1717 or 828-1718; www.haciendagripinas.com. 2 swimming pools. Check-out 11am. M-Th and Su singles $82; doubles $110; F-Sa $98/126. AmEx/MC/V.) Those who want to stay in town have one choice—**Hotel Posada Jayuya ❸,** C. Guillermo Esteves 49. The back entrance is accessible from C. Libertad, parallel to C. Guillermo Esteves. Wicker furniture, TV, and bar in the lobby give way to neat, tile-floored rooms. Textured murals decorate the walls. (☎828-7250. Small pool. Fridge, TV, and A/C. Doubles $69; extra person $10. AmEx/MC/V.)

The restaurant at **Parador Hacienda Gripiñas** ❸ has a wonderful view over a peaceful valley. This *mesón gastronómico* creates an exceptional dining experience—its glass-ceilinged central room holds a tree in the middle. Dishes include traditional seafood and steak options. (Entrees $11-19. Open daily 8am-10pm.) The up-and-coming owner of **Tainy Cafe's** ❶ has plans for inner-tubing and campsites along his riverfront property. For now, his roadside sandwich stand with covered picnic tables is a good place to get a bite to eat just outside of Jayuya on Rte. 539 Km 0.2. (☎828-3353. Sandwiches $5.)

◙ ❀ SIGHTS AND FESTIVALS. The **CEDETRA (Development and Labor Center)** complex, Rte. 144 Km 9.3, holds a variety of Taíno artifacts and contemporary artesanal work. Constructed in 1989, the bulbous **Museo El Cemí** was designed to look like a *cemí*, a Taíno religious image carved in stone. Don't worry if the building looks a little amorphous—there are at least 20 different theories about what the *cemí* was designed to look like. Inside visitors will find Taíno artifacts and replicas, including an *espátula vomita*, a spatula that the Taíno people used to induce vomiting before they took hallucinogenic drugs. (☎828-1241. Open M-F 8am-4:30pm, Sa-Su 10am-3pm. Free.) Completely unrelated, but on the same property, **Museo Casa Canales** houses one of Jayuya's most important families. Built in the late 19th century by Don Rosario Canales Quintero, the town's first mayor, the house also served as a residence for his son Nemesio Canales Rivera, a legislator and humorist who aided in the legal emancipation of women. Don Rosario's daughter Blanca Canales, the leader of the revolution of October 30, 1950, also resided there. The house was abandoned while she served her prison term, but in the early 1990s CEDETRA painstakingly reconstructed it in its original form. (☎828-4094. Open Sa-Su 10am-5pm. $1, under 12 $0.50.) The nondescript building in back holds the **CEDETRA exhibition hall** and a small *artesanía* souvenir shop. The kiosks across the path provide a venue for **local artisans** to sell their work on weekends and holidays. Finally, near the kiosks,

the **Museo de Café** displays coffee-related antiques. Despite the extensive work put into the CEDETRA complex, the most impressive sight lies about 1 mi. down the road. **La Piedra Escrita,** Rte. 144 Km 7.7, is a huge rock in the middle of the creek covered with Taíno petroglyphs. A new wooden ramp leads down to the rock, which locals use as a diving board into the surrounding creek.

Within the city center yet another cultural monument honors the island's Taíno heritage. From the plaza, hike up the steep staircase to reach a bust of the *cacique* Jayuya (Jayuya Taíno chief). Behind the bust, the small locked building contains the **Puerto Rican Indian tomb,** the bones of a Taíno indian lying on a bed of dirt accumulated from each of the island's 78 municipalities. Unfortunately, the monument is often locked and difficult to see. Behind the tomb the Puerto Rican Department of Culture maintains a small **cultural center,** C. San Felipe 25, with an assortment of antiques, broken Taíno artifacts, and reproductions. (☎828-2220. Spanish only. Open M-F 8am-noon and 1-4:30pm. Free.)

Jayuya's largest festival is the annual **Festival Nacional Indígena** (National Indigenous Festival), celebrated over 3-5 days in mid-November. The festival focuses on Taíno culture with indigenous dances, *batey* (a ritual ball game), and reproductions of an indigenous town. Check at **CEDETRA** for details.

UTUADO

Utuado's highlights are its rich Taíno roots and forward-thinking eco-development of its natural surroundings. The town reflects its colonial history, with a Spanish central plaza and American fast-food joints on the outskirts. Many visitors come to see the archaeological excavation, begun by two American archeologists in 1915, which is shedding light on this ancient social center of Taíno life. For those without any interest in the archaeology of Puerto Rico's early inhabitants, Utuado is a great place to experience the adventurous side of the Puerto Rican rainforest.

E⁊ TRANSPORTATION AND PRACTICAL INFORMATION. *Públicos* leave early in the morning for **Arecibo** (45min., $2) from Ave. Esteves and C. Israel Malaret Juarbe. The city center is divided by a river. Rte. 123 becomes **Avenue Esteves** and leads to the plaza. On the other side of the river, Rte. 111 runs parallel to the river and becomes **Avenue Fernando Luis Rivas**. **Tourist information** and hand-drawn maps are available at the **Centro de Arte, Cultura y Turismo,** C. Doctor Cueto 10, several blocks west of the plaza on the river side of the road. **Banco Popular,** C. Doctor Cueto 93, is before the tourist info center, heading away from the plaza. (☎894-2700. 24hr. ATM. Open M-F 8am-4pm.) The **police station** is on C. Sampson, at the corner of the plaza uphill from the main church. (☎894-3022. Open 24hr.) The **CDT** (Centro de Diagnóstico y Tratamiento), at C. Betances 2, acts as the local **hospital,** across C. Betances from the main church on the plaza. (☎894-2288. Open 24 hr.) Free **Internet** is available at the **Biblioteca Pública** across the street from the Centro de Arte, Cultura y Turismo. The **post office,** Ave. Fernando Luis Rivas 41, is on Rte. 111 at the south end of town. (☎894-2490. General Delivery. Open M-F 8am-4:30pm, Sa 8am-noon.) **Postal Code:** 00641.

⌐▐ ACCOMMODATIONS AND FOOD. If you just want a place to crash, look no further than **Hotel Riverside ❷,** Ave. Fernando Rivas 1, near the intersection of Rte. 111 and Rte. 123 above a Chinese restaurant. This tiny hotel has small rooms but manages to fit in a fridge and a TV, and the price is right. (☎562-7619. A/C. Doubles $40; 6-person room $60. Cash only.) The folks at **Valle Indígena Area de Acampar ❶,** Rte. 111 Km 14, allow travelers to camp in their large yard overlooking the river. Call well ahead as it can be difficult to catch the owner and the gate may be closed. (☎894-9434. $10 per tent. Cash only.) For lakefront luxury, visitors should head to **Los Piños Lake Resort ❸,** at the intersection of Rte. 140 and Rte. 613, on Lago Caonillas. The recently renovated villas contain sitting rooms, kitchens, and bedrooms. The resort has its own restaurant and bar. Classical music or jazz concerts liven things up twice a month, and a spa based on Taíno herbal aromatherapy is in the works. (☎894-3481 or 894-3464. $75, better view $85, additional person $15. AmEx/MC/V.) In town, there are plenty of *cafeterías* and fast-food joints, but to take advantage of Utuado's natural surroundings, head out of town to **Jungle Jane's Restaurant ❹,** at the remote Casa Grande Mountain Retreat. This *mesón gastronómico* serves *comida criolla* in a former coffee plantation. Candlelit tables on a balcony overlooking the forest with *coquís* chirping in the background create a romantic mood. (Entrees $12-25. Open M-F 8-10:30am and 6-9pm, Sa-Su 8-10:30am, noon-4pm, and 6-9pm. AmEx/D/MC/V.) Ravenous adventurers will appreciate the diversity (*mofongo,* spaghetti, pizza) of the menu and reasonable prices at **La Familia ❷,** Rte. 111 Km 12. (☎894-7209. Entrees $6-15. Open M and W-Th 11am-9pm, F-Sa 11am-11pm, Su 1-10pm. MC/V.)

◱ SIGHTS. Utuado is surrounded by natural wonders and historical sites on a prodigious scale. The island's largest cave system, the most extensive Taíno site, and the world's biggest telescope are all accessible from this one small town. **◪Tanamá Expeditions** leads exhilarating hiking/kayaking excursions along subterranean rivers, the overgrown bamboo forests of the **Tanamá Trail,** and the enormous **Arecibo Observatory.** These trips require good physical health and basic hiking equipment, but the owner provides specialized equipment, lunch, and even a place to stay the night before. Trips range from 3½hr. hiking and tubing trips through the 700 ft.-long Arco Cave ($58, including lodging) to two-day journeys that include traversing a bioluminescent cave and hiking the Tanamá Trail ($250, check with owner about necessary camping equipment). The tour includes **free lodging** (shared basic rooms with bathrooms or camping space) at the owner's house/office. (Continue past Parque Caguana to Rte. 111 Km 14.5, then turn left on Rte. 602 and follow signs to the office at Km 1.3. ☎894-7685. www.puertoricoadventures.com. Cash only.)

Parque Indígena Caguana is the largest site of Taíno ruins on the island, which leads archaeologists to believe that it once served as a social, religious, or ceremonial center. Supposedly the Taínos came down the Río Tamaná, then chose to settle in this spot when they saw that the surrounding mountains had the shape of their religious icon, the *cemí.*

IN THE PEOPLE'S HOUSE

When the same mining companies that helped to topple Chilean President Salvador Allende came to Puerto Rico looking to mine in the region around Adjuntas, a local civil engineer put his foot down. Alexis Massol González founded **Casa Pueblo** (The People's House, without the leftist connotations) to organize a series of door-knocking campaigns, concerts, and demonstrations. Over a period of 15 years these convinced González's neighbors, and eventually the whole of Puerto Rico, that digging over a dozen mile-wide pit mines in the collective water source would be a big mistake. In 1995, the organization succeeded in overturning the mining plans, but it was for González's continued work with Casa Pueblo that he received the Goldman Environmental Prize in 2002. Recently, the organization secured the protection of over 50,000 acres of forest, spanning a tract between in Adjuntas and Barranquitas. Casa Pueblo divides its activities between promoting public education, protesting environmental abuses, and taking part in ecological research studies. The organization is funded entirely by the sales of its coffee, Café Isla Madre, and accepts volunteer groups on the weekends for various projects.

(More information is available at www.casapueblo.org or C. Rudulfo González 30 in Adjuntas. ☎829-4842. Open daily 8am-4:30pm.)

Carbon dating techniques suggest that the first settlement here took place as early as AD 1200. The **Institute of Culture** maintains the site today, which means that it has much better infrastructure than other Taíno sights, and friendly workers frequently provide unofficial, free guided tours. Even without a tour it's enjoyable to wander around the picturesque botanical garden and attempt to identify the petroglyphs in the rocks. A museum at the beginning provides the basics of Taíno culture. (Rte. 111 Km 12.3 west of Utuado. ☎894-7325 or 894-7305. Open daily 8am-4:30pm. $2, ages 6-12 $1, under 6 and 60+ free.)

ADJUNTAS

This fruit- and coffee-exporting town has not developed much tourist infrastructure, but boasts affordable accommodations and unique eateries. It is also a gateway to the Bosque Estatal de Guilarte, and home of one of the most successful ecological activism projects in Puerto Rico.

TRANSPORTATION. From Jayuya, take Rte. 123 south into town, where it becomes **Calle Doctor Barboza** and leads to the plaza. From the Ruta Panorámica, Rte. 123 north becomes C. Rodulfo Gonzalez, which runs one-way along the plaza. These two roads run the length of the town and are perpetually clogged with traffic. It's best to park near the plaza and walk around town.

PRACTICAL INFORMATION. The **Oficina de Turismo** attached to the Ayuntamiento building at one corner of the plaza has limited information. (☎829-5000 ext. 247. M-F 8am-4:30pm.) **Police** (☎829-7800) are available 24hr. at C. San Joaquín just off the right-hand side of the plaza, facing the church. The **hospital,** CDT (Centro de Diagnóstico y Tratamiento), is two blocks east of the plaza at C. Doctor Fendini 4. (☎829-2860. 24hr.) Visitors will find an ATM machine at the **Banco Popular** on C. San Joaquín on the plaza. (☎829-2120. M-F 8am-4pm, Sa 9am-1pm.) Free **Internet** is available at the public library on C. César Gonzalez behind the church. (☎829-5039. M-Th 8am-8pm, F 8am-4:30pm, Sa 10am-1:30pm.) The **post office,** C. Luis Muñoz Rivera 37, is a block left of the plaza, facing the church. (☎829-3740. M-F 8am-4:30pm, Sa 8am-noon.) **Postal code:** 00601.

ACCOMMODATIONS AND FOOD. The cheaper of the only two options is the **Hotel Monte Río ❷,** C. César Gonzalez 18. It offers a pool, bar, and simple rooms with bed and futon for $50. (☎829-0766. TV. A/C.) The much more elaborate **Parador Villas Sotomayor ❸,** Rte. 123 Km 37.6, a few hundred meters up Rte. 602 from Rte. 123, is a popular vacation destination. *Villas* with bedroom, bathroom, and kitchenette are spread around a grassy area with basketball, tennis, and swimming pool. (☎829-1717 or 829-1774. TV, A/C. Doubles $85; more for multiple bedrooms.) Horse rental ($25 per hr.), bicycle rental ($5 per hr.), and **campground ❶** ($30 plus $5 per extra person, access to pool included) are also available.

On the town plaza, **Esquina de la Amistad ❶,** C. Rodfulo Gonzalez 56, bakes *pan de hogaza* (homestyle bread) every morning that draws customers from the whole region. (Pastries $0.50-0.70, bread $1-2. Open 5:30am-11pm daily.) Old men smoke their cigars at **La Playita Coffee House ❷,** 3 Rodulfo Gonzalez, marked by the sign "Lechonera La Playita," around the corner from Casa Pueblo, away from the plaza. A bar and a couple of pool tables round out the relaxed atmosphere. (☎316-9095. *Comida criolla* entrees $5-10. M and W-Su 9am-midnight.) Surprisingly, Greek fast food is available at **Gyros Cafe ❷,** C. Rodulfo Gonzalez 36, along with pizza and ice cream. (☎ 829-1684. 9am-10pm daily.) The **Villas Sotomayor ❸** also has a restaurant serving *comida criolla*. (Breakfast $3-5. Lunch $9-13. Dinner $9-22. Open daily 8am-10am and noon-10pm.)

◉ SIGHTS. ▨**Casa Pueblo,** C. Rodulfo Gonzalez 30, is the epicenter of Puerto Rico's ecological activism movement (see **The People's House,** p. 305). The house includes displays on the group's community projects—ranging from the 15-year struggle to prevent open-pit mining in the town's watershed to more recent studies on Puerto Rican rainforests. A collection of butterflies and various agricultural experiments fill the backyard. The gift shop sells the group's coffee, **Café Madre Isla,** which pays for the entire operation's expenses. Larger groups should call ahead about the possibility of volunteering for a weekend at the coffee plantation. (☎ 829-4842. Open daily 8am-4:30pm. Free.)

Southwest of Adjuntas, the Ruta Panorámica winds through **Bosque Estatal de Guilarte,** a protected area composed of several distinct units of land. Visitors coming from the east first pass Lago Garzas, a popular **fishing** spot. Farther west, the official forest entrance is marked by a patrol unit at the intersection of Rte. 131 and Rte. 518. Drive up the hill across from the office to reach the **DRNA office,** which provides information about the forest and nearby **swimming holes.** The **Área Recreativa,** at the end of a short path from the DRNA office, has a *mirador* (scenic overlook) with superb views of the surrounding valley. (☎ 829-5767. Open M-F 7am-3:30pm, Sa-Su 9am-4:30pm.) The only **marked trail** in the forest is a slippery 30min. path leading up to the peak of **Monte Guilarte.** The trailhead is 75 ft. from the guard station, next to a private driveway across the road from a ramshackle roadside eatery near the dead-end of Rte. 131. To make use of the wilder eastern segment of the forest, visitors will need to arrange a trip with either the DRNA officer or another local guide—the only trails date to before the reserve was established and require local knowledge. The highlight of Guilarte is its exceptional **cabins ❶.** Guilarte has bathrooms, rustic showers, trash cans, running water, and fire pits. (Cabins $20, bedding not provided.) To stay here you must have a DRNA permit and a reservation (see **Camping,** p. 42).

MARICAO

The remoteness and rugged terrain of this coffee-producing town have preserved it in a bygone age. As possibly the only town on the main island without any fast-food restaurants, Maricao offers a rare glimpse of what many Puerto Rican towns used to be like. It is surrounded by forests important to migrating birds and, in the winter, bird-watchers come here to catch a glimpse of the migrating flocks. Maricao's largest festival, the **Fiesta del Café** (Coffee Festival) is held on the weekend of George Washington's birthday in mid-February, and includes traditional music, coffee samples, drama shows, *artesanía*, and folkloric dances.

⁊ PRACTICAL INFORMATION. Tourist information is available at the **Oficina de Relaciones Públicas** on the plaza. (☎ 838-290. M-F 8am-4:30pm.) The **police** are located in the outskirts down on Ave. Luchetti 14. (☎ 838-2020. Open 24hr.) Across the street from the police is the **hospital,** Ave. Luchetti 9. (☎ 838-2100. Open 24hr.) An ATM is available at the **Banco Popular** on C. Luis Zuzuarregui, across the street from the **post office,** at C. Luis Zuzuarregui 9. (☎ 838-3605. General Delivery available. M-F 7:30am-4pm, Sa 7:30am-11:30pm.) **Postal code:** 00606.

⁊⁊ ACCOMMODATIONS AND FOOD. It's possible to camp or stay in concrete cabins at the private **Parque Nacional Monte de Estado ❶,** Rte. 120 Km 13.0, which borders on the Bosque Estatal de Maricao. Families vacation here and make use of the pool, playground, bathrooms, and grills near the cabin. Because no camping is allowed in the nearby state forest, the camping is pricey. Budget travelers would do much better to bring some friends and split a cabin. (☎838-5652 or 838-5632. Bathrooms, running water, pool. Office open daily 8am-4:30pm. Campsites $55; Cabins $65, up to 6 people.) **Parado Hacienda Juanita ❹**, Rte. 105 Km 23.5, is an attractive mountain *parador*. This 19th-century coffee plantation centers on a lush courtyard garden, and the grounds include a swimming pool, tennis court, and restaurant with a collection of farm implements on display. (Take Rte. 120 east of town, then turn on Rte. 105. ☎838-2550; www.haciendajuanita.com. Cable TV, wireless Internet. Singles $102; doubles $133. Prices include dinner, breakfast, and tax. AmEx/MC/V.)

Even travelers not staying at Hacienda Juanita can enjoy the idyllic setting and stylish dining room the *parador's* **La Casona de Juanita ❸**. Like most *mesones gastronómicos*, this restaurant serves succulent *comida criolla* on a back porch that makes you feel like you're sitting in the middle of the forest. (Entrees $9-18. Wine $20-180. Open M-Th and Su 8am-9pm, F-Sa 8am-10pm.) Those passing through town can grab a quick bite to eat at **El Buen Café ❶**, on the plaza. This is the type of place where locals congregate to discuss weather, politics, and the mistakes of the Spanish-American War over a Medalla beer. There is no written menu, but you shouldn't pay more than $6-7 for a sandwich or a plate of *comida criolla*. (☎838-4198. Open M 6am-3pm, Tu-W 6am-10pm, Th-Su 6am-midnight. MC/V.)

🄶 **SIGHTS.** Maricao is a magnet for birdwatchers from around the world as many species of birds take a break along their annual migratory route in the **Bosque Estatal de Maricao** between November and March. DRNA officers at the visitors center, Rte. 120 Km 16.2, can direct visitors to one of three trails, each of which descends less than a mile from the visitors center. Serious hikers will want to inquire with the DRNA office in San Juan (p. 100) to arrange a private guide for longer hikes on unmaintained trails in the forest. (☎838-1040 or 838-1045. M-F 7am-3:30pm, Sa-Su 8am-3:30pm.) On the way to the DRNA office from the private Monte del Estado campsite, visitors can stop at the **Torre de Observación** to delight in views of the entire western half of the island. (Open 8am-4pm. Free.) Maricao is also known for providing seed fish for the island's artificial lakes. **Los Viveros Fish Hatchery**, Rte. 410 Km 1.7, raises fish in several large pools to populate artificial lakes around the island. (From the east, turn right at the sign for Los Viveros and continue to the end of Rte. 410. ☎838-3710. Open to the public Th-Su 8:30-11:30am and 1-3:30pm. Free.) **La Gruta San Juan Bautista,** Rte. 410 Km 0.3, a tiny waterfall with a Catholic shrine, makes a nice stop on the way to Los Viveros.

APPENDIX

CLIMATE

The biggest climatic variations in Puerto Rico are between the mountainous areas (represented below by Barranquitas) and the coastal plains. In general, Puerto Rico's weather is beautiful year-round.

Temp. (°C/F) Precipitation (mm)	January			April			July			October		
	°C	°F	mm	°C	°F	mm	°C	°F	mm	°C	°F	mm
Arecibo	23.8	74.8	120.7	24.7	76.5	14.8	26.9	80.4	111.8	26.5	79.7	142.8
Barranquitas	20.2	68.4	83.9	21.7	71.1	105.7	23.7	74.7	99.9	23.2	73.8	216.4
Fajardo	24.3	75.7	94.1	25.6	78.1	106.2	27.7	81.9	147.5	27.0	80.6	215.1
Mayagüez	23.8	74.8	56.7	24.9	76.8	141.5	26.5	79.7	261.3	26.2	79.2	255.9
Ponce	24.4	75.9	25.3	25.6	78.1	54.3	27.7	81.9	67.2	26.9	80.4	150.8
San Juan	25.0	77.0	75.3	26.3	79.3	94.9	28.1	82.6	4.5	27.7	81.9	139.9

SPANISH QUICK REFERENCE

PRONUNCIATION

Spanish pronunciation is pretty straightforward; Puerto Rican Spanish is a bit more complicated. Puerto Ricans have a notoriously strong accent and tend to speak very rapidly. Some also have a tendency to drop of the ends of words—for example, "buenos días" becomes "buen día." In all Spanish each **vowel** has only one pronunciation: *a* ("ah" in father); *e* ("eh" in pet); *i* ("ee" in feet); *o* ("oh" in oat); *u* ("oo" in boot); *y*, by itself, is pronounced the same as Spanish *i* ("ee"). Most **consonants** are pronounced the same as in English. Important exceptions are: *j*, pronounced like the English "h" in "hello," and *ñ*, pronounced like the "ny" in "canyon." *Ll* theoretically sounds like the English "y" in "yes," but in Puerto Rican Spanish it frequently comes out like "s" as in "pleasure." *R* at the beginning of a word or *rr* anywhere in a word is trilled. *H* is always silent. *G* before *e* or *i* is pronounced like the "h" in "hen"; elsewhere it is pronounced like the "g" in "gate." *X* has a bewildering variety of pronunciations: depending on dialect and word position, it can sound like English "h," "s," "sh," or "x." *B* and *v* are often pronounced somewhere in between a "b" and a "v."

Spanish words receive stress on the syllable marked with an accent ('). In the absence of an accent mark, words that end in vowels, "n," or "s" usually receive stress on the second-to-last syllable. For words ending in all other consonants, stress falls on the last syllable. The Spanish language has masculine and feminine nouns, and gives a gender to all adjectives. Masculine words generally end with an "o": *él es un tonto* (he is a fool). Feminine words generally end with an "a": *ella es bella* (she is beautiful). Pay close attention—slight changes in word ending can have drastic changes in meaning. For instance, when receiving directions, watch for the distinction between *derecho* (straight) and *derecha* (right).

LET'S GO SPANISH PHRASEBOOK

ESSENTIAL PHRASES

ENGLISH	SPANISH	PRONUNCIATION
Hello.	Hola.	OH-la
Goodbye.	Adiós.	ah-dee-OHS
Yes/No.	Sí/No.	SEE/NO
Please.	Por favor.	POHR fa-VOHR
Thank you.	Gracias.	GRAH-see-ahs
You're welcome.	De nada.	DAY NAH-dah
Do you speak English?	¿Habla inglés?	AH-blah een-GLAYS
I don't speak Spanish.	No hablo español.	NO AH-bloh ehs-pahn-YOHL
Excuse me.	Perdón.	pehr-DOHN
I don't know.	No sé.	NO SAY
Can you repeat that?	¿Puede repertirlo?	PWEH-day reh-peh-TEER-lo

SURVIVAL SPANISH

ENGLISH	SPANISH	ENGLISH	SPANISH
Good morning.	Buenos días.	I'm sick/fine.	Estoy enfermo(a)/bien.
Good afternoon/evening.	Buenas tardes/noches.	I'm fine, thanks.	(Estoy) bien, gracias.
How are you?	¿Cómo está?	Is the store open/closed?	¿La tienda está abierta/cerrada?
What's up?	¿Qué pasa?/¿Qué tal?	How much does it cost?	¿Cuánto cuesta?
What is your name?	¿Cómo se llama?	That is very cheap/expensive.	Es muy barato/caro.
I don't understand.	No entiendo.	Do you accept traveler's checks?	¿Acepta cheques de viaje?
Again, please.	Otra vez, por favor.	I'm hungry/thirsty.	Tengo hambre/sed.
What (did you just say)?	¿Cómo?/¿Qué?	I'm hot/cold.	Tengo calor/frio.
Can/Could you speak more slowly?	¿Puede/Podría hablar más despacio?	I want/would like...	Quiero/Quisiera...
How do you say (beer) in Spanish?	¿Cómo se dice (cerveza) en español?	It's/That's fine.	Está bien.
Who?	¿Quién?	Let's go!	¡Vámonos!
When?	¿Cuándo?	What?	¿Cómo?
Why?	¿Por qué?	Because...	Porque...
Where?	¿Dónde?	Stop/That's enough.	Basta.
Where is (the bathroom)?	¿Dónde está (el baño)?	Maybe/Perhaps.	Tal vez.
Where can I make a phone call?	¿Dónde puedo hacer una llamada de teléfono?	Look!/Listen!	¡Mira!

YOUR ARRIVAL

ENGLISH	SPANISH	ENGLISH	SPANISH
I am from (the US/Europe).	Soy de (los Estados Unidos/Europa).	What's the problem, sir/madam?	¿Cuál es el problema, señor/señora?
I have nothing to declare.	No tengo nada para declarar.	I lost my baggage/passport.	Se me perdió mi equipaje/pasaporte.
Please do not detain me.	Por favor no me detenga.	I don't know where (the drugs) came from.	No sé de donde vinieron (las drogas).

GETTING AROUND

ENGLISH	SPANISH	ENGLISH	SPANISH
How do you get to (the público station)?	¿Cómo se puede llegar a (la terminal de guaguas públicas)?	Could you tell me what time it is?	¿Podría decirme qué hora es?
Does this público go to (Río Piedras)?	¿Va este guagua para (Río Piedras)?	Where is the bathroom?	¿Dónde está el baño?
How long does the trip take?	¿Cuánto tiempo dura el viaje?	Where can I check e-mail?	¿Dónde se puede chequear el correo electrónico?
Please let me off at (the zoo).	Por favor, déjeme en (el zoológico).	I would like to rent (a car).	Quisiera alquilar (un coche).
What bus line goes to...?	¿Cuál línea de autobuses tiene servicio a...?	How much does it cost per day/week?	¿Cuánto cuesta por día/semana?
I am going to (the airport).	Voy para (el aeropuerto).	Are there student discounts available?	¿Hay descuentos para estudiantes?
Where is (Fortaleza) street?	¿Dónde está la calle (Fortaleza)?	On foot.	A pie.
How near/far from here?	¿Qué tan cerca/lejos está de aquí?	I'm lost.	Estoy perdido/a.

DIRECTIONS

ENGLISH	SPANISH	ENGLISH	SPANISH
(to the) right	a la derecha	(to the) left	(a la) izquierda
straight ahead	derecho	turn (command form)	doble
next to	al lado de/junto a	across from	en frente de/frente a
near	cerca (de)	far from	lejos de
above	arriba	below	abajo
traffic light	semáforo	corner	esquina
street	calle/avenida	block	cuadra

ON THE ROAD

ENGLISH	SPANISH	ENGLISH	SPANISH
car	carro, auto	public bus/van	guagua
stop	pare	slow	despacio
lane (ends)	carril (termina)	yield	ceda
entrance	entrada	seatbelt	cinturón de seguridad
exit	salida	(maximum) speed	velocidad (máxima)
(narrow) bridge	puente (estrecho)	dangerous (curve)	(curva) peligrosa
narrow (lane)	(carril) estrecho	parking	estacionamiento, parking
toll (ahead)	peaje (adelante)	dead-end street	calle sin salida
authorized public buses only	transporte colectivo autorizado solamente	only (traffic only in the direction of the arrow)	solo
slippery when wet	resbala mojada	rest area	área de descansar
danger (ahead)	peligro (adelante)	do not park	no estacione
do not enter	no entre	do not turn right on red	no vire con luz roja
north	norte	south	sur
east	este	west	oeste

ACCOMMODATIONS

ENGLISH	SPANISH	ENGLISH	SPANISH
Is there a (cheap) hotel around here?	¿Hay un hotel (económico) por aqui?	Are there rooms available?	¿Tiene habitaciones libres?
Do you have any singles/doubles?	¿Tiene habitaciones sencillas/dobles?	I am going to stay for (four) days.	Me voy a quedar (cuatro) días.
I would like to reserve a room.	Quisiera reservar una habitación.	I'll take it.	Lo tomo.
Can I see a room?	¿Puedo ver una habitación?	I need another key/towel/pillow.	Necesito otra llave/toalla/almohada.
Are there cheaper rooms?	¿Hay habitaciones más baratas?	The toilet/shower/sink is broken.	El baño/la ducha/el lavabo está roto.
Do they come with fans/kitchen/windows?	¿Vienen con abanicos/cocinas/ventanas?	My bedsheets are dirty.	Mis sábanas están sucias.
(The cockroaches) are biting me.	(Las cucarachas) me están mordiendo.	Dance, cockroaches, dance!	¡Bailen, cucarachas, bailen!

EATING OUT

ENGLISH	SPANISH	ENGLISH	SPANISH
breakfast	desayuno	lunch	almuerzo
dinner	comida/cena	drink (alcoholic)	bebida (trago)
dessert	postre	Bon appetit!	¡Buen provecho!
fork	tenedor	knife	cuchillo
spoon	cuchara	cup	copa/taza
napkin	servilleta	Do you have hot sauce?	¿Tiene salsa picante?
Where is a good restaurant?	¿Dónde está un restaurante bueno?	Table for (two), please.	Mesa para (dos), por favor.
Can I see the menu?	¿Podría ver la carta/el menú?	Do you take credit cards?	¿Aceptan tarjetas de crédito?
This is too spicy.	Es demasiado picante.	Disgusting!	¡Guácala!/¡Qué asco!
I would like to order the eel.	Quisiera el congrio.	Do you have anything without meat?	¿Hay algún plato sin carne?
Delicious!	¡Qué rico!	The check, please	La cuenta, por favor.

EMERGENCY

ENGLISH	SPANISH	ENGLISH	SPANISH
Help!	¡Socorro!/¡Ayúdame!	Call the police!	¡Llame a la policía!
I am hurt.	Estoy herido(a).	Leave me alone!	¡Déjeme en paz!
It's an emergency!	¡Es una emergencia!	They robbed me!	¡Me han robado!
Fire!	¡Fuego!/¡Incendio!	They went that-a-way!	¡Fueron por allá!
Call a clinic/ambulance/doctor/priest!	¡Llame a una clínica/una ambulancia/un médico/un padre!	I need to contact my embassy.	Necesito comunicar con mi embajada.
I will only speak in the presence of a lawyer.	Solo hablaré con la presencia de un abogado.	Don't touch me!	¡No me toque!

MEDICAL

ENGLISH	SPANISH	ENGLISH	SPANISH
I feel bad/better/worse/fine.	Me siento mal/mejor/peor/bien.	Call an ambulance.	Llame para una ambulancia.
I have a headache/stomachache.	Tengo dolor de cabeza/estómago.	It hurts here.	Me duele aquí.
I'm sick/ill.	Estoy enfermo(a).	I think I'm going to vomit.	Creo que voy a vomitar.
What is this medicine for?	¿Para qué es esta medicina?	I haven't been able to go to the bathroom for (four) days.	No he podido ir al baño en (cuatro) días.
Where is the nearest hospital/doctor?	¿Dónde está el hospital/doctor más cercano?	I have a cold/a fever/diarrhea/nausea.	Tengo gripe/una calentura/diarrea/náusea.
I'm allergic to...	Soy alérgico(a)...	Here is my prescription.	Aquí está la receta médica.

INTERPERSONAL INTERACTION

ENGLISH	SPANISH	ENGLISH	SPANISH
Pleased to meet you.	Encantado(a)/Mucho gusto.	This is my first time in Puerto Rico.	Esta es mi primera vez en Puerto Rico.
What is your name?	¿Cómo se llama?	My name is Carlos.	Me llamo Carlos.
Where are you from?	¿De dónde es?	I am going to the club.	Voy al club.
I love you.	Te quiero.	I have a boyfriend/girlfriend/spouse.	Tengo novio/novia/esposo(a).
How old are you?	¿Cuántos años tiene?	I'm (twenty) years old.	Tengo (viente) años.
Do you have a light?	¿Tiene fuego?	I'm gay/bisexual.	Soy gay/bisexual.
No more (rum) for me	No más (ron) para mi.	Do you come here often?	¿Viene aquí a menudo?
What's wrong?	¿Qué te pasa?	Would you like to go out with me?	¿Quiere salir conmigo?

NUMBERS, DAYS, AND MONTHS

ENGLISH	SPANISH	ENGLISH	SPANISH	ENGLISH	SPANISH
0	cero	20	veinte	last night	anoche
1	uno	21	veintiuno	weekend	fin de semana
2	dos	22	veintidós	morning	mañana
3	tres	30	treinta	afternoon	tarde
4	cuatro	40	cuarenta	night	noche
5	cinco	50	cincuenta	month	mes
6	seis	100	cien	year	año
7	siete	1000	mil	early/late	temprano/tarde
8	ocho	1 million	un millón	January	enero
9	nueve	Monday	lunes	February	febrero
10	diez	Tuesday	martes	March	marzo
11	once	Wednesday	miércoles	April	abril
12	doce	Thursday	jueves	May	mayo
13	trece	Friday	viernes	June	junio
14	catorce	Saturday	sábado	July	julio
15	quince	Sunday	domingo	August	agosto
16	dieciseis	today	hoy	September	septiembre
17	diecisiete	tomorrow	mañana	October	octubre
18	dieciocho	day after tomorrow	pasado mañana	November	noviembre
19	diecinueve	yesterday	ayer	December	diciembre

APPENDIX

SPANISH GLOSSARY

abajo: below
abanico: fan
adelante: ahead
aduana: customs
aeropuerto: airport
agencia de viaje: travel agency
agua: water
aguas termales: hot springs
ahora: now
ahorita: in just a moment
aire acondicionado: air conditioning (A/C)
a la orden: at your service
al gusto: as you wish
alcaldía: mayor's office
amigo/a: friend
área de descansar: rest area
arriba: above
artesanía: arts and crafts
artesano: artisan
auto: car
avenida: avenue
ATH: ATM
bahía: bay
balneario: public beach
baño: bathroom
barato(a): cheap
barrio: neighborhood
béisbol: baseball
biblioteca: library
boletería: ticket counter
boleto: ticket
bomba: African-influenced music popular in Loíza
bonito(a): pretty, beautiful
Boricua: an affectionate term for a Puerto Rican
Borikén: Taíno name for Puerto Rico
borracho(a): drunk
bosque estatal: state forest
buen provecho: bon appetite
bueno(a): good
buena suerte: good luck
buenos días/buenas tardes/ buenas noches: good morning/ afternoon/evening
burro: donkey
caballero: gentleman
caballo: horse
cabaña: cabin
cafetería: a small, informal restaurant
cajeros: cashiers
calle: street
cama: bed
cambio: change
camino: path, road, track
camión: truck
campo: countryside
capilla: chapel
caro(a): expensive
carretera: highway
carril: lane
carro: car
casa: house

casado(a): married
cascada: waterfall
catedral: cathedral
ceda: yield
centro: city center
centro vacacional: government-sponsored vacation center
cerca: near, nearby
cerro: hill
cheques de viaje: traveler's checks
chico(a): boy/girl
cigarillo: cigarette
cine: movie theater
cinturón de seguridad: seatbelt
ciudad: city
coche: car
cocina criolla: Puerto Rican food
coliseo: coliseum, stadium
colmado: small store
comedor: dining room
comida criolla: regional dishes
comida típica: traditional Puerto Rican food dishes
con: with
consulado: consulate
cordillera: mountain range
CPN: Compañía de Parques Nacionales (National Parks Company)
correo: post office
cuadra: street block
cuarto: a room
cuatro: four, or a traditional Puerto Rican instrument similar to a guitar
cuba libre: rum and coke
cuenta: bill, check
cuento: story, account
cueva: cave
curva: curve
damas: ladies
derecha: right
derecho: straight
desayuno: breakfast
despacio: slow
dinero: money
disco: dance club
doblar: to turn
DRNA: Departamento de Recursos Naturales y Ambientales
dulce: sweet
edificio: building
embajada: embassy
embotellada: bottled
emergencia: emergency
entrada: entrance
español: Spanish
esquina: corner
estacionamiento: parking
estacionar: to park
estadio: stadium
este: east
estrecho: narrow

estrella: star
extranjero: foreign/foreigner
farmacia: pharmacy
feliz: happy
fiesta: party, holiday
finca: farm, ranch
friaje: sudden cold wind
fumar: to smoke
gandules: green pigeon peas
gobierno: government
gordo(a): fat
gracias: thank you
gratis: free
gringo: American (sometimes derogatory)
guagua: van
guanábana: soursop
habitación:room
hacienda: ranch
hola: hello
hombre: man
iglesia: church
impuestos: taxes
independentistas: supporters of the Puerto Rican independence movement
inglés: English
isla: island
izquierda: left
jarra: 1-liter pitcher
jíbaro: a man from the countryside
ladrón: thief
lago/laguna: lake
lancha: launch, small boat
larga distancia: long distance
lavandería: laundromat
lejos: far
lento: slow
librería: bookstore
luz: light
mal: bad
malecón: seaside boardwalk
maleta: luggage, suitcase
mar: sea
máxima: maximum
mercado: market
mesón gastronómico: traditional restaurant endorsed by the Puerto Rican Tourism Company
mirador: an observatory or lookout point
muelle: dock
museo: museum
música (folklórica): (folk) music
nada: nothing
nevera: refrigerator
niño(a): child
norte: north
nueces/nuez: nuts/nut
Nuyorican: someone of Puerto Rican descent living in New York
obra: work of art, play
oeste: west

APPENDIX

oficina de turismo: tourist office
panadería: bakery
parada: a bus or train stop (in San Juan "parada" is an old trolley stops that no longer exist; however, the term is still used for giving directions)
parador: "country inn" endorsed by the Puerto Rican Tourism Company
pare: stop
parque: park
pasaporte: passport
peaje: toll
pelea de gallos: cockfight
peligroso/a: dangerous
playa: beach
plena: a form of Puerto Rican music that originated in sugar plantations around Ponce
población: population
policía: police
por favor: please
públicos: public vehicles
pueblo: town
puente: bridge
puerta: door
puerto: port
reloj: watch, clock
río: river
ropa: clothes
sábanas: sheets
sabor: flavor
sala: room
salida: exit
salsa: sauce, a type of music and dance
santos: small hand-carved wooden religious figurines
seguro: insurance
semáforo: traffic light
semana: week
Semana Santa: Holy Week
sexo: sex
sí: yes
sin salida: dead end
SIDA: AIDS
solo/solamente: only
soltero(a): single, unmarried
supermercado: supermarket
sur: south
Taínos: Native Americans living on Puerto Rico
tarifa: fee
té: tea
tembleque: coconut milk custard
termina: ends
tiburón: shark
tienda: store
tiple: traditional Puerto Rican instrument similar to a guitar
turismo: tourism
turista: tourist
valle: valley

vejigante mask: a colorful mask with horns used during carnaval festivals
velocidad: speed
ventana: window
vereda: trail, path
vino: wine
virar: to turn
volcán: volcano
zoológico: zoo

FOOD GLOSSARY

acerola: West Indian cherry
aguacate: avocado
ajo: garlic
a la plancha: grilled
alcapuria: meat-filled fried plantains
almejas: clams
amarillos: sweet, fried plantains
arepas: corn dough patties, sometimes filled with meat, cheese, or vegetables
arroz: rice
arroz con dulce: sweet rice pudding
asada: roast
asopao: stew, thick soup
atún: tuna
avena: oatmeal
bacalaíto: flat fritter fried in codfish oil
batidas: smoothies or milkshakes made from fresh fruit
bistec empanado: breaded Spanish steak
bistec/bistek/biftec: beefsteak
bocaditos: appetizers (at a bar)
café: coffee, cafe
caldo: soup, broth, or stew
camarón: shrimp
cangrejo: crab
carne: red meat
carrucho: conch
cerveza: beer
chapín: trunk fish
chicharrón: bite-sized pieces of meat
chillo: red snapper
china: orange
chuletas: pork chops
churrasco: breaded steak
coco: coconut
empanadilla: stuffed fritter
empanado: breaded
encebollado: with onions
ensalada: salad
flan: egg custard
fresa: strawberry
frijoles: beans
frito: fried
fruta: fruit

gandules: green pigeon peas
guanábana: soursop
guayaba: guava
guayaba con queso: guava with cheese
guineo: banana
habichuelas: beans
helado: ice cream
hervido(a): boiled
hielo: ice
huevo: egg
huevo frito: fried egg
jamón: jam
juey: crab
jugo: juice
langosta: lobster
leche: milk
lechón: roast pork
lechuga: lettuce
limber: frozen fruit juice
mantequilla: butter
manzana: apple
mayonesa: mayonnaise
mariscos: seafood
mofongo: mashed plantain typically filled with meat
mojo: traditional sauce with garlic, lemon, and olive oil
ostiones: oysters
pan: bread
pana: breadfruit
pan mallorca: sweet bread
panqueques: pancakes
parcha: passion fruit
parilla: grilled (as in meat)
pavo: turkey
pechuga de pollo: chicken breast
pera: pear
pescado: fish
picante: spicy
piña: pineapple
pinono: fried plantain wrapped around ground beef
piña: pineapple
piragua: snow conepollo
plátano: plantainqueso
pollo: chicken
pulpo: octopus
queso: cheese
queso suiza: swiss cheese
refrescos: refreshments, soft drinks
sándwich: sandwich
sorullito: fried corn sticks
tocineta: bacon
tomate: tomato
tortilla española: Spanish omelette
tostadas: toast with butter
tostadas francesas: French toast
tostones: dry, fried plantains
trago: mixed drink/shot
tres leches: sweet, moist cake
vegetales: vegetables

INDEX

MAP INDEX

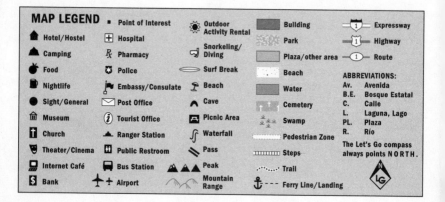

MAP LEGEND

- Point of Interest
- Hotel/Hostel
- Camping
- Food
- Nightlife
- Sight/General
- Museum
- Church
- Theater/Cinema
- Internet Café
- $ Bank

- ✛ Hospital
- ℞ Pharmacy
- Police
- Embassy/Consulate
- Post Office
- Tourist Office
- Ranger Station
- Public Restroom
- Bus Station
- Airport

- Outdoor Activity Rental
- Snorkeling/Diving
- Surf Break
- Beach
- Cave
- Picnic Area
- Waterfall
- Pass
- Peak
- Mountain Range

- Building
- Park
- Plaza/other area
- Beach
- Water
- Cemetery
- Swamp
- Pedestrian Zone
- Steps
- Trail
- Ferry Line/Landing

- Expressway
- Highway
- Route

ABBREVIATIONS:
Av. Avenida
B.E. Bosque Estatal
C. Calle
L. Laguna, Lago
PL. Plaza
R. Río

The Let's Go compass always points NORTH.